Political science
a comparative introduction

Rod Hague

Martin Harrop

Shaun Breslin

WORTH PUBLISHERS

Political Science
Second Edition

Library of Congress Catalog Card Number: 98–84776

ISBN: 1–57259–722–4

Printing: 1 2 3 4 5 – 02 01 00 99 98

Worth Publishers
33 Irving Place
New York, N.Y. 10003

Political Science

A Comparative Introduction

2nd edition
....
Fully Revised
& Updated

**Rod Hague,
Martin Harrop
& Shaun Breslin**

First edition 1982
Reprinted three times
Second edition 1987
Reprinted six times
Third edition 1992
Reprinted five times
Fourth edition 1998

Published by
MACMILLAN PRESS LTD
Houndmills, Basingstoke, Hampshire RG21 6XS
and London
Companies and representatives
throughout the world

ISBN 0–333–69631–X hardcover
ISBN 0–333–69632–8 paperback

A catalogue record for this book is available from the British
Library.

This book is printed on paper suitable for recycling and made
from fully managed and sustained forest sources

10   9   8   7   6   5   4   3
07   06   05   04   03   02   01   00

Printed in Malaysia

Summary of contents

Contents

List of tables, figures, boxes, exhibits, country and regional profiles

Boxes

Exhibits

Country and regional profiles

Preface

Rewriting this book to incorporate the recent transformation of the political world has proved to be both challenging and stimulating. Dramatic changes in the contexts, procedures and agendas of governments since the last edition have required a full rewrite of every chapter to the extent that this is essentially a new book. In addition to detailed revisions, we have also taken the opportunity to update the book's organizing framework. In place of the distinctly elderly three worlds perspective, we base our discussion in this edition around three dimensions along which countries can be arrayed: democratic–authoritarian, consolidated–transitional and developed–developing.

Of these, the democratic–authoritarian dimension is the most central for our purposes. Now that most countries are governed by passably democratic means, the new chapter on democracy seeks to present the growing diversity within the democratic family. For example, we discuss Asian models of democracy and those ambiguous regimes we characterize as semi-democratic. Of course, as good comparativists we must also adapt Kipling's question and ask: what know they of democracy who only democracy know? So throughout the book, examples of current authoritarian regimes and past totalitarian episodes complement the focus on democracy.

The consolidated–transitional dimension allows us to meet the criticism that the study of comparative government tends to the static. This edition pays more attention to the politics of transition, examining countries moving not just from authoritarian to more democratic government but also from arbitrary to more constitutional rule and from state-run to more market-led economies. The postcommunist countries, with their varied combinations of collective progress and individual suffering, offer dramatic insight into the problems of building both

state and civil society in a post-totalitarian setting. In addition, we have sought to capture the broader work on transitions to democracy, a literature which in our view is the outstanding recent achievement of comparative political research.

Studying regimes in motion also has a pedagogic advantage. It allows us to breathe new life into the foundation of our discipline and the heart of this book: the study of government institutions. John Stuart Mill's comment on constitutions applies to institutions generally: 'men did not wake up on a summer morning and find them all sprung up'. Modern institutional design may have begun in Philadelphia in 1787 but it did not reach its peak until the final decades of the twentieth century. The democratic revolution has forced constitutions to be written and institutions to be re-engineered. A presidential, a parliamentary or (most likely) a dual executive? A plurality, a proportional or (most likely) a mixed electoral system? A federal, an intergovernmental or (most likely) a mixed model for the European Union? These questions have migrated from the examination room into the real world of politics, where they are answered in an equal hurry and often amid comparable uncertainty. We live – or should that already read 'we have lived'? – through an exciting moment of convergence between institutional theory and political practice.

The developed–developing dimension is perhaps more of a background feature than a major theme. Nonetheless, in the chapter on the global context we emphasize how a country's location on this continuum continues to structure the choices available to its rulers. We draw attention to the growing diversity of countries (even developing ones) within the international political economy. We note also the increasing significance which all states must attach to national economic performance in an open global economy. Many developed states, once centrally involved with warfare and welfare, now find themselves playing a more managerial role, seeking to enhance the competitiveness of private corporations. This shift in the state's agenda both alters and weakens its functional significance and leads to many of the institutional developments we examine in Part 3.

In these core institutional chapters, we have sought to address classic topics in a contemporary fashion. Broadly, we find that the shape of democratic politics is continuing to evolve as mass parties, fixed ideologies, large public sectors and expensive welfare states begin to crumble. In place of those twentieth-century totems comes the more complex, fragmented and negotiated politics of a new century. Dominant and two-party systems fall by the wayside, as multiparty systems and coalition governments become the norm. The role of mass parties in linking society to the state declines as single-issue groups gain ground. In the bureaucracy, public corporations give way to regulatory agencies, issue networks replace policy communities and contractual networks are superimposed on Weberian hierarchies. In the legislature, more work is done sitting down, as specialist committees supplement stand-up debate in the chamber. The shape of the state across its territory alters as new or revived subnational tiers of government acquire greater autonomy (hence the full chapter in this edition on federal, unitary and local politics). And a new generation of activist judges emerges, not just to arbitrate disputes between levels of government but also to nudge the state toward fuller protection of individual rights. We summarize all these trends as a shift, albeit with marked variations between countries in enthusiasm, pace and extent, from government to governance. Put another way, these developments represent a move from a British toward an American model for reaching – or sometimes failing to reach – collective decisions.

Extensive rewriting notwithstanding, this edition retains the purpose of its predecessors. We have sought to provide an accessible and up-to-date introductory text for courses in comparative politics, and for non-country-specific first-year introduction to politics courses. However, in response to the expansion of postgraduate work, and of projects at first-degree level, we have also added a more advanced

concluding chapter on the comparative method. Here we have attempted to draw on the comparisons made elsewhere in the book to offer an introduction to methodology for students undertaking comparative work; in particular, we highlight the underestimated virtues of the case study approach.

We are aware that the book is often used by students for whom English is a second language and we have therefore sought to abide by the textbook-author's golden rule: write clearly. We have also given the book a design make-over; we hope that the new features aid accessiblity without detracting from coherence. We should mention two additional benefits of a major rewrite: first, a refreshed set of references and, second, the potential to attempt future editions on a more regular basis.

We have set up a web site to support this edition. Please visit us at:

www.newcastle.ac.uk/~npol

It is our pleasure to thank the many people who have helped us. In our home department we have sought advice from James Babb, Simon Caney, Phil Daniels, Peter Jones, Ella Ritchie, Rod Rhodes and John Wiseman. Many helpful suggestions came from our publisher Steven Kennedy and from Vincent Wright of Nuffield College, Oxford. Our publishers' anonymous reviewers in both Europe and North America also offered wise counsel. Richard Mulgan of the Australian National University generously allowed us to read a typescript version of his *Politics in New Zealand* (Auckland: Auckland University Press, 1997, 2nd edn) and also dealt patiently with our queries arising. We owe a special debt to Reuven Hazan of The Hebrew University of Jerusalem; his cogent comments made a real contribution to several chapters. We thank Jocelyn Mawdsley and Bertram Welker for preparing the references and Paul Gliddon for the index. For help ranging from general suggestions to detailed comments, we would also like to thank:

Scott Bennett, Australian National University
Richard Dunphy, University of Dundee
Adrian Guelke, The Queen's University of Belfast
William Hale, School of Oriental and African
    Studies, University of London

Christine Hudson, Umeå University
George Jones, London School of Economics and
    Political Science
Tom Mackie, University of Strathclyde
Roy May, Coventry University
Chris Rudd, University of Otago
Gerry Stoker, University of Strathclyde
Ulf Sundhaussen, University of Queensland
Paul Taggart, University of Sussex

Finally, we would again like to invite comments on the book from teachers and students. Rewriting a text, like any reform, may achieve its primary goal but still bring about unwanted side-effects. We can correct minor errors quickly when the book is reprinted; and we will place major suggestions in a folder, already beginning to bulge, marked Fifth Edition. Please contact Martin Harrop at:

Department of Politics
University of Newcastle
Newcastle upon Tyne
England
NE1 7RU

Tel. 0191 222 7922
Fax 0191 222 5069
e-mail Martin.Harrop@ncl.ac.uk

Rod Hague
Martin Harrop
Shaun Breslin

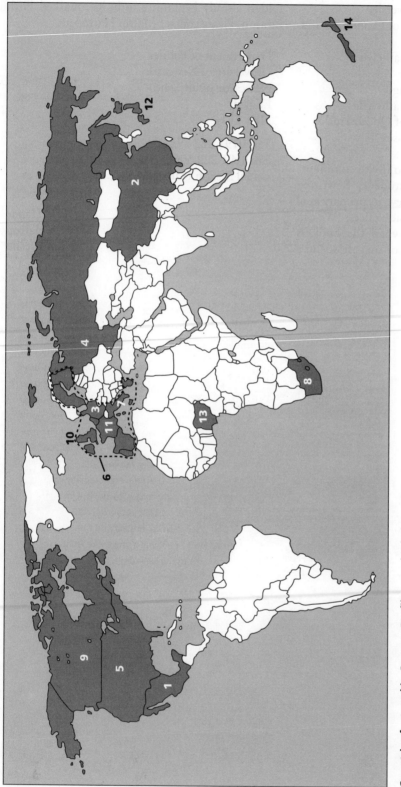

Countries featured in Country Profiles are shaded on map

For detail of Eastern and Western Europe see Maps 1.1 and 7.1

Map of the World

PART 1

FOUNDATIONS

In this part we set out the foundations of comparative government and politics. Chapter 1 introduces the core concepts of the subject, including politics, government and the state. Here we also outline the strengths of comparative analysis and introduce our classifications of states. We devote Chapter 2 to democracy: its origins, characteristics and forms. This chapter reflects the dominant position of democratic ideas, and to a growing extent democratic practice, in today's world. Chapter 3 examines the global context within which states operate. In an interdependent world we can no longer treat national governments as separate entities operating in isolation; rather, global forces impinge on states, providing both constraints on the operation of democracy but also new economic opportunities.

CHAPTER **1**

Comparative politics and government

In this book we examine how politics is organized in countries around the world. We focus on how nations solve the core political problem of making collective decisions. But we cannot jump straight into these issues. For just as what astronomers 'see' in the sky depends on the type of telescope through which they peer, so too does our interpretation of politics depend on the concepts through which we approach our topic. Indeed, in politics it often seems as though everyone has their own telescope – and claims that their own instrument is the best!

This point illustrates a key fact about studying politics. Our main concepts remain at the forefront of discussion in a way which does not normally apply to more scientific disciplines such as astronomy. Political analysis is far more than mere opinion; even so, conclusions vary with the analyst rather more than is comfortable for those who advocate a strictly scientific approach to the study of politics. *Comparative* politics, based on a range of countries, is especially suited to the task of revealing contrasting perspectives on our subject matter. So in this chapter we discuss some central concepts of our discipline, not so much to establish 'correct' definitions as to introduce our own interpretations.

Politics

To start at the beginning: what is politics? We can easily list, and agree on, some examples of political activity. When the American president and Congress start their annual tussle over the federal budget, they are clearly engaged in politics. When Chechnya declared its independence from Russia in 1991, its action was obviously political. When Greenpeace sent out a ship to a French nuclear test zone, it too was making a political point. The heartland of politics, as represented by such examples, is clear enough. However, the boundaries of the political are less precise. When one country invades another, is it engaged in politics or merely in war? Would politics occur if resources were unlimited? Is politics restricted to governments or can it also be found in families, universities and even seminar groups?

A crisp definition of politics – one which fits just those things we instinctively call 'political' – is impossible. Politics is a term with varied uses and nuances. Perhaps the nearest we can come to a capsule statement is this: politics is the activity by which groups reach binding collective decisions through attempting to reconcile differences among their members. We can draw out four points embedded in this definition:

- Politics is a *collective activity*, involving people who accept a common membership or at least acknowledge a shared fate. Robinson Crusoe could not practice politics.
- Politics presumes an initial *diversity of views*, if not about goals then at least about means. Were we all to agree all the time, politics would not be necessary.
- Politics involves *reconciling such differences*

3

through discussion and persuasion. Communication is therefore central to politics.

- Political decisions become *authoritative policy* for a group, binding members to decisions which are implemented by force if necessary. Politics scarcely exists if decisions are reached solely by violence but force, or its threat, is central to the execution of collective decisions.

Definition

Miller (1991, p. 390) defines **politics** as 'a process whereby a group of people, whose opinions or interests are initially divergent, reach collective decisions which are generally accepted as binding on the group, and enforced as common policy'. For Miller, the political process typically involves elements of persuasion and bargaining, together with a mechanism for reaching a final decision.

The necessity of politics arises from the collective character of human life. We live in groups which must reach collective decisions: about sharing resources, relating to other groups and planning for the future. We have no choice but to practice politics. So although the term 'politics' is often used cynically, to criticise the pursuit of private advantage under the guise of the public interest, politics is an inescapable feature of the human condition. Indeed, the Greek philosopher Aristotle (384–322 BC) argued that 'man is by nature a political animal'. By this he meant that people can only express their nature as reasoning, virtuous beings through participating in a political community.

Members of a group rarely agree, at least initially, on what course of action to follow. Even if there is agreement over goals, there may still be a skirmish over means. Yet a decision must be reached, one way or the other, and once made it will commit all members of the group. Thus politics consists in procedures for allowing a range of views to be expressed and then combined into an overall decision. As Shively (1995, p. 11) points out,

political action may be interpreted as a way to work out rationally the best common solution to a common problem – or at least a way to work out a reasonable common solution. That is, politics consists of public choice.

By debating the options, the quality of the final choice should improve; and the participants to the discussion should become both better-informed and more committed to the agreed course of action.

But of course politics consists of more than the disinterested pursuit of the collective good. Members of a group will share some interests but not others. Deciding to go to war is one thing; agreeing on who should be conscripted is quite another. Introducing a pension for senior citizens is one thing; working out whose taxes should be increased to foot the bill is another. A decision will affect all, and even benefit all, but not everyone will gain equally. Most often a course of action will produce both winners and losers. Here we arrive at the essence of our subject. Politics is about making decisions which impinge on both the shared and the competing interests of the group's members. Indeed some authors *define* political situations as those in which the participants mix common and competing interests. 'Pure conflict is war', writes Laver (1983, p. 1). 'Pure cooperation is true love. Politics is a mixture of both.'

So politics is the task of reconciling special interests in the pursuit of the common good. The British political theorist Bernard Crick (1992) advances this view with particular vigour. He asks: 'why call a struggle for power "politics", when it is simply a struggle for power?' Crick prefers to define politics as the 'activity by which differing interests within a given unit of rule are conciliated by giving them a share in power in proportion to their importance to the welfare and the survival of their community'. Crick's definition is somewhat extreme; it seems to dismiss the possibility of politics occurring at all in dictatorships. But he is surely right to stress that politics involves negotiation, bargaining and compromise.

Once reached, political decisions form authoritative policy for the group. In Easton's famous definition (1965a and b), 'politics is the authoritative allocation of values'. Public authority – ultimately, force – is used to enforce collective decisions. If you break the rules, the government may put you in prison; at any rate, it is the only body with the right to do so. And from government there is no escape. You cannot – in the contemporary world – choose a life without government.

Government and governance

Large groups develop special institutions for making and enforcing collective decisions. These bodies are the government. So government is technically the structure within which the activity of politics takes place; it provides the framework for politics. In popular usage, 'the government' refers just to the highest echelon of political appointments: in other words, to presidents and prime ministers, department heads and cabinet members. But in a broader sense the government consists of all those organizations charged with the task of reaching decisions for the whole community.

> **Definition**
> In Finer's words (1974), 'government is institutionalized politics'. Broadly, the **government** consists of institutions responsible for making collective decisions for society. More narrowly, government refers to the top political level within such institutions – that is, to presidents, prime ministers and department heads. **Governance**, by contrast, refers to the process of making collective decisions, a task in which government may not play a leading, or even any, role. In international relations, for example, no world government exists to resolve problems but many issues are resolved by negotiation. This is a case of governance without government.

We must distinguish between government and governance. An old word enjoying renewed popularity, governance refers to the activity, process or quality of governing. It points not to the structures of government but to the policies which are made and to the effectiveness with which they are carried out. A recurring theme of this book is that, at least in the consolidated democracies, government is giving way to governance. This means that collective decisions are no longer made by a single leader (say, the president) or by a single group (say, the cabinet). Rather, policies emerge from consultations between many affected interests. Further, policies are often modified when they are put into effect: those who implement policy take part in governance if not government. Governance – the task of managing complex societies – involves the coordination of many public and private sector bodies. In short, government is only one actor, and not always the leading one, in governance (Rhodes, 1996). But the governance theme does not just apply to developed countries. Many international agencies also suggest that effective governance is crucial to development. In an influential report, the World Bank (1997, p. 1) argued that 'the state is central to economic and social development, not as a direct provider of growth but as a partner, catalyst and facilitator'.

Yet it is the field of international relations which offers the best current examples of governance. The reason for this is clear: there is no world government, no institution making enforcable decisions for the world as a whole. Yet many aspects of global relations are regulated by agreement. One example is the Internet, a massive network of linked computers beyond the control of any one government or any one. Yet standards for connecting computers and data to the Internet are agreed; thus we can speak of the governance, but not the government, of cyberspace (Loader, 1997). International institutions have emerged to formulate rules in many other areas: for instance, the World Trade Organization works to reduce trade barriers. However, these organizations are certainly not governments; they have limited powers, especially in enforcement, and they lack a police force to enforce their will. So the emerging pattern, in international and perhaps also in national politics, is rules without rulers, governing without government. In a word: governance (Rosenau, 1992).

The state and sovereignty

Statehood is now the dominant principle of political organization. Except for the Antarctic, the world is parcelled up into separate states which, through mutual recognition, form the international system. The state is a unique institution. It stands above all other organizations in society. The state can legitimately use force to enforce its will and citizens must accept its authority as long as they continue to live within its borders. As Edelman (1964, p. 1) writes,

> the state benefits and it threatens. Now it is 'us' and often it is 'them'. It is an abstraction, but in its name men are jailed, or made rich on defense contracts, or killed in wars.

Understanding, and helping to control, the powers embedded in the state are prime tasks for students of comparative politics.

The state is a more abstract term than government. Broadly, statehood refers to the ensemble formed by government, population and territory. The French state, for example, is more than its government; it also encompasses the people and the territory of France. To bring out the distinction between government and state, note that all countries have someone who serves as head of state but that this person is not usually head of the government as well. European monarchs are examples: they symbolize the state but leave prime ministers to control the levers of power.

Definition

Sometimes used to mean the same as government, **the state** is better understood as a political community formed by a territorially-defined population which is subject to one government. The Montevideo Convention of 1933 regarded the capacity to enter relations with other states as one of four core features of states. The others were: a permanent population, a defined territory and a government (Rosenau, 1989, p. 17).

A central feature of the state is its capacity to regulate the legitimate use of force within its boundaries. The Russian revolutionary Lenin (1870–1924) put this most tersely, describing states as 'bodies of armed men'. And it is certainly true that when the power of the state is turned on its own people, gruesome brutality results (Exhibit 1.1). But the state is defined by the right, and not just the capacity, to employ force. As the German sociologist Max Weber (1864–1920) noted, the unique feature of the state is its integration of force with authority: 'A state is a human community that (successfully) claims the monopoly of the legitimate use of physical force within a given territory.' (Gerth and Mills, 1948, p.78). Any state must successfully uphold its claim to regulate the legitimate use of coercion within its domain. When the state's monopoly of legitimate force is threatened, as in a civil war, its continued existence is at stake. While the conflict continues, there is no legitimate authority. Society becomes stateless.

How did the state apparatus develop? The modern state emerged in Europe from the embers of feudalism. Under feudalism, monarchs were weak figures, sharing secular power with feudal lords and spiritual power with the Church. Administration and the economy operated locally, with little need for national regulation. However, this pattern changed during the sixteenth and seventeenth centuries. First in England and France, then in Prussia, Russia and elsewhere, monarchs succeeded in subordinating the landed aristocracy. Military forces came under the undisputed command of the crown. Warfare, taxation and statemaking went together; in its origins the European state was a war machine (Porter, 1994). As kings fought to acquire territory and population, royal bureaucracies developed to extract the resources needed for war and also to supervise (for example to pay and equip) the military. Finer (1997, p. 16) maintains that 'the raising and maintaining of military forces is the overwhelmingly most important reason for the emergence of the civil bureaucracy'. With the growth of bureaucracy, local patterns of administration and customary justice became more uniform within society, easing the development of national economies.

The doctrine of sovereignty provided the theoretical foundation for the emerging state. In his *Commentaries on the Laws of England (1765–70)*, the British jurist William Blackstone observed that 'there is and must be in every state a supreme, irresistible, absolute and uncontrolled authority, in which the right of sovereignty resides'. Blackstone's view summarized an account first developed by the French philosopher Jean Bodin (1529–96). Bodin defined sovereignty as the untrammelled and undivided power to make laws. Although Bodin's aim was to uphold the privileges of the French monarchy, the concept of sovereignty was subsequently reformulated for the democratic era. It came to express the doctrine that the state represented the collective will of the entire community. Louis XIV's 'L'état c'est moi' gave way to the American constitution's 'We the people'. Sovereignty, then, refers to the fount of authority in society and specifically to the body with law-making powers.

The law-making body within the state possesses *internal* sovereignty – the right to make laws applying within its territory. But sovereignty also has an *external* dimension (Scruton, 1996). External sovereignty is the recognition in international law that a state has jurisdiction (that is, authority) over

EXHIBIT 1.1

Power can kill: democide in the twentieth century

The power of a state, like that of a nuclear power station, is invaluable when contained but always carries the risk of catastrophe. Rummel (1997) coins the term 'democide' to describe a state which turns its weapons on its own people. He provides a list (right) of the ten most lethal governments of the century, as judged by the percentage of population killed. Rummell's solution to democide? Democracies, he notes, rarely fight each other and hardly ever kill their own people. In a democracy, the ballot replaces the bullet; it is absolute power which creates the conditions for democide. If Rummel is right, and his claim is plausible, the recent transition to democracy may make the twenty-first century a more peaceful place. We may be able to leave the twentieth century behind as a graveyeard for the 129 909 000 people killed by the very institution which should provide peace, law and order.

Country	Years	Rate[a] (%)	Total killed
Cambodia	1975–79	8.2[b]	2 000 000
Turkey	1919–23	2.6	703 000
Yugoslavia	1941–45	2.5	655 000
Poland	1945–48	2.0	1 585 000
Turkey	1909–18	1.0	1 752 000
Czechoslovakia	1945–48	0.5	197 000
Mexico	1900–20	0.4	1 417 000
USSR	1917–87	0.4	54 769 000
Cambodia	1979–87	0.4	230 000
Uganda	1971–79	0.3	300 000
World	1900–87	0.2	129 909 000

[a] per cent of its population that a regime murders each year, on average.
[b] survival odds for a Cambodian 1975–79 were 2.2 to 1.

a territory. This means the state is answerable for that jurisdiction in international law. External sovereignty matters because it allows a state to claim the right both to regulate affairs within its boundaries and to participate as an accepted member of the international system. In this way, the development of the international system of states has strengthened the authority of states in the domestic sphere.

> **Definition**
> **Sovereignty** refers to the ultimate source of authority in society. The sovereign is both the highest and the final decision-maker within a community.
> **Internal sovereignty** refers to law-making power within a territory; **external sovereignty** describes international recognition of the sovereign's jurisdiction over its territory. The phrase 'the sovereign state' reflects both dimensions.

Although the origins of the modern state lie in Europe, the form has now spread throughout the world. The end of Empire multiplied the number of independent states. The United States achieved independence from Britain in the eighteenth century; Latin American countries broke free from

Spanish and Portuguese control in the nineteenth century; and Asian and African colonies achieved statehood in the twentieth century, mostly after the Second World War. Within Europe itself the number of states continued to increase in the twentieth century. This growth resulted from the collapse of the Austro-Hungarian and Ottoman Empires after the First World War and then from the collapse of the Soviet empire in the early 1990s. In 1996, membership of the United Nations (an association of states, despite its name) stood at 185, of which 26 had joined since 1990 (Figure 1.1).

Yet many new states remain weak or 'soft', lacking the hard core which characterizes the strong states of Western Europe. Where the powerful European states were forged in war and territorial struggle, most of the newer states were born as the random offspring of decolonization. Especially in Africa, postcolonial states lack a precolonial national tradition on which to draw. The form of statehood has sufficed to secure external sovereignty and the international recognition flowing from it, but internally many new states lack strong governing institutions. In some respects they are not 'internally pacified'; local leaders or warlords provide whatever gover-

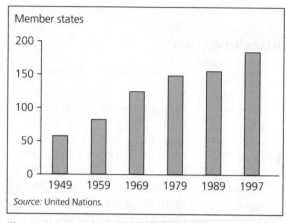

Figure 1.1 Number of states belonging to the United Nations, 1949–96.

nance exists (Sorensen, 1997). The presence of such quasi-states in Africa led Brunold (1994) to the provocative title for his book, *Africa Does Not Exist*. Even the United States, with more than two hundred years of independence, lacks the profound sense of statehood embedded in European countries with their history of monarchical and even absolute rule. As the poet Byron wrote, 'a thousand years scarce serve to form a state'.

At the start of the twenty-first century, even the strongest states must face the realities of interdependence. Territorially-based states must confront multinational corporations, financial flows and ecological problems which show no respect for national boundaries (see Chapter 3). In response to these issues, most states are now involved in a network of international organizations and agreements which compromise sovereignty. This process has gone furthest in the European Union, a loose federation of countries developed in the homeland of the modern state. Of course, states continue to operate; indeed, they are the indispensable building blocks of bodies such as the European Union. But states increasingly work through global and especially regional relationships which compromise traditional interpretations of sovereignty. States must recognize that old-fashioned notions of sovereignty, as propounded by Bodin and Blackstone, are now of little help. National sovereignty is still important in politics but partly as a populist myth.

Even within countries, the state is becoming less dominant in the final quarter of the twentieth century. As government gives way to governance,

identifying a sovereign power becomes more difficult. Since the 1980s, the danger of world war has receded, governments have reduced their involvement in economic production and some public welfare services have come to be viewed as unaffordable. In this new environment (new, at least, to Europe and New Zealand if not to the USA), so the role of the state has shifted from direct involvement in society to coordinating the work of other groups. These trends have been most obvious in countries making the transition from communism to democracy but they can also be observed within Western democracies. Like American presidents, states today must rely on their power to persuade. The state remains a unique institution in society but the idea of sovereignty becomes less and less relevant to understanding how it goes about its tasks of leadership, coordination and persuasion.

The nation

Nationality is a difficult but crucial term. It is both distinguishable from and related to the state. The word nation comes from the Latin, *nascire*, meaning 'to be born'. In the thirteenth century the term came to refer to ethnic groups such as the French and the Germans, as in these cases nations are often described and defended by reference to a common history, language or ethnic origin. However, nationality cannot be reduced to any one, or any combination, of these factors. Even language, which is one of the more reliable indicators, is far from infallible as a sign of nationhood. Switzerland, for instance, is indisputably a nation even though French, German and Italian are spoken there. Since nations are 'imagined communities', a nation can really only be defined as any group which upholds a claim to be regarded as such (Schöpflin and Hosking, 1997).

Definition

A **nation** is a people inhabiting a defined territory which seeks political expression of its shared identity, usually through a claim to statehood. **Nationalism**, the key ideology of the twentieth century, is the doctrine that nations are entitled to self-determination. The significance of nationalism is that it offers one answer to a question beyond the reach of democracy: who are 'the people' who are to govern themselves?

There is no one-to-one correspondence between nations and states. The United Kingdom, for example, is a multinational state. It contains England, Scotland, Wales and Northern Ireland within its borders. But the 15 successor states to the Soviet Union are probably the best examples of multinational states. These countries contain a total of over 100 nationalities, mixed within single states in politically-explosive combinations. In the Central Asian republic of Kazakhstan, no nationality is in the majority. Many successor states include a Russian minority, reflecting forced population shifts under communist rule. A total of 25 million Russians live beyond the borders of Russia itself, in what Russia terms the 'near abroad' (Brubaker, 1996).

Despite the existence of multinational states, nationality and statehood are linked. A nation is more than just another social group such as a race or a class. The nation, like the state, is intrinsically political. We can express this connection by suggesting that a nation is a people in search of a state. Thus, to describe French-speaking Canadians as a separate *nation* implies a demand for some form of statehood. In a similar way, to refer to the indigenous people of the Americas as Indian nations suggests a claim for a measure of self-government. Even though national claims to statehood do not always succeed, the idea of nationhood implies a claim to government.

Nationalism is the ideology which underpins these claims to self-rule. Nationalism's sole but crucial thesis is that nations have a right to self-determination, to govern themselves. The British philosopher John Stuart Mill (1806–73) was an early advocate of this position. He argued that 'where the sentiment of nationality exists in any force there is a *prima facie* case for uniting all the members of the nationality under the same government, and a government to themselves apart.' The American president Woodrow Wilson also promoted the idea of national self-determination at the end of the First World War. His principle provided the basis for redrawing the map of Europe in the peace settlement of 1919. The United Nations Covenant on Civil and Political Rights (1966) offered further support to national sef-government:

all peoples have the right to self-determination. By virtue of that right they freely determine their political status and pursue their economic, social and cultural rights.

As Tivey (1981) points out, nationalism has become the common ideology of the modern world, serving in particular as the gravedigger of empires.

The model of 'one nation, one state' is instinctively appealing. National identity can serve as political glue, providing a strong bond among the people living in a specific state. And where a sense of nationhood has been successfully harnessed to the state, as in France and even the United States, a single political community of enormous significance – the nation-state – has emerged. But using nationality as an adhesive to integrate states carries dangers in a world where international migration has increased cultural diversity within countries (Pesic, 1994). The risk is that civil and political rights will only be granted to people with the 'correct' national qualifications. The result is a two-tier society, with endemic conflict between majorities and minorities. Latvia, for instance, only grants citizenship to people fluent in the native language, a filter which leaves the once-dominant Russians in a difficult and marginal position. Israel is a Jewish state in which the minority Arab population (about 15 per cent of the total) continues to suffer outsider status. Further, asserting the right to self-determination may have the paradoxical effect of increasing civil conflict, at least if self-determination is understood as implying statehood (Sproat, 1997; Mahalingam, 1997). The contemporary challenge is to find ways in which national groups can co-exist within the framework of a single state. So far, the American experience with 'hyphenated Americans' – immigrants who retain their ancestral loyalties while also embracing the American creed – has proved difficult to repeat elsewhere.

Power

Power is the currency of politics. Just as money permits the efficient flow of goods and services through an economy, so power enables collective decisions to be made and enforced. Without power, a government would be as useless as a car without an engine. Power is the tool which enables rulers to achieve collective goals. How then should we define power?

One measure of power is simply the ability of a community to achieve its goals. In this sense, describing the United States as a powerful country simply means that it has the capacity to achieve many of its objectives. Notice that the emphasis here is on *power to* rather than *power over* – on the capacity to achieve goals, rather than to exercise control over other countries or people. This 'power to' approach is associated with the American sociologist Talcott Parsons (1967). He regarded power as the capacity of a government to draw on the obligations of its citizens so as to achieve collective purposes such as law and order and protection of the environment. The more powerful the government, the more effective it will be at achieving the goals of the community. For Parsons, then, power is a collective resource; the more, the better. The German-born political theorist Hannah Arendt (1906–75) made the same point when she defined power as 'not just the ability to act but the ability to act in concert' (1970, p. 44).

Definition

Power is the capacity to produce intended effects. In politics, power can be viewed benignly, as the capacity of a community to shape its own destiny. Power can also be seen as the ability of an individual or group to get its way against opposition. From this second perspective, we can say that A exerts power over B when A alters what B does – or even, some would argue, when A affects what B thinks or wants.

Parsons' view of power, though helpful and often ignored, is incomplete. Power, like politics, has a hard side. Politics is more than a technical task of implementing a vision shared by a whole society. It is also an arena of conflict over which goals to pursue. Thus we must also measure power by examining *whose* vision wins out. From this perspective, power consists of the ability to get one's way, to impose one's opinions, to overcome opposition. The underlying view of power here assumes conflict rather than consensus. In Dahl's famous definition (1957), power is a matter of getting people to do what they would not otherwise have done.

But what about actors who are so powerful that they prevent opposition from arising in the first place? Is this not the most subtle form of control of all? A president who controls the media so tightly that the public never learns about his theft of state assets will not face opposition on that score. A nuclear power station which leaks radioactivity will not face objections from the local community if the residents do not even realize they have been contaminated. Powerful actors can set the agenda of politics. Through their control of information, they can influence not the decisions which are reached but the topics which are raised.

To deal with this point, Lukes (1974) broadens the notion of power. Lukes suggests that power is exercised over people whenever their interests are ignored, even if these people are unaware that their interests have been affected. For Lukes, A exerts power over B when A affects B in a manner contrary to B's interests. So, the managers of the leaky power plant have exercised power even though the local inhabitants are unaware of the pollution and so do not object to it. Equally, a government which whips up patriotic fervour to improve military recruitment is still exerting power over the 'volunteers' – for how can it be in their interest to lay down their lives in a far-off field? Whether or not we regard these cases as examples of power, we must accept that manipulating people's knowledge and attitudes is the most efficient way to control them.

Authority and legitimacy

Authority is the right to rule. It exists when subordinates acknowledge the right of superiors to give orders.

Definition

Authority is the right to rule. Strictly, authority is the right to act, rather than the power to do so. However, authority creates its own power so long as people accept that the authority-figure has the right to make decisions. A **legitimate** system of government is one based on authority: that is, those subject to the state recognise its right to make collective decisions.

A general may exercise power over enemy soldiers but he does not have authority over them; this is restricted to his own forces. Yet authority is more than voluntary compliance. To acknowledge the authority of rulers does not mean you agree with their decisions. It means only that you accept their right to make decisions and your own duty to obey. Relationships of authority are still hierarchical. In politics, relationships typically combine elements of both power and authority.

The German sociologist Max Weber (1957, first published 1922) provided a path-breaking analysis of the bases of authority. He distinguished three ways of validating political power (Box 1.1). The first type is by reference to the sanctity of *tradition*. This authority is based on 'piety for what actually, allegedly or presumably has always existed'. Traditional rulers do not need to justify their authority (though they are certainly willing to enforce it). Rather, obedience is demanded as part of the natural order. Monarchs rule because they always have done; to demand a further justification is itself to challenge the basis of legitimacy. Traditional authority is usually an extension of patriachy – that is, the authority of the father or the eldest male. Weber offers a range of (traditional) examples:

> patriarchy means the authority of the father, the husband, the senior of the house, the elder sibling over the members of the household; the rule of the master and patron over the bondsmen, serfs, and freed men; of the lord over the domestic servants and household officials; of the prince over house- and court-officials. (Gerth and Mills, 1948, p. 296)

Traditional authority remains the model for many political relationships, especially in the developing world. In the Middle East, 'government has been personal, and both civil and military bureaucracies have been little more than extensions of the leader' (Bill and Springborg, 1994, p. 152). When an entire administration operates on the principle of traditional, patriachal authority, it is termed 'patrimonial'.

Charismatic authority is Weber's second type. Here leaders are obeyed because they inspire their followers, who credit their heroes with exceptional and even supernatural qualities. While traditional authority is based on the past, charismatic authority spurns history. The charismatic leader looks forward, convincing followers that the promised

---

BOX 1.1

Weber's classification of types of authority

Type	Basis	Example
Traditional	Custom and the established way of doing things	Monarchy
Charismatic	Intense commitment to the leader and his message	Many revolutionary leaders
Legal-rational	Rules and procedures – the office, not the person	Bureaucracy

---

land is within reach. Contrary to popular use, charisma is not for Weber an intrinsic quality of a leader; rather, it refers to how followers perceive their leaders. Such figures are seen as inspiring; they emerge in times of crisis and upheaval. Jesus Christ, Mahatma Gandhi, Martin Luther King and Adolf Hitler are examples. The role of Ayatollah Khomeini in transforming Iran after the fall of the Shah in 1979 is a more recent illustration. However, charismatic authority is short-lived unless it can be transferred to a permanent office or institution. 'It is the fate of charisma', wrote Weber (1957, p. 129), 'to recede with the development of permanent institutional structures'. This process is called the 'routinization' of charisma. Unusually for charismatic leaders, Ayatollah Khomeini succeeded in establishing a theocratic regime in Iran, dominated by the Islamic clergy, which continued after his death in 1989.

The third base for authority in Weber's scheme is called *legal-rational*. This is the opposite of charismatic authority. It means that obedience is owed to principles rather than individuals: in other words, government by rules. Authority inheres in a role or a position, not in an individual with charismatic or traditional powers. Weber believed legal-rational authority was becoming predominant in modern society and he was surely right. Indeed Weber's German homeland is the best example of a Rechtsstaat, an entire state based on law. One virtue of legal-rational authority is that it limits the abuse of power. Because it derives from the office rather than the person, we can speak of officials 'going beyond their authority'. Setting out the extent of an office-holder's authority reveals its limits, and so provides the opportunity for redress. In this way, legal-rational authority is a foundation of individual rights.

When the authority of a government is widely accepted, we describe it as 'legitimate'. Legitimacy is a similar idea to authority. The difference is simply that the term 'legitimacy' is normally used in discussing an entire system of government, whereas 'authority' often refers to a specific position. We speak of the legitimacy of a regime (system of government) but the authority of an official.

We need to make one final distinction: between legitimacy and legality. Legitimacy refers to whether people accept the validity of a law; legality denotes whether the law was made 'correctly' – that is, following regular procedures. Regulations can be legal without being legitimate. For example, the majority black population considered South Africa's apartheid 'laws' to be illegitimate, even though these regulations were made according to the country's then racist constitution. The same could be said of many laws passed by communist states: properly passed and even obeyed but not accepted as valid. Conversely, illegal action may be seen as legitimate by some sections of the population. Civil disobedience is one example, as with the American civil rights movement. Corruption, too, is often a legitimate part of politics even if it is technically illegal. 'You can make corruption illegal in Louisiana', said an old-time mayor of New Orleans, 'but you can't make it unpopular'. Corruption was integral to the state's politics. While legality is a topic for lawyers, political scientists are more interested in legitimacy: in how a regime gains and sometime loses the people's belief in its right to rule.

Why compare?

We have discussed politics and government but not, as yet, comparison. What does a comparative approach bring to the study of politics? Here we will outline four major virtues of the comparative approach, leaving a detailed discussion of the method to Chapter 16.

The first reason for comparison is the oldest, the simplest and the best. It is to find out more about the countries we know least about. In 1925, Munro described the purpose of his textbook on foreign governments as aiding 'the comprehension of daily news from abroad'. Because the focus of comparative politics is on states, background information about foreign governments not only helps to interpret new developments, it also enables us to view our own country in a fresh light. American students, for instance, are sometimes surprised to learn that their electoral system is one which most other countries have long since abandoned. Through comparison, say Dogan and Pelassy (1990), we discover our own ethnocentrism and the means of overcoming it. 'What should they know of England', asked Kipling in *The English Flag*, 'who only England know?'

The second reason for studying politics comparatively is to formulate and test hypotheses. Comparison enables us to develop and scrutinize such questions as: do plurality electoral systems (as in the USA and Britain) always produce a two-party system? Do revolutions only occur after a country has suffered defeat in war? As these questions illustrate, an hypothesis suggests a relationship between two factors: for instance between electoral and party systems, or between war and revolution. Verified hypotheses are valuable not just for their own sake, but because they can then help to account for the particular. Without comparison we would lack general knowledge of politics and therefore the ability to explain particular observations. As the American political scientist James Coleman tells his students, 'you can't be scientific if you're not comparing'.

The third reason for studying politics comparatively is that the generalisations which emerge sometimes have potential for prediction. If we find that the plurality method of election always produces a two-party system, we can predict that countries which switch to this formula will probably witness a fall in the number of parties represented in their parliaments. The term 'policy transfer' describes these attempts to learn from the successes (and avoid the fiascos) of other countries. Sometimes researchers choose to study specific countries precisely for their predictive value. Britain, for instance, was one of the first countries to travel down the privatization road; its journey now stimulates interest elsewhere. In the

1830s, to take an older example, de Tocqueville (1966 ed.) examined the United States because of his interest in politics in the new democratic age. America was his example but democracy was his subject:

> I confess that in America I saw more than America; I sought there the image of democracy itself, in order to learn what we have to fear or to hope from its progress.

In other words, America served as a prototype for a new form of politics.

The fourth advantage of comparison is that it improves our classifications of politics. Classification is a stepping stone on the journey to understanding. The Greek philosopher Aristotle (384–322) famously distinguished between government by the one (tyranny), the few (oligarchy) and the many (democracy). Armed with this scheme, Aristotle went on to examine the causes, characteristics and consequences of each type. Similarly, once we classify executives into presidential and parliamentary types, we can look at the origins and effects of each. But without a classification of governments, we have nothing to explain. In the remainder of this chapter, therefore, we introduce the key classifications which underpin this book. We distinguish between democratic and authoritarian states, between developed and developing states, and between consolidated and transitional states.

Democratic and authoritarian states

The contrast between democratic and authoritarian governments is the starting point for any classification of states. Democracy, in its various guises, is the most common form of government in the world today and we devote Chapter 2 to it. Here, we outline the main types of authoritarian rule; most feature in more detail later in the book.

The key feature of authoritarian government is that it denies the mass of the population any effective control over their rulers. Governments either keep the people out of decision-making altogether or just allow token opposition parties. The governing style is rough and ready, with rulers standing above, rather than controlled by, law. Authoritarian rulers do not heed individual rights; thus, authoritarianism is an illiberal, as well as undemocratic, form of rule.

> **Definition**
> Linz (1970) defined **authoritarian regimes** as
>
> political systems with limited, not responsible, political pluralism, without elaborate and guiding ideology . . . and in which a leader or occasionally a small group exercises power within formally ill-defined limits but actually quite predictable ones.
>
> **Totalitarian regimes** share the absence of pluralism but follow an explicit ideology and seek total control to implement their vision of a transformed society (on pluralism, see Chapter 7).

We should be wary, however, of exaggerating the similarities between authoritarian governments. As Box 1.2 shows, they form a more varied collection than do democracies. One dimension is whether an authoritarian government is led by a single figure (as with dictators), or takes a more collective form (as with military juntas – that is, councils). Aristotle made much of this distinction between government by the one and the few. However it needs to be supplemented by assessing the basis of rulers' power. Box 1.2 lists five kinds of authoritarian government: rule by monarchs, personal leaders, a dominant party, religious leaders and the military.

Besides the forms of authoritarian rule shown in Box 1.2, we must also introduce the idea of totalitarian government. This shares the nondemocratic character of authoritarianism but otherwise rests on different foundations. Totalitarian governments were mobilizing and revolutionary in character, committed to a total transformation of society. Where authoritarian leaders often wish to limit mass popular participation, totalitarian regimes sought to involve the masses in a reconstruction of society and even personality. In addition, where authoritarian rule is as old as history itself, totalitarianism was a philosophy of the twentieth century.

The two contrasting forms of totalitarian rule are fascism and communism. As ideologies, these are often placed on opposite wings, fascism on the extreme right and communism on the far left. Their theoretical goals certainly differed. Fascists favoured deference to a supreme leader (Hitler in Germany, Mussolini in Italy), while communists, in theory,

---

BOX 1.2
Forms of authoritarian government

• Ruling monarchs
These are now confined to remote Himalayan kingdoms such as Bhutan and some traditional societies of the Middle East such as Saudi Arabia. Buoyed by massive oil revenues, sovereign sheiks and sultans in the Middle East continue to rule in a personal fashion. Monarchs are found elsewhere, for example in much of Western Europe, but there democracy has reduced them to mere figureheads.

• Personal rule
This category of authoritarian rule developed from the experience of postcolonial societies in Africa (Jackson and Rosberg, 1982). Many personal rulers were 'hero-founders', charismatic figures who led the struggle for independence and then claimed an identity of interest with the nation they helped to found. Examples included Jomo Kenyatta (President of Kenya 1962–78) and Kenneth Kaunda (Zambia 1964–91). Personal leadership, often drawing on tribal traditions and relying on patronage, emerged naturally in African countries which were an artificial creation of European colonialists and therefore lacked strong governing institutions. However unlike ruling monarchies, personal rule lacks a succession procedure. Indeed the independence generation of African leaders has now disappeared, encouraging a transition toward democracy.

• Dominant parties
These are a form of authoritarian rule which tests the boundaries with democracy. The dominant party allows some electoral competition but it perpetuates its hold on power through control of the media, the resources of government and (if needed) the conduct of elections. The key feature of the dominant party is its control of public resources. This enables it to provide the framework of political competition; anyone wanting a share of the spoils must operate within its structures. Examples of dominant parties include Singapore's People's Action Party and Egypt's National Democratic Party. The grip of many dominant parties is now relaxing in response to democratic pressures.

• Rule by religious leaders
This is probably the least common form of authoritarian government. In modern times, Iran is the leading example. The Iranian revolution of 1979 led to Ayatollah Khomeini replacing the Shah as the country's ruler. Shi'ite Muslims, who form a majority in Iran, believe that the ulama (clergy) should rule directly and not rest content with advising secular rulers. These leaders draw on an Islamic philosophy which denies the separation, emblematic of the modern West, between religious and secular power. Although most countries with a Moslem majority are not Islamic states on the Iranian model, Islam influences the governance of some other nations: for example, Afghanistan, Libya, Pakistan and Sudan (Maley, 1997). It is also a source of conflict with secular rulers in such states as Algeria and Turkey. Islam provides the main remaining popular justification for authoritarian rule.

• Military rule
This was common in Africa, Asia and Latin America during the Cold War. The military frequently seized power in response to domestic political and economic problems and then remained there, with tacit or explicit support of the American or Soviet superpower. In office, military regimes followed a variety of paths. Some found the task of government beyond them; others used the national treasury to line their own pockets; and a few imposed a ruthless form of economic development. In the 1980s and 1990s, most ruling generals retreated to their barracks. Like personal rulers they were defeated by their limited success in office, the end of the Cold War and growing pressures for democracy.

---

advocated the goal of an equal and classless society. However, as systems of rule both forms employed totalitarian methods of control. And both sought to engage the masses not as masters but rather as servants of a political élite which sought to exploit the newly-discovered power of the state. We will briefly examine these two versions of totalitarianism.

More of an ideological impulse than a coherent system of government, *fascism*'s challenge ended with military defeat in 1945. Fascism was an extreme right-wing creed which glorified the nation (often defined in racial terms). Its theoretical purpose was to create an all-embracing nation-state to which the masses would show passionate commitment and submission. An autocratic ruler (führer or duce) and a single party would personify the state. State and nation were to become one. As Mussolini put it, 'everything in the state: nothing against the state: nothing outside the state'. Such ideas, the complete opposite of liberalism, underpinned Mussolini's fascist dictatorship of Italy and to a lesser extent Hitler's Nazi Party in Germany. Fascism was an attempt to use the power of the state, as revealed by the First World War, to revive the countries defeated in that conflict. It was the twentieth-century doctrine of nationalism taken to extremes (Eatwell, 1996).

The *communist* form of totalitarian rule proved to

be more coherent and resilient. Launched by the 1917 October Revolution in Russia, some 16 communist states (and a dozen more with dubious Marxist credentials) lasted until the late 1980s and early 1990s. In power, the communist system was heavily authoritarian. The ruling party could not be challenged effectively at elections and the party directed the government, ruling in the name of Marxism–Leninism. But communist rule was also strongly totalitarian. The party penetrated all aspects of life, dominating society to an unparalleled degree but thereby arresting social development. The party claimed to be building a new, equal and classless society and its transforming drive did initially deliver forced industrialization. However, the system then stagnated as the party sought above all to maintain its privileged position.

Communism collapsed in the USSR and Eastern Europe at the end of the 1980s, overwhelmed by a reform process initiated from the Soviet Union by Mikhail Gorbachev. Most of the surviving 'communist' states – principally China and Vietnam – have rejected Marx's original goals in favour of rapid economic development in which private enterprise plays a growing role. Symbolizing changing attitudes, China's pragmatic leader Deng Xiaoping (1902–1997) even declared, 'to get rich is glorious'. These modernizing communist regimes were never as totalitarian as the Soviet Union; now, they are best considered as authoritarian regimes with a monopoly party. Today, unreformed communism survives only in the form of shrivelled, isolated dictatorships as in North Korea and Cuba.

Communism's legacy is a brood of postcommunist countries which vary in political style and economic status (Table 1.1). Some, such as Hungary, are democracies with reasonably developed market economies. Others, such as the central Asian republic of Tajikistan, are developing countries with agricultural economies and limited democratic pretensions. The category of postcommunism cuts across the divide between developed and developing countries. Yet whether postcommunist countries are primarily industrial or agricultural, all such states have had to cope with the enormous problems inherited from the communist era. These included: distorted economies emphasising the military and heavy industrial sectors, severe pollution, large numbers of inefficient, loss-making state-owned enterprises, a massive black economy, poor tax collection, limited respect for law, endemic corruption, political cynicism, and economic collapse leading to mass unemployment in the initial shake-out after the end of communism. Most postcommunist states are now making progress with these problems; indeed a few are showing significant economic growth. However, the legacy of totalitarianism will continue to overhang social, economic and political development.

Consolidated and transitional states

Our second classification is whether states are consolidated or transitional. These ideas are less familiar than 'democratic' and 'authoritarian' so we must define our terms with care. A *consolidated* state is one in which the institutions of government are well-established and well-accepted. Political competition takes place within, but is not about, these institutions. All major players accept the rules of the political game. To use a word which will recur in this book, in a consolidated state the structures of power are 'institutionalized', providing a stable framework for political activity. Government institutions, the structure of the economy (public or private) and the relationship between the individual and the state are all well-established. It is important to note that a consolidated state is not static; indeed, the pace of change and transition can be rapid. However, a consolidated state accommodates change within an existing political framework. The peaceful transfer of power through elections is one means for building change on a foundation of stability.

Consolidated states are not necessarily democratic. Hereditary monarchies also possess a clear if irregular succession procedure. However the best contemporary examples of consolidated states are undoubtedly the developed Western democracies. The United States has operated with one constitution for more than 200 years (albeit maintained by force during the Civil War of 1861–65). The constitution sets out a set of values which underpins American society, legitimizing both individual rights and the market economy. The USA also illustrates how a consolidated regime can oversee a dynamic society. Despite constitutional stability, America is generally regarded as a fast-changing society. The point is that political consolidation provides a structure within which society and the economy can continuously evolve. We will discuss the notion of consolidation further when we examine transitions to democracy (Chapter 2).

> **Definition**
>
> A **consolidated state** provides an accepted framework for political competition. Governing institutions are well-developed, predictable and unchallenged. A **transitional state** is one which is seeking to establish or entrench a new form of government. In the contemporary world, the most common transition is from authoritarian rule toward democracy. However reverse movements also occur, as with military and fascist takeovers.

Transitional states are in a different situation. They are, by definition, moving from one form of rule to another. This is a challenging, unsettled and even explosive situation. The rules are made up as the game proceeds and actors matter more than institutions. In a consolidated regime, institutions typically dominate the political actors but during a transition the politicians themselves must craft new institutions. As Di Palma (1990, p. 9) says, 'whatever the historical trends, whatever the hard facts, the importance of human action in a difficult transition should not be underestimated'. Structures such as the executive and the legislature must become fully institutionalized – that is, they must acquire weight and autonomy, providing a framework rather than a topic for debate. But the participants realise that new institutions, once embedded, will entrench these gains and losses. So transition invariably creates winners and losers; the game of politics is played for high stakes. Yet even when a transition has occurred, the new regime will remain vulnerable to internal dissension and external attack. To consolidate, a transitional state must weather the hostility of the losers, and overcome the disillusionment which flows from inflated expectations.

The final decades of the twentieth century were a perfect time for studying political transitions. The most dramatic transition began with the collapse of communism at the end of the 1980s. This created 15 newly-independent states from the dissolution of the Soviet Union. Twelve Soviet satellites in Eastern

Table 1.1 Postcommunist states

State	Population, 1995 (million)
Eastern European states formerly under the control of the Soviet Union	
Albania	3.4
Bosnia–Herzegovina	3.2
Bulgaria	8.8
Croatia	4.7
Czech Republic	10.4
Hungary	10.3
Former Yugoslav Republic of Macedonia (FYROM)	2.2
Poland	38.8
Romania	23.2
Serbia and Montenegro	11.1
Slovakia	5.4
Slovenia	2.1
Total	123.6
States formed from the Soviet Union	
Armenia	3.6
Azerbaijan	7.8
Belarus	10.4
Estonia	1.6
Georgia	5.7
Kazakhstan	17.3
Kyrgyzstan	4.8
Latvia	2.8
Lithuania	3.9
Moldova	4.1
Russia	149.9
Tajikistan	6.2
Turkmenistan	4.0
Ukraine	51.8
Uzbekistan	23.1
Total	297.0

Source: CIA (1997).

Europe also became independent (see Map 1.1 and Table 1.1). All these countries faced massive challenges, particularly as most (including Russia and the Ukraine, the two largest) had no experience of democracy. The political problems which must be solved to consolidate a postcommunist democracy are immense. What can be done with the millions of state officials accustomed to a privileged life under the old regime? How can rulers retain the support of the population for a new system which immediately throws people out of work as loss-making factories close? The problems of transition are profound and we return to them in the next chapter.

Of course, the postcommunist world does not provide the only examples of transition. Latin American and African states are postmilitary, rather than postcommunist, societies. They face the difficulties of rebuilding civilian institutions after years, sometimes decades, in which such bodies were either abolished or treated with contempt by military strongmen. Healing the scars will be a long process.

Be it noted, transitions from democracy also occur. The collapse of democracy in some European countries between the wars, and military coups in the developing world in the decades after 1945, created postdemocratic regimes in which the task of consolidation fell to new authoritarian rulers. As the world moves towards predominantly democratic forms of government, it becomes more important to learn the lessons of these earlier transitions from democracy.

Developed and developing states

Classifying states by their system of government is insufficient for understanding comparative politics. The distinction between developed and developing countries, fundamentally an economic contrast, is just as important. Massive economic contrasts between countries yield contrasting political agendas for governments. For example, average income per head in the United States is almost 40 times greater than in Mozambique (see Table 1.2). Americans die from the diseases of affluence; people in Mozambique are killed by poverty. This is an extreme comparison but not a misleading one. In the least developed countries (LDCs) in Africa, for example,

millions have people have already died from hunger, disease and violence, and millions more face Hobbesian existences in conditions of accelerating environmental and social degradation: famines, chronic malnutrition, the collapse of health services, the erosion of education, reappearing endemic and epidemic diseases, AIDS, endemic criminal violence, civil wars and genocide. (Leys, 1996, p. 188)

Map 1.1 Postcommunist Eastern Europe

Table 1.2 Some subdivisions within the developed and developing worlds

Category	Definition	Examples (GDP per head, 1995)
Traditional developed countries	Advanced (post-) industrial societies	USA ($27 500), Japan ($21 300)
Newly industrial countries (NICs)	(Ex-)developing countries which have established a manufacturing capability and higher living standards	South Korea ($13 000), Mexico ($7 700)
OPEC countries	Members of the Organization of Petroleum Exporting Countries, some are wealthy but all are unequal	Kuwait ($17 000), Saudi Arabia ($10 100)
Middle income countries	Some development has occurred but inequality often still large. GNP per head at least $726 (World Bank definition, 1994)	Egypt ($2 760)
Least developed countries	The world's poorest countries. Limited manufacturing or literacy. Many are small African states.	Mozambique ($700), Niger ($500)

Note: GDP is gross domestic product, the total money value of all goods and services produced in an economy over a year. For comparison, gross world product per head in 1995 was $5,900.

Even to describe such countries as 'developing' involves a leap of faith.

Both the developed and the developing worlds are diverse. The developed world is perhaps the more straightforward, consisting at its core of countries with wealthy economies based on advanced manufacturing and service sectors. Knowledge and education increasingly serve as the driving force of economic growth. These countries also typically enjoy a long tradition of independent statehood and, in consequence, complex and elaborated institutions of government. Geographically, the developed world is concentrated on Western Europe, North America, Australia, New Zealand and Japan. One index of developed status is membership of the Organization for Economic Cooperation and Development (OECD), the club for rich countries.

To the established developed countries we must now add the newly industrial countries (NICs) such as Korea, Taiwan and Singapore. Since 1945 these have been among the fastest growing economies in the world. Even after the financial crises of the late 1990s, their overall affluence and the strength of their manufacturing sectors still exceeds that of some traditional developed countries. Certainly, the 'promotion' of the NICs from developing status shows how porous the developed/developing distinction has become. These newly-developed countries do not have the lengthy democratic traditions of the established developed countries. Nor, in many cases, are their economies yet fully open to international competition. However, many NICs have moved in a democratic direction, partly as a result of growing international contacts and pressures.

What of developing countries? Especially in the West, these tend to be defined by what they are not: non-developed, non-industrial, non-Western. Living standards are lower, sometimes tragically so, and the economy relies primarily on agriculture and on extractive industries such as mining. Exports are concentrated on a small range of commodities and manufacturing is small-scale, perhaps aided by routine assembly work for multinational companies. Educational standards are lower than in the developed world and literacy remains far from universal. Economic and social organization is still largely local, with limited penetration by the centre into outlying and especially rural areas. Most such coun-

> *Definition*
>
> **Development** is a difficult idea to define. Every country would prefer to be developed than developing but specifying the difference is partly a matter of opinion. Development implies growth, fulfillment and autonomy: the opposite of dependence. In economic terms (and this is the context in which we use the term), developed countries are taken to be industrial or postindustrial societies with high levels of income and education. Developing countries are a much more varied group but the least developed countries are marked by agricultural economies, limited urbanization, a small average income and low if improving literacy rates. To highlight the continuing impact of the colonial period on most of the 'developing' world, some authors prefer the term 'postcolonial' to 'developing'. (Hoogvelt, 1997)

tries are postcolonial in character, with economies which remain distorted by the supply of raw materials to the developed world.

Again, however, it is crucial to recognise the growing diversity within the broad category of 'developing country'. There is, for instance, a massive contrast between large middle-income states such as Brazil and Egypt, poorer but rapidly-growing economies such as China, and the least developed countries such as Niger. It is the least developed countries, including many small African states, which seem to be trapped in 'underdeveloped' status, with little prospect of achieving the rapid growth found in the larger developing countries of Asia and Latin America. Indeed the key question about developing countries is to explain these varied economic trajectories. Why have some achieved what Rostow (1971) called 'take-off' while others remain stuck on the runway, seemingly locked into a dependent relationship with the developed world? We examine this question in Chapter 3.

If the developed world consists of democracies old and new, what can we say about the the political complexion of the developing world? Certainly, the developing world contains most of the world's

surviving authoritarian regimes, from the ruling monarchs of the Middle East to the corrupt generals who run Nigeria. But the 1980s and 1990s witnessed a worldwide move towards democracy in developing countries. In Latin America, military dictators departed from formal positions of political power, replaced by rulers elected by more democratic means. In Africa, many personal rulers were replaced by governments elected in a somewhat more competitive fashion. As a result of this transformation the developing world now contains many of the world's newest democracies. However, the way that democracy operates in developing countries often differs markedly from procedures in the developed world. 'Semi-democracy', mixing democratic and authoritarian elements, is becoming more common. We explore this further in Chapter 2.

Key reading

> **Next step:** *Crick (1992, first pub. 1964) remains a lively and argumentative introduction to politics.*

Other excellent guides to politics include Dahl (1991) and Shively (1995). Governance is covered by Rosenau (1989) and Rhodes (1996). On the state, Hall and Ikenberry (1989) is a good starting-point, Dunleavy and O'Leary (1987) is comprehensive, while the World Bank (1997) offers the perspective of a key international agency on the state's role. Nationalism is examined historically by Breuilly (1993) and very accessibly by Kellas (1991). Boulding (1989) and Lukes (1974) provide contrasting perspectives on power; see Lukes (1986) for an edited collection. Watt (1982) provides an introduction to authority. On the distinction between developed and developing states, see Rostow (1971, 1987). Good accounts of politics in the developing world, such as Clapham (1985) and Bayart (1993), are probably the best sources on authoritarian rule. Jackson and Rosberg (1982) is the key account of personal rule in black Africa. Most texts on political ideologies, such as Heywood (1998) and Ball and Dagger (1995), cover communism and fascism.

Democracy

CHAPTER **2** |

limited forms emerging in much of the developing world. We must examine not just the underlying causes of the new democratic wave but also how politicians have gone about constructing their new regimes. And given continuing poverty in the developing world, we must ask whether democracy helps or hinders economic growth.

We live in a democratic world. Between 1975 and 1995 the number of democracies more than doubled from 36 to 78. At least half the countries of the world are now democratic and at least half the world's people now live in democracies. Both proportions are higher than ever before. In its current upsurge, democracy has expanded beyond its core of Western Europe and former colonies in North America, Australia and New Zealand. Democracy now embraces Southern Europe (for example Spain), Eastern Europe (for example Hungary), Latin America (for example Argentina), more of Asia (for example Taiwan) and parts of Africa (for example South Africa). The main refuges of authoritarian rulers are now Asia (notably China, Indonesia and Vietnam), the Middle East (for example Saudi Arabia) and Africa (notably Nigeria). All this amounts to a massive, and possibly irreversible, shift of the world's political landscape. Fukuyama (1989), for one, argues that the great conflict of ideas which dominated European and then world politics for 200 years after the French revolution has ended. Liberal democracy, and its ally the market economy, has triumphed.

Understanding the forms taken by democracy in today's world is therefore a central task. We must consider not just the version of democracy found in Western Europe but also the more contested and

Direct democracy

Democracy is a form of government, to be sure, but it is also an ideal, an aspiration and a standard. We cannot understand democracy simply by looking at examples, for judged against the democratic ideal even the most secure 'democracies' are found wanting. So what then is the core principle of democracy? The basic idea is self-rule: the word itself comes from the Greek *demokratia*, meaning rule by the people. Thus democracy – in its literal and richest sense – refers not to the election of the rulers by the ruled but to the denial of any separation between the two. The 'model' democracy is a direct democracy, a form of self-government in which all adult citizens participate in shaping collective decisions, in a context of equality and open deliberation. In a direct democracy, state and society become one.

The case for direct democracy is not just that those who are affected by decisions should have a say in making them. It is also that decisions reached by wide deliberation are likely to be better – more informed, more careful, more rational. This is because discussion allows the group to reconcile different interests, inform members about the issues and draw on the group's expertise. In short, debate enables people both to influence and to be influenced by the group. Thus decisions in a direct democracy are not necessarily or even best reached by voting. Indeed, the world's experience with mechanical instruments of direct democracy such as referendums is far from encouraging. Rather, the principle of direct democracy is to govern through seeking a consensus which emerges from careful deliberation of the options (Dryzek, 1990).

Ancient Athens is the classic example of a direct democracy. Between 461 and 322 BC, Athens was the leading city-state of Ancient Greece. Based on an area the size of Hong Kong it was small enough for all 40 000 citizens to meet together in an assembly, though rarely did more than half attend meetings. The assembly met around 40 times a year to settle issues put before it. Other offices (and there were about 1000) were filled by lot. These posts were rapidly rotated so that all citizens gained experience in the art of governing. Direct democracy was wide in scope: for example, military leaders were elected. Juries of several hundred people decided the fate of people accused of crimes; the jury that convicted Socrates of corrupting the young numbered over a thousand. As Dahl (1989, p. 18) writes,

> In the Greek vision of democracy, politics is a natural social activity not sharply separated from the rest of life . . . Rather political life is only an extension of, and harmonious with, oneself.

The democracy practiced by Ancient Athens had serious flaws. The vast majority of adults – including women, slaves and foreigners – did not qualify as citizens. If modern democracy is founded on the market economy, Athens was a democracy built on slavery; the labour of slaves created the time for the citizen élite to participate. In practice, orators and factions dominated debates. The lack of a permanent bureaucracy contributed to ineffective government, leading eventually to the fall of the Athenian republic after defeat in war. Finer (1997, p. 368) suggests that Athenian democracy was a dead end in that its functioning depended on a small city state which not only precluded expansion but was inherently vulnerable to predators: 'the polis was doomed politically if it expanded and doomed to conquest if it did not. It had to succumb and it did'. However, the Athenian model was crucial in establishing the democratic principle. Finer again:

BOX 2.1
Forms of democracy

Democracy
Broadly, rule by the people, or self-rule.

Direct (participatory) democracy
Citizens make decisions themselves, without representative institutions. This interpretation stresses the value of public discussion, both for the participants and for the quality of decisions.

Liberal democracy
Decisions are made by elected politicians who stand for the people (also called *representative government*). These elected leaders operate within formal limits designed to protect minority and individual rights. Such limits reflect the liberal goals of preserving individual rights and maximizing freedom of choice.

---

the Greeks invented two of the most potent political features of our present age: they invented the very idea of citizen – as opposed to subject – and they invented democracy.

Liberal democracy

The modern democracies of Western Europe, North America, Australia, New Zealand and Japan are usually called 'liberal democracies'. We can distinguish liberal from direct democracy in two ways. First, in a liberal democracy the people do not govern themselves Athens-style; rather, they elect politicians to do the job. The essence of liberal democracy lies not in self-government but in representative government. It is indirect rather than direct democracy. Second, a liberal democracy subjects the popular will to legal or constitutional limits. This is to protect individual rights to, for example, freedom of religion, speech and assembly. Power, even if acquired though fair election, can only be exercised within specified areas. Thus a liberal democracy is limited government.

But perhaps the real explanation for the success of *liberal* democracy lay in its provision of a framework for the development of the market economy. A system which protected private property but also enforced the rule of law provided fertile ground for commerce. As postcommunist economies have discovered, markets cannot flourish unless contracts, including property rights, are enforced. And where a thriving commercial sector does develop, it forms an independent source of power in society, further limiting the scope of government. Thus capitalism is integral to the liberal democratic mix.

To explore the contours of liberal democracy, we will examine its two core principles - representative and limited government.

Representative government

The achievement of representative government is the central achievement of modern politics. In its European homeland, it took several centuries (and as often as not a revolution) to consolidate representative institutions. Monarchs had to be brought under the control of the assembly. Then parliament, in its turn, had to be subjected to democratic election. Democratic elements had to be grafted onto ancient, predemocratic institutions of representation (Manin, 1997). Three main principles had to be conceded to bring about this transformation:

- *Freedom of expression*, to ensure that electoral choice was genuine
- *Popular sovereignty*, to establish that authority flowed from the ruled to the rulers
- *Political equality*, to give votes of equal value to all.

Viewed negatively, representative government appears as a mere shadow of direct democracy. More positively, it represents a triumphant compromise between élite rule and popular authority.

Definition

The idea of **representation** normally implies a principal and an agent, with the agent 're-presenting' the interests of the principal: for example, a lawyer representing a client in court. In representative government, decisions are reached by politicians elected to act on behalf of the voters. For a discussion of the varied forms of political representation, see Chapter 8.

The key strength of representative government is its practicality for large states. It resolves the problem of scale which bedevils direct democracy. The Athenians thought that the upper limit for a republic was the number of people who could gather to hear a speaker.

There is a case for saying that even this is too large. If politics is to be a true dialogue, giving everyone a chance to talk as well as listen, a group can surely be no larger than seminar size. But representative government allows even massive populations (such as 920 million Indians or 260 million Americans) to exercise some popular control over their rulers. And there is no upper limit. In theory, the entire world could become one giant representative system.

Representation also resolves the other democratic dilemma: how to combine popular preferences with expert judgment. In a direct democracy, open deliberation solves this problem: people learn about the issues through discussion which is central to the business of making a decision. But in representative government, this intensive method does not work. The population is too large, its interest in politics is too intermittent and the issues are too numerous. Instead, representative government limits the popular voice to determining *who* governs and allows these (presumably expert) politicians to decide *what* policies should be followed. It was for this reason that James Madison, an architect of the American constitution, believed a representative system was better, and not just more practical, than direct democracy. Representation, he thought, enabled the elected few 'to discern the true interests of the country'. Direct democracy, by contrast, was intolerant, unjust and unstable.

The theory of representative government owes much to Joseph Schumpeter (1883–1965), an Austrian-born economist who lived in the United States. Schumpeter accepted that élite rule was inevitable and desirable. But (and here is Schumpeter's contribution), he did not regard élite rule as incompatible with democracy. Rather he reinterpreted democracy as a system of *competing* élites. According to Schumpeter, the voter's role in a democracy is not, and should not be, to make decisions about the issues. Rather, the voter just selects from broad packages of policies and leaders prepared by rival parties. Schumpeter wanted to limit the contribution of ordinary voters because of his jaded view of their political capacity: 'the typical citizen drops down to a lower level of mental performance as soon as he enters the political field. He argues and analyzes in a way which he would recognize as infantile within the sphere of his real interests. He becomes a primitive again.'

Thus Schumpeter (1943, p. 269) was led to define democracy in purely procedural terms:

> the democratic method is that institutional arrangement for arriving at political decisions in which individuals acquire the power to decide by means of a competitive struggle for the people's vote.

In Schumpeter's view, this interpretation allows for the 'vital fact' of leadership. Direct democracy, based on continuing participation by active citizens, has given way to procedural democracy in which the citizen is passive. Democracy is simply a way of deciding who shall decide – a limited definition for a system whose watchword is practicality.

Limited government

Limited government is the second core characteristic of liberal democracy. Its purpose is to achieve the liberal goal of securing individual freedom – including freedom from unwarranted demands by government itself. Limited government is protective, seeking to protect not just minorities from majorities, but also the population from the rulers themselves. Liberal concerns about the abuse of power therefore qualify the exercise of democratic authority (Held, 1996). So liberal democracy qualifies the operation of the democratic principle itself.

Definition

The problem of **majority tyranny** arises because of the danger of the majority using its inherent power in a democracy to discriminate against minorities, ranging from ethnic groups to the very rich. **Limited government**, whether achieved through the constitution or through convention, is an attempt to address this difficulty.

Today we are likely to think of oppressed minorities – indigenous peoples, refugees, immigrants from another race – as the groups in most need of protection from an unsympathetic majority. And 'majority tyranny' is a particular danger where permanent majorities exist, as with Protestants in Northern Ireland. However, threatened minorities can also come from the top of the social scale. When the universal suffrage was emerging, property-owners and

the wealthy feared that democracy would bring about collective ownership and a massive redistribution of wealth (indeed, explaining why these threats never materialized is rather a puzzle). The élites of the time also believed that voters without property and education might lack the incentive and ability to use the franchise wisely. So, as insurance against 'democratic risk', conservatives sought to check the scope of popular rule. They achieved this by, for example, retaining a strong second chamber and ensuring legal protection for private property. Thus, limited government, and with it liberal democracy, is the outcome of a historical compromise. It is an uneasy but also creative synthesis of liberal and democratic principles.

All liberal democracies are based on representative and limited government. However, the weight given to these two principles varies. Today the USA, the most liberal of all the modern democracies, is the purest illustration of limited government, and this owes much to deliberate design. The founding fathers wanted, above all, to prevent tyranny. One of them, James Madison, wrote that 'the accumulation of all powers Executive, Legislative and Judicial in the same hands . . . may justly be pronounced the very definition of tyranny'. To prevent the government from acquiring too much power, the constitution set up an elaborate system of checks and balances between the institutions of government (Figure 2.1). Power checks power, to the point where it is often difficult for the government to achieve anything at all. The constitution contained the seeds of democracy but it placed government under law before government by all the people. American government was liberal before it was democratic. Many would argue that liberalism, not democracy, remains the guiding principle of American politics.

If the USA emphasises limited government, Britain gives priority to the representative element of liberal democracy. In Britain, a single party forms the government and holds extensive powers until the voters offer their verdict at the next election. Except for the governing party's sense of self-restraint, the institutions that limit executive power in the United States – such as a codified constitution – are absent. Instead the electoral rules give a secure majority of seats to a winning party. 'We are the masters now', trumpeted a Labour MP after his party's triumph in the British election of 1945. And a majority British

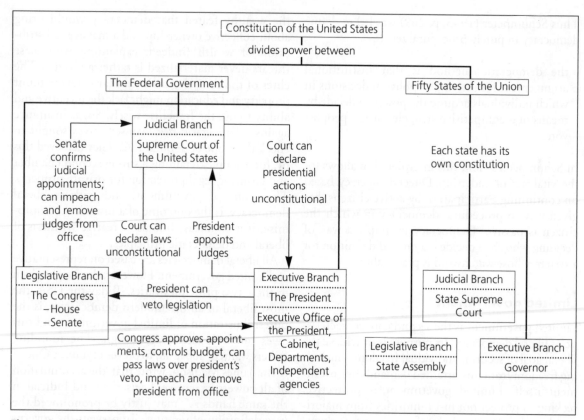

Figure 2.1 Liberal democracy: the US constitutional system

government is, in theory if not in practice, close to an elected dictatorship. The irony is that this concentration of power allowed the Labour government elected with a large majority in 1997 to introduce reforms (such as devolution to Scotland and Wales) which reduced its own direct power.

Before it introduced a more proportional electoral system in 1996, New Zealand was an even better illustration of a democracy in which governments claimed a mandate to do much as they liked. It is notable, though, that both Britain and New Zealand are considering reforms which would limit or eliminate majority governments. New Zealand has already adopted a more proportional electoral system while Britain is considering doing so. New Zealand adopted a Bill of Rights in 1990 while Britain proposes to incorporate the European Convention of Human Rights into UK law, allowing people to defend these rights in national courts. Such reforms strengthen, perhaps belatedly, the liberal aspect of these democracies.

Semi-democracy

As democracy has expanded beyond the Western world, so it has adapted to different conditions from those encountered in the West. Many developing countries are poor and unequal societies with little tradition of powerful representative insitutions. In these circumstances, the democratic principle has often been forced to coexist with authoritarian impulses. Democratic legitimacy is not wholly lacking; rather, it is acquired and exploited in dubious ways and often remains contested. The result is 'semi-democracy'. This hybrid is not new – Finer (1974) wrote about what he called 'facade democracy' – but it is becoming more prevalent. The crucial point is that we should not think of democracy and authoritarianism just as whole systems of government. Rather, each principle can provide pockets of power which can coexist, sometimes indefinitely, within the one political system. Semi-democracy is a cloth fashioned from mixed

EXHIBIT 2.1

Agreeing to avoid democracy: the case of central banks

Although it is instinctively appealing to believe that all collective decisions should be subject to democratic decision, many liberal democracies have restricted, or are restricting, the role of elected politicians in controlling the money supply, setting interest rates and implementing inflation targets. Both the German Bundesbank and the American Federal Reserve Board set and pursue their own monetary objectives, with the Bundesbank not even required to offer a full justification for its actions. The independence of the new European Central Bank will be enshrined in its constitution. More significantly, two democracies which traditionally gave most power to elected politicians, New Zealand and the United Kingdom, have now granted more autonomy to their central banks. Under the Reserve Bank Act 1989, New Zealand's Reserve Bank is required to pursue the single objective of controlling inflation without ministerial intervention (Mulgan 1997, p. 138). And greater independence for the Bank of England was one of the first acts of Tony Blair's Labour administration. The justification for the independence of central banks is not that it entrenches individual rights, the traditional argument for restricting democratic scope in a liberal democracy. Rather, the proposition is simply that central bankers will make a better fist of the job than elected politicians, who are prone to manipulate the money supply for short-term electoral reasons. Democracies are, it seems, concluding that democracy does not always yield sound policy.

Further reading: Dalziel (1993), Kettl (1986).

yarns. Crouch (1996, p. vii), for instance, shows how Malaysia's 'repressive–responsive' regime combines democratic and authoritarian features in a manner that 'provides the foundation for a remarkably stable political order'.

Definition

A **semi-democracy** blends democratic and authoritarian elements. In one form of semi-democracy, 'democratic despots' control the electoral process. Individual rights are violated and 'independent' bodies such as the media are carefully monitored. Kenya under President Moi is an example; in cases such as Singapore and Egypt, the controlling force is a party more than an individual. In the other form of semi-democracy, 'democratic puppets' are, despite their status as elected leaders, manipulated or constrained by other power-holders such as the military, ethnic leaders or criminal gangs. Several of the smaller postsoviet republics, such as Uzbekistan, fit this pattern.

One form of semi-democracy arises when a dominant party or leader sets the framework for political competition. In these conditions, opposition can survive but not flourish. One way of achieving this is through semi-competitive elections.

'Democratic despots' use control over money, jobs, contracts, pensions, public housing, the media, the police, the electoral system, the courts and if needed the election count to deliver success. Egypt and Tunisia are examples of countries where elections have long been semi-competitive. Such methods are often combined with effective governance and a favourable disposition toward a dominant ruler or party. For example, Singapore's People's Action Party may manipulate elections in its favour but it has also made Singapore a richer country, on a per person basis, than Britain.

Opposition can also be kept under control by intimidation. Semi-democracies are illiberal democracies in which policies are pushed through with scant concern for their impact on particular groups or communities. Institutions such as the assembly and the judiciary are cowed by the dominant force. This enables semi-democratic regimes to rough up their opponents and harass dissidents, tactics which are often wrapped in a nationalist cloak. In many postsoviet republics, for instance, politics is an extremely rough game, fought between rival clans which are not averse to using violence to make a point. Ordinary 'citizens' may have a vote and their rights are tolerably secure when the interests of the regime are not at stake. But citizens become accus-

BOX 2.2

Synonyms for semi-democracy

Political scientists use a range of terms to refer to what we call semi-democracy. These phrases include:

> authoritarian democracy
> contested democracy
> delegative democracy[1]
> *democradura*[2]
> electoral democracy
> facade democracy
> guided democracy
> illiberal democracy
> limited democracy
> low-intensity democracy
> partial democracy
> plebiscitary democracy
> presidential democracy[1]
> restricted democracy
> supervised democracy
> tutelary democracy[1]

[1] meaning a strong national leader (usually a president) is 'delegated' through elections to act as guardian for the nation (O'Donnell 1996).

[2] a Spanish blend of *democracia* (democracy) and *dictadura* (dictatorship).

tomed to the sound of gunfire. They know when to lie low.

In a semi-democracy based on a dominant party or individual, power is concentrated in a few hands. But there is another form of semi-democracy in which elected rulers have too little power. Here elected rulers are puppets rather than despots. In this version, 'power may be shifted to the military, bureaucracy or top business groups' (Case, 1996, p. 439). Thus elected politicians must continue to battle against military, ethnic, religious and regional leaders. Such people seek to maintain their established privileges and they claim more insight into the national interest than mere elected leaders. Such conflicts are signs of a contested democracy where elections are established but do not function as definitive statements of who should exercise final decision-making power. In Thailand, Turkey and Pakistan, among others, the military stand as a guardian of the nation, exerting a 'silent veto' over civilian decisions (Gills, Rocamora and Wilson, 1993, pp. 21–8). In many postmilitary democracies in Latin America, the armed forces continue to demand special privileges for their own sphere. These perks include seats in the cabinet and a guaranteed share of the budget.

In some postsoviet republics, too, the power élite shows little respect (contempt might be more accurate) for elected authority. The communist party may have reformed, and many state-owned enterprises may have been sold to the private sector, but the same people continue in power having changed nothing more than their hats. The group which ruled under communism continues in power, prospering by selling state assets to itself on the cheap: piratization rather than privatization. In such circumstances, the president is merely the mouthpiece of a dominant and corrupt élite, and elections are just plebiscites to confirm the élite's choice of top leader. Real power comes from patronage and from deals with regional and ethnic power brokers or even with criminal gangs. In this type of semi-democracy ('quarter-democracy' might be more accurate), power gives the capacity to take elected office but elected office does not add much power.

The ways of semi-democracy are a sobering reminder to those who take a naive view of the 'triumph of democracy'. Simplistic counts of the number of democracies do not tell the whole story. As quantity has increased, quality has fallen. Why is it, then, that so many new democracies turn out, on closer inspection, to be only semi-democratic? There are two answers, the optimist's and the pessimist's. The optimist's view is that semi-democracy is merely transitional, a temporary staging post in the world's pilgrimage from authoritarian rule to full democracy. This is certainly a possibility. After all, nearly all Western democracies passed through a stage of competitive oligarchy, meaning that the contest for power became open and legitimate before the vote became universal. Even in the United States, democracy took decades to establish. Also, a fully developed and open economy may prove to be incompatible with semi-democracy, which often operates 'crony capitalism' – that is, political leaders distort market allocations to bolster their own support.

But to assume that semi-democracy will turn out to be transitional is to stake a large bet on the future. And it would be a logical error to infer that because all current democracies were once semi-democratic, therefore all today's semi-democracies will eventually become fully democratic. It is prudent to

EXHIBIT 2.2

Is there such a thing as 'Asian democracy'?

Many Asian leaders reject aspects of the Western democratic tradition. They claim to be building a distinctive form of 'Asian democracy' (sometimes called 'illiberal democracy' in the West). For example, the rulers of Malaysia and Singapore explicitly reject the Western interpretation of liberal democracy based on individual rights. They favour an approach which gives more weight to Asian values, including respect for authority, avoiding public conflict and accepting the primacy of the group. Democracy is defined in almost familial terms, with the elected leader adopting a paternal style. The state leads society, and democracy therefore depends less on the independent groups and associations which provide the counterpoint to the Western state. The institutional consequences of 'Asian democracy' include a subservient media and judiciary. In addition, the police and security forces become more aggressive in their approach to criminals and dissenters.

The case for
The attempt to develop non-Western models of democracy derives in part from the natural cynicism of former subjects to their colonial 'masters'. Asian leaders reject what they see as imperialist attempts to 'universalize' the Western model. Dr Mahathir, Prime Minister of Malaysia, condemns Western democracies 'where political leaders are afraid to do what is right, where the people and their leaders live in fear of the free media which they so loudly proclaim as inviolable'. A former foreign minister of Vietnam exposed Western hypocrisy more bluntly: 'Human rights? I learnt about human rights when the French tortured me as a teenager'. Further, the Asian model has delivered economic growth by allowing leaders to focus on long-term modernization free from electoral pressures. Thus Prime Minister Goh of Singapore suggests that

> our government acts more like a trustee. As a custodian of the people's welfare, it exercises independent judgement on what is in the long-term economic interests of the people and acts on that

basis. Government policy is not dictated by opinion polls or referenda.

The case against
Critics allege that 'Asian democracy' is simply an excuse for failing to move beyond semi-democracy. Putzel (1997, p. 253) roundly declares that 'claims for "indigenous forms of democracy" appear to be no more than justifications for authoritarian rule'. And Brzezinski (1997, p. 5) suggests that 'the "Asian values" doctrine is nothing but a rationalization for a certain phase of historical development'. By this he means that through accidents of history Western societies have more experience with protecting individual freedom. Asia, Brzezinski suggests, is still playing catchup, both economically and politically. And the financial crisis which engulfed East Asia in 1997 will require most countries in the region to reduce the state's role in the economy, yielding a rather more liberal form of democracy. Finally, a Western human rights activist argues that democracy and human rights are inherently universal:

> There is nothing special about torturing the Asian way. Rape is not something that is done an Asian way. Rape is rape, torture is torture and human rights are human rights. (Vatikiotis 1996, p. 98)

Assessment
The debate on Asian democracy will not be resolved easily. It mixes analysis, ideology and colonial memories in an explosive combination. But two points are clear. The first is that Asia has never been a single category. China is authoritarian, Indonesia largely so, Singapore is a semi-democracy and Japan is a consolidated democracy. Second, rather than referring to 'Asian' democracy, it might be more useful to consider the kind of democracy best suited to economic development. The Western model may be appropriate for developed countries while the 'Asian' approach is more effective in countries which are still growing their industrial capacity.

Further reading: Bell (1995).

consider a more pessimistic account of semi-democracy: that it is a stable method of governing poor and unequal societies, particularly in a postcommunist era when blatant dictatorship has become unacceptable. When poverty coincides with extreme inequality, and when ethnic divisions are strong, the prospects of creating a democratic community of equals are slender (Gills, 1997). In practice, power remains with the rich, the landowners and other 'big men' who may exploit but can also offer a measure of protection to the poor. The institutions of the central state are often still weak and so therefore will be any democracy built upon them; semi-democracy may be the best that can be had. For such reasons, Case (1996, p. 464) concludes that semi-democracy is not 'a mere way station on the road to further democracy'.

Further, semi-democracy is usually sufficient for the ruling élite to meet the conditions of aid set by the World Bank, the IMF and donor governments. While these international bodies may welcome democracy, in practice they give higher priority to economic reform. The heart of the matter is that semi-democracy is a tacit, and possibly stable, compromise between domestic élites and international organizations.

Conditions of democracy

The problem of explaining why some countries are democratic, and others not, has long preoccupied political scientists. Why should India be a democracy while China is still governed by authoritarian rulers? Why has democracy proved to be stable in North America but intermittent (until recently) in Latin America? What, in short, are the conditions in which democracies emerge and flourish?

One approach to the conditions of democracy is the modernization framework, associated with Lipset. The central claim here is that affluence breeds stable democracy. In *Political Man* (1983, first pub. 1960), Lipset concluded that 'the more well-to-do a nation, the greater the chances that it will sustain democracy'. Like his many followers, Lipset used statistical data to support his thesis. He showed that stable democracies scored higher than did authoritarian regimes on such measures as income per person, literacy and the proportion of the population living in cities. More recent research confirms that the correlation between affluence and stable democracy still exists, though democracy can now consolidate at lower levels of national income. Huntington (1991), for instance, showed that the wealthier a non-democracy was in 1970, the more likely it was to have become democratic by 1989. Democratic transitions were concentrated on the middle-income countries of Latin America and Eastern Europe, not the poorest countries of South Asia and Africa. Summarizing the research stimulated by Lipset's theory, Marks and Diamond (1992, p. 110) describe the connection between affluence and democracy as 'one of the most powerful and stable relationships in the study of comparative national development'.

How exactly does affluence breed democracy? What are the mechanisms involved? Here the statistical work pioneered by Lipset is less helpful; his results show, but cannot in themselves account for, a correlation. Lipset did make a few suggestions. He thought that economic development and education encouraged a large middle class opposed to extremism. He also believed that a lower class living above absolute poverty would no longer be seen as inherently inferior by the upper class. In general, affluence seems to reduce inequality, temper class conflict and distribute power resources so widely that no single group can dominate all others (Vanhanen, 1997). All these are conditions which favour a democratic compromise.

The alternative approach to the conditions under which democracy develops is more historical. Within this tradition, the focus is on how societies manage the transition from an agricultural to an industrial society and the implications this has for the kind of political system which results. The pioneering work here is Barrington Moore's *Social Origins of Dictatorship and Democracy* (1966). Where Lipset concentrates on the impact of whether a society is modernized, Moore examines the legacy of how a society makes the great journey from agrarian to industrial status. Moore's method is comparative history; he asks why the route to modernity led Japan and Germany to fascism, Russia and China to communist revolutions, and England, France and the United States to liberal democracy. (Today, of course, all these countries except China are democratic. Thus from a contem-

EXHIBIT 2.3

Democracy without affluence/affluence without democracy

There will will always be exceptions to any generalization in comparative politics (except this one!). Lipset's link between affluence and democracy is an example. Among poor countries, India is the massive 'deviant case'. Since achieving independence from Britain in 1947, India has sustained the world's largest democracy despite extensive poverty, illiteracy and inequality. Randall (1997) attributes this unique achievement to three factors:

- The pluralistic Hindu religion
- The liberal norms instilled by British colonialism
- The remarkable if fading capacity of the Congress Party to integrate a fragmented society.

At the other extreme, oil-rich Middle East states such as Saudi Arabia and Kuwait have proved immune to democratic trends. This is despite levels of affluence per person which are among the highest in the world. But these countries have undergone unbalanced development in which oil wealth is controlled by a few ruling families, and much menial work is done by immigrant labour with few rights. Buttressed by a strong military, the traditional elite maintains a paternalistic and nondemocratic governing style. The deal which these rulers can afford to offer to their people is unique: no taxation, therefore no representation.

Exceptions such as India and Middle East oil states do not 'disprove' the existence of a relationship between national income and democracy. Rather, one value of the modernization thesis is precisely that it allows us to identify such exceptions in need of special explanation.

porary perspective Moore's analysis is best viewed as an analysis of how variations in the historical process of modernization produced contrasting routes to democracy).

Definition

The **modernization thesis**, associated with Lipset (1960), asserts that wealthier countries are more successful at sustaining democracy. This is because economic development reduces poverty and class conflict as well as bringing about an educated and tolerant middle class. The **historical approach** to democracy, linked with Barrington Moore (1966), argues that democracy is an outcome of a particular transition to industrial society. Specifically, the rise of the business class must not be arrested by either reactionary landowners or a powerful state.

The crucial factor is whether the emerging class of industrial employers can develop without being blocked. 'No bourgeoisie, no democracy', says Moore. So Moore, like many others, sees democracy as the political expression of capitalist development, a conclusion supporting Lipset's idea that a large middle class helps to stabilize democracy. England,

for example, followed a path of balanced modernization; neither the aristocracy nor the state could resist pressures for change. This freed the rising urban class of industrialists not only to develop economically but also to press for a more liberal, though not at that stage democratic, political system. Thus the business class emerged as a dominant force, establishing the principle of a market economy in which labour becomes just another commodity, freely bought and sold. The old feudal order, based on the fixed hierarchies of the countryside, fell apart. The individualistic foundations of liberal democracy were laid.

In many countries, however, this programme of capitalist development was blocked. Powerful landowners proved to be the main source of resistance. A landed aristocracy exploiting a dependent peasantry (for example through serfdom or other coercive devices) used its political power to prevent a gradual transition to an industrial society. In some countries the landowners sought a reactionary alliance with a powerful state; balanced modernization was prevented, democracy was impossible and political revolution became a likely outcome. The nature of this revolution varied, however. Where the peasantry could be mobilized, as in China, a communist revolution became possible. Where the peasantry was weak, the dominant reactionary class might eventually impose repression through fascism, as in Germany. Such revolutions delayed the development of democracy. Germany did not establish a liberal democracy, in its Western section, until fascism's defeat in 1945. And of course China remains an authoritarian state to this day.

Transitions to democracy

The wave of democratization since the 1970s has given political scientists a fine opportunity to observe democracy-building at first hand. This has led to a shift away from the broad modernization and historical approaches adopted by Lipset and Barrington Moore. Recent research has focused less on the underlying conditions of democracy, and more on the immediate tactics of transition. The intellectual problem here is to understand how the choices made by politicians in the move from authoritarianism affect the pace, form and outcome of regime change. This approach places more emphasis on human agency; history is not destiny and democracy must be crafted (Di Palma, 1990).

Dankwart Rustow (1970) established the field of 'transitology', the study of democratic transitions. Rustow's question was not, what factors encourage democratic stability? Rather he asked: how do politicians bring a democracy into being in the first place? And his answer, broadly, was that democracy is a bargain reached by conflicting groups which come to recognize the inevitability of power-sharing. Groups which recognise the impossibility of monopolizing power make do with a settlement which at least offers the chance to win office through elections. Although Rustow's approach was very different from Lipset's, he reached a similar conclusion: democracy is compromise. South Africa's transition from white rule is a textbook example. As Johnson and Schlemmer (1996, p. 9) comment, 'the three main parties hammered out an essentially liberal democratic constitution although none of them much believed in it'. Democracy's success, in South Africa and elsewhere, rested on being everyone's second choice: optimal for no-one, acceptable to everyone.

A major finding of transitology is the central role played by political élites. Even if democracy is made *for* the people, it is rarely made *by* them. Democracy is 'imposed' from above. On Latin America, Little (1997, p. 181) suggests that

> pressure from below was only rarely a factor in the democratization process. Where this took radical form (as in Guatemala and El Salvador) it led to a tightening of authoritarian control and only in Nicaragua in 1979 did popular protest succeed in overthrowing authoritarianism.

Indeed, Diamandouros *et al.* (1995, p. 403) even advocate 'a strategic demobilization of the masses during élite negotiations' so that élites can agree the transition in a calm atmosphere.

We can divide democratization into three phases: liberalization, transition and consolidation. In the liberalization phase, the authoritarian regime relaxes its controls, eases repression and permits more open political competition. Political prisoners may be released and media censorship reduced. For instance, in South Africa the white regime legalized the African National Congress and released Nelson Mandela from prison in 1990. Liberalization is most often triggered by a sense of failure within the authoritarian coalition itself as existing rulers recognize that the regime is declining in both effectiveness and legitimacy. Military defeat is a visible manifestation of this diminished capacity, as with Argentina's defeat in the Falklands (Malvinas) in 1982. In addition, the onset or prospect of a succession crisis (still to come in some authoritarian states in East Asia) also provides an opportunity for liberalization.

Even at this early stage, existing rulers begin to plot their own political (and sometimes personal) survival strategies. The balance between hardliners and softliners is particularly important here. Hardliners typically include people such as security chiefs and other extreme right-wingers who could expect to be out of a job (and possibly in jail) under a new regime. Softliners, by contrast, are willing to negotiate with the prodemocracy forces, hoping to find a niche in the new order.

Liberalization creates its own momentum. As political space opens, so the opposition gains strength; finally, the existing rulers realise their time is over. In South Africa, President de Klerk soon found his power leaking away to Nelson Mandela and the ANC. Mikhail Gorbachev may have set out to reform communism in the Soviet Union but he ended as its undertaker, overwhelmed by the reforming forces he himself had unleashed (Brown, 1996). Thus the scene is set for the transition proper to begin.

In the **transition** phase, the old regime is dismantled and democratic institutions are established. A democratic transition is complete when a freely-elected government is installed with sovereign authority. Transitions occur in two main ways (Linz, 1978). The most common is reform, which means the existing élites take the lead in initiating peaceful change. Examples include Spain after Franco (1975), Brazil after the army decided to step down (1985) and Hungary after the communists (1989). The other mode of transition is called rupture. Here, the opposition takes the initiative and the old regime, rather than collapsing from within, is destroyed from without, if necessary by violence. Rupture is an uncommon and uncertain road to democracy. In Romania, for instance, the Ceaucescu dictatorship was overthrown by violence in 1989. But ex-communists captured the revolution and their leader Ion Iliescu remained in power as president until defeated in an election in 1996 – a lengthy transition indeed.

Whether the transition starts by reform or by rupture, at some point round-table discussions take place between the relevant actors, within and without the government. These negotiations cover not just hardliners and softliners within the old regime but also moderate reformers (who respect the position of the previous rulers) and radical reformers (who prefer a complete break). These discussions typically take place outside the normal governing institutions, creating a fluid political situation within which both compromise and mistakes are possible.

In Eastern Europe, round-table talks took place between the old communists and national reform movements such as Solidarity in Poland. The key players around the reform table in South Africa were de Klerk's National Party and Nelson Mandela's African National Congress plus, eventually, the Inkatha Freedom Party. One specific form of round-table talks is the National Conference, a common

---

BOX 2.3
Stages in the transition to democracy

- **Liberalization**
The authoritarian élite relaxes its grip, allowing opposition to organize.

- **Transition**
The old regime is dismantled, a new system of government is agreed and founding elections are held.

- **Consolidation**
All major actors become accustomed to the new democracy, accepting it as the only game in town.

---

device in French-speaking Africa. A National Conference is a large meeting of all the major political forces which sets itself up as constitution-maker for the new order (Wiseman, 1996).

Whatever form the negotiations take, the outcome is normally a formal agreement between the contending players – hence the phrases 'negotiated' or 'pacted' transitions. Sometimes, the old regime simply gives in and accepts that the next election will be competitive: Hungary's peaceful transition from communism was an example. But the danger is that in the negotiations, elements of the old order will secure concessions which result in an incomplete transition. For instance, the military retains its traditional privileges in several new 'democracies' of Africa and Latin America. Reforming in stages may be the only viable strategy but it runs the risk of

---

BOX 2.4
Actors in the transition to democracy

Within the old regime:

- Hardliners (standpatters) oppose reform.
- Softliners are willing to negotiate over liberalization and/or democratization.

Within the opposition:

- Radicals favour a clean break; no compromise with the old regime!
- Moderates respect the difficulties of the old rulers and are willing to compromise.

diverting the transition into the siding of semi-democracy.

Consolidation is the final phase of democratization. A democracy has consolidated when it provides an accepted framework for political competition. As Przeworski (1991, p. 26) put it,

> democracy is consolidated when under given political and economic conditions a particular system of institutions becomes the only game in town and when no one can imagine acting outside the democratic institutions.

As President Havel noted in Czechoslovakia after communism's collapse, consolidation is a separate stage from transition: 'we have done away with totalitarianism but we have yet to win democracy'.

To consolidate, a democracy must offer the real prospect of an election victory for the opposition. This gives the opponents of the current rulers an incentive to accept the political system as a whole. And the acid test comes on the first occasion when an election does lead to defeat for the government. If the losers accept the voters' verdict, removing their hands from the levers of power, then democracy is well on its way to becoming 'the only game in town'. Thus the extent of democratic consolidation in South Korea was confirmed by the presidential election of 1997, which saw the first peaceful transfer of power to the centre-left in the country's history. The virtue of a peaceful transfer, once it has been achieved, it that it establishes the distinction between the system of government and the present incumbents. The outcome of consolidation is a system which is permanent precisely because rulers come and go by regular means.

Running counter to research on political culture, most scholars suggest that a consolidated democracy does not require the political élite to show a consensus around democratic principles. The requirement is that all the powerful actors must *abide* by the rules of the game even though they may not *believe* in them. They must see no realistic alternative to democracy. Thus the object of consolidators is not so much to win the hearts and minds of the antidemocrats. Rather the idea is to confine these dangerous tendencies to their lair. In these circumstances, opposition fades because it is unable to express itself. So consolidation is, in Rustow's apt term, a matter

---

BOX 2.5

Huntington's three waves of democratization

Wave	Period	Examples
First	1828–1926	Britain, France, USA
Second	1943–1962	India, Israel, Japan, West Germany
Third	1974–1991	Southern and Eastern Europe, Latin America, much of Africa

Note: the first wave was partly reversed between 1922–42 (for example in Germany, Italy and Poland) and the second wave similarly between 1958–75 (for example in much of Latin America and postcolonial Africa).

Source: Huntington (1991).

---

of 'habituation': 'democratic rules must be not so much believed in as applied'.

Transitions to democracy vary in difficulty. The first wave of democracies, such as Britain, Scandinavia and the United States, enjoyed a leisurely transformation, with the gap between liberalization and consolidation stretching over centuries. The extension of the suffrage occurred gradually, often without any clear notion that the outcome would be a representative democracy based on universal suffrage. Democracy was a result rather than an intention. But later waves of democratizers expected quicker results; and they had a democratic objective in mind from the start. After their defeat in the Second World War, for instance, Japan and West Germany moved rapidly from dictatorship to democracy. Modern transitions are compressed: managed revolution more than unplanned evolution. In view of this, it is remarkable that the new democracies so rapidly established since the 1970s have consolidated so successfully.

A major explanation of this accomplishment was a favourable global and regional context. The end of the cold war meant dictators could no longer hide under the skirts of a superpower. The collapse of communism destroyed the credibility of the major alternative to liberal democracy. Leading players such as the United States and the European Union, and sympathetic institutions such as the World Bank, began to promote democracy. Often, a favourable regional context also eased transition. Greece, Portugal and Spain – and more recently

Poland, Hungary and the Czech Republic – undoubtedly benefited from their position close to the heartland of European democracy. In a similar way, Mexico's emerging transition from semi-democracy owes something to its trading links with the USA, consolidated through NAFTA. Indeed Diamond (1997, p. 39) suggests that 'the greatest regional force for democratic consolidation in the Americas may well be the move towards regional free trade'. These global and regional factors allowed the third wave of democracy to function like a snowball, gathering momentum as it rolled round the world from one country to the next. Thus global forces underlie national transitions to democracy (Whitehead, 1996).

The ease of a transition to democracy is influenced by the nature of the previous regime. The shift from communist rule is particularly fraught because it involves a triple move: from communism to democracy, from a planned to a market economy and from arbitrary power to the rule of law. More than military regimes, communist rulers controlled all aspects of society. As a result, their postcommunist successors must encourage social institutions as well as consolidating a new political and economic order. They must aim to develop social capital at a time of political change, economic dislocation and nationalist assertion, a challenging project indeed.

While the focus of recent research has been on transitions to democracy, history also provides some instances of transitions *from* democracy (Linz and Stepan, 1978). The classic democratic breakdowns were Germany, Italy and Spain in interwar Europe. Military coups in Latin America during the 1970s are another instance. However it is rare for consolidated democracies to disintegrate; the democracies most likely to fall apart are ones that were never fully legitimate in the first place. For example, military coups in postcolonial Africa replaced liberal democratic forms which departing colonialists had constructed in haste, with little concern for long-term effectiveness. Similarly, in interwar Germany, the Weimar Republic overthrown by Hitler was never fully legitimate nor particularly effective.

When democracies do collapse, the underlying cause is often the same as for authoritarian regimes. The crucial factor is the inability of the government to resolve pressing problems, economic or military.

This suggests that the prognosis for democracy over the next few decades is favourable but not guaranteed. The future health of democracy depends on the continuing capacity of rulers to prevent or resolve social, economic and military problems. In the twenty-first century, there may be no coherent alternative to liberal democracy and the market economy. But this will not be enough to prevent demagogues from seeking to exploit the opportunities provided by disillusioned citizens, particuarly in ethnically-divided societies where national boundaries remain contested. Democracy may be partly 'self-legitimizing' in that people who help to shape decisions then feel obliged to abide by them. But democracy, like any other form of rule, will also continue to be judged by results. It must rely on its old friend, the market economy, to deliver the goods.

Democracy and development

For many people, development must take priority over democracy. A mother with a hungry child may cherish her vote but she must value food even more. So, to assess the value of democracy we must assess whether it contributes to or retards economic development. Can democracy and development go hand in hand or must we make a tough choice between them?

Clearly, some authoritarian regimes have generated rapid growth. In the twentieth century the main examples were communist governments in the first half and the Asian tigers in the second. As Sorensen (1993) suggests, economic development requires investment and nondemocratic regimes are well-placed to resist popular pressures for immediate consumption. Authoritarian rulers can create an economic surplus for long-term investment because they are better insulated from the political crosscurrents generated by rapid economic change. Simply put, they can ignore the losers. And nondemocratic governments can also provide the enormous intervention needed for rapid industrialization. Sorensen (1993, p. 65) again: 'in the twentieth century there was no case of successful economic development without comprehensive political action involving massive state intervention in the economy'.

We can illustrate these points by comparing the

Country profile **MEXICO**

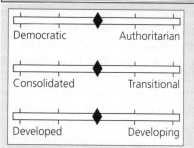

Population: 96m.
Gross domestic product per head:
$7 700.
Form of government: a federal and presidential republic.

Legislature: the 500 members of the Chamber of Deputies, the lower house, are elected for a five-year term. The 128 members of the Senate are elected for a three-year period, with four Senators per state.

Executive: the president, directly elected for a non-renewable six-year term, heads both the state and the government, choosing the members of the Cabinet. The PRI has won every presidential election it has contested.

Judiciary: headed by the Supreme Court of Justice, the judicial system mixes American constitutional principles with the civil law tradition. In practice, judges have been strongly influenced by the ruling PRI.

Party system: dominated by the PRI until the 1990s. Other major parties are the conservative National Action Party (PAN) and the left-wing Revolutionary Democratic Party (PRD).

Electoral system: 300 members of the Chamber represent single-member districts, the other 200 are elected by the list system of proportional representation. The Senate also operates a mixed electoral system.

'A watershed', 'a turning point', even 'a peaceful revolution' – these were some of the phrases used to describe the 1997 elections to Mexico's Chamber of Deputies. After a relatively free and fair election, the PRI lost its majority in the lower house for the first time in its history, winning only 239 seats. Mexico had entered unknown territory. It faced a period of French-style cohabitation between the powerful Presidency (still controlled by the PRI) and the legislature. More important still, the election represented the culmination of one lengthy phase of democratization in Mexico. It also created the possibility of further reforms.

Mexico's politics reflects its distinctive history. The PRI was founded in 1929, in the decade following the populist Mexican revolution. In the 1930s the PRI implemented progressive policies – including land reform – which gave the party enduring legitimacy. Gradually, however, socialist principles were diluted as the PRI established a classic semi-democracy based on patronage networks. The PRI distributed favours to its union and peasant organizations while repressing opposition and manipulating election results. In the 1950s and 1960s, the PRI seemed to have discovered what one observer described as 'the perfect dictatorship'.

However, three problems recurred:

- Continuing poverty for those excluded from the PRI network, reflected in periodic revolts.
- Increasing opposition from the expanding middle class created by economic growth.
- Occasional economic crises when the PRI placed its political objectives before sound economic policy.

With the political effectiveness of the PRI machine decaying, President Salinas (1988–94) initiated economic reforms, including privatizing major firms and opening the economy to international competition, not least through NAFTA. In contrast to the Soviet Union, where Gorbachev had initiated political reform before restructuring the economy, economic liberalization in Mexico preceded political change. As the PRI lost direct control of economic resources, so its powers of patronage declined and voters became free to support opposition parties. Independent trade unions began to form, outside the once-enveloping embrace of the PRI system. Further, by the 1990s, the PRI no longer felt able to manipulate electoral results. Indeed, President Zedillo (elected 1994) interpreted the 1997 elections as showing that 'Mexico has taken an irreversible, definitive and historic step towards the normalization of democracy'.

Mexico's gradual moves to democracy seem to have avoided what Baer (1993, p. 64) describes as 'the dilemma of all reforms from above, particularly in ageing regimes: how to avoid unleashing a revolution from below'. Thus the reform process has been managed with sufficient skill to keep the PRI in a strong, if less dominant, position. However, it remains to be seen how far Mexico will establish a *liberal* democracy, including for instance an independent judiciary. And question marks will continue to surround Mexico's democratic transition until the PRI finally accepts the loss of the presidency.

Further reading: Cook, Middlebrook and Horcasitas (1994), Cornelius (1996), Lawson (1997).
www.presidencia.gob.mx   www.pri.org.mx

fast growth achieved by communist China with the poor performance of democratic India. Both are large, populous and agrarian countries which achieved their current political status after the Second World War. Over the next 40 years, however, China's economy grew about twice as fast as India's. True, China's path of communist modernization involved the brutality of the Great Leap Forward, in which around 40 million people died in five years. Yet the sheer grinding poverty of India arguably leads to even more suffering. As Dreze and Sen (1989, p. 206) note,

> every eight years or so more people die in India because of its higher regular death rate than died in China's gigantic famine of 1958–61. India seems to manage to fill the cupboard with more skeletons every eight years than China put there in its years of shame.

Today, of course, authoritarian regimes do not adopt the communist model of forced industrialization based on a central plan. Yet even though China is now more market-oriented, it continues to combine authoritarian rule with economic growth. India's inferior economic performance must at least raise questions about the value of democracy to developing societies.

Several non-communist countries in Asia also developed economically in a political setting containing authoritarian features, offering more ammunition to those who consider democracy and development to be alternatives. Between 1960 and 1985, the high-performing economies of Hong Kong, Indonesia, Japan, Singapore, South Korea and Taiwan were six of the fastest-growing in the world. The governments of these states vary in the extent to which they rely on authoritarian mechanisms such as repression of dissent, martial law, anti-union legislation and abuse of the judiciary. For instance, Japan is a consolidated democracy, South Korea has moved strongly toward democracy while Indonesia retains strong authoritarian elements. Yet the East Asian tigers do share many features of what Chalmers Johnson (1987) calls the developmental state. Crucial among these features is stable rule by a political and bureaucratic élite which (just as Sorensen argues) constrains popular pressures for consumption. Cooperation between the public and

---

BOX 2.6
The developmental state

The main features of the developmental state are:

- Stable rule by a political and bureaucratic élite capable of overriding pressures for decisions which would reduce growth.
- Cooperation between the public and private sectors through a powerful planning agency.
- Heavy investment in mass education.
- Fairly equal distribution of the benefits of growth.
- A government which respects the market mechanism.

Source: Chalmers Johnson (1987).

---

private sectors, effected through a powerful planning agency, also exceeds the norm associated with Western liberal democracies. The idea of the developmental state, exemplified by the Asian NICs, codifies the proposition that rapid growth is best achieved by limiting democratic expression.

However, once a country reaches a certain level of economic development, continued authoritarian rule may reduce the pace of growth. The experience of the Soviet Union, for example, showed that a totally planned economy lacked the flexibility, innovation and focus on quality needed to avoid stagnation. The command economies of the communist bloc ended up in a cul-de-sac. And even the developmental states of Asia will need to place increasing reliance on the market if they are to maintain international competitiveness – which, it is often forgotten, was established in the first place with massive American aid. Indeed, the forced devaluation of several East Asian currencies in 1997 exposed the poor use many domestic banks had made of capital borrowed from abroad, taking the gloss off the economic performance of the NICs and also exposing the limits of the developmental state for open, advanced economies.

So the twentieth century showed that authoritarian rule can lead to rapid industrialization. However it also provided many examples of corrupt dictators inflicting enormous damage on their country's economy and people. Perhaps this is why the statistical evidence on the relationship between democracy and development is inconclusive. Most quantitative studies suggest that the type of regime has no consistent impact on economic performance (Inkeles, 1990; Przeworski and Limongi, 1993). The problem with such research is that the concept of authoritarian rule is too broad to pick up the particular styles of nondemocratic governance which create growth. In any event, the capacity of an authoritarian regime to extract a surplus for investment neither requires nor justifies the abuses of power and human rights which are an inherent risk of nondemocratic rule.

While some authoritarian rulers facilitated economic development in the twentieth century, in the twenty-first century liberal democracy may well provide a more successful route. Globalization has given developing countries access to new sources of capital through multinational corporations, overseas banks and agencies such as the World Bank. The 'surplus' needed for investment may no longer need to be wrung from a reluctant society. But foreign investors, in particular, are suspicious of the extensive bureaucratic controls which characterize developmental states; this was a major factor in the financial crisis which afflicted many Asian countries in 1997. In an interdependent world, it becomes harder for authoritarian rulers to 'get away' with a mode of forced development which offends the international community. Establishing at least an approximation to a liberal democracy eases a country's full entry to the world trading system – and this is now a precondition of substantial growth.

Conclusion: democracy in a global era

As countries become more integrated into a global community, so the idea of the autonomous, self-governing democracy recedes into history. What hope is there now for the Athenian model of citizens gathering together to decide their fate? Given that crucial economic decisions are now made outside the nation-state, what is the point of the people gathering together at all? At the very moment of democracy's triumph, is it being stripped of all significance by the forces of globalization?

The 'threat' posed by globalization has been asserted often enough. Guehenno (1995) notes that the demands of the global economy have transformed politics into management. He claims that

governments no longer make choices, they simply manage their country's engagement with global markets. He notes with distaste Margaret Thatcher's famous comment, 'there is no alternative'. According to Guehenno, this 'domain of inevitability' signifies the death of the polity as a forum of active citizens and by implication the end of democracy itself. In similar vein, the American political theorist Michael Sandel (1996, p. 202) writes,

self-government requires political communities that control their destinies, and citizens who identify sufficiently with those communities to think and act with a view to the common good. Whether self-government in this sense is possible under modern conditions is at best an open question.

Yet writing off democracy in this way is surely a mistake. An interdependent world is not necessarily undemocratic. The error lies in equating democracy with complete self-determination. If democracy could only exist in societies with total autonomy, we would be forced to conclude that it has never existed anywhere, an implausible conclusion indeed. Probably only imperial centres and superpowers have ever come close to this 'ideal' of complete autonomy, and then only for a limited time. All other states have always been strongly influenced from outside. Further, it would clearly be wrong to conclude that a small country like Switzerland (population seven million) is less democratic than a big one like the United States (population 258 million) simply because small countries are subject to more outside influences. Indeed, small democracies such as Switzerland often sustain a stronger sense of citizenship as they debate how to prosper in the shadow of larger neighbours. Statecraft, in democracies or otherwise, has always involved reconciling domestic populations to international pressures. What distinguishes democracies is that this adjustment is effected through persuasion and consent – and that if rulers fail in their effort, they are thrown out.

Key reading

> **Next step:** *Dahl (1989) is a magisterial account of democracy by a scholar who spent his professional life studying the subject.*

Other useful assessments of democracy include Arblaster (1994), the widely-used account by Held (1996) and, for a straightforward 'questions and answers' approach, Beetham and Boyle (1995). Two excellent readers on the global resurgence of democracy are Diamond and Plattner (1996) and Hadenius (1997). The classic works on the conditions of democracy are Lipset (1960) for the modernization approach, updated in Przeworski and Limongi (1997). See Barrington Moore (1966)

for the historical approach (updated in Rueschemeyer, Stephens and Stephens, 1992). Democratization has spawned an outstanding literature: O'Donnell, Schmitter and Whitehead (1986) is an excellent work, Potter *et al.* (1997) is a good text while Pridham (1995) is a collection of classic articles. For democratization in the developing world, see Luckham and White (1996). Bratton and van der Walle (1997) and Joseph (1998) examine Africa, Peeler (1998) considers Latin America while Bell (1995) discusses illiberal democracy in Asia. Sorensen (1993) is a balanced guide to democracy and development, while Chalmers Johnson (1987) considers the notion of the developmental state.

The global context

CHAPTER 3 | **The global context**

An interdependent world

In 1492, Christopher Columbus sailed across the Atlantic seeking a western passage to India. To his dying day, Columbus believed he had landed in India (hence, the West Indies) but he had in fact 'discovered' America. His epic voyage had momentous consequences. The conquest of the New World of the Americas by the European powers changed the nature of world politics. Empires had risen and fallen before but the European powers, with their ships, guns and trinkets, opened up the world to an unprecedented degree. Five hundred years later, even an explorer like Columbus would have been astonished at the world he had played a part in creating. Today, all national governments operate in an interdependent world. Aid, data, deals, disease, drugs, e-mail, food, genes, ideas, images, information, migrants, money, movies, music, pollution, radiation, refugees, software, students, technology, textbooks, tourists, values, weapons – all flow rapidly round the globe, giving national governments more challenges and more opportunities but also threatening their traditional authority.

To appreciate the complex world which states now inhabit, it helps to contrast two simplified models of interactions between states (Figure 3.1). In the restricted model A, these relationships operate through governments, with little direct contact between societies and no significant international organizations. Foreign policy, diplomacy, military intervention – these are the means of contact between countries. States are regarded as sovereign within their own territory and as the sole actors on the international stage. While always oversimplified, this model underlies the system of states which emerged in seventeenth century Europe and later spread to the entire world. It also provided the basis for a division of labour between students of international relations (who examined politics between states) and of comparative politics (who looked at politics within them).

However, the restricted model is clearly inapplicable to today's world. The emergence of a world economy, international organizations and global information-flows mean that the extended model B is now more accurate. As people and capital move around the globe, states find they no longer 'own' their people and resources. Further, information flows have become international, exposing even

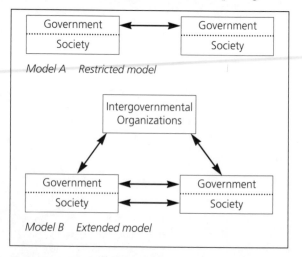
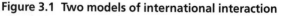

Figure 3.1 Two models of international interaction

people who do not travel abroad to competing values and perspectives. And in the international arena, governments must deal not just with other states but also with international organizations ranging from the United Nations to the Ford Motor Company. Contacts between countries now resemble a cobweb, with governments just one participant in an intricate network of interactions. Even if we do not accept that the world has moved *beyond* countries, we must acknowledge that the scale of interdependence *between* them is greater than ever before.

The question for this chapter is: how exactly does the cobweb of international relationships impinge on national governments? Our answer will involve a sharp distinction between the developed and the developing worlds. Western states, especially the larger ones, help to shape the rules of the international game while also retaining some autonomy from it. For these states, growing interdependence offers at least as many opportunities as constraints. By contrast, the rulers of developing states, especially the smaller ones, find themselves subject to external limits which make a mockery of traditional ideas of sovereignty. Yet in both the developed and the developing worlds, we will suggest, the state's role is evolving, not disappearing. Discussing the impact of the global economy, Grugel and Hout (1998) usefully suggest that

> the state has not lost significance as a result of global trends. Rather, the role of the state is evolving, as its strategies respond to the demands of globalization.

The changing state, not the disappearing state – that is our theme. In particular, states are becoming more coordinating bodies, seeking to ensure that their country's firms and people (or most of them) can prosper in an era of global competition.

To develop the theme of new roles for the state, our focus will be on three areas where interdependence matters most:

- The impact of international organizations, including the United Nations
- The growth of regions, both as free trade areas and as political institutions
- The contrasting effects of the global economy on developing and developed states.

BOX 3.1
What is globalization?

Waters (1996, p.3) defines globalization as 'a process in which the constraints of geography on social and cultural arrangements recede and in which people become increasingly aware that they are receding'. This has two implications. The first is a decline in the significance of territory in human affairs or, to put the point more dramatically, the annhiliation of space. The second is that the concept of globalization is in itself evidence of a trend. As Waters comments, '"globalization" can hardly be said to have begun before people realised the earth was a globe'.

Although the world has become more integrated since 1945, it would be wrong to suppose that globalization is entirely novel. As Krasner (1994, p. 13) comments, 'Globalization is not new … challenges to the authority of the state are not new … Transnational flows are not new'. Further, since globalization is a continuing process, we should not imply that we inhabit a world which is fully global.

International organizations and the state

International organizations are the most obvious form of interdependence. The UN, EU, APEC, OPEC, IMF, WTO, ILO – the acronyms are endless. The number of such bodies has grown enormously, particularly since 1960. Then there were around 1400 such institutions, but by 1993 there were over 5000 (of varying importance), far more than the number of states.

Definition
International organizations fall into two categories. The first is **intergovernmental organizations** (IGOs) whose members are states – examples are the United Nations and the North Atlantic Treaty Organization (NATO). The second category is international **nongovernmental organizations** (INGOs, usually called NGOs). These are interest groups whose members are individuals or private groups drawn from more than one country. Examples are Greenpeace, Oxfam and the Catholic Church.

Intergovernmental organizations (IGOs) are the major form of international institution. IGOs are established by treaty and usually operate by

Table 3.1 Types of intergovernmental organization (IGO)

Type	Example	Per cent of all IGOs in each category, 1992
Universal	United Nations	32
Regional	European Union	51
Single-purpose	International Atomic Energy Agency (IAEA)	18

Source: Shanks, Jackobson and Kaplan (1996).

consent, with a permanent secretariat to service the organization. They fall into various groups (Table 3.1), but for our purposes the problem is to assess the impact of this IGO network on states. The answer depends partly on the number of IGOs to which a state belongs. As Table 3.2 shows, West European states, which originated the state system itself, have most memberships. Most European states belong to several hundred IGOs. By comparison, countries with the fewest memberships tend to be those whose sovereignty is in dispute (for example Taiwan), very small countries (for example Liechtenstein), or impoverished developing countries devastated by internal conflict (for example Mozambique).

The impact of IGOs on states is a matter of controversy. One position is that IGOs play a significant role in global governance, enabling states to achieve common objectives in an interdependent world. Setting up an IGO creates a body with its own interests and an international perspective. IGOs may be created by states but, like children, they grow up to develop their own interests and perspectives. Further, IGOs can lead states to appreciate the extent of their common interests and reduce suspicion between them through achieving concrete results beneficial to all. That is, IGOs are confidence-building devices. They encourage wider cooperation, a point expressed in the idea of an 'international regime'. IGOs prosper because they are functionally useful: everyone gains from a world telephone network and from safer nuclear power plants (Mitrany, 1975, Jacobson, 1985). In particular, IGOs are necessary for addressing complex issues which cannot be solved by single states using traditional military means: 'you can't shoot the ozone hole'. If IGOs are irrelevant, asks Keohane (1994),

why do they last so long and increase in number? Advocates of this position note that even though most IGOs lack an enforcement mechanism, most states do comply with IGO decisions. Backsliding is unusual.

A second, more critical reading of IGOs is that they are mere decoration designed to conceal the continued pursuit of national self-interest. The argument is that IGOs do not govern states; rather, dominant states govern through IGOs. The 1991 Gulf War, for instance, was won by American forces protecting their country's oil supply. The United Nations label, secured by President Bush, was a convenient cover for the familiar pursuit of national self-interest. More generally, the developed West put in place the entire postwar system, including its trading regime, to benefit its own economic interests. Strong states only comply with IGO recommendations because they just commit themselves to what they are already doing (Downs, Roche and Baroom, 1996). Firm proof of IGO influence, measured by changes in what members do or by the ability of IGOs to resolve major disputes, is harder to come by. IGOs are 'empty vessels' into which members

Table 3.2 Countries with most memberships of intergovernmental organizations, 1992

Country	Memberships
France	441
United Kingdom	396
Germany	392
Netherlands	375
Denmark	373

Source: Shanks, Jackobson and Kaplan (1996) Table 6.

pour their national interests (Webber, 1997). So what we might broadly call a 'realist' position is that states, especially the leading ones, remain dominant, only agreeing in IGOs to what is in their national interest.

While this realist perspective may be overplayed, it is certainly the case that IGOs have several advantages for states. IGOs provide information and advice. They are useful for endorsing unpopular policies, providing national governments with both a conscience and a scapegoat: 'of course, we don't want to close your steel mill but the European Union insists on it'. IGOs also generate opportunities for collaboration and even, sometimes, for price-fixing. Many single-purpose organizations, such as the associations of oil, tin and coffee producers, are in effect trade associations for countries involved in producing a particular commodity. In addition, membership of universal organizations, especially the UN, confirms to all and sundry (including domestic opponents) that national rulers have acquired statehood and sovereignty. Joining the UN reduces vulnerability to external threats since the UN Charter expresses the principle of noninterference in domestic affairs. Thus UN membership is both a reflection and a tactic of political consolidation. In all these ways, IGOs help states.

That said, states must pay a price for the shelter provided by IGOs. While IGOs have their uses, they also impact on the state. At the very least, belonging to several hundred IGOs complicates the task of governance. States must arrange to pay their subscriptions, attend meetings, identify their national interests, consult with interest groups back home, initiate some proposals, respond to others and implement agreements. They must build coalitions behind their own proposals and against those which threaten their own objectives. These activities dilute the distinction between domestic and foreign policy. As Dehousse (1997, p. 40) writes, 'the time when "foreign policy" concerned only foreign ministries has gone for good. Most state institutions now attempt to conduct an external policy of their own'.

So IGOs increase fragmentation within national governments. In part this is because a club-like spirit often develops among ministers in 'their' IGO. For example, finance ministers – never popular at home – are among friends at bodies such as the

International Monetary Fund. Back home ministers stoutly defend the interest of their IGOs against attacks from other ministers (Bayne, 1997). Thus IGOs splinter the always fragile unity of national executives. Andeweg (1997, p.77) shows how

> European integration contributes to the fragmentation of national governments. Dutch Ministers of Agriculture, for example, have been eager to transfer powers from The Hague to Brussels. After all, in the European Council for Ministers, they meet only other Ministers of Agriculture, who are all convinced of the importance and needs of that particular sector, whereas in their national cabinets they confront ministers with other portfolios, and considerably more scepticism.

Especially in the European Union, many issues are settled at sectoral level – such as agriculture, finance or transport – leading some authors to question whether it is still sensible to think in terms of the position of 'a national government' at all. In a few cases, different ministries of the same government have been known to advocate contradictory positions in EU negotiations!

Given that IGOs tends to fragment national political systems, we must ask which governing institutions gain, and which lose, from increasing interdependence. The biggest winners are the executive and the bureaucracy: after all, these bodies provide the representatives who attend IGO meetings and conduct negotiations. Therefore they occupy pole position. Protective interest groups also benefit, since they provide their government with the expertise it needs to formulate a sensible negotiating position on specialist matters. IGOs virtually force cooperation between governments and interest groups, making friends of people who are often on opposite sides of the table within national politics. Any government, for example, would need to consult its Chemical Industry Association about an IGO proposal to ban a specific substance. So although IGOs lead to a more fragmented executive and bureaucracy, they also enhance the overall position of these core institutions against other bodies. More surprisingly, perhaps, the judiciary is also growing in significance as a result of IGO activity. IGOs contribute to the more judicial character of domestic politics since national judges can

EXHIBIT 3.1

Intergovernmental organizations and the world economy

The IGOs which have emerged to regulate the global economy according to the liberal principle of free trade merit special attention. The International Monetary Fund (IMF) and the World Bank were a product of a conference held at Bretton Woods, New Hampshire, in 1944 to organize the postwar economic order: hence the phrase, 'the Bretton Woods system'. These IGOs were set up by the most powerful states, including the USA, to establish 'rules of the game'. Four regional development banks, covering the Americas, Africa, Asia and Europe, support the work of the IMF and the World Bank. The underlying philosophy of these IGOs is to encourage world trade through improving the operation of market economies.

These institutions are important to students of comparative politics because they impinge on national governments. Their ability to grant or withhold loans gives them an oversight role over the least solvent states which amounts to veto power. A crucial test of the skill of the leaders of such countries is their ability to negotiate with these economic IGOs. It is true that middle-income developing countries can increasingly access private capital from overseas, thus bypassing the IGOs. Yet even here, as for the developed states, the IGOs remain important in providing an international seal of approval for a government's economic policies, thus lowering the cost of borrowing from any overseas source, public or private.

Consider the impact of the World Trade Organization (WTO). Its function is to provide a way of resolving trade conflicts between member states and to seek further reductions in tariffs and other barriers to trade. In practice, this means that members gain preferential access to each others' markets. With most countries requiring access to lucrative North American and European markets, membership of WTO is highly desirable. But in order to join, as Russia and China want to do, states must meet specific conditions. In essence, the price to governments of entering the global economy is to open their domestic market. Thus the WTO has leverage not just over its 120 members but also over the 70 or so states which have yet to join.

Further reading: Bayne (1997), Kahler (1995), Mansbach (1997, Ch. 12).

IGO	Full title	Function
IMF	International Monetary Fund	To promote international monetary stability and cooperation
IBRD	International Bank for Reconstruction and Development ('World Bank')	To promote economic recovery and development
WTO	World Trade Organization	To supervise and promote international trade

Note: the WTO was founded in 1995 to replace GATT (General Agreement on Tariffs and Trade) which, like the IMF and the World Bank, had been established at Bretton Woods (Jackson, 1998).

incorporate international agreements into their own decision-making. Also, some IGOs are themselves adopting a more judicial style.

So much for winners; what of losers? The biggest domestic loser from international integration is probably the legislature, which may only learn of an international agreement after the government has signed up. In some countries, Australia for one, international treaties are an executive preserve. Thus, the more treaties a government signs, the more it can bypass the assembly. If parliaments are to recover lost ground, they must rely on specialised committees of scrutiny. In Europe, for instance, the parliaments of all EU member states have now established European Affairs committees, even if these bodies are not yet sufficiently powerful to exert real impact. Political parties, too, seem to have fallen behind. Like assemblies, their natural habitat appears to be the nation state, not the international conference.

Like IGOs, nongovernmental organisations also impinge on national governments, particularly in developing countries where state authority is collapsing. This influence arises from the position some NGOs have achieved as executors of IGO, especially United Nations, policy. By the mid-1990s, over 10 per cent of all public development aid was distributed through NGOs, compared to less than 1 per cent in 1970 (Weiss and Gordenker, 1996). About 10 super-NGOs, including CARE, Save the Children and Oxfam, dominate the distribution of aid in complex emergencies. NGOs are more efficient and less corrupt than many domestic governments, especially those whose failure may have led to the crisis in the first place. They are also more sensitive to local conditions than multilateral military forces. All this gives NGOs considerable political clout in the least developed countries on which aid is concentrated.

In acting as UN subcontractors, NGOs in some respects *become* governments. For instance, NGOs coordinated primary education in northern Sri Lanka after civil war started there in 1987. In other cases the international community creates specific DONGOs (donor-organized nongovernmental organizations) to perform concrete tasks within countries. De-mining in Afghanistan is an example. As Mortimer (1997, p. 18) notes, these engagements

> often leave NGOs to take decisions with grave political or even military implications, which involve taking sides in a local struggle. The decision in 1994 to provide food and water to refugee camps on the Rwanda–Zaire border, controlled by the perpetrators of Rwandan genocide, is a clear example.

The role of NGOs as substitute states is one factor lying behind Fernando and Heston's claim (1997, p. 8) that 'NGO activity presents the most serious challenge to the imperatives of statehood in the

realms of territorial integrity, security, autonomy and revenue'.

The United Nations and intervention

In the crowded field of IGOs, the United Nations occupies a prime position. It is unique in combining general purpose status with virtually universal membership (currently 185, with neutral Switzerland the major non-joiner). The UN is a major forum for discussion on world problems, and is the starting point for most discussions of global governance. And, significantly, after the cold war it sent troops uninvited to several states facing civil war or other complex emergencies. These interventions in the domestic affairs of states must cause us to question the continuing vitality of national sovereignty. To what extent is the sovereignty of a state now conditional on its good behaviour, as judged by an emerging international community?

In theory, not at all. The UN's central purpose, as set out in its Charter (1945), is:

> to maintain international peace and security, and to that end: to take effective collective measures for the prevention and removal of threats to the peace.

The focus is clearly on international conflicts, not disputes within a state. The principle of non-intervention was explicitly enshrined in the Charter, partly to ease American entry into the UN. And for most of its history the focus of UN activity has been on keeping the peace in (or after) disputes between countries. Jackson (1989, p. 17) even likens the state system, as reflected in the UN's Charter, to a traditional club which assumes 'members are honourable fellows. Provided members conform to club rules in their outward conduct, their private lives are their own. Even skeletons in closets are their own affair'.

Yet despite the limits of its charter the UN has become more involved in domestic disputes, especially since the end of the cold war. The turning-point came with Security Council authorization for a US-led military expedition to expel Iraq from Kuwait in the Gulf War (1991). Of course, this was again a traditional international dispute but it did seem to open the prospect of a role for the UN in creating a new world order. The pace of UN operations quickened. By 1995, 60 000 blue helmets were deployed in 16 operations around the world. And of 11 UN operations set up between 1992 and 1995, nine were in response to internal civil conflicts (UN, 1995). Examples include Iraq (to protect the Kurds), Rwanda (to deter genocide) and Somalia (to distribute emergency aid). The motive was 'humanitarian intervention' usually following the failure of states amid civil war and ethnic violence. When the state has failed, as several have done in Africa, arguably there is no sovereignty left to violate. Some even argued that prevention is better than cure, and that intervention in collapsed states should be considered before human suffering becomes extensive. Again, we see how the discussion of intervention is focused on the weakest states in the developing world.

Definition

Humanitarian intervention occurs when the international community (or even a single state) intervenes in another country's domestic affairs in order to reduce immediate human suffering. The willingness to step in without invitation indicates some loss of faith in the norm of non-intervention on which the international system was traditionally based.

Somalia is an example where 'humanitarian disaster was the sole reason for the UN's intervention' (Mayall, 1996, p. 9). Tragic television images of starvation generated a public demand for the international community to 'do something'. Despite the limits of its Charter, the UN authorized military intervention to support the distribution of aid. The project was a disaster, revealing operational problems which may be inherent in such enterprises. An inadequate number of troops was despatched in 1992 after a long delay to carry out an unfamiliar humanitarian mission with insufficient local knowledge in a hostile situation where there was no state left with which to negotiate. An American helicopter killed about 200 civilians when crowds turned against UN troops fighting Somali militiamen, and the UN made clumsy efforts to capture local leader General Aideed, putting a price of $20 000 on his head. Finally, after a local warlord killed 20 Pakistani

---

BOX 3.2
When is intervention justified?

Drawing on a range of scholarly work, van Eijk (1997) suggests humanitarian intervention must pass the following tests before it is justified:

- **Importance**
The existence of a direct and extensive threat to fundamental human rights (for example the right to life).

- **No alternative**
No other means are available to improve the situation.

- **Support**
Intervention must have a wide base of support in the international community.

- **Reporting**
Intervention must be justified to the UN in advance.

- **Proportionality**
The extent of intervention must not exceed the demands of the situation.

- **Anticipated success**
Intervention must be able to make a constructive contribution to the situation.

- **Time**
Intervention must last no longer than is required.

---

soldiers serving with the UN, and a captured American pilot was paraded in public, the United States decided to quit. Although the mission was organized by the UN, when push came to shove the United States was prepared to act unilaterally. The entire UN mission folded in 1995.

So although intervention has become more common, its success remains limited. David Hannay (1996, p. 75), formerly British ambassador to the UN, sums up the dilemma of what he calls the 'CNN factor':

when the spotlight of publicity is on a particular international problem, two contradictory forces apply. First the cry goes out when faced with horrendous images of suffering that something must be done. Then, when intervention turns out to be messier and more costly than expected, the cry 'to bring the boys home' quickly follows.

As a result of these problems, initial optimism about building a new world order has given way to realism, even cynicism. By presidential directive, American involvement in UN operations is now restricted to short-term operations where a clear US interest is at stake. In the developing world, UN intervention is sometimes seen as recolonization; 'whose disaster is it anyway?' Further, the UN is unsuited to running, as opposed to legitimizing, military operations. It is an underfunded, decentralized and generally ineffective body. Even its Secretary General recognizes the need for reform. So the willingness of the international community to consider intervention in the affairs of states is not matched by the means to give effect to its purpose. A more successful model might be to subcontract military intervention to regional bodies, as with NATO's airstrikes into Bosnia to enforce the 1995 Dayton Peace Agreement. The difficulty here is that few regional security bodies possess NATO's organized fire power.

Yet despite the practical difficulties experienced by UN missions, something *has* changed. The more interventions there are, successful or not, the less convincing the traditional idea of national sovereignty becomes. Slowly the notion of international society, of a community of states sharing the values of democracy and human rights, gains strength. Even Boutros Boutros-Ghali was emboldened to say, when Secretary General of the United Nations, 'the time of absolute exclusive sovereignty has passed; its theory was never matched by reality' (United Nations, 1992). Absolute sovereignty may eventually be replaced by conditional sovereignty: that is, by the idea that a state's membership of the world system depends on good behaviour towards its own citizens. In the seventeenth century, the Dutch jurist Hugo Grotius (1583–1645) had argued that sovereignty is not the highest law (Tuck, 1979). Hoffman (1995, p. 35) is among those to recently reinforce this view: 'the state that claims sovereignty deserves respect only as long as it protects the basic rights of its citizens. When it violates them, the state's claim to sovereignty falls'. Oxfam takes a similar view: 'we do not accept that the principle of sovereignty should block the protection of basic rights, including the right to emergency relief and safety' (Harriss, 1995, p. 3). Sovereignty, it is argued, does not entitle a state to decline humanitarian aid, since the result is added suffering for the people who are the tangible expression of that state.

> **Definition**
> **Absolute sovereignty** is the notion that each state has unqualified jurisdiction over its territory.
> **Conditional sovereignty** makes this authority subject to the state observing principles such as protecting the rights of its people, for example to receive outside humanitarian aid. To embrace conditional sovereignty is to reject the notion that the state is the highest and final source of authority; in truth, it is a quiet way of burying sovereignty altogether.

A further step towards sidestepping state sovereignty has been taken by setting up international courts to try individuals directly for their alleged crimes, even if these were committed in the name of the state. The Nuremberg trials after World War II had established that individuals are responsible for their own acts in war. That view itself departed from the notion of treating states as the only subjects of international law. In the 1990s, the International Court of Justice set up new tribunals, the first since Nuremberg, to try people from Rwanda and former Yugoslavia suspected of genocide and other war crimes. One innovation of these new tribunals is that they indicted suspects who were not already in custody. However bringing these suspects to justice proved politically difficult. International snatch squads are not yet accepted and their use can stimulate a damaging reaction in the suspect's own community. Yet failing to capture indicted suspects, such as Radovan Karadzic in Serbian Bosnia, makes the international community appear weak. So far, the efforts made are typical of the uncertain and often ineffective way in which the international community has intervened in national politics. This is one reason why even though nonintervention may be declining as a *principle*, it will continue to dominate *practice*.

Regional organizations and the state

Regional organizations are an established form of IGO which have grown in significance, especially since the end of the cold war (see Box 3.3). As Gamble and Payne (1996a, p.249) write,

the turn to regionalism at the end of the 1980s coincided with the breakdown of the oldest regionalism in the global political economy, the division between the capitalist and the socialist worlds which developed after the Russian Revolution.

With the cold war over, states turned to their neighbours to find a means of responding to the new pressures of a freer and more global economy. It is noteworthy, for instance, that much of the expansion of international trade has been within regions rather than between them. Reflecting on these trends, Salvatore (1993, p. 10) suggests the world has 'already and possibly irreversibly moved into an international trade order characterized by three major trading blocs'. These are Asia, North America and Western Europe.

Definition

Regionalism refers to a deliberate attempts by states to create formal mechanisms for dealing with common issues. In Wyatt-Walter's words (1995, p. 77), regionalism is 'a conscious policy of states or sub-state regions to coordinate activities and arrangements in a greater region'. **Regionalization** refers to an undirected process of growing interdependence which originates from the actions of individuals, groups and corporations, rather than through national governments (Gamble and Payne, 1996, p. 250).

Even if regional organizations eventually become a threat to state power, they are initally an outgrowth of it. Regional integration, just like sucessful engagement with other IGOs, requires consolidated states. As Hurrell (1995) notes,

It is no coincidence that the most elaborate examples of regionalism have occurred in regions where state structures remain relatively strong and where the legitimacy of both frontiers and regimes is not widely called into question.

The European Union is a good example: strong states have come together, pooling some sovereignty,

to create a regional body with unique powers. By contrast, when a country faces severe internal tensions, it is unlikely to be able to build regional alignments. For example, the postsoviet republics which formed the Commonwealth of Independent States in 1991 were so preoccupied with domestic difficulties that they had little spare capacity to develop their association.

What does regionalism imply for the governance of states? Excluding the European Union, the domestic implications have so far been limited. Impact is restricted because the characteristic form of regional integration is the free trade area. Through this device, states attempt to gain the economic advantages of larger and more open markets but without sacrificing their political sovereignty. Thus modern regions tend to be looser arrangements than classic federations, which involved the participating units (such as the American states) pooling their sovereignty in a new central authority. While the European Union has inspired regional moves elsewhere, these other regions have not so far sought to replicate the EU's semi-federal status. Indeed, Alesina, Spolaore and Wacziarg (1997) suggest that once a free market is secured, there is no reason for further moves toward political integration. Thus the elaborate architecture of the European Union may prove to be a false model for the rest of the world. Certainly, it seems unlikely that the turn to economic regions at the end of the twentieth century will result in political federations of the type created a century or two earlier.

One specific problem which regional developments do pose for national governments is managing the domestic political implications of creating the new zone. The political set-up costs can be considerable. Establishing a free trade area may offer economic gains to each member country considered as a whole but the losers within each state will still complain. The general gains from increased trade are less visible than the damage caused to specific jobs, corporations and industries. Further, a free trade zone in itself is unlikely to inspire groups within a country to make sacrifices for some abstract national 'efficiency gain'. Of course, one way to solve this problem is by creating a sense of identity with the larger region. For instance, the European Union has made strenuous efforts to develop a European identity, paralleling the efforts of early nation-

BOX 3.3
Examples of regional organizations

Group	Date Established	Purpose	Members
Asia–Pacific Economic Co-operation (APEC)	1989	To promote trade and investment in the Pacific Basin	18 member states from the Asia Pacific: ASEAN members plus Australia, Canada, China, Hong Kong, Japan, New Zealand, Papua New Guinea, South Korea, Taiwan and the United States
Association of Southeast Asian Nations (ASEAN)	1967	To provide economic, social, and cultural cooperation among non-communist countries	Brunei, Indonesia, Malaysia, Philippines, Singapore, Thailand and now Vietnam
Benelux Economic Union	1958	To develop closer economic cooperation and integration	Belgium, Luxembourg, The Netherlands
Commonwealth of Independent States (CIS)	1991	To coordinate relations among members and to provide a mechanism for the orderly dissolution of the USSR	12 former members of the USSR
European Free Trade Association (EFTA)	1960	To promote the expansion of free trade in the non-members of the European Union	Iceland, Liechtenstein, Norway, Switzerland
European Union (EU)	1958*	Wide-ranging cooperation and integration	15 members
Gulf Co-operation Council	1981	To promote cooperation in economic, social, political and military affairs	Bahrain, Kuwait, Oman, Qatar, Saudi Arabia, UAE
North American Free Trade Association (NAFTA)	1994	To create a free trade area between its members	Canada, USA, Mexico
Nordic Council	1952	To promote regional economic, cultural and environmental cooperation	Denmark, Finland, Iceland, Norway, Sweden
South Pacific Forum	1971	To promote regional cooperation in political matters	16 members, including Australia, New Zealand and many Pacific Islands
Southern Cone Common Market (Mercosur)	1991	To increase regional economic cooperation	Argentina, Brazil, Paraguay, Uruguay and one associate, Chile

* Originally established by the Treaty of Rome as the European Economic Community.

Source: CIA (1997).

builders to create loyalties to new states. Yet so far regions lack the emotional pulling-power of nations. Our review of regional integration within the triad of Europe, North America and Asia will confirm some of the domestic political difficulties caused by regional innovation. In particular, it will show the state in characteristic modern pose, standing between international demands and sceptical electorates.

The European Union (EU)

Of all the regional organizations in the world today, the EU is the most developed. It has already acquired at least semi-federal status, pooling some of the sovereignty of its member states. But the journey towards integration has proved difficult, especially as public opinion in many countries has turned more instrumental. The effort to establish a

---

BOX 3.4

50 Years of the European Union

1951 Treaty of Paris signed by France, West Germany, Italy, Belgium, the Netherlands and Luxembourg. This set up the European Coal and Steel Commission (ECSC) which included a supranational High Authority.

1957 The ECSC members sign the Treaty of Rome, establishing the European Economic Community (EEC) and Euratom.

1965 The Merger Treaty combines the ECSC, EEC and Euratom.

1973 Britain, Denmark and Ireland join the EEC.

1979 The European Monetary System (EMS) is agreed, linking currencies to the European Currency Unit (ECU). First direct Europe-wide elections to the European Parliament held.

1981 Greece joins the EEC.

1986 Spain and Portugal join the EEC. Signing of the Single European Act, to streamline decision-making and set up a single market by 1992.

1992 Treaty of Maastricht launches provisions for economic and monetary union (EMU) and replaces the EEC with the European Union from 1993.

1994 Austria, Finland and Sweden join the EU.

1997 Treaty of Amsterdam agrees (subject to ratification) to extend the Union's role in justice and home affairs; to increase the authority of the European Parliament; and to address the problem of unemployment.

1999 Launching of European Monetary Union.

Note: nomenclature of the 'European Union' has varied over time, reflecting institutional and constitutional developments.

---

common currency is one illustration of the problems which EU initiatives cause within member states. The Maastricht Treaty of 1991 committed members (except Britain and Denmark) to establish a common European currency by 1999. To achieve this, member states had to ensure that their economies 'converged'. In practice, this meant each government had to reduce its budget deficit to a maximum of 3 per cent of gross domestic product; but deficit reduction caused considerable domestic opposition in many European states. For instance, when President Chirac called a general election in France in 1997, he described it as a referendum on the government's attempts to cut back the budget deficit in order to meet the Maastricht criteria. His government lost. The French public was unwilling to pay the price of closer European integration. Although the common currency project continues, further formal deepening of political integration within Europe remains in doubt. The EU will probably continue as a unique hybrid, combining elements of a genuine federation with a flexible intergovernmental alliance.

North American Free Trade Association (NAFTA)

This free trade area is unlikely to develop the strong drive towards political integration which has char-

acterized the EU. It is nonetheless a remarkable attempt to eliminate, over 15 years, trade tariffs between two developed states, the USA and Canada, and one developing economy, Mexico. NAFTA's combined market of 380 million people gives the association global significance. Yet as with the EU, both establishing and maintaining NAFTA have caused domestic political difficulties, particularly in the USA. In negotiating the compact, the American administration faced opposition from domestic producers and unions. They feared that free trade with Mexico would cause a migration of jobs to low-cost assembly sites (the *maquiladora* industries) on the Mexican side of the border. In a famous phrase, the independent politician Ross Perot referred to the 'great sucking sound' of jobs being pulled down to Mexico. The intensity of this debate within America illustrates the inherent problem of selling free trade areas to doubtful populations in democracies. NAFTA also illustrates the spillover effects of free trade areas. It has increased concern in the USA about labour rights and environmental standards in Mexico. It led to massive American aid for Mexico during its currency crisis of 1994–95. And the American administration has itself emphasised political spillover from the NAFTA, claiming that Mexico's continuing moves toward democracy are partly a by-product. It may well be that NAFTA will encourage some political *convergence* among its members even though (unlike the EU) political *integration* has never been on the agenda.

Asia-Pacific Economic Co-operation (APEC)

East Asia views the prospect of closed regional blocs in the Western hemisphere with concern. This is because exports to the West have provided the foundation of growth in East Asia. Precisely for this reason, initiatives to establish regional economic organizations in East Asia have been slow to emerge and limited in success. The most recent attempt is through APEC (Box 3.3), a loose grouping of states responsible for about half the world's output and trade. APEC's development reveals, in particular, the problems in welding a coherent region out of diverse materials. Its membership is wide-ranging in the extreme. Some members fear American values; many are concerned about China's military ambitions; and several long-standing sources of conflict (for example the status of Taiwan) remain unresolved. Despite the enormous potential of the Asia–Pacific region, there are no indications yet that coherent economic (let alone political) region-building is taking place. Indeed, the impetus behind APEC is not to create a region such as the EU with 'closed' characteristics. Rather the intention is to create an 'open' or 'benign' region: that is, a group of states which seeks to remove internal trade barriers while remaining committed to the expansion of free trade with the rest of the world. Open regionalism may prove a more accurate model for future regional developments than the institutional approach of the EU.

The global economy and developing states

For most developing countries the world economy is a given; they must play by rules shaped by more powerful states. A few developing states have established a successful place in the global economy, taking advantage of the gradual shift of the world's routine assembly and manufacturing away from high-cost Western producers. But the least developed countries remain in a dependent, postcolonial position, surviving by exporting basic foodstuffs or minerals in competition with other poor states. So far, then, one of the main effects of the global economy on the developing world has been to intensify the division between the genuinely 'developing' economies and the least developed countries.

East Asia is the renowned example of a region which seized the opportunities offered by a global economy. Between 1960 and the early 1990s, the region increased its share of gross world product from 4 per cent to over a quarter, a massive transformation. Under Japanese economic leadership, the East Asian 'tigers' (Hong Kong, Singapore, South Korea and Taiwan) became major exporters and offered foreign investors an appealing combination of cheap labour and stable politics. As countries such as Taiwan and South Korea became wealthier, so they in turn invested in other countries in the region. This pattern of development in East Asia was called the 'flying geese' model because the region's countries developed as a group, flying behind the leading goose of Japan (Cumings, 1987). By the same token, those countries which rose with Japan became vulnerable when its economy stumbled in the later 1990s.

But to date the experience of the least developed states has been far harsher than that of the East Asian tigers. Some countries, mainly in sub-Saharan Africa, are effectively 'out of the game' (Palan and Abbott, 1996, p. 184). These states are landlocked, remote, vulnerable to natural disasters, consist mainly of desert or possess populations which are illiterate or sick. In some African countries the population of working age is severely reduced by AIDS. In these circumstances even the cheapest labour and the steadiest politics will not attract investment from multinational corporations (MNCs). One limit of globalization is that so many of these least developed states are not part of the 'global' economy at all. Further, even those developing countries which do attract foreign investment find that it is concentrated on a few favoured regions within their territory.

Many commentators argue that the economies of the least developed countries are locked into dependence on rich countries. 'Dependency theory' suggests that the whole international economy inherently operates to the disadvantage of the developing world. Because the developed world is already economically advanced, it can maintain its advantage in producing higher-value manufactured goods.

EXHIBIT 3.2

The global economy

Economic developments drive interdependence. Trade grows apace while production and finance have broken free of national restraints. A global economy in which capital and knowledge are key resources poses enormous questions for states defined by their control over territory.

Of course, international trade is far from new; it is nearly as old as human history itself. As advocates of economic liberalism tirelessly point out, trade allows countries to specialize in areas where they are relatively efficient, thus enabling all participants to benefit. Trade can be a 'win–win' game. Yet while international trade may not be new, it is increasing at a faster rate than production. Between 1913–50, a period covering two wars and the depression, trade declined slightly as a proportion of world output. But in the decades after the war, and especially in the final quarter of the century, the proportion of world product traded between nations grew dramatically. Between 1990 and 1995 world merchandise trade grew at an annual average of 8 per cent, almost twice the rate of increase in world merchandise output. Factors contributing to this expansion were improved communications, lower transport costs, lower tariffs and a shift in government policies to supporting export-led growth.

Trends in the forms of trade are at least as important as increasing volume. The earliest forms of trade were generally carried out by or under licence from the state. In the twentieth century, stimulated by the industrial revolution and the growth of manufacturing, trade between national firms became dominant. In today's more global economy, the form of trade has changed again. A large and growing proportion of world trade – currently about a third – is conducted among divisions of the same multinational company. For instance, most of Japan's exports go to overseas divisions of its own companies (Katzenstein 1996, p. 135). *Inter*national trade is increasingly *intra*company.

The growth of intracompany trade reflects an explosion of foreign direct investment (FDI). FDI refers to a directly-owned investment made by a firm outside its home country, typically by establishing manufacturing plant overseas. For instance, Japanese car companies have made enormous investments in overseas markets. Between 1983 and 1990 world FDI expanded at an annual average of 34 per cent. By 1996, according to some estimates, FDI accounted for as much as a fifth of total world investment (Williams, 1997).

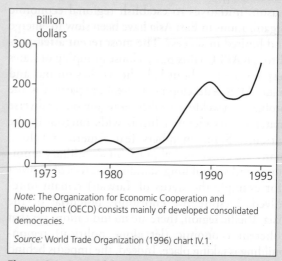

Note: The Organization for Economic Cooperation and Development (OECD) consists mainly of developed consolidated democracies.

Source: World Trade Organization (1996) chart IV.1.

Figure 3.2 Annual foreign direct investment by firms in OECD countries, 1970–93

Trade is the most obvious example of economic globalization but it is not the only illustration. Finance has become the most globalized of all economic functions, and unlike manufactured goods, money can be shifted electronically. Today, money washes around the world in far greater volume than is needed to support international trade. The amount of currency exchanged in a day exceeds the value of goods and services traded across borders in an entire year (Palan and Abbott 1996, p. 22). Money has been deterritorialized. The globalization of finance reflects three main causes:

- The increase in oil prices in 1973/74 which created an enormous quantity of petro-dollars to be recycled, principally from Middle-Eastern countries
- The revolution in communications which now allows financial prices anywhere to be displayed on computer screens anywhere

EXHIBIT 3.2

- The deregulation of financial markets, beginning in the 1980s, which permitted money to circulate with less government regulation.

Like trade, the way money flows round the world has also evolved. It is no longer routed through a few large banks but travels through a wide range of institutions, including private bodies recycling criminal gains. Just as MNCs can challenge states through their power in trade and production, so the sheer weight of money in global financial markets threatens national autonomy in setting exchange and interest rates.

Our picture of the global economy, then, reveals multinational companies leading the development of world trade and huge sums of money washing round the world in search of the highest return. We should not, however, fall victim to globalization fever. 'Globalization' does not embrace all countries, all companies or all economic sectors. Hirst and Thompson (1996) pour some beneficial cold water

over authors who have exaggerated the globalization of the world economy. Hirst and Thompson claim that:

- The world economy is in some ways no more integrated now than it was between 1880–1914
- Most multinational companies are not global but have a clear base in a specific country
- Foreign direct investment is not spread across the globe but is concentrated on a few developed economies
- Trade, investment and financial flows occur mainly within the triad of Europe, Japan and the USA
- This triad ('the G3' or group of three) retains the potential to control and regulate the 'global' economy.

Further reading: Hirst and Thompson (1996), Strange (1994), Stubbs and Underhill (1994).

The developing world is left to concentrate on primary products for which prices are low and volatile. Many economies in the developing world depend almost exclusively on exporting a single commodity to a single export market (Table 3.3). The result is unbalanced development, a pattern

which explains why a politician in Venezuela felt able to denounce oil, his country's major natural resource, as 'the devil's excrement'. Dependency theorists argue that what has emerged is not a neutral 'global economy' but rather a new form of economic colonialism in which the developed world shapes the

Table 3.3 The vulnerable economies, 1995

'Single commodity' exporters

Country	Commodity	Proportion of exports %
Algeria	Oil, natural gas	97
Uganda	Coffee	97
Nigeria	Oil	95
American Samoa[1]	Tuna fish	93
Guinea	Bauxite and aluminium	85

Exports to a dominant market

Country	Main Market(s)	Proportion of exports %
American Samoa[1]	USA	99
Djibouti	Somalia, Yemen	90
Niue	New Zealand	89
Puerto Rico	USA	86
Mexico	USA	82

[1] an unincorporated territory of the USA.

Source: CIA (1997).

structure of client economies in the developing world. This is not development but rather what Frank (1969) once called 'the development of underdevelopment'.

Definition

Conditionality is the practice of attaching strings to aid. Political conditionality might include a requirement to legalize opposition and hold competitive elections. Economic conditionality often takes the form of a specified **structural adjustment programme**, typically involving privatizing state companies, introducing more competition and opening domestic markets to overseas companies.

Certainly, the weaker the finances of a developing country, the more leverage international agencies can exert. IGO impact has been particularly strong in those countries most affected by the 1980s debt crisis. This arose when Western banks increased lending to developing countries which then failed to meet repayments. Although some larger states had regained international credit-worthiness by the mid-1990s, many of the least developed states remained in massive debt. As late as 1995, the developing world as a whole owed $1.5 trillion; interest payments stood at $232 billion per year. So the least developed states remain unable to bargain about the terms of any further financial aid. Bodies such as the World Bank and the IMF are generally willing to provide additional support but this debt restructuring is conditional on domestic economic reform, including privatization, reduced corruption, lower tariffs and more transparency in allocating government contracts.

Governments which build domestic political support by using the economy to reward their supporters find the injunction to reduce their control of the economy striking at the heart of their power. In effect, the international agencies require such countries to restructure their politics as well as their economy. Dr Mahathir, Prime Minister of Malaysia, likens the international political economy to 'a jungle of ferocious beasts' and claims that the IMF is willing 'to subvert our economy' in order to prove the validity of its own theories. However, Mahathir's assault on international agencies is largely a political tactic to increase his own domestic support. A few governments, such as Egypt in 1988 and Jordan in 1990, have sought to fight back by abandoning IMF restructuring and the aid linked to it. Politically, these states were unwilling to relinquish control over state-owned enterprises, to reduce government spending and to offer a larger role to MNCs. Significantly, though, both Egypt and Jordan later returned to domestic restructuring.

EXHIBIT 3.3

Bailing out Thailand

To help overcome the weakness of Thailand's currency, the international community (led by the IMF and Japan) offered a $16 billion loan to the Thai government in 1997. The conditions attached to the loan, some listed below, indicate just how far international institutions can influence domestic policy. It remains to be seen, however, how many of these conditions Thailand will implement. The suspicion is that some money will leak into dubious subsidies to firms that support the government. The politicians may calculate that as long as the loans are repaid somehow, no-one will worry about the small print; other Asian governments forced into the arms of international institutions will probably follow Thailand's lead.

- Keep foreign reserves above $25 billion.
- Raise value added tax (similar to sales tax) to 10 per cent.
- Keep inflation below 9 per cent.
- Halve the country's trade deficit.
- Balance the budget.
- Speed up privatization.
- Allow foreign ownership of banks.
- Let the currency float.
- Make government finances more transparent.
- End currency controls.

Further reading: 'Thai bailout: self-interest makes for cooperation', *Financial Times*, 12 August 1997. 'First in, First Out?', *Financial Times*, 24 February 1998.

Country profile THE PEOPLE'S REPUBLIC OF CHINA

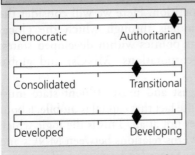

Democratic — Authoritarian

Consolidated — Transitional

Developed — Developing

Population: 1210m, the largest in the world.

Gross domestic product per head: $2900 (American estimate. Chinese figures may be understated to gain preferential treatment from organizations such as the World Bank).

Form of government: communist party dictatorship.

Assembly: a large unicameral National People's Congress, now including some representatives from Hong Kong. The Congress is party dominated but also includes some loyal non-party representatives (for example from national minorities).

Executive: formally headed by the premier. Real power lies in the Politburo (political bureau) of the Chinese Communist Party (CCP).

Judiciary: judges of the Supreme People's Court are appointed by the National People's Congress which is itself tightly controlled by the party.

Electoral system: members of the National People's Congress are chosen through indirect election via county and provincial congresses.

Party system: the CCP is the only significant party. Some small minor parties are permitted so long as they do not challenge the communist monopoly.

In 1978, the CCP embarked on a series of economic reforms that radically transformed the Chinese economy, setting it on course to become the largest in the world some time in the twenty-first century. The old state planning system was gradually dismantled, allowing market forces, previously condemned as a capitalist evil, to assume an important role. In the mid-1980s, China also abandoned its policy of disengagement from the international economy. Initially, economic contacts were restricted to four Special Economic Zones, so as to control the influence of overseas corporations. As foreign investment flooded in to these special areas, generating rapid growth, so the rest of the country opened to international contacts.

As a result of these reforms, China's economy has grown rapidly, increasing its share of global production. Between 1990 and 1995, growth in China averaged 12.8 per cent per year, compared to 2.8 per cent for the world as a whole. In 1995, China'a trade in goods and services was worth $289 billion, compared to just $21 billion in 1978. This remarkable growth reflects very low wages and high tax breaks to encourage investment. Indeed, nearly half of China's trade is 'processing trade'; China imports components from overseas and assembles them into finished goods for export. China's low costs have implications for all other countries. In the United States, for example, toy producers have lost market share to Chinese imports, prompting an attempted 'toycott' to protect American jobs.

China's entry into the global economy is a pivotal event; its consequences will be felt not just in the rest of the world but also within China itself. Rapid growth brings problems as well as benefits. Most foreign investment is in the costal strip, and significant income disparities exist between coastal areas and the interior. China's massive trade surplus with the USA has also led to American pressure for China to reduce subsidies to its own producers, and to allow American exporters greater access to the Chinese market. And the question arises of whether exploiting low production costs to achieve rapid short-term growth is the best strategy for China in the longer run. The work created is often low quality, offering little access to training and technology. Competition between China's provinces (and with other countries such as Vietnam) enables overseas companies to use the threat of moving production elsewhere to gain extra concessions, placing strains on the fragile unity of China itself. Indeed, some authors question whether China has a future as a single nation-state.

Further reading: Lieberthal (1995), Womack and Townsend (1996).
www.oop.gov.tw
www.insidechina.com
www.aweto.com/china

It is not only IGOs which impose conditionalities. Since the end of the cold war, bilateral aid has also become subject to specific conditions. During the cold war, competition between the American and Soviet superpowers gave developing countries considerable leverage; a promise of cooperation with one superpower was often enough to gain financial support with no questions asked. But the end of the cold war diminished the strategic value of small states, and Africa in particular suffered strategic marginalization. As a result, donor governments can now afford to attach strings to aid which may take the form of pressure for political change. For example, sanctions may be imposed on countries with poor human rights records (for example, China) or corrupt governments (Kenya). States which have invaded other countries (Iran), which sponsor international terrorism (Syria), which are ruled by undemocratic means (Libya) or which are still under communist control (North Korea, Cuba) find themselves isolated from, or entirely without influence within, the international system. Thus the attitudes of dominant countries directly affect the political situation confronting national leaders in poorly-regarded developing states. The worst cases become pariah states, kept out of the international community.

The global economy and developed states

The global economy presents states in the developed world with a more favourable balance of opportunities and threats. In particular, the countries with the largest domestic markets (Japan and the USA) still have a low (but still increasing) ratio of trade to national product. Exports make up just 10 per cent of gross national product in Japan and the United States, compared to 51 per cent for a smaller European economy such as the Netherlands. This gives the largest developed states some insulation from the world economy but also some impact on it, an enviable combination. But the pressures of the global market must be addressed by even the largest and most affluent states. An open trading world remorselessly exposes economic weaknesses which could be covered up in an era of national markets. Even the American manufacturing sector had to

undergo a painful period of restructuring in the 1980s to meet the challenge of overseas, especially Japanese, competition. Here we will consider the two major channels through which the global economy affects politics within developed states: multinational corporations (MNCs) and global financial flows.

Even the largest and most affluent state must confront the brute fact that capital is mobile, labour less so and states not at all. This is the logic which increasingly governs relations between MNCs and all governments. States (and regions within them) must compete to provide an attractive home for foreign direct investment. If they refuse to play the game, they pay the price of losing jobs and access to fresh technology. But the issue is not just about attracting new investment: MNCs can also obtain government money just by hinting that they might move existing plants elsewhere. When Ford threatened to stop making Jaguar cars exclusively in the UK, the British government found enough money to prevent the company from starting a production line in its American factories. MNCs also create tax competition between states by locating their profits where corporate taxation is low and their losses where taxes are high. For example, when the United States reduced its corporate tax rates in 1986, every country belonging to the Organization for Economic Cooperation and Development, except Switzerland and Turkey, followed suit within five years.

However, unlike the vulnerable states of the third world, the relationship between Western governments and MNCs is more balanced. MNCs must sell their products in the affluent and sophisticated markets of the developed world. Aware of their attractions, host governments can strike a deal. For instance, local MNC production may be subject to a requirement that local factories of the MNC buy a certain share of their resources from suppliers in the host country.

International financial flows are the other major way in which markets constrain policy-making in developed states. As one immodest foreign exchange dealer put it, 'basically, we are the world's government'. So how exactly is this influence exerted? Governments fund their debt by borrowing, often from overseas. The less confidence financial markets possess in a country's government or economy, the higher the rate of interest they will demand for lending to that country. The effect is to reinforce the strength of governments which are good house-keepers and to punish spendthrifts and money-printers. Democratic or not, any country integrated into the global market must accept its constraints. If you play the game, you accept the rules.

For example, the German government could tra-ditionally borrow money at lower cost than the British government, reflecting greater confidence in the deutschmark than in the pound. One advantage of the single European currency for weak member economies is that they can, in effect, shelter behind the deutschmark.

In similar fashion, the global financial system also influences currency values. The weight of money in the financial market is far greater than that in the vaults of central banks. If the market believes that a currency is overvalued, funds will move out of that currency, causing a decline in its value. The outcome may be an unwanted devaluation for those govern-ments which seek to maintain a fixed exchange rate. Sweden is a classic example. In 1992, international markets temporarily lost confidence in the Swedish economy, due to a large and growing budget deficit. Desperately trying to stave off a devaluation, the government dramatically increased short-term interest rates, made radical cuts in its budget, increased value added tax and cancelled two days paid national holiday. The measures failed to restore international confidence and the krona was allowed to float. The devaluation of several East Asian cur-rencies (including Malaysia) in 1997 is another example, and one which caused growing difficulties for domestic banks which had borrowed from abroad in order to invest, directly or indirectly, in a speculative property sector.

A final effect of economic globalization on devel-oped countries is to increase economic inequality within them. As inefficient producers go out of business, jobs go with them. Unskilled work moves out of the developed world to developing countries where wages are dramatically lower. Between 1986–90, the industrial countries captured 80 per cent of the world's FDI. By 1994, this had declined to 56 per cent. The result is endemic unemployment in many affluent states, particularly in those European countries where generous welfare provision

reduces the incentive to work for low pay. So the developed world is beginning to experience a pattern long familiar in poorer countries. Even as average incomes increase, so does the inequality of its distri-bution. In the United States, the income of the richest fifth of the population increased by 34 per cent between 1977 and 1988. By contrast, the poorest fifth faced a 10 per cent reduction. In Britain, economic inequality in 1997 was greater than at any time since 1887. For Thomas (1997), 'it is no longer enough to think only in terms of rich and poor states; we need to consider groups or classes of rich and poor people which crosscut state boundaries'.

We can draw a similar distinction between core and peripheral regions within a country. Core regions possess the location and skills needed to prosper from increases in trade; peripheral regions find themselves trapped in a cycle of decline. Eventually, we may find that the categories 'devel-oped' and 'developing' apply not to countries but to sectors and regions within them, producing massive new problems of political management for govern-ments increasingly hemmed in by global constraints. In such circumstances, the role of the state in mod-erating domestic conflict will be as crucial as ever. There is plenty of work left for states and there is no-one else able to do it.

Key reading

> **Next step:** *Waters (1995) is an accessible introduction to the debate about globalization.*

Kegley and Witkopf (1997) provide an excellent introduction to world politics. Blake and Walters (1992) is also a good intro-duction, particularly to development and underdevelopment. On international organizations, Bennett (1991) is a standard text, while Kratochwil and Mansfield (1994) is a useful reader. Mayall (1996) covers the UN's new interventionism. On regionalism, Gamble and Payne (1996b) is a good survey. Hurrell (1995) is an excellent analysis of regionalism and region-alization and a springboard to further study. Stubbs and Underhill (1994) is a helpful edited collection on international political economy. On globalization, Hirst and Thompson (1996) is a good place to start. Strange (1994) has generated considerable debate on how much power national governments retain in a global world.

PART 2

POLITICS AND SOCIETY

The relationship between politics and society has always preoccupied political thinkers. Government does not operate in isolation, unaffected by the society of which it forms part. For instance a society's culture and economy both help to explain its form of government. This part examines the major links between politics and society. Chapter 4 looks at the attitudes of people toward government while chapter 5 discusses their participation in it. The remaining chapters in this part examine how individuals and groups help to shape the political process: elections and voters (chapter 6), interest groups (chapter 7) and parties (chapter 8). Throughout this part, we need to bear in mind that the connections between society and state run both ways. Parties, especially, do not just reflect the public mood; they also help to set the agenda of debate.

Political culture

'The strongest is never strong enough unless he succeeds in turning might into right and obedience into duty.' So wrote Rousseau in the eighteenth century and rulers the world over have taken his saying to their hearts. For instance, the cult of Lenin in the Soviet Union required two- and three-year olds to sing nursery songs about Lenin; four- and five-year olds to decorate his portrait; and six-year olds to lay flowers at Lenin's statue (Tumarkin, 1997). Attempts to foster loyalty to the regime were not of course restricted to communist states; they are still found in all countries. Civics classes in American high schools and the deference to authority encouraged in many Asian countries are other ways in which states have tried to transform might into right, obedience into duty. To study how people view their country's politics is to investigate political culture. The notion of political culture does not refer to attitudes to specific actors such as the current president or prime minister, rather it denotes how people view the political system as a whole. This includes whether citizens see 'the system' as legitimate, with the rulers sustained by right as well as might. The building blocks of political culture are therefore the beliefs, opinions and emotions of individual citizens toward their form of government.

Political culture and political stability

A supportive political culture, sustained across the generations, contributes to the stability of political systems. A regime based on right is likely to last longer, not least because it is more effective than one relying on might alone. This impact of political culture on political stability is our first concern in this chapter. To illustrate the link consider Almond and Verba's classic work, *The Civic Culture* (1963). This study was based on surveys conducted during 1959–60 in the USA, Britain, West Germany, Italy and Mexico. Its purpose was to identify the political culture within which a liberal democracy was most likely to survive and develop.

Almond and Verba distinguished three pure types of political culture: the parochial, subject and participant. In the *parochial* political culture, citizens are only indistinctly aware of the existence of central government – as with remote tribes whose existence is seemingly unaffected by national decisions made by the central government. In the *subject* political culture, citizens see themselves not as participants in the political process but as subjects of the government – as with people living under a dictatorship. In the more familiar *participant* political culture, citizens believe both that they can contribute to the system and that they are affected by it.

> **Definition**
> Pye (1995, p. 965) defines **political culture** as 'the sum of the fundamental values, sentiments and knowledge that give form and substance to political processes'.

Almond and Verba's core idea was that democracy will prove most stable in societies where subject and parochial attitudes provide ballast to an essentially participant culture. This mix is termed the 'civic culture' (Figure 4.1). In this ideal combination, citizens are sufficiently active in politics to express their preferences to rulers but are not so involved as to refuse to accept decisions with which they disagree. In Almond and Verba's study, Britain, and to a lesser extent the United States, came closest to this ideal. In both countries citizens felt they could influence the government but often chose not to do so, thus giving the government a measure of flexibility.

Of course times move on. Since Almond and Verba's pathbreaking study many liberal democracies have hit turbulent waters: Vietnam, student activism, economic recession, the antinuclear movement, ecology groups, cutbacks in the welfare state. As Almond and Verba (1980) noted in an update of their original work, these events left their mark on Western political cultures. In Britain and the USA trust in government declined. Three quarters of Americans said in 1964 that they trusted the federal government 'to do the right thing'; by 1996, only a third did so. In Britain, the proportion trusting the government to put country before party fell from 39 per cent in 1974 to 22 per cent in 1996 (Figure 4.2). These figures show a shift away from the civic culture towards a more sceptical and instrumental attitude to politics. Yet, in America as in other consolidated democracies, governments continued to govern. In most of the democratic world rulers were able to privatize public corporations and reduce welfare provision without threatening the stability of the political system. Such discontent as

Per cent trusting the government 'most of the time'

Source: Nye, Zelikow and King (1997), Figure 3.1 and for the UK, Curtice and Jowell (1997), p. 91.

Figure 4.2 Trust in government in the United States and the United Kingdom, 1964–96

emerged focused more on the performance of governing parties and leaders than on the democratic process itself.

These points confirm that stable democracies have a bank of political capital which can sustain them through bad times. As Machiavelli (1469–1527) noted in *The Prince*, 'the prince should have the people on his side; if the contrary is true, there is no help in adverse moments'. Inglehart (1988) makes a similar point:

Even when democracy has no answer to the question, 'what have you done for me lately?' it may be sustained by diffuse feelings that it is an inherently good thing. These feelings may in turn reflect economic and other successes that one experienced long ago or learned about second hand as part of one's early socialization.

Putnam (1993) extends Almond and Verba's approach. Using Italy as his example, he shows how a supportive political culture directly enhances the performance as well as the stability of a political system. In their original work, Almond and Verba had portrayed Italy as a country whose people felt uninvolved in, and alienated from, politics. Putnam returns to this theme but pays more attention to diversity within Italy. He shows how the country's varying political cultures influenced the effectiveness

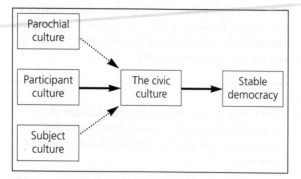

Figure 4.1 Almond and Verba's theory of the civic culture

of the 20 new regional governments set up by Italy in the 1970s. Similar in structure and formal powers, these 20 governments nonetheless varied greatly in performance. Some (such as Emilia-Romagna in the North) proved stable and effective, capable of making and implementing innovative policies. Others (such as Calabria in the South) achieved little. What explains these contrasts?

Putnam finds his answer in political culture. He argues that the most successful regions have a positive political culture, a tradition of trust and cooperation which results in high levels of what he terms 'social capital'. By contrast, the least effective governments are found in regions lacking any tradition of collaboration and equality. In such circumstances, governments can achieve little and the stock of social capital, already limited, will deflate further. But where does social capital itself come from? Like Almond and Verba before him, Putnam's answer is historical. Somewhat controversially, he attributes the uneven distribution of social capital in modern Italy to events deep within each area's history (Morlino, 1995). The more effective governments in the North draw on a tradition of communal self-government dating from the twelfth century. The least successful administrations in the South are burdened with a long history of feudal, foreign, bureaucratic and authoritarian rule. Thus in Putnam's analysis political culture becomes the

device through which the past influences the present.

Definition

Social capital refers to a culture of trust and cooperation which makes collective action possible and effective. As Putnam says, it is the ability of a community, to 'develop the "I" into the "we" '. A political culture with a fund of social capital enables a community to build political institutions with a real capacity to solve collective problems. Where social capital is scarce, even an elected government will be viewed as a threat to individual interests.

So far, we have examined the impact of political culture on government, but (and this is a point understated by Almond and Verba) the relationship flows in both directions. A civic culture contributes to the stability and effectiveness of democracy, but a democracy which literally delivers the goods engenders the supportive attitudes which will sustain the political system in the future. As Diamond and Lipset (1995, p. 751) write, 'for the long-run success of democracy, there is no alternative to economic stability and progress'. West Germany's success in translating its postwar economic miracle into favourable attitudes to its new democracy is testament to the power of economic performance to reshape political cultures. By contrast, postcommu-

---

EXHIBIT 4.1

Political culture in Kenya's Baraza

Political culture should be studied not just as an abstract category but also as a phenomenon which evolves in the actual practice of politics. Haugerud's research on Kenyan *baraza* (1995) is one of the few studies of political culture 'in motion'. *Baraza* are large public gatherings addressed by important officials known as the 'Wa-Benzi', big men who ride around in Mercedes-Benz cars. These élite figures speak from the platform to ordinary citizens who have travelled for miles on foot to attend the meeting. Ritual though they may be, these occasions are not an empty exercise for fooling the people; sharp, critical comments emerge from the crowd. But neither is the *baraza* an expression of a common

culture; after all, the inequality between those seated on the stage and those sitting on the bank is apparent to all. Rather, the *baraza* is a crossroads at which the national meets the local, and the powerful interact with the powerless. It is in such forums, suggests Haugerud, that political culture is shaped, confirmed and modified. Haugerud (p. 8) concludes that 'political culture is less rigid than the literature suggests. It is malleable and mobile, a matter of historical practice'. So political culture is not just an inheritance from the past. Rather, it continues to evolve through political practice.

Further reading: Haugerud (1995).

nist countries had to cope with economic collapse in their early years, an adjustment which inevitably tested the public's commitment to fledgling democracies. So it is important to recognize that political culture is itself shaped by a nation's history and economic performance.

Elite political culture

Although the impact of mass political culture on political stability has been debated widely, the significance of élite political culture has been addressed less often. Yet in countries with a parochial or subject political culture, élite political culture is primary. Even where mass attitudes to politics are well-developed, as in consolidated liberal democracies, it is still the views of the élite which exert the most direct effect on political decisions. As Verba (1987, p. 7) writes, the values of political leaders can be expected to have both 'coherence and consequences'; for instance, élites have been central to recent democratic transitions. In this section, we examine élite political culture, again focusing on its consequences for political stability.

Élite culture is far more than a representative fragment of the values of the wider society. Throughout the world the ideas of élites are distinct from, though they overlap with, the national political culture. For instance, elites generally take a more liberal line on social and moral issues. Stouffer's (1966) famous survey of American attitudes to freedom of speech, conducted in 1954, confirmed this point. Stouffer showed that most community leaders maintained their belief in free speech for atheists, socialists and communists at a time when the attitudes of the public were much less tolerant. Later surveys revealed a striking increase in the American public's support for free speech (Sullivan, Pierson and Marcus, 1982). Nonetheless, it was crucial to the cause of free speech in the United States that a majority of the political élite remained committed at a time when the principle was under strong attack from Senator Joe McCarthy's anti-communist witch-hunt (Fried, 1990). In a similar way, many leaders of postcommunist countries accept the need for a thorough transition to a market economy even while mass culture remains more sympathetic to the equality of poverty practised under communism.

> **Definition**
> **Élite political culture** consists of the beliefs, attitudes and ideas about politics held by those who are closest to the centres of political power. The values of elites are more coherent and consequential than those of the population at large.

One reason for the liberal and sophisticated outlook of élites is their standard of education; in many liberal democracies, politics has become a graduate profession. The experience of higher education nurtures an optimistic view of human nature, strengthens humanitarian values and encourages a belief in the ability of politicians to solve social problems (Astin, 1977). Indeed the contrast between the values of the educated élite and the least educated section of the population is a source of tension in many political cultures.

In assessing the impact of élite political culture on stability, three dimensions are crucial:

- Does the élite have faith in its own right to rule?
- Does the élite accept the notion of a national interest, separate from individual and group ambitions?
- Do all members of the élite accept the rules of the game, especially those governing the transfer of power? (Figure 4.3).

A major component of élite political culture is the rulers' belief in their own *right to rule*. The revolutions of 1989 in Eastern Europe illustrate how a collapse of confidence among the rulers themselves

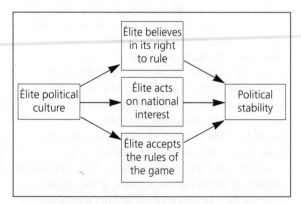

Figure 4.3 How élite political culture affects political stability

can lead to the fall of regimes. As Schöpflin (1990) points out,

> an authoritarian élite sustains itself in power not just through force and the threat of force but, more importantly, because it has some vision of the future by which it can justify itself to itself. No regime can survive long without some concept of purpose.

In the initial phase of industrialization, communist rulers had good reason to believe their new planned economies were producing results. But by the late 1980s progress had given way to decline: planned economies had reached a dead end. As even nominal support from intellectuals faded, so party officials began to lose confidence in their own right to rule. In the end, communist rule was toppled so easily because it had already been weakened from within. Élite values had ceased to underpin the system of government. Communist rulers were aware they they had become a barrier to, rather than a source of, progress.

For long-term stability, the political élite must accept and act on some interpretation of the *national interest*. At issue here is the attitude of rulers to the government posts they hold. Is public service seen as just that – a way of serving the national interest? Some national bureaucracies, from France to Pakistan, have seen themselves as guardians of the nation even to the point of protecting their country from 'mere politicians'. Often, however, the state is seen by its ruling élite as a seam of scarce resources to be mined for the benefit of the rulers, their family, their constituents and their ethnic group. In the developing world, where economic resources are scarce and state institutions are weak this approach often predominates. In postcommunist countries, too, officials who survived the collapse of the old order often gained personally from acquiring public assets in corrupt privatizations. This reflected a dog-eat-dog culture and a dismissive attitude toward the 'people's property'. It would be naive to suppose that politicians anywhere are guided solely by the national interest. However, at a minimum, élite values should not condone self-interested behaviour which threatens the collective good. When exposed, corruption should generate criticism rather than a mere shrug of the shoulders.

Perhaps the most critical dimension of élite political culture is the attitudes which politicians hold to the *rules of the game*. A range of possibilities exists here. Is élite competition absolute, as in countries such as Northern Ireland where 'gains' to one side (Protestant or Catholic) are thereby viewed as 'losses' by the other? In such circumstances there are no agreed rules which limit political competition. Or is strong party conflict moderated by agreement on the rules, as in Britain and New Zealand? The consequences of these attitudes to the political game are highly significant. Take America's Watergate scandal, during which President Nixon's supporters engaged in such illegal acts as break-ins and phone-taps against their Democratic opponents. This reflected the President's own stark view of politics: 'us' against 'them'. Nixon was willing to dispense with the normal rules to ensure that his enemies 'got what they deserved'. A democracy where such attitudes prevailed among the élite would have limited prospects of survival.

By contrast, when party or group leaders are willing to compromise to allow the expression of other interests and values, the prospects for political stability improve. Lijphart (1977) argued that an accommodating attitude among group representatives in divided societies such as Austria and Holland provided a recipe for stable government in the 1950s and 1960s. Then, religion still strongly divided these countries; however, party politicians representing the various communities accepted the right of each social group to a fair share of state resources. These groups – Catholic, Protestant and secular – were then left free to distribute these resources almost as their leaders wanted. This attitude of 'live and let live' successfully contained explosive divisions and showed the importance of élite values in contributing to the stability of democracies.

Political socialization

Political socialization is the means through which political culture is transmitted across the generations. It is a universal process. To survive, all societies must pass on the skills needed for people to perform political roles, varying from voting at an election to governing the country. The key point about socialization is that it is largely an uncontrolled and uncontrollable process. No matter how much rulers try (and try they do), they find themselves unable to dominate either the process or the content of socialization. By its nature, therefore, socialization serves to replicate the status quo. As a result political culture becomes a stabilizing force, providing a major barrier against planned change.

Definition

Political socialization is the process through which we learn about politics. It concerns the acquisition of emotions, identities and skills as well as information. The main dimensions of socialization are what people learn (content), when they learn it (timing and sequence) and from whom (agents). Most studies of political socialization derive from the primacy model – the assumption that what we learn when young provides a lens through which we interpret later experience.

Learning a political culture is very different from acquiring an academic skill, such as a knowledge of history. Formal education involves assimilating and learning how to use information transmitted from teacher to student in an educational setting. Political socialization is more diffuse, indirect and unplanned. It involves the development of political emotions and identities (what is my nation? my religion? my party?) as well as the acquisition of information. Political socialization takes place through a variety of institutions – the family, the peer group, the workplace – as well as formal education. It is as much influenced by the context of communication as its content. For example, childrens' attitude toward politics will be influenced as much by their experience of authority at home and at school as by what parents and teachers say their views should be.

The primacy view of political socialization is that basic political loyalties are formed when young. Childhood learning is 'deep learning' because it provides a framework for interpreting information acquired in adulthood. Core political identities are developed in *early childhood*, when the family is the crucial influence on the child. In *late childhood*, these attachments are supplemented by a marked increase in information. The main effect of *adolescence* is to refine the child's conceptual understanding, building on information already obtained. These three stages of socialization – early childhood, late childhood and adolescence – prepare the child for political participation in adult political life (Figure 4.4). Adult experiences will modify, but not usually transform, the outlook secured when young. The primacy model of socialization approach works best during stable eras such as the 1950s.

One example of the primacy model is Pye's (1985) analysis of Asian political cultures. Pye argues that

> the cornerstone of powerbuilding in the Asian cultures is loyalty to a collectivity. Out of the need to belong, to submerge one's self in a group identity, is power formed in Asian cultures.

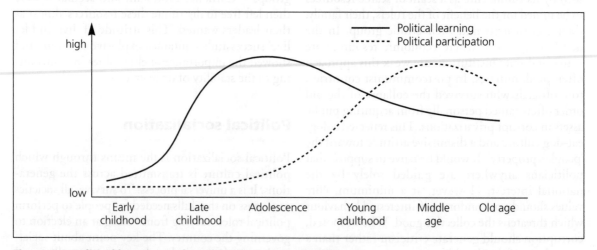

Figure 4.4 Political learning and participation across the life cycle

EXHIBIT 4.2

Socialized to kill: Africa's child soldiers

In a stable political system, studies of political social-ization can examine how children acquire the under-standing needed to fulfil normal adult roles such as voting. But where political authority has disinte-grated, and violence is the norm, children must learn survival skills: how to steal in order to eat, how to survive without parents and, in the case of Africa's child soldiers, how to kill without guilt.

Although the United Nations Convention on the Rights of the Child prohibits conscription of children under 15, boys have fought in guerilla armies in several African countries: for instance, Uganda, Liberia, Mozambique, Ethiopia and the Sudan. Estimates suggested there were about 200 000 child soldiers worldwide at the start of the 1990s.

Children make good fighters. Compared to adults they are quick learners, more obedient, less likely to run away, easier to confuse and more willing to fight without drugs. They can be fooled into thinking that adorning themselves with charms or special paint will protect them from enemy bullets. They are easier to drug, if needed, to reduce fear and inhibition. They do not expect pay but are often satisfied with food, a role and a gun. If they are first forced to kill their own relatives or set fire to their own village, they know they can never go back home but must throw in their

lot with the roving guerillas. Their individuality can be broken through torture and they can easily be rewarded for killing, with a simple smile or a quick hug. Thus they can be socialized to achieve higher levels of brutality than adults and so invoke more fear in the population. Adult soldiers can also use children as a shield, knowing the enemy will be less willing to attack.

Child soldiers are a new and hopefully a temporary phenomenon. Their existence is a symptom of col-lapsed states in which order has disintegrated, creating a generation of orphaned children who are easy prey for guerilla leaders. To stop the problem at source will require government control to be re-estab-lished, yet even if this political imperative is achieved an overwhelming task of 're-socialization' awaits. When children have been socialized to kill at a young age can they later learn to respect others, to give and receive affection and to listen to their conscience? And can people be found who are willing to give a year of their time after graduation to help with this task?

Further reading: Furley (1995). See also Dodge and Raundalen (1987), Kumar (1997) and Machel (1996).

But what is the origin of this need to belong and conform? Pye suggests that the answer lies in the experience of childhood. The Asian child finds unquestioned love and attention from the family: the child respects and does not question parental author-ity, leading to similar deference to political rulers later in life. This acceptance of benevolent leadership is supposedly characteristic of 'Asian democracy'.

Although most research on political socialization has focused on children, we must remember that the process is lifelong; basic political outlooks mature in response to events and experience and political learning does not stop at childhood's end

(Conover and Searing 1994). In the eighteenth century, Montesquieu (1949, first pub. 1748) observed that

> we receive three educations: one from our parents, another from our teachers, and a third from the world. The third contradicts all the first two teach us.

Some adult experiences such as foreign travel will be personal, but collective events such as depression and war will hold more political significance. Thus we can contrast the primacy model with an alterna-

Country profile GERMANY

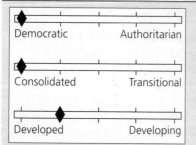

Democratic — Authoritarian

Consolidated — Transitional

Developed — Developing

Population: 84m.
Gross domestic product per head:
$17 900 (West Germany $21 100,
East Germany $6 600).

Form of government: a parliamentary federal republic.

Legislature: the 662-member Bundestag is the lower house. The smaller upper house, the Bundesrat, represents the 16 federal Länder (states).

Executive: the Chancellor leads a cabinet of between 16 and 22 ministers. A President serves as ceremonial head of state.

Judiciary: the Federal Appeals Court and the Federal Constitutional Court head the influential judicial system.

Electoral system: the Bundestag is elected through an additional member system which has now been adopted in over 20 other countries. Members of the Bundesrat are nominated by the Länder; hence, the Bundesrat is never dissolved.

Party system: the leading parties are the SPD (Social Democrats) and the CDU (Christian Democrats). The smaller FDP (Free Democrats) has often governed in coalition with one of the major parties. The Greens became significant in the 1980s.

The Federal Republic of Germany remains an economic superpower. Its skilled employees, based in capital-intensive factories, produce manufactured goods for sale at premium prices throughout the world. Germany's exports have exceeded its imports every year since 1955, and the country's 'economic miracle' supports extensive public services; both contributed to the growth in the legitimacy of the Federal Republic founded in 1949 upon the ashes of Hitler's Third Reich. Only in the later 1990s, as unemployment passed the four million mark, did the German economic model begin to look tarnished.

Seeking to avoid the political instability of the Weimar Republic (1919–33), which had contributed to the Nazi seizure of power, the framers of the postwar constitution made the Chancellor the key figure in the new system of government. The Chancellor determines government policy, appoints Cabinet ministers, heads a staff of 500 and can only be removed from office when parliament also demonstrates a majority for a named successor. Within a parliamentary framework, Germany offers a distinctive form of 'Chancellor democracy'.

Most of the Republic's six chancellors have been strong figures, further enhancing the status of the office. For example, Helmut Kohl (Chancellor since

1982) was the dominant force behind the rapid, peaceful and expensive unification of Germany following the dramatic opening of the Berlin Wall in 1990. Though unification has proved costly for West Germany, and required massive restructuring in the former German Democratic Republic, the result is the largest country in Western Europe. Germany is also strategically positioned at the heart of the European continent.

For students of political culture, the country's postwar history shows how the legitimacy of a political system can flow from successful performance. Between 1959 and 1988 the proportion of Germans expressing pride in their political institutions increased from seven to 51 per cent. Over a similar period, support for a multiparty system grew from 53 to 92 per cent. Although this success story has not been repeated so easily in the former East Germany, the emergence of a supportive public in the Federal Republic since 1945 offers hope to other transitional countries seeking to build a democratic culture.

Further reading: Conradt (1996), Smith, Paterson and Padgett (1996).
www.bundesregierung.de

tive recency model. This is the idea that current information carries more weight just because it is contemporary. What we see on television today matters more than submerged childhood memories. Adult reality packs more punch than childhood myths.

The recency approach works best during eras of rapid political change such as the 1980s and 1990s, but must also have some general merit since clearly political cultures *do* change, even if slowly. No generation understands politics in exactly the same way as its forebears. Indeed, generational turnover is undoubtedly a major mechanism of cultural change. As we will see in the next section, the 1960s generation with no memory of the Second World War developed distinct values which are proving highly significant as this cohort moves into positions of power.

Postmaterialism

One factor which helps to account for changes in political culture, at both mass and élite level, is postmaterialism. Although this notion applies primarily to affluent western societies since 1945, it is a useful example of the way in which political scientists have sought to understand how political cultures change.

From the late 1940s to the early 1970s, the Western world witnessed a period of unprecedented economic growth. 'You've never had it so good' became a cliché which summarized the experience of the postwar generation. This era was also a period of relative international peace, permitting a cohort to grow up with no experience of world war. In addition, the newly-completed welfare state offered increased security to many Western populations against the scourges of illness and unemployment.

According to Inglehart, this combination of affluence, peace and security led to 'a silent revolution' in the political cultures of Western democracies. As Inglehart (1997, p. 28) puts it,

the emphasis on economic achievement as the main priority is now giving way to an increasing emphasis on the quality of life. In a major part of

the world, the disciplined, self-denying and achievement-oriented norms of industrial society are giving way to an increasingly broad latitude for individual choices of lifestyle and individual self-expression.

A new generation of postmaterialists emerged – young, well-educated people whose concerns centre on lifestyle issues such as ecology, nuclear disarmament and feminism. Where older generations valued order, security and fixed rules in such areas as religion and sexual morality, postmaterialists de-emphasise political and religious authority, placing more emphasis on self-expression and flexible rules. Postmaterialists are élite-challenging advocates of the new politics rather than élite-sustaining foot-soldiers in the old party battles. They are more attracted to single-issue groups than to the broader packages offered by political parties. A loaf of bread does not satisfy postmaterialists; it must also be wholemeal and additive-free!

Based on extensive survey evidence, Inglehart showed that the more affluent a democracy, the higher the proportion of postmaterialists within its borders. In Europe postmaterialism came first to, and made deepest inroads in, the wealthiest democracies such as Denmark, the Netherlands and Germany. Thus the affluent Scandinavian countries (except Norway) have been unusually receptive to postmaterialist ideas (Knutsen, 1990). The United States was also in the first wave of postmaterialism. In the early 1970s, American postmaterialists were concentrated among yuppies – young, upwardly mobile urban professionals, especially those in the wealthiest state of all, California. Postmaterialism is less common in poorer democracies with lower levels of education: for example, Greece, Ireland, Spain and Portugal.

Definition
Postmaterialism is a commitment to radical 'quality of life' issues (such as the environment) which can emerge, especially among the educated young, from a foundation of personal security and material affluence. Postmaterialists participate extensively in politics but they are inclined to join elite-challenging promotional groups rather than political parties (Inglehart, 1997).

It seems likely that postmaterial values will become more prominent in the future. When Inglehart began his studies in 1970–71, materialists outnumbered postmaterialists by about four to one in many Western countries. But projections from the early 1990s suggest that by 2000 the two groups will be of similar size (Abramson and Inglehart, 1992), a major transformation in political culture. One reason for this changing balance is that education is the best single predictor of postmaterialism. Indeed 'postmaterialism' may amount to little more than the liberal outlook induced by higher education. If so, the expansion of education in the postwar era may prove to be a better explanation of postmaterialism than Inglehart's own emphasis on affluence and peace. In any event, educational standards are rising throughout the world and will continue to give a further push to postmaterialism. Demographic trends are also favourable. Since postmaterialism is least prevalent among the oldest and least educated generations, it should become more widespread as these older cohorts die off.

However the real impact of postmaterialism may turn out to be on élites rather than the mass public. Postmaterialists are an active, opinion-leading group, and already postmaterialism's shock troops are moving into positions of power, securing a platform from which their values can directly affect government decisions. So far the 1960s generation has retained touches of radicalism even as it secures the seductive trappings of office. For example, Bill Clinton (born 1946) offered a more liberal agenda to the American people than did his predecessor in the White House, George Bush (born 1924). These two men belonged to different parties, to be sure, but they also represented contrasting generations. In fact, Clinton was the first American President to be born after the second world war. A similar claim can be made about Britain by comparing Tony Blair (born 1953) with his predecessor John Major (born 1943). Here, the contrast in outlooks seemed even to exceed the difference in generations.

Religion and political culture

No discussion of political culture is complete without an assessment of religion. As a source of basic values, religion is an important component of political culture in many countries. This is because of religion's power to legitimate – or delegitimate – secular authority. Claiming to stand above the secular world, religion gives rather than receives legitimacy; religious leaders responsible for interpreting their creed can become at their most influential the guardians of a political culture.

Definition

Compared to political ideologies, **religion** has three linked qualities: transcendence, sacredness and ultimacy. 'Transcendence' refers to faith in a supernatural reality. 'Sacredness' describes those aspects of the world which are placed above the secular by virtue of their religious significance. 'Ultimacy' denotes a belief that religion answers ultimate questions about the meaning of life (Comstock et al., 1971).

This unique role has forced rulers to devote enormous attention to their relations with the 'spiritual estate'. Most often this takes the form of an established church supporting the political order, as with the Church of England. In Britain, for instance, the Archbishop of Canterbury places the crown on the head of a new monarch at the culmination of a coronation ceremony, symbolizing the church's gift of legitimacy. In Japan, similarly, Shinto rites are performed at the Emperor's funeral. These examples show how religion fits into a portrait of political culture as a force supporting the status quo. More interesting, perhaps, are those cases where religion drives the political culture in new directions, as with 'liberation theology' in Latin America and the rise of Islamic fundamentalism in the Muslim world.

In the premodern world, religion directly legitimized all aspects of society. As Smith (1970, p. 6) says, laws were treated as divine commands, the social pyramid was divinely ordained and education was the preserve of the church. Religion and government formed an integrated system; religion *was*, to a large extent, political culture. However, church and state later became distinct organizations, a division which ultimately enabled secular rulers to achieve a more independent position as the source of their authority switched from God to the people. Religion became just one element of political culture, and a declining one at that. This development formed part of the broader process of secularization. Until recently many authors interpreted the modern state as inherently secular; religion was viewed as a leftover from an earlier era. Religion meant underdevelopment; modern meant secular. In the extreme case communist states attempted to build a political culture from which religion was excised completely; religion was dismissed as an opiate for those unfortunates who had been forced to endure the evils of capitalism. Since religion had no role in bringing the people to socialism, it was suppressed in communist states.

Definition
Secularization denotes the declining space occupied by religion in political, social and personal life. It is often associated with modernity but as Weigel (1990) claims 'the unsecularization of the world is one of the dominant social facts of life in the late twentieth century'.

From today's perspective, the dismissal of religion as a premodern source of values was distinctly premature, and its role in contemporary political culture is far from residual. In Eastern Europe, postcommunist states permitted the expression of religious traditions which communism had failed to eliminate. In Africa, popular religions drawing on a range of cultural traditions have threatened the cozy relationships between official churches and the government (Haynes, 1996). And in the United States, the Christian right became a major political force in the 1980s, reflecting 'a yearning for a society where biblical precepts and saintly men would govern society' (Peele, 1984, p. 81). Drawing on the strong moral tone of American political culture, the leaders of this movement initiated a counter-movement against the unholy trinity of secularism, postmaterialism and liberalism.

In the developing world religion has become the culture of the dispossessed, and it is a major device through which those who feel distanced from society can articulate their frustration. Especially for poor people in highly unequal societies, religion is a powerful voice of political protest. Consider, for instance, liberation theology, a radical movement within the Catholic Church in Latin America in the 1970s and 1980s. Historically, the Catholic hierarchy in Latin America had supported conservative ruling élites, reflecting the traditional pattern of mutual aid between church and state (Medhurst, 1991, p. 190). Yet stimulated by the Second Vatican Council (1962–5), called by Pope John XXIII to renew the Church's role in the modern world, many Latin American theologians began to stress the importance of active commitment to the poor and oppressed. A few priests even drew on the Catholic tradition of the just-war to contemplate the overthrow of capitalism, a position which linked liberation theology with aspects of Marxism. Progressive Catholicism made an important contribution to Latin America's shift toward democracy in the 1980s (Sigmund, 1993).

Today, the most dramatic evidence of the continued importance of religion is the resurgence of Islam. The fastest growing religion in the world, Islam is predicted to have more than 1000 million adherents by the year 2000, second only to Christianity (Horrie and Chippindale, 1990, p. 1). Islam is the predominant religion in the Middle East and North Africa, and in a postcommunist and even postsocialist world it has become the major challenge to Western liberalism.

Islamic fundamentalism rejects foreign domination. The slogan 'neither East nor West' became a clarion call of the Iranian revolution and played a substantial role in the revival of Islam elsewhere. Today strong Islamic movements in developing countries are often a form of protest by people who have suffered most, but gained least, from economic growth linked to the West (Keddie, 1991, p. 304). The Islamic revival has provided a rallying cry behind which people in many developing countries can protest against the continued influence of the West on their societies. Islam is a non-Western view of the world that is always prone to become anti-Western, and it is prime evidence of the continuing power of religion to shape the political culture of the dispossessed. It illustrates the extent to which religion, like other forms of political culture, operates internationally, responding to inequalities between, not just within, nations (Esposito, 1997).

Yet there are of course internal theological divisions within Islam, notably between Shi'ite and Sunni Muslims. The Shi'ites, especially in Iran, believe that religion, politics and society are (and should be) linked. Religion is the foundation of all aspects of life and nothing, including law, is independent of it. Similarly, Islamic principles of submission to Allah provide the state with legitimacy. Thus religion and political culture merge, creating a single basis for authority and, in some ways, a contemporary form of totalitarianism. In the years following the Iranian revolution of 1979 these ideas were implemented with vigour; the ulama (the clergy) ruled directly, rather than through advising secular rulers. By contrast, Sunni Muslims allow greater space to secular rulers and law; Sunni Islam is diverse, flexible and accommodating. And Sunni Muslims, it is important to note, form a clear majority of the world's Islamic population.

Transforming political culture

In the mature democracies of the West, political culture largely reflects social values; the liberal democratic state is a servant, perhaps even a prisoner, of the society it governs. Totalitarian regimes, by contrast, had more ambitious goals. By definition they sought to transform political culture using all possible means. In Hitler's Germany, for instance, all textbooks had to conform to Nazi ideology and pupils were trained in arithmetic using examples based on 'the Jewish question'. Hitler was well aware of the potential of socialization; he said:

> When an opponent declares, 'I will not come over to your side', I calmly say, your child belongs to us already ... What are you? You will pass on. Your descendants, however, now stand in a new camp. In a short time they will know nothing else but this new community' (Rush, 1992, p. 93).

Even non-totalitarian rulers frequently seek to reconstruct political culture, developing mass values which will offer firmer support for their power. Such efforts rarely succeed in the way (or to the extent) that rulers hoped, but they can lead to unanticipated modifications of political culture. By examining three such efforts we can cast light on the resilience of political culture in the face of attempted reconstructions. Our cases are: communist states, post-communist states and postcolonial states.

Communist states

In the twentieth century, communist regimes made the most systematic effort at transforming political culture. Their starting-point was that the state must transform the way people think and behave. As Meyer (1983, p. 6) comments, communist revolutions were intended to be cultural revolutions. The ultimate goal was to create through education and persuasion a new communist man and woman, who would live in a classless, socialist, atheist society, lacking all the poisons inhaled under capitalism.

Take the Soviet Union and China as examples. In both countries the new communist rulers sought to increase mass participation in politics. The old feudal systems had been characterized by passive acceptance of authority – what Weber called traditional authority. To effect a revolution in political culture the communist citizen was to become an active participant in political life. Mass campaigns ensured that everyone became involved in politics. In China these activities ranged from participation in land reform programmes to campaigns against the 'three evils' – corruption, waste and bureaucratic red tape.

Yet the anticipated transformation of political culture never came about. Mass participation took on a purely ritual form, based on passive obedience to power rather than active commitment to communism. If you did not conform by taking part in political acts you ran the risk of being branded an enemy of the people; so you participated anyway but without commitment. Thus a dual political personality emerged. In his study of Russian political culture, White (1979, p. 11) developed the idea of 'two persons in one body'. The public person repeated the phraseology of the authorities when required and took part in ritual demonstrations of unity. But the hidden person retained a set of older attitudes towards politics and society. Fear created citizens who outwardly conformed but in reality adopted strategies designed to ensure their own survival.

The final collapse of communist rule in Eastern Europe in 1989 confirmed the failure of the ruling party to restructure political culture. The precommunist cultural heritage had outlasted official attempts to reconstruct it. Indeed, longstanding cultural traditions grew stronger by providing a focus of opposition to communist rule. In Poland, for example, the Catholic Church became the major source of opposition to the ruling party, and a strong counterweight to communist rule.

Postcommunist states

Just as the political cultures of Eastern Europe proved highly resilient to communist manipulation, so too are they providing difficult ground on which to establish stable democracies in the postcommunist era. Looking back, the initial collapse of communism now appears straightforward in comparison with the difficulties of building a democratic culture. When communism imploded at the end of the 1980s, no-one predicted that within five years reformed communists would have won a string of election victories, including wresting the Polish presidency from Lech Walesa, the revolutionary hero.

Why did the postcommunist transition to democracy prove so awkward? After all, the new regimes could claim to be more in tune with national political traditions than Soviet puppet leaders fronting regimes imposed by force of arms. One problem was that most of these 'national political traditions' were themselves non- or even anti-democratic. Tismaneanu (1995) describes the political cultures of the Asian republics as 'antidemocratic, antiliberal and ethnocentric'. The precommunist heritage simply offered weak foundations on which to build a democracy.

The cultural residue of communism further inhibited democratic consolidation. Far from creating the new man and woman, in reality communism had reinforced the selfish individualism needed to survive under authoritarian rule. Offe (1996, p. 218) describes this 'state of mind' as

> a combination of apathy, depletion of communal bonds, passivity, unwillingness to accept responsibility, atomization, lack of respect for formal rules, short-termism and a pervasive grab-and-run attitude to economic gain.

This is the learned behaviour of survival under arbitrary dictatorship; it will take time to change. In Putnam's terms, postcommunist cultures suffer from a chronic shortage of 'social capital'.

One consequence of these survival strategies is a cynical view of human nature. This in turn contributes to an emphasis on the need for strong, even authoritarian, leadership. Even East Germans, who showed widespread support for general democratic principles by the time of unification in 1990, remained sceptical about some of democracy's implications. Survey evidence showed that compared to West Germans, East Germans were unwilling to accept the pluralistic idea of competition between social groups. They were also less likely to give priority to individual rights over public order (Gabriel, 1996). Thus postcommunist populations may be particularly unwilling to embrace the *liberal* aspects of Western democracy. So the postcommunist experience shows that totalitarian regimes *can* influence a country's political culture, though often in unplanned and damaging ways.

Popular attitudes influenced the transition from communism in a further way. In the giddy moment of revolution, expectations ran away with themselves. With a measure of freedom achieved, the people expected affluence to follow, seemingly unaware of the magnitude of change needed to transform an inefficient state-run economy into a vibrant free market. Anticipating effortless wealth, many in Eastern Europe simply encountered long-term unemployment. As de Tocqueville noted long ago (1954 edn., p. 76), dashed expectations are politically more damaging than outright fatalism.

With their reserves of legitimacy built up over generations, established democracies in the West could have ridden out a similar crisis. Electorates would have voted their current rulers out of office without losing faith in the democratic system itself. However, the postcommunist states have had neither the time nor the success to build up savings in the Legitimacy Bank. Their initial reservoir of goodwill soon ran dry as factories closed and economies declined, and further, the small welfare safety net provided by communism had also gone. Despite the poor performance of communist economies the population had grown used to a measure of economic security: inexpensive housing, cheap food, jobs for everyone, subsidized transport. This is another way in which the communist phase did leave its mark on political cultures. It created expectations of a welfare safety net which did not, and probably could not, survive the transition to a market economy. Thus safety-net socialism presented another hurdle for postcommunist countries to overcome. This shows how political culture lags behind, and slows, the pace of change. As one frustrated politician said, 'When people had security, they wanted freedom; now they have freedom, they want security'.

Public opinion towards the new postcommunist system depends largely, indeed excessively, on its current performance. A striking finding of public opinion surveys in Eastern Europe is that attitudes to the system of government vary with assessments of current leaders; and that these ratings depend in turn on economic performance (McDonough, 1995). In other words, both politicians and the political system are judged instrumentally by their ability to literally deliver the goods. East European political systems lack political capital at the very time they need it most, in their vulnerable early years. The surprise is that they have survived as well as they have.

Postcolonial states

Where communist rulers sought to transform established national political cultures, politicians in much of the postcolonial world have attempted to construct a national culture where none previously existed. Many developing countries only emerged from colonial status after 1945, and the nation remains a weak focus of political identity in such societies, especially those in Africa. This reflects arbitrary borders inherited from colonial rulers who cared little for traditional, and often flexible, boundaries. The state, too, is weak, with limited penetration into the countryside; it provides only a limited focus for public attention. In Almond and Verba's terms, large parts of the postcolonial world face the problem of parochial political cultures.

The postindependence generation of leaders recognized this problem. They sought to nationalize fragmented political cultures, hoping this would strengthen the authority of the state. Primary education stressed allegiance to the nation rather than to the ethnic group. The mass media reported national as well as local events and frequently recalled memories of the heroic struggle for independence. To take a more recent example, the leaders of South Africa's new democracy used the

country's international sporting success to help nationalize a political culture previously ruptured by race.

Yet just as communist party states failed to create the new person, so too have most attempts at transforming political cultures in the postcolonial world achieved little. South Africa's success story is the exception, not the rule. Elsewhere in the postcolonial world, efforts at nation-building have now become little more than ritual. Primary school children may still wave the national flag when the Education Minister comes to visit but true nation-building is not achieved so easily.

Why have national political cultures failed to solidify? The inherent difficulty of reshaping a culture is the underlying problem. But the governments of new states face the additional problem of the continuing authority of traditional leaders. Because the institutions of the state are underdeveloped, central governments are often forced to administer localities through traditional leaders. In practice, this delegation contradicts nation-building efforts. For example, the Education Minister may supposedly visit an area to open a new modern school, but the real purpose is to cement an alliance with traditional local leaders. The effect is to reinforce the old ways rather than to help build the new state.

It is on these uncertain foundations that rulers in the postcolonial world have faced the added challenge of nurturing the democratic forms which emerged in the 1980s and 1990s. Three problems have presented themselves:

- Traditional cultures have proved to be a mixed blessing; in Africa, for example, indigenous cultures contain a strong element of deference towards the personal (though not unlimited) authority of traditional rulers. The democratic idea of authority flowing from the bottom up, and expressed in institutions rather than individuals, does not blend easily with these norms.
- The legacy of the struggle for independence can be unhelpful. This battle was a national rather than a democratic campaign; the mission was anticolonial more than prodemocratic. As Sithole (1993) notes, 'for all but a few leaders – Seretse Khama of Botswana and Dauda Jawara of The Gambia being the notable exceptions – the com-

mitment to democracy was a transitory one'. In other words, élite political culture was not democratic.

- The authoritarian governments which emerged soon after independence naturally increased popular cynicism about national politics. In particular, dictatorships stunted the growth of social organizations such as trade unions and voluntary groups which are an essential part of the democratic fabric (Chazan, 1993). A civil society will not flower easily in African conditions.

Yet, as in the postcommunist world, it would be wrong to argue that political culture rules out democratic consolidation in Africa. Historically, norms of public consultation and collective discussion coexisted with the authority of traditional leaders. Anyhow, as we have seen political culture is a variable, not a constant; it can flourish with sustained economic success. And experience with democracy can itself bring forth democratic attitudes (Diamond, 1993). Lemarchand's balanced conclusion (1995, p. 47) convinces: 'in the nations of Africa, democracy is neither inevitable nor impossible'.

Global political culture?

Most discussion of political culture has focused on its role within the state, but this tradition now needs supplementing. Like many aspects of politics, culture must now be viewed from a global perspective. Ideas and images know no boundaries; they travel faster than products and arguably have more impact.

In a major essay, Huntington (1996) argues that culture will be the dominant source of world conflict in the twenty-first century. He notes that the old bases of international conflict – between communism and capitalism, between the Soviet Union and the United States – are exhausted. Even national political cultures are losing ground in a global era. In Huntington's view, we will be left with 'a clash of civilizations', an irreducible division between the major cultural groupings of the world. These groupings are supernational but subglobal. Between the contradictory worldviews they repre-

---

BOX 4.1
The clash of civilizations?

Huntington divides the civilizations of the world into six or seven main groups. These are Western, Japanese, Islamic, Hindu, Slavic-Orthodox, Latin American and possibly African civilizations. These divisions pose special problems for torn countries located on the faultlines between cultures. Mexico (situated between the West and Latin America) and Turkey (on the border between the West and Islam) are examples of torn or split countries.

---

sent there is little common ground or room for compromise. As globalization proceeds, interaction and friction between civilizations will intensify, producing a high potential for conflict. Huntington notes, for example, how cultural kinship influences the choice of sides in contemporary conflicts: 'in the Yugoslav conflicts, Russia provided diplomatic support to the Serbs ... not for reasons of ideology or power politics or economic interest but because of cultural kinship' (1996, p. 28). Huntington is also doubtful of pragmatic efforts to switch civilizations; he suggests that the reason Australia cannot reinvent itself as an Asian country is simply that it's not. The same problem underlies Turkey's efforts to join the European family: critics claim that Turkey just does not share European culture.

Huntington's analysis appeals because it takes the analysis of political culture into the international realm. However, critics allege that he: (1) understates the vitality of the nation state, (2) mixes culture and religion in the confusing idea of a 'civilization', and (3) ignores the ability of some civilizations to evolve in response to contact with others (Kirkpatrick, 1993). Thus the clash of civilizations may be less strident than he suggests.

But even if we were to reject all Huntington's conclusions, there are certainly aspects of political culture operating on a regional, if not a global, scale. The postwar effort to build a united Europe has been led by a multinational élite with a strong commitment to the European idea. In Asia efforts at building regional institutions have been helped by cultural contrasts, not least the desire to catch up with the West. The Confucian tradition is also common to several countries in the region, contributing to the flow of business across national boundaries.

Yet even in an international context we should be wary of separating political culture from the blunter realities of power. Just as Marx claimed that national cultures reflect the interests of the dominant class, so too does 'global culture' bear the imprint of dominant countries. Global culture is primarily a Western product. American culture, in particular, has proved to be uniquely exportable: 'Macworld' is a place where we eat American food, watch American movies, and write books using American software. Global culture is not neutral between civilizations; it inevitably reinforces the strength of the leading power.

The media

The mass media are clearly one channel through which political culture is expressed and transmitted. Newspaper articles, television news, films and even advertisements project not just information about the world but also agendas, interpretations and opinions. At least in developed societies where media consumption is greatest, the media must be a significant mechanism of socialization for children and, at minimum, a major source of information for adults. Further, as families fragment and media channels expand, so the influence of mass communication increases.

Yet it is easy to become carried away with unsubstantiated assertions of media omnipotence. Two cautions are in order. First, personal interaction – whether within families or with friends and workmates – possesses an immediacy and impact which media communication, necessarily addressed to a mass audience, can never match. Personal relationships, especially within the family, remain the crucible of value-formation. Second, media content does not emerge from thin air. It is created by groups of people who have themselves been socialized into the political culture of their (fragment of) society. The assumptions which media professionals bring to their work reflect their own background and socialization. Just as a river does not create the water which flows along it, neither do journalists create all the perspectives which are implicit in their output.

> **Definition**
> **Mass media** refer to methods of communication which can reach large numbers of people simultaneously. Television and newspapers are the most important; others are posters, radio, books, magazines and cinema. An e-mail to a friend is personal, not mass, communication but sending a message to all members of a newsgroup is a form of mass communication.

Liberal democracies

The mass media remain most important in democracies, where journalists have greatest independence and their reports therefore carry most credibility. Even in democracies, though, the government always has a head start in media presentation. Statements by a president are always more newsworthy than those made by political opponents. In Britain, the activities of the Prime Minister generally receive more coverage than those of the Leader of the Opposition (Miller, 1990, Ch. 3). This bias can sometimes be a double-edged sword, magnifying government mistakes as well as achievements. Even so, media claims to cover all parties equally are best taken with a pinch of salt. The 'ins' have more potential to control their coverage than do the 'outs'.

In most Western democracies, television has now been the dominant medium for a generation (Table 4.1). Television provides a visual, credible and easily-digested source which reaches nearly every household, providing the main source of political information. In election campaigns, for instance, the television studio has become the main field of battle. The party gladiators participate through appearing on interviews, debates and talk-shows; the spectators participate through watching and, ultimately, voting. Local party activists, once the assault troops of the campaign, are now mere skirmishers. Television no longer covers the campaign; television *is* the campaign.

Yet it would be wrong to discount the political significance of the second mass medium, newspapers. The print media remain important participants in politics, not least because they are free of the close regulation still applied to many state-owned television networks. In Britain, Japan and Scandinavia, most people still read a national daily newspaper

(Table 4.1). However, in response to television the role of the press has changed from an information source to a provider of interpretation and opinion. Newspapers also influence the television's agenda: a story appearing on TV's evening news often begins life in the morning paper. Where newspapers are organized on a local or regional basis (as in New Zealand and the United States), they tend to be less significant for the mass public. The same point obviously applies where circulation is low (France, Italy). For example, daily newspapers in Italy are specialist products aimed at a small but politically sophisticated public.

What is the media's impact on how people vote in elections in liberal democracies? This remains a matter of controversy. In the 1950s, before television became preeminent, the reinforcement thesis held sway (Harrop, 1987). Party loyalties were transmitted through the family and, once developed, they acted as a political sunscreen protecting people from the harmful effects of propaganda. People saw what they wanted to see and remembered what they wanted to remember (Klapper, 1960). This interpretation proved to be a useful counter to bland assertions of media power. But reinforcement is an inadequate guide to the role of the media today. Party loyalties are now weaker, and television more pervasive, than in the 1950s.

Table 4.1 Media penetration and campaign coverage on television

	TV sets per 1000 people, 1994	Newspaper circulation per 1000 people, 1992	Campaign coverage on television		
			Paid political ads?	Free time to parties?	Leader debates?
Australia	484	244	Yes	Yes	Yes
Austria	475	358	Yes	Yes	
Belgium	447	221	Yes	Yes	Yes
Canada	626	226	Yes	Yes	Yes
Denmark	528	359	No	No	Yes
Finland	488	547	No	No	Yes
France	400	166	No	Yes	Yes
Germany	643	386	Yes	Yes	No
India	27	26	No	Yes	
Ireland	271	101	No	Yes	Yes
Italy	423	105	Yes	Yes	No
Japan	610	577	Yes	Yes	Yes
Netherlands	485	307	No	Yes	
New Zealand	372	321	Yes	Yes	Yes
Norway	423	548	Yes	Yes	Yes
Sweden	471	520	Yes	Yes	Yes
United Kingdom	434	393	No	Yes	No
United States	814	251	Yes	No	Yes

Source: LeDuc, Niemi and Norris (1996) Table 1.7. Newspaper readership is normally at least twice circulation.

> **BOX 4.2**
> *Reinforcement and agenda-setting theories*
>
> According to the **reinforcement** theory, the media conserve but do not change the political attitudes and behaviour of the electorate. Political outlooks are too entrenched to be swayed by media reports. According to the **agenda-setting** theory, the media (and television in particular) influence what we think about, though not necessarily what we think. The media frame the agenda but do not determine our reaction to their coverage.

For this reason, the agenda-setting view of media effects has gained ground. This claims that television directs our attention to the latest coup, drought or war even if it does not determine our reaction to these events. Newsworthiness comes to depend on the quality of the pictures; as a television news editor said, 'if it bleeds, it leads'. Thus Walter Lippman's (1922) view of the press is applicable to the media generally: 'It is like a beam of a searchlight that moves restlessly about, bringing one episode and then another out of the darkness and into vision'. In this way the media helps to shape political culture though its influence on day-to-day discussion.

Communist states

Under communism, the function of the media was to help the party in its efforts to reconstruct political culture. Specifically, the dual role of the media was propaganda and agitation. Propaganda instructed the masses in the teachings of Marx, Engels and Lenin and explained the party's mission; agitation sought to mobilize the masses behind specific policies such as increased production. To achieve both objectives, ruling communist parties developed an elaborate media network with radio, posters, cinema and television reinforcing each other. But the communist experience shows the limits of media power. A cynical public is not easily fooled. Some problems may have been disguised and national economic progress successfully exaggerated, but propaganda by itself was unable to transform political culture. Grandiose statements were too often contradicted by the grim realities of immediate experience. In any case, as communist states became inert, so propaganda became empty

ritual. Like the weather it was taken for granted and largely ignored.

Against this background the political time bomb of *glasnost* (Gorbachev's policy of openness) in the Soviet Union began to tick away. The more open the media became, the more information was released demonstrating the true scale of the Soviet Union's problems. Throughout the communist world, free media were inevitably far more damaging to the regime than in the consolidated democracies where resentments were aired in a context of legitimate government. As communist power waned, so the media discovered their vitality. Eager customers snapped up newspapers which had previously been left unsold. Official publications began to discuss reform; nonparty publications presented radical options to an intrigued, if bemused, public. International comparisons became more important; images of Western affluence were a potent stimulus for change throughout the communist world. The growing independence of the media was a crucial and irreversible stage in the liberalization of communist states, a phase which lay the groundwork for their final disintegration.

Postcommunist states

The media remained a vital forum of political communication in the postcommunist era. In contrast to the development of Western democracies, the leading figures in postcommunist states could exploit existing national media to reach the voters, thus avoiding the need to build elaborate party organizations. And postcommunist presidents and prime ministers showed little hesitation in ensuring they retained the lion's share of media resources. In the aftermath of communism's collapse, newsprint was scarce and somehow opposition publications were always last in the queue. Channels for production and distribution of unofficial publications were often primitive in the extreme. Journalists found it difficult to develop an American-style adversary relationship with politicians who had become national heroes in the struggle to expunge communism. Rulers often acted as though the ability to manipulate the media was a perk of office (which it was). In Russia, Boris Yeltsin's remarkable reelection in 1996, after all seemed lost, owed something to his decision to invite the head of the country's independent tele-

EXHIBIT 4.3

The global village: Disney über alles?

In communications terms, we live in a global village. The world has been compressed into a television set. In 1776 it took 50 days for news of the English reaction to the American Declaration of Independence to get back to the United States. In 1950 British reaction to the outbreak of the Korean War was broadcast in America in 24 hours. With advances in satellite broadcasting, reports filmed in Britain now take a mere 25 seconds to reach American TV screens (Flammang *et al*. 1990, p. 378). We now take for granted the almost immediate transmission of newsworthy events around the world. When the allied powers launched attacks on Iraq in the 1991 Gulf War, news reporters in Baghdad broadcast live to the world as the missiles whizzed overhead on their way (sometimes) to their programmed targets. CNN supplied coverage of the conflict around the clock and across the globe.

What difference has global communication made to national governments? In essence, it has created more open societies – it is now harder than ever for governments to isolate their populations from international developments. Even communist states found it difficult to jam foreign radio broadcasts aimed at their countries; the bricks of the Berlin Wall were unable to prevent radio and television signals from the West reaching the East. 'Spiritual pollution', as the Chinese call it, could not be avoided. Eberle (1990, pp. 194–5) commented that 'the changes in Eastern Europe and the Soviet Union have been as much the triumph of communication as the failure of communism'. For better or worse, in the global village all governments run the risk of being judged by the standards of the best.

The impact of the global village depends on whether a country is a sender as well as a receiver of communication. The prime example of a sender nation is the United States. Critics allege that American primacy in such fields as films and television enables it to spread American values in a form of cultural imperialism: Disney über alles. Coca-cola and American cigarettes are still statements of high fashion in Beijing, even as such symbols lose their appeal among health-conscious Americans. For governments in receiver countries, however, the impact of the global village is more threatening. Television is a window on the West, particularly for élite groups. Both television and radio also affect popular aspirations – mass communications increase awareness of inequalities within nations, between nations and, indeed, between the developed and developing worlds. In this connection, 'the revolution of rising expectations' is a useful, if rather glib, phrase.

Recent technological developments also facilitate underground opposition to authoritarian regimes. A small group with a fax machine and internet access now has the potential to draw the world's attention to political abuses, providing source material for alert journalists. Burma's military rulers, China's communist government and Saudi Arabia's ruling families have all suffered in this way from overseas groups. However, all these regimes currently continue in power. Of course, authoritarian regimes can and do control access to the internet by limiting the number of transmission routes into their own country. Further, minimal access to telephones and computers in many developing countries dramatically reduces the domestic impact of these new sources of information. But not even the most dictatorial government can control global information flows, the speed and detail of which have served to raise the political cost of domestic repression.

vision service to join his campaign staff (White, 1997, p. 55).

The existence of substantial media freedom is a major achievement of postcommunist politics, but this does not mean that all the old party organs have closed down. Some have shown remarkably ingenu-ity in adapting to new times. The most extravagant gymnastics came from the Russian journal *Party Life*, originally the turgid mouthpiece of the Central Committee of the Communist Party. Its new title is *Business Life* (Sakwa, 1996). But it would be wrong to suppose that the postcommunist media are now as free as those in the West. The reflex of rulers is still to control. For instance the Slovakian government quickly closed down critical newspapers when the country achieved independence in 1993.

Where private ownership of the media is established, the new entrepreneurs use their newspapers and television stations to push their own political agenda. In Russia, the leading banks own many leading newspapers and television stations, which dutifully propagate their masters' interests. Owners make deals to support particular (usually incumbent) politicians. Where Western media magnates such as Murdoch and Berlusconi have acquired power through their media, in postcommunist states economic wealth and political power have been used to acquire control over the media. The result is that truth-seekers again find themselves tuning in to foreign sources. Editorial freedom remains the exception; the postcommunist media are best viewed as pluralistic rather than independent. Further, journalistic standards remain low, reflecting decades in which reporters (often appointed by party patronage) did little more than reproduce party platitudes. Easy editorializing still takes priority over the hard graft of news-gathering (Dempsey, 1993, p. 281). Even when journalists do expose corruption and poor governance, nothing happens.

Developing countries

The mass media are less important in most of the developing world; national media are weak and official politics takes place within a smaller stratum of the population. In Asia and especially in Africa the media are still seen as agents of rule, touting the official line and encouraging the mission of development. Islamic states, in particular, reject the Western idea of a free press; instead they stress the media's role in affirming religious values and social norms.

Again we must distinguish between print and broadcast media. Newspapers are generally élite publications with circulation confined largely to the big cities. In Nigeria for instance, where about half the population is still illiterate, the circulation of daily newspapers is only one per hundred people (Mundt and Aborisade, 1996, p. 753). Editors may not operate under strict censorship but they are fully aware that it does not do to make too many enemies:

journalists and editors are high on the hit list when repression strikes. In Argentine and Chile in the 1970s they were imprisoned and tortured – or else they just 'disappeared'. In such circumstances self-censorship is an understandable reflex.

Television is more important for the mass public, especially for illiterate viewers. Latin America, with its privately owned and commercially operated television, is the best example. There television has long been a major political force. Mexico was one of the first countries in the world to introduce television and the Brazilian network TV Globo is the fourth largest in the world (Fox, 1988). This means that television appeal can be a major factor in presidential elections. Consider, for example, Brazil's election of 1989, won by Collor de Mello. Collor was a handsome 39-year-old former athlete with a 23-year-old wife. For two years before the election, TV Globo prepared the ground for Collor by using popular *telenovelas* (soaps) to portray a country drowning in corruption. The implication was that Brazil needed a political newcomer like Collos to perform a rescue act. So even the writers, actors and viewers of soap operas were participating in national politics.

Key reading

Next step: *Putnam (1993) is an influential study. Using modern Italy as his case, Putnam takes the study of political culture in new directions.*

Almond and Verba's *The Civic Culture* (1963) remains an excellent starting point but it needs to be supplemented by the follow-up, *The Civic Culture Revisited* (1980), edited by the same authors. On élite political culture, a comparative study focused on attitudes to equality is Verba (1987); for a general text, see Putnam (1976). The key source on postmaterialism is Inglehart (1971, 1990, 1997). A standard text on political socialization is Dawson, Prewitt and Dawson (1977). Nye, Zelikow and King (1997) examine the declining faith of Americans in their federal government. Eatwell (1997) is a collection focused on the political cultures of European countries. For postcommunist states see Tismaneanu (1995) and Volgyes and Barany (1995). On Russia specifically, see Vainshtein (1995) and Petro (1995). On the developing world see Diamond (1993). Of the limited work on religion and politics,

Westerlund (1996) is an excellent general collection. Haynes (1993, 1996) and Juengensmeyer (1993) cover religion and the developing world. Huntington (1993, 1996) is the source on the clash of civilizations; the 1993 article is followed by useful critiques. On the media, Berger (1991) covers the USA, Seymour-Ure (1991) looks at Britain, Kuhn (1997) surveys West Europe, while Skidmore (1993) examines the intriguing case of Latin America.

CHAPTER **5** # Political participation

A suicide bomber detonating an explosion on a crowded bus, an environmentalist lying in front of workers building a new road, a citizen contacting a legislator about a missing social security cheque – all are examples of individual participation in politics. This chapter examines general citizen involvement in politics; we reserve to the next chapter the specific case of participation through the ballot box.

Democratization in the 1980s massively increased the proportion of the world's population able to play a significant role in collective decision-making. Only a few regimes still deny the masses any formal political role at all: these are traditional regimes, where politics remains the exclusive preserve of a tiny élite (for example Saudi Arabia), and military governments which forego a democratic facade. Elsewhere the population is usually permitted, sometimes encouraged and occasionally required to express its political views.

The study of participation raises three main questions:

- What forms does participation take? What, for instance, is the balance between orthodox involvement and direct action, or between peaceful and violent protest?

- Who participates most in politics: the wealthy with most to protect, or the poor with least to lose? This issue reminds us that even when participation is widespread, it is never equal; some people and groups always exert more influence than others over government decisions.

- What have been the effects of the 'participation explosion' caused by democratization? That is, has involvement in politics led to an informed and public-spirited population, as the original advocates of democracy had hoped?

Definition
Political participation is activity by individuals formally intended to influence either who governs or the decisions taken by governments. Both the extent and forms of participation vary between types of regime. Liberal democracies characterized by voluntary participation are more participatory than most authoritarian regimes.

How people get involved in politics varies across regimes. Liberal democracies, totalitarian dictatorships and the developing world offer contrasting styles of engagement. In liberal democracies, *voluntary participation* is the norm. People can choose whether to get involved (for example by voting or abstaining) and how to do so (for example by joining a party or signing petitions). The main exception to the voluntary nature of participation is compulsory voting, found in a handful of democracies such as Australia and Belgium. By contrast, in totalitarian regimes, *regimented participation* is the norm. This involves the expression of support for, but not the selection of, government personnel and policy. Its main function is to mobilize the people behind the regime's effort to transform society, whether towards a communist or fascist ideal. Finally, the *patron–client relationship* is a typical form of participation in developing countries. Here low-status individuals offer political support to patrons such as employers, chiefs or religious leaders. In exchange, the patron offers a measure of protection such as a guarantee to supply food should the crops fail. This is manipulated participation in which the client must bend to the patron's will.

Liberal democracies: voluntary participation

The most striking fact about political participation in liberal democracies is how little of it there is. Voting in national elections is normally the only form of participation which engages a majority of the people (Verba, Nie and Kim, 1978, pp. 58–9). In some countries, especially in Scandinavia, most people also turn out for local elections. However, throughout the democratic world anything beyond

voting is the preserve of a minority of activists. Indeed the activists are outnumbered by the apathetics – people who neither vote nor even follow politics through the media.

In a renowned analysis, Milbrath and Goel (1977, p. 11) divided the American population into three groups, a classification which has since been applied to several other democracies. Their categories were: (1) a few *gladiators* (about 5 – 7 per cent) who fight the political battle, (2) a large group of *spectators* (about 60 per cent) who watch the contest but rarely participate beyond voting, and (3) a substantial number of *apathetics* (about one-third) who are withdrawn from politics (Figure 5.1). Milbrath's labels were based on an analogy with Roman contests, where a few gladiators performed in front of the mass of spectators but the apathetics did not even watch the show.

Early postwar investigations, such as Milbrath's, viewed participation as one-dimensional; the idea was that everyone could be arrayed at some point along a single scale of political activity. The gladia-

---

EXHIBIT 5.1

Participation in America: Verba and Nie's classic study

This classic empirical study of participation, based on a national sample of Americans interviewed in 1967, developed a number of techniques for measuring political activity which have since been adopted in other countries, often with similar results.

One of Verba and Nie's main contributions was to question the idea that Americans could be classified on a single scale of political participation. Certainly the authors confirmed the existence of Milbrath's gladiators, active in all ways, and of his apathetics who did not participate at all. But the in-betweens fell into more specialized categories. These included those who always voted but virtually never did anything else. Another group consisted of 'parochial participants' – people who contacted officials on individual problems but were otherwise inactive. Thus people varied in *how*, and not just in *how much*, they participated in politics.

More important, the authors showed the existence of a participation bias in America. Political involvement was greatest among people of higher social

status. At the time of the research, activists were more conservative than the public, especially on welfare issues. Conservative Republicans were especially participatory. Thus, even in a liberal democracy such as the United States, the currents of opinion surrounding decision-makers did not reflect the views of the public. The conclusion was that American politics exhibited a built-in bias to the right.

Thirty years on from Verba and Nie's study, the American debate on participation now centres on how to establish (or re-establish) a sense of community in the United States. Here too Verba and Nie offered useful insights. They showed how involvement in social organizations – what we now call 'civil society' – crosses over into political activity. They also speculated that 'the communities that appear to foster participation – the small and relatively independent communities – are becoming rarer and rarer'.

Further reading: Verba and Nie (1972).

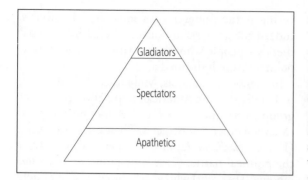

Figure 5.1 Patterns of participation in democracies

tors formed one extreme while the apathetics were found at the other. Those who engaged in the rarer forms of activity (for example contacting officials) were expected also to engage in the more popular modes (for example voting). However, later research showed that political involvement operates in several dimensions; that is, people can be politically active in different ways and some specialization does occur within the broad category of participation. This is especially so when we extend the analysis of participation to include protestors – those who specialize in direct action such as boycotts and marches. In Britain, whether a person engages in such radical acts tells us little about whether he or she votes a lot or a little, indicating a division of political labour between mainstream and unorthodox activists (Parry, Moyser and Day, 1992, p. 58). Paticipation today is multi-dimensional; people who score highly on one form of activity may not do so on others.

In every country political activists are anything but a cross-section of society. In most liberal democracies, as in the United States, participation is greatest among well-educated, middle-class, middle-aged white men. Furthermore the highest layers of political involvement show the greatest skew. As Putnam (1976, p. 33) says,

> The 'law of increasing disproportion' seems to apply to nearly every political system; no matter how we measure political and social status, the higher the level of political authority, the greater the representation for high-status social groups.

What explains this bias in participation towards upper social groups? Two main factors are at work: political resources and political interest. First, the members of high-status groups are well-equipped with relevant political resources. These include education, money, status and communication skills. Education gives access to information and, we trust, strengthens the ability to interpret it. Money buys the luxury of time for political activity. High status provides the opportunity to obtain a respectful hearing. And communication skills such as the ability to speak in public help in presenting one's views persuasively. Second, high-status individuals are just more likely to be interested in politics. No longer preoccupied with daily struggles, they can take satisfaction from engagement in collective activity. Also, the wealthy are more likely to be brought up in a family and attend a school, which encourage an interest in current affairs; adult participation reflects these early influences.

We can apply this framework for understanding participation bias to the question of why women are underrepresented at higher political levels; and there can be no doubt that women are still infrequent actors on the national political stage. In 1995, women made up just 11 per cent of the world's legislators, an increase on the figure of 7 per cent 20 years earlier but still a remarkably low proportion (Jacquette, 1997). As a group women still possess fewer political resources than men. They have less formal education (though this difference has reversed among the young in many developed states); childbearing and, often, homemaking responsibilities cut into political time; and women still lack the confidence needed to throw themselves into the hurly-burly of formal politics. In addition, of course, women still face the high hurdle of discrimination from sexist male politicians. These gatekeepers claim that women are 'unsuited' to politics – and then use the scarcity of women in high office to prove their point!

The emphasis of research on political participation is on explaining what distinguishes the gladiators from the spectators. But what about the apathetics, the people who do not participate at all? This group raises the emerging problem of political exclusion. The apathetics who do not participate are, in effect, excluded from the normal means by which citizens collectively shape their society. There are, suggest Verba, Schlozman and Brady (1995), three explanations for why people do not participate: because they can't (for example lack of resources such as time),

EXHIBIT 5.2

Women in the House

Everywhere, women are still in the minority in national parliaments. Even where their position is most favourable, as in Scandinavia, improvement stems from the 1970s and later. Three factors help to explain cross-national contrasts in female representation. The first, and most important, is the *electoral system*. Women do best under the party list version of proportional representation, a method which allows party officials to select a gender-balanced set of candidates. When New Zealand switched to a more proportional system in 1996, the proportion of women legislators increased from 21 to 29 per cent. A second variable is the *political culture*; Scandinavian countries have shown a uniquely strong commitment to gender equality (Nicholson, 1989). In Norway, for example, the leading parties introduced quotas as early as 1973, aiming to ensure that within each party each gender provides at least 40 per cent of elected representatives. And the third factor is the *turnover of legislators*. Low turnover, as for example in the United States Congress, creates a recruitment bottleneck which enables men, once elected, to remain in post for decades.

Further reading: Jacquette (1997), Karvonen and Selle (1995).

Table 5.1 Female representation in national parliaments

	Year	Women MPs %
Sweden	1994	40
Norway	1993	39
Denmark	1998	37
Netherlands	1994	31
New Zealand	1996	29
Germany	1994	26
Britain	1997	18
Canada	1993	18
Italy	1994	15
USA	1994	11
Ireland	1997	12
Australia	1993	8
France	1993	6

Note: in bicameral assemblies, figures are for the lower house.

Source: adapted from Norris (1993, p. 310, and 1996).

because they don't want to (for example they are disillusioned with politics), or because nobody asked (for example they are isolated from social networks that might draw them into politics).

The point is that the politically excluded are often also the socially excluded. A typical nonparticipant would be an unemployed young man with no qualifications, often from a minority culture and inhabiting a high-crime inner-city neighbourhood. Preoccupied with daily struggles, members of this underclass lack the resources and interest to participate in orthodox politics. Usually they are not on the electoral roll, often they do not watch the news on television, and rarely do they read a national newspaper. Ironically, those who suffer most from the problems of growing inequality in market societies are the people least able to articulate their plight to government. Their political activity, if any,

is often irregular and spasmodic, as with riots. More positively, political exclusion can also be the incubator of self-help groups. But such movements often maintain an arms-length relationship with official channels, with equal suspicion on both sides.

Definition
Political exclusion refers to those people who through occupying a marginal position in society are effectively excluded from participation in collective decision-making. Migrant workers, criminals, drug addicts and those who do not speak the native language are examples of groups which face this difficulty.

In the past, trade unions and socialist parties reduced the problem of political exclusion, at least in Western Europe. Such organizations provided a channel of entry into politics for working-class people who would otherwise have remained outside formal politics. Trade unions and mass parties help to turn apathetics into spectators and some spectators into gladiators. However today education, not the union or the party, is the avenue of advancement. Formal education does of course provide more people with the resources to take part in politics, and the graduate population in particular is politically active. But those who miss out on education find themselves in a difficult position, lacking the 'lift' that might have been provided to earlier generations by the labour union or the party machine. Many are left with nowhere to go and find themselves joining the politically excluded.

Communist states: regimented participation

For the classic example of regimented participation, we must look back to communist regimes, particularly in their earliest and most vigorous decades. At first glance, participation in communist states left liberal democracies in the shade. People in such states were far more active in politics than are citizens in liberal democracies, and mass participation in communist states always exceeded that in liberal democracies. Citizens sat on comradely courts, administered elections, joined para-police organizations and served on people's committees covering local matters. In China, they even helped in the campaign to kill off grain-eating sparrows. This apparatus of participation derived from the Marxist idea that all power at every level of government should be vested in soviets (councils) of workers and peasants. Marxist theory stressed self-government, so citizens in communist states had a wider menu of participation opportunities than their counterparts in liberal democracies.

> *Definition*
> **Regimented participation** is élite-controlled involvement in politics designed to express popular support for the notional attempt by the rulers to build a new society. Its purpose is to mobilize the masses behind the regime, not to influence the personnel or policies of the government.

However, the quality of participation did not match its quantity. Although the party's desire for popular participation may originally have been genuine, the impulse to safeguard party control proved to be stronger. Communist élites sought to ensure that mass participation always strengthened, and never weakened, the party's grip; so party members guided all popular participation. At regular

EXHIBIT 5.3

Regimented participation: China's sparrows

As every farmer knows, birds eat seeds. Most farmers accept the loss of part of their crop as an occupational hazard. Not so the Chinese Communist Party. In the early 1950s it decided to fight nature head on.

In an extraordinary exercise in mass participation, the population of China took up drums, pots and pans to create a nationwide cacophony. Whenever a sparrow landed for a rest, it was bombarded by noise and scared away. Eventually, the exhausted birds simply fell from the sky and died.

Unfortunately birds don't just eat grain; they are also partial to bugs and insects. With the bird population decimated in the cities, insect life flourished.

Faced with a near plague the authorities despatched teams to wage war on the insects by digging up their breeding grounds. But with the grass now gone, winter winds whipped up the soil creating dust storms across the cities of northern China.

But did this really matter? The communist party had realised its aim of involving the population in a mass campaign – no matter how ridiculous. For the party, the campaign was a success. Rather than the end justifying the means, the means had justified the unfortunate ends.

Further reading: for a more recent study of political participation in China, see Shi (1997).

meetings of women's federations, trade unions and youth groups, party activists explained policy to the people. The outcome was that communist parties directed political participation to an extent unknown in the democractic world.

Eventually, this tight control of participation harmed economic development. A complex industrial society calls for technical and administrative skills, proficiently applied, but experts need discretion to perform well. So, well before the collapse of communism in 1989 a participation crisis had developed in communist states. The system required, but could not allow, genuine participation by functionally important personnel. It also needed more than the sullen acquiescence of ordinary people. Eventually, some ruling parties did allow more participation but only in areas that did not threaten their monopoly of power. In particular, party leaders encouraged reforms that would revive ailing economies. Managers were given more say in policymaking and political participation became more authentic on local, specific and technical matters. But, crucially, these reforms were not matched in the sphere of national politics. Because no real channels existed for airing grievances, people were left with two choices: either to shut up and get on with life, or to express their views outside the system. For all the notional participation, communist governments chose to ignore the extent of popular opposition to their rule.

Postcommunism: building civil society

A change in form of government always requires the politically active population to learn new habits, but the transition from communism to democracy is especially acute. In postcommunist states, both élite and citizens need to learn that mass participation need no longer be a cynical exercise in manipulation by the rulers. Experience suggests that acquiring these new operating procedures is a difficult task. Establishing democratic institutions is one thing; unlearning old assumptions about the limited role for voluntary participation is another. Especially in postcommunist countries with no democratic tradition, mass participation still does not connect with the realities of power. A transition from communism

is only one aspect of creating a postcommunist democracy.

In the communist world the old style of regimented participation quickly disintegrated as these regimes fell apart. The demolition job carried out in the revolutions of 1989 revealed two related points about participation. First, the historic protests on the streets of the capital cities in Eastern Europe were historic because of their mere occurrence. Street demonstrations may be almost routine in Paris and Rome but similar events carried infinitely more weight in Prague and Bucharest. In a context of regimented participation, explicit protest became a revolutionary act. But, second, mass protests on the streets came late in the collapse of communism. They were not so much a cause of disintegration as a symbol of the party's loss of control and a trigger of its final collapse. The protestors buried communism more than they murdered it.

Once postcommunist regimes had been created, the task was to create more structured forms of voluntary participation through parties, elections and interest groups. This was difficult. The populations of many Eastern European states had experienced regimented participation under communist rule and seen mass participation on television during its collapse. However, they had little experience of voluntary participation as understood in the West. The same was true of political élites. In the Balkan states such as Bulgaria and Romania, as in the successor states to the Soviet Union, communist rule had simply continued an authoritarian political tradition. A stable system of voluntary participation would require the relationship between state and society to be completely recast, a long-term task far harder than merely breaking up the rotten timbers of the communist state.

The problem was to build a 'civil society', regulated by law but remaining separate from the state. Such a society provides opportunities for people to participate in collective activities which are neither pro-state nor anti-state, but simply non-state. Under communist rule, however, civil society had been demobilized. It had been stood down so that the rulers could directly control the individual: 'everyone was supposed to be the same – working for the state, on a salary, on a leash' (Goban-Klas and Sasinka-Klas, 1992). Civil society had been flattened by the bulldozer of the communist party because, as

Rose observes, 'communist rule transformed public opinion into private opinion'. Yet, as Diamond, Linz and Lipset note (1995, p. 28),

> civil society contributes in diverse ways to deepening, consolidating and maintaining democracy. It supplements the role of political parties in stimulating political participation and increasing citizens' political efficacy and skill.

Definition

Civil society consists of those groups which are 'above' the personal realm of the family but 'beneath' the state. The term covers public organizations such as firms, labour unions, interest groups and even (on some definitions) recreational bodies. Such institutions form part of the collective life of society, and of liberal democracy, but are voluntary in character and autonomous from the government. Italians put it this way: if the state is represented by the palazzo (the palace), civil society is found in the streets of the piazza (the square). Where a civil society is absent, as in totalitarian regimes, there are only two groups: rulers and ruled.

The notion of a civil society had played an important role in the critique of communist power developed by Eastern European dissidents in the 1980s. However, these thinkers had naturally tended to see civil society as an enemy of, not a complement to, state power (Szacki, 1995). To support civil society was to oppose the state. 'We want democracy, we don't want politics', proclaimed a slogan of the Romanian revolution. In similar vein, Konrad (1984, p. 66) wrote, 'a society does not become politically conscious when it shares some political philosophy, but rather when it refuses to be fooled by any of them'. Anti-politics proved to be more destructive than constructive. It provided a critique of communism but no basis for constructing postcommunist avenues of political participation. It may even have reinforced the natural cynicism towards politics instilled in Eastern European populations by their long experience of authoritarian rule.

Building a civil society remains a central task for most postcommunist regimes. The overthrow of the communist party has left a dangerous vacuum which, in the absence of a developed civil society, can easily be filled by nationalist demagogues hawking their crude wares. Even in the most consolidated postcommunist democracies such as Poland, political parties have not integrated society and state. They have tended to be loose, volatile coalitions representing few people apart from their own leaders. Further, the unbalanced character of many postcommunist economies, mixing massive state-owned enterprises with get-rich-quick entrepreneurs, has also worked against a vigorous civil society based on the institutions of capitalism.

So a civil society will not emerge spontaneously from the ashes of communism. Rather, it must be built, paradoxically, by manipulating the levers of state power themselves. An independent judiciary, respect for minority rights, the enforcement of contracts and the maintenance of law and order – all require active intervention by the state. Building a civil society requires participation by citizens in both state and nonstate institutions. Yet the economic crisis confronting the postcommunist countries has inevitably increased cynicism about politics. It has reduced political participation and reinforced the traditional belief that individuals must take care of themselves, relying on neither the state nor anyone else beyond the immediate family.

The developing world: patron–client relationships

Clientelism is a form of political involvement which differs from both voluntary participation in liberal democracies and the regimented routines of communist states. Although patron–client relationships are found in all political systems, the developing world provides the fullest examples of such relationships. Indeed in many developing countries they are often the main instrument for bringing ordinary people into contact with formal politics.

So what exactly are patron–client relationships? They are informal hierarchies fuelled by exchanges between a high-status 'patron' and some (often many) 'clients' of lower status. The colloquial phrase 'big man/small boy' relationships conveys the nature of the interaction. Lacking resources of their own, clients gather round their patron for protection and security. Political patrons control the votes of their clients and persuade them to attend meetings, join organizations or simply follow their patron around

Country profile **RUSSIA**

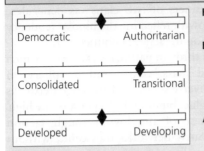

Democratic — Authoritarian

Consolidated — Transitional

Developed — Developing

Population: 148m (and falling slightly)
Gross domestic product per head:
$5300 (fell dramatically 1990–96).

Form of government: federation of 21 autonomous republics.

Executive: formally semi-presidential but with a strong presidency. The prime minister heads the Council of Ministers and succeeds the president if needed (no vice-president).

Assembly: the Federal Council (upper house) contains two members from each of 79 geographical units. The Duma (lower house) contains 450 members elected by an additional member system.

Judicial branch: based on civil law. Headed by a Constitutional Court and, for civil and administrative cases, a Supreme Court. Substantial lawlessness.

Natural resources: massive reserves of oil, gas, coal, timber and minerals but many are difficult to exploit.

Environment: extensive pollution, deforestation and contamination (including local radioactivity).

Russia is a vast country with an imperial and nondemocratic past. It is a place full of problems, potential and paradoxes. By area Russia is the largest country in the world, almost twice the size of the United States. The population includes 36 national groups with populations of at least 100 000. Russia's rulers have in the past been autocratic empire-builders, basing their imperial expansion on control of a serf society and (until the communist era) a rural economy. Thus Russia's experience with communist dictatorship represented a variant of a familiar authoritarian pattern. The communist party did, however, dominate society completely, more so than in nearly all other communist states. Internationally, the Union of Soviet Socialist Republics (USSR, 1922–91) was in effect a Russian empire.

Of all the postcommunist states, Russia raises the most interesting questions about the relationship between participation and democracy. For many observers a country with Russia's autocratic past cannot expect to develop the voluntary participation which supports stable liberal democracies. The country's history has bequeathed a political culture based on a fatalistic acceptance of strong leadership. This desire for a near-dictator was, it is claimed, reinforced by the economic decline and ethnic divisions of the early postcommunist years. Cynics suggest that Russia spent the twentieth century proving that communism did not work and intends to do exactly the same with liberal democracy in the twenty-first century. Brown (1989, p.19) notes that

because political cultures are historically conditioned, the long-term authoritarian character of the Russian and Soviet state constitutes a serious impediment to political change of a pluralizing, libertarian or genuinely democratizing nature.

Yet this assessment of the prospects for democracy in Russia may be too gloomy. In any large country, attitudes to politics are neither simple nor uniform. Among younger generations, and in the Moscow region, support for democracy is firmer. The desire for effective government in postcommunist Russia may be a short-term response to social breakdown, not an indicator of deep-seated authoritarianism. Russia's past may be nondemocratic but this does not prevent its people from learning from established democracies elsewhere. Further, by the mid-1990s Russia had succeeded in holding a series of reasonably free elections to both the presidency and the Duma. And despite monumental corruption, its economy was finally beginning to pick up. Whatever the future may hold for postcommunist Russia, it is surely too fatalistic to claim that an authoritarian past rules out the possibility of building democracy in Russia. The real question, perhaps, is just how democractic Russia's 'democracy' will prove to be.

Further reading: Petro (1995), Sakwa (1996), White, Pravda and Gitelman (1997), Woshinsky (1995, Ch.6).

in a deferential manner (this explains why political motorcades are so long). For example in Sri Lanka patrons with access to the resources of the state largely decide how ordinary people vote (Jayanntha, 1991). Patrons are landlords, employers, political entrepreneurs or most often ethnic leaders. Indeed, the elusive notion of an ethnic group can be partly understood as a large patron–client network for distributing favours.

Definition
Clientelism is a term used to describe politics substantially based on patron–client relationships. These relationships are often traditional and personal, as in the protection provided to tenants by landowners in developing countries. But they can also be more instrumental, as with the resources which machine politicians in American cities provided to new immigrants in exchange for their vote. Where clientelism is common, it can pervade the political culture, affirming the inequality from which it springs (Clapham, 1982).

Where patron–client relationships predominate, politics becomes personal and factional. The big men, such as government ministers and tribal leaders, control most resources and so acquire the most followers. In a developed patronage system with multiple levels, the president is simply the biggest man of all, compelled by political logic to distribute the most favours to satisfy his followers and maintain his precarious status as the 'highest of the high'. As Bayart (1993, p. 226) says, 'the copious thefts from state funds by competing networks makes it all the more important for the president of the republic to enrich himself if he is to affirm his authority over other networks'. Political success brings more followers who require more favours. Since patrons compete to distribute favours, escalation is built-in and the result, in extreme cases, is that the government simply runs out of money or at least has recourse to printing more of it. One reason why African presidents accepted the austerity programmes imposed by international organizations in the 1980s is that they helped to rein in spending ministries in which patronage had run riot.

Africa is particularly rich in examples of patronage politics, and Senegal is a textbook case (Bayart, 1993, p. 211). There, the phrase 'to make politics'

just *means* to be a devotee of a faction leader and to work for him. National politics consists of a conflict between the leaders of two clans (as Senegalese factions are known), reflecting the bipolar tendency which is common in factional politics.

Participation through patronage is a device which links élite and mass, centre and periphery, in unequal and diverse societies. Patronage networks act as political glue, binding the 'highest of the high' with the 'lowest of the low' through faction membership. Such networks transcend, without nullifying, inequalities of wealth, status and power. Thus inequality provides the fertilizer in which patron–client relationships flower. Poverty means the poor are vulnerable and need protection; inequality means the rich have the resources to provide it in exchange for political allegiance.

The developing world: trends in participation

As in communist states, mass participation in politics has a chequered history in the developing world. In much of sub-Saharan Africa, the postwar struggle for independence had created mass movements based on an ethos of participation; the nationalist party provided a vehicle through which people could participate in politics. However, in practice this engagement was often limited and in any case the mobilizing culture and associated party structures soon decayed after independence. In many African states participation withered. Kashfir (1976) referred to 'departicipation' and the 'shrinking political arena'. For example only one in four voters took part in the Nigerian general election of 1983 shortly before the military takeover. The military regimes which often replaced mobilizing independence movements were suspicious of popular participation, and often they did not even bother with the facade of pompous rallies and 'spontaneous' outbreaks of support which had been a speciality of communist rulers.

It was not until the end of the 1980s that democratization, and with it more genuine forms of participation, returned to sub-Saharan Africa. The prodemocracy movements of most African states in the late 1980s represented a remarkable coming-together of political participation by a range of social groups (Wiseman, 1995, p. 5). Prominent among them were church leaders and professional associations of lawyers, journalists, students and medical staff. These bodies had always maintained some distance from the state; they formed the glimmerings of the civil society on which a stable liberal democracy is founded.

More often than in Latin America, mass political participation in strikes or street demonstrations was the key which unlocked the door leading to political reform. Benin was the pioneer. There, students marched out of classes in the national university in 1989 demanding payment of overdue scholarships, and later in the year civil servants and schoolteachers threatened a general strike for non-payment of salaries. These protests initiated a period of reform which culminated in the electoral defeat of President Kerekou in 1991 (Bratton and van de Walle, 1997, p. 1). Where Benin led the way, other African countries followed. In Malawi, the effects of a strike in 1992 at a Lonrho factory rippled through the country. Civil servants stopped work and demonstrators took to the streets, burning offices of the ruling party and looting state-owned supermarkets. As Venter (1995, p. 159) says,

> these strikes and demonstrations marked a rite of passage for the country. At last the people had found their voice and one could sense that a major psychological barrier had been swept away. In fact, the crack had widened in the granite edifice of the Malawian regime and the process of change now seemed irreversible.

Developing countries which achieved independence in the nineteenth century (mainly in Latin America) have also followed a chequered participation history. Mass participation has often been demanded but, until recently, rarely achieved in anything like a stable form. Economic development, which has generally progressed further in Latin America than in Africa, produced an urban middleclass and proletariat. Both groups demanded entry into the political system. These demands encountered a haughty response from Latin America's conservative, aristocratic élites. Except in Costa Rica and Venezuela, which have been fairly stable throughout the postwar era, the result was political instability. Military governments and civilian oligarchies confronted, and occasionally gave way to, populist movements from the lower-middle and working classes.

However, in the 1980s the generals of South America went into retreat, and civilian regimes based on voluntary participation were established throughout Latin America. By 1990 Bolivia had witnessed three orderly transfers of power between civilian presidents. These new regimes were based on more stable forms of popular participation than has been the case with earlier waves of populism, leading George Bush to prophesy in 1990 that 'in Latin America the day of the dictator is over'. If reformed economies continue to grow, and the fruits of this prosperity reach beyond the grasping arms of the wealthy, this prediction should prove justified.

Yet in both Latin America and Africa the development of a civil society, and with it extensive voluntary participation, is likely to be a slow process. In South America, economic inequality and a strongman tradition (both in government and in the countryside) help to maintain patron–client relationships even in an era of formal political equality. As in postcommunist states there is also some tradition of 'antipolitics' represented in new social movements. Born out of the struggle to survive under often brutal authoritarian rule, these groups tend to be outside the state rather than channels for engagement with it. In Africa the difficulty of deepening voluntary participation lies in the core problem of poverty which narrows horizons to issues of survival. Limited education, particularly illiteracy, is another negative factor for voluntary participation. Further, in smaller African states the national government itself has limited functions and weak penetration beyond the capital. National media barely exist so that even passive participation through following political news is impractical. Such participation as emerges, at least beyond voting in an occasional election, is likely to be directed towards informal politics such as ethnic networks. These factors all suggest that voluntary participation in the new democracies of Latin America and Africa is unlikely to match the undemanding levels of consolidated democracies. Participation will fail to bridge the gap between national politics and the mass population, thereby strengthening semi-democracy.

In many East Asian regimes, too, participation tends to be controlled and monitored by semi-democratic governments, often ruling through the vehicle of a dominant party. 'Soft authoritarianism' does not reduce popular participation to the empty rituals of communist states but neither does it permit the untrammelled expression of conflicting ideas as found in, say, the United States. Rather, the national goal of economic development is regarded as sacrosanct. Challenges to this 'shared' objective – by radical students, fledgling ecology movements or trade unions – can be harshly repressed. Since the national leader, dominant party and/or the bureaucratic élite are the vehicle for implementing the national vision, any threat to these wielders of power is dealt with equally harshly. In some countries, however, this pattern is gradually giving way to more open participation. For example, as South Korea becomes more affluent so a better-educated and more middle-class population has begun to test the implicit limits of political discourse. But traditions of deference to elders and rulers, reinforced by the governing élite itself, still give a tentative flavour to political opposition which is not found in the consolidated democracies of the West.

New politics

In 1996, 325 000 Belgians, 3 per cent of the country's population, marched through Brussels in a peaceful protest against an inadequate public investigation into a sexually-motivated child murder. This White March (white was worn as a symbol of purity) was an example of new politics. In Belgium as in many other Western democracies, new politics has mounted a major challenge to the 'official' system. It represents a style of participation which deliberately seeks to distance itself from the established channels, thereby questioning the legitimacy as well as the decisions of the government. Advocates of new politics are willing to consider new forms of participation: demonstrations, sit-ins and sit-downs, boycotts and political strikes. In some democracies, including West Germany and Italy, unorthodox participation in the 1960s and 1970s extended further, to include violent activities such as terrorism and kidnapping.

These unorthodox modes of participation are usually in pursuit of broad, not class-based, objec-

---

BOX 5.1

Old and new politics

	Old politics	New politics
Organization	Formal	Informal
Attitude to political system	Supportive	Critical
Vehicle of participation	Parties	Single-issue groups
Style of participation	Orthodox	Unconventional
Concerns	Interests	Values
Breadth	National	Global
Motives	Instrumental	Expressive
Typical age	Middle aged	Younger

---

tives: for example, nuclear disarmament, feminism and the protection of the environment. New politics is as concerned with making statements and expressing identities (for example the gay movement) as with achieving precise legislative objectives. If political parties exemplified old politics, informal single-issue movements define new politics. Tarrow (1994) even speaks of the emergence of a 'movement society' in which new politics becomes the normal mode of participation as the traditional institutions of government lose weight.

The question raised by these new modes of participation is how they relate to the orthodox political system. At one level, the whole rationale of new politics is to threaten the dominance of existing elites. It provides a 'people's challenge' to the iron triangles of government, protective interest groups and mainstream parties. Yet except for their youth, the unconventional activists of the 1960s resembled the orthodox activists of an earlier era. The exponents of new politics are primarily well-educated, articulate people from middle-class backgrounds – exactly the same types who are to be found in the council chambers of local government and the meeting rooms of political parties. And more than a few leaders of the new politics are switching to orthodox politics as they age; many a protest activist of the 1960s turned into a political leader in the 1990s and 2000s. Indeed, for all the apparent differences between new and old politics, one function of the new politics has been to provide a training ground for future national leaders.

In any case, new politics, like the postmaterialism from which it partly springs, remains a minority sport. Surveys conducted in eight Western democracies in 1974 showed that less than half the population said they approved of more extreme forms of protest such as occupations, rent strikes and blockades. In this survey the most radical countries were Italy and the Netherlands; the Austrians were most cautious. Across all countries the young were most likely to be protestors (Marsh, 1990). The political impact of new politics should not lead us to exaggerate its scale.

Definition

Social movements are defined by Tarrow (1994, p. 4) as 'collective challenges by people with common purposes and solidarity in sustained interaction with élites, opponents and authorities'. Unlike parties, social movements do not seek state power. Rather, they aim to bypass the government through a self-help ethos.

The developed world holds no monopoly over new politics. Hiding under the label of 'new social movements' (NSMs), new politics has also become a significant feature in parts of the developing world. Encouraged by development agencies and in Latin America by radical Catholicism, social movements sought to carve political space for themselves by asserting their identity as indigenous peoples, gays, feminists and ecologists (Escobar and Alvarez, 1992). As in the developed world, NSMs arose more from opposition to the state than from any desire to become part of it. In contrast to the West, however, new politics in the developing world is also the territory of the poor, as people facing acute problems of daily life organize to improve their conditions. The urban poor organizing soup kitchens, the inhabitants of shanty towns lobbying for land reform, the mothers whose sons 'disappeared' under military rule – all are examples of this flowering of popular political activity which occurred in the 1970s and 1980s. Sociologically, such activists are very different from the postmaterialists who lead the new politics in the Western world.

Fluid in organization and democratic in ethos, these movements seek to retain their social charac-

ter. They aim to influence but also remain separate from formal political institutions. They play the state without aiming to occupy it (Watson, 1990). The movements attach importance to education (for example, through medical advice for mothers) so that people can acquire more control over their own lives. Such movements prosper when the state lacks either the desire or the resources to help those living on the margins of society. However, the reluctance of the movements to engage with formal politics limits their long-term national significance; local and small-scale in origin and character, they often lack policy sophistication, particularly on national economic issues. Indeed the democratic transition has taken some wind from the sails of NSMs. In Uruguay, for example, 'democracy brought, by a curious twist, the disappearance of many grass-roots movements that had been active during the years of dictatorship' (Canel, 1992, p. 290).

Revolutions

The forms of participation we have examined so far operate within a specific framework. Voters in democracies casting their ballot, marchers in communist states demonstrating 'support' for their rulers, villagers in developing countries doing the bidding of their local landowner – in all these cases, ordinary people participate through taking on clear but also limited roles in the political process. Yet occasionally, of course, political conflict extends to the governing framework itself, and the entire political order becomes a matter for dispute. When the existing structure of power is overthrown, usually by violence, and this leads to a long-term reconstruction of the political, social and economic order, we can speak of a revolution. While a coup simply involves the forcible replacement of one set of rulers by another, a revolution entails broad and deep alterations in social, economic and political organization. Revolutions are rare but pivotal events. The major instances – France, America, Russia, China, Iran – have substantially defined the modern world.

The collapse of communism in Eastern Europe in 1989 leading on to the fall of the Soviet Union in 1991 is a recent example of revolutionary change. In most countries these were negotiated revolutions; Czechoslovakia's Velvet Revolution is a case in point.

Popular protest on the streets of Eastern European capitals in the summer of 1989 came late in the downfall of communism; protest served to bury a system which had, in effect, already died. But in bringing about the end of the cold war, and initiating major restructuring in postcommunist societies, 1989 certainly qualifies as a year of revolutions. Communism's disintegration confirms that revolutions should be known by their impact as much as the manner of their inception; a peaceful revolution is a revolution nonetheless (Holmes, 1997, p. 35).

> **Definition**
> Skocpol (1979, p. 4) defines **social revolutions** as 'rapid, basic transformations of a society's state and class structures; and they are accompanied and in part carried through by class-based revolts from below'. Goldstone (1991, p. 37) suggests revolutions consist of three overlapping stages: state breakdown, the ensuing struggle for power and then the crucial reconstruction of the state.

The French revolution

Our scrutiny of revolutions must begin with France in 1789, as this was the first and most important revolution of modern times. Indeed, it is no exaggeration to say that the modern concept of revolution developed from the French experience. What, then, were the contours of this landmark episode? Before 1789, France still combined an absolute monarchy with feudalism. Governance was a confused patchwork of local, provincial and royal institutions. However, in the 1780s the stormclouds gathered: the old regime came under stress as the monarchy became virtually bankrupt, and in 1788 a poor grain harvest triggered peasant revolts in the countryside and discontent in the cities.

The revolution was initiated after the Estates General was convened in May 1789 for the first time in over 150 years. The assembly was called in an effort to protect aristocratic privileges. However, the Third Estate, representing the people, withdrew and declared itself to constitute the National Assembly. When the Bastille fortress was stormed in July – only seven prisoners freed but a symbol of despotism overthrown – the revolution was underway. There followed a half-decade of radical reform in which,

amid enormous violence known as The Terror, the old institutions were demolished and the foundations of a modern state laid down. The monarchy was abolished in 1791; two years later Louis XVI was executed. In the 1790s assorted attempts to build a constitutional monarchy, a republic and a parliamentary government failed. Eventually Napoleon instituted a period of authoritarian rule lasting from 1799 to 1814. Universal male suffrage was not adopted until 1848 and the conflict between radicals and conservatives embedded in the revolution remained important to French politics for the next two centuries.

Despite its mixed outcomes, the epochal significance of the French revolution cannot be doubted. It established the future shape of liberal democracy – popular sovereignty, a professional bureaucracy, a market economy and a liberal ideology. Politically it destroyed absolute monarchy based on divine right and curtailed the traditional powers of the aristocracy. Economically, by weakening aristocratic control over the peasantry, the revolution helped to create the conditions under which market relations could spread and capitalism would eventually emerge. Ideologically the revolution was strongly secular, fathering liberal ideas of individual rights enforceable through codified law. The revolution was also powerfully nationalist: the nation became the transcendent bond, uniting all citizens in patriotic fervour. The shockwaves of the French revolution reverberated throughout Europe as ruling classes everywhere saw their very existence imperilled.

Marx and the communist revolutions

Although the orginal meaning of revolution had been for rulers to 'revolve' in power without any change in the underlying political structure, the French case revealed revolutions in their modern guise as agents of progress. This perspective was further developed in Marx's theory of revolution, an account which exerted profound influence on both academic study and political practice. Karl Marx (1818–83) viewed revolution as inescapable. He argued that revolution involved the transformation of society from one mode of economic production to another – from feudalism to capitalism (as in France), or from capitalism to socialism (as, Marx hoped, in the future). The entire movement of history was inevitable and would culminate in the creation of a communist utopia.

Marx's theory was based on a materialist reading of history. He argued that the prevailing economic system always creates conflict in society between ruling and exploited classes. Members of the exploited class become increasingly alienated from the existing order and are drawn together by an emerging class consciousness. Once the exploited class achieves sufficient unity, it rises up and over-throws the ruling class. The distribution of power is transformed as the exploited class take its destiny into its own hands and begins a new historical epoch based on a new mode of production. Just as the French revolution enabled the new merchants and manufacturers to seize power from a dying aristoc-racy, so Marx believed that in capitalist societies the working class would eventually destroy the system which exploited them. Treated as a commodity, and suffering from a declining standard of living, the working class would eventually fulfill its historic role as capitalism's gravedigger. The communist revolu-tion would initiate a new, rational and progressive era of distribution according to need.

Marx's contribution was expressed in terms which were both deterministic and idealistic. Even so, he succeeded in drawing attention not just to the economic factor in revolutions but also, more broadly, to the way revolutions can dispose of a political order which has become a fetter to progress. But his account also created paradoxes of its own. If a revolution is inevitable, should activists just sit back and wait for it to arrive? If capitalism must mature before it enters its phase of decline and becomes ripe for overthrow, why did the major com-munist revolutions of the twentieth century – in Russia in 1917 and in China ending in 1949 – occur in some of the weakest links in the capitalist chain? Part of the answer, surely, is that revolutionary situ-ations may arise whenever, and for whatever reason, a state loses its legitimacy and governing effective-ness. And in both Russia and China, hard-nosed practitioners were on hand to seize the moment. Lenin and Mao Zedong did more than just lend a helping hand to historical forces; they helped to make revolutions happen.

In Russia, Lenin (1870–1924) attached great sig-nificance to political organization in fomenting rev-olution. He developed the notion of the vanguard party, an élite body of revolutionaries which claimed to understand the long-term interests of the working-class better than that class itself. 'Give us an organization of revolutionaries and we shall overturn the whole of Russia', he declared in 1902. Without such a party, Lenin thought, the working class could only develop limited 'trade union consciousness'. From his realpolitik perspective Lenin may have been justified in dismissing left-wing communism as 'an infantile disorder'. Even so, critics allege that his notion of the vanguard party prepared the ground for the regimented participation which became such a stultifying feature of communist states.

In China, Mao Zedong (1893–1976) adapted Marxism to a peasant society without an established working class of any sort. Marx had regarded the peasantry as a reactionary class with no revolution-ary potential; and even Lenin viewed peasants as no more than a dispensable ally. But Mao recognized the revolutionary potential of the Chinese peasantry. China's peasants were spurred into revolutionary activity as their situation worsened after the arrival from 1839 of Western powers such as Britain and France. But nationalism also played a major part in the Chinese revolution. Between 1931 and 1934 the communists downplayed their policy of class war. Instead they built their policies around anti-Japanese sentiment. As such, the rise to power of the com-munists in 1949 can be seen as a victory for nation-alist ideology. In relying on the peasantry and nationalism, we can see how far Mao deviated from Marx's original ideas. Schwartz (1960) concludes that the political thought of Mao Zedong was so divorced from the original writings of Marx that Mao could hardly be called a Marxist at all.

Social psychological and structural theories

The twentieth century vastly increased the world's stock of revolutions (Box 5.2). Confronting these examples, political scientists have sought to develop general explanations of revolution which extend beyond Marx's focus on class conflict. The social psychological account is perhaps the most promi-nent of these non- (or even anti-) Marxist approaches: it seeks to identify what motivates indi-viduals to participate in revolutionary activity. Why

BOX 5.2

A century of revolutions

Country	Date	Outcome
Mexico	1910	A populist revolution leading to rule by a dominant party, the PRI
Russia	1917	The first communist state
Turkey	1922	A secular nation-state built from the ruins of the Ottoman Empire
China	1949	The communist People's Republic of China, led by Mao Zedong
Iran	1979	An Islamic state led by Ayatollah Khomeini
Eastern Europe and the Soviet Union	1989/91	Collapse of communist rule

do some people sometimes feel so strongly about politics that they are willing to give time, energy and ultimately their lives to achieve change?

In his study of the French revolution, Tocqueville (1966, first pub. 1856) had noted that grievances patiently endured become intolerable once the possibility of a brighter future crosses the population's minds. In the 1960s this insight was developed by advocates of the social psychological approach. One of the main exponents of this new school was Gurr (1980). He argued that relative deprivation was the key to revolutions; when there is a difference between what people perceive they are receiving (value capability) and what they feel they are entitled to (value expectations), collective violence may result. The most explosive situation is when a period of rising expectations is followed by a decline in the ability of the regime to meet those demands. This combination creates a revolutionary gap between expectations and reality. Davies (1962) sums up the implications of this approach: 'revolutions are most likely to occur when a prolonged period of economic and social development is followed by a short period of sharp reversal'. This hypothesis is known as the J-curve theory (Figure 5.2).

Davies suggests that relative deprivation helps to account for the Russian revolution in particular. Although Russia became a military power in the nineteenth century, it remained a poor country with a serf economy and government by an autocratic Tsar. However, the Tsar did institute important reforms between 1860–1904, including improved rights for the peasantry, the introduction of a modern legal system, state-sponsored industrializa-

tion and a general liberalization of society. But these reforms served only to enhance a sense of relative deprivation; the peasants were legally free but most remained burdened by debt. Furthermore, expectations raised by political reforms were then dashed by the Tsar's inability to push ahead with further, more radical changes. Reform oscillated with repression in a perfect formula for fostering relative deprivation. Though an attempted revolution failed in 1905, the hardships imposed by Russia's involvement in the First World War created another revolutionary opportunity in 1917. This time the chance was taken. The Bolsheviks exploited the opportunity and established the world's first communist state.

Relative deprivation is certainly a background

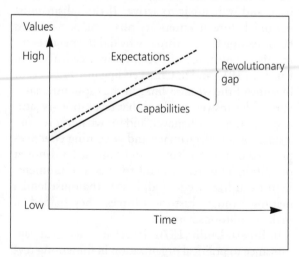

Figure 5.2 The J-curve theory of revolutions

factor in many revolutions. Peasant frustrations, in particular, were involved in the French, Russian and Chinese revolutions. The contribution of the social psychological approach lies in demonstrating that how people perceive their condition is more important than the actual condition itself. To analyse the exploitation of the peasantry is one thing; but to understand the conditions under which resignation transmutes into violence is altogether a more challenging and useful project. Yet although the social psychological account provides an interesting insight into the conditions of political instability, it seems incapable of explaining revolutionary progress and outcomes. Whose discontent matters? Why does discontent sometimes lead to an uprising but sometimes not? How and why do uprisings turn into revolutions? How is discontent channelled into organized opposition movements? Why is such opposition usually suppressed but sometimes not? How do the new revolutionary leaders consolidate their hold on power?

Given these weaknesses, the study of revolutions has turned away from broad psychological theories and returned to more fine-grained historical examination of a small number of cases. Skocpol's (1979) influential discussion of the French, Russian and Chinese revolutions was an example of this fresher approach. For Skocpol, the causes of revolutions cannot be found in the motives of the participants. What matters are the structural conditions – the relationships between groups within a state and, equally important, between states. The background to revolution is provided by a regime that is weak internationally and ineffective domestically. The classic revolutions occurred when a regime had already lost its effectiveness and well-organized revolutionaries succeeded in exploiting peasant frustration with the old regime.

In these circumstances the actual seizing of power can be quite straightforward. The real revolution begins as the new rulers develop and impose their vision on society and, in particular, opposition groups. Revolutions do not stop with the taking of power, as the social psychological theory seemed to imply, but often only start at this point. Thus Skocpol says much about how discontent is mobilized into political activity and how that activity turns into a revolutionary transformation. She thereby confirms one of the key points about revolutions: that their nature is expressed in their consequences rather than their causes.

Key reading

> **Next step:** *Verba, Scholzman and Brady (1995) is a major study of participation in America, building on a generation's worth of previous research.*

Milbrath and Goel (1977) is still a useful text. The classic empirical study is by Verba and Nie (1972) on the United States. For a comparable British investigation see Parry, Moyser and Day (1992). The major comparative studies are Verba, Nie and Kim (1978) and, on unconventional participation, Barnes and Kaase (1979), summarized in Marsh (1990). Dalton and Kuechler (1990) is a good collection on social movements; see also Tarrow (1989). Escobar and Alvarez (1992) is an excellent collection on social movements in Latin America. The literature on participation in postcommunist societies is still fragmentary; on Russia, see Sakwa (1996, Ch.5). For participation in the developing world, standard works are Huntington and Nelson (1976), Eisenstadt and Lemarchand (1981) and Clapham (1982). For participation in African transitions, see Bratton and van de Walle (1997, Ch.4). On revolutions, see Skocpol (1979) for a classic analysis and Goldstone, Kurr and Moshiri (1991) for twentieth century revolutions specifically.

Elections, voters and public opinion

On 27 April 1994, Primrose Ngabane, a 58-year-old black domestic employee, voted in South Africa's first nonracial election. To cast her ballot (she voted for the white-led National Party), she had to walk several miles, take a long bus journey and a group taxi, and queue outside the polling station for several hours (Reynolds, 1994, p. i). Primrose Ngabane's commitment was typical of millions of people throughout the world who acquired the right to vote in the final quarter of the twentieth century. Democratization has drawn ordinary people into the political process via competitive elections. In countries like South Africa, this involved extending the right to vote to previously disenfranchised groups. In the postcommunist world, the democratic revolution took the form of adding real choice to what had previously been charade elections. As a result of these changes, competitive elections are now more central to national politics in more countries than ever before.

To understand elections, we must unravel both the forces shaping individual choice and the role of elections in the political system. At the *individual* level, the task is to understand the forces shaping the voter's choice. Why, for instance, was Primrose Ngabane one of about 4 per cent of blacks to vote

for the National Party? How did the National Party manage to gain almost half its support from nonwhites? Such questions involve the study of voting behaviour, a field of politics which, with the arrival of the sample survey, has exploded since 1945. At the level of the *political system*, the task is to understand the wider significance of elections. What are the consequences of elections for the system of government? For example, the South African contest of 1994 was a classic example of a 'founding election', a high-turnout affair which establishes the legitimacy of a new regime.

> **Definition**
> An **election** is a competition for office based on a formal expression of preferences by a population. These opinions are then combined into a collective decision about which candidates have won.

Competitive elections

There are two views about the role of elections in liberal democracies: the bottom-up and top-down theories (Harrop and Miller, 1987). By reviewing these, we will cover the main functions of competitive elections. The bottom-up theory is the more orthodox, and it stresses the extent to which competitive elections render governments accountable to the governed. The last election decides who governs; the thought of the next election influences how they do so. Competition between parties forces them to respond to the views of the electors, attuning state to society. From this perspective, then, the key function of competitive elections is to channel communication upwards from voters through to parties and governments.

BOX 6.1
A classification of competitive elections

1. *Founding* election
The result confirms the legitimacy of a new regime, acting as a referendum on democracy. These elections are often transitional in that the broad coalition which fights, and often wins, the founding election later falls apart.

Examples: South Africa, 1994; the initial postcommunist elections in most of Eastern Europe, 1990.

2. *Realigning ('critical')* election
This changes the underlying strength of parties and redefines the relationships between parties and social groups. Full realignment, usually lasting for at least a generation, often takes place over two or three critical elections.

Example: American presidential elections in the 1920s and 1930s which forged the Democratic New Deal coalition.

3. *Normal* election
The result expresses the balance of long-term party loyalties

in the electorate as a whole. The party leading in party identification wins.

Example: Democratic presidential election victories in the USA.

4. *Deviating* election
The natural majority party loses the election due to short-term factors, such as a faltering economy or an unappealing candidate.

Example: Republican presidential election victories in the USA.

5. *Dealigning* election
The major parties lose support but no new cleavage emerges to supplant the existing system. Common in Western democracies.

Example: the British election of February 1974 in which the minority Liberals gained ground in a protest against the major parties.

This is a conventional picture but it has not gone unchallenged. Top-down theorists such as Ginsberg (1982) are more critical of the electoral process in liberal democracies. Ginsberg argues that 'competitive' elections are, in reality, devices for expanding the power of the élite over the population. Elections incorporate potential dissenters into the political system, reduce popular participation to a mere cross on a ballot and encourage people to obey the state without limiting its autonomy. Elections give a feeling of choice to voters, although one restricted to a few broad packages of proposals. This 'choice' serves to enhance the authority of governments over the voters. So the top-down perspective suggests that choice and accountability are not the key functions of elections. Rather, their leading role is to increase the legitimacy of ruling élites; to add to the authority, effectiveness and stability of the state; and also to educate the voters about élite concerns. 'Since the nineteenth century', notes Ginsberg, 'governments have ruled *through* elections even when they have sometimes been ruled *by* them'.

Our view falls between these two perspectives. Competitive elections are, we think, best seen as an *exchange* of influence between élites and voters. Elections are like a forge, in whose heat, noise and

glare rulers strive to shape power into authority. But elites gain added authority only in exchange for responsiveness to voters; they do not win something for nothing. Equally, the voters gain influence over government decisions but only in exchange for obedience to decisions they only partly shape. Overall, competitive elections expand the authority of government while reducing the likelihood of that authority being misused. They benefit both rulers and ruled.

Of course, competitive elections vary in significance. Some are political earthquakes, restructuring the party landscape for a generation or more. Others produce barely a tremor on the body politic, simply returning the existing government to power for another term. One useful way of classifying competitive elections is to categorize them by their significance. Box 6.1 outlines the main types of competitive election, as judged by their political significance.

Semi- and non-competitive elections

Strange as it may seem, elections are not always com-

BOX 6.2

Forms of semi- and non-competitive election

1. Dominant party

This is a semi-competitive form; it permits a facade of competition. However, the ruling party exploits patronage, corruption, control of the media and when necessary ballot-rigging to ensure its own continued hold on power. It is a form characteristic of semi-democracies, for example Egypt and Singapore.

2. Candidate-choice

This is also a semi-competitive form; it allows some choice of candidates but not of party. It was found in the less authoritarian communist states (for example Poland) and in some one-party systems in the developing world (e.g Kenya under KANU).

3. Acclamatory

This is a non-competitive form with only one candidate; any 'choice' is restricted to the nomination phase. It was found in totalitarian regimes, for example the Soviet Union.

---

petitive. Sometimes they are stage-managed affairs, presenting an illusion of choice but with the winner known in advance. In a few cases they are acts of acclamation rather than choice, with just one official candidate presented to the voters – and woebetide any elector who fails to support this nominee (Box 6.2). So how do these less competitive elections work? And what functions, if any, do such 'choiceless elections' perform?

The most common form of semi-competitive election is that controlled by a *dominant party*. Such elections mix choice and control in the characteristic fashion of a semi-democracy. The ruling party uses all the advantages of office (and these include effective governance and a high-visibility leader) to ensure its reelection. Patronage is the party's key resource; it is used either to reward loyal voters directly, as with the old party machines in American cities, or to provide local notables with jobs, contracts, access, influence, status and money. In exchange, these local big men deliver the vote of dependent clients in their patch. Sometimes voters simply hand over signed ballots for local patrons to fill out. When a Brazilian voter enquired who he had voted for, his patron replied, 'Now son, never ask me that kind of question and above all do not forget that the vote is secret'. In some developing countries (for example, Morocco), votes are simply bought and sold, with political entrepreneurs offering job lots to whichever party offers the best price. Since vote selling is a significant source of money for poor people, criticising the practice is politically impossible in countries such as Morocco.

Dominant parties also exploit their control over both the media and the administration of the election. Opposition candidates find they are disqualified from standing; that electoral registration is inefficient in their areas of strength; that they are rarely permitted to appear on television; that they are harassed by the police; and that their leaflets and even their votes are mysteriously lost. The opposition loses heart because it knows its function is always to oppose but never to win.

Mexico's Partido Revolucionaria Institucional (PRI), one of the world's most successful vote-winning machines, was the classic example of a party which ran semi-competitive elections. By virtue of winning the last 11 presidential elections, the PRI became a 'party of the state', giving it unique access to resources which it could pass out through its intricate patronage network (Cornelius, 1996). Semi-competitive elections remain widespread in Africa. The goal of many African Presidents, such as Arap Moi in Kenya, is to 'dodge democracy' by using elections to legitimize their power without threatening it (Macdonald, 1996). So far, many of these 'democratic despots' have succeeded in this delicate task.

In general, though, semi-competitive elections are becoming harder to manage. Domestically, population shifts to the cities take voters away from rural areas where patrons are most powerful. Internationally, Western countries and aid organizations have become less forgiving of obvious fraud now that the cold war is over. Privatization of state corporations means the governing party has less patronage (jobs and contracts) to distribute to its supporters. Even in Mexico the PRI now tolerates cleaner elections; in 1997 it lost its majority in the Chamber of Deputies, a result which the party would simply not have permitted in earlier times.

EXHIBIT 6.1

What is a free and fair election?

Observers from overseas are now a common sight during elections in democratizing countries, and their job is to report on whether an election was indeed democratic. But what is a 'free and fair' election? In a report commissioned by the Commonwealth Parliamentary Association, two Canadian election officers (Gould and Jackson 1995, p. 36) suggest that the key test is whether 'the will of the majority of voters is expressed freely, clearly and knowledgeably, and in secret'. Specifically:

A free election is an electoral process which respects human rights and freedoms, including:

- Freedom of speech
- Freedom of association
- Freedom to register as an elector, a party or a candidate

- Freedom from coercion
- Freedom of access to the polls
- Freedom to vote in secret
- Freedom to complain

A fair election is an electoral process with a level playing field, including:

- Non-partisan administration of the election
- Constitutional protection of electoral law
- Universal suffrage and accessible polling places
- Balanced reporting by the media
- Equitable access to resources for campaigns
- Open and transparent counting of the vote
- Equitable and noncoercive treatment of parties, candidates and electors by the government, the police, the military and the judiciary.

Further reading: Kumar (1998).

While semi-competitive elections preserve an illusion of choice, non-competitive contests are more brutal. They were found in one-party, especially communist, systems and there was no pretence that the ruling party could be defeated or even opposed through elections. Rather, the purpose of such 'contests' was, in theory, to confirm the party's continued support among the people. In practice, such elections demonstrated the party's power to get out the vote, confirming its dominance over society.

Acclamatory elections were the purest form of non-competitive election and they allowed no choice at all, not even between candidates supporting the one party. The offical candidate was simply presented to the electorate for ritual endorsement. The communist Soviet Union was the classic example; an old Soviet joke had a reporter announcing that a burglar had broken into the Kremlin and stolen next year's election results! Elections by acclamation were grim, ritualistic affairs, irrelevant to the real politics taking place within the party. They were an opportunity for the party's agitators to lecture the population on the party's achievements and to demonstrate their control by getting people out to vote on election day. Far from expressing popular influence over the rulers, acclamatory elections articulated the élite's continuing hold over the population. Contemporary examples are confined to decaying communist dictatorships. In Cuba, for example, 601 candidates were put up for election to the National Assembly in 1998; and there were exactly 601 seats to be filled.

Candidate-choice elections were a more liberal form of controlled election, and were characteristic of Eastern Europe in the 1970s and 1980s. Such contests allowed more candidates than seats, particularly at local level, thus giving voters a small measure of choice. But all candidates supported the communist party; the 'choice' was between candidates committed to the same cause. However, as communist control began to weaken such elections could easily become an arena of opposition. In Poland the communists introduced a reform which permitted Solidarity, the independent movement led by Lech Walesa, to contest one third of the seats in the parliamentary elections of June 1989. Solidarity won every one of these seats. In theory, the communists retained a clear majority in the assembly; in reality, their back was broken. Two months later, Poland had the first postcommunist prime minister in Eastern Europe.

Electoral systems: scope, franchise and turnout

An electoral system is a set of rules for conducting an election. Normally we think of an electoral system in terms of the procedures for translating votes into seats. But there are three broader – and prior – issues. These are: the scope of elected office (which offices are elected), the extent of the franchise (who can vote) and turnout (who does vote). In discussing these topics we use countries with competitive elections for illustrations.

A key feature of an electoral system is its scope. Which offices are subject to election is as fundamental as who has the right to vote. Compare the United States and Britain: the USA is unique in its massive range of elected offices, ranging from president to dogcatcher. This reflects a strong tradition of self-government, particularly at local level. In Britain, by contrast, voting has traditionally been confined to elections for the House of Commons, the European parliament and local councils (however, the Labour government elected in 1997 did introduce elected parliaments to Scotland and Wales). Similarly, Australians engage in much more electing than New Zealanders.

Other things being equal, the greater the number of offices subject to competitive election, the more democratic a political system becomes. However, there are dangers in electionitis. One is voter fatigue, leading to a fall in turnout and the quality of choice. In particular, the least important elections tend to become second-order contests – that is, their outcomes reflect the popularity of national parties even though they do not install a national government. For example, elections to the European parliament become referendums on *national* governments, although their supposed purpose is to elect a member for the *European* parliament. In many democracies local elections function in a similar way, as tests of national party strength. The difficulty with second-order contests is that they snap the link between performance in office and the voters' response (Anderson and Ward, 1996). Effective local administrations may be thrown out for no better reason than the incompetence of their party colleagues at national level.

The franchise (who can vote?) is another important element of the rules governing elections. In

Table 6.1 Average turnout in elections to the lower house, 1960–95

90% and over	81–90%	71–80%	70% and below
Australia	Denmark	Canada	India
Austria	Germany	Finland	Russia
Belgium	Israel	France	Switzerland
Italy	Netherlands	Ireland	USA
	New Zealand	Japan	
	Norway	Spain	
	Sweden	UK	

Source: Franklin (1996), Table 8.1.

most democracies, the franchise now extends to nearly all citizens aged at least 18. In many countries the age qualification was reduced from 21 in the 1960s or 1970s. The remaining exclusions are criminals, the insane and non-citizen residents such as guest workers. However this 'universal' franchise is fairly recent, particularly for women. Few countries can match Australia and New Zealand where women have been electors since the start of the twentieth century; elsewhere women often did not win the vote until after the Second World War. In a few countries, Kuwait included, women remain disenfranchised. Minority groups have also suffered discrimination until recently. The Canadian Inuit were only enfranchised in 1950; and Aborigines were unable to vote in Australia's 'whitefella' elections until 1962. In the American South, poll taxes and literacy tests served to deny the vote to Southern blacks until the mid-1960s.

A universal suffrage does not guarantee a full turnout. Consider the United States again: in presidential elections barely one in two Americans of voting age cast a ballot. In 1996, turnout fell below 50 per cent, denting the legitimacy of the winner. Turnout is respectable among those registered to vote; the problem lies in persuading Americans to register at all. Lijphart (1997) suggested that the United States should adopt compulsory voting (as in Australia and Italy, among others) as a way round this problem. However, it is a moot point whether compulsory voting is a contribution to, or a denial of, democracy. Apart from the United States, most Western countries achieve a level of turnout at national elections exceeding 75 per cent (Table 6.1). Other influences on turnout, at the level of both the electoral system and the individual, are shown in Box 6.3.

Electing assemblies

Most controversy about electoral systems centres on the rules for converting votes into seats, and such rules are as important as they are technical. The same set of votes can be combined in different ways to produce contrasting outcomes. Hence electoral systems represent the inner workings of democracy; a point of particular importance in parliamentary systems where assembly elections determine the party composition of the government (p. 207). Political compromises have delivered some remarkable systems. Hungary's method, it is claimed, is so complex that no-one has yet been found who understands all its intricacies. In this section we examine the rules for translating votes into seats in elections to the legislature (Box 6.4, p. 103). The key distinction here is between nonproportional systems and proportional representation (PR). Nonproportional systems are the simplest, and are based on the old idea of electing a person or people to represent a specific territory: for example, a Canadian MP or the two American senators per state. There is no attempt to reward parties in proportion to the share of the vote they obtain; instead, 'the winner takes all'.

Nonproportional systems take one of two forms: plurality or majority. In plurality (also called 'first-past-the-post') systems, the winning candidate is simply the one who receives most votes in a particular district, constituency or riding (all these terms refer to the unit of territory which elects a representative). A plurality of votes suffices; a majority is unnecessary. Despite its simplicity, the plurality system is rare and becoming rarer. The main survivors are Britain and British-influenced states such as Canada, various Caribbean islands, India and the United States.

The crucial point about the plurality method is that it usually gives a substantial bonus in seats to the party which leads in votes. In parliamentary systems, this encourages government by a single party with a clear majority in the assembly. To see why, consider an extreme case in which the Reds defeat the Blues by one vote in every district. Despite the closeness of the vote, the Reds win all the seats while the Blues win none at all. An extreme example, of course, but one which demonstrates the inherent bias of a method which offers *all* the representation of a particular district to the *one* party which tops the ballot. In essence, the plurality method is a giant conjuring trick, pulling the rabbit of majority government out of the hat of a divided society. In Britain, for instance, a majority in the popular vote for a single party is exceptional but a secure parliamentary majority for the winner is customary.

The other form of nonproportional system is the majoritarian method. As its name implies, this requires a majority of votes for the winning candidate, normally achieved through a second ballot. If no candidate wins a majority on the first round, then an additional ballot is held, usually a runoff between the top two candidates. Many countries in Western Europe used majority voting before switching to PR early in the twentieth century. The system is also used in parts of Eastern Europe. For democrats, the argument for a majoritarian system is intuitively quite strong: namely, that no candidate should be elected without being shown to be acceptable to a majority of voters.

There is another, and rather unusual, way of

achieving a majority outcome in a single ballot. This is the Alternative Vote (AV), used for Australia's lower house, the House of Representatives. AV takes into account more information about voters' preferences than simple plurality voting (Box 6.4). AV is periodically recommended by electoral reformers in Britain, where its main effect would be to transfer seats from the Conservatives to the centre Liberal Democrats (Dunleavy, 1997, p. 153). For this reason, it may prove attractive to the Labour government elected in 1997 on a promise of a referendum on electoral reform.

We move now from nonproportional systems to proportional representation. PR is the norm in Western, and now Eastern, Europe; it also predominates in Latin America. It is based on the idea of representing parties rather than territory. Thus PR is more recent than nonproportional systems; it is a creature of the twentieth-century age of parties. The basic idea is straightforward and plausible: seats should be gained in direct proportion to votes. In a perfectly proportional system, every party would receive the same share of seats as of votes; 40 per cent of the votes would mean 40 per cent of the seats. Although the mechanics of PR are designed with this end in mind, in fact most 'PR' systems are not perfectly proportional. They usually offer at least a modest bonus to the largest party, though less than most nonproportional methods.

Since a single party rarely wins a majority of seats under PR, majority governments are unusual and coalitions become standard (unusually, the ANC won a majority of seats in the 1994 South African election, the first fought under PR in that country). Because PR usually leads to postelection negotiations in parliament about which parties will form the next government, it is best interpreted as a method of selecting *assemblies* rather than governments.

How does PR work? The most common method, by far, is the list system. The principle here is that the elector votes for a list of the party's candidates rather than for just a single candidate. The number of votes won by a party determines how many candidates are elected from that party's list. The order in which candidates appear on the list (usually decided by the party itself) governs which people are elected to represent that party. For example suppose a party wins 10 per cent of the vote in an election to a 150-seat assembly. That party will be entitled to 15 MPs, who will be the top 15 candidates on its list. So list voting is party voting. This method therefore weakens the link between the representative and a particular constituency.

List systems vary in how much influence they give voters over which candidates they can vote for from a party's list. At one extreme stand the closed party lists used in Portugal, South Africa and Spain. Voters there have no choice over candidates; they simply vote for the party they prefer. This gives party officials at the centre enormous, perhaps excessive, control over political recruitment. At the other extreme lie the free party lists used in Switzerland and Luxembourg. In these countries electors can, if they wish, vote for candidates drawn from the lists of different parties. Most countries give voters at least some choice between candidates from a party's list, a procedure which in application gives some advantage to celebrities. However, the natural (because simplest) procedure is for electors to vote for a party's entire ticket.

To achieve a proportional outcome, PR systems must use constituencies returning several representatives. There is no way of proportionally dividing one representative between several parties. But just how many representatives are elected for each constituency, a number known as the district magnitude, is a critical influence on how proportional PR systems are in practice (Lijphart, 1994, p. 49). The more members per district, the more proportional the outcome can be. In a few countries, for example the Netherlands and Israel, the whole country serves as a single large constituency, permitting exceptional proportionality. By comparison Spain is divided into 52 constituencies, each returning just seven members, thus producing a less proportional outcome overall. Indeed the Spanish Socialists have managed to win a majority of seats with just 40 per cent of the vote, confirming the boost which even proportional systems give to winners (Gallagher, 1997, p. 116). Especially when there are just three or four members per district, small parties may not gain a single seat even with a respectable share of the vote. The largest parties pick up the spare seats and are overrepresented in the assembly.

Most list systems add an explicit threshold of representation below which small parties receive no seats at all. Thresholds help to protect the legislature

BOX 6.4
Electoral systems: assemblies

PLURALITY AND MAJORITY SYSTEMS – *'winner takes all'*

1. Simple plurality – 'first past the post'
Procedure: Leading candidate elected on first and only ballot.
Where used: 13 countries (for example UK, USA, Canada, India, Thailand).

2. Absolute majority – alternative vote ('preferential vote')
Procedure: Voters rank candidates. If no candidate wins a majority of first preferences, the bottom candidate is eliminated and these votes are redistributed according to second preferences. Repeat until a candidate has a majority.
Where used: Australia (House of Representatives).

3. Absolute majority – second ballot
Procedure: If no candidate has a majority on the first ballot, the two leading candidates face a runoff.
Where used: Mali, Ukraine.

Note: In elections to France's National Assembly (lower house), all candidates who receive more than 12.5 per cent of the votes on the first ballot go through to the second round. The candidate with most votes wins this additional ballot.

PROPORTIONAL SYSTEMS – *seats obtained by quota in multimember constituencies*

4. List system
Procedure: Vote is cast for a party's list of candidates though in most countries the elector can also express support for individual candidates on the list.
Where used: 24 countries (for example Israel, Scandinavia, most of continental Europe, including Eastern Europe, and most of Latin America).

5. Single transferable vote (STV)
Procedure: Voters rank candidates in order of preference. Any candidate needs to achieve a set number of votes (the quota) to be elected. Initially, first preferences only are counted. Any candidates over the quota at this stage are elected. Their 'surplus' votes (that is, the number by which they exceeded the quota) are then distributed to the second preferences shown on these ballot papers. When no candidate has reached the quota, the bottom candidate is eliminated and these votes are also transferred. These procedures continue until all seats are filled.
Where used: Irish Republic, Malta, some Australian states, Estonia (1990 only) – and Cambridge, Massachusetts.

MIXED SYSTEMS – *combining single-member seats with PR*

6. The Additional Member System (AMS) – also known as the Mixed Member System (MMS) and Mixed Member Proportional (MMP).
Procedure: Some seats are elected on a territorial/plurality basis and others by PR. Usually the latter acts as a top-up to secure a proportional outcome overall. Electors normally have two votes, one for the territorial election and the other for the PR contest.
Where used: 11 countries (for example Germany, Hungary, Italy, Japan, Russia and New Zealand).

Note: the figures for the number of states employing each method are not based on all countries but just on the 53 democracies covered in Leduc, Niemi and Norris (1996).

---

from extremists. Many Eastern European countries adopted a threshold, usually of 4 or 5 per cent, when they switched to PR for their postcommunist elections. New Zealand's threshold for its new mixed member proportional system is also 5 per cent, high enough to restrict representation in the legislature to six parties after the 1996 election.

What is the relationship between electoral systems and party systems? This remains a matter of controversy. In a classic work, Duverger (1954) claimed that the plurality method strongly favoured a two-party system while PR contributed to a multiparty system. At the time, the plurality system was associated with strong, decisive government; PR was found guilty by its association with unstable coalition governments. But in the 1960s a reaction set in against attributing weight to political institutions such as electoral systems. Writers such as Rokkan (1970) adopted a more sociological approach, pointing out that social cleavages had produced multiparty systems in Europe long before PR was adopted early in the twentieth century. PR did not

EXHIBIT 6.2

The best of both worlds? The additional member system (AMS)

Plurality and PR systems are usually considered alternatives yet the hybrid additional member system (AMS) seeks the best of both worlds. Germany provides the model. There, half the seats are filled by plurality voting in single-member seats, thus retaining the representative–constituency link. However the other half are allocated to parties with the aim of producing a proportional result overall. The compromise nature of AMS encouraged other countries to experiment with similar methods. Twenty-five countries, covering about 16 per cent of the world's population, now use various forms of AMS. These include Senegal, Japan, Taiwan, Mexico, Venezuela, Italy and New Zealand. AMS has prospered in postcommunist Eastern Europe, and it has been adopted in Russia, Hungary, Croatia, Lithuania and Albania.

Further reading: Blais and Massicotte (1996), Elklit and Roberts (1996).

cause a multiparty system; rather it was adopted because it was the only electoral system which would satisfy all the interests and parties of divided societies (the same point applies to postcommunist Europe). More recently Lijphart (1994) has suggested a middle position. He believes that plurality systems nearly always deliver parliamentary majorities but that electoral systems are only one of several influences on the number of parties achieving representation.

Much ink has also been used on a related issue: the question of which is the 'best' electoral system. In truth there is no such thing, and different methods work best in different circumstances. For example, in countries with intense social divisions such as Northern Ireland and South Africa, PR will provide at least some representation for parties based on minority groups so reducing the risk of majority tyranny. But where regular changes of government occur under a majority system, as in Great Britain, this argument for PR loses much of its force. Over time, the swing of the pendulum gives each party its turn in office – *proportional tenure* without *proportional representation*.

Nonetheless, PR did gain respectability in the decades after the Second World War. Far from producing political instability, as those who observed Hitler's Germany had thought, PR contributed to continuity of policy in postwar Europe. The same parties often continue in government for decades, with slight variations in their coalition partners. By contrast, the plurality method can thrust parties in and out of office. This is because the outcome in seats amplifies, in an erratic fashion, the result in votes. Canada is a good example. In 1984, the Conservatives won three-quarters of the seats on just half the vote. Nine years later they were decimated in an astonishing election which reduced them to just two seats despite retaining 16 per cent of the vote (Table 6.2). Under PR, the Conservatives would have retained more than this toehold in parliament.

The coruscating case of the Canadian Conservatives confirms the bias of the plurality method against small parties with evenly-spread support, and this distortion has become more obvious as minor parties have gained ground. In the British election of 1987, the Alliance of Liberals and Social Democrats won just 3.5 per cent of the seats for 22.6 per cent of the vote. The Canadian New Democratic Party suffers in a similar, if less extreme,

Table 6.2 The Canadian election of 1993

Party	Votes %	Number of seats
Liberal	42	178
Conservative	16	2
New Democratic Party	7	8
Reform	19	52
Bloc Quebecois	14	54

Note: In the 1997 election, again won by the Liberals, the Conservatives secured 21 of the 301 seats with 19 per cent of the vote.

way: in 1993, its share of seats was much less than its share of votes (Table 6.2). By contrast, small regional parties (such as Britain's nationalists and Canada's Bloc Quebecois) can benefit under the plurality method from the geographical concentration of their support. Thus the plurality method does not discriminate against all small parties; rather, it tends to encourage political fragmentation by favouring small parties with a strong local base.

If the plurality system gives too little weight to smaller parties with even support, PR arguably gives small parties too much power. Under PR, smaller parties are often in a pivotal position in postelection coalition negotiations; their bargaining power exceeds their representation in the assembly. They may be able to form a stable alliance with either major party although, in practice, ideology restricts the range of feasible partners. In addition, advocates of decisive government argue that coalitions tend towards the lowest common denominator, acting as a barrier against radical but necessary change. For better or worse, it is difficult to see a figure such as Margaret Thatcher emerging as a compromise coalition leader after an election fought under PR.

In practice, electoral systems tend to persist once established in the founding election; parties elected under one system have no incentive to change to another. When countries do change their electoral system, it is usually because a series of governments is considered to have failed. Electoral reform is uncommon but not unknown; Japan, Italy and New Zealand changed their electoral system in the 1990s. All three countries adopted the fashionable additional member system. In Japan, the object was to reduce the significance of money in elections by ending an unusual system which forced candidates from the same party into competition with each other. Yet factionalism and even corruption continue to inhibit real policy debate. Reformers in Italy wanted to escape from the unstable coalitions produced by PR and to encourage a small number of large parties which would alternate in power, British-style. Yet the first government produced under Italy's new electoral law lasted just eight months, hardly a model of political stability. In New Zealand, the motive was to reduce the unrestrained power of the single-party governments produced by the plurality method. The 1996 election did indeed lead to a coalition yet it remains to be seen whether

this will improve the governance of New Zealand over the long term. Electoral reform does not always deliver the desired effects yet it will almost certainly lead to unintended consequences. The passion of electoral reformers notwithstanding, changing the rules does not always improve the quality of the political game. Electoral reform is no cure-all. As Gallagher (1997, p. 124) concludes, 'it is all too easy to use an electoral system as a scapegoat for a general malaise'.

Electing presidents

In comparison with parliamentary contests, the rules for electing presidents are straightforward. Unlike seats in parliament, a one-person presidency cannot be shared between parties; the office is indivisible. So PR is impossible. As Figure 6.1 shows, 61 of the 91 directly-elected presidents in the world are chosen by a majority system. And of these, the vast majority (49) are selected by a majority run-off, meaning that if no candidate wins a majority on the

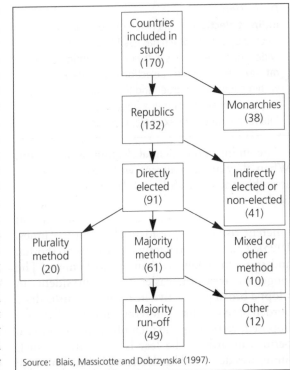

Source: Blais, Massicotte and Dobrzynska (1997).

Figure 6.1 Methods for selecting presidents

first round an additional ballot is held allowing voters to choose between the top two candidates. France is an influential example of this system. The next most common method is by plurality: the candidate with most votes on the first and only round wins. This technique saves the bother of two ballots but the winner may receive only a small share of the vote. In the Bolivian election of 1997, to take an extreme illustration, General Banzer won with just 20 per cent support.

As Figure 6.1 also shows, almost a third of presidents manage to avoid the perils of direct election. Many of these are chosen via indirect election where a special body (which may itself be elected) chooses the president, thus acting as a buffer against the whims of the people. The United States was once an example: the Founding Fathers opposed direct election of the president. Fearing a surfeit of democracy, they set up an electoral college for the purpose with delegates selected by each state legislature as it saw fit. Today, of course, America has embraced direct election, with the electoral college surviving only as a relic of the eighteenth century.

Definition

Indirect election occurs when officeholders are elected by a body which has itself been chosen by a wider constituency; it is a device for limiting democratic expression. Indirect election was widely used within communist parties and the device is also employed in elections to the upper house in some federal countries: for example, Germany.

The timing of presidential elections is important. When they are concurrent with elections to the assembly, the successful candidate is more likely to be drawn from the same party as dominates the legislature. This reduces the fragmentation which is an inherent risk of the presidential executive (Jones, 1995). The presidential term is normally no shorter, and sometimes longer, than for parliament. The longer the term, the easier it is for presidents to adopt a broad perspective free from the immediate burden of re-election. But term limits are often also imposed, restricting the incumbent to one or two periods in office. The fear is that without such limits presidents will be able to exploit their unique position to remain in office too long. The USA introduced a two-term limit after Franklin

Roosevelt won four elections in a row between 1932–44. As with other institutional fixes, term limits solve one problem at the cost of creating a new one: lame-duck presidents lose clout as they near the end of their term. For instance, the Korean financial crisis of 1997 coincided with the end of the president's non-renewable six-year tenure, adding to uncertainty. Also, presidents subject to term limits sometimes seek to alter the constitution in order to permit their own re-election. This has been a regular source of friction in much of Latin America. Box 6.5 gives some examples of the range of restrictions which countries place on presidential re-election.

Voting behaviour

Given that voters have a choice, how do they decide who to vote for? Although this is the most-heavily studied question in all political science, there is no single answer. The nature of electoral choice varies across voters, countries and time. As a broad summary, electors in postwar Western democracies have moved away from group and party voting towards voting on issues, the economy and party competence. Franklin (1992) describes this process as 'the decline of cleavage politics and the rise of issue voting'.

For two decades after the war most studies of electoral behaviour disputed the intuitive proposition that voters do 'choose' which party to support. An influential theory of electoral choice, originally developed in the United States in the 1950s, argued that voting was an act of affirmation rather than choice (Campbell *et al.*, 1960; Markus and Converse, 1979). In America, voting was seen as an expression of a deep-seated, long-lasting loyalty to a party. This party identification was acquired initially through one's family, reinforced through membership of politically-uniform social groups (for example workmates) and confirmed by life-long electoral habit. Electors learned to think of themselves as Democrats, Republicans or, in a minority of cases, as Independents. This view of the voter is variously called the socialization, Michigan or party identification model. Mulgan (1997, p. 268) offers a good summary:

BOX 6.5
Methods for electing presidents: some examples

Country	Electoral system	Term (years)	Re-election permitted?
Argentina	Electoral college	6	After one term out
Brazil	Run-off	5	After one term out
Finland	Plurality*	6	Yes
France	Run-off	7	Yes
Ireland	Single transferable vote	7	Two term limit
Mexico	Plurality	6	No
Russia	Run-off	5	Two term limit, then a term out
United States	Electoral college	4	Two term limit

* If no candidate wins a majority in the popular vote, selection is by an electoral college.
Source: adapted from Jones (1995b).

like sports fans cheering on their team, voters with strong partisan preferences welcome the opportunity to express their support and to share in the party's performance, even when they know their own support will not affect the outcome.

Definition

Party identification is a long-term attachment to a particular party which anchors voters' interpretations of the remote world of politics. Party identification is often inherited through the family and reinforced by the elector's social milieu. It influences, but is separate from, voting behaviour. The stability of party identification was used to explain the continuity of Western party systems in the 1950s and 1960s.

In Europe, where social divisions ran deeper, voting was seen as an expression of loyalty to a social group rather than a party. The act of voting affirmed one's identification with a particular religion, class or ethnic group. Thus electors thought of themselves as Catholic or Protestant, middle-class or working-class; and they voted for parties which explicitly stood for these interests. Social identity anchored party choice. But whether the emphasis was placed on identification with the party (as in the USA) or with the social group (as in Europe), voting was viewed more as a reflex than as a choice. In reality, the electoral 'decision' was an ingrained habit.

Models of party and group voting assumed a stable rather than a volatile electorate. Such theories explained why most people did not change their votes, not why a few people did. This approach was fair in the relatively static and apolitical 1950s but it became less appropriate in the 1960s and 1970s. A major electoral trend in postwar democracies has been partisan dealignment – the weakening of the ties which once bound voters, social groups and political parties tightly together. Even compared with the late 1960s and early 1970s, the proportion of party identifiers has fallen by 6 percentage points in both the United States and the Netherlands. It has declined by 9 points in Britain and Germany and by a massive 17 points in Sweden (Holmberg, 1994, p. 106).

What caused this decline in party loyalties? Why have voters really begun to choose? One factor is government failure: the decay of party loyalties is not uniform but tends to be focused on periods of disillusionment with major parties (for example the USA during the Vietnam war). Another influence is the declining ability of social cleavages to fashion electoral choice. Class and religious identities were fundamental to the outlook of older generations but they are less relevant to young, well-educated people living in urban, mobile and more secular societies. Class voting, in particular, has declined throughout the democratic world; Dalton (1996, p. 324) concludes that 'class-based voting ... currently has limited influence in structuring voting choices'. Parties have developed more of a catch-all character and television has also made a difference. It is more neutral than newspapers and directs attention to politicians more than parties. Also, many younger voters are more attracted to single-issue groups than to the established parties, which are seen as slow-moving and part of the official system. All this has led to an increase in electoral volatility and to the emergence of new parties with a more radical complexion, such as the Greens.

Definition

Partisan dealignment refers to the weakening of bonds between (a) electors and parties, and (b) social groups (for example classes) and parties. In most consolidated democracies, such links have declined in strength but they have not disappeared; electorates are 'dealigning' rather than 'dealigned'.

The decay of group and party voting has led political scientists to focus on the question of how voters do decide. The emphasis now is on four newer factors: political issues, the economy, party leaders and party image. Fiorina's theory (1981) of retrospective voting is crucial here. Retrospective voting means casting one's ballot in response to government performance, and is a phrase which tells us much about the character of contemporary voting behaviour. Electors do form a general assessment of the government's record – and, increasingly, they vote accordingly. A vote is no longer an expression of a lifelong commitment, rather it is a piece of business like any other. The elector asks of the government, 'what have you done for me (and the country) lately?' Retrospective voting helps to explain why economic conditions as reflected in unemployment and inflation figures have such a strong impact on the popularity of governments (Norpoth, 1996). More voters now proceed on the brutal assumption that governments should be punished for bad times and perhaps also rewarded for economic advance. Rather than staying with parties come what may, more voters now judge by results.

In this newer, more volatile and pragmatic era, electors assess the general competence of the parties seeking office. Increasingly, they ask not just what a party proposes to do but also how well it will do it. Now that parties are less rooted in ideology and social groups, their reputation for competence in meeting the unpredictable demands of office is a crucial marketing asset. So party image becomes crucial. In particular, the electoral significance of the party leader is probably increasing, stimulated by television's dominant position in political communication (McAllister, 1996). Through its leaders and more generally via its conduct of the campaign, any serious party must convey the impression of being government-ready. More than ever, a reputation for competence and credibility is the foundation of electoral success.

This provides the backgound in which political marketing, as plied by the new breed of spin doctors, has emerged. These professionals do not seek to bombard the voters with paid advertising in the manner of a consumer goods company. Political communication is a distinct form of marketing, largely because its wars are fought on the battlegound of news reports rather than commericals. Rather, as the term 'spin doctor' implies, the art lies in gaining the most sympathetic treatment of the issues which are most favourable to one's party. The skill is to generate trust in one's own side – and especially to create doubts about one's opponents. Given volatile and sceptical voters, credibility is the cardinal objective.

Referendums

Elections are instruments of representative democracy; the role of the people is to decide who will decide. Referendums, and similar devices such as the initiative and the recall, are devices of direct democracy; they enable the voters to decide issues themselves. Yet in practice referendums do not always live up to their democratic pretensions; sometimes they are just instruments of control by the élite. Napoleon, Hitler and other dictators used referendums (often called plebiscites in a nondemocratic context) to boost their authority, somewhat denting the case of those who advocate direct democracy for large countries.

Even democratic governments often secure the desired result of referendums by controlling their timing and wording. For instance, in 1997 the British government only held a referendum in Wales on its devolution proposals *after* a similar vote in Scotland, where support for devolution was known to be firmer. This trick of timing worked, just. Further, referendums can be contained by limiting their impact. In Italy, referendums can only vote down existing laws; it is then parliament's job to introduce replacement bills. And, of course, rulers can simply ignore the result of a referendum. In 1980, Sweden voted to decommission its nuclear power stations. In 1997, they were all still running. For better or worse, referendums often produce conservative results showing a reluctance by the voters to embrace radical change. In Switzerland, for example, the voters have consistently supported the country's international isolation, confirmed by what Kobach (1997) calls the 'thunderous rejection' of UN membership in a decisive referendum in 1986.

Many democracies now make some use of referendums. Of the 728 national referendums held in the world between 1900 and 1993, 65 per cent occurred after 1960. Their subject matter falls into three main categories:

- Constitutional issues (such as changing the electoral system in Italy and New Zealand)
- Territorial issues (such as the decision to join a federation or allow more autonomy to provinces)
- Moral issues (such as temperance, divorce and abortion).

Significant recent referendums include those in South Africa in 1992 in which the white minority voted to end apartheid, and in Canada (also 1992) in which the electorate rejected further devolution of power to the country's provinces (Butler and Ranney, 1994, p. 4). But few democracies make more than occasional use of the device. Heavy users are Australia, Denmark, France, New Zealand and especially Switzerland. Between 1945 and 1980, most referendums in the Western world occurred in Switzerland (Lijphart, 1984).

Although the United States has never employed a referendum at national level, traditions of direct democracy are strong in many states and localities. The western states, especially California, make widespread use of referendums and initiatives. For instance, Proposition 13 in 1978 limited property taxes in California; it was the first of the modern taxpayers' revolts. California is also one of the 15 American states to use the recall. Adopted early in

---

BOX 6.6

The referendum, initiative and recall

Referendum – a vote of the electorate on an issue of public policy such as a constitutional amendment.

Initiative – a procedure which allows a certain number of electors to initiate a referendum on a given topic.

Recall – allows a certain number of voters to demand a referendum on whether an elected official should be removed from office

Source: Cronin (1989).

---

the twentieth century, the recall has achieved little. The normal tenure of elected officials is rarely cut short (Cronin, 1989).

Referendums and other instruments of direct decision-making live uneasily in the house of representative democracy. Their main benefit is to provide a double safety-valve. First, a referendum allows a government to put an issue to the people when for some reason it is incapable of reaching a decision itself. Like a plumber's drainrods, the referendum is a device for resolving blockages. Second, where the initiative and the recall are permitted, aggrieved citizens can use these devices to raise issues and criticisms which might otherwise go unheard. But these benefits are easily hijacked: by dictators seeking to reinforce their own position, by wealthy companies waging expensive referendum campaigns on issues in which they have an economic interest, and by illiberal majorities seeking to legitimize discrimination against minority groups. The world's experience with referendums suggests that proposals for direct democracy based on electronic voting should be approached with scepticism (Budge, 1996). Even though technology renders direct democracy possible in large societies through mechanical push-button voting, what is possible is not always desirable.

Public opinion

Sir Robert Peel, twice Prime Minister of Britain in the nineteenth century, defined public opinion as 'that great compound of folly, weakness, prejudice, wrong feeling, right feeling, obstinacy and newspaper paragraphs'. Many modern politicians are equally cynical about public opinion but this does not prevent them from being acute observers of it. Public opinion matters, and nowhere more so than in consolidated democracies where academics and journalists dissect the findings of regular opinion polls. Even in the new democracies of Eastern Europe, opinion polls rapidly emerged to provide a detailed, and rather depressing, account of growing disillusionment with new regimes.

Definition

Public opinion refers to the aggregate views of the politically-relevant population on the politics of the day. Key dimensions of public opinion are: reach (what proportion of the population forms the 'public'?), salience (how much does an issue matter to people?), direction (what is the public's preference on an issue?) and momentum (is an issue, party or candidate gaining or losing support?)

The reach of public opinion is especially important. In liberal democracies public opinion extends to virtually the entire adult population. Nearly all adults have the vote, their views are represented in frequent polls and elected politicians have an incentive to study the findings. Even here, though, a minority underclass exists which rarely votes, lives in no-go areas for pollsters and does not follow politics at all. Public opinion does not reach the politically excluded. In authoritarian regimes, of course, national politics engages far fewer people, even as spectators, and therefore public opinion shrinks. In developing countries, too, the sector which is significant for national politics may not extend far beyond well-educated people in the major cities.

What, then, is the political impact of public opinion in democracies? In a sense public opinion pervades all policy-making; it forms part of the environment within which politicians work. Thus public opinion sits in on many government meetings even though it is never minuted as a member. In such discussions public opinion performs one of two roles, acting either as a prompt ('public opinion demands we do something about traffic congestion') or as a veto ('public opinion would never accept restrictions on car use'). Thus, as

Qualter (1991, p. 511) writes, 'while public opinion does not govern, it may set limits on what governments do'.

But there are three factors limiting the influence of public opinion, even in consolidated democracies:

- The impact of public opinion declines as issues become more detailed. Voters are more concerned with goals rather than means, with objectives rather than policies. 'What policies politicians follow is their business; what they accomplish is the voters' business' (Fiorina, 1981). A few important objectives preoccupy the public but most policies are routine and uncontroversial. Here organized opinion matters more than public opinion.
- The public is often surprisingly ill-informed, and this, too, limits its impact. Most Americans, for example, are unable to name their member of Congress (Flammang, 1990, p. 230). Similar findings from other democracies confirm the ignorance of large sections of the public, especially on foreign policy issues remote from ordinary life. Limited knowledge is another reason why public opinion functions more often, and more appropriately, as an agenda-setter than as a policy-maker.
- Public opinion can evade tradeoffs but governments cannot (though they sometimes try). The public may endorse the principle (for example cleaner air) but not will the means (for example restrictions on using cars). So even in the most democratic of countries, government by opinion poll remains a far-off dream – or nightmare.

Opinion polls

The idea of public opinion has gained further currency as opinion polls have developed to measure it. Indeed there are few areas in politics where a concept (public opinion) is so closely linked to its measurement (the opinion poll). So how accurate are polls and what contribution, if any, do they make to the operation of democracy?

Although the public itself remains resolutely sceptical of public opinion polls, their accuracy is now well-established, at least in predicting election outcomes. In the United States, the average error in

Country profile **THE UNITED STATES**

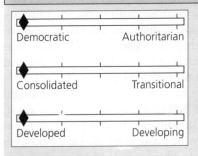

Democratic — Authoritarian

Consolidated — Transitional

Developed — Developing

Population: 266m.
Gross domestic product per head:
 $27 500.
Form of government: a presidential,
 federal republic.

Legislature: the 435-member House of Representatives is the lower house. The 100-member Senate, perhaps the most influential upper chamber in the world, contains two directly-elected senators from each state.

Executive: the president is supported by a massive apparatus, including the 350-strong White House Office, and the Executive Office of the President, numbering around 2000. The Cabinet is far less significant than in, say, Britain.

Judiciary: a dual system of federal and state courts is headed by the Supreme Court. This nine-member body can nullify laws and actions which run counter to the Constitution. America has a strongly legal culture.

Electoral system: the plurality method is still used; there is little pressure for, or possibility of, change.

Party system: the Democratic and Republican parties show extraordinary resilience, despite periodic threats from third parties. Their survival reflects ideological flexibility, the electoral system and their entrenched position in law.

The United States is the world's remaining superpower. This status is based partly on its 'hard power': a large population, a massive economy and the capacity to deliver military force anywhere. Yet America's 'soft power' is also significant. The USA benefits from a leading position in education, science, information technology, communications, entertainment and professional services. Its culture, brand names and language have universal appeal. Above all, America retains a faith that it is 'bound to lead' (Nye, 1990). With the rise of Japan and the European Union, the United States may no longer dominate the world but it remains by far the single most important power.

The internal politics of the United States is therefore of vital interest. Ironically, the world's No.1 operates a political system intended to frustrate decisive policy-making. By constitutional design, power is divided between federal and state governments. The centre is itself fragmented between the executive, legislature and judiciary. American politics takes the form of 'hyper-pluralism' in which reforms are more easily blocked by interest groups than carried through by a disciplined party. The president, the only official elected by a national constituency, finds his plans obstructed by a legislature which is among the most powerful (and decentralized) in the world. Major reforms such as the New Deal require a major crisis, such as the depression, to bring forth that rare consensus which generates rapid reform. Except in times of crisis, Washington politics is a ceaseless quest for that small amount of common ground on which all interests can agree.

Similar paradoxes abound in the American experience with elections. The United States has over 500 000 elected offices, more than anywhere else, yet turnout is low for most of them including the presidency. A premise of equality underlies elections yet Southern blacks were effectively denied the vote until the Voting Rights Act of 1965. The 'log cabin to White House' ideal is widely accepted but money is increasingly necessary, if not sufficient, for electoral success. Many states use devices of direct democracy but there has never been a referendum at national level. Ironically, the United States, a country with a strong culture of political participation, seems now to be suffering a 'crisis of community' as political participation declines. The causes of this predicament are difficult to establish but one factor may be television. Generations raised on television are less active in society (Putnam, 1995). Since the television era came to the United States first, there may be lessons here for the future of electoral participation in other countries.

Further reading: McKay (1997), Wilson (1997).
www.fec.gov
www.whitehouse.gov

predicting the major parties' share of the vote at national elections between 1950 and 1988 was a mere 1.5 per cent. Accuracy is similar in other democracies. Counter-intuitive it may be, but 1000 people carefully selected for an opinion poll can accurately represent the whole population. A well-selected sample will certainly provide a more reliable guide to public opinion than relying on either the self-selected readers who answer write-in polls in magazines or the listeners who call radio discussion shows. In fact, opinion polls have transformed our knowledge of public opinion, creating new opportunities for political scientists to study how opinions vary between social groups, between countries and, perhaps most usefully, over time.

> ### Definition
> An opinion poll (or sample survey) is a series of questions asked in a standard way of a systematically-selected sample of the population. The term **opinion poll** usually refers to short surveys on topical issues for the media; a **sample survey** involves a more detailed questionnaire, often conducted for government or for academic researchers.

Opinion polls contribute to the democratic process in three ways.

- They bring into the public realm the voices of people who would otherwise go unheard. They are the only form of participation, apart from the ballot box itself, in which all count for one and none for more than one.
- Polls are based on direct contact by interviewers with the public; they get behind the group leaders who claim to speak 'on behalf of our members'.
- Polls enable politicians to keep in touch with the popular mood and give some insight into the reasons for election results. In short, opinion polls oil the wheels of democracy.

Yet it would be wrong to overstate the value of opinion polls in defining the 'mood of the people'. Just like students taking a test, interviewees answer the questions but they do not set them. Party officials and journalists in the capital city commission polls and set the pollsters' agenda. The concerns of the political élite, caught up in the intricacies of day-to-day politics, contrast with those of ordinary people. An example of diverging agendas is the economist who conducted an opinion poll about inflation, only to discover that many people thought, correctly, that it meant blowing air into tyres!

More seriously, people may not even have thought about the topic before answering questions on it. They may give an opinion when they have none; or agree to a statement because it's the easiest thing to do ('yea-saying'). This leads to the criticism that opinion polls construct, and even shape, public opinion at the same time as they measure it. The public opinion poll is an invaluable tool for the student of politics, but it is prudent to remember that opinions are always expressed in a social context which shapes the views expressed. The well-dressed interviewer with her official-looking clipboard was one such context; the telephone interview with a distant stranger is another.

Key reading

> **Next step:** *LeDuc, Niemi and Norris (1996) is an excellent comparative study of elections and voting, reviewing a wide literature.*

Harrop and Miller (1987) provide a general overview of elections and voters. On electoral systems, Farrell (1997) is a current introduction. For the impact of electoral systems on party systems, see Lijphart (1994). Ginsberg (1982) is a stimulating top-down view of competitive elections. Franklin, Mackie, Valen *et al.* (1992) is a comparative study of voting trends. On the United States see Asher (1988) for presidential elections generally, and Pomper *et al.* (1997) for the 1996 election. Gallagher (1997) is the best short survey of electoral systems and voting in Western Europe. For Britain, Denver (1994) and Norris (1997) are accessible starting-points. On elections in the developing world, see Diamond, Linz and Lipset (1989, Vols. 2 and 3). On referendums see Butler and Ranney (1994), Cronin (1989) and Gallagher and Uleri (1996). On public opinion, Stimson (1991) is an impressive analysis of American trends. Public opinion polls are covered generally by Butler (1996); for America see Crespi (1989) or Mann and Orren (1992), and for Britain, Broughton (1995).

Interest groups

There is a story, possibly true, that New Zealand Prime Minister Sid Holland was woken by a phone call from an irate woman who could not find a plumber willing to come out in the middle of the night to fix a leak. A plumber soon arrived on her doorstep thanks to Holland's direct intervention (Du Fresne, 1989). Another story – undeniably true – is that in 1989, the major cities of Eastern Europe filled with people expressing their profound dissatisfaction with communist rule, demonstrations that accelerated the collapse of communism in Europe. Both examples show people acting on their interests, whether these are individual complaints or broad concerns about the legitimacy of government. Politics and interests are inseparable: politics is about decisions, and interests are involved whenever any actor stands to gain or lose from a decision.

Organized interest groups developed in Western democracies in a series of waves, stimulated both by social change (such as industrialization) and by the expansion of state activity (such as public welfare). Periods of social change raise new problems while an active government gives people more hope of, and gains from, influencing public policy. Table 7.1 summarizes the development of interest groups in the United States. Most Western nations have followed a similar course, creating the mosaic of independent group activity which makes up civil society.

> **Definition**
>
> **Interest groups** (also called pressure groups) are 'organizations which have some autonomy from government or political parties and … try to influence public policy' (Wilson, 1990). Interest groups seek to influence government but, unlike political parties, they do not aspire to control it. In nearly all countries, interests are transmitted from society to the state. Studying the extent and means of this 'interest articulation' is essential to understanding a country's politics.

The range and influence of modern interest groups raises awkward questions about the distribution of power in democracies. Consultation between government and interest groups is now constant and intimate, and groups provide governments with the information and technical advice needed to make sensible policy. In exchange, favoured groups acquire 'insider' status and thus the potential to influence decisions at an early stage. Despite only representing small minorities, interest groups are deeply entrenched in policy-making, certainly more so than many supposedly 'sovereign' parliaments. Interest group activity creates a system of functional representation operating alongside electoral representation. The question is whether these groups are simply an expression of the democratic right to organize in defence of interests. Or are they, as Lowi (1969) contends, 'a corruption of democratic government?' In short, do interest groups help or hinder democracy?

Although interest groups are now fundamental to politics, there is a puzzle about how they develop in the first place. In his influential book, *The Logic of*

BOX 7.1

Waves of interest group formation in the United States

Period	Description	Examples
1830–60	Founding of first national organizations	YMCA and many abolitionist groups
1880–1900	Founding of many business and labour associations, stimulated by industrialization	National Association of Manufacturers, American Federation of Labor
1900–20	Peak period of interest group formation	Chamber of Commerce, American Medical Association
1960–80	Founding of many environmental and public interest groups	National Organization for Women, Common Cause

Source: Hrebenar and Scott (1990), pp. 13–15. See also Wilson (1973).

Collective Action (1968), Olson argued that people have no reason to join groups when the fruits of the group's efforts are available to nonmembers as well as members. Why should a worker join a union when the wage rise it negotiates goes to all employees? Why should a company pay a fee to join an industry association when the benefits the group obtains will help all the firms in that sector? The smart move, surely, is to be a 'free rider' and gain the reward without paying the cost. Olson suggests that free riders do hinder collective organization. He argues that interest groups will only emerge in specific conditions. These are when membership is compulsory (for example the closed shop) or when groups offer selective benefits, marked members only, rather than collective goods for the constituency at large.

Olson's analysis poses the problem of collective action – the difficulty of organizing rational actors to achieve what is in their collective interest. He helps to explain why attracting members to new groups is often a thankless task, particularly when the benefits are spread among many people, as with consumer and ecology groups. However, the brute fact is that new groups do emerge and grow; and that some people, such as postmaterialists, are willing to work for collective goals. Although healthy air is an example of a collective good which cannot be restricted just to some people, green groups have grown enormously in recent decades. Perhaps this is because members receive

the selective benefits of developing their skills and meeting new people, as well as contributing to a shared goal which is dear to their hearts (Moe, 1980).

Although most research on interest groups concentrates on their role in specific countries, it is crucial to recognize the emerging international dimension to their work. Environmental and aid charities now operate on an international scale, lobbying and assisting intergovernmental organizations and even, some argue, providing the basis for a global civil society. Globalization has also helped to rebalance traditional interests within countries. For example, firms and unions normally seated on the opposite side of the table may come together to demand restrictions on foreign imports. Equally, governments and trade associations may work together to influence such bodies as the European Union. The emergence of international bodies such as the EU, and regimes such as the Whaling Commission and the World Bank, has given interest groups an extra lever with which to influence national governments. In this more complex environment, even states have become interest groups seeking to influence international bodies. The result is that most political actors are now both lobbyists and lobbied. To an ever increasing extent, everyone in politics is a lobbyist. Understanding politics is a matter of finding out who is lobbying whom, by what means, with what resources and with what success.

Classifying interest groups

We can classify interest groups by whether they are based on communal or associational relationships. Communal ties are acquired by birth, not voluntary membership. The clearest example is the family but the term also covers ethnic, linguistic and caste relationships. At the other end of the scale are associational ties, formed for specific, instrumental purposes. Here, people come together for shared but limited aims such as joining a wildlife conservation society. The interest group system in any society largely reflects the relative weight of communal versus associational ties. Communal relations are more important in the developing world, associational relations in the developed world. Figure 7.1 shows four types of group – customary, institutional, protective and promotional – arranged by their position on this communal–associational scale. Classifying groups on this scale offers insight into both the nature of their demands and the manner of their pursuit.

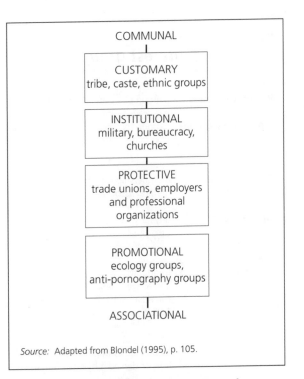

Source: Adapted from Blondel (1995), p. 105.

Figure 7.1 Classifying interest groups on the communal–associational dimension

> *Definition*
> **Communal** relationships are those into which people are born. They are found in bonds of family, kinship and ethnicity. These do not always take a political form but conflicts based on communal ties are intense and difficult to resolve. **Associational** ties are more pragmatic, based on people coming together to pursue a shared but narrow interest. Because these interests are more limited, groups based on them are pragmatic and generally accommodating.

Customary groups

These are groups which are not created for specific purposes but are simply part of the social fabric. They fall at the communal end of the spectrum. Customary groups have become more important to politics, especially in the postcommunist world where ethnic and religious identities provide a major focus. Examples of such conflicts include Muslims and Christians in former Yugoslavia and indigenous majorities versus the Russian minority in the Baltic states. In the Western world, Protestants against Catholics in Northern Ireland is one example of a particularly violent conflict between customary groups; other instances are the divisions between settlers and indigenous peoples in the Americas, Australia and New Zealand.

In many developing countries, for example much of Africa, customary groups based on kinship and ethnicity are the major channel for distributing state resources. Politicians and officials are expected to use their office to benefit 'their' customary group. A customary group defines a way of life; where this is threatened, either by other groups or even by the rights which a liberal democracy offers to all its citizens, political conflicts ensue which are difficult to resolve. Unlike, say, a professional association, customary groups are not formally organized. Instead they are represented through parties, protest or even violence.

Institutional groups

These are large formal institutions which are not founded to exert political pressure but are often drawn into the political arena. Churches, corporations, trade unions and universities are examples.

BOX 7.2
Classifying interest groups

AIMS		**BENEFICIARIES**	
Protective groups	a group of – defends an interest, e.g. trade unions	**Collective**	benefits go to both members and nonmembers, e.g. trade unions win pay increases for all workers in a plant, whether union members or not
Promotional groups	a group for – promotes a cause, e.g. environmental groups		
SUPPORT			
Closed groups	membership is restricted, e.g. medical associations	**Selective**	only group members benefit e.g. cheap insurance for union members
Open groups	anybody can join, e.g. environmental groups	**ORIENTATION**	
		National	groups aim to influence national governments, e.g. housing groups
STATUS			
Insider groups	frequently consulted by government and actively seek this role, e.g. Canadian Bankers' Association, British National Farmers' Union	**International**	nongovernment organizations (INGOs, e.g. Greenpeace) aim to influence bodies such as the EU, international regimes and global public opinion.
Outsider groups	not normally consulted by government – either does not seek such a role, or denied it by government.		

Source: Adapted from Matthews (1989).

Institutional groups have an established role in society which gives them independent authority and a role in carrying out policy. Where would an industrial policy be without the support of industry? Where would educational policy be without teachers? Another form of institutional group is found within government itself in public bodies such as bureaucracies, the military and local government. Bureaucrats always want to extend their sphere of influence; the military always claims a new weapon is essential to winning the next war; cities always claim that law and order will break down without more money.

Even in authoritarian systems, where independent interest groups are outlawed or controlled, institutions within government may still be able to express their opinions before decisions are made. Such institutional groups articulate their interests from *within* government, and therefore do not need special bodies to represent them. Even so, they can still contribute to communication between society and the state. For instance, the army may articulate the concerns of one specific ethnic group or class.

Protective groups

Sometimes called sectional or functional groups, these are formally-organized groups which exist to protect the material interests of their members, from physicians to lecturers. Protective groups are what first come to mind when we think of 'interest groups'. Trade unions, employers' organizations and professional associations are prime examples. Such groups are founded to influence government and they have sanctions to help them achieve their goals. Workers can go on strike, for instance. Protective groups seek selective benefits for their members and insider status with relevant government departments (box 7.2). Because they represent clear economic interests, protective associations are often the most influential of all interest groups.

One contrasting form of protective interest is the geographic group. These arise when the interests of people living in the same location are threatened, for instance by a new highway or a hostel for ex-convicts. Because of their negative stance – 'build it anywhere but here' – these are called NIMBY groups (Not In My Back Yard). NIMBYs often succeed in blocking change but unlike other protective groups they are usually temporary, falling apart once their battle is over.

Promotional groups

Sometimes called attitude, cause or campaign groups, these are set up to promote ideas, identities, policies or values. Examples include pro- and anti-abortion groups; organizations combating pornography; and ecology groups. The classic promotional groups are not primarily concerned with their members' personal welfare or material interests. Rather, they promote a broad conception of the public interest; for example, Common Cause in the USA. Associations which seek to change social attitudes towards particular groups, such as the women's movement or the gay lobby, are also best considered as promotional groups, even though they also represent partial interests. Lacking both the resources and the access available to protective groups based on the economy, promotional groups use publicity as their stock in trade. Their target is society as much as government. Promotional groups are most significant in liberal democracies, with their participatory cultures and open media. Indeed, the growing number and influence of promotional groups since the 1960s, especially in the United States, have been major trends in interest group politics. This growth reflects the rise of new politics and postmaterialism.

Channels of access

How are interests communicated to political decision-makers? What are the channels through which this process takes place? There are a range of alternatives, varying from personal petition to the ruler (the Saudi king still dispenses personal justice to petitioners) to elite connections (called 'the old school tie' in Britain and *guanxi* in China). Figure 7.2 sets out three of the regular mechanisms of group influence found in consolidated democracies: direct dealings with government, indirect influence through political parties and indirect influence through public opinion. We discuss each of these before addressing the less conventional channel of direct action.

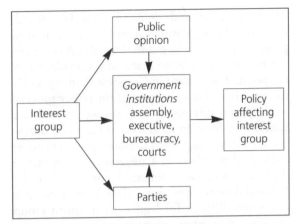

Figure 7.2 Channels of interest group influence

Direct dealings with government

Ultimately, all interest group activity addresses government, either directly or indirectly. Direct contact focuses on the bureaucracy, the legislature and the courts.

In liberal democracies, the *bureaucracy* is the main pressure point. Interest groups follow power and it is in executive offices that detailed decisions are made. As Matthews (1989, p. 217) comments,

> the bureaucracy's significance is reinforced by its policy-making and policy-implementing roles. Many routine, technical and 'less important' decisions, which are nonetheless of vital concern to interest groups, are actually made by public servants.

The broad contours of policy, as set by elected politicians, are difficult for even the most powerful interest groups to control; shrewd protective groups therefore focus on the small print. On such matters, most Western governments follow a convention of discussion with organized opinion through consultative councils or committees. Often the law requires such consultation. Even in France where the higher bureaucracy prizes its autonomy, extensive dialogue takes place between groups and civil servants. As long ago as the 1970s there were no fewer than 500 councils, 1200 committees and 3000 commissions, all bringing together groups and the bureaucracy at national level.

Assemblies are an additional channel through

which interests and demands can be voiced. However, the legislature's significance for interest groups depends on its political weight. A comparison between the United States and Canada makes the point. The American Congress (and especially its committees) is a vital part of the policy process; weak party discipline and strong committees combine to form an ideal habitat for lobby operations. Interest groups exert substantial influence over individual members of Congress and committee decisions, and large financial contributions by Political Action Committees (PAC) mean that it is politically difficult for legislators to spurn group demands. By contrast, party voting is normal in the Canadian parliament. In Canada, as in most Western democracies, lobbyists therefore concentrate their fire on the executive (Pross, 1993, p. 145).

If interest groups feel ignored in the policy making process, they may still be able to challenge decisions in the *courts*. In the European Union, an interest group which is unsuccessful at home can take its case to the European Court of Justice. In the United States, business corporations routinely subject government statutes and regulations to legal challenge. Class actions (legal cases covering many people with the same grievance) are common. But America has a strongly legal culture; in other countries the courts may be growing in importance but they still tend to be an arena of last resort. In Australia, for instance, the requirement for litigants to prove their personal interest in the case hinders legal action; the wider interests of society or the group do not suffice (Matthews, 1989).

Indirect influence through political parties

In theory, parties and interest groups play distinct roles: parties aim to occupy positions of power while interest groups seek influence only. Yet despite these contrasting missions, relationships between parties and interest groups can be extremely close. Some political parties are simply an offshoot of interest groups. The British Labour and Australian Labor parties were essentially creations of the trade union movement though these ties have now weakened. Interest groups can blur into (or sometimes turn into) political parties: thus environmental groups in many countries have spawned green parties, and,

equally, ethnic groups can spawn parties to represent their interests. In Romania, for instance, the Hungarian Democratic Union virtually monopolizes support from the Hungarians in Transylvania (Dellenbrant, 1993, p. 157). Some highly specialized parties are really interest groups in disguise, seeking to defend a cause rather than to obtain a share of power. But where coalitions are usual, small parties can end up with a minister or two: agrarian parties in Scandinavia and some religious parties in Israel have won a share of government in this way. Such 'interest parties' are growing in number, using their party label to generate publicity and privileges for a narrow cause.

> ### Definition
> **Interest parties** are small parties which aim for seats in parliament to pursue more specific objectives than governing. Examples include pensioners' and car-owners' parties. Interest parties are also found in postcommunist countries where parties have developed to reflect narrow agrarian, religious and ethnic interests.

Many interest groups prefer to hedge their bets rather than develop intimate links with one specific party. So looser, pragmatic links between parties and interests are the norm. This has always been the case in the USA where business and organized labour gravitate towards the Republican and Democratic parties respectively. But these are partnerships of convenience, not indissoluble marriages. The traditional maxim of the American trade union movement has been to reward its friends and punish its enemies, wherever these are found. Business, despite its ideological affinity with the Republican party, still contributes heavily to the election coffers of many Democratic members of Congress. A hefty donation ensures a hearing when a company takes a problem to Congress. Most interest groups give more to incumbents; they do not waste money on no-hopers, even if these doomed candidates are standing for the 'correct' party.

Indirect influence through the mass media

Press, radio and television provide an additional resource available to interest groups. By definition, messages through the media address a popular audience rather than specific decision-makers. Thus the media are a central focus for promotional groups seeking to steer public opinion. Ecological groups mount high-profile activities, such as seizing an oil rig to prevent it from being sunk, to generate footage shown on TV across the world. Such groups view the media as sympathetic to their cause (Table 7.1). Traditionally, the media are less important to protective groups with their more specialized and secretive demands. What food manufacturer would go public with a campaign opposing nutritional labels on foods? The confidentiality of the committee room is a quieter arena for fighting rearguard actions. But even protective groups seek to influence the climate of public opinion, especially in political systems where assemblies are important. In the United States, most protective groups have realized that to impress Congress they must first influence the public. Therefore groups follow a dual strategy, going public and going Washington. Interest groups in other democracies are beginning to follow suit. Slowly and uncertainly, protective groups are emerging from the undergrowth into the glare of publicity.

Direct action, protest and violence

Direct action is most often the resort of customary groups denied formal access to government. At least until the nineteenth century, the masses were excluded from recognized channels of political influence. Outbreaks of violence were, and may still be, the only way of expressing grievances by people who have lost hope in government. This is not just a historical phenomenon as many established democracies also experience public disorder: inner-city riots remain endemic in England and the USA, for instance. Such behaviour is often taken to imply irrationality and frustration rather than calculated action; yet direct action can also be focused in its goals. As we noted at the start of this chapter, massive, if usually peaceful, popular protest signalled the end of communism in Eastern Europe. International terrorism, centred on the Middle East, has also proved to be an effective way of using the media to attract global attention to a group's cause (Schmid, 1989). Increasingly, the use of coercive tactics is carefully planned to coincide with

Table 7.1 Methods of political action used by European environmental groups	Groups often using action %
Public action	
Media contacts	86
Mobilizing public opinion	72
Conventional action	
Contacts with the executive	53
Contacts with parliament	53
Contacts with local government	45
Participation in government bodies	41
Formal meetings with the executive	36
Contacts with party leaders	11
Challenging actions	
Protest actions	25
Court actions	20
Non-cooperation with government	13

Note: based on interviews in 1985/86 with 69 organizations in 10 Western European countries.

Source: Dalton (1994), Table 8.2.

legitimate methods. Orthodox and unorthodox methods form a single repertoire of action. French and Belgian farmers resort to roadblocks and violent demonstrations not as their sole political tactic but as a means of putting additional pressure on the authorities.

With their history as outsider groups, ecological groups also engage in protest activity. But demonstration fatigue can reduce the willingness of supporters to engage in protest and of the media to report it. As the leader of one ecological group said, 'protest has no value in itself; it only captures media attention and other actions are necessary to carry through policy change' (Dalton, 1994, p. 197). Promotional groups which have established good relations with government need to exercise enormous care with any form of direct action. Any protests which embarrasss the government will

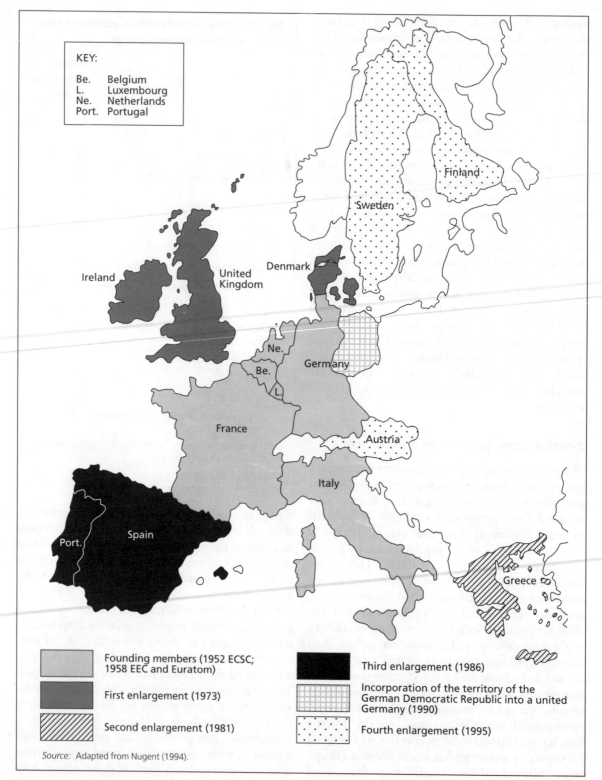

KEY:

Be.   Belgium
L.   Luxembourg
Ne.   Netherlands
Port. Portugal

Founding members (1952 ECSC; 1958 EEC and Euratom)

First enlargement (1973)

Second enlargement (1981)

Third enlargement (1986)

Incorporation of the territory of the German Democratic Republic into a united Germany (1990)

Fourth enlargement (1995)

Source: Adapted from Nugent (1994).

Map 7.1 The European Union

Regional profile THE EUROPEAN UNION

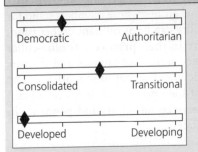

Democratic — Authoritarian

Consolidated — Transitional

Developed — Developing

Population of member states: 369m
Gross domestic product per head:
15 942 purchasing power units (by
the same measure USA equals 22 422
and Japan equals 19 078).

Form of government: a unique
regional body in which policy is made
partly by European Union (EU) institutions and partly through negotiations
among the member states, which
retain considerable independence.
Executive: the Council of the European
Union composed of heads of government provides political drive. The
powerful European Commission
divided into 17 directorates initiates
legislative proposals.
Assembly: the unicameral European
Parliament has 626 members directly
elected from each country for a five-
year term. The number of MEPs from
each country reflects its population.
Though growing in significance, the
Parliament still lacks full control over
the Commission, the budget and
even legislation.
Judicial branch: the influential
European Court of Justice, composed
of one judge from each member
country, has successfully developed
the constitutional underpinnings of
federalism.
Members: Austria, Belgium, Denmark,
Finland; France, Germany, Greece,
Ireland, Italy, Luxembourg, The
Netherlands, Portugal, Spain,
Sweden, UK.

The European Union is the most developed example
of regional integration in the world. Unusually
among regional bodies, the EU has developed institutions which resemble the architecture of national
governments. It has a parliament (of sorts) and an
influential Court of Justice. The heart of the EU,
however, is the European Commission (an EU body)
and the Council of Ministers (an intergovernmental
body). The tension between these bodies – between
the EU as a cohesive actor and the EU as an arena for
negotiation between member states – is central to its
functioning.

The EU's emergence owes much to Europe's long
history of conflict. After the 1939–45 war, many
European leaders set out to create a unified continent within which war would no longer be feasible.
The goal was to build a United States of Europe.
However, economic factors also played their part.
European economies needed to be rebuilt after the
war and then, to achieve economies of scale, integrated into a large, single market.

More recent members, notably Britain, have emphasized the economic basis of the Union while rejecting
the idea of a federal Europe. Mrs Thatcher expressed
this position in 1988: 'willing and active cooperation
between independent sovereign states is the best
way to build a successful European Community'. In
developing this line, Britain has exploited the continental notion of subsidiarity to argue that decisions
should be taken at the national level wherever
possible.

The development of the EU has encouraged interest
groups to adopt a Europe-wide perspective. About
3000 professional lobbyists were registered at EU
headquarters by 1990, many just keeping an eye on
developments for their clients. Over 500 European-
wide interest groups exist, mainly federations of
national groups. Around half are based on specific
industries (for example, pasta makers). However
many groups possess few resources and they experience difficulty in taking positions acceptable to all
their members. Increasingly, therefore, national
interest groups lobby directly in the EU, often
working in partnership with their home government.
Other lobbying comes from regional and local governments within member states. Outside bodies,
such as Japanese trade associations and American
multinationals, are also active. Most lobbyists focus
on the Commission, a small body which relies heavily
on interest groups for its information and expertise.

Further reading: on the EU, see Nugent (1994). On
lobbying in the EU, see Mazey and Richardson (1993).
europa.eu.int

quickly lead to the group being left out of real dialogue over policy within the inner circle.

What makes interest groups influential?

The key factor in determining the collective influence of interest groups is the nature of the political system. In consolidated democracies, the expression of interests is unhindered and encouraged by competition between parties, allowing groups to play off one party (or candidate) against others. Groups flourish when power is divided, thus giving several access points. The classic instance is the United States where the separation of powers has made Washington the interest group capital of the world. Authoritarian regimes belong at the other extreme. Rulers exert tight control over the expression of unofficial interests, and expressing independent goals may invite reprisals. In such conditions, influence is restricted to institutional groups within the government and high-status technical professions such as science and medicine.

What gives some interest groups more influence than others? The answer depends on the sanctions the group can apply, and on its legitimacy, membership and resources. *Sanctions* reflect a group's usefulness to those in power. Thus protective groups (such as an industry association) have more impact than promotional groups (such as an ecology movement). Since the re-election of governing parties depends partly on economic success, any protective group based on the economy can demand a hearing. Indeed, governments are likely to consider the impact of any proposals on the economy even without explicit attempts at influence from protective groups. Multinational companies are in a particularly strong position to influence a national government. Such firms have the sanction of taking their investments (and their jobs) elsewhere. As economies become more open, so multinational corporations acquire a stronger bargaining position in direct dealings with government, supplementing the national trade associations which traditionally articulated the interests of their member firms.

The degree of *legitimacy* achieved by a particular group is also important. The aphorism 'What is good for General Motors is good for America'

encapsulates this point. Interests which enjoy high prestige are most likely to prevail on particular issues. Professional groups whose members stand for social respectability can be as militant on occasion, and as restrictive in their practices, as blue-collar trade unions once were. But lawyers and doctors escape the public hostility that unions attract. The high standing of such professions helps to explain why they have retained substantial independence in running their affairs.

> **Definition**
> **Density of membership** refers to the proportion of those eligible to join a group who actually do so. High density allows the group to claim more authority and gives the group more bargaining power with government.

A group's influence also depends on its *membership*. This is a matter of density as well as sheer numbers. What proportion of those eligible to join actually belong? A high density adds clout, as with the nearly complete membership which many medical associations achieve among physicians. But low density reduces influence, especially when an occupation is fragmented among several interest groups. For instance, American farmers divide between three major organizations with lower total coverage than Britain's National Farmers' Union. The declining density of trade union membership in the final quarter of the twentieth century undoubtedly weakened labour's bargaining power (Table 7.2). In the European Union, breadth of membership is especially important for lobbying organizations. Groups operating in Brussels need to show they are backed by national associations in all member countries. Only then will the Commission listen. Members' intensity of support is also important since commitment determines how far the members of a group are willing to go in support of its objectives. Here customary groups have a natural advantage. In an extreme case, some members of militant nationalist and ethnic groups may be willing to kill, and be killed, in pursuit of their objectives. The same cannot usually be said for members of chess clubs.

The financial and organizational *resources* available to an interest group are fundamental, and money obviously helps. The National Rifle Association

Table 7.2 Density of trade union membership (workers belonging to a trade union, 1995)

	Per cent	Trend 1985–95
Sweden	91	Up
Italy	44	Down
South Africa	41	Up
Australia	35	Down
UK	33	Down
Germany	29	Down
New Zealand	24	Down
Japan	24	Down
USA	14	Down

Source: International Labour Office, Labour Report (1997).

(NRA) in the USA illustrates this point. With an annual budget of $40 million, the NRA employs 275 full-time staff. The coalition of gun control groups cannot match the NRA's 'fire power'. Yet even in the USA, hard-up but skilful campaigners can generate free publicity and wide public reaction. Ralph Nader's Crusade for Car Safety in the 1960s was an early example. As a rule, financial resources are rarely decisive; the skill with which resources are used matters just as much. The NRA is again a good example in the way it uses its extensive funds to good effect. In a matter of days it can blitz members of Congress with millions of 'spontaneous' letters, faxes and e-mail from its members.

Policy communities and issue networks

In the democratic world, many interest groups are in virtually daily contact with government. So the question arises, what is the nature of such relationships? This is the core issue in the study of interest groups, bearing on the question of whether groups express or subvert democracy. Here we review two interpretations of the relationship between groups and governments, based on the contrasting ideas of policy communities and issue networks. As we will see, the 'policy community' idea is implicitly critical of groups, the 'issue network' idea less so.

Definition
A **policy community** is a close-knit group, consisting primarily of civil servants and leaders of insider groups. The members of the policy community settle detailed issues in their policy area in a confidential and depoliticized atmosphere of trust, based on shared interests. Policy communities are also termed 'subgovernments'. An **issue network** is a contrasting depiction of the links between interest groups and government. It implies a looser and larger collection of players whose impact depends on what they know as well as whom they know. If a policy community has the intimacy of a village, an issue network shows the more impersonal character of a large town.

The metaphor of a policy community views the relationship between interest groups and the state as warm and snug. The term implies that the actors involved in detailed policy-making in a particular sector (especially interest group leaders and senior public officials) form their own small village. Everyone knows each other, uses given names and tries not to upset each other. Over time, the participants develop shared working habits and common assumptions about what can be achieved. The actors learn to trust each other and to respect each other's confidences. Shared interests predominate: for instance, the farmers' association and the Agriculture Department seek ever larger subsidies from the public purse. Business is done behind closed doors to prevent political posturing and to allow a quiet life for all. As in all communities, insiders are sharply distinguished from outsiders. Everyone inside the community wants to keep outsiders where they belong: outside. The golden rule is never to upset the apple cart.

American political scientists used the term 'iron triangle' to describe policy communities. The three points on the triangle are executive agencies, interest groups and congressional subcommittees. These became an exercise in mutual back-scratching: the *committee* appropriated funds which was spent by the *agency* for the benefit of *interest group* members. For instance, Defense Subcommittees in Congress authorized the Defense Department to purchase costly weapons from arms manufacturers. Every point on the triangle benefitted. This was a game without losers – except for the taxpayer who rarely knew what was going on. Iron triangles were also called 'subgovernments', implying that policy was made in an independent compartment of power. The effect of a series of subgovernments was to fragment policy-making.

To portray the links between groups and governments in terms of policy communities is to criticize the working of liberal democracies. Such communities may make policy by consultation and consensus but many such communities amount to little more than conspiracies against the taxpayer. It is therefore fortunate, perhaps, that policy communities are beginning to decay in many democracies. Today, policies are subject to more scrutiny by the media; new consumer groups protest loudly when they spot the public being taken for a ride; and international comparisons can expose national inefficiencies. Also as issues become more complex, so more groups are drawn into the policy process, making it harder to stitch together secret deals among a few insiders. In the United States where this trend has gone furthest, the committee barons who used to dominate Congress have lost much of their power. The iron has gone out of the triangle; now influence over decisions depends on what you know as well as who you know.

Reflecting these trends, the talk now is of issue networks. These refer to the familiar set of organizations involved in policy-making: government departments, interest groups and legislative committees. However, an issue network does not imply the familial relationships suggested by the term 'community'. In an issue network, the impact of an interest group varies from issue to issue, depending on its expertise. As Heclo (1978, p. 102) put it,

the notion of iron triangles and subgovernments presumes small circles of participants who have succeeded in becoming largely autonomous. Issue networks, on the other hand, comprise a large number of participants with quite variable degrees of mutual commitment ... it is almost impossible to say where a network leaves off and its environment begins.

The mutation of policy communities into issue networks reflects a shift to a more open policy-making style in which cozy deals are harder to sustain. Clearly, the idea of issue networks enables us to portray policy-making more positively. More interests participate in decisions, the bias toward protective groups is reduced, new groups can enter the debate and a sound point carries more weight.

Pluralism and corporatism

To appraise the political significance of interest groups we must now consider their function in the political system as a whole. This means broadening the debate beyond policy communities and networks. That debate asks how policy is made in specific sectors: for instance, in agriculture, education or transport. In this section we move on to consider the overall role of interest groups in politics. Again, political scientists have developed two models: pluralism and corporatism. While corporatism is in general decline, some democracies – notably the United States – have always been closer to the pluralist model.

The debate between pluralists and corporatists goes to the heart of a central question in politics: the relationship between society and the state. Pluralists see society dominating the state; corporatists view the state as leading society. At one level this difference is descriptive, reflecting contrasting assessments of the flow of influence between government and interest groups. But at another possibly deeper level, the debate is ideological. Pluralists see the task of government as responding to interests expressed to it. Corporatists, by contrast, favour an organized, integrated society in which the state offers leadership in pursuit of a vision shared with society.

Pluralism

The pluralist view dominated early postwar accounts of interest group activity. Pluralism sees politics as a competition between a multitude of freely-organized interest groups. These compete for influence over a government which is willing to listen to all the voices it can distinguish in the political din. Under pluralism, society dominates the state which becomes little more than an arena for competition between interest groups. For Bentley (1908), an American pioneer of this approach, 'when the groups are adequately stated, everything is stated. When I say everything, I mean everything'. All kinds of interests – customary, institutional, protective and promotional – have their say before the court of government. Groups compete on a level playing field, with the government showing little bias either towards interests of a particular type, or to specific groups within that type. As interests emerge, new groups form to represent them; there are few barriers to entering the political market.

Because many people belong to more than one interest, the temperature of political conflict remains low. Most groups restrict themselves to a single sector so there is healthy fragmentation across the range of government activity. Indeed the central tenet of pluralism is that there is no single dominant élite. So pluralism depicts a wholesome process of dispersed decision-making in which interest groups ensure government policies reflect the diversity of modern society. Dahl (1993, p. 706) summarized the strengths of pluralism, suggesting that groups

> served to educate citizens in political life, strengthened them in their relations with the state, helped to ensure that no single interest would regularly prevail on all important decisions, and, by providing information, discussion, negotiation and compromise, even helped to make public decisions more rational and more acceptable.

Definition
Literally 'rule by the many', **pluralism** refers to a political system in which numerous competing interest groups exert strong influence over a responsive government. However each group concentrates on its own area (for example education, medical care) so no élite dominates all sectors. New groups can emerge easily, bringing further competition to the political marketplace.

Both as an ideal and as a description of how politics works, pluralism draws on American experience. In the USA, interest group patterns come closer to the pluralist model than anywhere else. As de Tocqueville (1954 edn) wrote in the 1830s, 'in no country in the world has the principle of association been more successfully used, or applied to a greater multitude of objects, than in America'. Petracca (1992, p. 3) makes the point more succinctly: 'American politics is the politics of interests'.

Nowhere else are interest groups so numerous, visible, organized or successful. The USA hosts the largest single interest group in the world: the American Association of Retired Persons, with 28 million members. Thousands of other groups, ranging from Happiness of Motherhood Eternal to the United Autoworkers of America, seek to influence policy at federal, state and local levels.

Promotional groups, in particular, have established a firm foothold in the USA. Citizens' groups lobby for all kinds of public interest causes, from monitoring nuclear power stations to reducing interest rates on credit cards. Over 500 groups focus on environmental protection alone. This kaleidoscope of activity reflects Americans' constitutional right 'to petition the government for a redress of grievances'. It also reflects the weakness of parties and the government's long history of distributing resources to favoured interests rather than through European-style universal programmes. But the key factor in the strength of American interest groups is the dispersed nature of government itself. The separation of powers allows many points of access to interest groups. Congressional committees, government departments and even the White House seek allies among interest groups in the struggle to impose their agenda on Washington's unruly policy process.

Critics of the pluralist model allege that it idealizes political decision-making. Harrison (1984, pp. 69–70) points out that some interest groups are so large that they have become internally oligarchic, with leaders representing themselves rather than their largely apathetic memebers. Further, some interests are inherently difficult to mobilize: for example, illegal immigrants, people with learning disabilities, or the homeless. In any case, some groups are wealthier and better organized than others so that the pluralist ideal of equal representation for all groups is far from reality. As Schattschneider famously put it, some interests are organized into politics – but others are organized out (Mair, 1997).

Underlying these criticisms is the assumption that the vigorous interplay of pluralism is mere froth on the body politic. In the United States, for instance, pluralist competition operates within an unquestioned acceptance of broad American values favouring the free market and the pursuit of individual self-interest. The entire political discourse works within a narrow ideological range, shaping and limiting the demands expressed. This particular criticism of pluralism reflects a view of power which emphasises non-decisions and agenda-setting.

Corporatism

Where pluralism implies competition between groups, corporatism emphasizes coordinated relations between certain key groups and the state. Corporatism refers to decision-making by negotiation between the government and a few powerful interest groups. These privileged groups normally include peak associations representing industry and labour – for example, the Federation of German Industry and the German Federation of Trade Unions. Though formally accountable to their members, the main role of the peaks is to carry their members with them after agreements have been struck with the government and other national groups; corporatism is a top-down approach.

Definition

Corporatism is a relationship between the state and interest groups in which major decisions on domestic matters emerge from discussion between the government and a few leading protective groups, especially business associations and trade unions. In return for their influence, the interest groups are expected to ensure the compliance of their members. Unlike pluralism, corporatism assumes a state-led hierarchy of groups and that favoured interests can deliver the acquiescence of their large membership.

Under corporatism, negotiations between the state and recognized groups take an administrative, technical form. Policy-making is depoliticized and electoral representation becomes less important. Corporatism also implies a hierarchy of groups, with the government dealing with the influential peak associations, which then pass decisions down the line. So in contrast to pluralism, which emphasizes an upward flow of preferences from group members to their leaders and then on to government, corporatism stresses the downward flow of influence. The state retains a leadership role. Also, whereas pluralism is the absence of planning, corporatism is an attempt by the state and dominant interests to develop a coherent approach. Corporatism therefore

requires a high level of social and political organization.

An example will add colour to this outline. Just as the United States exemplifies pluralism, so Austria reveals many corporatist features (Fitzmaurice, 1991). At least until the mid-1990s, many of Austria's major economic and social decisions emerged through a system called Economic and Social Partnership. This brought all the major economic interests into an elaborate network which in turn connected to the government, the parties and the bureaucracy. At the pinnacle of this partnership stood the Party Commission. This was an entirely informal network (no offices, no rules) which nonetheless made decisions affecting the whole working population. It set price limits, ratified wage increases and was an important forum for discussing economic policy. Final decision-making in the commission often ended as a face-to-face talk between just two people: the president of the Chamber of Commerce, representing capital, and the president of the trade union federation, representing labour. Except during war or other crises, it is inconceivable that a pluralistic country such as the United States could ever reach decisions in such a centralized way.

Corporatism can work in Austria because all working people belong to statutory and centralized chambers of commerce, labour and agriculture. In general, corporatism is most likely to take root where national interest groups possess a high density of membership and extensive authority over their members. The Scandinavian nations, Austria and the Netherlands fit these conditions well (Box 7.3). In all these countries, there is a tradition of compromise and consultation between government and interest groups. Indeed Denmark has been termed 'the consulting state' because of the extensive negotiations between the government and the 2000 or so national groups. Bukst (1993, p. 110) describes Denmark as 'one of the most organized countries in the world'. But one factor favouring corporatism was particularly important in Austria. The country had experienced bitter conflict between the wars, and after 1945 both major groups, Catholic and socialist, sought negotiation and compromise. Corporatism was a form of consensus politics designed to forestall any repetition of social breakdown.

BOX 7.3
Selected European and North American countries grouped by the extent of corporatism, mid-1990s

Most corporatist	**Least corporatist**
Austria	Canada
Denmark	United Kingdom[†]
Switzerland	United States
Germany	
Finland	
Belgium	
Ireland*	

Many features of corporatism
Norway
Sweden
The Netherlands

A few features of corporatism
France
Italy

* Ireland's social pact, beginning in 1987 and now called the Programme for Competitiveness and Work, gives tax cuts and a say in economic policy to trade unions in exchange for voluntary wage restraint. This scheme has so far proved consistent with rapid economic growth.

[†] Twenty years earlier, the United Kingdom would probably have been placed in one of the more corporate categories, indicating the volatility of this particular classification.

Source: Modified from expert assessments in Lijphart and Crepaz (1991).

In the 1980s and 1990s, corporatism came under attack. Even in Austria, those who felt left out of the system began to voice their protest, and Austria's extreme right Freedom Party became one of the most successful populist parties in Western Europe. However, it was in the Anglo-American world where corporatism was never more than half-hearted that the heaviest blows were struck. As early as 1982 the American political economist Mancur Olson had claimed that corporatism was a form of political sclerosis, reflecting the gradual accumulation of power by sectional interests. Corporatism was viewed as harmful to both economy and society, because it invited excessive state intervention and over-reliance on the state. The carefully-crafted consensus between government, capital and labour was held to inhibit the continuous economic changes needed to remain competitive in an increasingly global economy.

This intellectual sea-change led to a political assault on the power of entrenched interests. Reforms began in Britain and the United States in the 1980s during the Thatcher and Reagan administrations. While this attack was focused on the privileges of organized labour, some large companies were also hit by more vigorous competition policy, more open markets and a growing emphasis on competitive tendering in the public sector.

Economic change, particularly the decline of heavy industry with its strong unions, large companies and powerful trade bodies, accelerated the decay of corporatism. However the countries which have gone furthest in reducing the power of special interests were those that were least corporatist to begin with. It remains to be seen how far most continental European countries, with their long history of corporatist thinking and the inherent value placed on governing by consensus, have either the desire or the ability to change their ways.

Interest groups in communist and postcommunist states

The role played by interest groups in both communist and postcommunist states provides a sharp contrast with their position in liberal democracies. The evolution of interest groups in communist states was especially interesting. All authoritarian regimes seek to insulate themselves from group pressures but communist states went furthest in aiming to impose their vision on all aspects of society. In contrast to pluralist systems, communist states were party-led, not society-dominated. Groups served the party, not the other way round, and society was to be moulded, controlled and developed by the party.

Interest articulation by freely-organized groups was inconceivable. Communist rulers sought to harness all organizations into 'transmission belts' for party policy. Trade unions, the media, youth groups, professional associations – all served the party in the great cause of communist construction.

However, the capacity to articulate interests did increase as communist regimes evolved. The use of coercion and terror declined while conflict over policy became more visible. Institutional groups such as the military and heavy industry had always carried weight but they became more important as economies matured and decisions became more technical. The more open struggle which developed in the 1970s and 1980s involved inputs from below; issues were no longer resolved by ruthless imposition. Sectional interest began to be openly expressed, particularly in Poland, Hungary and Yugoslavia. However one sharp contrast with Western pluralism remained: ruling communist parties tried to restrict interest articulation to safe technical matters. They continued to crack down vigorously on dissent which went beyond these confines. The objectives of the communist state remained beyond criticism. Thus 'socialist pluralism', to the extent that it existed, remained far more limited than its Western counterpart.

Despite the best efforts of communist regimes, independent groups did eventually emerge. They played an important role in challenging communist authority in Eastern Europe. Charter '77, an organization calling for human rights in Czechoslovakia, was the forerunner of Civic Forum, which eventually replaced the communists. Above all, in Poland, the trade union organization Solidarity (supported by the Roman Catholic Church) emerged in 1980 to assert the interests of Polish workers. Nine years later, Solidarity took over the reins of government from the communists. However, groups such as Solidarity were not interest groups in the Western sense; they began as *de facto* opposition parties and then became broad social movements or popular fronts. They sought to replace rather than to influence communist rule. Their historical task was pivotal, if short-term, and went far beyond anything of which a narrow interest is capable.

With the collapse of communism, interests were suddenly expressed openly to the government. One major aspect of interest articulation in the postcom-munist world is the speed with which organizations have formed around nationalist, ethnic and religious bonds. These communal groups, long suppressed under communism, have proved to be a potent force for instability in Eastern Europe. Nationalist forces brought about the disintegration of Czechoslovakia, the Soviet Union and Yugoslavia. Institutional groups have also continued to carry considerable clout. The managers of state-owned enterprises have been a major force in postcommunist politics. Initially, they slowed the process of privatization, often abusing their monopoly power to slow the growth of private firms. Later, public sector managers exploited their insider position to obtain ownership of their enterprises, often at knockdown prices and sometimes using illegal means: more piratization than privatization. The revolutions of 1989 dismantled communist political structures but the political overhang of the state's dominant position, especially in industry, will remain for decades.

Few postcommunist states are developing along Western pluralist lines. Especially in the republics formed from the Soviet Union, most protective interest groups are still underdeveloped. Their membership is limited and they have not established the regular but regulated links with government found in consolidated democracies. Many state assets are still being sold, often in a chaotic way, which gives politically-connected entrepreneurs the chance to acquire wealth through dubious deals with political power-holders. The links between business and politics are close but corrupt, operating through individuals rather than interest groups. Just as under communism, politics and the economy continue to form a single field of action. All that has changed is the myths: what was once done in the name of constructing socialism is now done (by much the same people) in the context of building a market economy.

As Russia's postcommunist experience shows, pluralism cannot function without a reasonably strong and impartial state. When the state itself is corrupt, then so too are the business interests that depend upon it – and even in many postcommunist economies most large companies are probably still state-dependent. When the state itself is divided between independent ministries, with little effective co-ordination from a central body, fiefdoms become

EXHIBIT 7.1

The seven-bankirshchina: economic interests in postcommunist Russia

Russia is the best, because most extreme, example of the tendency for links between business and politics in a postcommunist setting to operate through powerful firms and individuals rather than interest groups. The separation between public and private sectors, so central to the organization of interests in the West, has not emerged in Russia. Instead private entrepreneurs compete for the wealth which can be extracted from the rusting hulk of state-owned industry. Ruthless businessmen, corrupt public officials and jumped-up gangsters make deals in a transitional environment where the communist order has collapsed but no new structure of regulation has emerged – or at least is not implemented. For a

period in the mid-1990s, many observers felt that a handful of well-connected bankers had substantially captured the Russian state, a phenomenon called *seven-bankirshchina* (the reign of the seven banks). These financiers pulled the strings of their political puppets, using them to obtain public assets on the cheap and then dispensing with the politicians by exposing their weaknesses on media networks owned by the bankers. No wonder that in a survey of business executives in 1996, Russia was named the most corrupt country in the world. In a sense, Russia's economy is *too* competitive: for where else do entrepreneurs regularly kill each other?

self-serving and often corrupt. When the government's deeds do not match its policies, interest groups have little incentive to form to influence policy. Instead, a netherworld of plunder and bandit capitalism emerges – and will continue until the state can establish and enforce clear rules governing business-to-business and business-to-state transactions.

Interest groups in developing states

In traditional societies little interest articulation occurs because the mass of the population falls outside the formal political process. However, almost all societies in the developing world are now transitional. Traditional ways of life are giving way to urbanization, industrialization, cash-crop agriculture, monetary exchanges, formal education and growing penetration by the mass media. As these changes proceed, so the pattern of interest organization alters. For instance, peasant leagues and trade unions appear, reflecting emerging political cleavages. The conditions for the organized articulation of interests are created.

But pluralist representation is hampered by weaknesses of organization, finance and membership.

Strong ethnic and tribal loyalties also inhibit the growth of formal groups. Interest articulation still operates on an individual basis, through patron–client networks. Furthermore, landowners and business operators rarely rejoice when peasants and workers begin to organize. They are far more likely to plan reprisals and press the government to marginalize such activity. They prefer the 'divide and rule' strategy of dealing with individuals rather than organized groups.

How do rulers respond to these new demands? One strategy is to repress organized group activity completely. Where civil liberties are weak and many groups are still new, this is a feasible approach. The strategy of repression was, for example, adopted by many military regimes. On the other hand, authoritarian rulers may seek to manage the expression of these new interests, seeking to incorporate them. That is, rulers may allow interest organization but try to control it. By enlisting part of the population, particularly its more modern sectors, into officially sponsored associations, rulers hope to accelerate the push toward modernization. This approach is common in countries following the corporate Roman Law tradition (for example in Latin America) which require groups to achieve legal recognition before they can operate.

Before the promarket economic reforms of the

1980s and 1990s, Mexico was a case in point. The ruling party (the PRI) was itself a coalition made up of labour, agrarian and 'popular' sectors. Trade unions and peasant associations had access to the leadership of the PRI, which was willing to provide resources such as subsidies and control over jobs. In effect, Mexico became a giant patron–client network – corporatism for a developing country. The system was over-regulated, giving so much power to civil servants and PRI-affiliated unions as to deter business investment, especially from overseas.

But the system is now in rapid decline; as the market sector has expanded, so the patronage available to the PRI has declined. For example, an independent National Workers Union emerged in 1997, claiming that 'the old mechanisms of state control are exhausted'. But even when the PRI network was at its strongest, life could be hard in Mexico's highly unequal society. With hardship and discontent endemic, workers and peasants regularly broke away from their associations. These independent movements then faced continual harassment from the combined forces of the state, the party, employers and officially-favoured unions. Thus Mexico under the PRI's exclusive control exhibited both corporate techniques of policy-making and the tensions these techniques failed to resolve.

Key reading

Next step: *Wilson (1990) is a clear and straightforward introduction to interest groups.*

Many of the best studies of interest groups continue to be about the United States; see the reader edited by Cigler and Loomis (1991), the collection by Salisbury (1992) and the text by Hrebenar and Scott (1990). On Britain, Smith (1995) is a brief, helpful introduction; Marsh and Rhodes (1992) is an influential account of issue networks. For a comparative perspective on interest groups in the Western world see Thomas (1993) or Richardson (1993). On corporatism, Williamson (1985) is a helpful guide; for a trenchant critique of corporatist ways see Olson (1982). On postcommunist Russia see Cox (1993) and Sakwa (1996, Ch.8).

Political parties

The evolution of parties

'In this book I investigate the workings of democratic government. But it is not institutions which are the object of my research: it is not on political forms, it is on political forces I dwell.' So Moisei Ostrogorski (1854–1919) began his pioneering comparison of party organization in Britain and the United States. Ostrogorski was one of the first students of politics to recognize that parties were becoming a vital force in the new era of democratic politics: 'wherever this life of parties is developed, it focuses the political feelings and the active wills of its citizens' (Ostrogorski, 1902, p. liii).

Ostrogorski's supposition that parties were growing in importance was fully justified: the twentieth century proved to be the century of parties. In Western Europe, mass parties emerged to battle for the votes of newly-enlarged electorates. In communist and fascist states, ruling parties monopolized power in an attempt to reconstruct society and the people within it. In the developing world, nationalist parties became the vehicle for driving colonial rulers back to their imperial homeland. In all these cases, parties succeeded in drawing millions of people into the national political process, often for the first time. The mass party was *the* mobilizing device of mass politics in the twentieth century.

Definition
Political parties are permanent organizations which contest elections, usually because they seek to occupy the decisive positions of authority within the state. Unlike interest groups, which seek merely to influence the government, serious parties aim to secure the levers of power. In Weber's phrase, parties live 'in a house of power'.

In standing between the people and the state, parties became, and largely remain, integral to the operation of modern political systems in four ways:

- Parties function as agents of *élite recruitment*. They serve as the major mechanism for preparing and recruiting candidates for public office. If you want to lead your country, you must first persuade a party to adopt you as its candidate.
- Parties serve as agents of *interest aggregation*. They transform a multitude of specific demands into more manageable packages of proposals. Parties select, reduce and combine interests. They act as a filter between society and state, deciding which demands to allow through their net.
- Political parties still serve as a *point of reference* for many supporters and voters, giving people a key to interpreting a complicated political world.
- The modern party offers *direction to government*, performing the vital task of steering the ship of state. Crucially, parties provide leadership to government.

Party organization

The study of internal party organization is a classic topic which has recently returned to favour. This is especially true of Western Europe where parties are strongest (American parties are distinctive and will serve as a counterpoint to European examples through this chapter). Consider the work of Panebianco (1988). He believes that the key questions to ask about parties are organizational. How is power distributed within the party? What is the relationship between leaders, members and parliamentarians? The answer to these questions, Panebianco claims, must be historical. He places special emphasis on a 'genetic' account of party development, by which he means to stress the importance of the party's 'founding moment' in dealing out the power cards between the elements of party organization. These 'continue in many ways to condition the life of the organization even decades afterwards'.

Adopting a historical approach leads to a distinction between élite, mass and catchall parties (Box 8.1). This classification captures the origins of parties and also tells us something about their contemporary character. *Elite* (or caucus) parties are 'internally created'. They are formed by cliques within an assembly joining together to reflect common concerns and then to fight effective campaigns in an enlarged electorate. The earliest parties were of this élite type: for example, the Conservative parties of Scandinavia and Britain which emerged in the nineteenth century. The first American parties, the Federalists and Jeffersonians, were also loose élite factions, based in Congress and state legislatures.

Definition

The word **caucus** means a closed party meeting, usually for strategy or nomination purposes. The term is usually used in the context of legislative parties, where the caucus formed by the members representing a specific party in effect forms that party's top committee (as traditionally in Australia and New Zealand).

Mass parties originate outside the assembly, in groups seeking representation in the legislature for their interests and goals. The working-class socialist parties which spread across Europe at the turn of the twentieth century were prime examples of these externally-created parties. Such parties acquired an enormous membership and sought to keep their representatives in parliament on a tight rein. Stimulating other parties to copy their techniques, these socialist parties exerted tremendous influence on European party systems in the twentieth century. The United States, almost uniquely among the older democracies, never developed mass parties.

Catch-all parties are not new organizations. Rather, this term describes the outcome of an evolutionary path followed by many élite and mass parties in response to conditions after 1945. Catch-all parties seek to govern in the national interest rather than as representatives of a single social group. They are dominated by their leaders who communicate with the voters through television rather than indirectly via a large, active membership. Catch-all parties seek electoral support wherever they can obtain it; their purpose is not to represent but to govern. The catch-all party is a response to a political system with a mobilized electorate, in which governing has become technical and in which electoral communication is through the media. The transformation of several radical socialist parties into leader-dominated social democratic parties is perhaps the most important example of a shift from mass to catch-all parties. Another is the broadening of Christian Democratic parties (for example the CDU in Germany) from catholic defense organisations to broader catch-all parties of the centre-right. America's parties, it might be argued, went straight from élite to catch-all status, missing out the mass stage.

A central feature of party organization is the relationship between the parliamentary party and the party organization. Parties are complex organizations, with legislators in the assembly and officials at party headquarters needing to develop a way of working together. The party leader, a strong figure in both the parliamentary party and the external organization, provides a bridge between the two worlds. However, the balance also reflects a party's orgins. In élite parties, with their origins in the assembly, the parliamentary party normally dominates. But mass parties, especially socialist ones, tra-

BOX 8.1
Models of party organization

	Élite ('caucus') party	Mass party	Catch-all party
Emergence	19th century	1880–1960	After 1945
Origins	Inside the assembly	Outside the assembly	Developed from existing elite or mass parties
Claim to support	Traditional status of leaders	Represents a social group	Skill at governing
Membership	Small, élitist	Large card-carrying membership	Declining; leaders become dominant
Source of Income	Personal contacts	Membership dues	Many sources, including state subsidy
Examples	19th century liberal parties, many postcommunist parties	Socialist parties	Modern Christian and Social Democratic parties in Europe

Source: modified from Katz and Mair (1995).

ditionally sought to keep their parliamentary brothers and sisters on a stricter leash. In practice, though, elected representatives have always exercised considerable discretion. In the United States, to take an extreme case, the parties in Congress are virtually independent of weak national party institutions. Members of Congress ask what their party can do for them, not what they can do for their party. In a few countries the position of individual MPs is strengthened by the constitutional requirement of the 'free mandate'. This is a requirement, to quote Austria's constitution, that legislators 'shall be bound in the exercise of their function by no mandate' (Müller, 1994, p. 70). At least in theory, the party organization is unable to dictate to its representatives in the assembly.

Yet the relationship between the two wings of the party is far from one-sided. The party organization retains some useful 'power cards'. State financial aid normally goes to the party bureaucracy, not to the party in parliament. And only party officials can cope with increasingly technical tasks such as recruiting members and fighting elections. In particular, the media war of a modern election has reduced ordinary members of parliament to peripheral status; if they ever were big shots in the campaign, they are no longer. As politics becomes more professional, so the technicians in the extra-parliamentary organization regain some clout.

Given the central role of parties in political recruitment, candidate selection is a crucial aspect of party organization. As Schattschneider (1942)

put it, 'the nominating process has become the crucial process of the party. He who can make the nominations is the owner of the party'. So who does control candidate recruitment? How does an ambitious politician go about winning a party's endorsement for election to the legislature? These are important issues since in most parliamentary systems those subsequently elected to the assembly often form the pool from which top national leaders emerge. In most democracies, candidate selection is a decentralized procedure involving a major role for local parties and an increasing one for individual members. Indeed, 'many parties now afford their ordinary members a greater voice in candidate selection than was once the case' (Mair, 1994, p. 15). The most common requirement for a prospective parliamentary candidate is to win selection by constituency parties which operate under the supervision of party headquarters (for example the major parties in Britain and Denmark). The next most frequent format is national selection after consideration of suggestions from lower levels (for example the major parties in Japan and the Netherlands). In either case, then, nomination is certainly not the exclusive preserve of the party élite at the centre.

Israel is a a striking example of what Hazan (1997a, p.95) calls 'dramatic democratization' in candidate selection. Israel's major parties have introduced the primary system previously associated with the United States, and party members now select all the candidates to be included on their party's

EXHIBIT 8.1

Why are American parties so weak?

'If I could not go to heaven but with a party, I would not go there at all.' Thomas Jefferson, 1789.

Parties in the United States are much weaker than those in Western Europe, Australia and New Zealand. Outside Washington, parties barely seem to exist between elections. There is no system of individual membership. Even presidential candidates seem to impose themselves on a party more than they emerge from within the party. Members of Congress, especially in the Senate, would not take kindly to being instructed on how to vote by their party. To be sure, the Republican and Democratic parties are securely entrenched, with a history dating back to the 1850s. However, they are anything but the cohesive, organized actors found in most consolidated democracies. Why so?

Part of the answer is that the United States achieved suffrage for most white males before industrialization. So the question of securing political representation for industrial workers did not arise. This worked against the development of a tightly-organized mass party of the left, coming from outside the formal political system and seeking to transform it. In turn, the absence of a socialist party meant that the Republicans did not have to respond by developing a mass organization themselves.

But three other factors contribute to the weakness of America's parties. First, the decentralization of political power – between federal and state governments, and between the White House and Congress – encourages fragmentation within the parties. Second, the diversity of American society also works against cohesive parties. Third, the ideology of 'Americanism' is also so strong that it leaves little room for other political ideologies to emerge around which strong parties could develop.

Further reading: Epstein (1986), Hernnson (1994).

national list at the general election. Members vote for up to 20 candidates from a long tally of hopefuls. Inevitably candidates with good name recognition score highest, driving politicians to publicity-seeking initiatives and reducing the coherence and effectiveness of the parties themselves. The result, Hazan concludes, may be to transform the Knesset from an assembly of parties into an assemblage of individuals.

Definition
Primary elections enable a party's supporters to decide which candidate will represent their party at a subsequent general election. Primaries are widely used in the United States, where they were introduced to reduce the dominance of party bosses. However, many observers now claim that the primary system takes too much control away from the party, destroying its cohesion.

As Mair (1994) also notes, 'more and more parties now seem willing to allow the ordinary members a voice in the selection of party leaders'. Of course, American parties have long selected their presiden-

tial candidates through party conventions; and in Canada both the Liberals and the Conservative have used a similar method for selecting their leaders since the 1920s. But the franchise for leadership elections is broadening in other countries too. In Britain, the three largest parties – Conservative, Labour and Liberal Democrat – all now give rank-and-file members at least some say in choosing their leader. The traditional method of giving members of parliament exclusive control over selecting the party leader is declining, a trend which places more emphasis on the ability of candidates to reach out to a larger audience through the media.

Social base and ideology

The base of Western European parties in the social structure gives them a secure foundation. Major parties not only persist through time but also show remarkable continuity in the shares of the vote they obtain. As Bartolini and Mair write, 'the century of mass politics in Western Europe can be seen as a century of electoral stabilization, showing a funda-

---

BOX 8.2

Major stages in the development of Western European societies and their impact on parties

1. The national revolution

This refers to the original construction of the state as a territory governed by a single central authority (Lipset and Rokkan, 1967). Though fought many centuries ago, modern party systems still show the scars of these violent state-building battles. Even today many parties represent outlying territories, usually opposing a pre-eminent party representing the core region. In Britain, Labour and Liberals represent the peripheral areas, with the Conservatives currently confined to their core region around London. The other aspect of the national revolution, conflict between state and church, proved even more important in generating parties. As the modern state developed, it came into conflict with the Catholic Church which sought to defend its traditional control over 'spiritual life'. This conflict continued into the twentieth century in many European countries, with anticlerical parties (notably the communists) and Christian Democratic parties emerging, particularly in Catholic nations.

Types of party created: regional (5), religious (6).

2. The industrial revolution

The emergence of an industrial society exerted a profound influence on parties, and the initial effect of industrialization was to sharpen the divide between city and countryside. As the rural economy began to decline, agrarian parties formed to defend rural interests in Norway, Sweden and Finland. But industrialization exerted another deeper and (excepting the USA) nearly universal effect. It stimulated the emergence of socialist parties to represent the interests of the new urban working class.

Types of party created: agrarian (4), socialist/communist (3,7).

3. The postindustrial 'revolution'

Western democracies have now become largely postindustrial, with education and knowledge replacing capital and manufacturing as key resources. The main impact of this postindustrial 'revolution' has so far been within parties of the left. New generations of graduates, with an international outlook, have challenged the older echelons of left-party members with their roots in the trade unions. In the United States this division led to physical violence between old and new outside the 1968 Democratic convention at Chicago. Younger and better-educated generations have also provided a healthy pool of activists for the new green parties which have now emerged in most Western democracies (Parkin, 1989). Green candidates have won election to parliaments in several democracies, including Austria, France, Germany, Italy, Portugal and Sweden.

Types of party created: green parties (10).

Note: the numbers in brackets cross-refer to Von Beyme's classification in Box 8.3. (p. 136).

---

mental bias toward stability' (1990, p. 287). Most parties have core supporters located in particular segments of society, which provide a solid, long-term grounding. These links between parties and social groups usually develop at crucial points of conflict in a country's history. Such moments define new social cleavages (that is, divisions) from which parties emerge and which they then reinforce, producing what is often called a 'frozen' party system (Lipset and Rokkan, 1967). So to explain the social base of parties, we must again don the historian's robes. Box 8.2 shows the three main cleavages from which Western European parties have emerged. As always, the American experience is distinctive.

The waves of social change described in Box 8.2 produce counter-currents which are powerful in their own right. Social change always creates losers as well as winners, and the resulting tensions can lead to the emergence of extreme, often short-lived, protest parties (Lipset, 1983). These parties can easily flourish in an unsettled society, offering simple 'solutions' to irreversible changes. One example of these movements of protest is the racist parties which emerged in many Western European countries in the 1960s and the 1970s. Based on poorly-educated segments of the urban working-class, these parties used the growth of immigrants and guest workers to 'explain' their supporters' sense of insecurity in a changing world. The main illustration is from France where the National Front (FN), led by Jean-Marie Le Pen, remains well-established. An early example from the United States is George Wallace's campaign for the presidency in 1968. Fighting on a racially-charged law-and-order ticket, Wallace won 13.5 per cent of the vote as candidate for his own American Independent party. Ignati (1992, p. 1) interprets recent European extreme right parties (ERPs) as a counter-revolution to the postindustrial revolution. He suggests that

> the Greens and ERPs are respectively the legitimate and the unwanted children of the new politics; as the greens came out of the Silent Revolution, the ERPs derive from a reaction to it, a sort of 'silent counter-revolution'.

Definition
Protest parties exploit popular resentment against the government or the establishment, usually by highlighting specific issues such as high taxes or a permissive immigration policy. They are often short-lived 'flash parties' which fall as quickly as they rise. Their leaders are often charismatic but usually inexperienced. A significant and well-established example is France's National Front.

BOX 8.3
Von Beyme's classification of parties in Western democracies

Type of party	Emerged in opposition to
1. Liberal	Conservatives
2. Conservative	Liberals
3. Workers	Industrial employers
4. Agrarian	Industrial society
5. Regional	Central authority
6. Christian	Secular society
7. Communist	Social Democrats
8. Fascist	Democracy
9. Protest	Bureaucracy and the welfare state
10. Green	Unsustainable economic growth

Note: parties are listed in approximate order of foundation, oldest first.

Source: von Beyme (1985).

To summarize this section, we can draw on von Beyme's (1985) attempt to classify contemporary parties by ideology (Box 8.3). Just as Panebianco suggests that a party's organization reflects its 'founding moment', so Von Beyme emphasises that the ethos of a party reflects the underlying conflicts from which it originates. Parties develop an ideology to rationalize and justify their particular concerns; and these principles, once adopted, acquire deep significance for the activists. For instance, even if green parties broaden their agenda in the twenty-first century, it is inconceivable that their original ecological concerns could disappear from their agenda. Not all Von Beyme's ideological groups or *familles spirituelles* are found in any particular country. However, traces of most groups can be found in the complex multiparty systems of continental Europe. Even in two-party systems such as Britain and the United States, many of von Beyme's groups are discernible as tendencies within the major parties.

We should end this section with a caveat. The links between society and parties are weakening, and the conflicts of class and religion which fuelled party systems have softened. The anchors of voter loyalty are slipping. New generations of educated voters prefer to enter politics through single-issue cause groups, not political parties. Television and the internet allow for communication between leaders and voters without any need for party activists to serve as intermediaries, leading Seisselberg (1996) to postulate the emergence of new media-based 'personality parties' such as Silvio Berlusconi's Forza Italia. In the final quarter of the twentieth century, these factors led not just to the emergence of catchall parties but also to a decline in the membership of established parties, especially in the 1970s and 1980s (Table 8.1). In Australia, where membership has always been low because compulsory voting reduces the need for activists to get out the vote, major party membership halved from four per cent of the electorate in 1967 to two per cent in 1996 (Bean, 1997, p. 111). In New Zealand, the drop was even more dramatic: Labour's membership fell from around 80,000 in the early 1980s to under 10,000 in 1993 (Mulgan, 1997, p. 249). Lacking a steady flow of young members, the average age of party members increased. By the late 1990s, the mean age of members of Germany's Christian Democratic Union had reached 54; Britain's Conservatives were just as elderly. The classic European mass membership party, based on mobilizing specific social groups, will certainly need to continue to adapt if it is to prosper in the new century.

As parties' links with society have weakened, so they have come to depend more on the state for their sustenance. In particular, state funding of parties is now virtually universal in democracies (Katz, 1996, p. 130). In Austria, Denmark, Finland, Norway and Sweden, state funding for national parties exceeds or equals their recorded income from other sources.

Table 8.1 Trends in party membership in European democracies, 1960s–80s

	Party members as a per cent of the electorate	
	Beginning of 1960s	End of 1980s
Austria	26	22
Sweden	22	21
Denmark	21	6
Finland	19	13
Norway	16	14
Italy	13	10
UK	9	3
Netherlands	9	3
Belgium	8	9
Germany	3	4

Source: Mair (1994), Table 1.1.

Only in the Netherlands, the UK and the USA do membership contributions clearly exceed funding from the public purse (Mair, 1994, p. 10). Since most state support goes to the leading parties, the effect is to reinforce the status quo. For these reasons, the state and the top levels of major parties are tending to converge into a single system of rule: the 'party state'. Given these tendencies, it is perhaps no wonder that the ordinary member feels remote from this process and has been drifting away from parties to the purer satisfactions of the single-issue group.

Party competition

To understand the political significance of parties, we must go beyond examining them individually. Just as a football game consists of the play between two teams, so a party system consists of the interaction between competing parties. Competition encourages the diffusion of innovations in party organization, fund-raising and election campaigning. Equally, legal regulation – particularly strong in the United States – applies to all parties. It is a property of the party system as a whole.

A party system can be said to be strong or institutionalized when:

- The rules governing electoral competition are stable.
- The major parties have deep roots in society.
- All significant political actors (for example the courts and the military) accept the legitimacy of parties.
- Parties have strong organizations and their own resources.

Western Europe is the homeland of institutionalized party systems; Latin America is an example of a continent where party systems have traditionally been weak (Mainwaring and Scully, 1995).

> **Definition**
> A **party system** denotes the interaction between the significant political parties. In a democracy, parties respond to each others' initiatives in competitive interplay. Also, all the parties in a country are influenced by the political and constitutional system of which they form part.

The classic study of how parties compete is Anthony Downs' *An Economic Theory of Democracy* (1957), one of the most influential works of social science published since the Second World War, an impact which derives from Downs' elegant theoretical approach (Grofman, 1996). While the author's assumptions are often criticized as too simple, we should recall his own advice: 'theoretical models should be tested primarily by the accuracy of their predictions rather than by the reality of their assumptions'.

Downs assumes that in the political market, parties and voters act in a rational, self-interested way. So he defines a party as 'a team of people seeking to control the governing apparatus by gaining office in a duly constituted election'. In other words, in pursuit of power parties seek to maximize their vote. The question Downs raises is: what policies should parties adopt to maximize their vote?

To answer this, Downs assumes that voters' policy preferences can be represented on a single left–right scale (Figure 8.1). The left end of the scale represents full government control of the economy; the right

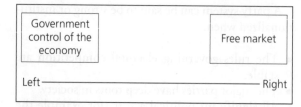

Figure 8.1 Downs' single dimension of party competition

end, a completely free market. In reality, public opinion is more complicated than this; contrast von Beyme's 10 different ideological families with Downs' single dimension. However Downs' left–right dimension is present in nearly all Western democracies, even if it is just one of several cleavages (Budge, Robertson and Hearl, 1987). It is a reasonable starting-point.

How vote-maximizing parties will position themselves depends on the distribution of public opinion along the left–right scale. In his most famous scenario, Downs imagines that public opinion forms a symmetrical, bell-shaped distribution around the midpoint (Figure 8.2). Again, this assumption is simple but plausible: more people are probably found at the centre than anywhere else. In these circumstances, vote-maximizing parties in a two-party system will converge at the midpoint. A party may start out at one extreme but it will move toward the centre because there are more votes to be won there

than there is support to be lost to abstention at the extremes. Once parties have converged at the midpoint, equilibrium is reached; they have no incentive to change their position.

Of course, different distributions of public opinion can produce different incentives for parties. Consider, for instance, another possible if less common scenario: a society polarized between two extremes (Figure 8.3). Here the parties would not converge at all, since if they did so they would be in danger of losing more extreme votes to abstention than they would gain from the thinly-populated centre. Each party remains with its troops, glaring across at its opponents.

When more than two parties are allowed into the model, the possibility arises of 'blackmail' parties forming to force a major party back toward an extreme. Thus, many protest parties aim to remind 'them', the big parties, not to forget 'us', the ordinary folk. Downs uses an American example to illustrate this point: the States' Rights Party of 1948. This party gained just 2.4 per cent of the vote in the presidential election. However its purpose was not to win the election but rather to threaten the Democrats because of their liberal policy on civil rights.

How accurate are the predictions from Downs' model? In reality, do parties tend to converge on the centre? Often, they do. Bill Clinton and Tony Blair are just two examples of leaders who have won elec-

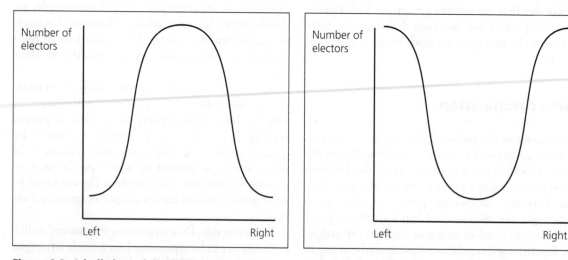

Figure 8.2 A bell-shaped distibution: parties converge at the centre

Figure 8.3 A polarized society: parties remain at the extremes

tions by steering their parties to the middle ground. Leaders who move their party away from the centre generally meet with less success. Examples of failed extremists from the United States include Barry Goldwater, Republican candidate for the presidency in 1964, and George McGovern, Democratic candidate in 1972. Both leaders were led astray by their party's zealous activists. In his campaign, Goldwater argued that 'extremism in the defence of liberty is no vice'. That may be so but his campaign also showed that extremism in pursuit of the White House is no virtue.

What qualifications should we introduce to Downs' model? The main point is that the narrowness of his assumptions can, in three ways, lead him astray:

- Voters judge not just what parties propose but also their likely skill at putting ideas into effect. Margaret Thatcher was probably always to the right of most British voters but she won elections because voters respected her determination. Downs does not allow for this possibility of strong leaders appealing to the public because of their ability to get things done (Green and Shapiro, 1994).
- Downs ignores the extent to which parties influence their voters' own policy preferences. Many electors use their party identification precisely as a compass to guide their own policy views. This means that if a party changes its policies, so too (within reason) will many of its voters. Because parties are 'preference-shaping', they have more flexibility in the electoral market than Downs implies.
- Downs construes party motives a shade rigidly. To assume that parties are just office-seekers may fit the pragmatism of the American two-party system. However in the more complicated and ideological party systems of continental Europe, parties compete over policy and not just for office. For example, in European countries governed by coalitions (especially Scandinavia), the choice of partners is influenced by agreements over what policies the coalition will follow. Parties seek to influence policy; they do not follow the goal of power at any cost.

Our conclusion, then, is that a simple model is a virtue but a simplistic model is a vice; Downs's theory is both.

Party systems in democracies

Downs's model of party competition represents, indeed inspired, a theoretical strand of research into party systems. But general models are unable to capture the substantial variation in how party systems operate in different countries (Box 8.4). Indeed, the nature of its party system reveals much about the character and functioning of any democracy. At one extreme stands the dominant party system where a single party provides a constant element in government, as in Japan. Rather like ageing heavyweights, these dominant parties are past their prime but must still be treated with respect. A second species, equally threatened by political change, is the two-party system. Here two parties become constant sparring partners, engaged in an endless battle for power – as in the United Kingdom. However, the most common format today is a multiparty system. In this version, preeminent in Europe, a number of the parties represented in the assembly join together to make a coalition government. Multiparty systems are centred around a search for common ground but, as we will see, they do not always provide dynamic governance.

Dominant party systems

Here one party is a constant component of the executive, governing either alone or in coalition. Dominant parties can exist in either a democratic context (for example Japan) or in more authoritarian settings (for example Egypt). The key difference is that a dominant party operating in a democracy permits genuine electoral competition; thus, electoral defeat is at least a possibility. Japan under the conservative Liberal Democrats (LDP) is a classic case. Until the LDP suffered a temporary loss of its monopoly of office in 1993, Japan was often described as a 'one and a half' party state. The LDP did not engage in ballot-rigging or intimidation, devices used by dominant parties in semi-democracies. But the constant tenure in office of the LDP did lead to the rather corrupt meshing of state and party which characterizes such systems. The LDP

BOX 8.4
Party systems in democracies

Type	Definition	Example
Dominant party system	One party is constantly in office, either governing alone or in coalition	Japan (Liberal Democrats), India (Congress)
Two-party system	Two major parties compete to form single-party governments	Great Britain (Conservative and Labour), United States* (Democratic and Republican)
Multiparty system	The assembly is composed of several minority parties, leading to coalition government	Scandinavia

* However, divided government means one party can control the presidency while the other has a majority in either or both houses of Congress.

used state patronage to reinforce its strength, passing out resources such as campaign funds to its candidates through party factions. Indeed, personalized factions within the ruling LDP became the main form of political competition, reducing the focus on policy choices.

The role played by the Christian Democrats (DC) in Italy until 1992 in some ways resembled the position of Japan's LDP. The DC was a leading player in all 47 Italian governments between 1947 and 1992. It was a patronage-based, Catholic catchall party which derived its political strength from serving as a bulwark against Italy's strong communists. The DC slowly 'colonized' the state, with particular ministries becoming the property of specific factions. The party used its control of the state to reward its supporters with jobs, money and favours, with little regard for the public purse. This patronage network spun across the country, providing a measure of integration between the affluent North and the backward South (LaPalombara, 1987). However the system was static, even antiquated, and eventually fell apart.

Many other dominant parties have declined, although they have not suffered the DC's rapid death. In Israel, for instance, the Labour (Mapai) party dominated political life for 30 years from the state's inception in 1949. Mapai, and in particular its leader David Ben-Gurion, benefited from their links with the founding of the state. However, in 1977 the right-wing Likud bloc became the largest group in the Knesset (parliament). For the next 15 years, Likud headed coalition governments, including a period of a national unity coalition with

Labour. Today, Likud and Labour provide the major poles of a highly competitive party system.

India provides another instance of a dominant party losing its preeminence. Indian politics has been led since 1947 by the Congress Party, a broad-based left-of-centre party which has emphasized secularism in a nation riven with religious conflict (Mishra, 1994). As with Israel's Labour Party, Congress's preeminence owes much to its role in establishing an independent state. To maintain its dominant position, Congress relied on a pyramid of class and caste alliances to sustain a national organization in a fragmented society. However Congress is now less able to dominate Indian politics, partly because of growing religious tensions (also evident in Israel), and it did not participate in the coalition formed after the 1998 election. As its status has declined from dominant party to large party, so the shadow which Congress throws across Indian politics has shortened.

An important feature of nearly all dominant parties is factionalism. Lacking an effective challenge from other parties, the competitive impulse reasserts itself within the framework of the leading force. A party faction is an organized, self-aware group which enjoys some stability of membership. Although factions are often thought to be less legitimate than parties, they are a means for restraining party leaders. In Japan, factions are based on spoils. This resulted from an electoral system which, until the reform of 1994, forced candidates from the same party to compete against each other for election in constituencies which each returned several members but where the elector only had one vote. A faction leader

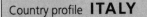

Country profile **ITALY**

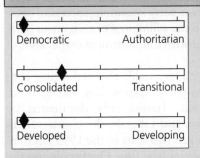

Democratic — Authoritarian

Consolidated — Transitional

Developed — Developing

Population: 57m.
Gross domestic product per head:
 $18 700.
Form of government: parliamentary,
with an indirectly-elected president who can play a role in government formation.

Legislature: the Chamber of Deputies (630 members) and the Senate (315) are elected simultaneously by popular vote for a maximum of five years. A bill must receive the positive assent of both houses and (as in Australia) the Cabinet is equally responsible to both chambers, producing a strongly bicameral legislature.

Executive: the Prime Minister formally appoints, but cannot dismiss, the members of the large Cabinet.

Coalition requirements limit the PM's choice. An 800-strong Office of the Prime Minister provides support, which has given PMs more influence over the machinery of government.

Judiciary: based on the civil law tradition, Italy has both ordinary and administrative judicial systems. A 15-member Constitutional Court has powers of judicial review.

Electoral system (1994): an additional member system, with three-quarters of both houses elected by simple majority and one-quarter proportionally.

Between 1992 and 1994, a political earthquake hit Italy leading many commentators to refer to the end of the First Italian Republic. A dominant and stable party system – a partyocracy – fell apart, a meltdown without precedent in the democratic world (Gundle and Parker 1996, p. 1). Still the largest party in 1992, the Christian Democrats (DC) had ceased to exist two years later. Its old sparring partner, the communists, had already given up the ghost, largely reforming as the Democratic Party of the Left (PDS) in 1991. Why then did this party-based system collapse?

Donovan (1995, p. 3) suggests that five catalysts initiated the destruction of Europe's oldest ruling elite. These were:

- The collapse of communism
- The success of the new Northern League in the 1990 regional elections, opening up the possibility of real political change
- Referendums on electoral reform in the early 1990s which revealed public hostility to the existing order
- Vivid attacks on the partyocracy by Francesco Cossiga (President 1985–1992)
- *Tangentopoli* ('kickback city', referring originally to Milan), the word used to describe the exposure of political corruption by a newly-assertive judiciary.

Like many other dominant parties, the DC's reliance on patronage also came under pressure from the global economy and, in Italy's case, the European Union.

Although the disintegration of the old system was
decisive, Italy's new order is still consolidating. The election of 1994, the first fought under a new electoral system designed to reduce fragmentation, yielded a remarkable government of populist right-wing parties headed by media magnate Silvio Berlusconi. This government collapsed after seven months, the victim of traditional coalition infighting, and it was replaced by an astonishing government of technocrats (experts, lawyers and academics). Remarkably, this crisis government contained no parliamentary representatives at all, but it nonetheless survived for a whole year. The next election, in 1996, did produce signs of consolidation. Two major alliances emerged: the centre-left Olive Tree Alliance and the more right-wing Liberty Pole. The Olive Tree Alliance, committed to restoring the state's tottering finances, formed a government led by former academic Romani Prodi. But within 18 months Prodi was forced into a brief tactical resignation in an attempt to force his ex-communist coalition partners to support his reforms.

So far, then, changes to the electoral and the party system have not ushered in a new era of stable government. Yet Italy's old mass parties have disappeared for ever, replaced by the looser, leader-dominated parties which are characteristic of new democracies of the 1990s. The rapid decline of the DC showed just how vulnerable and outdated its form of dominant party rule had become.

Further reading: Donovan (1995), Gundle and Parker (1996), Zariski (1993).

would help to provide a candidate with resources to win an election, expecting loyalty in return. The additional member system introduced for 1996 was an attempt to rein in these financially-based factions.

Two-party systems

These are defined by Mair (1990, pp. 420–2) as

> those in which two parties of equivalent size compete for office, and where each has a more or less equal chance of winning sufficient electoral support to gain an executive monopoly.

In two-party systems, the leading contenders regularly alternate in office, resulting in clear accountability to the electorate but also running the risk of adversary politics. One of the few remaining examples of this rare, possibly doomed, species is Britain, where the Conservative and Labour parties compete for power. However even in Britain, the centre Liberal Democrats now offer some limited support for the Labour government elected in 1997.

Why has the two-party system entered a period of decline? In complex societies, a two-party system is an artificial creature, sustained largely by the plurality electoral system. Duverger's Law says that 'the simple majority single ballot [plurality] system favours the two-party system'. Thus the recent shift away from the plurality method, as in New Zealand and South Africa, has damaged the prospects of two-party systems.

Definition

Adversary politics was a phrase introduced by Finer (1974) to describe party competition in Britain. Finer considered that British party politics took the form of 'a stand-up fight between two adversaries for the favour of the lookers-on'. This endless battle, he believed, caused ineffective governance. However, single-party government based on a secure parliamentary majority does permit radical change, as in Britain under both Margaret Thatcher and Tony Blair.

Further, the new democracies, as in Eastern Europe, have all rejected the model of a two-party system based on the plurality method, in favour of a multiparty system based on proportional represenation. PR offers representation in the assembly to more parties and minority interests, a valued feature in low-trust societies. By contrast, for all the adversarial froth of a two-party system, its successful operation depends on the willingness of each major party to trust the other with sole control over the levers of power.

Yet even where a favourable electoral regime continues, the two-party system has lost ground. Consider Canada. Traditionally dominated by the Conservatives and Liberals, the Conservatives were reduced to just two seats in the 1993 election. Two regional parties (the Bloc Quebecois and the Reform party) emerged as the main opposition to the Liberals. Even Britain has long been a 'two and a half' party system. In 1997, the Liberal Democrats made a further advance in seats: their total of 46 (7 per cent) was the highest for a third party in over 50 years. And in the United States, where the two-party system remains entrenched, independent candidates emerge periodically to impinge on presidential contests. In 1992, for instance, the billionaire Ross Perot secured 19 per cent of the vote. The case for still calling these countries two-party systems is that minor parties rarely win sufficient seats to influence government formation (Sartori, 1976). In contrast to multiparty systems, coalitions are unusual in two-party systems.

Multiparty systems

These are characterized by proportional representation, a system which normally precludes any single party from winning a majority of seats in the assembly. The result is government by coalition. Since multiparty systems are becoming the norm in democracies, it is important to examine their character and functioning. In particular, how effective are they in delivering sound goverance?

Answers to this question have evolved over time, largely in response to variations in economic performance. Traditionally, multiparty systems were held to produce weak and unstable government with confused accountability to the electorate – if things went wrong, which party or parties in the coalition should be blamed? The party composition of government often changed in response to shifting alliances within parliament; therefore, elections (and electors) were marginalized. For instance, Finland averaged a government per year in the 30 years after 1945. Sometimes, elections in multiparty systems were extremely slow in delivering any government at all. After the Dutch election of 1972, six months elapsed before a workable coalition emerged. All this is far removed from the concentration of power in a single-party cabinet in Britain, or the focus of responsibility on the White House in the United States.

But opinions of multiparty systems became more positive in the 1960s as the postwar recovery of continental economies took hold. In practice, coalition government did not lead to inconsistent, vacillating policies. In Scandinavia, for instance, coalitions were composed of parties with a similar ideological persuasion. Coalitions come and go but without threatening continuity of policy. Policy is formed by consensus. This contrasts with two-party systems, such as the United Kingdom, where each new government would set about reversing the policies of its predecessor. Careful, cautious coalition government was, it was claimed, best-suited to the governance of complex societies.

However, the link between multiparty systems and weak government resurfaced in the 1990s. This reinterpretation reflected the tough 1990s agenda: cutting the government's budget deficit, privatizing state-owned companies and reducing welfare expenditure. The more parties there are in a government, it was argued, the harder it became to reach agreement on a programme of reform. It was the traditional two-party systems, notably Britain and New Zealand, which pursued the new policies with most energy. Continental Europe tended to lag behind, leading to doubts about whether multiparty systems were sufficiently flexible to produce the rapid policy changes needed to adapt to a global economy. Blondel (1993), for one, argued that

> the consensus mode of politics is not well-equipped to lead to long-term strategic action … its value appears to lie primarily in its ability to handle deep social cleavages rather than policy development.

The conclusion, perhaps, is that multiparty systems produce continuity of policy which is helpful when the economy is growing naturally, but are less successful at reviving economies which have fallen on hard times.

Parties in semi-democracies

In a semi-democracy, democratic legitimacy is not wholly lacking but is acquired and exploited in dubious ways. One device used to manage many semi-democracies is a dominant party. Unlike the dominant party in democracies such as Japan, the dominant party in a semi-democracy is willing to manipulate the electoral process to secure its own hold on power. Elections are neither completely free nor completely fair. But unlike the dominant parties in wholly authoritarian regimes (for example ruling communist parties), dominant parties in semi-democracies do allow a measure of real competition – as long as it does not threaten the status quo. Thus the task of a dominant party in a semi-democracy is to maintain its own position, relying on genuine support where possible but manipulated support where necessary. This is a time-consuming task, carrying the danger of distracting the rulers from effective governance.

We can use Singapore to illustrate how dominant parties operate in semi-democratic settings. The People's Action Party (PAP) has ruled Singapore since the island achieved independence from Britain in 1959, and the PAP held all the seats in parliament between 1968 and 1981. Like many dominant parties, PAP was headed by a powerful leader who served as a father figure for the nation – Lee Kwan Yew served as Prime Minister from 1959–90. But unlike some dominant parties, the PAP has outlasted its founder. In 1997 it still won 81 out of 83 seats, leading the new Prime Minister to claim that the voters 'had rejected Western-style liberal democracy'. PAP continues to manipulate public opinion by limiting media freedom. It also runs smear campaigns against opposition figures; government-inspired libel and tax fraud suits have bankrupted several opposition politicians.

PAP's attitude to the electorate is a characteristic blend of threat and benevolence. In the 1997 campaign, for instance, it threatened to deny housing estate improvements to districts which did not support its candidates. This intimidation was so effective that most PAP candidates went unopposed.

But PAP also provides effective governance; Singapore is a classic example of the Asian 'developmental state' in which a modern economy has been built on the foundations of tight political control. This commitment to economic development, enabling the country to by-pass the East Asian financial crash of the late 1990s, gives the PAP continued confidence in its right to rule. Any sucessful dominant party needs a national agenda which can be used to justify both its hold on power and its periodic departures from strict democratic principles.

As in democracies, so dominant parties in semi-democracies are facing increasing problems in maintaining their position in a more democratic world. Economic pressures to reduce the public sector, stimulated by international organizations such as the World Bank, are reducing the supply of patronage which provided the fuel for dominant parties. Just as one-party systems gave way to dominant parties, now these too are being supplanted by multiparty systems operating in genuine democracies. In the 1980s, for instance, Mexico's PRI initiated major economic liberalization, thereby reducing its direct control over the resources which served as the building blocks of its power. Even dominant parties which have always been more sympathetic to the private sector – such as Singapore's PAP – may find themselves falling victim to their own economic success. As Lipset argued, a wealthy and educated citizenry may become increasingly frustrated with the tight control exercised by a dominant party.

Parties in authoritarian regimes

Although political parties are found in most authoritarian regimes, their role contrasts sharply with their position in liberal democracies. By definition, authoritarian rulers limit open competition; therefore, there is at most one party and its purpose is to express the will of the dominant élite. Parties in authoritarian regimes pass communication downwards, serving as agents of propaganda and control. There are, however, some functions which are shared by parties in both authoritarian and democratic regimes. The most important are recruiting people to the political élite and directing the activities of the state.

A few authoritarian regimes still get by with no parties at all. These are either *preparty* or *antiparty* states. Preparty states are most commonly found in the Middle East; for example, Saudi Arabia, Jordan and Kuwait. In these traditional monarchies, a ruling family dominates and parties have yet to emerge or be permitted. In an antiparty state, by contrast, existing parties are banned when a new regime takes over – military rulers are the main example. After seizing power, the generals often quickly abolish parties, claiming that the nation can no longer afford the bickering and corruption associated with them (an alternative tactic of military rulers is to ban all parties bar their own puppet organization). Yet when the political thaw comes, and the generals retreat to their barracks, parties emerge again. So an antiparty system has become an unstable form, always prone to fall apart.

> **Definition**
>
> **Democratic centralism** was a key feature of communist party organization. It was based on two principles. The first was that lower levels had always to accept the decisions made by higher levels (the centralism dimension). The second was that higher levels were elected by the level immediately below, forming a pyramid of indirect election (the democratic dimension). But only one person would be nominated for each election; and in reality this candidate was chosen from above. So in practice 'democratic centralism' was centralism without democracy.

The characteristic form of authoritarian rule is the one-party system, where the single party becomes the instrument for the exercise of power. We can use ruling communist parties as the classic example of the institutionalization of power in a monopoly party. The party achieved its domination through a range of means. It controlled all the top jobs in government, acted as a watchdog over society, vetted appointments to all positions of responsibility and carried out agitprop (agitation and propaganda) activities. Coercion, and the fear of it, also helped the party to achieve its goals. The secret police were the main instrument of repression, as with the feared NKVD (later KGB) in the Soviet Union. The KGB used a vast network of informers to identify, and then eliminate, 'class enemies' and 'poisonous weeds'.

Where this system of social control operated fully, as in the Soviet Union most especially under Stalin, it provided probably the most systematic penetration of society that any political party anywhere has ever achieved. The elaborate hierarchy of communist parties served to strengthen top-down control (see Figure 8.4 for the Chinese case). At the base of the party stood many thousands of small cells. At the pinnacle stood a ruling politburo (literally, political bureau) which directed the party's work. Behind a facade of elections to higher levels, the structure formed a rigid, centralized pyramid.

Of course, we should not equate communist states with a one-party system. Many non-communist authoritarian rulers have also relied on a single party though without achieving the total control and tight internal organization found in totalitarian states. Consider, for example, the countries of the developing world which achieved independence in the 1950s and 1960s. The fight against colonialism did produce some nationalist movements which mobilized the population. Kwame Nkrumah's Convention People's Party (CPP) in Ghana (formerly the Gold Coast) was an example. Once these movements achieved power, they soon put a stop to party competition. 'Western' democratic models were held to be irrelevant to developing countries; the nationalist party became the personal vehicle of the country's hero-founder. But banning other parties did not prevent the fragile unity of the nationalist party from collapsing once power had been achieved. Ethnic and regional identities took precedence over party loyalties. When a coup finally overthrew Kwame Nkrumah, his party simply disappeared with him. So ruling nationalist parties proved to be far more fragile than communist parties. Indeed many post-colonial authoritarian regimes were governed more by personal rule than by a cohesive party. Many 'one party' states in the developing world became, in reality, no-party systems. They stood in sharp contrast to the disciplined party rule found in communist societies.

But like communist states the one-party systems of the developing world have not been immune from the worldwide trend towards democracy. As authoritarian regimes have given way to new democracies, so one-party systems have declined. With a few exceptions (China is the most important), ruling communist parties have virtually disappeared,

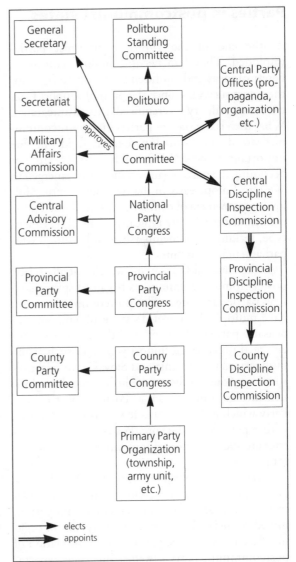

Figure 8.4 Organization of the Chinese Communist Party

exposed as hollow dictatorships. Even many of the looser one-party systems in the developing world have been replaced by multiparty systems. This change in developing countries has been prompted partly by international pressures and partly by the ageing of the first generation of independence leaders whose personal vehicles these parties were. At the very least, one-party authoritarian regimes are giving way to semi-democracies with a dominant party.

Parties in postcommunist states

At the end of the 1980s, communist parties imploded. They had become hollow, enfeebled, bereft of ideas and confidence, unable to fight for their own survival – once the prop of support from the Soviet military was removed, they disintegrated. What then is the state of parties in the postcommunist world? The situation remains fluid but one important trend is discernible: parties are not becoming the mass organizations which emerged in Western Europe early in the twentieth century following its own era of democratization. Rather, postcommunist parties are typically of the élite, caucus type, lacking mass membership and strong extraparliamentary structures.

As the national movements which initially seized power from the communists began to split, many new parties appeared. The postcommunist states have multiplied the world's stock of agrarian and peasant parties. Also, many ethnic parties have emerged to represent minority groups, such as the Hungarians in Romania and Slovakia, or Estonia's Russians. Some of these were little more than glorified interest groups, such as Poland's Beer Lovers' Party which in 1991 won a few seats in parliament with 3 per cent of the vote. Postcommunist countries are short of many things but they do not lack for parties.

Initially, many observers expected that the new postcommunist party systems would settle down into a few Western-style mass membership parties, linked to social cleavages. The emergence of organized parties would be part of the consolidation of postcommunist party systems. But such expectations proved false. Many new parties are classic 'internal parties' – that is, loose coalitions of a few deputies in the national parliament. The deputies find value in a party label for fighting elections but otherwise these parties lack clear ideology. Few of them have acquired strong organization. As Steen (1995, p. 13) says about the Baltic countries, 'the parties are more like campaigning institutions before elections than permanent institutions propagating ideology'. In that respect, postcommunist parties follow the American rather than the Western European model.

The failure to penetrate society reflects the incentives facing party leaders. Parties in the Czech Republic, Poland, Hungary and Slovakia already receive generous state subsidies, eliminating the financial need to build a dues-paying membership. Why should leaders expand their party's membership if the result is simply to build a potential threat to their own position? After all, the mass media already exist in postcommunist states to provide a channel of communication with the electorate. So large numbers of local activists are unnecessary. And since voting has already extended to the whole population, there is no need for mass parties to emerge to demand the suffrage. A mass membership, and the organization to go with it, is simply unnecessary in postcommunist conditions.

In any case, the communist legacy means that politicians are widely seen by voters as the problem rather than the solution. A suspicious political culture provides difficult soil in which to grow a mass party. As Marody (1995, p. 267) says of Poland, 'politicians are engaged mainly in solving the problems produced by themselves'. This problem of mobilizing demobilized voters is hard to overcome. For such reasons, Kopecki (1995, p. 515) suggests that 'parties in East-Central Europe are likely to develop as formations with loose electoral constituencies, unimportant membership and a dominant role for party leaders'. They will be élite parties rather than mass parties, led by political entrepreneurs unconstrained by a large party membership. Lewis (1996, p. 6) offers a similar judgement: 'recognisable counterparts of the great historic parties of Western Europe and other democracies may never emerge in East-Central Europe'. Instead, the leader-dominated, media-focused style of parties in the postcommunist world may offer clues about how parties in the consolidated democracies will themselves evolve as the twenty-first century unfolds.

Definition

Successor party is the term used to describe the new parties which formed in postcommunist states from the old ruling communist parties. The Social Democrats in the Czech Republic and Poland are examples. Reflecting their organization and membership, several successor parties achieved a remarkable electoral recovery in the mid-1990s. Ideologically, they accepted the end of communism but they did question the speed of transition to a full market economy.

Ironically, the organizational weakness of the new parties allowed the communist successor parties to stage an unpredicted comeback in several countries. In the early to mid-1990s, successor parties won presidential or parliamentary elections in Poland, Hungary and Russia. They also secured 20 per cent of the vote in the former East Germany. The living corpse of communism had risen from its uneasy grave, brought back to life in a popular protest against the mass unemployment of the early post-communist era. This political rebirth, surely the most astonishing in the history of parties, owed much to the communists' organizational inheritance – of money, property, facilities, people and expertise. The popular perception of the successor parties as organized and purposeful proved electorally crucial in a chaotic environment.

The successor parties exploited their organizational advantages skilfully, claiming to offer the best of the old (safety and security) without seeking to reimpose a planned economy. Ideologically, it seemed, the communist leopard really had changed its spots. Re-elected to power in Poland in 1993, the successor Democratic Left Alliance (SLD) pressed ahead with privatization and pension reform, encouraging the economy's recovery from the shock of transition. Yet (and here we come to another twist in a remarkable journey) the success of the successor parties may itself prove to be temporary, a product of economic decline in the aftermath of communism's collapse. In 1997, the Polish successor party was voted out of office – this time to a revived Solidarity, the same movement which had originally brought down the communist regime. In the same year Bulgarians swept away what many had come to call the 'red trash' which had been re-elected in 1994 on a promise of painless reform. In the Eastern European countries where market economies become entrenched, and the living standards of the majority begin to improve, so the desire for a return to 'the good old days' will weaken, especially among younger generations. Successor parties may survive and even prosper but only by demonstrating their commitment to a postcommunist agenda. In a situation of flux at least one point is clear: the traditional form of totalitarian communist rule has gone for ever, born and died in the twentieth century.

Key reading

> **Next step:** *Mair (1990) – a fine collection of classic articles.*

The literature on parties is outstanding, especially for Western Europe. Standard works include Lipset and Rokkan (1967) on the social base of parties, Sartori (1976) on party systems, Kircheimer (1966) on catch-all parties and Bartolini and Mair (1990) on the stabilization of European electorates. Von Beyme (1986) is a fund of information, particularly on party ideologies. Two modern comparative collections, both influenced by Panebianco (1988), are Lawson (1994) and Katz and Mair (1994). Wolinetz (1997) gathers over 20 articles. For a critique of Downs's 'rational choice' approach, see Mavrogordatos (1987). Lewis (1996) covers postcommunist parties; Randall (1988) examines parties in the developing world.

PART 3

THE STRUCTURES OF GOVERNMENT

We examine here the key institutions of national government: assemblies, the executive, bureaucracies, the military and the police. In nearly all political systems, these are the core structures through which policy is shaped and power is exercized. We then turn to territorial politics, reviewing the relationships between central, provincial and local levels of government. But we begin this part with a chapter on constitutions and the legal framework. Always significant in liberal democracies, constitutions and the judiciary are growing in political significance as more governments come to operate within the rule of law.

Constitutions and the legal framework

Law and politics

At first sight, law and politics make strange bed-fellows. The concept of law conveys an image of resolving disagreements in the calm atmosphere of the courtroom, while politics, by contrast, summons up a sharper picture in which power rather than law is the basis of conflict resolution. Yet in reality law and politics are closely connected. Indeed, the development of Western politics has been an attempt to ensnare absolute rulers in the threads of legal restraint. In the words of A.V. Dicey, the nineteenth-century British jurist, the object was to substitute 'a government of laws' for a 'government of men'. A legal order, affording both protection for individual rights and a means of resolving disputes between citizens and state, is the major accomplishment of liberal politics. As the seventeenth-century English philosopher John Locke put it, 'wherever law ends, tyranny begins'. The rule of law also provides a framework for the development of a contract-based market economy. From this liberal perspective, law is not so much separate from politics as an achievement of it.

In the twentieth century, law and politics diverged as academic disciplines but there is a need now to recombine them. One reason for this is the explosion of constitution-making after 1945, first among the newly-independent states of Africa and Asia, then among postauthoritarian states in Europe and Latin America. In addition, several liberal democracies – including Belgium, Canada, the Netherlands, Portugal, Spain and Sweden – have adopted new constitutions since 1970. We begin this chapter with a discussion of constitutions.

Growing 'judicialization' of political life is another reason for recombining the study of law and politics. Throughout the Western world, the willingness of judges to step into the political arena has increased – judicial activism is no longer primarily an American phenomenon. We assess the role of the judiciary in the second part of this chapter. The 'legalization' of international politics is the final reason for bringing law and politics back together. More international contacts bring forth a demand for more regulation. Global issues such as migration, trade, transport and the environment are all addressed within a framework of hard and soft law. We look at international law in the final section of the chapter.

Constitutional rule

To understand the political role of constitutions we must examine the idea of constitutional rule (also called constitutionalism). This refers to the rule of law. The British jurist A.V. Dicey defined this important if imprecise term as

---

BOX 9.1
Legal distinctions

Natural and positive law
'Natural law' refers to normative principles of right conduct which may or may not be reflected in 'positive law', the law of the land.

Basic and statute law
'Basic law' is entrenched in that it overrides ordinary 'statute law' passed by the legislature. Constitutions are often expressed in basic law.

Civil and criminal law
'Civil law' resolves disputes between, and initiated by, private persons. 'Criminal law' covers acts that the state has defined as illegal and which it is therefore willing to prosecute.

Constitutional and administrative law
'Constitutional law' sets out the structure of government and the rights of citizens. 'Administrative law' covers the exercise of power by the bureaucracy, particularly in relation to citizens.

Roman and common law
'Roman law' is an extensive system of codified law which is prevalent in continental Europe. It dates back to Justinian, Roman Emperor 527–65. European Union law is influenced by the Justinian codes. The more flexible 'common law', used mainly in Britain and the USA, evolves from judges' decisions in particular cases. These judgments create predictability by setting influential precedents.

Flexible and rigid constitutions
'Flexible constitutions' have the same status as statute laws. They can be amended in the same way or even (as in Britain) by the evolution of conventions. The only way to amend a 'rigid constitution' is through special procedures beyond those required for ordinary laws.

Hard and soft law
'Hard law' establishes legally binding obligations; 'soft law' codifies informal norms of expected behaviour. Soft law is widespread in the international arena.

---

the absolute supremacy or predominance of regular law as opposed to the influence of arbitrary power … it means, again, equality before the law, or the equal subjection of all classes to the ordinary law of the land. (Dicey, 1959, first pub. 1885)

In Europe, the rule of law was therefore a means for overcoming feudalism, under which rights were not universal but depended on one's position in the social hierarchy.

Crucially, the rule of law also entitles those citizens affected by a government action to challenge that act in independent courts – and to expect that the executive will abide by the court's rulings. Constitutional rule is therefore a constraint on government, including democratic ones (hence the radical criticism that constitutions are nothing more than 'the rule of the dead over the living'). It developed to restrain authoritarian rulers but offers equal cover to minorities which are threatened in a democracy by zealous majorities. In these ways, constitutional rule forms the cornerstone of liberal democracy.

The United States is the prime illustration of a constitutional order. The country was built on the foundations laid down by the Founding Fathers in Philadelphia in 1787. The constitution produced

there, the world's first explicit written constitution, became America's political Bible. Its central ideas – limited government and a dispersal of power – are etched into America's culture, creating not so much principles to be debated as a framework within which political debate takes place. Further, the Supreme Court has become the most influential judicial institution on earth since it secured (some time after its inception) the role of settling constitutional disputes. Constitutionalism suffuses the daily operation of American politics.

Britain, by contrast, is an example of a democracy in which constitutional government has been less secure. Partly, this arises because the constitution is neither codified in a single document nor entrenched in basic law. Rather it is an unfixed constitution with conventions which are, in Marshall's striking metaphor (1984), 'as slippery as procreating eels'. More important, as Prosser (1996) points out, the traditions of monarchy still inhibit the development of the British constitution. Although the monarchy now has little if any direct political power, in law people are still to an extent treated as 'subjects'. This has delayed the development of clear rights for citizens. Until recently, for instance, it was impossible for people to sue many public institu-

EXHIBIT 9.1

What is liberalism?

The liberal ideas of individual rights and limited government by consent form the rock of Western political thought. Liberalism developed in the eighteenth and nineteenth centuries as part of the modern reaction against feudal remnants and aristocratic privileges. The liberal ethos remains rational and progressive, valuing individual responsibility and equality of opportunity (but not reward). As the ideology of limited government and individual initiative, liberalism provided the underpinnings of the now-triumphant market economy. Hence, in uneasy alliance with democracy, liberalism dominates politics at the start of the twenty-first century. Historically, liberalism has disposed not just of the conservative notion of a natural social hierarchy but also of the socialist preference for extensive state provision. But threats to liberalism's pre-eminence remain: from radical feminism, Islam, nationalism and a competing emphasis on the group and the community rather than the individual, especially in Asia but increasingly in the West as well.

tions since these bodies represented the monarchy. And since the monarch is technically the source of law, she cannot herself be subject to it. Treated as subjects, people often behaved accordingly, failing to assert those rights scattered about in common law.

From this perspective, Britain still lacks fully constitutional government. The Labour government elected in 1997 promised to remedy some of these 'weaknesses' by, for example, incorporating the European Convention on Human Rights (1950) into domestic law. It is ironic that while the rule of law is often considered a British bequest to its former colonies, notably India, Britain itself has relied on practice more than rules to sustain fair treatment of its own people.

> **Definition**
> **Constitutional rule** is government by law. It places limits on the scope of government, sets out individual rights and creates opportunities for redress should the government exceed its authority. Constitutional rule is a defining feature of liberal thinking which predominates in the West and especially in the United States.

Nearly all countries have constitutions but only some have constitutional rule. This is because constitutional rule is a cultural as much as a legal notion (Franklin and Baun, 1995). It refers to an acceptance of the rule of law by the political élite, without which the constitution itself is dead in the water. Authoritarian regimes rarely dispense with a consti-

tution but frequently this is just a fig-leaf intended to cover arbitrary power. Thus a constitution without a supportive culture, especially among the élite, is of limited value.

Communist regimes provided a useful contrast to the Western tradition. They explicitly rejected the Western idea of constitutional rule with its emphasis on limited government, individual rights and private property. What does the Western tradition amount to, asked the communists, other than an affirmation of the status quo? In communist states, constitutions were of little moment – nothing could hinder the party's task of building socialism, and the party's mission was too important to be subject to formal limits. So communist regimes were party-led rather than constitutionally-limited, a point asserted in the constitutions themselves. For instance, the Chinese constitution grants specific rights to all but adds that these freedoms are conditional on supporting socialist principles, including the dictatorship of the proletariat. In a major contrast with Western thought, people can lose their individual rights for several years if they are found guilty of failing to support core principles – a yellow card for political incorrectness. Besides emphasising the supremacy of the party, communist constitutions also stressed social and economic rights such as the right to work.

Against the hopes of Western liberals, the fall of communism has not led to constitutional government throughout Eastern Europe. Many postcommunist countries, especially the successor states to the Soviet Union, have simply swapped one nonconstitutional order for another. Acherson (1995

p. 14) has referred to 'postcommunist one-party police states, where semi-free economies nourish seething corruption'. Until the election of a reforming government in 1997, the governing coalition of Romania consisted

> of populist, nationalist, collectivist or otherwise unreconstructed elements who lacked the intent to embark on a Western-style democratic and constitutional transformation. (Pogany, 1996, p. 584).

Even in its Western heartland, the idea of constitutional rule faces fresh challenges. In particular, multiculturalism poses acute difficulties (Slaughter, 1994). Many ethnic and cultural groups demand formal recognition and protection of their status: for example, indigenous peoples, religious minorities and women. However, the idea of group rights rests uneasily alongside the Western tradition of equal rights for all individuals (Jones, 1994). This problem is especially acute when the group wants a measure of self-government, including the right to control its members in a way which runs against the liberal spirit of the national constitution. For instance, some groups may insist on a religious education or arranged marriages for their children, or on different (unequal?) treatment for men and women. Such demands do not fit easily into a liberal framework. To take another example, many indigenous peoples in the Americas do not accept private ownership of land (as absurd, they say, as buying the air), yet the notion of private property is integral to the Western constitutional order (Boldt, 1993). Constitutional recognition of group, as opposed to individual, rights is alien to the Western liberal tradition.

Constitutions

We can look at constitutions in two ways. The first reflects their historical role in the West of limiting the state's power over its citizens. For the Austrian liberal Friedrich Hayek (1960), a constitution was nothing but a device for limiting the power of government. In similar vein, Carl Friedrich (1937) defined a constitution as 'a system of effective, regularized restraints upon government action'. Reflecting this approach, a Bill of Rights now forms part of nearly all written constitutions. The first Bill of Rights comprises the 10 amendments appended to the American consti-

tution in 1791. This covers such rights as freedom of religion, speech, the press, assembly and (more ominously) the 'right of the people to keep and bear arms'. Recent constitutions tend to be more ambitious in their statements of rights, imposing duties on rulers such as fulfilling citizens' 'rights' to work and to medical care. An extreme case is the Brazilian constitution of 1988 (Howard, 1993). This lengthy document made so many extravagant promises that special revising sessions of Congress were needed in 1993 and again in 1997 to tone down its commitments. But Brazil's response to its luxuriant constitution was unusual. More often, grand pledges made in a flourish of constitution-making are just ignored when it comes to working out who should pay.

> **Definition**
> A **constitution** sets out the formal structure of government, specifying the powers and institutions of central government, and the balance between central and other levels of government. In addition, constitutions specify the rights of citizens and in so doing create limits on and duties for the government.

The second, surprisingly neglected role of constitutions is to set out the structure of government. Described by Duchacek (1973) as power maps, constitutions prescribe the formal distribution of authority within the state. Constitutions set out the pathways of power, showing the procedures for making laws and reaching decisions. A constitution is therefore a form of political engineering, to be judged like any other construction by how well it stands the test of time. Thus the American constitution, still going strong after more than 200 years, must be judged a triumph. It sets out a classic division between executive, legislature and judiciary, all operating in a federal framework. Sartori (1994, p. 198) argues that the defining feature of a constitution is this provision of a frame of government. As he says, 'a constitution without a declaration of rights is still a constitution, whereas a constitution whose core and centerpiece is not a frame of government is not a constitution'.

The typical constitution contain several parts (Duchacek, 1991). A *preamble* seeks popular support for the document with a stirring declaration of principle, often adapted from America:

We the people of the United States, in order to form a more perfect union, establish justice, insure domestic tranquility, provide for the common defense, promote the general welfare, and secure the blessings of liberty to ourselves and our posterity, do ordain and establish this constitution for the United States of America.

An *organizational section* then sets out the powers of the various institutions of government. A *bill of rights* covers individual and perhaps group rights, including access to legal redress, and thereby sets limits on government. Finally, *procedures for amendment* define the rules for revising the constitution.

A traditional distinction contrasts written and unwritten constitutions. Yet no constitution is wholly unwritten; even the 'unwritten' British and New Zealand constitutions contain much statute and common law. A contrast between codified and uncodified systems is more useful. Most constitutions are codified – that is, they are set out in detail within a single document or body of laws. The constitution of Germany, for instance, is laid down in the Basic Law ratified in 1949. The constitutions of Britain, New Zealand and Israel are unusual in that they are not formalized in this way.

Procedures for amendment are important. Most constitutions are rigid; this makes them more acceptable to the various interests involved in their construction. Specifically, a rigid framework limits the damage should political opponents obtain power, for they too must abide by the values embedded in the constitutional settlement. A rigid constitution also offers the general benefit, much prized by liberals, of predictability to those subject to it. By contrast, the main benefit of a flexible constitution is its adaptability to changing conditions. In New Zealand, this flexibility permitted a recasting of the country's electoral system and government administration in the 1980s and 1990s. For better or worse, in many other countries such radical changes would have required constitutional amendment.

In practice, though, many 'rigid' constitutions are more adaptable than they seem. Take the United States. At first glance the American constitution looks highly inflexible – amendment requires two-thirds majorities in Congress and ratification by three-quarters of the states. Yet the constitution still responds – not so much through formal amendment as through changing judicial interpretation. The Supreme Court has become skilled at adapting an old document to new times. Thus one contrast between rigid and flexible consitutions is that in the former the judiciary manages evolution while in the latter politicians take the lead.

Frequent amendment is a sign of a political system (and a constitution) under stress. Too many alterations are self-defeating, since they reduce the sense that the constitution offers a settled formula for rule. Despite this, several liberal democracies, especially Belgium and Canada, have experienced regular constitutional changes in response to conflicts between language groups. Constitutional amendment can reflect such problems but seems unable, by itself, to resolve them.

Making constitutions

As the English political theorist John Stuart Mill (1991, first pub. 1861) wrote in rather gendered terms, constitutions 'are the work of men ... Men did not wake up on a summer morning and find them sprung up'. How then do constitutions come into being? Most often, they form part of a fresh start after a period of disruption. Such circumstances include regime change (for example the collapse of communism), reconstruction after defeat in war (for example Japan after 1945), external imposition (for example the influence of the Soviet Union on Eastern Europe after 1945) and independence (for example much of Africa in the 1950s and 1960s). The 1980s and 1990s were busy times for constitution-makers: 17 new ones were introduced in Eastern Europe between 1991 and 1995, and over 30 in Africa during the 1990s (Vereshchetin, 1996).

Constitutions, then, are documents intended to create and mark a new regime; but they are rarely born of celebration. Most often they are products of crisis; who would favour a new constitution if everything were going well? Usually, constitutions are compromises hammered out between political actors who may recently have been in conflict and who continue to distrust each other. They are fudges and truces, wrapped in fine words (Weaver and Rockman, 1993). Examples of such negotiated set-

Country profile SOUTH AFRICA

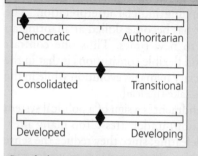

Population: 45m (annual increase 2.3%).
Gross domestic product per head: $4 800.
Unemployment: about 33 per cent.
Racial composition:

Whites 14%
Coloured 8%
Indian 3%
Blacks 75%

Form of government: a democracy with an executive president and entrenched provinces.
Legislature: the National Assembly, the lower house, consists of 350–400 members elected for a five-year term. The president cannot dissolve the assembly. The weaker upper house, the National Council of Provinces, contains 10 delegates from each of the nine provinces.
Executive: a president heads both the state and the government, ruling with a cabinet. The National Assembly elects the president after each general election. The president cannot normally be removed while in office.
Judiciary: the 11-member Constitutional Court decides constitutional matters and can strike down legislation. Power of appointment rests jointly with the president and a special commission. The Supreme Court of Appeal is the highest court of appeal on nonconstitutional matters.
Electoral system: the National Assembly is elected by proportional representation. Provincial legislatures appoint members of the National Council.
Party system: the African National Congress (ANC, 63% of the vote in 1994) was the traditional centre of resistance to apartheid. The National Party (NP, 20%) was the traditional vehicle of white rule. The Inkatha Freedom Party (10%) is the Zulu party.

South Africa's transformation from a militarized state based on apartheid to a more constitutional order based on democracy was one of the most remarkable political transitions of the late twentieth century. The fact that the transition was largely peaceful, defying all predictions of an 'inevitable' bloodbath, was the most astonishing fact of all.

Since white settlers came to South Africa in 1652, the country had been run by whites on the basis of exploiting black labour. After 1945, the system of apartheid (apartness) institutionalized these racial divisions. Apartheid defined the three races of white, coloured and black and outlawed not just marriage but even sex between Europeans and non-Europeans. This unique system of institutional racism was presented as necessary to defend white freedom against the communist threat.

Apartheid's survival into the 1990s showed that governments based on brute power can last a long time. Yet change was inevitable at some point. Externally, the EU and the United States imposed sanctions while the collapse of communism destroyed the regime's bogeyman. Within South Africa, advanced capitalism (in which money is all) proved increasingly incompatible with apartheid (in which race is all). Black opposition to apartheid led by the African National Congress began to encompass armed, and not merely nonviolent, resistance. As so often, modest changes introduced in the 1980s merely stimulated demands for

more and faster reform. In 1990, ANC leader Nelson Mandela was released after 26 years in prison, symbolizing recognition by the white rulers that the time had come to negotiate their own downfall. Four years later, Mandela became President of a government of national unity, including the white-led NP, after the ANC won the first multiracial elections on a turnout of 86 per cent.

In 1996, agreement was reached on the final constitution, to take full effect in 1999. The constitution had taken two years to negotiate, reflecting hard bargaining between the ANC and the NP. The final 109-page document inevitably reflected the interests of the dominant ANC. It included a bill of rights covering education, housing, water, food, security and human dignity – including the right of every child to a name. The NP expressed its general support despite reservations which led to its withdrawal from government.

It remains to be seen how liberal South Africa's democracy will prove to be, given the country's history of conflict, its continuing inequalities, unemployment and lawlessness. Yet South African politics, more than most, should be judged against what preceded it. By that test the achievements of the new South Africa are remarkable indeed.

Further reading: Deegan (1998), Rich (1994), Johnson and Schlemmer (1996).
www.truth.org.za

EXHIBIT 9.2

Rules of prudence for constitution-makers

Drawing on the work of Abbe Sieyes, a propagandist of the French Revolution, McWhinney (1981) suggests the following rules of prudence for constitution-makers:

- Keep the constitution short
- Don't try to solve short-term problems
- Keep the constitution neutral in party political terms
- Leave the drafting to lawyers
- Be modest in ambition if society is divided
- Don't attempt to legislate the impossible
- Don't make the constitution too rigid
- What works elsewhere may not work in your country

- Changing one institution will affect others
- Society can only absorb limited change at once

The interesting point is how often constitution-makers ignore these tips (rule 2 especially). Most constitutions resemble Australia's: vague, contradictory and ambiguous (Lucy 1989, p. 271). This is because drafters are more concerned with a short-term political fix than with establishing a structure which will last forever. In the cut and thrust of constitution-making, McWhinney's tips are easily forgotten.

Further reading: McWhinney (1981).

tlements include blacks and whites working on the 1996 constitution for South Africa, trying to coax a democracy out of the unpromising history of near slavery.

Even the American constitution of 1787 has been described as 'a thing of wrangles and compromises. In its completed state, it was a set of incongruous proposals cobbled together. And furthermore, that is what many of its framers thought' (Finer, 1997, p. 1495). Conceived in crisis and delivered by compromise, the danger is that a constitution will not grant the new rulers the authority needed for effective governance. The American constitution, for instance, divides power to the point where its critics allege that the 'government', and specifically the president, is virtually incapable of governing (Cutler, 1980). Some constitutions do no more than pass the parcel of unresolved political problems to later generations.

A key question about constitutions is: when do they succeed in creating a stable political framework? Essentially, it seems, when they do not attempt too much. The spirit as well as the letter of the constitution is more likely to prosper when the constitution reflects dominant interests and values. The American constitution established a limited central government, 'created' as President John Adams put it, 'out of the grinding necessity of a reluctant nation'. Had it created a more powerful centre, as

some founders wanted, the constitution might well have sunk under opposition from independent-minded states and settlers.

Conversely, the liberal-democratic constitutions which departing colonialists bequeathed in the 1950s to the new states of Africa and Asia failed because they did not take account of social inequalities and nondemocratic cultures. It was naive to suppose that Western constitutions would export to the different conditions in the developing world; many were soon suppressed by authoritarian rulers. Fresh starts became false starts. However, the widespread 'redemocratization' of these states after the cold war reveals a partial, and more soundly-based, return to constitutional government, particularly in Latin America.

The goal of constitution-making is to give new rulers the tools to govern effectively. Yet, and here we come to the essence of the founders' craft, this goal needs to be reached without alienating any of the groups involved in setting up the constitution, including those which fear they are destined for opposition. This is a delicate balancing act. A comparison of the Italian constitution of 1948 with the French settlement of 1958 makes the point. While both constitutions have survived, the Italian one proved to be less successful. The hallmark of the Italian constitution is *garantismo*, meaning that all political forces are guaranteed a stake in the political system. Thus the document establishes a strong bicameral assembly and extensive regional autonomy. These checks on power were intended to prevent the prewar dictatorship from recurring. In practice, *garantismo* contributed to ineffective government and ultimately to the collapse of the 'First Republic' between 1992 and 1994.

By contrast, the constitution of the Fifth French Republic sought to concentrate rather than to check power. This was in reaction to the executive instability which had beset the Fourth Republic. In France, the objectives of a curbed assembly and a strengthened executive were clearly achieved, even through the imaginative solution of a hybrid executive, mixing presidential and parliamentary government, can still cause difficulties. But the French constitution survived because, unlike Italy's, it did encourage effective government.

Judicial review and constitutional courts

Constitutions are no more self-implementing than they are self-made. Some institution must be found to apply the constitution, striking down laws and practices which offend its principles. This review power has fallen to the judiciary. For better or worse, judicial review gives unelected judges a unique position both in and above politics – the judiciary can override the decisions and laws produced by democratic governments. Indeed, India's Supreme Court can even override amendments to the constitution itself. Judicial power, furthermore, is only partly limited by the constitution itself, for interpretation inevitably varies with the temper of the times. As the American Chief Justice Hughes once remarked, 'we live under a constitution. But the constitution is what the judges say it is'. Often the judges cannot agree among themselves on their interpretation of the constitution; only a quarter of judgments reached by the nine justices of the American Supreme Court are unanimous (Hodder-Williams, 1996, p. 20). Basking in their privileged position, constitutional courts express a liberal conception of politics, restricting the power not just of rulers but also of the elections which generate them. Judicial review both stabilizes and limits democracy.

> **Definition**
> Smith (1989) defines **judicial review** as 'the power of ordinary or special courts to give authoritative interpretation of the constitution which is binding on all the parties concerned'. This covers three main areas: ruling on whether specific laws are constitutional, resolving conflict between the state and citizens over basic liberties, and resolving conflicts between different institutions or levels of government.

In reality, judicial power is far from unqualified. For one thing, constitutions themselves do restrict what judges can plausibly say about them. Justices are only 'unfree masters' of the document whose values they defend (Rousseau, 1994, p. 261). More important, the impact of a court's judgments depends on its status among those who carry out its decisions. After all, a court's only power is its words; the purse and the sword are found elsewhere. So courts must consider the broad climate of opinion within which they operate. Thus, as O'Brien (1993 p. 16) concludes of the American Supreme Court,

the Court's influence on American life is at once both anti-democratic and counter-majoritarian. Yet that power, which flows from giving meaning to the constitution, truly rests, in Chief Justice White's words, 'solely upon the approval of a free people'.

Judicial review may limit majority rule but it does this by implementing liberal democracy.

As Smith (1989) notes, the function of judicial review can be allocated to either ordinary or special courts. Australia, Canada, India and the USA are examples of the former approach, with the highest court acting as a court of appeal for the entire judicial system. In the USA, the constitution vests judicial power 'in one Supreme Court, and in such inferior Courts as the Congress may from time to time ordain'. Constitutional issues can be raised at any point in the ordinary judicial system, with the Supreme Court selecting for arbitration those cases which it selects as having broad significance.

Continental Europe (both East and West) favours special constitutional courts, separate from the ordinary judicial system. These courts are a recent but, it seems, a successful innovation. In Western Europe they were adopted after 1945 in, for instance, West Germany, Austria, Greece, Spain and France. To a degree, such courts have become the 'third chamber' of politics. Shapiro and Stone (1994, p. 405) suggest that 'in the context of executive-dominated legislative processes, the impact of constitutional courts may at times overshadow that of parliaments'. With the collapse of communism, constitutional courts have now spread to most post-communist regimes; for example Russia, Hungary and Poland. They are a success story in the mixed history of postcommunist constitutions. The Hungarian Court, for instance, has made significant judgments on such topics as capital punishment, abortion and private property.

> ### Definition
> **Constitutional courts** are special courts, separate from the normal judicial process, which can pronounce broadly on constitutional issues without needing the opportunity provided by a specific case. These courts are more political and less judicial in style than those courts of appeal, such as the American Supreme Court, which head the standard judicial hierarchy.

In Germany, the activist Federal Supreme Court wields remarkable influence. With political power still under a cloud after 1945, the decisions of the Court have impinged on such areas as abortion, university reform and funding political parties. Between 1951 and 1990, the Court judged that 198 federal laws (nearly 5 per cent of the total) contradicted the Basic Law (Keating, 1993, p. 276). In framing new bills, German policy-makers anticipate the likely reaction of the Court, and Kommers (1994) argues that the German Court's influence is fully the equal of America's Supreme Court. Germany and the United States are both legalistic cultures but the German Federal Court has the advantage of operating within a society more accepting of regulation.

In France, the *Conseil Constitutionel* (Constitutional Court) has also become a significant force. Originally intended to help the executive control the legislature, it has now assumed the power to restrain the executive. It asserted its right to invalidate unconstitutional legislation – and did so in about

half the 70 bills on which it passed judgment between 1981 and 1986 (Kesselman, Krieger and Allen, 1987 p. 184).

But it is the American Supreme Court which provides the original example of judicial review. Ironically, the constitution itself does not specify the court's role of adjudicating constitutional disputes. Rather, this function was gradually acquired by the justices themselves, with *Marbury* v. *Madison* (1803) proving decisive. Though its activities take legal form, the Supreme Court's function is broadly political – in a real sense it presides over America's constitutional system. It is responsible for protecting the constitutional rights of individuals; it also reviews the constitutionality of both congressional statutes and executive actions. Its judgments can be far-reaching. For example, a single ruling in 1982 (*Immigration and Naturalization Service* v. *Chadha*) invalidated portions of no fewer than 49 statutes. The Court has also imposed significant checks on the presidency. In 1974, for example, it ruled that President Nixon should surrender tape recordings of confidential discussions about the Watergate affair. This decision effectively sealed the president's fate.

Like most judicial bodies, the Supreme Court favours the doctrine of *stare decisis* (stand by decisions made – that is, stick to precedent). Sometimes, though, the Court does boldly overturn its own legal precedents. This 'inconsistency' has proved to be a source of strength, enabling the court to adapt the constitution to changes in national mood. For example, after its rearguard struggle against the New Deal, the court conceded the right of the national government to regulate the economy.

At times the Court has deliberately changed its mind and sought to lead the nation. The most important of these initiatives, under the leadership of Chief Justice Warren in the 1950s and 1960s, concerned black civil rights. In its major and unanimous decision in *Brown* v. *Topeka* (1954), the Court outlawed racial segregation in schools, dramatically reversing its previous policy that 'separate but equal' facilities for blacks fell within the constitution.

Despite *stare decisis*, the Court has at times seemed to sympathize with Viscount Snowden's critique of precedents:

EXHIBIT 9.3

A quiet revolution: the European Court of Justice

The European Court of Justice was a founding institution of the European Community. Set up in 1952, its purpose is 'to settle conflicts between the states, between the organs of the Community, and between the states and the organs' (Nugent 1994, p.41). It consists of one judge appointed from each member state for a renewable six-year term. In selecting judges, broad experience is more important than judicial expertise, though appointments are less politicized than in the American Supreme Court. Eight advocates-general support the justices by doing much of the detailed work. Since 'justice delayed is justice denied', a Court of First Instance has been added in an effort to speed decisions.

From the 1960s to the 1980s, the Court played a remarkable role in converting the treaty of Rome into a constitution for Europe. It achieved this by advancing three linked doctrines: direct effect, direct applicability and primacy. In 1963, the Court established in Van Gend en Loos the doctrine of *direct effect*. This means that European law applies directly to individuals and that national courts must enforce it. The Court also strengthened the range of EU instruments which are *directly applicable* to member states without any need for corresponding domestic legislation. The Court also established the *primacy* of European over national law, even when the 'offending' national law is embedded in the country's constitution. Like the American Supreme Court in its early decades, the Court's decisions consistently strengthened the authority of central institutions.

Weiler (1994 p. 510) argues that the European Court played a major role in imposing a European regime that resembled the constitutional order of a federal state. He concludes:

> to an extent unprecedented in other international organizations, states have found themselves locked into this regime and unable to enjoy the more common international legal compliance latitude. Interestingly, member state courts, legislatures and governments seemed to accept the constitutional order 'imposed' by the European Court with a large measure of equanimity – a veritable 'quiet revolution.'

In the 1990s, however, several governments (not just Britain's) woke up to the Court's influence and began to question both its procedures and any further expansion of its authority.

Further reading: Dehousse (1998), Weiler (1994).

All human progress has been made by ignoring precedents. If mankind had continued to be the slave of precedent, we should still be living in caves and subsisting on shellfish and wild berries.

The Supreme Court of the 1980s and 1990s is more conservative but can still assert itself.

Judicial activism

With the worldwide movement to more democratic and constitutional government, judges have acquired more political scope. In Pakistan, a country governed by the military for almost half its history, the Supreme Court even charged the Prime Minister with contempt in 1997, precipitating a political crisis. But judicial assertiveness is seen most often in consolidated democracies. For instance, the Australian High Court under Sir Anthony Mason (Chief Justice 1987–95) boldly uncovered 'implied rights' in the constitution which had gone undetected by its timid predecessors. The Dutch Supreme Court has produced important case law on issues where parliament seemed unable to legislate, such as abortion, strikes and euthanasia. The Israeli Supreme Court has considered appeals from Palestinians that in specific instances the military had exceeded its authority in the occupied territories. Throughout the Western world, judicial intervention in public policy has grown, marking the shift from government to governance (Tate and Vallinder, 1995).

What explains the judicialization of politics? The central factor seems to be the declining scope of other political institutions and ideologies, leaving space which the judiciary has been willing to enter and claim as its own. Thus it is the changing nature of politics, rather than developments within the judiciary itself, which are key. For instance, the trust of the Israeli public in political parties has declined though confidence in the judiciary remains high (Edelman, 1995, p. 408). The decay of left-wing ideology has also allowed more judicial scope. Socialists were always suspicious of judges, believing them to be staunch defenders of the status quo and to lack democratic legitimacy. So in Sweden, for instance, the declining strength of social democracy has given more room to a traditionally restrained judiciary (Holmstrom, 1995). In Britain, limiting the royal prerogative, which allowed the state to claim to be above the law, has also given more opportunities to the judges. Throughout the democratic world, interest groups, parties and rights-conscious citizens have become more willing to continue their struggles in the judicial arena. Finally, international conventions have given judges an extra lever they can use to break away from judicial restraint. Documents such as the United Nations Universal Declaration of Human Rights (1948) and the European Convention of Human Rights (1950) have given judges a quasi-judicial foundation on which to construct what would once have been viewed as excessively political statements.

> **Definition**
> **Judicial activism** refers to the willingness of judges to venture beyond narrow legal decisions so as to influence public policy. It is the opposite of **judicial restraint**. This more conservative philosophy maintains that judges should simply apply the law (including the constitution), irrespective of policy implications and the judge's own values. The two terms developed in connection with the American Supreme Court but they have wider applicability in an era of judicial politics.

Of course, judicial activism has proceeded further in some democracies than in others. In comparative rankings of judicial activism, the United States always comes top (Figure 9.1). The USA exhibits all the features which contribute to judicial activism. These include: a written constitution, federalism, judicial independence, no separate administrative

MOST ACTIVE

United States
Canada
Australia
Germany
Italy
Israel
Japan
France
United Kingdom
Sweden

LEAST ACTIVE

Source: Adapted from Holland (1991, p. 2).

Figure 9.1 Levels of judicial activism in selected liberal democracies

courts, easy access to the courts, a common law tradition, high esteem for judges and limited government (Holland, 1991, p. 7). The United States *is* a contract and an army of lawyers will forever quibble over the terms.

Fewer of these conditions are met in Britain, a country which is one of the few democracies to operate without judicial review. There, parliamentary sovereignty clings on and judges have to find other means of bringing politicians to heel. However, even in Britain judicial activism is increasing, largely reflecting European influence, and British judges have proved to be willing accomplices of the European court as it has sought to establish a legal order applicable to all member states. In addition, the national judiciary has grown in confidence as it has witnessed the government losing cases in the European Court (Woodhouse, 1996 p. 439). The emergence of a younger generation of judges, and some public squabbles between the judiciary and Conservative ministers over sentencing policy, also encouraged judges to become less subservient.

Other democracies with a tradition of judicial restraint have also begun to move in an activist direction. Consider Canada and New Zealand. In Canada a Charter of Rights and Freedoms was appended to the constitution in 1982, which gave judges a more prominent role in defending individual rights. In the ten years after the Charter was introduced, the Supreme Court nullified 41 statutes, showing a particular interest in protecting the rights of those accused of crimes (Morton, 1995, p. 58).

New Zealand introduced its Bill of Rights in 1990, protecting 'the life and security of the person' and also establishing traditional democratic and civil rights (for example the right to vote and freedom of belief, association and movement). However, judges in New Zealand are unable to strike down legislation which violates the Bill of Rights. To protect the hallowed sovereignty of parliament, MPs merely receive advice from the Attorney-General on whether legislative proposals are consistent with basic rights (Mulgan, 1997, p. 178). Britain is adopting a similar half-way house in incorporating the European Convention of Human Rights into UK law. The New Zealand approach shows that judicial activism can be accommodated even in countries with the most potent traditions of parliamentary sovereignty.

Judicial independence and recruitment

Liberal democracies accept judicial independence as fundamental to the rule of law. In Britain, as in the American federal judiciary, judges hold office for life during 'good behaviour'. Throughout continental Europe the judiciary is more closely controlled by the state than in Britain or the USA, but judges still remain secure in their tenure. After the war, judges appointed during the fascist era in Italy and Germany proved embarrassingly hard to remove. Of course, an independent judiciary is not necessarily a neutral judiciary. Judges generally see their task as upholding dominant values so as to stabilize society. The narrow recruitment base of the judiciary – heavily male, white and middle-class – reinforces this conservative disposition.

Judicial independence raises the problem of how to choose judges. Box 9.2 shows the four main methods. Which format is preferred depends on the weight given to judicial independence, on the one hand, and responsiveness to public opinion or party balance, on the other. Co-option by other judges is the surest guarantee of independence but democratic election, as practised in some American states,

offers more (even excessive?) responsiveness to popular concerns.

For courts charged with judicial review, selection normally involves a clear political dimension. In the USA, the Supreme Court is so important that appointments to it (nominated by the president but subject to Senate approval) are key decisions. Senate ratification now normally involves a set-piece battle between presidential friends and foes. The judicial experience and legal ability of the nominee may matter less than ideology, partisanship and a clean personal history. In South Africa the President of the Republic appoints senior judges, after consulting a Judicial Services Commission which includes representatives from both the legal profession and the legislature. In European states, members of constitutional courts are usually selected by the assembly, though in Romania and Bulgaria the president also selects some members. Thus political factors influence court appointments, precluding a sharp distinction between the legal and the political.

Once appointed, judges continue to develop their approach. This means the tenor of their decisions cannot always be predicted on appointment. The classic example is Earl Warren: he became Chief Justice of the American Supreme Court in 1953 but dismayed President Eisenhower with his liberal rulings. Eisenhower later described the appointment as 'the biggest damn fool mistake I ever made'. The crucial point here is tenure. While American justices hold office for life, subject to 'good behaviour', the constitutional courts of Europe usually limit their judges to one term of seven to nine years. This reflects the more political environment of an exclusively constitutional court and limits the impact of a single justice.

The judiciary in authoritarian regimes

Judicial independence had no role in communist states. There, the judiciary became an instrument for forcing through a totalitarian reconstruction of society. Under Stalin, Soviet justice showed no procedural impartiality. Vague catchall offences – 'socially dangerous tendencies', 'enemy of the people' – ensnared those suspected of opposition to the regime. During the 1950s and 1960s in China,

BOX 9.2
Methods of selecting judges

Method	Example	Comment
Popular election	Some states in the USA	Produces responsiveness to public opinion but at what price in impartiality and competence? May be accompanied by recall procedures
Election by the assembly	Some states in the USA; some Latin American countries	This method was also formally used for senior judges in communist states but in practice the party picked suitable candidates
Appointment by the executive	Britain, Supreme Court judges in the USA (subject to Senate approval)	'Danger' (?) of political appointments though most judges will be appointed by an earlier administration
Co-option by the judiciary	Italy, Turkey	Produces an independent but sometimes unresponsive judiciary

the police dominated the legal system using the courts as educational devices to warn citizens against bad behaviour. Judges in communist states were selected for their 'party-mindedness' and were expected to put this 'virtue' to good effect in court.

Yet as with many other aspects of communist politics, this situation was already altering before the 1989 revolutions. Even authoritarian regimes can discover the advantage of applying the rules consistently. When one citizen sued another, or even when one enterprise sued another, the interests of the communist party were best served by resolving the issue through law. The courts therefore observed a measure of 'socialist legality'. In China, too, laws became more precise after the hiatus of the Cultural Revolution. Especially after Mao's death, rules were drawn up for investigating crimes and prosecuting suspects. Law could prevail as long as the party was not directly involved.

In noncommunist authoritarian regimes, rulers continue to keep the judiciary on a tight leash, at least on cases with political overtones. In Indonesia, President Suharto is effectively above the law. The Ministry of Justice administers the courts and pays judges' salaries; the justices understand the implications. Many nondemocratic regimes make extensive use of Declarations of Emergency which are exempt from judicial scrutiny. Once introduced, such 'emergencies' drag on for years, even decades. Judicial procedure is often rigged in favour of state prosecutors; a common tactic is to make use of special courts which do the regime's bidding without much pretence of judicial independence. Like many

authoritarian rulers, President Fujimori of Peru finds military courts useful for this purpose. Fujimori is also inclined to sack 'unsatisfactory' judges, a policy taken to extremes by Egypt's President Nasser in 1969. He got rid of 200 in one go: the 'massacre of the judges'.

This general pattern of judicial subordination to authoritarian executives becomes even more marked under military rule. The Argentine Supreme Court, for instance, routinely accepted rulings made by technically illegal military governments. The generals controlled the means of coercion and the judges adjusted their decisions to suit. In Uganda, an extreme case, President Amin had his Chief Justice shot dead. Authoritarianism and the rule of law are incompatible; black robes are poor protection against a drawn sword. Yet the willingness of judges to raise their heads above the parapet is often an early sign of the liberalization which precedes the final collapse of arbitrary power.

Administrative law

Where constitutional law sets out the fundamental principles governing the relationship between citizen and state, the separate field of administrative law covers the rules governing this interaction in detailed settings. As government has grown, so administrative law has expanded. Typical questions asked in administrative law are: was an official empowered to make a particular decision (that is, competence)? Was a decision made in the correct way (for example with adequate consultation)? What should be done if a decision was incorrectly made or had undesirable results (that is, liability)? Such questions arise in all modern states; and liberal democracies seek lawlike answers. While the traditional focus of administrative law is on the actions of central and local government, its scope can also extend, somewhat uneasily, to public corporations and agencies working under contract to government.

Definition

Administrative law sets out the specific principles which govern the making of decisions by public sector bodies, principally the bureaucracy. For instance, the decisions of British civil servants must (a) be within their authority, (b) be made by a fair procedure, and (c) accord with natural justice. Administrative law also sets out the remedies for a breach of such principles.

The flavour of administrative law is conveyed by its content, covering such areas as immigration disputes, planning applications, tax matters, public employment and social security. It is in these concrete areas that the citizen is most likely to experience bureaucratic high-handedness. Such topics have no clear analogy in private or commercial law and therefore need separate treatment.

There are three ways of handling the problem of regulating the administration (Box 9.3). The first, found in continental Europe, is to establish a separate system of administrative courts. France is the most influential example of this *separatist* approach. The *Conseil d'Etat* (Council of State) stands at the apex of an elaborate system of administrative courts. All administrative decisions taken by ministers and their officials are subject to review by the Council. Through its own case law, the Council has developed general principles regulating administrative power. The government consults the Council on all proposed legislation. The prestige of the Council and the publicity given to its rulings enable it to check executive power even in a country with a strong state tradition (Dreyfus, 1990, pp.142–3).

The second solution, favoured in Anglo-American countries with a common law tradition, seeks to deny the distinction between public and private law. The idea here, rarely fulfilled in practice, is that one general system of law should apply to both public

---

BOX 9.3

Methods for judicial regulation of the bureaucracy

Method	Definition	Example
Separatist	Special codes and courts	France
Integrationist	Rely on ordinary law and courts	Anglo-American countries
Supervision	A procurator assesses the legality of administrative acts	Russia

Source: Bell (1991).

---

and private transactions. For instance, employment in the public sector can be regulated by exactly the same laws covering the private sector; no special codes are needed. One strength of this *integrationist* approach is that it avoids boundary disputes between ordinary and administrative courts. This is becoming more of an issue now that the public sector contracts out many tasks to private firms, raising problems for the separatist philosophy. Also, one type of law requires just one court system. Above all, the integrationist philosophy reflects a modest conception of the public sphere. The state abides by the same laws as its citizens.

In reality, special courts are rarely avoided entirely. Even the United States has courts dedicated to tax, military and patent issues. And if there are no special courts, administrative tribunals develop in their stead. These tribunals, dealing for instance with appeals involving employment law or social security regulations, are relatively informal. They are quicker, cheaper and more flexible (though often more secretive) than the courts. In Britain, tribunals rather than courts resolve most administrative cases.

The third approach to formal regulation of the bureaucracy is through *administrative supervision*. Peter the Great introduced this device in Russia in 1722; it is now used throughout Eastern Europe. An officer known as the procurator supervises the legality of administrative acts and can suspend decisions pending judicial or other resolution. Russia revived the role of procurator in 1992. We should distinguish here between the procurator and the ombudsman. The ombudsman is a Western invention whose function is not to make administrative law but to investigate allegations of maladministration in individual cases. The procurator's role is broader, encompassing principles as well as cases.

International law and regimes

International law is often dismissed as irrelevant to the 'real world' of politics. The argument is that without a sovereign power to enforce it, international law is nothing more than moral persuasion. 'Where there is no common power, there is no law', wrote the English philosopher Thomas Hobbes (1588–1679). Yet just as we concluded that intergovernmental organizations can exert some influence on states, so too must we acknowledge the role now played by international law. Its sheer density, both hard and soft, is shown by the 10 000 or so agreements registered at the United Nations. These cover such areas as international trade, the environment and human rights. In general, states obey this intricate cobweb of rules. As Henkin (1968, p. 47) writes, 'almost all nations observe almost all international law and almost all of their obligations almost all of the time'. Indeed international law probably achieves greater compliance than does national (or, as international lawyers call it, 'municipal') law. So the lack of Hobbes's sovereign has not prevented the emergence of a law-governed international society (Bull, 1977).

> **Definition**
> **International law** is the system of rules which states and other actors regard as binding in their mutual relations. It derives from treaties, custom, accepted principles and the views of legal authorities. The term 'international law' was coined by the English philosopher Jeremy Bentham (1748–1832) in 1780.

For four reasons, international law must receive attention from students of comparative politics:

- It helped to define the division of the world into the states which form our subject: states were the only, and remain the major, units of international law. Through international law, states reinforced their dominant position in the modern world, and it is through participation in an international

legal community that 'statehood' is formally acquired.

- International law forms part of national law, often without any special mechanism of incorporation. Many constitutions are explicit on this point. The German constitution (1949) states that

> the general rules of public international law are an integral part of federal law. They shall take precedence over the laws and shall create rights and duties for the inhabitants of the federal territory.

South Africa's new constitution (1999) also requires judges to favour interpretations of domestic law which are consistent with international law. Even where judges are not obliged to apply international law, they are increasingly disposed to do so. For instance, the decision by the Australian High Court in the Mabo case (1992) to recognize a native title to land drew on the 1975 Western Sahara ruling by the International Court of Justice (Scott, 1997).

- International laws can apply directly to individuals. The famous illustration here is the Nuremberg War Crimes Tribunal in 1946. The tribunal declined to accept the defence that 'I was just obeying the orders of the state'. The laws of the European Union also apply directly not just to the governments but also to the citizens of member countries.
- International agreements constrain national policy-makers. These accords set out objectives (for example reducing carbon dioxide emissions) which national governments must – or at least should – put into effect. Interest groups can use these accords as a stick with which to beat backsliding governments. When states fail to abide by conventions they themselves have signed, for example in the area of human rights, individuals can in principle seek remedy through the courts, both national and international.

An example from Australia illustrates this last point and also draws out some broader domestic implications of international law. When Australia ratified a protocol to the International Covenant on Civil and Political Rights in 1991, Nick Toonen, a gay rights activist, lodged a complaint against Tasmania's prohibition of sexual behaviour between males. Tasmania remained resolute but the federal government in Canberra passed a liberalizing law, overriding provincial legislation. This shows how international agreements can impinge not just on the relationship between governors and governed, but also on the balance between different levels of government. Indeed, critics allege that Australia's federal government could in theory use its expanding treaty commitments to interfere in virtually any area of activity which, under the national constitution, is supposedly reserved to the states (Scott, 1997).

Where does international law come from? Traditionally, the four sources were:

- Treaties
- Custom
- General principles accepted by civilized nations
- Legal authorities.

The statutes of the International Court of Justice (ICJ) from which this classification derives require the justices to apply these sources when reaching decisions. However, the ICJ was set up in 1946 and today's world requires a broader interpretation of international law. For instance, declarations (but not resolutions) of the UN usually receive legal status. Bodies which codify law, such as the International Law Commission (1947), also help to develop it. More generally, 'soft law' consists of standards and objectives agreed at international level. Such norms may not fit the traditional categories of law but they do guide how states behave.

The developing picture, then, reveals international law merging with the general politics of interdependence. Political scientists employ the term 'international regime' to capture this trend towards intergovernmental policy-making in particular sectors. A regime is a broader idea than an institution; and its fruits include but go beyond law. The regime's collaborative activities may be focused on an institution such as the International Civil Aviation Organization or the International Maritime Organization; however, the essence of an international regime lies in shared norms and mutual expectations, not in a formal organization. Clear examples of such regimes include international trade, finance, air transport, whale conservation and nuclear energy.

Definition
International regimes consist of 'governing arrangements constructed by states to coordinate their expectations and organize aspects of international behaviour in various issue areas' (Kratochwil and Ruggie, 1994, p. 7). This means that in specific areas – such as international trade – specialists from various states and nonstate bodies collaborate on treaties, conventions and declarations.

In an international regime, specialists acting with the authority of (but operating at one remove from) their home government seek to establish standards and policies regulating their particular issue area. Debate within the web of conferences which gives tangible expression to the idea of a 'regime' is a technical affair involving participants from a range of organizations who develop relationships of trust and reciprocity. Crucially, the policy-makers in a regime enjoy substantial autonomy from their political masters. As long as negotiators do not cause trouble back home, they will acquire considerable latitude. Thus, in international regimes, the policy-makers form their own club whose members know, or believe they know, what needs to be done. Subject to the overriding political priorities of their governments, members seek progress toward their shared goals. Often governments are pleased to do their bit, and to be seen doing it, especially when the cost is low. After all, collegiality helps to build up credits in the international community, allowing rulers to feel more secure in their sovereignty precisely because they are accepted as full participants in international regimes.

Key reading

Next step: *the special issue of* Political Studies *(1996) is an excellent survey of constitutionalism.*

Rosenfeld (1994) is an alternative source on constitutionalism; Greenberg *et al.* (1993) examine the links with democratic transitions. Duchacek (1973) and Bogdanor (1988) remain useful sources on constitutions generally. Maddex (1997) is a compilation of 80 constitutions. Howard (1993) covers constitution-making in Eastern Europe. On the judiciary, Holland (1991) and Tate and Vallinder (1995) are cross-national studies.

Hodder-Williams (1996) is a useful comparative essay, focused on the USA and the UK. O'Brien (1993) and Shapiro (1990) concentrate on the American Supreme Court. On international law, Bull (1977, Ch.6) is a good starting point. Kratochwil and Mansfield (1994) provide a selection of readings on international organization. Useful web sites include Human Rights Watch (www.hrw.org) and, for primary documents including constitutions, wiretap.spies.com.

Federal, unitary and local government

The word 'territory' means the area ruled by states. So governing always has a territorial dimension. Rulers need to extract resources from their territory while also retaining the willingness of the population to remain within the orbit of the state.

To achieve these ends, the modern state consists of a remarkably intricate web of organizations including (1) the central government, (2) its field offices in cities, towns and villages, and (3) subnational governments such as elected regional and local authorities. These bodies engage in a continuous effort to extract resources from, provide services to, and maintain the support of the population they both serve and control. But this web has been changing shape since the 1980s, with new or revived subnational governments gaining ground as the national authority finds itself increasingly strapped for cash. This renaissance of regional and provincial governments gives added point to studying the distribution of power across the state's domain. We begin this chapter by examining the two solutions to the territorial organization of power – federal and unitary government. We then consider local government, arguably the level at which the buck really does stop, and assess its changing style of operation.

Federalism

In a federation such as the United States, legal sovereignty is shared between the federal government and the constituent states. A federal constitution creates two layers of government, with specific functions allocated to each. The centre takes charge of external relations – defence, foreign affairs and immigration – and some common domestic functions such as the currency. The functions of the states vary from one federation to another but typically include education and law enforcement. Residual powers may also lie with the states, not the centre. Significantly the existence and functions of the states are entrenched; they can only be modified by amending the constitution. It is this protected position of the states which distinguishes federations from unitary governments. In a unitary system, sovereignty resides solely with the centre and lower levels exist at its pleasure. Further, in nearly all federations the states have a guaranteed voice in national policy-making through an upper chamber of the assembly, in which each state normally receives equal representation.

Definition

Federalism is the principle of sharing sovereignty between central and provincial (or state) governments; a **federation** is any political system which puts this idea into practice. A **confederation** is a weaker link between the component parts. In a confederation, the central authority has little power and unanimity may be a condition of collective action.

Federalism is a common solution to the problem of arranging the territorial distribution of power (Elazar, 1996, p. 426) counts 22 federations in existence today. These contain some two billion people or 40 per cent of the world's population. Federalism is particularly common in large countries, whether size is measured by area or population. Four of the world's largest states by area are federal: Australia, Brazil, Canada and the United States. Of the 25

BOX 10.1
Federalism: who gets to do what?

Allocation of functions	Definition	Example
Exclusive jurisdiction	Functions allocated entirely to one level of government	Canadian provinces have exclusive jurisdiction over education
Concurrent jurisdiction	Functions shared between levels of government	In Canada, both the national and provincial governments can pass laws dealing with agriculture
Residual powers	The level of government which, by default, controls functions not specifically mentioned in the constitution	The 10th amendment to the United States constitution states, 'the powers not delegated to the United States by the constitution, nor prohibited by it to the States, are reserved to the states respectively, or to the people'.

provinces in India's federation, ten contain more than 40 million people. As a form of geographical pluralism, federalism is attracting attention from countries seeking to maintain the unity of the state in multiethnic and multinational societies (Smith, 1995). Federalism seems to promise the economic and military advantages of size while maintaining, even encouraging, more local identities. Federalism, its advocates claim, permits diversity within unity and is thus an important model for a world of strong national and ethnic identities.

Federations should be distinguished from confederations. In the latter, the central authority remains the junior partner and is dominated by the component states. Confederal relationships may appeal where culturally-diverse members seek the benefits of scale (for example a larger market) without closer union. The classic instance of a confederation is the short-lived system adopted in 1781 in what is now the United States. The weak centre, embodied in the Continental Congress, could neither tax nor regulate commerce. It also lacked direct authority over the people. It was the weakness of the Articles of Confederation that led to the drafting of a federal constitution, and to the creation of the United States proper, in 1787.

A more recent example of a toothless confederation is the Commonwealth of Independent States (CIS), set up in 1991 by former republics of the Soviet Union. Azerbaijan's president dismissed the CIS as 'a mere soap bubble – pretty on the surface but empty inside' (Kux, 1996). At least at this early stage, the member states of the CIS are too preoccu-pied with internal problems to be capable of creating a true federation.

The origins of federalism

Federalism is a complex, legalistic and always conscious creation; usually it emerges from a voluntary compact between previously autonomous states. This was the case in the United States when the representatives of 13 states met in Philadelphia in 1787 to create the world's first and most influential federation. Similar conventions, influenced by the American experience, took place in Switzerland in 1848, Canada in 1867 and Australia in 1897/98 (Table 10.1). But elsewhere, in Latin America and some British colonies, federalism was imposed from without rather than created from within. Imposed federations have little prospect of creating a stable devolution of power from the centre. Many of the federations cobbled together by Britain as it shed colonial responsibilities soon fell apart: for instance, the short-lived East African Federation comprising Kenya, Tanzania and Uganda. In India, however, federalism has provided a means for holding together a large and diverse country.

The emergence of federations raises an obvious question. Why should autonomous governments ever agree to cede some sovereignty to a new federal authority? After all, power like money is difficult to acquire and for that reason is rarely given away. The answer is that a federation represents a decision to invest rather than renounce power. Federalism is a

EXHIBIT 10.1

The European Union: federation or confederation?

Distinguishing federations from confederations can be difficult. Consider the European Union (EU) where a case can certainly be made for regarding it as a true federation. Its well-developed institutions include a powerful Commission, an influential Court and a parliament which is directly elected by the citizens of member states. EU decisions must be implemented by member states; and these decisions apply directly to citizens. There is no provision for member states to withdraw from the Union.

So the EU has certainly involved some pooling of sovereignty by its members, yet it also lacks the insti-

tutional architecture of an orthodox federal state. As Scharpf (1996) argues, a fully federal Europe would require the Commission (as the executive) to become accountable to the parliament. It would also need the Council of Ministers (representing the member states) to become a second chamber, like the American Senate. But there are few signs of such developments. The EU continues to involve a strong element of intergovernmental decision-making. It is a unique hybrid, far more than a free trade area but still less than a true federation. This ambiguous status seems set to continue in the new century.

gamble: some autonomy is given up in the expectation of greater benefits to come. Specifically, Riker (1975, 1996) argues that federations emerge when there is an external threat. The American states, for instance, joined together in 1789 partly because they felt themselves to be vulnerable in a predatory world. When large beasts lurk in the jungle, smaller creatures gather for safety. The American statesman Benjamin Franklin (1706–90) put this point well when he said, 'we must all hang together or most assuredly we shall all hang separately'. Alternatively, the partners may believe that a federation will itself be able to behave aggressively in the international arena. In Canada, for example, the framers wanted to expand their political and economic influence to

the northwest in response to American expansion up the Pacific coast. With the end of the cold war, and a decline in the frequency of wars between countries if not within them, this military motive for forming federations is currently rather weak.

Riker may be taking too narrow a view of the motives for forming federations. Sometimes, the reasoning has been economic rather than military; for example Australian and American federalists felt that a common market would promote economic expansion. Although the federal status of the European Union is open to question, its development also owed much to the desire for a large internal market. Indeed, the Union was originally called the European Economic Community or, in popular

Table 10.1 Some federations in consolidated democracies

	Year established as a federation	Area (sq km, thousands)	Population (million, 1995)	Number of states
United States*	1776	9373	266.0	50
Canada*	1867	9976	28.1	10
Switzerland	1874	41	7.2	26
Australia	1901	7687	18.1	6
Germany*	1949	357	82.0	16
India	1950	3288	943.0	25
Belgium	1983	30	10.1	3

* For profiles of these countries, see p. 111 (USA), p. 171 (Canada) and p. 66 (Germany).

Country profile CANADA

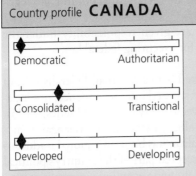

Democratic — **Authoritarian**

Consolidated — **Transitional**

Developed — **Developing**

Population: 28m.

Gross domestic product per head: $24 400.

Main groups: British origin 40%, French origin 27%, other European 20%, indigenous 1.5%, other 11.5%.

Form of government: a federal parlia-mentary democracy, with 10 provinces. Most Canadians live in Ontario or Quebec.

Legislature: the 301-seat House of Commons is the lower chamber. Most unusually for a federation, the 104 members of the Senate, the upper chamber, are appointed by the Prime Minister, not selected by the provinces.

Executive: the Prime Minister leads a Cabinet, selecting ministers with due regard for provincial representation. A Governor General serves as cere-monial figurehead.

Judiciary: Canada employs a dual (federal and provincial) court system, headed by a restrained Supreme Court. In 1982 the country intro-duced the Canadian Charter of Rights and Freedoms.

Electoral system: a plurality system with single member districts. This produces massive swings and distor-tions in representation in the Commons.

Party system: the party system is strongly regional, with the governing Liberals dominating the key province of Ontario. The main opposition parties are now the Western-based Reform Party and the Bloc Quebecois. Almost wiped out in 1993, the Conservatives recovered to win 21 seats in 1997, mostly in the Atlantic Provinces (p. 104).

Canada is a large country with a relatively small pop-ulation. Its landmass is the second largest in the world but its population is little more than a tenth of its powerful American neighbour. Most Canadians live in urban settlements in a 100-mile strip border-ing the United States. Canada's economy depends heavily on the USA, a relationship reinforced by the formation of the North American Free Trade Association in 1994.

Reflecting British influence, Canada's constitution, originally set out in the British North America Act of 1867, established parliamentary government in a centralised federation. Since 1867, 'Canada has moved from the highly centralized political situation of 1867 to one of the most decentralized federal systems in the world' (Landes 1995, p. 101). This reflects the central issue of Canadian politics: the place within it of French-speaking Quebec. The origins of this division go back to the founding of the country. From the sixteenth century, France and then Britain colonized the territories of Canada, then inhabited by around ten million indigenous people. Britain finally defeated the French in 1759.

For many Francophones, Canada consists of two founding peoples – the British and French – whose status should be equal. This is taken to imply that Quebec should be more than just one among the 10 provinces of the federation. Since the 1960s a revived nationalist party in Quebec has sought to implement this vision. However the federal response has been to decentralize power to all 10 provinces, not just Quebec. This is an understandable response – the danger of 'asymmetric federalism' in which one province receives special treatment is that it just breeds resentment in the rest of the country. This explains the defeat of the Lake Meech Accord of 1987 which proposed constitutional recognition of Quebec's special status. The Accord fell because two provinces refused to endorse it.

In Quebec itself, the Parti Quebecois, elected to power in 1994, held a provincial referendum in 1995 on 'sovereignty association' for Quebec. This would have combined political sovereignty for Quebec with continued economic association with Canada. The proposal lost but by the narrowest of margins. For now, the issue of constitutional reform is exhausted as Quebec belatedly turns its attention to improving its economy.

Yet as Williams (1995, p. 69) writes,

despite all Canada's domestic turmoil, it is endowed with a responsive federal system. Over time this has created a good safe place to raise a family and earn a crust, the ultimate test of a state's obligations to its citizens'.

Further reading: Watts (1996), Williams (1995). info.ic.gc.ca/opengov/commons/

parlance, 'the common market'. However, just as there are currently few military reasons for forming new federations, so the economic case has also faded. States are increasingly finding that the advantages of scale can be obtained by creating a free trade area without sacrificing political sovereignty. For example, the East African Federation has now reformed as the Commission for East African Cooperation, aiming to create a single market for its 75 million people.

Federations are useful for bridging ethnic diversity, and a federation is a way of incorporating such differences within a wider political community. People who differ by descent, language and culture can nevertheless seek the advantages of common membership in a federation (Forsyth, 1989, p. 4). For example, federalism in Switzerland integrates 23 cantons, two and a half languages (German and French, plus Italian), and two religions (Catholic and Protestant). Belgium is another instance of ethnic federalism. Its rebirth in 1983 as a federal state reflected a desire to give more self-government to French- and Dutch-speaking cultures in a linguistically-divided country.

European federalism, as found in Austria, Germany and Switzerland, has different origins from the American form. Federalism in the USA is based on a contract in which the states came together to create a central government with limited functions. By contrast, European federalism (particularly in Germany) rests on the idea of cooperation between levels of government. Such solidarity expresses a shared commitment to a united society; federalism displays organic links which bind the participants together. The moral norm is solidarity and the operating principle is 'subsidiarity'. The idea here is that decisions should be taken at the lowest level possible but with the central government offering overall leadership.

In Germany, all the Länder (states) are expected to contribute to the success of the whole; in exchange, they are treated with respect by the centre. Three procedures encourage this 'collaborative federalism':

- Both the federal government and the Länder can legislate in several areas of concurrent power (for example, transport and public ownership).
- The centre passes 'framework laws', outlining policies which are then fleshed out in Land legislation.
- The Länder are given responsibility under the constitution for executing federal law.

Unlike the United States, German federalism from its inception has stressed interdependence, not independence, between the two levels (Hoetjes, 1993). Imposed by the allies in 1949 as a barrier against dictatorship, federalism has built on regional traditions to become an accepted part of the country's political order. However, growing economic inequalities have led the richer Länder, notably Bavaria, to complain about the use of equalization grants to help poorer provinces like Saarland.

While federalism is usually a compact between separate units recognizing a common interest, it is also possible for a unitary state to restructure as a federation. This is still a rare occurrence and Belgium is the main example (Fitzmaurice, 1996). First established in 1830, Belgium has been beset by divisions between French- and Dutch-speaking regions. Constitutional revisions in 1970 and 1980 devolved more power to these groups and in 1983 Belgium finally proclaimed itself a federation. Other democracies have decentralized power to lower levels while stopping short of the reallocation of sovereignty required to create a federation. For example, Spain after Franco and South Africa after apartheid both introduced strong regions but without formally embracing the federal formula. In Britain, setting up parliaments in Scotland and Wales will move a multinational but historically centralized state in a similar direction.

So federalism can be achieved either by giving powers to a new central authority or by transferring them from an existing national government. Indeed the two processes can occur together. While Belgium was devolving power *downwards* to French-speaking Wallonia and Dutch-speaking Flanders, its national government also remained a firm supporter of shifting functions *upwards* to the European Union. This double leakage of power away from the national level raises the question of whether national governments in federal countries such as Belgium now have any good reason for existing at all.

Federal–state relations

The relations between federal and state governments are the crux of federalism and two points are crucial. First, a federal framework creates an inherent conflict between the two levels and indeed between the states themselves. Struggle inheres in a federation, reinforced by the inevitable uncertainties of the constitution. Second, intergovernmental relations, like all good partnerships, evolve over time. Despite the fixed constitutional framework, in practice federations show surprising flexibility and even dynamism.

Most federal systems have witnessed growing interdependence between the two tiers. The United States illustrates this trend. The Founding Fathers favoured dual federalism, in which each level was separate and autonomous in its sphere. Perhaps always a myth, dual federalism has long since disappeared, overwhelmed by the demands of an integrated economy and society. It has been replaced by a system of intergovernmental relations in which federal, state (and local) governments work together. In such areas as education, transport and the environment, policy is made, funded and applied at all levels of government. In Canada, this mingling is called 'executive federalism'.

> **Definition**
> **Dual federalism** means that the national and state governments in a federation retain separate and independent spheres of action. In reality, the main feature of contemporary federations is not the separation of functions but rather the extent of interdependence betwen levels. The phrase **intergovernmental relations** (IGR) refers to these complex political, administrative and financial interactions between levels of government. IGR is most elaborated in federations but is also found in notionally unitary states.

In most federations, the central government tended to gain influence until the final decades of the twentieth century. Partly, this reflected the centre's financial muscle. The flow of money became more favourable to the centre as income tax revenues grew with the expansion of the workforce and a rise in living standards (income is invariably taxed mainly at national level because otherwise there would be too many opportunities for people and corporations to move to low-tax states). By contrast, the states must depend for their independent revenue on sales and property taxes and these sources have grown more slowly than income tax.

This shift in financial strength is seen in Australia, where about 60 per cent of the states' total revenue now comes from the federal government. Until President Reagan introduced sharp cuts in the early 1980s, the American states had depended on revenue transfers from the federal government for around a quarter of their outlays. Even this relatively small proportion gave Washington significant financial leverage which it exploited to the full.

> **Definition**
> **Fiscal federalism** refers to the financial flows between central and provincial governments. The central government grew in financial power through most of the twentieth century. However in several federations the low-tax environment of the 1990s forced the national government to reduce its support to the states.

The enhanced authority of the centre in federal systems has been more than a financial matter. More than anything, it reflects the emergence of a national economy demanding overall planning and regulation. To take just one example, a modern economy requires an effective transport system but individual states have little incentive to pay for road networks which will benefit other states as well as their own. So the central government must plan and fund, if not build and operate, the national road system. Wars and economic crises have also strengthened the central authority; additional powers, once acquired, tend to be retained.

By the end of the 1980s, however, budget deficits at national level forced central governments to become less generous in their support of the provinces. As an American Treasury Secretary said, revenue-sharing ended 'because there was no revenue left to share'. The fiscal resurgence of the American states, based on growing revenues from sales taxes and the requirement of many state constitutions for administrations to run balanced budgets, enabled them to rediscover some autonomy. State policies became more creative and innovative, extending to important social issues such

BOX 10.2

Financial transfers from the federal government to states

Form of transfer	Definition
Categorical grants	For specific projects (e.g. a new hospital)
Block grants	For particular programmes (e.g. for medical care)
Revenue-sharing	General funding which places few limits on the recipient's use of funds
Equalization grants	Used in some federations in an effort to equalize financial conditions among the states. Can create resentment in the wealthier states.

as welfare reform and education. Walker (1991, p. 130) referred to 'the renaissance of the states' as they again became 'laboratories of democracy'. This caused some irritation at the centre, as when Massachusetts launched a boycott in 1996 of firms trading with military-led Burma. Critics felt the state's action had compromised both America's internal market and Washington's control of foreign policy.

Constitutional courts have generally acceded to central initiatives, particularly when justified on grounds of national emergency. In the rulings of the US Supreme Court, federal law prevailed over state law during most of the twentieth century. For instance, the Court declared in *Garcia* v. *San Antonio Metropolitan Transit Authority* (1984) that the federal government could require local authorities to set minimum wage levels. In this case, the Court ruled that restrictions on federal intervention were a matter for the political rather than the judicial process. In Australia, decisions of the High Court have favoured the centre to the point where some commentators regard federalism as sustained more by political tradition than by judicial command. Of the major Western federations, only Canada has seen a long-term drift away from the centre. However, by the 1990s there were signs that courts in a number of federal systems were seeking to restore at least some autonomy to the states. In the USA a more conservative Supreme Court has favoured lower tiers of government, contributing to the renaissance of the states.

So the crucial feature of most contemporary federations (as indeed of unitary states too) is interdependence rather than independence. Domestic policies, at least, involve a complex patchwork of government agencies: central, provincial and local. The centre has broad goals but, in contrast to unitary states, it is unable to dictate to subnational governments. Indeed states can sometimes organize themselves into an effective pressure-group. They can then press for more resources from the centre, as with the Governors' Conference in the United States. Other political actors, particularly parties and interest groups, can also provide a measure of integration between levels of government. All this is a long way from the Founding Fathers' desire for separate layers of government, each supreme and independent within its own sphere.

Assessing federalism

What assessment can we give of the federal experiment? At a minimum, federalism is clearly a viable form of government. It has lasted in the United States for over 200 years and has also provided a measure of unity in linguistically-divided Switzerland. But federalism has more to be said for it than mere longevity. It is a natural arrangement for large states such as the United States, India and even perhaps Australia. It provides for checks and balances on a territorial basis, keeps some government functions closer to the people, and allows for the representation of difference (for example ethnic diversity). The existence of several states produces healthy competition and opportunities for experiment. Citizens and firms also have the luxury of choice: if they dislike governance in one state, they can always move to another. Finally, federations can secure the political, military and economic bonus which accrues to big countries.

But federalism also has weaknesses (Box 10.3); it may be a viable system but it can also be ineffective and inefficient. It is inherently complex. Decisions are slow to emerge, requiring a consensus between central and provincial levels. After a gunman ran amok in Tasmania in 1996, killing 35 people, Australia experienced some political problems before it tightened gun control uniformly across the country. By contrast, unitary Britain acted quickly when a comparable incident occurred at Dunblane

BOX 10.3
Federalism: strengths and corresponding weaknesses

Strength	Weakness
Encourages competition and innovation between states	... but citizens are treated differently in different states
Entrenches the power of the states	... but this can be used to exploit minority groups within the states
Entrenches the status of states	... but nonterritorial groups are not given this protection
Can contain conflict between groups	... but can entrench and thus strengthen these same conflicts
Encourages government by consent	... but can delay necessary change

primary school in Scotland. Further, federalism complicates accountability, with opportunities for politicians to pass the buck to the other level. Critics also allege that federalism, in Germany for instance, has become geographical corporatism – that is, it enables the Länder to hold the central authority hostage, producing what the Germans call *reformstau*, meaning reform blockage.

Overall, the difficulty with federalism is that it distributes power by territory when the key conflicts in society are social rather than geographical. Australia is typical in this respect:

> Australia is culturally and regionally heterogeneous, but these social divisions are not essentially represented by current state boundaries. Differences between the states do not equate with the fundamental cleavages in Australian society. (Wilcox, 1989, p. 152)

Despite their claim to represent social diversity, federal states do not formally incorporate 'minority' groups such as women and indigenous peoples into the federal framework. In the United States, the racial cleavage is not represented by dividing the country into 50 predominantly white states; indeed the white-dominated South was for a long time the main beneficiary of federalism. Where social and territorial divisions largely coincide – as in the

Canadian conflicts between French- and English-speakers, and between the Eastern and Western provinces – a federal arrangement is more justifiable.

Federalism holds out the tempting prospect of reconciling difference in a larger unity. Yet as civil war in Yugoslavia confirmed, federalism has no formula for conjuring harmony out of ethnic conflict (Forsyth, 1989, p. 5). It is a nice question whether federalism has contributed to divisions within states more than it has contained them.

As with other political institutions, evaluations of federalism depend on taking a view of the proper balance between the concentration and diffusion of political power. Should power rest with one body to allow decisive action? If so, federalism is likely to be seen as an obstacle and impediment – as an anti-majoritarian and therefore an anti-democratic device. Or should power be dispersed among a range of actors so as to reduce the danger of tyranny, including majority dictatorship? If so, federalism will be viewed as an indispensable technique for protecting the liberty of the people.

Unitary government

Most contemporary states are unitary, which means that sovereignty lies exclusively with the central government. Subnational authorities, whether regional or local, may make policy as well as implement it but they do so by permission of the centre. In theory, the national government could abolish lower levels if it wished. Unitary states emerge naturally in societies with a history of rule by sovereign emperors and monarchs, such as Britain, France and Japan. Unitary structures are also the norm in smaller countries, particularly those without strong ethnic divisions, for example Scandinavia. In Latin America, with its focus on centralized presidential rule, nearly all the smaller countries are unitary.

But the location of sovereignty is rarely an adequate guide to political realities and unitary government is not necessarily centralized in its operation. Indeed in the 1990s many unitary states attempted to push responsibility for more functions (including fund-raising) onto lower levels. In practice, unitary states, just like federations, involve constant bargaining between levels of government. In Europe, these multi-level games extend beyond

---

BOX 10.4

Methods for distributing power away from the centre

Method	Definition	Illustration
Deconcentration	Central government functions are executed by staff 'in the field'	Almost 90 per cent of US federal civilian employees work away from Washington, D.C.
Decentralization	Central government functions are executed by subnational authorities	Local governments administer national welfare programmes in Scandinavia
Devolution	Central government grants some decision-making autonomy to new lower levels	Regional governments in France, Italy and Spain

Note: Deconcentration and decentralization can be found in federal as well as unitary states.

---

the state to include the European Union.

Developments in democratic Spain test the boundary line separating federal and unitary states. Spanish regions were created rapidly in the transition to democracy following General Franco's death in 1975. Seeking to integrate a centralist tradition with strong regional identities, Spain's constitution-makers created a system in which the country's 'autonomous communities' (that is, regions) could decide their own level of autonomy. The 'historic communities' of the Basque Country and Catalonia, quickly followed by Galicia, were the first to receive their 'Statutes of Autonomy'. Spain's compromise delivered quasi-federalism within the frame of a unitary state. This was a messy but politically effective solution for a country which has always needed to reconcile a strong centre with assertive regions.

As far as formal relationships are concerned, we can distinguish three broad ways in which unitary states can disperse power from the centre (Box 10.4). The first, and least significant, is *deconcentration*. This is purely a matter of administrative organization; it refers to the (re)location of central government employees away from the capital. The case for a deconcentrated structure is that it spreads the work around, enables field offices to benefit from local knowledge and frees central departments to focus on policy-making. The second, and politically more significant way of dispersing power is through *decentralization*. This means delegating policy execution to independent bodies, traditionally local authorities but also (and increasingly) a range of other agencies. In Scandinavia, for instance, local governments have put into effect many welfare programmes designed at national level. The third and

most radical form of power dispersal is *devolution*. This occurs when the centre grants decision-making autonomy (including some legislative powers) to lower levels. In the United Kingdom, for instance, Northern Ireland possessed a devolved assembly until the British government abolished it in 1972. Similar bodies are now being set up for Scotland and Wales and any settlement of the Northern Ireland problem will surely involve reestablishing a devolved assembly there. In theory, Britain will probably remain a unitary state because control over the constitution will continue to be exercized from Westminister. In practice, the newly-devolved British state may be no more centralized than some federations.

In practice, there is a balance of political resources between central and subnational governments in unitary states. The relationship is usually one of interdependence rather than dominance. Indeed financial pressures at national level in the 1980s and 1990s encouraged local authorities to fund a somewhat higher share of their total spending. Thus the balance of power between levels of government cannot be simply read off from a country's unitary or federal character. Understanding this balance requires a closer examination of intergovernmental relations within unitary states.

Central–local relations in a unitary state tend to one of two models: dual or fused. Under a *dual* system, local governments retain freestanding status, setting their own internal organization and employing staff on their own conditions of service. Staff tend to move horizontally – from one local authority to another – rather than vertically, between central and local government. Ultimate authority

---

BOX 10.5
The balance of power between central and local government

The resources of local government typically include:

- control over policy implementation
- responsibility for directly providing public services such as health, education and welfare
- some revenue-raising power
- a local electoral mandate.

Against this must be set the resources of the centre:

- control over legislation, including (in unitary states) the right to abolish or modify local government
- provision of much local authority finance
- setting administrative standards for service provision
- popular expectations that the national government should solve problems
- greater legitimacy from higher turnout at elections.

---

rests with the centre but local government employees do not regard themselves as working for the same employer as civil servants based at the centre. Traditionally, Britain was regarded as an example of a dual system, though centralization in the 1980s and early 1990s reduced its distinctiveness.

Under a *fused* system, by contrast, central and local authority are joined in an office such as the prefect. This is a central appointee who oversees the administration of a particular community and the prefect normally reports to the Ministry of the Interior. In theory, a prefectoral system signals central dominance by establishing a clear unitary hierarchy running from national government through the prefect to the local authorities. France is the classic example of this fused approach. Established by Napoleon early in the nineteenth century, the system consists of 96 departments, each with its own prefect and elected assembly. The framework is uniform and rational but in practice the prefect must cooperate with local councils rather than simply oversee them. The prefect is now as much an agent of the department as of the centre, representing views upwards as well as transmitting orders downwards. Although the powers of the prefect have declined, the French model remains influential. Many other countries have adopted it, including all France's ex-colonies and several postcommunist states.

A final factor affecting the central/local balance in unitary states is the extent to which local politicians participate directly in national politics. France is again an interesting case. There, national politicians often become or remain mayor of their local town, helping the locality to defend its interests at national level. This technique also provides a way of side-stepping unhelpful prefects. In other countries, it is less common for politicians to simultaneously straddle the two worlds though local government may still be a launching pad for a national political career.

Definition
A **dual** system of local government (as in Britain) maintains a formal separation of central and local government. Although the centre is sovereign, local authorities are not seen as part of a single state structure. In a **fused** system, characteristic of strong states such as France, a centrally-appointed prefect supervises local authorities. The localities, although possessing considerable autonomy in practice, form part of a uniform system of administration applying across the country.

Nearly all unitary states have developed at least one level of government (often called counties in Northern Europe) which stands between central and local authorities. France, Italy and Spain have introduced elected regional governments. The smaller Scandinavian countries took a different route, strengthening and refurbishing their traditional counties (Sharpe, 1993, p. 1). Even a small country like New Zealand has developed 12 elected regional councils. A standard pattern now is to have three levels of subnational government – regional, provincial and local – as in France and Italy (Table 10.2). Regional and provincial levels are 'intermediate' governments which form the 'expanded middle' of modern states. The result is a multi-tier system which reduces the contrast between unitary and federal arrangements. Whatever the formal structure, constant negotiation between levels of government has become a permanent feature of territorial governance in every developed state.

What caused this renaissance of regional governments? The answer was a mix of cultural, economic and political factors (Sharpe, 1993). The cultural factor was regional ethnic nationalism, as with the

Table 10.2 Subnational government in some unitary states

	France	Italy	Japan	Norway
Regional level	22 regions	20 regions	–	–
Provincial level	96 departments	94 provinces	47 prefectures	19 counties
Local level	36 433 communes	8 074 communes	3 200 municipalities	448 municipalities

Note: figures are from about 1987.

Sources: Norton (1994, Table 1.2). Norway: Hansen (1993, p. 155).

Basque Country in Spain. There as to a lesser extent in Italy, such nationalisms had previously been suppressed by dictatorships, but they reemerged naturally in the transition to democracy. Economic factors included unequal growth: as economies develop, peripheral regions tend to lose ground compared with core regions, a process accelerated in Europe by the single market. This creates resentments which regional parties can exploit in their campaign for more self-government. Politically, regional government is a natural cry of opposition parties which then (sometimes!) feel committed to carrying out their schemes when finally elected to office. Finally, a new layer of elected government also creates more offices for political parties to occupy, a form of political inflation.

In Europe, where regionalism has been concentrated, the European Union has also played a part. It has stimulated regions to lobby for aid through the European Regional Development Fund (ERDF). Regions have been further encouraged by the EU's policy of distributing aid directly to them, rather than through member states. This squeeze on central governments has encouraged regional nationalists to postulate a 'Europe of the Regions' (see p. 179) in which the EU and the regions exert a pincer movement on national power.

Although regional governments can pass laws in their designated areas of competence, their main contribution has been in economic planning and infrastructure development. In the Spanish region of Valencia, for example, the authority has sought to improve telecommunications, roads, railways, ports and airports. These tasks are beyond the scope of small local authorities but beneath the national vision of the central government. Using regional taxes, loans and central grants, French regions in particular have exerted leverage over lower-level

departments, even though regions remain the poor relation in financial terms (Loughlin and Mazey, 1995). In Italy, too, regional authorities outside the South have made a notable contribution, with some left-wing parties determined to display their competence through showpiece governance. Although institutional reforms often fail to achieve their goals, the introduction of regional governments is widely considered to have been a success.

Local government

Local government is universal, found in federal and unitary states alike. It is the lowest level of elected territorial organization within the state. Variously called communes, municipalities or parishes, these bodies express both the virtues and the vices of their limited scale. At their best, local governments represent natural communities, remain accessible to their citizens, reinforce local identities, act as a political recruiting ground, serve as a first port of call for citizens with a problem and distribute resources in the light of local knowledge and needs. Yet local governments also have characteristic weaknesses. They are often too small to deliver local services efficiently, they lack financial autonomy and they are easily dominated by local élites.

The perpetual 'problem' of local government is: how to marry local representation with efficient delivery of services. As Teune (1995a, p. 8) notes,

> there never has been a sound theoretical resolution [at local level] to the question of democracy and its necessity for familiarity, on the one hand, with the size and diversity required for prosperity, on the other.

EXHIBIT 10.2

A Europe of the Regions?

This idea attracts many regional nationalists. The notion is that the European Union and the regions gradually become the leading policy-makers, out-flanking central governments which are left with little (well, less) to do. The EU encouraged such aspirations by introducing a committee of the Regions and Local Communities in 1988; this body is composed of subnational authorities. Although this committee is only consultative, its mere existence indicates the growing pressures facing states in maintaining historic claims to exclusive sovereignty over 'their' territory (Jones and Keating, 1995).

This dilemma is probably insoluble and can lead to frequent reorganizations by higher authority. Various schemes have been adopted to counter the inefficiencies of small scale. One is for local governments to collaborate with their neighbours. For instance by 1994 the 36 000 communes in France had arranged themselves into 18 000 consortia for such purposes as supplying water and electricity. Of these collaborations, 2100 were multipurpose (Stevens, 1996, p. 161). Another approach is to set up special-purpose authorities, often formally separate from the system of territorial government. Elected school boards in the United States, and the old road boards in New Zealand, are examples.

More radically, local government can cease to deliver services altogether, becoming instead an interest group for voicing community needs at higher level. This has been the inevitable fate of many French communes, most of which still have under 500 inhabitants. Elsewhere, the trend over most of the twentieth century was for local govern- ment to increase in population size, especially in urban areas. Sweden, for example, had 2500 communes in 1952; by 1969 this had fallen to just 278. Increased size also reduces the problem of 'the free rider' – people who use but do not pay for community resources. An example is commuters who work in the city but contribute nothing to its upkeep because their home (and their property taxes) lie outside city boundaries.

One issue which has attracted attention in the organization of local government is the role played by elected mayors. In some countries, including Britain and parts of the United States, the mayor is a ceremonial post, usually offered by the other councillors as a reward to a colleague with long service. Real power rests with the council or, as in parts of the USA, with an appointed city manager. However, under the 'strong mayor' system, the mayor acts as a directly-elected chief executive, providing a focal point for local government and stimulating public interest in its activities. For instance, in the person-

EXHIBIT 10.3

The case for local government, as made in 1842

William Swanson, Attorney General of New Zealand, outlined the advantages of local government in his preamble to the ordinance establishing local boroughs in his country in 1842. His case, that local government is the most efficient and effective way of meeting local needs with the added advantage of preparing participants for higher office, remains relevant today:

Whereas it is necessary that provision should be made for the good order, health and convenience of the inhabitants of towns and their neighbourhoods:

And whereas the inhabitants themselves are best qualified, as well by their more intimate knowledge of local affairs as by their most direct interest therein, effectually to provide the same:

And whereas the habit of self-government in such cases hath been found to keep alive a spirit of self-reliance and respect for the laws, and to prepare men for the due exercise of other political privileges:

Be it therefore enacted ...'

Further reading: Bush (1980, p. 13).

alist political culture of Latin America, the high visibility of the mayor has encouraged ambitious politicians to use the office as a stepping stone in their political careers (Nickson, 1995, p. 70). Slovakia, too, has experienced some success with elected mayors in the postcommunist era. The perceived success of strong American mayors such as New York's Rudy Giuliani has encouraged Britain to consider introducing elected mayors, for example in London, as a way of reviving a demoralized local government sector. Italy introduced such a system in 1993.

But not all mayors can become local folk-heroes. In some European countries, for example France, the mayor has responsibilities as a representative of the state as well as the locality. Thus French mayors, although appointed by the council, cannot be dismissed by them. Indeed, in the Netherlands mayors are still appointed by the central government though with sensitivity to local concerns; as with American city managers, the office is regarded as managerial rather than political, with appointment to a larger municipality seen as a successful career move (Andeweg and Irwin, 1993, p. 160).

The new world: whatever works is best

The style of local government differs sharply between the new world (for instance, the USA, Canada, Australia and New Zealand) and the old world of Europe. In the new world, local government has a pragmatic, utilitarian character. Local authorities were set up as needed to deal with 'roads, rates and rubbish'. Special boards (appointed or elected) were added to deal with specific problems from mosquito control to licensing, harbours and land drainage. The policy style was pragmatic and apolitical: 'there is no Democratic or Republican way to collect garbage'. Indeed special boards were often set up precisely to be independent of party politics, providing early forms of governance. The consequence is diversity in organization. For instance, the USA is governed at local level by a smorgasbord of over 80 000 cities, counties, school districts, townships and special districts.

In the United States, Canada and Australia, the variety of local government is reinforced by federalism. In federations, local government is a responsi-

bility of the states, not the centre. So in effect the United States has 50 different local government systems, one for each state. In Canada, the provinces have been especially keen to maintain control over 'their' local charges, seeing off various attempts by the centre to deal directly with the municipalities. Generally, federalism focuses attention on the national/provincial relationship, with local government rated least important. One paradox of many federations is the low status of local government within them.

Definition

Special-purpose boards are functional authorities set up to deal with specific problems in a local area. They are separate from but linked to elected local councils based on territory. Members are generally appointed. However, many of the 15 000 school districts in the United States are elected.

Europe: representing community

In most of Western Europe, local government has a higher status than in the new world. This position derives from its role in representing historic communities and is reflected, in two ways, in an entrenched constitutional position. First, national constitutions normally mandate some form of local self-government. Sweden's 'Instrument of Government' is an example. It roundly declares that 'Swedish democracy is founded on the freedom of opinion and on universal and equal suffrage and shall be realized through a representative and parliamentary polity and through local self-government' (Jones, 1993, p. 121). Second, local authorities normally enjoy 'general competence': the authority to make regulations in any matter of concern to the area. Germany's Basic Law, for instance, gives the *gemeinden* (municipalities) 'the right to regulate under their own responsibility and within the limits of the law all the affairs of the local community'. All this reflects the European doctrine of subsidiarity – the idea that matters should be dealt with at local level whenever possible.

In a European context, English local government is the great exception. Despite a long history of local administration, English councils are notably underpowered. They are protected neither by provincial governments (Britain is a unitary state), nor by constitutional entrenchment (Britain lacks a codified constitution), nor by the power of general competence (councils can only do what central government explicitly permits). Local authorities have long been seen as providers of central services, to be judged by cost-effectiveness rather than by their ability to represent natural communities. This explains why the population served by English local authorities is uniquely large (Table 10.3).

> **Definition**
> **General competence** is the authority of local governments to make regulations in any matter of concern to the area. These regulations must be consistent with national law. The power of general competence signals the status of local government within the political system; where local government can only perform those functions explicitly granted to it by the centre, as in England, its status is weak.

Always vulnerable, England's local authorities were reduced to virtual servant status by 18 years of assertive Conservative rule beginning in 1979. Over this period, the British government centralized power at a time when many European democracies were devolving it. No wonder Britain declined to support the European Charter of Local Self-Government, adopted by the Council of Europe in 1985. The Labour government elected in 1997 seeks to restore the morale of local government but faces the danger that doing so will reduce its capacity to enforce its own agenda, for example pushing for improved educational standards.

Functions

What do local governments do? Broadly, their tasks are two-fold: providing local public services (such as refuse collection) and implementing national welfare policies (Box 10.6). As Teune (1995b, p, 16) says, 'local government is where the day-to-day activity of politics and government gets done'. However, a static description of functions fails to reveal how the role of local government evolved in the 1990s. The major trend has been for municipal authorities to reduce their direct provision of services by delegating tasks to private organizations, both profitmaking and voluntary. In Denmark, for example, many local governments have set up 'user boards' in

Table 10.3 Average population of elected local authorities in selected European countries

Country	Average population of local authorities (lowest level)
England	127 000
Scotland	91 620
Ireland	41 910
Sweden	30 000
Netherlands	17 860
Belgium	16 740
Finland	10 646
Norway	9 145
Germany	7 240
Italy	6 800
Spain	4 700
France	1 500

Source: Norton (1991, Table 2.2).

primary schools. These boards are given block budgets and the authority to hire and fire staff (Bogason, 1996). In some American cities, private firms located in an area have taken over much of the responsibility for funding and even organizing improvements to local services such as street-cleaning.

In this way the local authority's role is changing from a provider to an enabler. The council does not so much provide services as ensure that they are supplied. This enables the authority to become a smaller, coordinating body, more concerned with governance than government. More organizations become involved in local policy-making, many of them functional (for example school boards) rather than territorial (for example county councils). Reflecting this trend, the role of citizen in local government may be evolving from *voter* at elections to a *customer* for specific services (for example care for the elderly). This shift represents an important transition in conceptions of how local governments should go about their task of serving their communities.

BOX 10.6
Typical powers of local authorities

Cemeteries	Recreation
Economic development	Refuse disposal
Environmental protection	Roads
Fire service	Social assistance
Homes for the elderly	Social housing
Libraries	Tourism
Local planning	Water supply
Primary education	

Source: Norton (1991, Table 2.3).

Definition
The enabling authority is a term used to summarize one vision of local government. Such an authority is concerned with coordinating the provision of services and representing the community both within and beyond its territory. Its role is strategic, with specific services contracted out to private agencies, whether voluntary or profit-making.

One priority of the enabling authority is to promote inward investment. Rather than acting as the instrument of the welfare state, many local governments (especially cities) now place more emphasis on economic development, seeking to identify and promote whatever competitive advantages their area may possess. Whether the aim is to attract transnational companies or individual tourists, local authorities find themselves competing with each other, replicating on a smaller scale the international battle between states. In Japan, for instance, 'local governments have begun to take on the character of a real estate agent as they bustle about, wooing factories in the name of regional development' (Junnosuke, 1995, p. 270).

Cities lead these developments. As Goldsmith and Klausen (1997) comment,

> cities from Barcelona to Boston, Melbourne to Manchester, have engaged in place marketing designed to make their territory attractive to mobile middle classes and firms as they try to improve their position in the world urban economic order.

But the politics of the city has always loomed large in local government; indeed, local government began in European towns in the eleventh and twelfth centuries. Towns were the cradle of local government, civil society and an independent business class, and they have continued to provide the base for commerce and taxes as well as new ideas, parties and social movements.

Indeed, world cities such as London, Tokyo and New York have partly escaped from their national moorings (Knox and Taylor, 1995) and today they march to the drum of global finance, not national politics. Large border conurbations (such as Vancouver, Seattle and Portland) in effect form a single transnational unit (Kresl and Gappert, 1995). The sheer size of many modern cities also gives their local governments intrinsic importance: the populations of New York (9 million) and Los Angeles (9 million) exceed that of most countries and London's gross domestic product exceeds that of Sweden or Belgium. Pressures on land have also given city authorities, with their planning powers, a pivotal role in urban development. At the same time, however, cities have also created extra problems for national governments in the postwar period. Urban decay and depopulation have attracted the attention of national governments. Financial transfers from the centre have increased direct coordination between central and city governments, thus bypassing provincial and regional authorities with their more rural and conservative bias. For good reason, then, the study of urban politics occupies a special place in the analysis of local government (Keating, 1991).

Postcommunism: doing what it can

Under communism, local government was functionless and spineless – and often deliberately kept so by frequent reorganization. Party officials, not elected councillors, wielded the real power. The struggles of local governments to become established in the postcommunist era therefore provide a cameo of institutional development amid the difficult inheritance of a collapsed dictatorship. In the former Soviet republics (and to a lesser extent in Eastern Europe) local government was massively unprepared for the postcommunist era. 'We are starting from less than zero', complained a city official in Kiev, the capital of Ukraine (Campbell, 1996, p. 41).

Often local officers worked from buildings which were still technically owned by the communist party; authorities had little revenue, and the central government was preoccupied with survival and had no money to give to local governments. Previously state-owned industrial enterprises had no tradition of paying taxes to anyone, least of all to a mere local authority. The state-owned enterprises which had built large blocks of flats simply handed over their decaying properties to the local council, which inherited a large repair bill and tenants accustomed to artificially low rents. Despite chronic under-resourcing, local officials were left to pick up the enormous welfare problems created by industrial collapse.

Local governments had to resolve these difficulties in the context of societies which had gone without authentic local social organization for at least a generation and in which turnout at local elections soon became embarassingly low. In one Polish local election district in 1991, the only elector who turned up was a candidate – and he voted for someone else. The task of creating a civic society between the central government and the citizen was inevitably long-term. Intermediate levels of government between the centre and the localities are still being created. Unlike consolidated democracies, local government initially had had no regional bodies to provide support. In the absence of clear public authority, many cities were taken over by feuding criminal gangs.

In countries with a pluralist tradition and a less severe history of communism (notably Hungary but also Poland and the Czech Republic), local government did begin to take root, usually drawing on pre-communist traditions. The pattern here was more evolutionary and less revolutionary, helped by the desire of the Eastern European states to achieve membership of the European Union. Indeed local authorities began to achieve more success than remote national governments in wresting taxes from local firms and citizens. But, in general, the challenge of running a local authority in a postcommunist state was, to say the least, daunting.

Key reading

> **Next step:** *Smith (1995) is a thoughtful collection assessing the contribution which federalism can make to a world of growing ethnic conflict.*

On federalism, useful comparative collections are Burgess and Gagnon (1993), and, from a European perspective, Hesse and Wright (1996). Elazar (1996) provides an enthusiast's overview while de Villiers (1995) covers some under-researched federations. Of the older works, Riker (1975) and even Wheare (1963) are still worth reading. For Canada specifically, see Taylor (1993) or Rocher and Smith (1995). Sharpe (1993) is the standard source on regional government in Europe, best supplemented by Jones and Keating (1995) on regions and the EU. Collections on local government include Teune (1995a), a special issue of the *International Political Science Review* (1998) and Chandler (1993). Norton (1994) examines local government in nine countries. For urban politics specifically, see Keating (1991) and Pierre (1995). Two edited collections on local government in postcommunist states are Coulson (1995) and Gibson and Hanson (1996).

CHAPTER 11 | Assemblies

Assemblies as representative institutions

Assemblies are symbols of popular representation in politics. They are not governing bodies, they do not take major decisions and usually they do not even initiate proposals for laws. Yet they are still the foundation of both liberal and democratic politics. This importance rests on what parliaments stand for rather than what they do. As Olson (1994, p. 1) writes,

> legislatures join society to the legal structure of authority in the state. Legislatures are representative bodies: they reflect the sentiments and opinions of the citizens.

Assemblies are, in potential and often in reality, the authentic representative of the people's will. For this reason they help to 'mobilize consent' for the system of rule (Beer, 1982). As representative democracy spreads throughout the world, so more assemblies are gaining the political weight which comes from standing for the people.

To appreciate the representative role of assemblies, it is helpful to consider their origins in medieval Europe. Their purpose then was to represent the various estates – the clergy, the nobility and the towns – into which society was divided. As these orders became more important in the thirteenth and fourteenth centuries, so kings began to consult estate leaders on issues of war, administration, commerce and taxation. Myers (1975, p. 23) describes how these early assemblies developed:

> the leading members [of estates] might appear in the assemblies either by virtue of their office or status, or because of election. At first the composition and functions of such assemblies were very ill defined and fluid, but gradually they solidified into increasingly definite forms which, in a traditionally-minded society, came to be regarded as customary and therefore respected.

So European assemblies were representative bodies long before they became legislatures with the sovereign right to pass laws.

Definition

An assembly is a multimember representative body which considers public issues. Its main function is to 'give assent, on behalf of a political community that extends beyond the executive authority, to binding measures of public policy' (Norton, 1990a, p. 1). The words used to denote these bodies reflect different aspects of their representative role: 'assemblies' meet, 'parliaments' talk and 'legislatures' pass laws. We use these three terms interchangeably.

By contrast, in new republics such as the United States, Congress was given the right to legislate from the start. The first section of the first article of the American constitution states: 'All legislative powers herein granted shall be vested in a Congress of the United States'. James Madison, an architect of the American constitution (and of American political thought) declared that 'in republican government, the legislative power necessarily predominates'. And so, in the United States, it did.

In authoritarian regimes, the representative role shrinks and the assembly's significance declines. Some dictators dispense with parliaments altogether; others keep them as shadow institutions, allowing only short sessions or packing them with government appointments. Yet assemblies are difficult to extinguish completely; they are resilient creatures. In 1990 only 14 out of 164 independent states had no assembly. Of those 14, only five (traditional dynastic states in the Arabian Gulf) had no experience of assemblies at all. Even authoritarian rulers value the appearance of public consent which assemblies provide.

cohesive collective body. It will also be in constant danger of being taken over by more coherent actors such as parties or even by its own committees. This was one reason why communist rulers preferred large assemblies. Such bodies were so unwieldy that much of their work had to be delegated to committees where the party kept a tight grip.

Where assemblies consist of two chambers the upper house is normally the smaller, thus gaining the advantage of intimacy. Indeed, the 'nexus clause' of the Australian constitution requires the upper house to be half the size of the lower chamber. A seeming exception is Britain's House of Lords, an upper chamber with 1200 members, although most of these are hereditary peers who rarely show up. The 'working house' is 300–400 in size, smaller than the Commons (659 members).

Structure of assemblies

Only two things, claims Blondel (1973), can be said with certainty about every assembly in the world: how many members and chambers it has. Both are important aspects of parliamentary structure. But a third factor, the committee system, is perhaps the most important influence on how modern parliaments work. In this section, we examine all three features of assembly structure.

Assembly size

By size, the smallest assembly in the world, with a mere 12 members, is in the South Pacific island of Tuvalu. As Tuvalu's population is only 8624, it has far more representatives per head than most other assemblies. At the other extreme, the National Peoples' Congress in China, the world's most populous nation, has almost 3000 members. As these examples suggest, a large population generally means a large assembly (Figure 11.1).

Midsize assemblies are often the most effective. On the one hand, a very small chamber – say, under 100 – offers opportunities for all deputies to have their say in a collegial environment. But it may also impose heavy workloads on members, allow insufficient specialization, fail to represent all social interests, and be of limited value in political recruitment. On the other hand, a very large chamber – say, more than a few hundred – will be unable to act as a

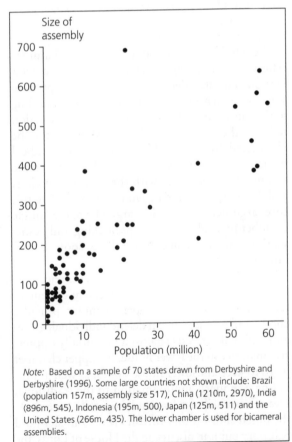

Note: Based on a sample of 70 states drawn from Derbyshire and Derbyshire (1996). Some large countries not shown include: Brazil (population 157m, assembly size 517), China (1210m, 2970), India (896m, 545), Indonesia (195m, 500), Japan (125m, 511) and the United States (266m, 435). The lower chamber is used for bicameral assemblies.

Figure 11.1 Population and assembly size

Number of chambers

About three in four assemblies in today's world have only one chamber (Derbyshire and Derbyshire, 1996, p. 58). This proportion has increased since the war, and several liberal democracies have abolished their second chamber, notably New Zealand (1950), Denmark (1954) and Sweden (1971). Unicameralism is most common among newer, smaller and unitary states, especially in Africa and the Middle East. Some postcommunist states also have single chamber assemblies.

> **Definition**
> Most assemblies today are either **unicameral** (one chamber) or **bicameral** (two chambers). A bicameral legislature consists of a lower chamber (the first chamber, often called the House) and an upper chamber (the second chamber, often called the Senate). The lower chamber is directly elected; the members of upper chambers are chosen by a range of methods.

The choice between one and two chambers reflects contrasting visions of democracy. Unicameral parliaments are justified by an appeal to a majoritarian reading of popular control. According to this, an assembly based on direct popular election reflects the popular will and should not be obstructed by a second chamber. As the radical French cleric Abbé Sièyes (1748–1836) wrote, 'if the second chamber agrees with the first, it is useless; and if it disagrees, it is dangerous'. In addition to this core argument, it is also argued that a single chamber precludes the petty politicking and point-scoring which becomes possible as soon as two houses exist.

The defenders of bicameral parliaments reject this logic. They emphasise the liberal element of democracy, arguing that the upper chamber provides checks and balances. It can defend individual, group and regional interests against a potentially oppressive majority in the lower house. An upper chamber helps to keep the lower house honest as well as providing a modern approximation to the traditional idea of a council of elders (and, hopefully, wisers). As the nineteenth-century British Prime Minister Lord Salisbury put it in discussing the House of Lords, the upper chamber 'represents the permanent, as opposed to the passing, feelings of the nation'. Thus the second house plays a restraining and revising role, providing a natural home for sober second thoughts. Specifically, it can make useful revisions to bills, delay intemperate legislation, adopt a broad view of national problems and reduce the workload of the lower chamber.

Above all, a second chamber can guarantee a voice in parliament for distinct territories within the state. Thus all major federal systems provide for an upper chamber or 'states' house' to represent the component provinces. This provides particular reassurance for small states which otherwise fear that they might be overwhelmed in the lower house, where representation is based on population. The United States is the classic example. In the Senate each state has two senators irrespective of population; Alaska with about 500 000 inhabitants has the same representation as California with a population exceeding 25 million. Australia, a federal system with just six states, grants 12 senators to each (plus two each to the Northern and Capital Territories). The German Bundesrat offers three to six seats to each Lander, according to population. Membership is still weighted towards the smaller states but not to the same extent as in, say, Australia.

Whether federal or unitary, a bicameral structure raises the question of how the membership of each chamber should be chosen; some divergence in selection procedure is needed if the chambers are not simply to replicate each other. Generally, the members of the upper house are given longer tenure. In the United States, the Founding Fathers gave senators a long six-year term, expecting them to exhibit, in James Madison's words, 'superior coolness ... and wisdom' compared to their colleagues in the House. By and large they have done just that. In contrast, the entire membership of the House of Representatives must stand for re-election on a demanding two-year cycle. Critics allege that representatives are too busy securing their own future to have time to worry about their country's (King, 1997).

The four main principles of selection to the upper house are, in order of popularity: direct election, appointment by the government (sometimes for life), indirect election through regional or local governments, and heredity (for examples, see Table 11.1). Some countries mix and match these tech-

Table 11.1 Selection to the second chamber

Country	Chamber	Size	Method of selection
Australia	Senate	76	Direct election by PR in each state
Britain	House of Lords	about 1200*	Mixture of inheritance and government appointment
Canada	Senate	104	Appointed by Prime Minister
France	Senate	321	Indirect election via départements#
Germany	Bundesrat	69	Appointed by state governments
India	Council of States	245	Indirect election via state assemblies, except for eight presidential nominees
Japan	House of Councillors	252	Direct election by a mixed member system
USA	Senate	100	Direct election by plurality voting in each state

Notes:
* of whom 300–400 regular attenders form 'the working house'.
# units of local government (100 in total).

See also: Tsebelis and Money (1997), Ch.2.

niques. Thus Britain is the only country still to rely on heredity, but even there lords who inherit their title now sit alongside government appointees. And the Labour government elected in 1997 proposed finally to end the right of hereditary peers to vote in the upper chamber. As the method of appointment moves away from election, so in a democratic age the danger grows that the upper house will lose authority and effectiveness. In Canada, despite its federal structure, senators are appointed by the Prime Minister; the Senate has been condemned as a dumping-ground for old politicians. Oddly, though, many members of Britain's political class retained some affection for the unreformed House of Lords.

Modern bicameralism takes weaker and stronger forms. In the more common weaker version, the upper chamber is subordinate to the lower chamber but retains some powers to delay legislation or force its reconsideration. Weak bicameralism is inherent in two-chambered parliamentary systems. As Wheare (1968, p. 201) argued, parliamentary government 'encourages, if indeed it does not require, the supremacy or at least the superiority of one chamber over another.' Britain is an example. The House of Commons is the dominant partner: ministers and governments emerge from the lower chamber and remain accountable to it. Further, the Commons – like most lower chambers – dominates consideration of financial bills. However, their lord-

ships are not entirely toothless; they can still delay nonfinancial legislation for a year.

Just as assemblies with two chambers are less common than those with one, so strong bicameralism is less frequently encountered than weak bicameralism. Under strong bicameralism the two chambers have broadly equal powers, but this is rather rare and largely confined to federal states such as Australia, Germany, Switzerland and the United States (Italy is a non-federal example). The American Congress is the best illustration. The Senate plays a full part in the country's complex legislative and budget-making process, with most bills ending up in a joint committee of both houses. Conflict and even deadlock between the two chambers is a real possibility. Thus a government's programme may face real restraints and decisive policy-making becomes difficult, requiring a broad consensus between the executive and both chambers of an exceptionally assertive assembly.

Committees

Given the complexity of many modern issues, a powerful assembly needs a well-developed committee structure if it is to exert real influence. As Kashyap (1979, p. 321) observed, 'a legislature is known by the committees it keeps'. Committees are small workgroups of members, created to cope with

EXHIBIT 11.1

Can a government be accountable to two chambers? Australia's constitutional crisis of 1975

'A cabinet, it would seem, must be responsible to one chamber. It cannot be responsible to two.' Wheare's comment (1968) is the conventional reading of why bicameralism is weak in parliamentary systems. If a government were equally accountable to two chambers, it might be caught in the grip of contradictory pressures. To forestall such crises, one chamber, normally the lower house with its popular mandate and control over the budget, emerges as the focus of government accountability.

But Australia provides an interesting exception. In 1975 the Senate (where the Labor Party had lost its majority) refused to pass the money bills proposed by Labor Prime Minister Gough Whitlam. Despite this loss of control the Prime Minister refused to resign, claiming that his responsibility lay to the lower house only. Instead, Whitlam advocated a new election for half the Senate. The Governor General of Australia – in effect, the head of state – rejected this opinion. He argued that the constitution stipulated that the executive should be accountable to both chambers. Drawing on the theoretical powers granted to him under the constitution, the Governor General proceeded to dismiss Whitlam from office and to appoint the opposition leader as a caretaker Prime Minister. In an election held later in the year, the Labor Party lost its majority in the lower house.

This remarkable sequence of events was not just a crisis of Australia's constitution. It was also 'a crisis of federalism, a crisis of the party system, a crisis of responsible government, even a crisis of democracy' (Jaensch 1992, p. 81). Whatever the constitutional niceties, today it is accepted that the Governor General was wrong to dismiss a Prime Minister whose party had been fairly elected. Yet many observers also acknowledge that the Senate's action in refusing to pass a budget was both impudent and imprudent.

the volume of business in the house. Their functions are threefold:

- to consider bills and financial proposals
- to scrutinize government administration and past expenditure
- to investigate general matters of public concern (Box 11.1).

A strong committee system largely defines a 'working' (committee-oriented) as opposed to a 'talking' (chamber-oriented) assembly.

Definition

In a **talking assembly**, such as the British House of Commons, floor debate is the central activity; it is in the main chamber that major issues are addressed and reputations are both won and lost. In a **working assembly**, such as the American Congress, the core activity takes place in committee. There, legislators shape bills, authorize expenditure and scrutinize the executive (Loewenberg, Patterson and Jewell, 1985).

The American Congress is again unique in the impact of its committees. Although unmentioned in the constitution, committees rapidly became vital to Congress's work: 'Congress in its committee rooms is Congress at work', wrote Woodrow Wilson over a century ago, and this is still true today. In 1994 the Senate alone had 20 permanent standing committees plus 87 subcommittees. In both chambers committees are uniquely well-supported, employing over 3500 policy specialists. In the absence of dominant parties, committees decide the fate and shape of most legislation. So autonomous did these 'little legislatures' become that they reduced the overall coherence of Congress. Their chairs became Congressional lions, powerful and protective of their own territory. By the early 1990s, party leaders sought to rein in the committees, settling issues outside the committee structure and developing 'megabills' which were impossible for any one committee to digest. But even after this latest wave of reforms, the American Congress remains an institution defined by its numerous, open and specialized committees.

Committees have less influence on legislation in party-dominated assemblies. In the British House of Commons, for instance, government bills are examined by standing committees which largely replicate party combat on the floor of the chamber (Box 11.1). These committees, unlike those of Congress, do not challenge executive dominance in framing legislation. They are unpopular, unspecialized and under-resourced. However, like many other legislatures the Commons has expanded its system of select committees of scrutiny. These now shadow all the main government departments, helping to probe government policy and to monitor its implementation. The members of a select committee can develop a shared outlook which at least moderates the war of the parties still waged on the floor of the House. In the context of a parliament which remains under the firm control of the executive, Norton (1997, p. 166) suggests these select committees 'mark a remarkable advance in terms of parliamentary scrutiny'.

The Australian Parliament confirms the importance of parties to the operation of the committee system. In the House of Representatives, interest in committee service has been weak; indeed, until 1993 many bills were not even examined in committee (Uhr, 1997). By contrast, in the Senate the number of committees has increased and nearly all backbenchers have served on at least one. What explains this difference? The answer is that the House of Representatives is more party- and executive-dominated: parliamentary committees are less important for ambitious backbenchers than party committees. The Senate, elected by proprotional representation since 1948, is less dominated by the government and provides a stronger check on the executive; its committees provide good footholds for resistance. Thus the Australian example shows that effective committees are most likely when the governing party does not dominate the relevant chamber.

When the political style is less adversarial and policy emerges through agreement, influential committees can coexist with strong parties. In the German Bundestag (lower house), party discipline is firm but the committee members have more regard for objectivity than point-scoring. Scandinavian politics, also characterized by coalition governments, is similar. Its governing style is 'committee parliamentarianism', which means that influ-

---

BOX 11.1

Types of parliamentary committee

Type	Definition
Standing committee	Permanent bodies which subject bills to detailed consideration
Select committee	These scrutinize the executive and conduct special investigations. Often one for each main government department
Joint or conference committees	These iron out differences between the bills passed by the two chambers (bicameral assemblies only)

---

ential standing committees negotiate the policies and bills on which the whole parliament later votes. In Sweden, for instance, committees modify about one in three government proposals and nearly half these changes are substantial. The figures for Norway and Finland are comparable (Sjolin, 1993, p. 174). Thus committees become the vehicle for the extensive consultation which underlies policy-making in Scandinavia.

In Canada, committees traditionally played only a limited role in a party-dominated and generally inactive House of Commons. But the famous bells incident in 1982 encouraged reform of parliament, including its committees. As a way of putting pressure on the government, the Conservative opposition had refused to take part in a vote: parliament was paralysed for 15 days as the division bells rang (White, 1991, p. 413). Subsequently, committees were granted permanent staff and other support services. However, high turnover and absenteeism continue, reflecting members' frustration at their limited influence on policy (Price and Mancuso, 1995, p. 226).

Apart from the party system, the key to the influence of committees lies in their expertise. This is itself a product of four factors: specialization, permanence, intimacy and support. Committees with *specialized responsibilities* and a clear field of operation are most likely to develop the expertise needed to challenge government proposals. Similarly, permanent committees with *continuity of membership* will develop a fund of knowledge which is impossible for committees created anew each session. *Intimacy* emerges from small size. Particularly when meetings take place in private, a small group setting can encourage cooperation and consensus. *Support*, finally, refers to the use of qualified staff to advise committees. Significantly, all four of these factors are present in the American Congress.

Functions of assemblies

The key functions of modern assemblies are representation, deliberation and legislation. Even a dictator ruling largely by decree is likely to allow his assembly to go through the motions of representing the people, debating issues and passing bills. Other functions, crucial to some parliaments but not all, are: making governments, authorizing expenditure, scrutinizing the executive and providing a channel of élite recruitment and socialization. We discuss each function in turn.

Representation

One interpretation of representation is that the assembly should be *a microcosm* of society. The idea here is that the assembly should be 'society in miniature', reflecting its diversity. Such an assembly would balance men and women, rich and poor, black and white, even educated and uneducated, in the same mix as in society. It would implement the interpretation of the legislature as a body which could stand for society, replicating its goals and diversity. Yet, ironically, achieving this mirror of society would require interfering with the normal process of election. A microcosm could only be achieved by quota, not election. Communist states, for instance, ensured high levels of representation of peasants, workers and women. But this was at the price of noncompetitive elections. Indeed, a true microcosm is best obtained by random selection, dispensing with elections altogether (as with juries). Also, to prevent the representatives becoming untypical of society, they would need regular replacement. In practice, the assembly as microcosm is an impractical ideal – if it is an 'ideal' at all.

The idea of the legislature as a 'deliberative assembly' stands at the other extreme to the micro-cosm view. A deliberative legislature should represent the interests of the whole nation; and the representatives themselves should seek to apply exceptional knowledge and intelligence to public problems. Elected politicians are not mouthpieces but trustees chosen to use their judgment in a broad, independent way. The heyday of the *trustee* assembly was in the eighteenth and nineteenth centuries, before the rise of disciplined parties.

While a strong element of deliberative representation remains, today representation in most assemblies operates by *party*. Victorious candidates owe their election primarily to their party and they vote in parliament largely according to their party's dictates. Further, in parliamentary regimes it is the party balance in the assembly which decides the composition of government. So the members of the assembly represent their party more than a specific social group or even the country as a whole. Representation by party is most strongly entrenched in British-influenced systems. In Britain itself the radical politician Richard Cobden (1804–65) claimed that he had seen many MPs reduced to tears during debates but none to changing their vote. In New Zealand, Labour members must sign a pledge committing them to abide by the decisions of the party caucus. In India, an extreme case, members lose their seat if they vote against their party (Mitra, 1996, p. 700). Slowly, MPs are becoming less reliable 'lobby fodder' but they are still defined, first and foremost, by their party label.

Elsewhere, party discipline is combined with at least some independence for members. In France and Germany, for instance, party obligations must be reconciled with the constitutional statement that members of the legislature owe allegiance to the nation and not to any group within it. In practice, members of parliament suffer from role conflict and must form their own interpretation of representation, balancing the demands of country, party, constituency – and conscience.

Deliberation

While representation is the core purpose of assemblies, deliberation follows close behind. Public discussion of national issues is a hallmark of parliaments. In 'talking assemblies' such as Britain's and New Zealand's, this deliberation takes the form of

Edmund Burke and the trustee role

The British conservative Edmund Burke (1729–97) gave the classic exposition of the representative's trustee role. Elected member of parliament for Bristol in 1774, Burke admitted in his victory speech that he knew nothing about the constituency and had played little part in the campaign. But he continued:

> Parliament is not a congress of ambassadors from different and hostile interests; which interests each must maintain, as an agent and advocate against other agents and advocates; but Parliament is a deliberative assembly of one nation, with one interest, that of the whole; where, not local purposes, not local prejudices, ought to guide, but the general good, resulting from the general reason of the whole. You choose a member indeed; but when you have chosen him, he is not a member for Bristol, but he is a member of Parliament.

debate in the chamber. In Britain, most issues of moment eventually make their way to the floor of the House of Commons. Questions of war and peace, of the rise and fall of governments, of turning points in national affairs, are debated there usually with passion and sometimes with flair. Skene (1989, p. 188) regards deliberation as 'by far the most important' function of New Zealand's party-dominated legislature. At any one time, as few as 4000 people are listening to the continuous live radio broadcasts of these debates. Even so, these deliberations set the tone for national political debate. Floor debate forms part of a continuous election campaign.

Most assemblies adopt a less theatrical approach to deliberation. In working assemblies such as the American Congress and the Scandinavian parliaments, deliberation takes the form of policy debate in the committee room. The style here is more careful and detailed. Even so, committees are still serving as a 'policy refinery', not necessarily initiating policy but at least examining proposals, investigating issues, issuing reports and making recom-

mendations. Particularly when such deliberation occurs in public, ministers have to anticipate parliamentary reaction to their ideas.

Legislation

Most constitutions explicitly assert the legislative function of parliaments, signifying the triumph of a liberal model of politics. The end of absolute executive power is affirmed by giving to parliament, and it alone, the right to make laws. Arbitrary government by presidential decree is replaced by a formal procedure for law-making based on a representative assembly (Figure 11.2).

In reality, legislation is rarely the function where assemblies exert most influence; this is partly because most governance does not involve law-making. Because passing bills is a slow and cumbersome process, governments prefer to rule through more flexible devices: making regulations, establishing priorities and allocating money. Legislation is often unnecessary and is usually a last resort; its importance to modern governance is easily exaggerated. In any case, in executive- and party-dominated parliaments, bills (proposed laws) pass through the assembly without being initiated or even transformed by it. Several English-speaking assemblies show this pattern. In Australia, the government treats the legislative function of parliament with virtual contempt; on a single night in 1991 it aimed to put 26 bills through the Senate between midnight and 3.00a.m. A New Zealand Prime Minister once boasted that an idea he had while shaving could be on the statute book by the evening, truly a case of slot-machine law. In Britain, 97 per cent of bills proposed by government between 1945 and 1987 became law. As Rose (1989, p. 173) says, 'laws are described as acts of Parliament but it would be more accurate if they were stamped "Made in Whitehall"'. In these party-dominated parliaments, the legislative function reduces to quality control: patching up errors in bills prepared in haste by ministers and civil servants. Thus in practice the government takes on the function of preparing bills while the lower chamber informally adopts the revising role which formally belongs to the upper house.

In a few parliamentary systems, particularly in smaller countries like Switzerland, for instance,

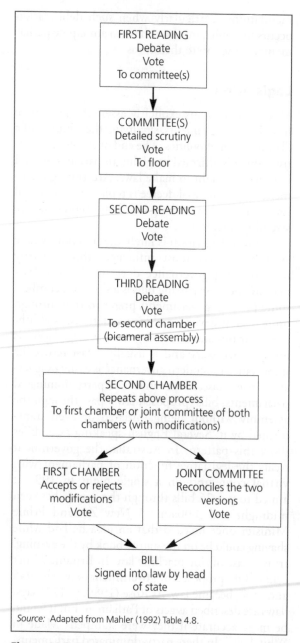

Figure 11.2 Typical steps in making a law

In Israel's increasingly fragmented party system, most laws passed by the 13th Knesset (1992–96) were initiated by private members. This is a rare case where the executive in a parliamentary system is the source of only a minority of the laws passed by the assembly (Hazan, 1997b). With parties still developing in Eastern Europe, individual deputies there also have a fair chance of seeing their proposals or at least their amendments pass into law. A weak party system permits both legislators and the legislature more autonomy in the business of lawmaking.

But it is in the presidential system of the United States that the assembly achieves maximum autonomy in the legislative process. Separation of powers limits executive influence in Congress, a constitutional fact which is often reinforced by 'divided government'. This means that one party controls the White House while the other has a majority in either or both houses of Congress. It is true that even in the United States, most serious bills originate in the executive. However, they are usually transformed in Congress if indeed they do not expire in its maze of committees. 'You supply the bills and we work them over', a member of Congress said to an administration official. America's uniquely pluralistic lawmaking process means that, crises apart, a bill will only prosper if it does not cause offence to powerful interests. Inevitably, this reduces the coherence of the legislative programme. As President Kennedy said, 'It is very easy to defeat a bill in Congress. It is much more difficult to pass one'. The collapse of President (and Hilary) Clinton's proposals to reform the country's patchwork system of medical care is an example of the difficulties of legislating even when the need for change is widely recognized. So the American experience suggests that an assembly which really does control the legislative process is a mixed blessing.

> **Definition**
> **The 90 per cent rule** is a summary description of the legislative process which approximates the situation in many assemblies. The rule maintains that about 90 per cent of bills come from the executive, and that around 90 per cent of its bills become law. The United States is the most striking exception both to the 90 per cent rule and to the executive dominance of the legislative process which underpins it.

the executive and the legislature work closely together in the initiation and passage of legislation ... A bill may originate in either house of the federal assembly on the initiative of any member, or it may be proposed by the federal council, or it may be requested by a canton. (Laundy, 1989, p.70)

Authorizing expenditure

This is one of the oldest functions of parliament and of the lower house in particular. The origin of European parliaments lay in the monarch's need for money. This requirement enabled the lower chamber to establish the right to raise grievances before granting supply (revenue) to the rulers. In Britain, this tradition continued until recently with 'supply days' during which the opposition could raise any issues it wanted.

The power to authorize spending may be one of parliament's oldest functions but in many democracies it has become purely nominal. Like the legislative function, it forms part of the myth rather than the reality of parliamentary power. Indeed lack of real financial control is a major weakness of the modern assembly: the executive prepares the budget which is then reported to parliament but rarely modified there.

In many countries (including Britain and New Zealand) parliament cannot initiate its own expenditure proposals; it can only approve or reject spending proposed by the government. Parliamentary approval is largely after the fact, serving to confirm complicated budget compromises worked out between government departments. Once the budget reaches the assembly (or, more often, special committees), it is usually a done deal. If the assembly began to unpick any part of the budget, the whole package would fall apart. In Israel, since 1996, if the legislature does not pass a budget within 90 days it is dissolved and new elections are held.

Australia is an extreme case of government control over the budget. Emy and Hughes (1991, p. 361) describe the political realities:

> there is no suggestion of the House of Representatives ever 'refusing supply' since control over the whole process of financial appropriations is firmly in the hands of the executive. Only they may propose to spend money ... Moreover, it seems members of the House themselves lack both the knowledge of, and an interest in, the financial procedures which are, ultimately, crucial to the concept of parliamentary control.

Certainly any assembly which seeks to control or even influence the budget must develop expertise among its members and specialist support staff.

The United States is, yet again, exceptional. Congress remains located near the centre of the confused tangle which is American budget-making. All money spent by executive departments must, under the constitution, be allocated under specific spending headings approved by Congress. Following the 1921 Budget and Accounting Act which required the president to present an annual budget to Congress, financial control did shift towards the executive. However, Congress fought back. In the 1970s it created a Congressional Budget Office in an attempt to match the expertise available on the executive side.

The result is that the annual American budget has become an elaborate game of chicken: the executive and the legislature each hope the other will accede to its own proposals before the money runs out and federal employees have to be sent home without pay (this does happen). This is a rather alarming method of budget-making; it is evidence for the proposition that the finances of the modern state are too important to be left to the assembly's many hands.

Making governments

In parliamentary systems the assembly makes, and sometimes breaks, governments. The executive governs only while it retains the confidence of the assembly; parliament remains the sovereign body.

This is in contrast to presidential systems, where the chief executive is directly elected by the people and cannot normally be removed from office. The sovereignty of the assembly in a parliamentary system does not mean that it dominates government-making. In countries using the plurality electoral system, one party normally achieves a clear majority in the legislature; this party then automatically forms the government and from then on needs only the continued support of its own backbenchers to remain in office. So the government is selected *through* parliament rather than *by* it.

> **Definition**
>
> A **minimum winning coalition** (MWC) is a phrase used in analysing coalition governments formed in assemblies where no single party has a majority of seats. The term describes the smallest number of parties which can together command a bare majority in the assembly and therefore form a government. Theory suggests that coalitions should be MWCs, since including additional parties in a coalition would simply dilute the number of government posts each of the participating parties obtains. In practice, though, many coalitions contain more parties than are needed for a MWC (Riker, 1962).

Elections held under proportional representation rarely produce a parliamentary majority for a single party; so coalitions become inevitable. In this situation the assembly becomes the crucial political arena, providing the context for complex and protracted bargaining between the parties. The initiative clearly lies with the party with most seats. However, small swing parties (so-called because they can form a majority government in combination with any of several larger parties) can also strike a hard bargain. In the end a coalition will emerge, most often containing the minimum number of parties needed to make a viable government. Often the government which emerges will not even have a majority in the assembly; minority cabinets account for about one in three postwar governments in parliamentary systems (Strom, 1990, p. 8). They are viable as long as a majority cannot be mustered to vote them out of office.

Once a coalition has formed, the ruling parties must treat backbenchers with respect lest they lose the support of members on whom their government depends. When a coalition government does fall through a vote of no confidence, the focus moves back to the assembly. A new coalition composed of a fresh combination of parties often emerges without another election. This explains why some European countries have had more governments than elections since the war: these cases include Belgium, Denmark and Italy. Finland, an extreme case, got through 33 governments in the 32 years after 1945. Even where government is by coalition, the assembly does not itself govern but it does provide the forum for government-making.

Scrutiny

Scrutiny (or oversight) of the executive is one of the most useful functions of the modern assembly. It enables parliament to monitor the activities of the government, checking the quality of governance. To emphasise the scrutiny function is to accept that the executive, not the legislature, must govern. However the assembly can restate its key role as representative of the people by acting as a watchdog over the administration. Effective scrutiny can compensate for the relegation of the assembly's legislative and expenditure functions to largely nominal status. But there is a difficulty here. Effective scrutiny requires parliamentary committees to be given powers to gather information and interview decision-makers. Yet most rulers remain reluctant to grant these rights; scrutiny remains a contested function which most assemblies are still struggling to develop. The main techniques of oversight are:

- questions and interpellations
- emergency debates
- committee investigations.

Questions and interpellations

Oral and written questions are mainstays of oversight in Britain. In 1987, for example, members of the House of Commons asked a total of 73 000 questions. All ministers must face the Commons from time to time; prime minister's Question Time occurs once a week. In other countries, questions have lower status. French ministries often fail to answer questions at all, and in the Australian House of Representatives ministers give long prepared answers to questions from their own side so they have little time for opponents' queries. Many other parliaments, including Finland, France and Germany, favour the interpellation, a more substantial form of question.

> **Definition**
>
> An **interpellation** is an enquiry of the government, initiated by the opposition, which is followed by a debate and usually a snap vote on the assembly's satisfaction with the answers given. This technique, often linked to a vote of no confidence, brought down several governments in the French Third and Fourth Republics.

Country profile **UNITED KINGDOM**

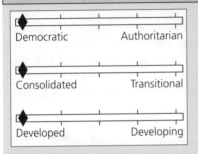

Population: 58.5m.

GDP per head: $19 500.

Form of government: a parliamentary democracy, with a hereditary monarch playing a largely ceremonial role.

Legislature: the House of Commons (659 members) is the dominant chamber. The House of Lords (which mixes hereditary peers with government appointments) acts in a revising and restraining capacity.

Executive: the Cabinet is the top decision-making (or at least decision-ratifying) body; however, the Prime Minister selects and dismisses Cabinet members. Much policy is formed outside the full Cabinet, either in Cabinet committees or in informal groups led by the Prime Minister.

Judiciary: based on the common law tradition. The absence of a codified constitution and the doctrine of parliamentary sovereignty have restricted the scope of the judiciary. However, Britain's membership of the European Union has placed the government under new legal obligations which have given judges more room for initiative.

Electoral system: national and local elections still use the plurality system. More proportional methods are gradually being introduced, beginning with elections to the European parliament, with a referendum to be held on electoral reform for national elections.

Britain is a consolidated democracy whose political system is nonetheless in transition. Traditional models portrayed Britain as a centralized, unitary state; as a two-party system; as an exemplar of parliamentary sovereignty in which ministers were held to account by the assembly; and as a political system whose uncodified constitution offered little formal protection of individual rights. Yet the accuracy of all these images is now under review, only partly as a result of the election in 1997 of Tony Blair's modernizing Labour administration.

The centralized and even the unitary character of the United Kingdom has been put in question by creating elected assemblies for Scotland and Wales. The two-party system has been challenged by the rise of the centre-left Liberal Democrats. Parliamentary sovereignty has been dented by British membership of the European Union and a more assertive judiciary. Ministerial accountability has been complicated by the delegation of government tasks to semi-independent agencies (p. 230). And individual rights will receive more protection from incorporating the European Convention of Human Rights into British law.

The new era of transition in British politics is certain to impinge on its assembly. Traditionally, Britain's parliament (the oldest in the world) mixed omnipotence and impotence in a seemingly impossible combination. Omnipotence, because parliamentary sovereignty, allied to an uncodified constitution, meant there could be no higher authority in the land. Impotence, because the governing party exercised tight control over its own backbenchers, turning parliament into an instrument rather than the holder of power.

Today, parliament's position is becoming less clear-cut. The tired rituals of adversary politics in the Commons have become less convincing, not least for the 260 new MPs elected in 1997. The notion that parliament still possesses some abstract quality called 'sovereignty' still carries weight but, like many assemblies, Britain's legislature runs the risk of being left behind by the pace of political change. But not all developments are negative. MPs themselves have become more professional and committed; the era of the amateur MP is over. And new select committees have begun to enter the debate over policy.

To strengthen its position in an evolving political system, parliament will need to step further down the road of reform. Besides its traditional function as a talking assembly, the legislature will need to become a more effective working body. To influence a more complex decision-making process, committee reports must offer strong arguments and well-researched recommendations. Yet even as parliament tries to broaden its repertoire, it will surely continue to do what it has always done best: acting as an arena for debating issues of central significance to the nation, its government and its leaders.

Further reading: Norton (1993), Searing (1994).
www.parliament.uk
www.number-10.gov.uk

Emergency debates

Most parliaments make provision for these exchanges; they are a high-profile way of calling the government to account. In Britain and most of the Commonwealth such debates take place under the technical rubric of a motion to adjourn the House, a nondescript format for dealing with issues of major importance. Normally a minimum number of members, and the Presiding Officer (Speaker), must approve a proposal for an emergency debate. The event normally ends with a vote – and a government win.

Committee investigations

These are the major device for detailed oversight. The American Congress is the exemplar here: many tasks delegated to the federal bureaucracy are formally allocated by the constitution to Congress, a fact which gives Congress exceptional powers of supervision. The sheer extent of committee oversight is remarkable. On defence issues alone, for instance, 14 committees and 43 subcommittees of Congress held hearings in 1988, creating a large and possibly excessive burden on the Pentagon (Laffin, 1994, p. 184). However even in the USA oversight by committee has limits. It can only cast light on a few corners of the vast bureaucracy – routine watchfulness does not add to the status of committee members and Congress often micromanages departments rather than setting broad targets. Even so, Congress's level of oversight remains unique.

Recruitment and socialisation

The final function of assemblies is to recruit, socialize, train and assess political leaders. Members of the legislature form a pool of talent from which decision-makers emerge. In parliamentary systems where government ministers are usually drawn from the assembly, the legislature becomes the key channel of recruitment to political office. By contrast, in presidential systems, parliament is less crucial as a recruiting agent. In the main, recent American presidents have been drawn from state government rather than from Congress.

Particularly in parliamentary systems, the assembly is a proving ground in which ambitious backbenchers make their mark and in which ministers' stock rises or falls. Writing on Britain, Rose (1989, p. 172) argues that

> the Commons' first function is weighing the reputations of men and women. MPs continually assess their colleagues as ministers and potential ministers. A minister may win a formal vote of confidence but lose status if his or her arguments are demolished in debate.

The House of Commons, like many lower houses, is a parade ring in which contestants for higher office must regularly display their talent.

In liberal democracies, parliament helps to socialize new entrants to the political élite. Observers have pointed to the speed with which the House of Commons absorbed and 're-educated' many firebreathing socialists who entered Parliament after 1918. More recently, assemblies in the new assemblies of Spain and Portugal served to bring together people of different ideologies and background, and reduce hostility between them. By integrating major political actors and power groups within society, parliaments can regulate – if not resolve – conflicts between them (Liebert, 1990, p. 13).

The members: who they are, what they do

Assemblies are bound by detailed procedures, but the political behaviour of the members helps to define the assembly's style. Changes in the operation of parliament often reflect an influx of new members: we cannot understand legislatures without looking at legislators. Who are the members and what do they do?

In every democracy, the profile of parliamentarians is statistically unrepresentative of the wider society: no legislature is a microcosm of society. Reflecting wider patterns of political participation, democratic assemblies are still dominated by well-educated, middle-aged white men. As Berrington (1995, p. 429) says,

> almost every study of legislators in Western democracies shows that they come from more well-to-do backgrounds, are drawn from more prestigious and intellectually satisfying back-

Table 11.2 Occupational backgrounds of members of the lower house 1990–92 (per cent)

	Australia	Canada	France	New Zealand	USA	UK
Law	11	19	6	14	35	13
Administration	8	10	20	–	–	11
Politics	11	1	–	–	11	7
Business	22	25	6	26	10	26
Education	18	15	26	12	11	16
Journalism	2	5	3	–	5	7
Medicine	4	4	12	3	1	1
Agriculture	–	5	3	15	4	2
Manual	10	–	3	5	1	10
Not available/other	14	16	21	25	22	7

Source: Norris (1995, Table 1).

grounds and are much better educated than their electors.

Generally, representatives of right-wing parties come from business, especially finance, while education provides a fruitful recruiting ground for parties of the left. In the United States, law is the most common professional background (Table 11.2). Throughout the world, a surprising number of representatives are drawn from highly political families, suggesting that politics is in danger of becoming, to some extent, an occupational caste.

Many parties on the left are making a determined effort to increase female representation (p. 83). However this is difficult to achieve when candidates are selected locally (as in Britain and the USA) rather than centrally (as under list systems of PR). Authoritarian regimes often produced more 'representative' assemblies but this reflects tight party control of the nomination process and the limited political significance of the legislature. In practice, a socially representative assembly has been a sign of an impotent institution. For instance, Egypt's constitution stipulates that half its deputies must be peasants or workers: in reality, this is simply a way of keeping troublesome teachers and left-wing lawyers out of the legislature. Communist assemblies included higher proportions of women and workers, yet as assemblies have become more significant in the post-

communist era so the representation of these groups has fallen.

Increasingly, the career politician is coming to dominate the most prestigious Western parliaments. The local farmer, the loyal trade unionist, the prominent business executive – all are losing ground to the professional politician for whom politics is a full-time career. Often, the career politician will have no background in any work other than politics. A typical trajectory begins as a legislator's research assistant, moves on to local politics and culminates in a prized seat in the national parliament.

What are the consequences of the rise of the career legislator? On the one hand, such members are assiduous, hardworking and ambitious. They burrow away in committees, serve their constituents, influence public policy and understand how to develop their own career. On the other hand, as Berrington (1995, p. 446) comments, 'the career politician does not know when to leave alone'. An assembly peopled by career politicians is a 'restless, assertive institution' (King, 1981). It lacks the ballast of people for whom politics is not all-consuming and the judgment of those with work experience outside politics. After all, politics is not inherently a technical profession. Perhaps assemblies can still benefit from a few colourful amateurs who can offset the dark suits of the career politician.

> people committed to politics. They regard politics as their vocation, they seek fulfillment in politics, they see their future in politics, they would be deeply upset if circumstances forced them to retire from politics. In short, they are hooked.

Most assemblies have witnessed an increase in the number of career politicians. However, the tradition of the amateur survives in assemblies where members are poorly paid, have little to do, are barred from re-election or are frequently removed by the voters.

BOX 11.2
Backbench roles in Britain's House of Commons

- **Policy advocates** seek to influence national policy.
- **Ministerial aspirants** seek a post in government.
- **Constituency members** stress service to the locality and the people in it.
- **Parliamentarians** work for the esteem of the institution.

Source: Searing (1994).

Of course, not all career politicians achieve, or even aspire to, high office. Once the chance of promotion has gone, members must find other sources of satisfaction. Some pour their energy into helping their constituents, others become stalwarts of the assembly, propping up the institution and sometimes its bars. Researchers have sought to classify these varying ways in which members interpret their role; for instance, Searing's classification shown in Box 11.2 is based on a study of British MPs. Searing finds that the role of policy advocate now predominates in the Commons although many members give priority to a job in the government. The less ambitious emphasise working for their constituents or the esteem of parliament. Although many MPs mix and match roles – for example, ministerial aspirants may also need to be policy advocates – interview-based research like Searing's does show that assemblies cannot be understood solely through institutional analysis. The institution provides a setting in which individual men and women follow diverse objectives.

Of course, career politicians can only flourish in parliament when re-election prospects are good; if members are turfed out after each election, no parliamentary career is possible. This does happen. In Mexico, for instance, legislators cannot be re-elected once their six-year term is complete. Such term-limits are commonly used in Latin America in an effort to forestall the emergence of a self-serving élite. The goal is not always achieved and the price is considerable: reduced party cohesion within the congress and a diminished status for assemblies

already overshadowed by assertive presidents (Carey, 1996). In Canada, re-election is permitted but large electoral swings condemn many MPs to defeat. Three-quarters of MPs serve less than eight years and most members are political tourists, on vacation from other more satisfying careers (Laponce, 1994).

But such cases are exceptional. In most parliaments, re-election rates are high – and nowhere more so than in Taiwan whose members of parliament were elected permanently until 1991. The success rate of incumbents in winning re-election is over 85 per cent in Denmark, Germany, Japan, New Zealand and the USA. It is around 60 per cent in France, Great Britain and Israel (Somit, 1994, p. 12). Average length of service reaches 20 years in the

Table 11.3 Average length of service in national parliaments

	Years
United Kingdom	20
Japan	15
New Zealand	12
United States (House)	12
United States (Senate)	11
Israel	11
Germany	8
Denmark	8
France	7
Canada	6

Source: Somit (1994, p.13).

UK and 15 years in Japan (Table 11.3), which is certainly sufficient time to develop a parliamentary career. Indeed, the question is whether the incumbency effect (the electoral bonus to sitting members arising from their visibility and access to resources) damages assemblies. In the United States, for instance, members spend so much time 'bringing home the pork' for their districts that they can lose sight of national problems. Voters rate the performance of their own member of Congress highly; they are more sceptical about the effectiveness of Congress as a whole. One danger of virtually automatic re-election is that parliaments become inward-looking, lacking the new ideas which fresh blood can provide.

Assemblies in new democracies

The transition to democracy provides opportunities for assemblies to assert themselves. Since parliaments embody the idea of representation, we should expect their stature to grow in newly-minted democracies. And the status of legislatures has undoubtedly risen in almost all the new democracies, at least compared to their enfeebled position under authoritarian regimes.

However, parliaments are not always central actors in the transition itself; more often they are products of, rather than participants in, the change of regime. In other words, the new political system emerges from an élite agreement made outside an institutional framework. The assembly's structure and powers become a topic for negotiation; the legislature is not itself an actor in the process. Further, once the new democracy has consolidated, legislatures become subject to the same pressures which lead many commentators to speak of 'the decline of parliament' in established democracies. The revival of assemblies in new democracies therefore tends to be fleeting, a theme we can develop by reviewing the assembly's role in transitions in Southern Europe, Latin America and Eastern Europe.

Southern Europe
Here parliaments had to recover from highly subordinate positions, particularly under the antiparliamentary fascist regimes in Italy and Spain. In Spain, exceptionally, the Cortes did become the major

arena for debating reforms, including the new constitution, between 1977–8. Parliament played a key role in developing the new democratic system because it 'was the only meeting place for the democratically-minded. At the outset of democracy, it was the place where all the advocates of renewal met' (Giol *et al.*, 1990, p. 96). Yet once the new democracy consolidated, the esteem of parliament soon declined and the Cortes became dominated by disciplined parties and strong leaders. Parliament played a less crucial role in the other Southern European transitions (Italy, Portugal and Greece); it remains a weaker institution than elsewhere in Western Europe. Pridham (1990, p. 246) notes that one feature of the new party-led democracies of Southern Europe is the limited expectations held of their parliaments.

Latin America
The position of assemblies in Latin America has undoubtedly strengthened in the postmilitary era. However, parliaments have rarely achieved more than marginal status and institutionalization remains limited; overall, their position is weaker than in Southern Europe. In part this reflects the strong man tradition of political leadership; the president crowds out the legislature. A common tactic is to deny deputies even the most basic facilities. In Nicaragua, for instance, deputies do not have individual offices, and they are forced to hold committee meetings in the open air (Close, 1995, p. 56). Reflecting these constraints, many legislators are of low calibre, a weakness reinforced by the tradition and sometimes the stipulation of rapid turnover. Many deputies remain more concerned with gaining patronage than shaping policy. Even in a more democratic era, the realistic goal facing Latin American assemblies is not to gain sovereignty but rather 'to restrain the prince and discipline the powerful' (Chalmers, 1990).

Eastern Europe
Some assemblies in Eastern Europe, such as Poland's and Hungary's, were beginning to achieve modest grievance-raising and policy-influencing powers even before the collapse of communist rule. This experience undoubtedly helped such legislatures to acquire more weight in the postcommunist era. In several ways, postcommunist parliaments are in a

favourable position to influence legislation and policy. Unlike Southern Europe, political parties and interest groups remain weak, giving legislators exceptional autonomy in their work. Yet this potential is only partly realized. High turnover, limited calibre, poor support and weak internal procedures limit the assembly's ability to confront assertive executives (Agh, 1996). As in Southern Europe, the general esteem of East European parliaments declined sharply once the immediate crisis of transition was over. 'When burning problems have to be resolved', says Karasimeonov (1996, p. 58) of the Bulgarian National Assembly, 'people have difficulty accepting the parliament as a place of strife and useless debates'. And as in Latin America, presidents are no friends of parliaments. In Russia, President Yeltsin often disregarded the Duma; at one point, he even denied the legislature the funds needed to buy paper on which to print its laws.

Definition

A parliament is **institutionalized** when:

- It deals effectively with legislation
- It has a well-developed internal organization (for example committee system)
- It abides by its own rules
- It achieves an accepted place in the political system.

Institutionalization is a key task of new parliaments. James Madison noted this problem during the first American Congress when he complained that 'every day, we suffer from the want of precedents'.

The decline of assemblies?

The decline-of-parliament thesis maintains that assemblies in consolidated democracies are losing power to the executive. Weighing up this thesis provides a suitable way of rounding off this chapter. Consider, first, the arguments for the idea that parliaments have been marginalized: assemblies have, it is claimed, lost control of the legislative process. Bills pass through the assembly on their way to the statute book but their origins lie elsewhere: in the executive, the bureaucracy and the interest groups. This argument is an old one. As early as 1921, the British historian Lord Bryce (p. 370) had claimed that

'general causes ... have been tending to reduce the prestige and authority of legislative bodies'. He referred specifically to the growth of disciplined parties and the increased complexity of policy-making, both of which strengthen the executive. More recently, Petersson (1989, p. 96) concludes that 'every description of the form of government of the modern state seems to end up with a discouraging conclusion about the actual role of parliament'. For their sharpest critics, parliaments have become political museum-pieces.

Growing interdependence between countries poses additional problems for assemblies. Parliaments are creatures of the state; they are poorly adapted to a global era. How can national parliaments grapple with a world of international trade, intergovernmental deals, complex treaties, intricate diplomacy and war? The executive is where the action is. True, the American Congress is still heavily involved in international trade and foreign policy, in effect setting itself up as legislature for the world. However, as we have seen thoughout this chapter, Congress is a unique case.

Consider the European Union as an example of interdependence. Its growing authority has weakened national parliaments: assemblies only learn about European Commission decisions or agreements between member states after the fact, and by then it is too late. Thus, assemblies are in a weaker position than with national legislation where bills must at least pass through the assembly's hands on their way to the statute book. The solution, of course, is for the European Parliament to develop a more powerful role within the European Union, providing the check on the Commission that domestic legislatures cannot provide. But the European Parliament remains rather feeble. As Nugent (1994, p. 206) comments, it 'does not have full legislative powers, its budgetary powers are circumscribed and it cannot overthrow a government'.

However, to speak of the decline of assemblies in a global era is, in three ways, too simple:

- Parliaments continue to perform such functions as representation and recruitment.
- The alleged 'golden age' of parliaments was as long ago as the mid-nineteenth century; and there is little firm evidence demonstrating that parliaments have lost further ground, at least to

national governments, since 1945 (Sjolin, 1993, p. 160).

- Most important, it is possible to identify a few ways in which assemblies are growing in importance.

Parliaments are becoming more significant as arenas of debate, as intermediaries in transitions from one political order to another, as raisers of grievances and especially as agencies of oversight. Televising proceedings has made assemblies a more significant arena for deliberation. Moreover, where the American Congress led the way in equipping assembly members with the staff and resources to do their jobs professionally, other legislatures are belatedly following suit. In the assemblies of Western Europe, backbench members have become more assertive: party leaders can no longer expect well-educated career politicians to be totally deferential (Norton, 1990b). Specialized committees, and members with a driving interest in policy, are increasingly successful in contributing to the debate over policy.

Our conclusion, then, is that the role of parliaments is changing rather than declining. Law-making is but one aspect of the modern assembly's role. Indeed, it can be argued that the main responsibility for legislation should not rest in the assembly, given the instability to which assembly-dominated regimes have been prone. What could be more odd, asked the nineteenth-century English writer, Walter Bagehot, than government by public meeting? What assemblies can do is to oversee the executive, forcing politicians and civil servants to account for their actions before a body which still possesses a unique capacity to represent the nation.

Key reading

Next step: *Norton (1990a) is a helpful volume, drawing together the most influential writings on legislatures.*

Olson (1994) and Mezey (1979) offer comparative treatments of assemblies. On bicameralism, a major if sometimes demanding source is Tsebelis and Money (1997). The comparative approach is carried forward by Damgaard (1993) on the Nordic parliaments. For comparative studies of assemblies in democratic transitions see Liebert and Cotta (1990) on Southern Europe, and Agh (1994) or Olson and Norton (1994) on Eastern Europe. Committees are examined comparatively in Longley and Davidson (1998). For studies of parliaments in specific regions see Norton (1990b) on Western Europe, and Close (1995) on Latin America. Searing (1994) is an impressive analysis of the roles adopted by British MPs. On the European Parliament, see Jacobs and Corbett (1992). The most intensively studied legislature is the American Congress, and Mayhew (1974) and Fenno (1978) are classics. Davidson (1992) is an edited collection on the post-reform Congress, while King (1997) skilfully argues the thesis that American politics requires members of Congress to pay excessive attention to their own re-election.

The political executive is the core of government. Governing without an assembly or judiciary is perfectly possible, but ruling without an executive is impossible. But what exactly is the political executive? The term refers to the political leaders who form the top slice of government; it is the energizing force of government, setting priorities, making decisions and supervising how they are carried out. Hence the executive, which makes policy, must be distinguished from the bureaucracy, which puts policy into effect. The executive is chosen by political means, for example by election, and can be removed by the same method. The executive is accountable for the activities of government; it is where the buck stops.

> Definition
>
> The **executive** is the political tier at the apex of government. It is charged with directing the nation's affairs, supervising how policy is carried out, mobilizing support for its goals and providing both ceremonial and crisis leadership. In liberal democracies, the executive takes a presidential, parliamentary or dual form.

The categories of liberal democracy and authoritarian rule are defined by how the executive operates. Liberal democracies have succeeded in the delicate task of subjecting executive power to constitutional limits. These restrain the exercise of power and set out rules of succession to executive office. Both in theory and in practice, political leaders in liberal democracies are accountable for their conduct.

In a pure authoritarian executive, by contrast, constitutional and electoral controls are either unacknowledged or ineffective. The outward forms of elected government may be adopted but they do not constrain the exercise of power. In practice, authoritarian executives are unaccountable – human rights are neither recognized nor respected, and violence may be inflicted on political opponents. Power is far from total; indeed, the authoritarian ruler may have a lower capacity to steer society than elected rulers in a liberal democracy. But the scope of rule is limited only by political, not constitutional, realities.

In liberal democracies, executives fall into three groups: presidential, parliamentary and dual. In *presidential* systems, of which the USA is the leading example, the chief executive is elected independently of the assembly and for a fixed tenure. Presidents are elected by, and remain responsible to, the electorate. In the *parliamentary* type, found in most of West Europe as well as Australia, Canada and New Zealand, the head of government leads a council of ministers which emerges from the assembly and continues in office just so long as it retains the support of the legislature. An elected president or hereditary monarch serves as ceremonial head of state. The *dual* (or semi-presidential) executive mixes the two pure types. Here, a powerful elected president coexists with a prime minister accountable to the assembly. This dual executive, exemplified by the Fifth French Republic, has been adopted in many postcommunist states. We will examine each of these three forms before turning to the authoritarian executive.

Presidential government

The world contains many presidents but few examples of presidential government. All tin-pot dictators can style themselves 'president' and many do so. However, the existence of a self-styled president is not a sure sign of presidential government. Presidentialism proper is a form of constitutional rule in which the president acts as chief executive, using the authority derived from direct election and governing with an independent legislature (Figure 12.1). This definition excludes not only arbitrary dictators but also elected presidents whose duties are purely ceremonial, as in many parliamentary systems. Presidential government is rare, confined largely to the United States, where the system began, and Latin American countries influenced by the USA. Just as Europe is the fount of parliamentary government, so the home of presidentialism is the Americas. To understand presidentialism, therefore, we must examine how the American system operates in practice.

The United States constitution tersely states that 'the Executive Power shall be vested in a President of the United States'. He (and all have been men) is chosen by popular election, operating through a nominal electoral college, for a four-year term. Under a constitutional amendment of 1951, presidents are limited to two terms of office. During his tenure, the president can only be dismissed through impeachment by Congress for 'high crimes and misdemeanours'. Just as Congress cannot normally remove the president, neither can the president dissolve Congress and call new elections. This separation of executive and legislative institutions distinguishes presidential from parliamentary government.

For the framers of the American constitution meeting at Philadelphia in 1787, the issue of the executive posed a dilemma. They quickly agreed that a single executive was needed for 'decision, activity, secrecy and despatch'. Yet they also wanted to avoid anything which might prove to be a 'foetus of monarchy'. After all, the American revolution had just rid the new nation of England's George III. The founders' creative solution was the presidency, an office which would offer energy to government in a republic in which Congress was expected to play the leading role.

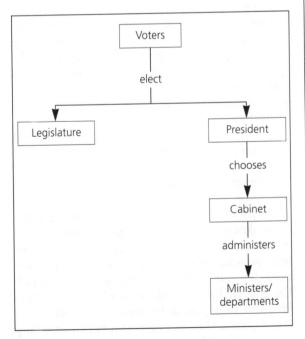

Figure 12.1 The presidential executive

Definition

The presidential executive consists of three features:

- Popular election of the president (to provide legitimacy).
- Fixed terms of offices for the president and the assembly, neither of which can be brought down by the other (to forestall arbitrary use of power).
- The president directs the government and makes key appointments to it.

See: Shugart and Carey (1992), von Mettenheim and Rockman (1997).

Although the American presidency is often seen as a symbol of power, the institution was designed as part of a concerted attempt to control executive pretension. The smallprint of the constitution hems in the office with restrictions. The president is commander in chief but Congress retains the power to declare war. He makes government appointments but only with Senate approval. He recommends to Congress 'such measures as he shall judge necessary and expedient' but is offered no means to ensure his proposals are accepted. He can veto legislation but

EXHIBIT 12.1

Joint presidencies

Being president, we might think, is a one-person job. Indeed, Lijphart (1992) defines the presidential system so as to exclude the possibility of a multi-person presidency. Yet directly-elected joint presidencies have been tried in several countries, notably Uruguay, Cyprus and Bosnia, in an effort to represent within the executive the major interests of a divided society. In Uruguay, the original idea was to give all the leading strong-men a stake in power; in Cyprus, to give representation to both the Greek and Turkish communities; and in Bosnia, to reflect the interests of Moslems, Croats and Serbs. The performance of these collegial executives is hard to judge. As a system of last resort, they are only adopted in difficult circumstances which would test any form of government. In Bosnia, which established its triple

executive in 1996 after a bitter ethnic war, a collegial system was the only form of government acceptable to all sides. Its success lay in its mere existence.

Country	Period	Executive structure
Uruguay	1952–66	A nine-member National Council of Government with a rotating chair.
Cyprus	1960–63	A dual structure with a Greek President and a Turkish Vice-President, each with a veto in foreign affairs.
Bosnia	1996–	A tripartite presidency consisting of a Croat, Moslem and Serb.

Congress can in turn override his objections. Congress, not the president, controls the purse strings. President Kennedy summarized the peculiar ambivalence of the office:

> the president is rightly described as a man of extraordinary powers. Yet it is also true that he must wield those powers under extraordinary limitations.

Two points flow from the president's constitutional position. First, to describe the relationship between the president and Congress as a 'separation of powers' is misleading. In reality there is a separation of institutions rather than of legislative and executive powers. President and Congress share the powers of government: the president seeks to influence Congress but cannot dictate to it. This separated system, as Jones (1994) calls it, is subtle, intricate and balanced. It reflects a successful attempt by the founders to build checks and balances into American government.

Second, in a system of shared control presidential power becomes the power to persuade (Neustadt, 1980). As President Truman said, 'the principal power that the president has is to bring people in and try to persuade them to do what they ought to do without persuasion'. In this task of persuasion,

the president has three options: going Washington; going public; and going international (Rose, 1991):

- 'Going Washington' involves the president in wheeling and dealing with Congress and its members, assembling majorities for his legislative proposals.
- 'Going public' means the president uses his unrivalled access to the mass media to influence public opinion and persuade Washington indirectly; Ronald Reagan was a master of this strategy.
- 'Going international', finally, reflects American involvement in world affairs. Every president now spends most time on foreign relations and national security issues.

Whichever route(s) the president takes, his task is persuasion.

The paradox of the American presidency – political weakness amid the trappings of omnipotence – is reflected in the president's support network. To meet presidential needs for information and advice, a conglomeration of supporting bodies has evolved. Collectively known as the Executive Office of the President, these provide far more direct support than is available to the chief executive in parliamentary systems. Yet this apparatus of advice has often

---

BOX 12.1
Presidential government: advantages and disadvantages

Advantages

- The president's fixed term provides stability in the executive
- Popular election of the chief executive is democratic, enabling citizens to vote both for president and for members of the legislature
- The legislature is not charged with supporting or bringing down a government, thus enabling it, in principle, to judge bills on merit
- The separation of powers encourages limited government and thus protects liberty
- Elected by the country at large, presidents take a national view and seek to cajole the assembly into doing likewise.

Disadvantages

- The danger of deadlock when executive and legislature disagree

- Fixed terms of office are too inelastic; 'everything is rigid, specified, dated', wrote Bagehot
- A one- or two-term limit wastes the experience and ability of a good president. Not infrequently, presidents seek to amend the constitution so as to continue in office
- Only one party can win the presidency; everyone else loses
- Politicians with the public appeal to win elections are often political outsiders who make poor chief executives
- Too much depends on one person. The popular focus on the president, exaggerated by television, leads to unrealistic expectations
- Evidence suggests presidential democracies are less likely to consolidate than parliamentary democracies (Stepan and Skach, 1993). In particular, a frustrated or ambitious president may become a dictator.

Sources: Linz (1990), Mainwaring and Shugart (1997a).

---

proved to be a weakness. Many advisers are political outsiders, appointed by the president at the start of his tenure before his eye for Washington's politics is set. Far from helping the president, advisers sometimes end up undermining his position. The Watergate scandal in the 1970s destroyed the presidency of Richard Nixon; the Iran–Contra scandal in the 1980s undermined the reputation of Ronald Reagan. One problem is that the presidential system lacks a strong Cabinet to offer a counterbalance to personal advisers. In the USA, Cabinet meetings are little more than a presidential photo-oppportunity. Department heads follow their own agenda, not the president's. This is in sharp contrast to the parliamentary executive in which the cabinet is the collective apex of the decision-making process.

The experience of Latin America democracies such as Chile, Venezuela and Costa Rica confirms the conclusion that presidents are in a weak position unless they can succeed in mobilizing support from other branches of government. Even though Latin America has a stronger tradition of personal rule than the United States, its democratically-elected presidents have experienced difficulty in getting legislation through a hostile assembly (non-elected

presidents on the continent have often dispensed with assemblies altogether but these are not presidential systems as we have defined them). Indeed, as the status of legislatures has risen with democratization, so presidents have found the problems of effective governance increasing. In Latin America (as in South Korea), many presidents face the additional hindrance of a one-term limit, meaning they become lame ducks as their tenure proceeds. Mainwaring's conclusion (1992, p. 113) is sobering for those who equate presidential rule with strong government: 'effective executive power is almost indispensable if democracy is to thrive, yet the history of presidential democracies in Latin America has often been one of immobilized executives'. Many strong men have ended their careers as weak presidents.

It is for such reasons, suggests Linz (1990, p. 127), that presidential government has proved to be 'less conducive to democratic stability' than parliamentary rule. Indeed, Linz argues that the United States is the only unbroken example of presidential rule in a democracy. He believes that the presidential system places too large and risky a bet on the ability of one leader to overcome the divided powers which are built into the system. Further, the president's fixed tenure reduces the ability to change leaders in response to new circumstances. Linz therefore recommends the more flexible parliamentary order, particularly to new democracies with deep political cleavages and many political parties.

Parliamentary government

Where the presidential executive is separate from the assembly and independently elected, the parliamentary executive is organically linked to the legislature (Figure 12.2). The government emerges from the assembly and can be brought down by a vote of no confidence. By the same token the government can, in most cases, dissolve the assembly and call fresh elections. If the paradox of presidentalism is executive weakness amid the appearance of strength, the puzzle of parliamentary government is to explain why effective government can still emerge from the mutual vulnerability of the assembly and the executive.

> **Definition**
> **Parliamentary government** has three main features:
>
> - The governing parties emerge from the assembly. Government ministers are usually drawn from, and remain members of, the legislature.
> - The executive is collegial, taking the form of a cabinet or council of ministers in which the prime minister was traditionally just first among equals.
> - The head of the government (called prime minister, premier or chancellor) and the cabinet can be dismissed from office through a vote of no confidence by parliament. The post of prime minister is usually separate from that of head of state.
>
> Source: Lijphart (1992).

If the United States is the classic instance of presidentialism, Britain is the most influential example of parliamentary government. After an election the party which wins a majority of seats in the House of Commons forms the government; the leader of the winning party becomes Prime Minister (PM) and selects 20 or so parliamentary colleagues to form the cabinet. The cabinet is the formal lynchpin of the system; it is the focus of accountability to parliament and even the strongest PM cannot govern without its support. The cabinet meets weekly, chaired by the PM. Government accountability to the assembly is tight. All ministers, including the PM, must regularly defend their policies 'in the house'; the opposition will demand a vote of no confidence whenever it senses an advantage from launching an attack. However the government's majority normally offers in-built protection against such assaults. The monarch sits above the entire political process, meeting regularly with the PM but rarely if ever intervening in political decisions.

The party system and parliamentary government

The party system is the crucial influence on the operation of parliamentary government. Where a single party holds a majority in the assembly (as in Britain), government is stable and decisive, perhaps even excessively so. But where no party wins a parliamentary majority (as in most of continental Europe), coalition governments are slower to form and quicker to fall. So, in effect, parliamentary government has two variants, depending on the party system. These two forms merit separate discussion.

Single party government

In the British case, party is the bridge between cabinet and assembly. Through party discipline, the executive dominates the assembly, controlling its agenda and timetable. The cabinet is officially the top committee of state but it is also an unofficial meeting of the party's leaders. As long as the senior party figures represented in the cabinet remain sensitive to the views of their backbenchers (and often even if they do not), they can control the Commons. Each party has a Whip's Office to ensure backbenchers (ordinary MPs) vote as the party's leaders require. Even without the attentions of the Whips, MPs will generally toe the party line if they want to become ministers themselves. In a strong party system such as Britain's, showing too much independence is an unwise career move.

The importance of party to the effective operation

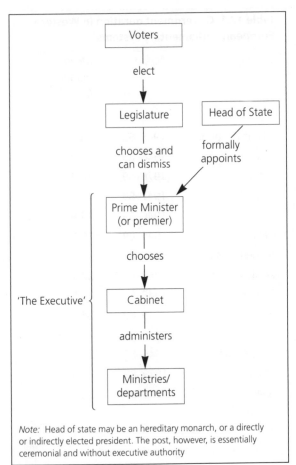

Figure 12.2 The parliamentary executive

of parliamentary government is seen even more clearly in other British-style systems. In New Zealand, for instance, open defiance of a caucus (parliamentary party) decision by an MP 'would constitute grounds for expulsion from the party and is tantamount to a formal expulsion' (Mulgan, 1997, p. 114). In Australia, a cabinet is more a meeting of the ruling party than of the government. Cabinet is captured by party. So where the executive can count upon disciplined majority support in the assembly, as in these Westminster systems, government can be decisive.

Coalition government

Throughout Western Europe (and since 1996 in New Zealand), proportional electoral systems enable a range of parties to secure seats in the assembly; a majority party is unusual if not unknown. In this more complex situation of a fragmented legislature, government becomes more uncertain and cautious. After an election the outgoing government remains as a caretaker administration until a coalition emerges which is acceptable to the legislature; the same applies when a government falls mid-session. Forming a government can take several months of hard bargaining. Typically, the head of state appoints the leader of the largest party as *formateur*, to form an administration (Figure 12.3). The *formateur's* task is made more difficult if a formal vote of investiture is required, demonstrating majority support for the new government, as in Belgium, Italy and Sweden. The job is simpler if the new government just has to avoid a vote of no confidence.

Coalition government can be unstable. In extreme cases, such as Italy's First Republic and France's Fourth, government duration was measured in months rather than years (Table 12.1). But we should not exaggerate this point. Coalitions can be long-lasting (by the same token, single-party admin-

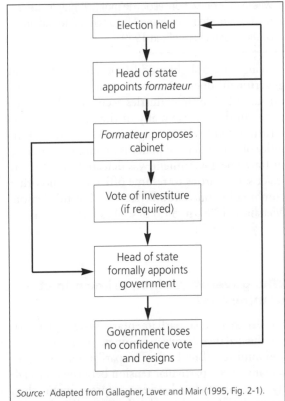

Figure 12.3 Building coalition governments

istrations in countries such as Britain do not always last their full course). In Germany coalition government has proved fairly durable helped by the constructive vote of no confidence, now also adopted in Hungary. In Ireland, coalitions have been sustained by the exceptional party loyalty of MPs and by the single-minded commitment of governing parties to their own survival in office. As a rule, coalition governments last longest when: (a) the participating parties have a parliamentary majority and a compatible ideology, (b) the coalition is based on a small number of parties, (c) the economy performs well and, linked to these points, (d) the government remains popular in the country (Warwick, 1994, p. 9).

Definition

The constructive vote of no confidence requires an assembly to select a new prime minister before it can dispose of the incumbent. The purpose of this rule is to reduce government instability where coalitions are the norm. The device comes from Germany, where only one Chancellor (Helmut Schmidt in 1982) has been ousted by this method since the founding of the Federal Republic in 1949.

In any case, a slight modification of the parties in government does not constitute a political earthquake in European countries accustomed to coalitions. In due course many of the same characters return, often to the same ministries, so that continuity of personnel and policy is maintained. Indeed, in Italy one government was defeated only for the exact same parties to resume office when no other combination proved to be feasible. For this reason, Mershon (1996, p. 549) describes Italy as a case of 'transitory cabinets staffed by permanent incumbents'.

Who governs: cabinet, prime minister or ministers?

Governance in a parliamentary system depends on the balance between cabinet, prime minister and ministers (Box 12.2). The parliamentary executive involves a particular tension between collegiality and hierarchy, between a preeminent chief minister and a ministerial college of political equals. The general trend is for prime ministers to acquire

Table 12.1 Government duration in Western European parliamentary systems

Country	Period	Mean duration (months)
France (Fourth republic)	1945–58	4.7
Italy	1948–89	8.3
Portugal	1976–89	10.3
Finland	1947–89	10.5
Belgium	1946–89	14.8
Denmark	1945–89	19.0
Netherlands	1946–89	21.4
West Germany	1948–89	22.1
Sweden	1948–89	24.5
Norway	1945–89	24.8
Austria	1945–89	26.3
United Kingdom	1945–89	28.0
Spain	1979–89	30.4
Ireland	1948–89	30.7

Source: Warwick (1994), Table 1.1.

more weight in relation to the cabinet. This reflects three factors:

- Increasing media focus on the premie
- The international role of the chief executive in a global era
- The growing need for coordination of policy as governance becomes more complex (King, 1994a).

Finland provides an exceptionally clear case of *cabinet* government. By law, the Finnish State Council is granted extensive decision-making authority and in 1988, for example, it handled 4472 agenda items in 81 formal sessions (Nousiainen, 1994, p. 91). Both the Prime Minister and individual ministers are subject to constraints arising from Finland's complex multiparty coalitions. Prime Ministers (who last only two years on average) are little more than chairs of council meetings; they find

---

BOX 12.2
Models of power in the parliamentary executive

Model	Definition	Example
Cabinet government	The Cabinet determines policy, with ministers and even the prime minister acting within a collegial framework	Finland
Prime Ministerial government	The Prime Minister is the dominant figure, using the cabinet to announce decisions and dealing directly with individual ministers	Germany
Ministerial government	Ministers take major decisions within their specialist areas, with little overall co-ordination	Italy (First Republic)

---

their authority further squeezed by an influential elected President. Individual ministers also find their hands tied by their party and its coalition agreements.

At the other extreme, Germany's constitution emphasises hierarchy rather than collegiality among government ministers. Germany is an example of *prime ministerial* government, called chancellor democracy in Germany. Accountability to the Bundestag (lower house) is mainly channelled through the chancellor. He answers to parliament; ministers answer to him. The strong position of the chief executive derives from the Basic Law of the Federal Republic. This states that the 'chancellor shall determine, and be responsible for, the general policy guidelines'. The powerful Chancellor's Office has a large staff of about 500. The status of the job has been further enhanced by a series of (sometimes literally) heavyweight incumbents. Just six chancellors have held office since the Federal Republic was established in 1949. The strength of the chancellor diminishes the role of the cabinet, and many matters are despatched there without discussion. For instance, the key decisions about German reunification were made by Chancellor Kohl and simply reported to the cabinet.

In many parliamentary systems the sense of collective responsibility within the executive is even more limited. In extreme cases, the result is *ministerial* government. For instance, the Italian constitution enjoins collective responsibility of the Council of Ministers to parliament but in the First Republic this was notably lacking. Inter-departmental coordination of policy was notoriously weak and conflict became endemic. The underlying problem was that the parties were extremely factionalized. These

factions tended to colonize different ministries, which were thus at odds with departments belonging to other factions. Prime ministers were in no position to impose coherence on this fragmented executive; they were often anonymous figures whose main virtue was their acceptability to all the parties in the coalition.

Ministerial government is also found, in more constructive form, in countries where technical expertise is valued. In the Netherlands, for instance, departments guard their traditional independence, are staffed by specialists and recruit their own staff. They would not take kindly to orders from the Prime Minister. Ministers serve with the prime minister, not under him (Andeweg, 1991). In Germany, Sturm (1994, p. 82) reports,

> a justice minister should be trained in law while a minister responsible for the family and the young should not be a batchelor. As a rule defense ministers should have served in the armed forces.

The Ministers of Finance, Interior and Justice cannot be overruled on proposals affecting their departments, provided the chancellor sides with them (Andeweg, 1997, p. 60). The combination of a powerful chancellor and specialized ministers reduces the extent to which cabinet acts as a collegial and coherent body.

The strength of any prime minister depends critically on control of cabinet appointments. British prime ministers have exceptional room for maneuver: subject to some constraints of party balance they form a government of their choosing from the talent available in the parliamentary party. Only a handful of senior figures possess such stature

EXHIBIT 12.2

Israel's directly-elected Prime Minister

The essence of parliamentary government is that the cabinet, and the prime minister, emerge from the assembly and depend on its continued confidence for their tenure. In 1996, however, Israel introduced direct election of its Prime Minister, in effect adding a presidential element to a parliamentary system. Unlike a true presidency, the prime minister can still be removed from office by majority vote of the Knesset (parliament). But this is a suicide pill for members since it automatically generates new elections for the assembly as well as for the Prime Minister.

The reform was introduced to raise the status of the premier's office and speed up the process of coalition formation. Israel's pure form of proportional representation gives seats in the Knesset to many parties, which would then squabble over which one should be awarded the prize of Prime Minister. With that issue now settled by the voters, it was hoped that governments would form faster and become more cohesive. It was also anticipated that direct election might reduce the number of parties in the Knesset since extensive ticket-splitting was not expected.

The initial results, however, were disappointing. The first contest in 1996 divided the country on a central issue – the peace process – and did not deliver a clear mandate. The new Prime Minister, Benjamin Netanyahu, won by a margin of less than 1 per cent. The number of parties in the Knesset, far from declining, actually increased. The cabinet remained fragmented, containing members from six parties, and for the first time in Israel's history the Prime Minister's party was in a minority in cabinet. A more prudent reform than direct election of the Prime Minister might have been to make the electoral system less proportional, so as to exclude small extreme parties from the Knesset altogether.

Further reading: Arian (1996, 1997), Hazan (1996, 1997b).

or experience as to be too important – or too dangerous – to be excluded. King (1994b) calls these 'the big beasts of the jungle'. Moreover, what prime ministers give they may also take away; cabinet reshuffles are frequent. Further, British prime ministers, unlike many others, can restructure government so as to vary the number of ministries.

But where coalition government is the norm, the autonomy of the prime minister is reduced. In many European countries the distribution of ministerial posts is the result of bargaining between the coalition partners, with each party filling its share from its own nominees. In Japan under LDP rule the same principle applies, but operating within the party's factions. In these conditions the premier's role is diminished, with ministers owing more loyalty to their party or faction leader than to the prime minister.

Whether or not the role of cabinet is declining, it is certainly evolving. As government has grown, so too has the number of ministers. In Canada, the cabinet reached the unwieldy size of 40 by 1987, reflecting the representation principle which requires the various provinces and linguistic groups

to be included in a strongly federal cabinet. Elsewhere cabinets have been kept to a more manageable size, usually around two dozen, by excluding some ministers from cabinet. This creates an outer ministry alongside the inner ministry of cabinet members. To belong to 'the ministry', to use a New Zealand phrase, does not guarantee a seat round the cabinet table. Canada has now introduced the device of non-cabinet ministers to pare the size of its cabinet.

The crucial development in the operation of cabinets has been the emergence of cabinet committees as key decision sites. These committees often develop during and after wars, reflecting the volume and urgency of business. In most countries, full cabinet now acts mainly as a ratifying body – an umpire rather than a decision-taker. Decisions made by Australia's nine cabinet committees can only be reopened in full cabinet with the approval of the Prime Minister. New Zealand has around 12 committees, including an influential one which examines overall strategy. So cabinet government, to the extent that it still exists, has become government by the cabinet system, with the real decisions made in cabinet committees. Indeed, even these commit-tees now largely ratify decisions fixed up before the committee meets.

Heads of state and parliamentary government

One of the hallmarks of a parliamentary system is, in Bagehot's classic analysis, the distinction between the 'efficient' and 'dignified' aspects of government (Bagehot, 1963, first pub. 1867). 'Efficient' leader-ship, as we have seen, rests with the cabinet, premier and ministers. Dignified or ceremonial leadership centres upon the head of state, either a titular presi-dent or a constitutional monarch.

In an era of popular sovereignty, royal heads of state remain surprisingly numerous, particularly in Europe and Asia. Half the countries of Western Europe, for instance, are constitutional monarchies (Box 12.3). In some former British colonies such as Canada, a governor-general appointed by the Queen on the recommendation of the prime minister acts as a stand-in for the monarch. But the duties of most modern monarchs are ceremonial: banquets without end. For example, Jeanne Sauvé, Canada's governor general between 1984 and 1990, awarded 1921 medals, gave 427 speeches and travelled 573 000 kilometres on offical business (Landes, 1995, p. 135). Such worthy activity does take some pressure off prime ministers, creating more time for them to concentrate on the political aspects of their job.

Royal influence can be real in fragmented politi-cal systems undergoing change. In the 1970s, King Juan Carlos helped to steer Spain's transition to democracy. More recently, the King of Belgium played a conciliatory role in his country's long march to federal status; the King once famously declared, 'I am the only Belgian'. Senelle (1996, p. 281) claims that

> were it not for the monarchy as symbol of the cohesion of the kingdom and therefore the visible incarnation of federal loyalty, the Belgian experi-ment would be doomed to failure.

Perhaps national divisions explain why the Belgian king still has 'more real power than almost any European constitutional monarch and perhaps as much as a constitutional monarch can decently

---

BOX 12.3

Some royal heads of state in par-liamentary democracies

Country	Head of state	Accession
Belgium	King Albert III	1993
Denmark	Queen Margrethe II	1972
Japan	Emperor Akihito	1989
Netherlands	Queen Beatrix Wilhemina Armgard	1980
Norway	King Harald V	1991
Spain	King Juan Carlos I	1975
Sweden	King Carl XVI Gustav	1973
United Kingdom	Queen Elizabeth II	1952

---

exercise' (Fitzmaurice, 1996, p. 87). In 1990, for instance, King Baudouin declined to sign an abortion bill into law. The ingenious compromise was to declare the monarch 'unable to reign' for 36 hours, during which time the cabinet assumed the king's functions and signed the bill.

Where parliamentary systems take a republican form, an elected or appointed president acts as titular head of state. Sometimes the president is directly elected by the population, as in Austria, Ireland and Portugal; in other cases the chief of state is elected by parliament or by an electoral college. This body usually comprises the national legislature plus representatives of regional or local government, as in Germany, Greece, India and Israel. But the duties of even elected presidents are largely hon-orific, with presidents using their public position only occasionally to nudge the political agenda towards problems receiving inadequate attention from the politicians. Even directly-elected presidents in parliamentary systems are expected to speak for the nation as a whole, leaving the detailed politics to parliament. One reason for the success of Mary Robinson (President of Ireland, 1990–97) was pre-cisely her ability to capture a *national* mood of a modernizing country.

The dual executive: presidents *and* prime ministers

Presidential and parliamentary executives are straightforward – one top leader, whether prime minister or president, is the fulcrum of the government. With the dual executive we enter more complex and varied territory. The dual executive combines an elected president with a prime minister and cabinet accountable to parliament. The president usually has special responsibility for foreign affairs and can also appoint ministers (including the prime minister), initiate referendums, veto legislation and dissolve the assembly. Whatever the specific powers (and they vary between countries), the president in a dual executive is *in* rather than *above* politics. This distinguishes the dual executive from a parliamentary system in which an elected president plays a ceremonial role.

The dual executive is a hybrid. Indeed in a commonly-used phrase Duverger (1980) refers to the dual system as the 'semi-presidential executive'. Its purpose is to marry within the executive the national focus of an elected president with a prime minister who responds to the specific interests represented in the assembly. As a two-headed system, the dual executive creates an invitation to struggle between president and prime minister. Despite the dangers of political competition, clashing egos and tangled accountability, the dual executive is growing in popularity. An established form in France and Finland, the dual executive has proved attractive to postcommunist regimes.

> **Definition**
> **The dual executive** combines an elected president performing political tasks with a prime minister who heads a cabinet accountable to parliament. The prime minister, usually appointed by the president, is responsible for day-to-day domestic government (including relations with the assembly) but the president retains an oversight role, responsibility for foreign affairs, and can usually take emergency powers. The best-established examples are France and Finland; the system has also been adopted in postcommunist states.

France

If the United States exemplifies the presidential system, the French Fifth Republic provides the model for the dual executive. Established in 1958 to overcome political instability, the constitution created a presidency fit for the dominating presence of its first occupant, General Charles de Gaulle. Directly elected since 1962, the president serves for an unusually long period of seven years. De Gaulle argued that 'power emanates directly from the people, which implies that the Head of State, elected by the nation, is the source and holder of that power'.

Accordingly, the president is granted an extensive array of reponsibilities. He appoints the Prime Minister, presides over the Council of Ministers, signs decrees, appoints top civil servants and three members of the Constitutional Council, is commander in chief, can call referendums, dissolve the assembly, exercise emergency powers and has special responsibility for foreign affairs (Meny, 1990, p. 198). In pursuing these roles, the president is supported by an influential personal staff in the Élysée Palace. So far, all five Presidents have sought to govern in expansive style. As Meny comments, there is probably no other Western country where the president would expect not only to exemplify the national will but also to have the final say on prestige building projects in the capital.

> **Definition**
> **Cohabitation** occurs in a dual executive when the president's party is opposed by a majority in the assembly. This situation, which has occurred three times in the French Fifth Republic, intensifies competition between president and prime minister. It has also arisen in postcommunist Poland.

What of the prime minister in France's dual executive? Appointed by the president but accountable to parliament, the prime minister's task is never easy. He or she (Edith Cresson was PM 1991–92) directs the day- to-day work of the government, operating within the style and tone set by the President. Since the government remains accountable to parliament, much of the Prime Minister's work focuses on managing the National Assembly. The ability of the assembly to force the Prime Minister and the Council of Ministers to resign after a vote of censure is the parliamentary component of the dual executive.

The crucial relationship in the dual executive is between the president on the one hand, and prime minister and assembly on the other. While the constitution may give control of foreign affairs to the

Country profile **FRANCE**

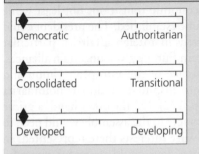

Population: 58m.

Gross domestic product per head: $20 200.

Form of government: a unitary democratic republic, headed by an elected president. The current Fifth Republic was established in 1958.

Legislature: the lower chamber, the National Assembly, contains 577 directly-elected members. The 321 members of the Senate are indirectly elected, a third at a time, through local government for a long nine-year term. The legislature is weaker than in many democracies.

Executive: France's distinctive dual executive combines a strong president, directly elected for seven years, and a prime minister who leads a Council of Ministers accountable to the assembly.

Judiciary: French law is still based on the Napoleonic Codes (1804–11). The Constitutional Court has grown in significance during the Fifth Republic.

Electoral system: a two-ballot system is used for both presidential and assembly elections, with a majority needed to win on the first round. The last experiment with PR was in 1986 for the National Assembly.

Party system: left–right conflict remains central to French politics, though parties have been less stable. The system has become largely bipolar, with well-defined coalitions of the left and right contesting the second ballot. Jacques Chirac won the Presidency for the Gaullist RPR (Rally for the Republic) in 1995. The Socialist Party under Lionel Jospin was the dominant partner in the left's victory in assembly elections in 1997. The extreme right-wing National Front is also significant.

Just how different is modern France? Traditionally, France has been portrayed as a country with a paradoxical combination of a strong state and a history of political instability. The case for French exceptionalism can be stated in three words: the French revolution. Of course, the shock-waves of the revolution of 1789 reverberated throughout Europe as the destruction of absolute monarchy laid the groundwork for the emergence of modern, secular nation-states. But the revolution created a distinctive ethos within France itself. Like other states built on revolution, notably the United States, France is an idea as well as a country. But in France the myths remain contested. The legacy of the revolution is not just a disputed creed of liberty, equality and fraternity. It is also a widespread belief in the ability of the state to implement its ideas rationally, even against opposition from a diverse and sometimes hostile society. The result, it is claimed, is a strong but unstable political system characterized by haughty bureaucrats, extensive regulation, limited pluralism and a political culture which combines dependence on, with hostility towards, the state.

Yet French uniqueness certainly declined, and possibly disappeared, in the second half of the twentieth century. Rapid modernization, urbanization and industrialization created a more conventional and consolidated democracy. The retreat from empire left France, like Britain, as a middle-ranking European power. Membership of the European Union encouraged the French political class to negotiate and compromise with its new partners. France's governing architecture of a dual executive remains distinctive but it works: policies are formed, decisions are reached. The party system has settled and even the judiciary has acquired some weight. 'The revolutionary impulse is exhausted', concludes Hayward (1994, p. 32). France today seems to be a normal country, preoccupied with the workaday question of finding jobs for all its people.

So contemporary France is no longer a revolutionary society. But to portray France as just another country is to go too far. Inherited traditions still condition the way France approaches its typically European combination of a cosseted workforce and mass unemployment. Public discourse still tends to assume that the state must be capable of creating new jobs while protecting the rights of existing workers. *Dirigisme* (state direction), suggests Wright (1997), has evolved rather than disappeared. And while France has become less distinctive, French culture itself remains intolerant of difference. France today is a consolidated democracy, certainly, but perhaps not yet a fully *liberal* democracy.

Further reading: Morris (1994), Stevens (1996), Wright (1989, 1997).
www.premier-ministre.gouv.fr/som.htm

president and reserve domestic policy to the prime minister, an interdependent world does not permit such pigeon-holing. France's relationship with the EU, for instance, encompasses both foreign and domestic affairs. Presidents and prime ministers therefore need to work together, a task made easier when the party in the Élysée Palace also has a majority in the assembly. This was the case from 1962–86 and in these circumstances presidential power tended to flourish; incumbents extended their reach to, and perhaps even beyond, constitutional limits. However, between 1986 and 1988, and again from 1993 to 1995, socialist President Mitterrand confronted a conservative assembly. After the 1997 parliamentary election the situation was reversed: a Gaullist President, Jacques Chirac, had to work alongside a socialist Prime Minister, Lionel Jospin. In such periods of cohabitation, presidential power tends to shrink as prime ministers assert their constitutional duty to 'determine and direct the policy of the nation'. Crucially, though, cohabitation has not led to a crisis of the regime. The French experience shows that the dual executive can provide stable government even when president and prime minister belong to different parties.

Postcommunist states

In the early 1990s, experts on France's double-headed executive were flown to Eastern European capitals to advise fledgling democracies on the design of their new governing institutions (Keeler and Schain, 1997, p. 84). All Eastern European countries have adopted a French-influenced dual executive in which presidents exercise a highly variable but often extremely significant role. In operation, the postcommunist executive often deviates sharply from the French model, either because of presidential assertiveness or because institutions have not fully consolidated. Yet the French model of a semi-presidential executive proved more exportable than either America's pure presidential, or Britain's pure parliamentary, system. Communism's collapse has considerably increased the number of dual executives in the world.

To postcommunist states, the dual executive seemed to promise the best of both worlds. On the one hand the president could symbolize national unity in uncertain states, adopt a national perspec-

tive, restrain extreme strands in the assembly and generally steer the country through the trauma of political and economic transition, not least while assemblies became established. The president could also act decisively in foreign affairs, a particular concern in Eastern Europe given uncertain alliances, the nearby presence of the European Union and sometimes even disputed national boundaries (Bunce, 1997, p. 172). On the other hand, a prime minister accountable to the assembly would need to consider the diverse interests there represented. In addition, the president could represent powerful organs of state while the assembly expressed the concerns of society. Finally, in low-trust political systems, building in divisions within the executive seemed to offer a further check on the abuse of power.

The constitutional position of Eastern European presidents varies (Box 12.4). Generally, the more eastern countries (including here the successor republics to the Soviet Union) have the strongest, most personalized and least accountable presidents. The Russian super-president is particularly powerful. Indeed, Gorbachev complained that Russia's 1993 constitution gave Boris Yeltsin more power than even the tsar had exercised before the revolution. 'Tsar Boris' has sought to govern partly by decree, thus bypassing parliament altogether. Not for nothing did Yeltsin jokingly refer to himself as 'Boris the First'. Conversely, the parliament of the Czech Republic, the most Western of the postcommunist states, has rebuffed attempts by President Vaclav Havel to secure more powers. The prime minister Vaclav Klaus proved to be the more influential figure, despite Havel's prestige as the leader of Czechoslovakia's velvet revolution. Hungary, too, is moving toward a true parliamentary system.

To date, the main feature of the dual executive in postcommunist states has been conflict, sometimes magnified by personal hostility between president and prime minister. In Slovakia, relations beween President Michal Kovac and Prime Minister Vladimir Meciar deteriorated to such an extent that Kovac sued the PM for libel. The pair refused to meet face to face for 14 months before April 1996. This damaging conflict was one reason why the European Union declined to open negotiations on Slovakia's accession. Throughout the postcommunist world, presidents and prime ministers have

BOX 12.4
Presidential powers in Eastern Europe

	Directly elected?	Nominate PM and dissolve assembly?	Emergency powers?	Authority over foreign and defence policy?	Introduce bills?
Bulgaria	Yes	Yes	Yes	Yes	No
Czech Republic	No	Yes	No	No	No
Hungary	No	Yes	Yes	Yes	Yes
Poland	Yes	Yes	No	Yes	Yes
Romania	Yes	Yes	Yes	No	No
Slovakia	No	Yes	No	No	Yes

Source: Baylis (1996). See also Budge, Newton *et al.* (1997), pp. 239–44.

engaged in turf wars to establish the extent of their own powers. Presidents such as Lech Walesa in Poland were certainly not content with a ceremonial role; several, Walesa included, threatened to establish their own parties and most sought to build their own staffs of advisers to act as a counterweight to the government apparatus controlled by the prime minister.

Two interpretations can be offered for the conflictual nature of the dual executive in postcommunist Europe. The first is that jousting between presidents and prime ministers will continue unabated because personalities are more important than institutions in the politics of Eastern Europe: postcommunist governments are less rule-bound – less institutionalized – than those in the West. Politicians are concerned with power and voters with their daily struggle; neither group cares greatly for constitutions. In Belarus the president initiated a referendum in 1996 to extend his term of office and to give him greater powers over both the assembly and the constitutional court. Parliament responded by proposing to abolish the presidency altogether. Further East, in the central Asian republic of Uzbekistan, the presidency is even more personalized:

> power resides as much in the person of the president as in the office. The Uzbek presidency is not just a formal power position; it is also the center of an extensive informal network of regionally-based, patron–client ties. The president is, in effect, the chief patron. (Easter, 1997)

The second, more optimistic account of institutional conflict in the East European dual executive is that initial sparring is just a sign of a new system of government bedding down. After a few more rounds, the balance between president and prime minister will be established one way or the other. Constitutional uncertainties (and even contradictions, for postcommunist executive structures were designed in a hurry) will be resolved by custom and the courts.

A compromise view combines these two accounts. It already seems clear that the countries of Central Europe are moving towards a clear parliamentary system while those further East, especially the post-Soviet republics, remain dominated by strong-arm, semi-accountable presidents. The dual executive may prove to be a transitional form of government in many postcommunist states.

The executive in authoritarian states

The authoritarian executive, like the accountable executive, spans a wide range. It covers rule by absolute and limited monarchs, military juntas (councils), priests, communist parties, fascist parties and personal dictators. At the risk of painting an over-stark portrait, the central feature of most authoritarian executives is weak institutionalization, leading to struggles over succession and the supremacy of politics over policy.

Typically, arrangements for decision-making are

less well-developed than in accountable executives. Structures vary more with the style of the leaders and respond more to the balance of power within the political élite. In China, Deng Xiaoping gave up all his official posts in state and party in 1984 but his political preeminence continued into the (and his) nineties. Many forms of authoritarian rule are prone to personality cults. Absolute rulers, in particular, regard themselves as personal rulers of their country, presenting themselves as a national hero (which indeed some once were). Lacking the constraints of an accountable or collegial executive, and surrounded by fawning courtiers, the cult of personality can reach absurd, even tragic, proportions.

One consequence of weak institutions is the lack of a succession procedure (except for hereditary monarchies). This weakness produces a struggle among potential successors, not just after the leader's exit but also in the run-up to it. The absence of rules governing replacement of the élite is a major reason for the periodic instability of authoritarian regimes. As a result, many leaders find themselves preoccupied with politics rather than policies. Political survival is a greater problem for authoritarian than for accountable rulers. An American president is given a four-year contract, renewable once; authoritarian leaders keep their job for just as long as they can ward off rivals. Thus they must mount a constant watch for threats from competitors and be prepared to neuter those who are becoming too strong. Further, the price of defeat is high; politics can be a matter of life and death. When an American president is ejected by the voters, he can retreat to his library to write his memoirs; ousted dictators risk a harsher fate. By necessity, then, the governing style is prone to be ruthless. The ruler needs allies but must also prevent them from becoming a threat. So favourites come and go and political management, rather than policy leadership, is the core task.

Communist states illustrated these themes. True, such states did have a clear structure of government, headed by a presidium which was an inner steering body of a larger Council of Ministers which was itself formally 'elected' by the parliament. The chairman of the presidium was, in effect, prime minister, leading the communist equivalent of the cabinet. But in practice the ruling communist party dominated the formal institutions of the state, with leading figures in the party also taking on top state positions. Although the party was supposed to drive the government forward, in practice the communist executive fell victim to personality cults, policy inertia and instability.

The non-accountable character of the communist executive explained two of the weaknesses that contributed to its ultimate collapse: slow turnover at the top and the lack of a succession procedure. As McCauley and Carter, (1986, p. 1) said, 'biology was the mid-wife of change'. But biology worked slowly and irregularly. In the Soviet Union, Stalin's rule may have lasted for over 30 years but that of Yuri Andropov (General Secretary of the Soviet Communist Party, 1982–4) survived for less than two. Until the emergence of Gorbachev in 1985, slow turnover restricted policy innovation, reflecting cautious, unimaginative leadership intent just on preserving its own power. The paradox of the political executive in communist party states was that strong, authoritarian leadership was insecure in tenure and uncertain in succession.

The Soviet Union under Joseph Stalin was an extreme, but important, case of a personalized dictatorship in a communist setting. Stalin had become undisputed ruler of the Soviet Union by 1929 and remained so until his death in 1953. He adopted policies of rapid, forced industrialization and the collectivization of agriculture. Resistance was ruthlessly crushed, with millions of people despatched to gulags (prison camps), many to die there. Political opponents were purged, convicted in show trials and/or killed. Propaganda was unremitting. Political power was highly centralized and the economy operated on a command rather than a market basis, both characteristic features of totalitarian rule. Although the West was glad enough of Stalin's support during the war, he intensified his dictatorship after the victory in 1945, directing some purges of national minorities, Jewish cultural leaders and 'foreign influences'.

The question remains of how far the potential for Stalinism was inherent in communist doctrine, and how far its origins lie in Russian autocratic traditions or even in the weaknesses of Stalin himself: abused as a child, he proved to be a manipulative and vindictive adult. Certainly, most communist regimes were less Stalinist than the Soviet Union. And even the Soviet Union began a process of destalinization

EXHIBIT 12.3

When illness strikes: government by the infirm

The young and the healthy may run for high office but their ambition is rarely achieved until late middle age. By this time leaders are often unfit and becoming prone to serious illness. As Post and Robins (1993, p.xii) write, 'aging, ailing leaders are not a rare exception – illness and disability are frequently guests and occasionally permanent residents in the throne room'. Elderly leaders are a particular problem in governments lacking a recognized succession procedure (for example communist states), and in those based on seniority (for example Japan, China). But the problem of declining energy among the very old is probably less serious than that of impaired judgment in late middle age brought about by drugs and mental illness. This is less obvious than physical infirmity and, by its nature, poor judgment is rarely recognized by leaders themselves. Indeed, strong egos are often the last to acknowledge their declining powers. Excuses are always to hand; the heavy-drinking Winston Churchill always claimed that he 'took more out of the cognac than the cognac took out of him'.

How well, then, do governments cope with the problem of the ailing leader? The answer is, poorly; few countries publicly assess the medical condition of candidates for office. In any case, once in power even healthy leaders find the pressure of work encourages them to take sedatives for sleep and stimulants for work. When medical problems do exist, it is not only the leader who engages in denial; often, their followers refuse to accept that the Great One is sick. Even if the illness is known at court, the tendency is to close ranks, keeping the condition secret. Physicians are often accessories to such conspiracies, following the easy route of placing their duty of confidentiality to their patient before the 'health of the nation'.

Although the sick leader is often a greater problem in presidential systems, the health-conscious USA does relatively well by international standards. Medical reports on presidential candidates, for example, are circulated. In any case, the two-term limit reduces the period by which the country can be governed by the 'living dead' (one argument for term limits is that they reduce the chance of rule by the sick). Further, the 25th amendment (1967) allows the vice-president, together with the heads of executive departments, to certify that the president is unfit for office and to replace him until the president declares a readiness to return to the fray. Yet no system is foolproof. After Ronald Reagan regained consciousness following an operation for cancer, his advisers considered that his ability to understand a short prepared statement announcing his resumption of power was sufficient evidence of his lucidity. Becoming President is a monumental challenge; remaining so, it seems, depended on nothing more than the ability to read out two sentences. Perhaps more probing examination might have revealed early signs of the Alzheimer's disease which tragically destroyed the former President's mental functioning after he left office.

Examples of drug use by office-holders

Leader (Position)	Period in office	Drug use
Mohammad Reza (Shah of Iran)	1941–79	Psychoactive drugs to alleviate cancer treatment
John Kennedy (American president)	1961–63	Steroids to treat Addison's disease
Winston Churchill (British Prime Minister)	1940–45/ 1950–55	Alcohol and barbiturates
Anthony Eden (British Prime Minister)	1955–57	Amphetamines
Adolf Hitler (German Chancellor)	1933–45	Barbiturates, narcotics, cortizone, cocaine (after 1944) plus numerous quack remedies such as extract of bull testes

Further reading: L'Etang (1980), Park (1986), Post and Robins (1993), Gilbert (1998).

soon after the dictator's death. Yet whatever the explanation for Stalinism, his rule indicates the dangers of personal dictatorship, especially in a country lacking a tradition of limits on power (Medvedev, 1972).

The recent wave of democratization has reduced the number of authoritarian executives in the developing world but many examples can still be found. Personal rule remains central to politics in the Middle East, for example in Saudi Arabia (Bill and Springborg, 1994, Ch.5). In Islamic countries such as Iran where religion and politics are intertwined, rule continues to be strongly authoritarian. Thus shahs, sheikhs and sultans continue to rule in the traditional patriachal fashion identified by Weber. Sultans rule more than they govern. Advancement within the ruler's circle depends not on merit but on closeness to the sovereign and his network of advisors, relatives, friends, flatterers and guards. Public and private are not sharply distinguished; each forms part of the ruler's sphere. Government posts are not secure but are occupied on good behaviour, demonstrated through unquestioned loyalty to the ruler's interests. Such systems of personal rule have survived for centuries, limiting the development of strong government institutions. The paradox is that personal rule itself constitutes a stable system, providing an exception to the general theme of political instability in the authoritarian executive.

Personal rule was also central to African politics. In poor societies with weak states, and possessing strong tribal traditions, it was natural for leaders to emerge who were adept at using the coercive and financial resources of the regime to reward friends and punish enemies. Other government institutions lacked the weight to provide a check on personal rule. The incentives of patronage and the risks of non-cooperation with the government ensured that assemblies were docile, elections were uncompetitive and the courts unassertive. Such conditions again favoured personal rather than institutional rule. For instance, President Mobutu governed Zaire for more than thirty years after coming to power in 1965, surviving on a mixture of corruption and cunning. Described as a 'walking bank balance in a leopard skin cap', Mobutu never distinguished between the

state's finances and his own. Those opponents he could not buy off he had killed. While this is an extreme example, many other African presidents also ruled in a highly personal way. Indeed, many continue to do so, now operating under the more acceptable conventions of semidemocracy.

Although personal leaders were rarely properly accountable in a constitutional sense, they were tightly constrained by other *political* actors. These included: the military, leaders of ethnic groups, landowners, the business class, the bureaucracy, students, multinational companies, foreign governments, ex-presidents and factions in the leader's own court. To survive, leaders had to distribute the perks of office so as to maintain a viable coalition of support. This was a challenge which left little room for concern over broader issues of national development. Personal rulers were far from absolute rulers. Inadequately accountable in a constitutional sense, these personal rulers (like most authoritarian executives) were highly constrained in other ways.

Key reading

> **Next step:** *Lijphart (1992) is an excellent reader on parliamentary and presidential government.*

Linz and Valenzuela (1994) and Mainwaring and Shugart (1997b) are rewarding analyses of the political executive, focusing on the strengths and weaknesses of the presidential form. Elgie (1995) covers a range of democracies in his account of political leadership. On the American presidency, see Rose (1991), Jones (1994) and the classic by Neustadt (1980). Mainwaring (1992) covers presidencies in Latin America. Comparative studies of parliamentary government include Weller, Bakvis and Rhodes (1997), Laver and Shepsle (1994) and on Western Europe, Heywood and Wright (1997). For cross-national comparisons of Prime Ministers see Jones (1991) and Weller (1985). On the dual executive, the original source is Duverger (1980); see Baylis (1996) and Taras (1997) for post-communist states. On personal rule, Jackson and Rosberg (1982) consider Africa, Bill and Springborg (1994) examine the Middle East, and Clapham (1985, Ch. 4) offers a general account. Finally, Brooker (1995) assesses twentieth-century dictatorships.

The bureaucracy

What is the bureaucracy?

The bureaucracy is the state's engine room. It consists of permanent salaried officials employed by the state to advise on, and carry out, the policies of the political executive. The bureaucracy is indispensable to modern government yet, lacking the legitimacy of election, it has always aroused controversy. The central themes of this debate are responsiveness and efficiency. On responsiveness, the question is how can civil servants be made accountable to the politicians they notionally serve? And on effectiveness, the issue is how in the absence of a competitive market can we ensure that the bureaucracy does its job with efficiency and economy? The theme of value for money became particularly prominent in the era of lean government in the 1990s.

Delimiting the bureaucracy raises some tricky issues of definition. Reflecting the complexity of modern government, public employees have a range of employment relationships with the state (Figure 13.1). The broadest term is the *public sector*, also called the public service or public administration.

This covers all those whose salary comes directly or indirectly from the public purse. However, the public sector includes several areas not normally counted as part of the civil service, such as local government officers, teachers, public corporations and the armed forces. *Civil servants* proper are normally defined as employees directly paid by the national exchequer, subject to the state's conditions of service (including access to its pension scheme) and engaged in shaping or more commonly implementing government decisions. Just to complicate matters, a few countries such as Germany extend civil service status to teachers, even though this group works at one remove from the government.

> **Definition**
> The **bureaucracy** consists of salaried officials who conduct the detailed business of government, advising on and applying policy decisions. In contrast to the personal advisers surrounding a ruling monarch, a modern bureaucracy is a public institution with recruitment on merit and an emphasis on the consistent application of clear rules to individual cases. The word 'bureaucracy' comes from the Old French term, *burel*, meaning the cloth used to cover a writing desk or bureau.

In any one country, the number of civil servants with a direct *policy-advising* role, the group of special interest to students of politics, is no more than a few thousand. In all modern societies most civil servants work in the field, applying policy away from the decision-making centre. Traditionally, the core mandarins (to use the old Chinese term for high-level bureaucrats) formed a special grade in the civil service, often filled by able graduates recruited straight from university. However, some countries have now introduced more flexible practices at this

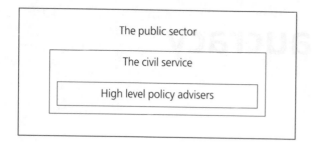

Figure 13.1 Delimiting the bureaucracy

highest level, making more use of short-term contracts and open recruitment. Examples include the Senior Executive Services established in the United States (1978), Australia (1984) and New Zealand (1988).

While the word 'bureaucracy' is often used descriptively as a synonym for the civil service, it is also employed in a more abstract way as a model for organizing public administration. The analysis of bureaucracy presented by the German sociologist Max Weber (1864–1920) is preeminent here (Gerth and Mills, 1948). Weber's model will be a point of reference throughout this chapter, and its main points are as follows:

- Bureaucracy involves a carefully defined division of tasks.
- Authority is impersonal, vested in the rules that govern official business. Decisions are reached by methodically applying rules to particular cases; private motives are irrelevant.
- People are recruited to serve in the bureaucracy based on proven or at least potential competence.
- Officials who perform their duties competently have secure jobs and salaries. Competent officials can expect promotion according to seniority or merit.
- The bureaucracy is a disciplined hierarchy in which officials are subject to the authority of their superior.

Weber's central claim was that bureaucracy made administration more efficient and rational; he believed that it was the means by which modern industrial efficiency could be brought to bear on civil affairs. To quote Weber himself:

the fully developed bureaucratic apparatus compares with other organizations exactly as does the machine with non-mechanical modes of production. Precision, speed, clarity, knowledge of files, continuity, discretion, unity, strict subordination, reduction of friction and of material and personal costs – these are raised to the optimum in the strictly bureaucratic administration.

For Weber, the ideal bureaucracy was a fine piece of administrative machinery but, like any device, it needed to be subjected to human control.

The evolution of bureaucracies

The idea of administrative efficiency is not unique to modern or Western thought. In China from about 165 BC officials were selected by competitive recruitment, based on a testing literary examination. Chinese administration employed ideas of hierarchy, official statistics and written reports long before Weber developed his model. Indeed Gladden (1972, p. 227) argued that the bureaucracy of imperial China 'contributed more than anything else to the staying power of Chinese civilization'.

However, it was the evolution of bureaucracies in Western Europe which contributed most to modern thinking. In Europe, clerical servants were originally agents of the royal household, serving under the personal instruction of the ruling monarch (Raadschelders and Rutgers, 1996). Many features of modern bureaucracies – regular salaries, pensions, open recruitment – arose from a successful attempt to overcome this idea of public employment as personal service to the monarch. Indeed, the evolution of royal households into twentieth-century Weberian bureaucracies was a massive transformation, intimately linked to the rise of the modern state itself. It was a transition from patriachy to bureaucracy, a story of the depersonalization of administration as the royal household was converted into the royal service and then into public service (Hyden, 1997, p. 243).

In the new world, however, civil service development was more pragmatic. Lacking the long state tradition of Western Europe, 'public administration' was considered a routine application of political directives. In the United States, the spoils system ('to the victor, the spoils') was employed until the end of the nineteenth century. This allowed new presidents, among others, to reward their campaign supporters with federal posts ranging all the way down to postal clerk. The spoils system continued until 1883 when the Pendleton Act created a Civil Service Commission to recruit and regulate federal employees. Thus a merit-based bureaucracy began to emerge as the spoils system declined.

In the twentieth century, bureaucracies reached their zenith. The depression and two world wars vastly increased government intervention in society. The welfare state, completed in Europe in the decades following the second world war, required a massive investment in a Weberian bureaucracy to pass out grants, allowances and pensions in accordance with complex eligibility conditions set by politicians. By 1980, public employment accounted for almost a third of the total in Britain and Scandinavia, though much of the expansion had occurred at local level.

However, the final quarter of the twentieth century witnessed declining faith in government and, more to the point, deteriorating public finances. In the 1970s, some projections suggested that governments might eventually go bust. Seizing on this fiscal crisis, right-wing politicians such as Ronald Reagan and Margaret Thatcher called for, and to an extent delivered, a reduced role for the state. Privatization, and a sharper focus on results in what remained of the public sector, signalled a changing style of bureaucratic operation away from strict Weberian guidelines.

Recruitment and the representative bureaucracy

Recruitment to bureaucracies has evolved in tandem with the development of the civil service itself. The shift from patrimonial to Weberian bureaucracies was a transition from recruitment by personal links with the ruler to open selection on merit. Jobs became available, at least in theory, to the whole population. Even though these reforms occurred in most democracies as long ago as the late nineteenth century, recruitment to the civil service remains an important theme. Selection methods and employee profiles are scrutinized more carefully than in the private sector. Further, what counts as 'merit' still varies between countries, revealing subtle contrasts in conceptions of a civil servant's role.

> **Definition**
> In a **unified** (or **generalist**) bureaucracy, recruitment is to the civil service as a whole, not to a specific job within it. Administrative work is conceived as requiring intelligence, education and appropriate personal skills but not technical knowledge. By contrast, a **departmental** (or **specialist**) approach recruits people with specialist knowledge to a specific department or job. Unified bureaucracies are career-based while departmental civil services are job-based.

Britain exemplifies the unified (*generalist*) tradition, pushing the cult of the amateur to extremes. Administration is seen as the art of judgment, born of intelligence and honed by experience. Specialist knowledge should be sought by bureaucrats but then treated with scepticism; experts should be on tap but not on top. Recruiters look for general ability, not technical expertise. Other countries with a strong state tradition and a high-status bureaucracy, such as France, Germany and Japan, also adopt a unified approach but with more emphasis on technical training. France is a notable example, where recruitment to the civil service is through competitive examinations to a particular corps, such as the Diplomatic Corps or the Finance Inspectorate. These Corps offer their own specialized post-entry training. For example, members of the administrative corps are trained at the prestigious *École Nationale d'Administration* (ENA). But the seemingly technical basis of this training is rather misleading. Although civil service recruitment is in theory to a specific corps, it is in reality as much to an élite ('the *Enarques*') which encompasses both public and private realms. Even within the civil service over a third of corps members are working away from their home corps at any one time; the *Enarques* are far more than narrow technicians sticking to their knitting.

Some unified civil services stress one particular form of technical expertise: law. In many European countries with a codifed law tradition, a legal training is common among higher bureaucrats. Germany is a good illustration. Over 60 per cent of top German civil servants are lawyers, compared to just 20 per cent in the United States. The German model has influenced other countries, notably Japan, where the recruitment base is narrower still. Most of those who pass through the 'dragon gate' examination for recruitment to high-level positions in the Japanese civil service are graduates of just one department: Tokyo University's law school.

In a *departmental (specialist)* system, recruiters follow a different philosophy. They look for specialist experts for individual departments, with more movement in and out of the civil service at a variety of levels. This model is common in countries with a weak state in which the administration lacks the status produced by centuries of service to predemocratic rulers. The United States, New Zealand and the Netherlands are examples. In the Netherlands, each department sets its own recruitment standards, normally requiring training or expertise in its own area. Once appointed, civil servants usually remain in this department for their entire career (Andeweg and Irwin, 1993, p. 176). The notion of recruiting talented young graduates to an élite, unified civil service is weak or non-existent.

Irrespective of differences in recruitment philosophy, the social background of senior civil servants is always unrepresentative of the general population. In the Western world, the typical high-level civil servant is a male graduate, from an urban background and from a middle or upper-class family that was itself active in public affairs. Of course, many of these qualities are also found among politicians; however, the skew is greater in the bureaucracy (Box 13.1). These findings have disturbed advocates of a 'representative bureaucracy', a term introduced by Kingsley (1944), an American scholar who claimed that the middle-class composition of Britain's civil service exploded the myth of its supposedly neutral bureaucracy. By implication, the same argument could be applied to other countries.

Definition

The theory of **representative bureaucracy** claims that a civil service recruited from all sections of society will produce policies that are responsive to the public and, in that sense, democratic (Meier, 1993, p. 1). **Passive representation** exists when the demographic profile of the bureaucracy matches that of the population. **Active representation** occurs when civil servants take the same decisions as would be made by the represented – that is, the public.

However, it is far from clear that the narrow social background of civil servants does produce the prejudice against the left which Kingsley claimed to detect. On the one hand, where civil servants are allowed to pursue political careers, as in France, they frequently join parties of the left. A third of the *Enarques* elected to the French National Assembly in 1978 were members of the Socialist Party. The dominant *Enarque* ideology was centrist; bureaucrats were as sceptical of the far right as they were of the far left. A crossnational survey in the 1970s found that this middle-of-the-road attitude was common among senior civil servants in other Western democracies (Aberbach *et al.*, 1981).

On the other hand, a more recent survey in Australia did find that younger civil servants working in central government favoured the radical pro-market reforms then getting under way (Pusey, 1991). This new generation, many of whom had degrees in economics, rejected the bland centrism of its elders. It appears that class background is too broad a base from which to predict the outlook of senior bureaucrats. Generation, degree subject and

---

BOX 13.1

Background characteristics that favour entry into bureaucratic and political elites

	Senior posts in public administration	Senior posts in political parties
Male	✓✓	✓✓
University education	✓✓	✓
Middle or upper class family background	✓✓	✓
Family involved in public affairs	✓	✓
From an urban area	✓	–

✓✓ indicates a strong advantage
✓   indicates a weaker advantage
–   indicates little effect

Source: Adapted from Aberbach *et al.* (1981), p. 80, reporting findings from a study of élite recruitment in seven liberal democracies.

the wider climate of the times are just as important. Broadening the class base would not, then, necessarily lead to radical changes in bureaucratic decisions.

However, there are three other arguments that can be made for a bureaucracy which reflects the social profile of the population (van der Meer and Roborgh, 1996).

- Civil servants whose work involves direct contact with specific groups may be better at the job if they also belong to that category. Language is the most obvious example but the point can be extended to ethnicity and gender (note that this point applies more to street-level bureaucrats than to top-level mandarins).
- A civil service balanced between particular groups, such as religions or regions, may enhance stability in divided societies.
- Democracy is said to involve government by, and not just for, the people. A representative civil service, involving participation by all major groups in society, may therefore help to defuse the inherent tension between democracy and bureaucracy.

Such arguments did lead to affirmative action programmes in some countries, notably the United States, in the 1970s and 1980s. Considerable efforts were made to ensure that the profile of employees matched that of the wider population. Canadian governments, concerned since the 1960s to improve recruitment from francophones, also extended their recruitment efforts to women, Aboriginal peoples and those with disabilities. However, such affirmative action schemes never achieved the same popularity in Europe, perhaps because they would have involved accepting the inadequacy of the constitutional requirement of neutrality imposed on some civil services. Even in North America, attitudes were ambivalent, reflecting a tension between social engineering and the fundamental bureaucratic principle of merit-based recruitment. In any event, affirmative action schemes lost momentum in the more conservative 1990s.

How the public sector is organized

Here we examine the detailed organization of government activity, looking at how the cogs of the administrative machine are arranged. The central distinction is between departments which form the stable core of central government, and agencies operating at one or more removes from departments.

Departments

A dozen or more government departments (or ministries) form the centrepiece of modern bureaucracies. The United States has 14 departments, each headed by a Secretary of State appointed by the President. The Netherlands has 13 while Canada, always prone to political inflation, has over 20.

Most countries follow a similar sequence in introducing departments. The first to be established are those performing the core functions of the state: finance, law and order, defence and foreign affairs. These ministries are often as ancient as the state itself. In the United States, for instance, the Departments of State, Defense, Justice and the Treasury each date from 1789. At a later stage countries add extra ministries to deal with new functions. Initially these are usually Agriculture (1889 in the USA) and Commerce (1913), followed later in the

---

BOX 13.2

The organization of government: departments, divisions and agencies

Government department or ministry
An administrative unit over which a minister exercises direct management control. Usually structured as a formal hierarchy and often established by statute.

Division, section or bureau
An operating unit of a department, responsible to the minister but may have considerable independence in practice (especially in the USA).

Agency
Operates at one or more removes from the government, in an attempt to provide management flexibility and political independence.

twentieth century by welfare departments dealing with social security, education, health and housing.

Reflecting Weber's principles, departments are usually organized in a clear hierarchy. A single minister has overall responsibility but in large departments may be supported by junior ministers with responsibilities for specific divisions. A senior civil servant, often called the Secretary, is responsible for administration and for forming the crucial bridge between political and bureaucratic levels (in Japan this person is called the vice-minister, reflecting the high status of top bureaucrats there). Table 13.1 shows the elaborate structure of German ministries, a fine illustration of Weber's quasi-military chain of command. It would be wrong, however, to suppose that working practices correspond exactly to such organization charts, with their reassuring image of information moving smoothly up and down the administrative pyramid. In Germany, the 2000 sections of the federal ministries possess a concentration of expertise that enables them to block or at least circumvent changes proposed from on high. And the top minister may also be able to circumvent the civil service by seeking advice from political advisers, as in the French cabinet system.

Bureaus

The United States is the great exception to the principle of hierarchy in departments. American departments are more like multinational corporations, containing many divisions jostling within a single shell. Departments are merely the wrapping around a collection of disparate bureaus and it is these bureaus which form the main operating units of the federal government. For example, within the Department of Health and Human Services it is divisions such as the Social Security Administration and the Family Support Administration which administer specific federal welfare schemes. Some bureaus are even older than the department in which they are located. The Bureau of Land Management, successor to the General Land Office, still has records signed by George Washington (Fesler and Kettl, 1996, p. 89). Bureaus have their own traditions, clients and support base in Congress; it is Congress, not the president, which creates and funds bureaus. And what Congress gives it can (and occasionally does) take away. Reporting formally to the

Table 13.1 The structure of Germany's Ministry of Economics

Position	Number of positions	Service level
The minister	1	—
State secretaries	2	Political officials
Department heads	8	Political officials
Subdepartment heads	30	Higher service
Section heads	171	Higher service
Section assistants	457	Higher service
Caseworkers	610	Elevated service
Clerical/secretarial	810	Intermediate service
Messengers etc.	277	Lower-level service

Note: In Germany, 'political officials' are tenured civil servants who must be transferred to another job of suitable status if not retained by their minister.

Source: Conradt (1995), Table 8.1.

President, bureau chiefs spend much of their time ensuring their operational independence from the White House.

Agencies

The defining feature of public agencies is that in theory they operate at one remove from government departments, with a formal relationship of at least semi-independence. In Germany, for example, three prominent agencies are: the *Bundesbank*, a legally independent central bank; the *Treuhandanstalt*, which managed the disposal of state-owned enterprises inherited from East Germany; and the Federal Labour Institute, which administers unemployment insurance. However 'public agency' is an umbrella term covering institutions which vary in their labels and their relationships with both the executive and the legislature (box 13.3). We will examine two major forms of agency found in many democracies: government corporations, a form now in decline, and regulatory agencies, which are still growing in number.

BOX 13.3
Types of public agency

Government corporation
A state-owned enterprise established by statute to sell goods and services, with no private shareholders. Examples included Britain's nationalized companies, Canada's Crown Corporations, Australia's public enterprises and the U.S. Postal Service.

Government holding company
A state-owned organization established to acquire shareholdings in other enterprises. An example is Sepi (*Sociedad Estatal de Participaciones Industriales*) in Spain. These are an alternative device to government corporations for securing public control but like government corporations they are now threatened by privatization.

Regulatory agency
An organization whose function is to oversee non-state activity in areas where a public interest is at stake, for example private monopolies, financial services, medical research. Usually operating at one remove from government, regulatory agencies are a characeristic mode of modern governance.

The device of the *public corporation* originated in the Australian state of Victoria, where it was prized as a great contribution to state socialism. Enthusiasm for the form reached its peak in Britain's Labour government of 1945-51. This administration nationalized a raft of industries including coal mines, electricity, gas and the railways. Herbert Morrison, a minister in the postwar Labour administration, believed these nationalized industries could combine business efficiency with public accountability. In most cases he was eventually proved wrong: although some economies of scale may have been present in the early years of public ownership, political interference led to overstaffing and underinvestment. In Britain, most public corporations were sold back to the private sector during Conservative rule between 1979–97. This policy of privatization is now being copied in other countries with a tradition of public ownership, with telecommunications normally the first to go private.

In much of continental Europe, rulers preferred to acquire a shareholding in private companies rather than take them directly into public ownership. The state formed special *holding companies* for this purpose. In Spain as late as 1997, Sepi was still the country's largest industrial conglomerate, controlling firms with over 120 000 employees. This group was modelled on Italy's IRI (Institute for Industrial Reconstruction). In Italy, as elsewhere on the continent, these massive but sprawling holding companies were seen as, and probably were, a positive vehicle for development in the 1950s and 1960s. Now, plagued by patronage appointments, weak management and divided accountability to a number of government departments, they are considered ripe for reform. The director of Sepi anticipates that he will be out of a job by the year 2001, by when he hopes all the enterprises he controls will have been privatized.

Even in a world of privatized industry, huge swathes of commercial and social activity are and will remain subject to detailed control by *regulatory agencies*. Examples include adoption, broadcasting licenses, restraining private monopolies, drug licensing and nuclear energy. Far from declining, public regulation is growing in scale, reflecting increased knowledge of the consequences of commercial activity (for example environmental damage) and the need to regulate newly-privatized monopolies (for example water suppliers). Britain, for instance, has well over 100 regulatory bodies, employing over 20 000 people and costing around £1 billion ($1.5 billion) per year. The media entrepreneur Rupert Murdoch even claims that regulation represents socialism's comeback trail: 'socialism is alive and well, and living in regulatory agencies'.

The hope, at least partly reflected in reality, is that independent agencies will act as a buffer between the government and the regulated bodies, reducing the excessive intervention which held back many government corporations. Even France, a bastion of state power, has established an independent *Autorité de Regulation des Télécommunications* (ART) to supervise the liberalized telecommunications sector, including the partly-privatized France Telecom. However, the danger of all such agencies is that they come to serve the interests of those they supervise. The risk of regulatory capture is acute when the subjects of regulation are private corporations, which invariably have more expertise, staff, money and above all lawyers than their regulator.

As the state retreats from the direct provision of goods and services, and concentrates more on overseeing private firms, so the issues involved in designing an appropriate regulatory regime come to the fore. A comparison between the United States and Britain reveals some of the issues: consider the utility industries, for example energy and telecommunications. In the United States many regulatory commissions are the responsibiliy of the states, complicating the environment for national private corporations which must cope with a raft of regimes. A common technique is the multi-member commission, covering a range of industries and operating through public hearings. The general policy has been to cap the profits which monopoly utility companies are permitted to make.

By contrast, Britain has adopted separate (and secretive) regulatory bodies for each industry: one for electricity, another for water, a third for telecommunications. In contrast to the USA, national scope offers the potential for more coherent regulation. However, the existence of separate agencies for each industry reduces the ability to apply lessons from one sector to another. Each British 'Offer' (office of regulation) is run by an individual director, rather than operating through a many-headed commission. British regulation also operates under a more sophisticated principle than the American idea of profit-capping. British regulators cap prices rather than profits, thus allowing increased profits from efficiency gains to accrue to the companies themselves. This gives companies more incentive to streamline their operations but can lead to political damage all round when profits become 'excessive'. These issues of regulatory design illustrate the increasing complexity of modern governance, showing how far democratic states are departing from Weberian hierarchies.

Controlling the bureaucracy

To understand how to ensure political control of the bureaucracy we must address the sources of its influence. Why is there a danger of power leaking from ministers to civil 'servants'? The answer is found in five features of the bureaucracy: its expertise, permanence, ingrained habits, control of implementation and special interests.

- *Expertise*   A government department is a large, multi-tiered organization, containing enormous knowledge and experience in its specialist area. Since ministers must depend, at least to an extent, on the advice and information presented by their civil servants, the bureaucracy possesses potential agenda-setting power. It can decide which information should be presented and which should be suppressed.

- *Permanence*   Civil servants' tenure is more secure than that of the politicians who head ministries, so top civil servants will have had more experience in their field than their ministers. Especially in parliamentary governments, ministers are regularly moved up, down, sideways or out. This gives bureaucrats an incentive to resist change; they just hang on until the minister goes away. Further, when there is a vacuum at the top, power gravitates to the permanent bureaucracy. If ministers are unwilling to govern, whether because of a political crisis or just weak leadership, civil servants can, will and must.

- *Ingrained habits*   Departments develop their own ways of proceeding, their own priorities and their own house view. They acquire links with other departments and interest groups, to which they are bound by ties of tradition, informal agreeements and personal relationships. These ingrained habits can be difficult for ministers to overcome or even penetrate.

- *Control of implementation*   Because bureaucrats implement political decisions, they can bend policy not just to conditions in the field but also to their own concerns. This is unavoidable because civil servants need discretion if they are to carry out policies effectively.

- *Special interests*   Bureaucracies are often viewed as expansionist organizations, seeking to increase their size, staff and scope of operations. In particular, top civil servants are often portrayed as wanting to maximize their organization's budget; this is taken to be the equivalent of the entrepreneur's goal of optimizing profits (Niskanen, 1971). But ministers may not share these special interests. They may be part of a right-wing administration which seeks to reduce government spending by reigning in departmental empire-building.

Political control by ministers

To counteract bureaucratic power, liberal democracies have developed a range of techniques (Box 13.4). Hierarchical control by a minister is the classic Weberian solution but is conditioned by three other factors: the reach of political appointments, norms of ministerial responsibility and the use made of ministerial advisers.

The reach of political appointments

In theory, the greater the number of political appointments to a department, the easier it is to ensure political control. The extent to which political appointments extend into the bureaucracy varies substantially. An American president appoints around 3000 people, and a career civil servant there will find several layers of political appointees blocking access to the cabinet secretary. In Germany, civil servants who are responsive and sympathetic to the ruling party are moved into sensitive administrative positions. This tendency to staff important ministries with loyal and sympathetic civil servants is even more marked in Finland (Vartola, 1988, p. 126). In Britain, by contrast, only the ministers who head departments are politically appointed; the rest of the ministry consists of permanent professional civil servants. Yet is is far from clear that ministerial control is reduced as a result. In fact, senior civil servants welcome political direction; they recognize the unique authority which the minister possesses as a member of an elected government. More political appointments does not necessarily enhance political control.

The use of political advisers

Political control of the bureaucracy can be aided by providing ministers with personal advisory staff. Although – indeed, because – such gurus are not part of the department's permanent staff, they can act as their minister's eyes and ears, proferring alternative and politically-attuned advice. The Executive Office of the President and the White House Office of the American presidency are the fullest expression of this approach. They form a counter-bureaucracy within the political system – one much more likely to be ideologically or politically driven than the formal bureaucracy. Such advisers may help to

> ### BOX 13.4
> ## Modes of control over bureaucracies
>
> | Formal | Informal |
> |---|---|
> | Political direction by ministers | *External* |
> | | Mass media scrutiny |
> | Scrutiny by the assembly | Public opinion |
> | Scrutiny by the judiciary | Interest group scrutiny |
> | Ombudsmen | |
> | Performance standards | *Internal* |
> | Ministerial control | Professional standards |
> | | Anticipated reactions |
> | | Peer-group pressure |
> | | Conscience |
> | | Competition between departments |
>
> *Source:* Adapted from Nadel and Rourke (1975, Table 1).

control bureaucratic power but, as American political scandals revealed in the 1970s and 1980s, they create their own problems of control. Advisers are subject neither to election nor to vetting by Congress. The danger is that they are too dependent on their patron, preferring to offer blandishments rather than home truths.

A preferable system, perhaps, is the French *cabinet* (not to be confused with the cabinets which form the apex of the government in parliamentary systems). A French *cabinet* is a group of about 15 to 20 people who form the minister's personal advisory staff and work directly under his or her control. *Cabinets* provide the minister with ideas and help in liaising with the department, other ministries, the party and the constituency. However, in contrast to the United States most *cabinet* members come from the civil service and return to it after a spell of a few years with their minister.

Norms of accountability

The more accountable civil servants are for their acts, the more their influence can be identified if not necessarily controlled. Bureaucrats can easily escape both political and public scrutiny when, as in Britain, ministers alone are formally responsible to parliament for the actions of their officials. So civil servants can, in effect, exert power without being subject to external accountability. Fortunately, perhaps, the British stress on the anonymity of higher civil servants is not matched in other liberal democracies. In the United States, bureaucrats appear before congressional committees. American public officials are also likely to give more candid replies than their inhibited British counterparts, who make a profession of being 'economical with the truth'. Paradoxically, containing bureaucratic power may be easier when, as in the USA, that influence is openly acknowledged.

Other forms of control

While ministers are an essential source of drive and coherence for departments, there are other formal means of bureaucratic oversight aimed at increasing the responsiviness of civil servants not just to politicians but also to ordinary people. These devices include the courts and legislative scrutiny, both of which are used prominently in the United States. The courts are routinely used to appeal bureaucratic decisions while congressional committees provide detailed, if selective, scrutiny of their agencies.

A more recent addition to the armoury is the Ombudsman, a watchdog first introduced in Sweden and then emulated in New Zealand, followed later by other European countries. Assigned to investigate complaints of maladministration, ombudsmen must have strong powers of investigation if they are to succeed. So far, governments outside Scandinavia have proved reluctant to grant this facility. As a result, the standard letter from an ombudsman reads, 'I regret I do not have the authority to investigate your complaint'.

Definition

An **ombudsman** is a public official who investigates allegations of maladministration in the public sector. These watchdogs originated in Scandinavia but they have been emulated elsewhere though often with more restricted jurisidiction and resources.

A final tool for controlling the bureaucracy is to set formal performance standards for departments, for example in the time taken to reply to letters from the public. This is the approach adopted with the Citizen's Charter in Britain. The Charter is toothless but the mere threat of being labelled substandard may offer some stimulus to improved performance.

Informal pressure can also be brought to bear on the bureaucracy. Public opinion, especially when aroused by organized interest groups, can act as an informal ombudsman within the system. A vigorous mass media can also act as a check and balance on the bureaucracy: regular television programmes, for example, now specialize in exposing public scandal and bureaucratic ineptitude. However, these exposés rarely lead to structural reform; the specific case may be resolved but the complacency of the bureaucracy often continues. In France,

> despite a legislative framework that provides a potentially impressive degree of open government, and continuous efforts over the past decade to render the administration less forbidding, the image of the administration remains one of remoteness, complexity and arcane procedures. (Stevens, 1996, p. 150)

Other informal controls are internal to the bureaucracy. One is competition between departments, where spending ministries must compete against each other for money, with a finance ministry often keeping tight control over the money box. Liberal democracies also rely on the internalized professional norms – the conscience – of civil servants. If they are subject to undue political pressure they can complain to their union (if they are a member), leak stories to the media (if they dare), or complain through an official but anonymous whistle-blowing system (if it exists).

The new public management

'Government is not the solution to the problem; government is the problem'. This famous declaration by Ronald Reagan is one inspiration behind the new public management (NPM), a creed which swept through the Anglo-American world of public administration in the 1980s and 1990s. NPM represents a powerful critique of Weber's ideas about bureaucracy. It has attracted many specialists who do not share the ideological perspective of Ronald Reagan, it is spoken of warmly by international bodies such as the OECD and it has led to radical change in the public sectors of Australia, Canada, the United Kingdom and especially New Zealand.

Osborne and Gaebler's *Reinventing Government* (1992) was an exuberant statement of the new approach. Subtitled 'how the entrepreneurial spirit is transforming the public sector', this American best-seller outlined ten principles which government agencies should adopt to enhance their effectiveness (Box 13.5). Where Weber's model of bureaucracy was based on ideas of efficiency drawn from the Prussian army, Osborne and Gaebler are inspired more by the freewheeling world of American business.

The authors cite with enthusiasm several examples of public sector organizations which have followed their tips. One is the California parks department which allowed managers to spend their budget on whatever they needed, without seeking approval for individual items of expenditure. Another is the public convention centre which formed a joint venture with private firms to bring in well-known acts, with each side sharing both the risk and the profit. The underlying theme in such anecdotes is the gains achievable by giving public servants the flexibility to manage by results (that is, 'managerialism'). And the significance of this, in turn, is the break it represents with Weber's view that the job of a bureaucrat is to apply fixed rules to cases. For its supporters, NPM is public administration for the twenty-first century; Weber's model is dismissed as history.

While Osborne and Gaebler provide a convert's handbook, Hood (1996, p. 271) offers a more dispassionate and comparative perspective (Box 13.6). Hood shows that the Anglo-American democracies, plus Sweden, have made most progress in implementing the new philosophy. By contrast, Germany, Japan and Spain are among the countries showing least interest. It seems that the traditional power and status of the bureaucracy in these countries has so far prevented the diffusion of NPM. A particular problem is that the status and duties of civil servants are entrenched in extensive legal codes, making radical change impossible without legislation.

For advocates of NPM, New Zealand is the perfect laboratory. Since 1984, successive governments – first Labour and then National – have revolutionized the structure, management and role of

---

BOX 13.5

Steer, don't row! Osborne and Gaebler's 10 principles for improving the effectiveness of government agencies

- Promote *competition* between service providers.
- *Empower* citizens by pushing control out of the bureaucracy into the community.
- Measure performance, focusing not on inputs but on *outcomes*.
- Be driven by goals – *missions* – not by rules and regulations.
- Redefine clients as *customers* and offer them choices - between schools, between training programmes, between housing options.
- *Prevent* problems before they emerge, rather than offering services afterwards.
- *Earn* money rather than simply spend it.
- *Decentralize* authority, embracing participatory management.
- Prefer *market* mechanisms to bureaucratic ones.
- *Catalyze* all sectors – public, private and voluntary – into solving community problems.

Source: Osborne and Gaebler (1992).

---

the public sector. A remarkable coalition (perhaps even conspiracy) of economic theorists in the Treasury, senior politicians from both major parties and business leaders came together to ram through many unpopular but far from ineffective reforms. One feature of the 'New Zealand model' is its massive use of contracts (Boston, 1995). This goes far beyond the standard fare of using private firms to supply local services such as garbage collection. It extends to engaging private suppliers in sensitive areas such as debt collection. By such means, the Department of Transport reduced its direct employees from around 5000 staff in 1986 to less than 50 in the mid-1990s, a remarkable reduction. The Ministry of Women's Affairs was cut to just 37 staff (Mulgan, 1997, p. 145). Many employees may simply have been redeployed to the private sector, but even so such reductions demonstrate the feasibility of containing bureaucracies supposedly driven by the desire for endless expansion of their scope and budgets.

In New Zealand, contracts are not just used in links with the private sector. They are also widely

---

BOX 13.6

Components of the new public management

- Managers are given more discretion but are held responsible for results.

- Explicit targets are set and used to assess results.

- Resources are allocated according to results.

- Departments are 'unbundled' into more independent operating units.

- More work is contracted out to the private sector.

- More flexibility is allowed in recruiting and retaining staff.

- Costs are cut in an effort to achieve more with less.

Source: Hood (1996).

---

used *within* the public sector to govern the relationships between purchasers (for example the Transport Department) and providers (for example Transit New Zealand, responsible for roading, and the Civil Aviation Authority, charged with air safety and security). Even within a single department, ministers and senior civil servants agree a contract on what the civil servant should achieve, with bonuses to follow if targets are achieved. 'Contractualism' within the public sector is an additional step, and a more direct challenge to Weber's model, than simply contracting out services to the private sector.

What lessons can be learned from New Zealand's ambitious innovations in public administration? Mulgan (1997, p.146) offers a balanced assessment. He concludes that

> the recent reorganization of the public service has led to greater clarity of government functions and to increased efficiencies in the provision of certain services to the public. At the same time, it has been expensive in the amount of resources consumed by the reform process itself and also in the added problems of coordination caused by the greatly increased number of individual public agencies.

The New Zealand experiment raises a new issue. Are there are *any* inherently governmental functions which should still be performed directly by the state?

Even if the state ensures a service is provided, is there any reason why the public sector itself should serve as supplier? Should firms run prisons? Should private agencies be paid to investigate crimes? Can small wars be contracted out to mercenaries? Can, will or should government become a virtual state, reduced to nothing more than a set of contracts? The American General Accounting Office suggests one limit to contractualization. It argues that policy-making, and the ability to supervise contracts, are 'inherently governmental'. As Sturgess (1996, p. 69) puts it, 'the state must retain the capacity to make up its mind'.

Definition

An **inherently governmental function** is one that the state should provide directly and not contract out to third parties. For instance, making key decisions about foreign policy would normally be considered inherently governmental; collecting the garbage would not.

The key political issue raised by NPM and the contract culture is accountability. When something goes wrong with a service provided by an agency operating under contract to government, who should take the blame: the supplier or the department? In Britain, parliament has traditionally held ministers to account for all the actions carried out in their name. As *The Times* wrote in 1977, 'the constitutional position is both crystal clear and entirely sufficient. Officials propose. Ministers dispose. Officials execute'. Yet under the Next Steps programme (named after the title of an influential government report published in 1988), most British civil servants were working by 1994 in one of about 100 semi-independent agencies (O'Toole and Chapman, 1995). In theory, the minister sets the policy and the agency carries it out. But when a political storm blows up – when convicts escape from prison or the child support agency pursues absent fathers too zealously – it is still ministers who are hauled before parliament. Knowing this, ministers are inclined to interfere with operational matters, thus contradicting the original purpose of the reform. Agency managers discover that they are not free to manage after all, with damage to morale.

The problem of accountability in a reformed civil service leads Campbell and Wilson (1995, p. 287)

BOX 13.7
Government by contract: for and against

The three theoretical advantages of using contracts to supply governnment services (whether via contracting-out or contracts within the public sector) are:

- Separating the purchaser ('the principal') and the provider ('the agent') means standards must be specified and independently monitored. In a traditional bureaucracy a lower-level official or division is just told to get on and perform a function.
- In bidding for a contract, providers must attempt a precise assessment of costs. If successful in their bid they are then able to strip out unneccesary expenditure, often by reducing labour costs.
- A contract holds out the possibility of replacing one provider with another who is cheaper, better or preferably both. So competition should keep the agent up to the mark.

Against these advantages must be set five dangers:

- The cost of drawing up the agreement – the transaction cost – may exceed the benefit gained.
- Contracts may drive down commitment. Staff may be unwilling to go the extra mile if it is not in their performance agreement to do so.
- Agents may engage in opportunistic behaviour, exploiting their position to advance their own interests rather than those of their principal. In other words, contractors may cut corners to increase profit. This is known as the 'principal/agency problem'.
- Departments lose the fund of experience – the collective memory – which comes from conducting projects in house. How successful can a ministry be in monitoring a job it has never done itself?
- The public may distrust contractors.

Further reading: On transaction costs, see Williamson (1975). On the principal/agency problem, see Vickers and Yarrow (1988).

---

to suggest that 'a huge hole now exists in the operation of British democracy'. Public servants are becoming more responsive downwards, to their users, and less accountable upwards, to their political masters. Control is melting away from the minister's office to a diffuse set of agencies. Weber's hierarchy of control based on direct provision by departments is giving way to a looser network based on persuasion rather than order-giving (Rhodes, 1996). Governance is replacing government. In devolved political systems such as the USA, or in countries such as Sweden which have long used independent agencies, this is nothing new. But for previously centralized countries, notably Britain and New Zealand, the political implications of NPM are profound. Members of parliament wedded to the idea of accountability to the assembly are not pleased to discover that their cherished sovereignty has passed into history.

Communist and postcommunist bureaucracies

Two differences separated administration in the communist world from the first world. One was

scale: communist administration extended into society to an extent unknown in the west. The other was that in the communist world, the bureaucracy was far more politicized. The essence of communist rule lay in combining bureaucratic and political rule in one gigantic system.

The sheer scale of the bureaucracy under communism flowed from the totalitarian character of its guiding ideology. To achieve its theoretical mission of building a new society, the party had to control all aspects of development, both economic and social. Most obviously, the private sector disappeared and the economy became an aspect of state administration. In the extreme case of the Soviet Union virtually every farm, factory and shop formed part of the bureaucracy. The shop assistant, the butcher, the electrician – all were employees of the Union of Soviet Socialist Republics. This required one army of administrators to do the work and another to provide coordination. The Soviet Union became the most bureaucratic state the world had ever seen.

How did the ruling party control the bureaucratic army it created? In essence, it sought to dominate the bureaucracy in the same way that it controlled the armed forces: by ensuring its own people were in key posts and by requiring all office-holders to pay at least lip-service to party goals. At the highest levels of the bureaucracy, party membership was the norm. All the leading posts within the administrative machinery were staffed by leading party members – in effect, the ruling party told itself what to do. But even if lower bureaucrats were not party members, they were still expected to contribute to achieving precise and demanding targets. Serving the party's interests became the key to promotion. Fear of dismissal – or, under the brutal excesses of Stalin, of death – ensured that bureaucrats either met their targets or at least pretended that they had done so. In its extreme form, then, the totalitarian bureaucracy was a system energized by fear.

Yet precisely because the party set such demanding targets, nepotism and corruption flourished. Goals were often arbitrary and dealings outside the formal system were needed to stand a chance of achieving objectives. Reasons could always be found for dismissing bureaucrats who had fallen out of favour; they were bound to have broken the rules in some way. But the imperative of 'building socialism' meant there could be no appeal to an administrative tribunal for unfair dismissal. Communist states could not waste time on procedures: if you were demoted or dismissed, that was it. So political survival skills became paramount; a lower official would latch on to superiors who offered protection. In a bureaucracy fuelled by fear, many petty tyrants flourished. Meanwhile, the top dogs jostled for control between themselves. Whole regions, industries and ministries were run as the personal fiefdoms of these lords of the bureaucracy. They remained secure in their position as long as the results flowed (never mind how) and the political winds remained favourable.

The collapse of communism was not just the end of communist government. It was also the disintegration of an over-extended, all-pervasive bureaucracy. Inevitably, this leaves a debilitating legacy for the postcommunist era. Because the communist party and the bureaucracy were so intertwined, the collapse of the party creates a hole in the state apparatus. National politicians are busy fighting their own political battles and have no time for detailed supervision of the state administration. Indeed the penetration of the state through the country falls away, leaving entire regions and provinces in a semi-independent position. In extreme cases, officials

only receive their salary on an irregular basis, forcing them to find ways of supplementing their income.

One method is to exploit the massive bank of formal regulations inherited from the communist, and even the precommunist, era. Numerous permits are often still required to start a new business; and with domestic and overseas entrepreneurs queuing up, an official stamp becomes a valuable commodity. One result of postcommunism, suggests Crawford (1996, p. 105), is simply that the price of bribes went up. All sorts of exemptions might be granted. To take a minor example, in Russia, currently the world leader in corruption, some sports clubs were for a period permitted to recoup lost government grants by importing alcohol and tobacco duty-free. And public officials were quick to grant themselves all permits needed to start their own businesses. Thus the bureaucracy fails to become a device for regulating a new, free market. Rather it offers a random mixture of haphazard taxes and licensed bounty. In the Wild East, bureaucrats and sometimes even entire ministries simply keep for themselves any money they raise in taxation. Thus the willingness of ordinary people to pay taxes falls. A vicious circle of decline emerges, based on ever-growing distrust between bureaucracy and people.

So *post*communist bureaucracies are still in a *pre*Weberian stage – they do not operate by the consistent application of formal regulations. The bureaucracy is extensive but weak, a damaging combination since social and economic development needs a clear regulatory environment. Holmes (1996, p. 51) gives some examples of how markets need an effective bureaucracy: records of transactions (for example of land transfers) must be kept, contracts must be enforcable by prompt access to law, and infractions of trespass and patent law must be punished. Yet, as Holmes goes on to say,

> how can a government impose order on a disorderly society if the government's own agents are themselves infected with disorder – if they will neither obey instructions nor follow the law? How can a stable legal framework, essential for functioning markets, be established in a country where all things, including public officials, are for sale?

Some postcommunist states, particularly the Czech Republic, Hungary, Poland and Slovenia, have made considerable progress in overcoming these problems. Hungary, for example, has managed a smooth transition to a functioning postcommunist bureaucracy. Generally, the transition to a market economy regulated by a competent bureaucracy is smoother in postcommunist countries which

- Had a shorter experience of communism
- Always regarded communism as a forced imposition by the Soviet Union
- Aspire to membership of the European Union
- Experienced less severe authoritarian rule in the precommunist era
- Made progress in deregulating their economy even while communist rule continued.

Overall, these factors distinguish the countries of Eastern Europe from the former republics of the Soviet Union, including Russia.

Bureaucracy and development

In examining the role of the bureaucracy in developing societies, the crucial question is the relationship with economic growth. Is the bureaucracy a force for, or a brake on, development? The answer is that the role of the bureaucracy is often variable but always important. It can act as a catalyst for growth but more often it has held back development, crowding out the private sector.

One problem confronting many developing countries is that their bureaucracy still reveals the footprint of colonialism. During the colonial period, overseas rulers imposed bureaucracies on their territories which reflected the culture of the imperial centre, and these styles survive to this day. Kingsley (1964, p. 303) describes how

the *fonctionnaire* slouched at his desk in Lomé or Cotonou, cigarette pasted to his underlip, has his counterpart in every provincial town in France; and the demeanor of an administrative officer in Accra or Lagos untying the red tape from his files would be recognizable to anyone familar with Whitehall or, more specifically, with the Colonial Office.

Whether the mannerisms were French or English,

many native civil servants adopted the aloof and élitist style of their colonial masters.

The process of grafting a modern administrative system onto a traditional political culture has produced bureaucracies that depart sharply from Weber's ideas, especially in Africa. Ties of kinship still pervade many developing societies: civil servants are expected to use their privileged positions to reward their families and ethnic group, which have often made great sacrifices to ensure that one of their number receives the education needed for a government job. Such behaviour, which the Western eye sees as corrupt, is interpreted as fulfilling moral obligations. Public office becomes an opportunity for personal enrichment; the state becomes a device by which the administrative and political class extracts reources from society for its own benefit. The poorer the country and the more dominant the state in its economy, the greater the pressure to use the state as the route to personal wealth or at least security. These problems are compounded by chronic unemployment which has led to excess labour being absorbed into government. As a result bureaucracies are overstaffed, leading to bureaucratic behaviour which parodies Weber's model. Initiative is stifled, formal procedure is rigidly followed and authority is not delegated. The result is that the bureaucracy cannot act as an effective instrument for achieving the economic and social changes to which regimes are notionally committed.

Yet despite the dangers of an over-exteneded state, the bureaucracy has undoubtedly played a positive role in those developing countries which have experienced rapid economic growth. In the 1950s and 1960s, for instance, the bureaucracy helped to foster economic modernization in several Middle East regimes. Usually this was in conjunction with the military and a strong national leader such as Abdul Nasser (President of Egypt, 1956–70). These regimes have now lost their reforming drive as bureaucracies have come to stifle the private sector, rendering their economies less attractive to foreign investors.

More recently, the most prominent examples of the bureaucracy's contribution to development came from the high performing economies of East Asia, particularly Japan. The concept of the developmental state, largely based on Asian models, placed special emphasis on the bureaucracy. A powerful

Country profile **JAPAN**

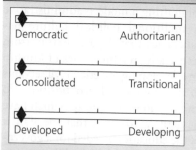

Democratic — Authoritarian

Consolidated — Transitional

Developed — Developing

Population: 125m.
Gross domestic product per head:
   $21 300.
Form of government: unitary parliamentary state with a ceremonial Emperor.
Legislature ('Diet'): the 500 members of the House of Representatives are elected for a four-year term. The smaller upper house, the House of Councillors, is less significant.
Executive: an orthodox parliamentary executive, with a cabinet and prime minister accountable to the Diet. Senior bureaucrats play a crucial role in policy-making.
Judiciary: the 15-member Supreme Court possesses the power of judicial review under the constitution of 1946 but has proved to be unassertive.
Electoral system: under the additional member system introduced for 1996, 300 members of the lower house are elected in single-member constituencies while the other 200 are elected by proportional representation. Although the new system was designed to reduce corruption and increase policy debate, turnout in 1996 fell seven points to 60 per cent.
Party system: postwar Japanese politics has been dominated by the conservative Liberal Democratic Party (LDP). It monopolized power from its formation in 1955 until 1993 and has participated in coalition rule since 1994. In 1996, the LDP won 239 seats, with the main opposition no longer coming from the Social Democratic Party of Japan (15 seats) but from the tax-cutting New Frontier Party (156) and the new reformist Democratic Party of Japan (52).

Contained in a series of islands the size of Montana, and lacking all major natural resources, Japan's 125m people have built the second largest economy in the world. From the ashes of defeat in the Second World War, Japan by the early 1990s had become the world's largest creditor nation and donor of economic aid. How was this transformation achieved?

Specific historical factors were part of the answer. After the war, American aid, an undervalued yen, cheap oil and the procurement boom caused by the Korean War all contributed to economic recovery. Yet Japan took remarkable advantage of these favourable circumstances, focusing its initial efforts on heavy industry but eventually becoming the world's leading producer and exporter of more sophisticated industrial and consumer goods.

'Japan, Inc.' was a popular (and populist) explanation of the country's success. According to this, the ethnically homogenous Japanese were driven not just by memories of wartime hunger but also by a shared desire to catch up with the West. A more sophisticated explanation was institutional. Although the country's post-war constitution was an American-imposed liberal democracy, in practice the political system was dominated by business. This enabled long-term investment to proceed by repressing any popular demands for rapid increases in domestic consumption; hence the Japanese paradox of 'a rich country with poor people'.

The bureaucracy certainly played a major role in post-war reconstruction. Senior civil servants retain close links with both party politicians and big business. Bureaucrats must retire at the age of 55 and many then go on to second careers – either as politicians or on the boards of companies. Thus, the dominant Liberal Democratic Party (conservative in all but name), the bureaucracy and big business are entwined through interlocking connections. They form a ruling élite though one which is now declining in coherence.

The professional economic bureaucracy, and in particular the Ministry of International Trade and Industry (MITI), was a key force behind Japan's success. As postwar reconstruction began, MITI targeted specific growth industries such as cameras, and these were shielded from overseas competition until they became competitive. MITI operated mainly through persuasion, thus reducing the risk of major mistakes.

In the 1990s, Japan's economy suffered prolonged asset deflation and even the once-dominant LDP was forced into coalition. State-led deflation painted the bureaucracy in a harsher light than did state-led growth. But in the earlier postwar decades, Japan was a preeminent example of how a small, meritocratic bureaucracy, operating largely on the basis of persuasion, can guide economic development.

Further reading: Johnson (1995); Kim *et al.* (1995); Flanagan and Reed (1996).
www.kantei.go.jp
bekkoame.or.jp

bureaucracy was needed to ensure that long-term investment occurs, despite political pressures for short-term benefits. Thus, in Japan 'the politicians reign but the bureaucracy rules'. The Japanese civil service is accorded high status, attracts able recruits through open competition and motivates them with the thought of plum post-retirement jobs in the private sector. As Johnson (1995, p. 68) writes, senior bureaucrats form part of 'the economic general staff, which is itself legitimated by its meritocratic character'. The crucial point is that the bureaucracy in a developmental state generally works with the market rather than seeking to replace it (as under communism) or to crowd it out (as in much of Africa and the postcommunist world). The danger with this model, as some East Asian states began to discover at the end of the twentieth century, is that bureaucractic leadership is more effective at building an industrial economy than at continuing to manage it once it becomes mature and open to international competition. In Indonesia, for example, the Asian financial crisis of the late 1990s exposed the extent to which investment patterns had been distorted by 'crony capitalism', with access to capital depending on bureaucratic and political contacts rather than the anticipated rate of return.

Key reading

Next step: *Peters (1995) is a clear and genuinely comparative introduction to bureaucracy.*

Heady (1996) is an alternative to Peters. Bekke, Perry and Toonen (1996) is a lively edited collection. Page (1992) is a comparative study adopting a Weberian approach. Osborne and Gaebler (1993) is an enthusiast's account of the new public management, while Hughes (1994) is more academic but still positive. See Ranson and Stewart (1994) for a heavy dose of British drizzle. For particular countries and regions, see Fesler and Kettl (1996) on the United States, Dowding (1995) on the United Kingdom, Campbell and Wilson (1995) on Britain viewed comparatively, Boston (1995) on New Zealand, and Flynn and Strehl (1996) on Europe. For Japan, Johnson (1995) is an influential interpretation. Wallis (1989) examines the role of bureaucracy in third world development. Linz and Stepan (1996) comment perceptively on postcommunist bureaucracies.

The military and the police

All modern governments must come to terms with 'the state in uniform'. The military and the police monopolize the legitimate use of force; they are the visible expression of the state's capacity to use brute power to maintain its authority against external and internal threats. Yet who is to prevent the army from turning its tanks on the politicians or the people? Who is to prevent the police from taking the law into its own hands? Who is to prevent the secret police from exploiting its lack of accountability? Who, in short, is to guard the guards?

Controlling the military

The two main approaches to controlling the armed forces are the liberal model, based on a depoliticized military which accepts civilian supremacy, and the penetration model which seeks to imbue the military with the values of the political elite (Box 14.1).

The liberal model

In the liberal model favoured by democracies, the role of the military is to implement the defence policy adopted by the civilian leadership. The armed forces do not formulate policy; politics is not the generals' business. Civilian preeminence is asserted by placing politicians at the top of the military hierarchy. Thus the American constitution states that, 'the president shall be Commander in Chief of the Army and Navy'. The civilian leadership makes decisions on military engagement and resourcing. The task of the armed forces is to offer advice before such decisions are reached, especially on the feasibility of achieving objectives by military means, and above all to implement decisions once they have been agreed. The military ethos is professional, not political. The armed forces should be primarily concerned with their technical fighting ability; and on these matters the politicians should show due deference to the experts in violence. Thus each side respects, without seeking to dominate, the other.

It is unrealistic to expect that the military should have no involvement in domestic politics; controlling the military is a two-way street. The implicit deal is that the soldiers will stay in their barracks as long as their interests are given due weight in policymaking. Even in liberal democracies, the military remains a powerful institutional interest. Again, the American experience is illustrative. Although there is no serious question of the American military posing a direct challenge to the supremacy of the elected government, military leaders are skilful players of Washington's political game. With the support of arms manufacturers, military leaders have won enormous funding from a compliant Congress for weapons whose sophistication and cost sometimes exceeds their military value. Senior officers make full use of their standing and their technical knowledge in their participation in the National Security Council (the body which advises the president on foreign policy) and in appearances before Congressional committees. Through their dealings with the media, the armed forces have also demon-

---

BOX 14.1
Models of civilian control over the military

Model	Definition	Example
Liberal	A depoliticized and professional military accepts civilian control	Consolidated democracies
Penetration	A politicized military shares the goals of the leaders. Security services keep a close watch on military personnel	Communist states

---

strated considerable skill in mobilizing public opinion behind their cause. At the highest level, generals and admirals are inevitably politicians in uniform; they spend more time politicking than fighting.

The effectiveness of the military lobby was enhanced during the cold war when Western governments perceived a clear and present danger to their security. Thus the end of the cold war posed a challenge to civil–military relations in the democratic world. Governments faced popular expectations of a peace dividend; that is, a reduction in military spending with the savings used either to cut taxes or to increase public spending in other areas (Figure 14.1). The ability of Western democracies to manage this reduction in military resourcing reveals the extent to which the liberal model has been accepted, not least within the military itself. The division between the various branches of the armed forces also proved useful for managing decline; it forced military chiefs into competition to minimize the damage to their own service.

The liberal model of civil–military relations has emerged slowly as part of the evolution of liberal democracies; it cannot be transplanted quickly. To succeed, it requires a consolidated state which shows competence in governing a complex society and which enjoys legitimacy among the population. In these circumstances, still far from universal, the military will have neither the inclination nor the opportunity to seize power from civilian rulers.

The penetration model

The penetration model of civilian control is based on imbuing the armed forces with the political ideals of the ruling party. In the communist world, where penetration was most extensive, the role of the military was not just to defend the state from foreign aggression but also to pursue the transformative goals of the party. The Soviet Union was the classic instance of penetrative control, providing a model which was copied throughout the communist world. The Soviet communist party went to extreme lengths to ensure the political reliability of the armed forces, even at the cost of weakening its efficiency as a fighting force. For example, Stalin's paranoid purge in 1937–38 of 'politically unreliable' officers virtually destroyed the Red Army's professional leadership. Less extreme measures were employed in all communist states. At each level within the military command structure, a political commissar (reporting to higher officials in the party) kept a watchful eye on proceedings. Nearly all career soldiers belonged to the party or the Young Communist

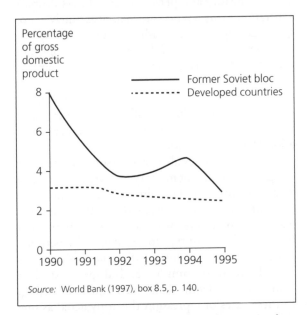

Source: World Bank (1997), box 8.5, p. 140.

Figure 14.1 Military expenditure by former Soviet bloc and developed countries, 1990–95.

EXHIBIT 14.1

Controlling the military: the case of Saudi Arabia

Control through penetration is seen most clearly in communist states but is not confined to them. It is a feature attempted by many authoritarian regimes, though not always successfully. In the patrimonial regimes of the Middle East, top military commanders are selected because they are close confidants of the ruling political groups. Islam legitimizes this interpenetration since it does not separate political, military and religious leadership. Saudi Arabia is a leading example of successful containment of the military by a noncommunist authoritarian government. The techniques used by Saudi's ruling families combine buying the support of the military and maintaining tight control just in case. Specifically:

- Military intelligence officers report directly to the royal family.
- Soldiers are formally prohibited from engaging in politics.

- The National Guard provides a counterweight to regular forces.
- Military command is highly centralized but the bases themselves are scattered around remote areas.
- Soldiers are regularly rotated around bases.
- Some air bases are placed under the army's control to limit the power of the air force.
- The military receives over 10 per cent of the country's considerable annual product.
- Staff are extremely well-paid for doing very little. Indeed most officers are reputed to be seriously unfit.

So successful are these techniques that resurgent Islam poses more of a threat than plump generals to Saudi's princes.

Further reading: Khatani (1992).

League. Ordinary conscripts were given intensive political indoctrination; the armed forces were supposedly 'schools for socialism'. Finally, the security agencies also undertook extensive surveillance of 'unreliable' individuals within and without the armed forces.

Military leaders gained immense power and influence in all communist states. In the Soviet Union, senior officers formed a three-headed ruling class with party leaders and the secret police. The top personnel of these 'three sisters' enjoyed special privileges such as holiday homes, access to foreign imports and extra medical care. No waiting in queues for officers of the Red Army; for them, communism had already arrived. No wonder the Soviet Union was described as 'militarized socialism' (Colton, 1990).

So civilian penetration of the army resulted not only in the party inserting itself in the army, but also in the army gaining a place within the party. This interlocking is most evident in China, where the party and military became closely intermingled. When as in China revolution occurs as the result of a protracted military (and especially guerrilla)

struggle, party and military become almost indistinguishable. Both sets of leaders are bound together by a shared history and personal ties. China's People's Liberation Army has never seen itself as purely a professional fighting force. Rather, its top figures believe that they have a right and a duty to be involved in politics. When Jiang Zemin became first among equals in China's civilian leadership after the death of Deng Xiaoping in 1997, one of his problems (or opportunities?) was his lack of the close contact with the army which came naturally to the earlier generation of revolutionaries.

Communist states also provide some of the most dramatic examples of military intervention to crush a domestic threat to the regime. China is again a case in point. During the Cultural Revolution, the army was used to restore order after political turmoil brought the country to a standstill between 1966–69. Then in June 1989, the military was brutally used to murder and disperse student demonstrators from Tiananmen Square in Bejing. In these cases of repression the army acted as one element in a ruling élite that encompassed party, state and military.

Military coups

When politicians fail to master the threat from their armed forces, particularly from the army which is the largest branch and the one most suited to domestic intervention, a coup may result. Yet the military coup, leading to government by soldiers, is primarily a twentieth-century, and even post-1945, event. As Pinkney (1990, p. 7) writes,

the involvement of soldiers in politics is not new, and can be traced back at least as far as Roman times. The phenomenon of military government, in the sense of a government drawn mainly from the army and using the army as its main power base, is much newer and belongs essentially to the last 50 years.

In the developing world, and especially postcolonial countries, generals soon seized power from civilian rulers – and then from other generals. In sub-saharan Africa, 68 coups occurred between 1963 and 1987 (Magyar, 1992, p. 233), and as late as 1987, half the countries of Africa were under military control. In Latin America, only Mexico and Costa Rica have been immune from military government in the postwar period, the latter by virtue of abolishing its army after a civil war in 1948. In most but not all of these cases the military withdrew from formal rule in the 1980s, transforming the pattern of government around the world.

Definition

A **military coup** is a seizure of political power by the armed forces or sections thereof. The term conjures up images of a violent, secretive and unwelcome capture of power against the opposition of civilian rulers. In fact, most coups replaced one military regime with another, many involved little if any loss of life, and some were more or less invited by the previous rulers.

The clustering of military coups, and later disengagement, suggests some common factors must have been at work. The most important of these was the cold war. During this period many developing countries became pawns on a global chessboard dominated by the United States and the Soviet Union. Each superpower sought allies and did not enquire too closely into the background, civilian or military, of the rulers of a particular country. Ruling generals might lack support in their own country but they could survive, at least for a period, through the political, economic and military backing of a superpower.

Simple contagion, both from one country to another and within a single country over time, was another major factor behind coups. Once the military had seized power in all the surrounding states, it was natural for generals in the remaining island of civilian rule to wonder whether they were missing a trick. And when a country had experienced one coup, it was likely to suffer more. Coups bred counter-coups as military takeover became, in some countries, a standard means of élite replacement.

Definition

The **cold war** refers to the competition between the United States and the Soviet Union which lasted from the late 1940s to the collapse of the Soviet Union in 1991. Falling short of open war, the cold war often reached a high intensity of confrontation, particularly before detente began in the late 1960s. The cold war was a conflict between superpowers, reinforced by conflicting ideologies and heightened by the capacity of each side to destroy the other. The end of the cold war brought about by communism's fall was an event of first magnitude. It released the waves of globalization, regionalization, nationalism and democratization which characterized the politics of the 1990s.

Beyond these international factors of the cold war and contagion, we can distinguish between society-centred and military-centred motives for coups. Society-centred factors refer to features of the wider society (including the government) which, while they did not directly involve the armed forces, did provide a reason or pretext for military intervention. Such factors included economic decay, social conflict and government corruption, all of which contributed to the loss of legitimacy by civilian rulers. Indeed, a decline in the effectiveness and legitimacy of government was a key condition underlying most coups. This society-centred perspective was captured by Magyar's comment (1992, p. 234) that 'coups are like vultures which pick on dead prey'.

Society-centred factors were important reasons for coups in both Africa and Latin America. In the many small states of Africa, one society-centred factor was simply the ease with which the army could seize power. With central government centred on a few offices in the capital, and probably only one state-controlled radio station to capture, seizing power was fairly simple. A handful of tanks supported by a few hundred troops would suffice. In such circumstances, a coup became a tempting proposition for an ambitious and frustrated general. So the inherent fragility of African states helped to explain their vulnerability. Society-centred factors were also central to the long history of coups in Latin America. The army most often stepped in when the temperature of political conflict rose too high, and in particular when the left seemed to be gaining the upper hand in its continuous struggle with conservative élites.

But features internal to the military were also relevant in many cases. In a military-centred coup, officers responded to a threat, real or perceived, to the corporate interests of all or part of the military. These included: inadequate or unstable funding of the armed forces, political interference, late payment of wages, lack of a career path for ambitious soldiers, ethnic divisions within the military, mutinies by lower-level officers, poor barracks or even inadequate food. In reality, society-centred and military-centred motives for coups were often linked. The difference was that in a society-centred coup, the forces sought to save the country; in a military-centred coup, the soldiers aimed to save themselves.

Military government

Seizing power was the easy part. A coup was nothing more than the capture of the state by the most organized section of its employees (Clapham and Philip, 1985). Once installed in office, the real problems began. New military leaders attempted to resolve the underlying problems which had brought their tanks to the presidential palace. However, they usually lacked the political background, experience and sometimes the ability of those they replaced. The first lesson learned by new military rulers was that governing is difficult, especially in the poor, sometimes bankrupt, countries in which coups tended to occur. Military rulers responded to their challenges in a range of ways, from honest attempts to refloat the ship of state to monumental corruption which

served only to sink the state altogether. The only clear feature of military regimes was their lack of respect for civil rights and individual freedoms; though this of course extends to many authoritarian civilian governments too.

Inclusionary and exclusionary regimes represented the two extremes of military rule (Remmer, 1989). In the former, the military leaders tried to build a base of support among the political class – and even on occasion the wider population – often by exploiting the population's respect for a strong leader. Civilian politicians were represented in a cabinet and the bureaucracy continued to make important decisions. Such inclusionary military regimes were often organized on presidential lines, based around a strong personal ruler attempting to build a strong country (Munck, 1989). The modernizing regime of Abdel Nasser in Egypt was an example. Nasser came to power in a coup in 1952, became president in 1956 and remained there until his death in 1970. Inclusionary military regimes often underwent a process of civilianization, becoming instances of presidential rather than military government. This was again the case in Egypt, which has turned into a state dominated by the bureaucracy rather than the military. Another example of a military leader broadening his support was Colonel Juan Peron in Argentine. He came to power in a coup in 1943 and undertook a populist programme of state-led industrialization based on a strong trade union movement and a commitment to social welfare for the urban working class.

In the more common exclusionary military regime, the generals limited popular participation in politics. In Chile between 1973 and 1989, General Pinochet suppressed all potential sources of popular opposition. He exterminated, exiled or imprisoned thousands of labour leaders and left-wing politicians, concentrating power in the hands of his ruling military clique. The standard institutional form of an exclusionary regime was the junta (council), a small group made up of the leader of each branch of the armed forces. In Chile, for instance, Pinochet himself acted as chief executive while a classic four-man junta representing the army, navy, air force and national police performed legislative functions. In Burma (Myanmar), a military junta – absurdly rebranded in 1997 as the State Peace and Development Council – seized power in 1988. It is

Country profile **NIGERIA**

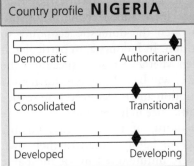

Population: 104m.
Gross domestic product per head: some estimates suggest as high as $1300 but inequality is marked.
Main groups: Hausa-Fulani in the north, Yoruba in the southwest and Ibos in the southeast. These groups make up about 65 per cent of the population.
Religions: Muslim 50%, Christian 40%, traditional religions about 10%.
Form of government: military rule since 1983. Civilian institutions are weak; the National Assembly is suspended and judges are appointed by the military.
Territorial basis of power: federal, with the number of states increasing from 12 in 1967 to 30 currently.

'On 15 July, 132 Ogoni men, women and children, returning from their abode in the Cameroons, had been waylaid on the Andoni River by an armed gang and cruelly murdered, leaving but two women to make a report. The genocide of the Ogoni people had taken on a new dimension. The manner of it I will narrate in my next book, if I live to tell the tale.'

These words were written in prison by Ken Saro-Wiwa (1995, p. 238) on 17 May 1994. On 10 November 1995, Saro-Wiwa and eight others were hanged by order of Nigeria's military leaders. Saro-Wiwa, a writer and activist, had been an outspoken critic of the Nigerian government. Although his execution stimulated massive international publicity, the military continues to govern, endlessly delaying a promised transition to civilian rule. This is despite the advantage of oil which provides about 95 per cent of the country's exports. So why is Nigeria one of the few military governments to survive in Africa? Why is the country a deviant case?

One answer is oil itself. This creates enormous resources – $220bn worth of exports in 25 years – which have been corruptly appropriated through the armed forces and the state. Oil money keeps the military regime afloat and permits massive misgovernance. In a 1996 survey of company directors, Nigeria was rated the second most corrupt country in the world after Russia. Oil means that political loyalties are simply bought and sold. When the oil price fell, the economic pain fell on civilian groups, leading to continuing political cynicism which makes the generals fearful for their own safety should civilian rule be restored. Oil also gives Nigeria a bargaining chip which weakens the efforts of the international community to encourage reform.

Ethnic diversity superimposed on provinces operating in a federal framework is also a factor. Reflecting the colonial policy of divide and rule, the federal government became an arena for conflict between regions and ethnic groups leading to civil war in 1967. With gains for one group defined as losses for others, the interests of the country are lost in a fog of spoils. In short, the generals are out for what they can get.

Whether oil and ethnic divisions are a sufficient explanation for military rule in Nigeria is debatable; after all, South Africa's successful transition to democracy overcame even more severe enmities. But South Africa had Mandela and de Klerk. By contrast, Nigeria has suffered poor political leadership, with ruthless schemers showing no interest in improving the cynical terms of Nigerian politics. Indeed, General Abacha, Nigeria's military leader, has severely weakened the effectiveness of the military in the process of protecting his own back.

But deviant cases rarely show staying power. In the longer term, the options for Nigeria seem to be democratization or disintegration. Either someone or some event will break the logjam preventing democratic reform or the country will fall apart into its component parts.

Further reading: Diamond, Kirk-Greene and Oyediran (1997).

chaired by the commanding general of the army; the chief of intelligence acts as secretary. This particular junta has followed a ruthless exclusionary strategy, disbanding the assembly and governing under a martial law which permits all private organizations to be investigated by the council.

How effective were military governments in stimulating economic development? Relying on their monopoly of force, and lacking immediate accountability, military governments should have been able to pursue a long-term developmental agenda. Some inclusionary military regimes attempted this, providing a military version of the developmental state. Nasser's Egypt was again a good example. He broke the power of wealthy landowners by setting ceilings on landholdings while also investing heavily in measures to improve rural health and agricultural productivity. The result is that today nearly all Egyptians have access to safe water, a considerable achievement (Lesch, 1996, p. 615).

Indonesia is a more severe example of economic growth under authoritarian military rule. General Suharto became president in 1968 after the army destroyed the old regime by the brutal device of murdering the regime's supporters: about half a million in all. Over the next two decades, Indonesia became the eighth-fastest growing economy in the world, helped by rising demand for oil, its major export. The military imposed political order while the bureaucrats prepared the ground for an injection of foreign capital, much of it in or through military-connected enterprises. Through these means, Suharto established a dominant system of rule which went beyond, even if it always relied on, military foundations (Vatikiotis, 1993).

Burma provides an example of economic growth under even more merciless army rule. Recognizing the country's tourist potential, as well as the potential wealth of its oil and gas fields, the junta has destroyed inconveniently-sited villages (often peopled by ethnic minorities) before making massive deals with overseas companies. In the era after the cold war, surviving military regimes like Burma's do so, in part, by ruthlessly exploiting the opportunities provided by a global economy.

However, military-led modernization eventually causes difficulties of its own. The economy becomes more sophisticated and new social groups and gen-

erations emerge to challenge authoritarian rule. Multinationals and international economic organizations seek to open the domestic economy to genuine competition. In Indonesia, in particular, it remains to be seen whether Suharto's successors (he was born in 1921) will be able to hold his regime together as corruption and trade protection reduce international confidence in his regime.

But only a handful of military governments reached the stage of falling victim to their own success. Most were uninterested in, or incapable of, imposing a development strategy on society; many acted in a way which precluded further growth. Particularly in Africa, where the state already dominated the formal economy, military rulers pursued a policy which resembled that of the government they replaced: exploiting the state's resources to reward their own supporters. Aware of their own uncertain tenure, the generals also took care to squirrel away wealth for themselves. Some military governments (such as Mobutu's in Zaire) were no more than kleptocracies – government by thieves. The result was public over-spending, especially on bloated armed forces and on favoured ethnic groups. In Somalia, for instance, the army increased from 3000 personnel at independence in 1960 to 120 000 in 1982.

Definition

A **collapsed** or **failed state** is a territory in which the central government has lost the capacity to rule. Laws are not made, taxes are not extracted and order is not maintained. The state disintegrates and power is exercised by whoever can acquire and retain the means of coercion in a particular area – armed bands, invading troops, army divisons, clan leaders. Warlords emerge to offer protection and pillage to their followers. Most examples are from Africa in the 1980s and 1990s: for instance, Zaire in the dying days of Mobutu's dictatorship (Zartman, 1995).

In extreme cases, often linked to the seizure of power by lowly officers from lowly tribes, military rule not only failed to contribute to development but actively contributed to state collapse. Misrule by army despots transforms soft states into collapsed states; public authority disintegrates and society is divided into competing clans and military bands. Invading armies often spot a chance to annex territory, striking at the soft underbelly of the country's periphery. Thus authority is further divided, economic activity breaks down and people live by subsistence and barter.

In Uganda, for example, ex-boxer Idi Amin Dada (who ousted the civilian ruler Milton Obote in a coup in 1971)

> destroyed a state that was still being made, a state groping with rudimentary tasks of broadening its authority over an uncertain territory, against a backgound of scarce resources and unrefined administration. (Khaidagala, 1995, p.35)

Amin was a crude tyrant who relied on a narrow tribal base, damaged the economy by expelling many Asians and launched a foolhardy invasion of northern Tanzania. The eventual result was civil war. The collapse of Liberia under Master-Sergeant Samuel Doe, a member of the low-status Krahn tribe, was similar in its essentials. In other cases the military contributed to state collapse through internal divisions, with junior officers leading rebellions against military governments and resulting in civil war. Stalled coups, in which the rebels are prevented from reaching the capital but retain control of some outlying territory, can have the same result. The grim realities of life in collapsed states are powerful ammunition for those who argue that any political order is better than none.

Military withdrawal

The 1980s saw the military return to their barracks. First in Latin America and then in Africa, military governments handed power back to elected civilian leaders. By the end of 1990 Latin America had no military regimes at all. One recent study found only seven unambiguous examples of military government remaining in the world, mainly African states such as Nigeria, Gambia and Sierra Leone (Derbyshire and Derbyshire 1996, p. 50). True, the military often remains a substantial, even leading, political force in many 'civilian' regimes. This position is sometimes even institutionalized through a National Security Council containing a mix of military and civilian representatives, as in Pakistan and Turkey. But it is still important to ask

---

BOX 14.2
Some conditions for successful military withdrawal

- Withdrawal must be orderly; all elements of the armed forces must agree or a military faction may stay in power.
- Arrangements must be made to protect the safety of the departing generals; officers who fear prosecution may cling to power.
- The generals must feel that the corporate interests of the military will not be unduly threatened by a return to civilian rule.
- An organized civilian authority, such as a political party, must be available to take up the reins of power.

Further reading: Sundhaussen (1985).

---

why the generals were willing to remove their hands from the formal levers of power. Why has the sword returned to its sheath? Why are clubs no longer trumps?

Changes in the international environment were a major factor. Just as military governments prospered during the cold war, so they shrivelled after its close. As Wiseman (1996, p. 4) writes,

> authoritarian African political leaders [such as the military] were more strongly placed to resist the pressures of African democrats when they could turn to outside pressures to help them stay in power.

During the cold war, military rulers could obtain the support of a superpower on the basis of no questions asked. Now conditionality rules the roost. Aid and technical assistance flow to civilian regimes that adopt democratic forms and offer at least some protection to civil rights. International bodies such as the World Bank stipulate market-based economic policies which do not sit comfortably with military rule. The USA's immense economic leverage in Central and South America was successfully applied to military regimes in Bolivia, El Salvador and Guatemala. And just as contagion accelerated the diffusion of military coups in the 1960s and 1970s, so also did it encourage generals to return to their bases in the 1980s and 1990s. So the retreat of the military must be seen in the context of international pressures to introduce democratic, and not merely civilian, governments.

However, some military rulers periodically passed power back to civilians even before the current wave of democratization. Since 1932, for instance, Thailand has experienced 14 coups, many leading only to short periods of military rule. Thailand is a classic example of the military acting as a guardian of national life. A coup became the device for replacing civilian leaders when the existing rulers suffered a loss of authority. The Thai military has high status in society (reinforced, unusually, by its political role) while representative institutions, especially parties, remain weak. Although the last coup was in 1992, the armed forces remain active, insisting for example on prime ministerial support for a new constitution during a political crisis in 1997. In supervised democracies such as Thailand's the armed forces retain a watching brief over civilian rule, showing how the end of military rule does not signal the end of military influence.

If a coup requires brute force, handback is a more delicate task. In politics as in war, nothing is more difficult than a well-ordered retreat (Box 14.2). The problem underlying withdrawal is that long periods of army rule lead to an interweaving of civilian and military power which is not quickly unravelled. Senior officers may be accustomed to seats in the cabinet, to a high level of military expenditure, to running the security agencies independently of civilian control, to making money from defence contracts and to exemption from civilian justice. These expectations often survive the transition to civilian rule. Indeed a Faustian pact may be needed to entrench some of these privileges before the military is willing to go. In Chile, for instance, General Pinochet ensured military autonomy was secured in the new constitution before handing power back to civilians in 1980. The armed forces were exempted from prosecution in civilian courts and retained the role of guarantors of the 'institutional order' and 'national security' (Luckham, 1996, p. 149). Ecuador's armed forces are guaranteed 15 per cent of the country's oil revenues until 2010. Such military-led transitions, characteristic of Latin America, help the shift to, but weaken the depth of, the postmilitary democracy.

The military in transitional states

The transition from military to civilian rule is straightforward in one sense: by the end, the army has usually made its own decision to get out. But what problems are raised by keeping the army at bay during transitions from one *civilian* regime to another, such as the transition from communism to postcommunism? Here the military is on the outside looking in, potentially a dangerous situation. Recent transitions have succeeded in keeping the army at bay, reflecting a declining desire among military officers to take the formal reins of power. Aguero (1995) notes several factors which help to keep the military quiescent in these civilian-led transitions:

- Élite unity is important in preventing an 'opening' from developing for the army
- Civilian supremacy over the military should be asserted gradually
- Consolidation of the new regime eventually (but not initially) requires the military to offer positive support for the new order. This is best achieved by giving the armed forces the resources and the autonomy to pursue purely military goals effectively.

Spain's democratic transition after the death of General Franco in 1975 is an example of successful management of the military during a civilian transition. The problem there was that an army oriented to domestic politics formed part of Franco's 'poisoned legacy' (Preston, 1990). As Heywood (1995, p. 58) notes, 'the dictator deliberately sought to instil in the armed forces a narrow preoccupation with internal rather than external threats to Spain', thereby building upon a tradition of military intervention which dated back to the nineteenth century. Officers formed a privileged caste with strong antidemocratic values. It is no surprise, then, that the military came close to aborting the birth of democracy in Spain. Indeed, it was remarkable that the only coup attempt – in 1981 – was an ineffectual affair by junior officers. Yet in Spain the time for coups has now passed. From 1982 a socialist government succeeded in stengthening civilian control and modernizing the armed forces' organization and equipment. Joining the North Atlantic Treaty Organization (NATO) in 1986 gave further impetus

EXHIBIT 14.2

The military in postcommunist Russia

Russia's armed forces provide a magnified illustration of trends applying to much of the postcommunist world. In Russia, an enormous if fragmented military sector confronted a divided and politicized state. As Donnelly (1993) comments, 'large bureaucratic institutions continue to function irrespective of the lack of government; by mid-1992, the armed forces hierarchy was increasingly determining its own agenda'. Under the constitution, the military come under the specific control of the president rather than serving as agents of the state as a whole. But the reality was that the military, together with the security services, formed a massive, diverse and substantially independent empire. In border regions commanders pursued their own foreign policies. Throughout Russia officers exploited for commercial gain the legacy of the leading role played by the military in the Soviet economy, forming a new military–industrial complex. Militarized capitalism replaced militarized socialism. Officers such as General Lebed became national figures, challenging the authority of President Yeltsin.

All this reinforced the declining effectiveness of the armed forces in strictly military terms as the quality of personnel and equipment declined. In 1994 the disastrous 'invasion' of Chechnya, which had proclaimed its independence from Moscow, further damaged morale. During the campaign some conscripts were even reduced to begging for food. As Sakwa (1996, p. 320) concludes, 'the attempt to sculpt a lean and professional Russian army out of the bloated Soviet defense establishment at a time of economic crisis would inevitably be long and arduous'.

---

for Spain's military officers to address professional rather than political concerns. Heywood concludes that by the 1990s 'the distant rattling of sabres may still be heard on occasion but it elicits little reaction from the Spanish public'.

In some other new democracies the problems of managing the military remain considerable. The status of the armed forces invariably suffers as democracy consolidates yet military decline must be accomplished in a context of inexperienced civilian leadership, limited resources and the absence of a clear military mission after the cold war. Living in decaying barracks and surrounded by rusting tanks (or in Russia by the radioactive hulks of nuclear submarines), there is a danger that disillusioned officers will sit around dreaming of the good old days – and of how to restore them. As Kohn (1997, p. 153) argues, 'how the transition to civilian control is managed will be crucial in determining the fate of democracy around the world'. We can examine these problems in more detail by looking at two cases: postcommunism and Latin America.

Postcommunism

As with other aspects of the transition from communism, the role of the military was changing before the final implosion of party rule. In Hungary, for instance, a large-scale reduction of the armed forces was already under way. In the collapse of communism in 1989, the elaborate structure of penetrative control by the communist party largely fell apart of its own accord. But the new leaders faced a tricky issue: what to do with officers closely linked to the old order? Should they be retained for their expertise or sacked, even prosecuted, for their past roles? In most countries the policy was a combination of compulsory retirements plus a pragmatic decision to forget the past. In Hungary, for example, forced retirement was restricted to generals in charge of the army's political departments. The defence minister pointed out that it was impossible to dismiss the entire armed forces: 'an army, just like a people, cannot be relieved of duty' (Agocs, 1997, p. 87).

In other respects, the military was left to fend for itself. Previously subject to intense penetrative control by the party, the armed forces suddenly found themselves left to their own devices. Civilian rulers had more pressing problems to confront and in any case they often lacked the expertise to offer coherent leadership to the armed forces. The new Hungarian defense minister was typical. He said that nothing in his previous life 'not one moment of it, suggested that I would end up here. I was not preparing for this position and always pursued other goals'. Initially, there was little attempt to develop the national military strategies much needed after the end of the Soviet empire.

In practice, the overall military budget was cut severely but officers were left to manage as best they could, producing such farces as the Czech parachute regiment which did not have enough parachutes to go round! Pauperization of the armed forces led to increasing use of military resources for profit-making activities, for example weapons trafficking. In these demoralized conditions lawlessness within the forces became a growing problem, not least through bullying of conscripts. Suicides increased. In Russia, over 100 soldiers committed suicide or were killed by their 'colleagues' in 1997 alone. For the first time, problems such as these were widely reported by a more independent media, contributing to a further loss of morale.

Latin America

While postcommunist states have little experience of military coups, the same cannot be said for Latin America. There the initial task for postmilitary regimes was to prevent another round of military intervention 'in defence of the country'. With few external threats, politicians were keen to keep the soldiers busy by involving them in civilian activities ranging from highway construction to the war against drugs. But officers resisted policing duties, fearing the corrupting effect of involvement in drug wars as well as the civilian unpopularity which might arise from enforcing domestic law and order. The armed forces remained keen to protect their remaining privileges, resisting the full implications of the liberal model. The issue of human rights abuses under military governments, and the continuing absence of effective judicial control of the forces, proved particularly sensitive. Given such continuing tensions, Farcau (1996, p. 159) concludes that 'tried and true motivations for military intervention in politics still exist'.

Yet this judgment may be too cautious. In a world of democratic politics, market-based economies and growing trade links with the United States, the probability of a return to direct military rule in Latin America has fallen sharply. In Paraguay, an attempted coup failed in 1996 when Brazil made it clear that the price of military rule would be expulsion from the Mercosur trade grouping. Further, as time passes, so the number of officers with direct experience of organizing coups has declined; time-served coup-crafters are becoming scarce. Participation in international peacekeeping missions has also given some armies something to do. And a number of civilian administrations have shrewdly reduced the number of military bases close to the capital, making coups more difficult to execute. Hunter (1997, p. 475) argues that even when the military secured an entrenched position in the new democracy, 'the competitive dynamic unleashed by democracy can be expected to drive the military to retreat further before an advancing civil and political society'. In the future, concludes Millett (1996, p. 298), any coups in Latin America are likely to be short-term interventions, by invitation only, and following a prolonged period of ineffective civilian rule. Even then the army may be reluctant to take over. In the future the problem may be to persuade the generals to move in rather than to keep them out.

The police

Although the military is sometimes used by governments to deal with domestic disorder, its primary function is to pursue national defence. Except for cases of severe civil disorder, the task of upholding and enforcing the laws of the land belongs to the police. As with the military, problems of accountability and control arise. The danger is that the strong professional norms of the police degenerate into a 'canteen culture' – male-dominated, authoritarian and racist – which leads to the abuse of power. The task is to design mechanisms of civilian control which do not threaten the crime-fighting ability of the police. In the democratic world, the two main ways of organizing policing are represented by the Anglo-American and continental European models.

(Box 14.3)

Definition

As a noun (that is, an institution), **the police** refers to an organized body, authorized to use force in specified conditions in order to maintain domestic order and identify offenders. As a verb (that is, a function), **to police** means to supervise the activity of a group. All societies must perform the policing function; large and modern societies allocate this function to specialized police institutions.

The Anglo-American model

In both Britain and the United States, the transformation of community self-policing into professional and specialized police forces, with a measure of national coordination, was an integral part of the development of the modern state. The major developments came early in the nineteenth century, stimulated by industrialization and the resulting growth of crime and disorder in enlarged cities. The formation of Sir Robert Peel's London Metropolitan Police in 1829 was the key innovation, serving as a professional model for the New York force established in 1845 (though in practice American forces remained more closely linked to local politics than did British forces).

In the Anglo-American model, the dominant policing tradition remains strongly local or bottom-up (Box 14.3). The American system remains astonishingly fragmented, reflecting distrust of national power. Local police forces are controlled by elected or appointed police chiefs. Most of America's 40 000 police forces employ fewer than 25 officers. There are five levels of public policing: federal, state, county, city and borough. The United States also makes considerable use of private or semi-private forces, for example to police parks and campuses. Decentralized policing is perhaps the most striking example of localized governance in the United States. Yet it is far from self-evident that such fragmentation provides an effective structure for catching villains.

In Britain, the balance between central and local control is embodied in a tripartite division of authority. The three points on the triangle are: central government, represented by the Home Office (interior ministry); 40 local police authorities, composed of councillors and magistrates, each of which supervises policing in a particular area; and chief constables (the chief of police) who deliver the policing service in each authority's area and retain considerable autonomy over tactics and priorities. The system is complex but workable, reflecting a compromise between local and national interests.

In the twentieth century, moves were made to encourage national coordination of policing in both Britain and the United States. For example, Britain's National Reporting Centre established after the 1972 miners' strike enabled the Home Office to move police forces round the country. Governments in both countries also used their financial power to encourage local forces to develop specialist units dealing with criminal investigation, drugs, tactical weapons units, crowd control and public order. And central governments also attempted to set broad professional standards for the police. Thus the United States, for instance, established a Commission on

---

BOX 14.3

Policing democracies: Anglo-American and continental European models

	Anglo-American model	Continental European model
Source of legitimacy	Community	State
Organizational structure	More local	More centralized
Main function	Crime control	Crime control and general administration
Style	Civilian	Often military
Examples	UK, USA	France, Spain

Accreditation for Law Enforcement Agencies in 1979. However, local policing remains deeply entrenched, both as a structure and as a value, in the Anglo-American model.

The continental European model

In most of continental Europe the police have always been a more national force, operating as agents of the central state rather than the local community: a state police but not a police state (p. 251). This reflects and contributes to a strong state tradition. In these top-down systems, the police fall under the direct control of central government and as such perform a wide range of administrative functions, such as issuing passports and driving licences, thus leading to larger forces (Figure 14.2) and to more frequent contact with citizens.

France and Spain illustrate this top-down model. In France, small local forces perform only a minor role in enforcing the law: the major players are two national forces, the *Police Nationale*, under the civilian control of the Ministry of the Interior, and the *Gendarmerie Nationale*, under the military control of the Ministry of Defence (Horton, 1995). The *Gendarmerie*, dating back to 1791, is organized along military lines, with *gendarmes* based in barracks and operating in a regimented fashion, with little discretion. Crimes are investigated with more concern for the rulebook than catching the culprit. Spain has an even stronger tradition of top-down policing, reinforced under Franco's dictatorship (1939–65). Indeed the two national forces – the military Civil Guard and the hated Armed Police – became symbols of Franco's authoritarian rule. The

Civil Guard provided the base for the attempted coup against Spain's fledgling democracy in 1981 (Heywood, 1995, p. 66). Reform of these forces is a continuing concern of the country's post-Franco rulers.

Attempts to transplant one model of policing to a country with different traditions rarely succeed, showing the limits of lesson-drawing in comparative politics. After the Second World War, the United States sought to impose its own system of local policing on Japan in an attempt to defuse the awesome power acquired by the Tokko or Special Higher Police ('If you say "Tokko", even a crying child falls silent', wrote one Japanese scholar). Yet in 1954, soon after the Americans left, the Japanese passed a new law which strengthened central control though without restoring Tokko to its previous position. American-style local policing was, it seems, not for export.

Global and local policing

The police are an excellent example of the pressures towards an approach which is simultaneously both more global and more local. On the one hand they must respond to the internationalization of serious crime, most of it drug-related. On the other hand the police must develop, or at least maintain, their role in the local community, investigating individual crimes and responding sensitively to the distress of the victims.

With criminal activities routinely crossing national boundaries, the need for international cooperation in policing increases. In extreme cases this takes the form of one country making military

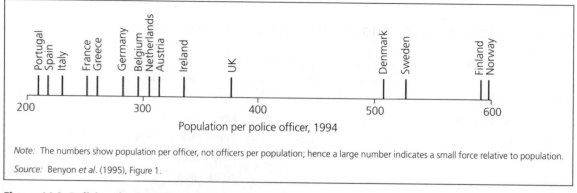

Note: The numbers show population per officer, not officers per population; hence a large number indicates a small force relative to population.

Source: Benyon *et al.* (1995), Figure 1.

Figure 14.2 Policing democracies

EXHIBIT 14.3

Policing Japanese style

Although Japan's police operate under national control, the integration of the force into the local community is a distinctive feature of its policing style. Indeed Bayley (1982) regards Japan as an exemplar of an 'Asian' policing style also found in China, Malaysia and Korea.

Japanese officers are assigned to one of 15 000 'police boxes' (small offices) or residential police stations, which act as a grass-roots link between police and society. Police officers are expected to visit all the families under their jurisdiction during the year, a feat requiring the consumption of immense amounts of tea. Japanese citizens accept that their lives will be closely monitored by the local officer. The neighbourhood police officer – known as *omawari-san* (honorable Mr Walkabout) – is a common visitor to family homes and local employers. Police officers are respected members of the local community in Japan but their policing style would be unacceptable in more individualistic cultures such as the United States.

But the Japanese method of maintaining law and order also has its harder side. Anyone who is arrested faces a tough time. Interrogations are not recorded, suspects can be detained for 23 days without charge and nearly all those charged are convicted by the courts. It may be this, as much as Mr Walkabout, which explains why Japan's crime rate is only about one hundredth that of the United States. Certainly, the lack of emphasis on the rights of suspects and the accused is one reason for supposing that Japan's form of democracy is distinctly illiberal.

Further reading: Mawby (1990, Ch.7), Ritchie (1992, Ch.9), Tipton (1990).

incursions into another. American attempts to hit the narcotics trade at source by seizing drugs barons in Central America are a case in point. Such police actions are usually performed by military or quasi-military units. However, cooperation rather than confrontation is more common in the fight against international drug-dealing, terrorism and trafficking in people. From its headquarters in France, Interpol (International Criminal Police Organization) has become the main instrument of police cooperation across borders. Nearly all countries are members. Interpol is a rare instance of a body which has evolved into an international organization, complete with an assembly and executive committee, without the stimulus of an international treaty (Anderson, 1989).

Europol, a separate body to Interpol, was created for information exchange in 1996. Occupying fortified quarters in The Hague, it consists of liaison officers from the EU's member states, each of whom has an office which remains part of the sovereign territory of the member state. This eccentric arrangement reflects political sensitivities; even in Europe, governments see control of a police force as the realization of sovereignty (Benyon, 1996). The absence of a common criminal justice system also prevents Europol from becoming a truly European police agency. As one of Europol's directors said, 'you still can't commit a Euro-murder'. Indeed, the development of a net of informal bilateral agreements between national police forces may inhibit the emergence of a truly European policing agency (Anderson *et al.*, 1995). Crime remains more international than those who police it.

Clearly, countries with national police forces find it easier to engage in cross-border cooperation than do those with localized policing systems such as the United States. But the decentralized Anglo-American policing model is more effective at responding to increased pressures towards a more local, community-oriented policing style. The police are increasingly expected to adopt a proactive approach, seeking to prevent as well as investigate crime through advisory services to the community. More and more, the police are expected to confront the consequences of crime, offering or arranging for counselling to victims. Such activities are unlikely to come naturally to a military barracks-based force, especially when officers are deliberately drawn from outside the local area.

EXHIBIT 14.4

Policing the Internet

Policing the Internet illustrates the difficulties of controlling crime beyond frontiers. Cybercrime takes various forms: obscenity (for example child pornography), trespass (for example hacking into unauthorized sites) and theft (for example stealing intellectual property or making illegal use of credit cards). Yet it is difficult for national police forces to investigate crimes which may originate on the other side of the world. Apart from the need for greater international cooperation, three other problems arise in policing the Internet:

- Most legal systems are based on the premise that crime takes a physical form; intellectual property rights are often inadequately protected in law.
- Police officers themselves are often poorly trained to investigate virtual crime.
- The Internet is inherently difficult to monitor; criminal acts cannot easily be tracked to their source.

Some authoritarian governments (for example Singapore, China and Vietnam) have sought direct control, forcing users to register with the government and monitoring traffic coming into the country. But such censorship is aimed at limiting political dissent rather than crime. For now, the Internet will continue to operate on an anarchic mixture of limited, self- and no policing.

Further reading: Loader (1997), Wall (1997).

Community policing is impossible to achieve in divided societies where the legitimacy of the regime is disputed. In South Africa under apartheid, minority white power meant that the black population was fully aware of the role of the police – and its army allies – as an instrument of racial domination. The South African Defence Forces (SADF) took over policing functions in the most troubled areas; indeed it was part of the formal duties of the SADF 'to assist the police in preserving internal order' (Brewer *et al.*, 1996, p. 178) and the police themselves adopted a paramilitary character. In Northern Ireland, too, the Catholic minority has always lacked confidence in the local police force, of whom nine out of ten are Protestants. Once such a situation exists, joining the police can be seen as an act of betrayal, thus reinforcing a separation between police and locality which is incompatible with community policing. Thus the question of recruitment to the police, as to other public services, is always sensitive and sometimes controversial.

The secret police

Surveillance raises difficult questions about the limits of police activity. The question is not whether surveillance should take place – anti-terrorist operations are accepted as legitimate – but rather who should be watched and who should authorize such observation. Defining an 'enemy of the state' is difficult. Terrorists are 'enemies' but what about eco-warriors or anti-nuclear campaigners who break the law in pursuit of principle? Surveillance is inherently difficult to monitor because it is, by its nature, secret. People may suspect that they are under investigation but if the intelligence agencies are doing their jobs properly, surveillance is difficult to prove. So secret policing is the least accountable area of police operations.

Surveillance can easily cross ill-defined boundaries. If judgments on who is a legitimate target for police surveillance are made by politicians, they may be too free with permission and even authorize investigation of their political opponents. However, the greater danger is that surveillance agencies will defy political control altogether. In the United States, J. Edgar Hoover, the legendary Director of the FBI 1935–72, exploited his powerful position to keep files on over a million people, including Marilyn Monroe (1400 pages of information) and Albert Einstein (1427 pages). In Britain in the mid-1970s, a few rogue elements in the security services sought to destabilize Harold Wilson's Labour government – the very body that was supposed to control the intelligence agencies.

In authoritarian regimes, the police are nearly always an agent of political repression. In these cases surveillance of the population can be both overt and covert. *Overt* surveillance is often carried out by civilian informers: in China, neighbourhood committes keep close tabs on the activities of their neighbours. It is common to see the old women of a neighbourhood sitting outside, knitting for the grandchildren – and quietly noting any visitors to the area. After the suppression of the 1989 democracy movement in Beijing, activists were often turned over to the police by members of their own family. The party ensured such cases were widely reported in the press. Similarly, Saddam Hussein's Iraqi regime has been described by exiled dissidents as one in which the entire population informs on itself. Clearly these cases justify the label 'police state'.

Definition

A **police state** is a system of rule in which the police wield arbitrary power in a repressive and totalitarian political system. The operation of a police state depends on overt and covert surveillance; this foments fear and hinders organized opposition. Examples of police states include Nazi Germany and communist (and to an extent postcommunist) Russia. A police state should be distinguished from the German term, **polizeistaat**, which refers to a more benign system in which police carry out administrative functions beyond law enforcement.

Covert surveillance reinforces the hold of the police. As well as using civilian informers, members of the security police infiltrate social institutions such as the workplace, reporting back to their superiors on potential trouble-makers. The true extent of this penetration by the secret police in communist states only became apparent with the collapse of communism. Files found in the Stasi (secret police) offices in East Germany covered six million people, half the adult population. The headquarters of the Romanian secret police, the Securitate, also contained extensive intelligence information covering about one in four of the population. Indeed the Securitate played a major role in maintaining Ceauscescu's rule and was one of the few political

forces to resist his overthrow. Covert surveillance succeeds by creating a climate of fear since no-one knows who is a spy. The only sensible course of individual conduct is to keep your head down and trust no-one.

In communist states the secret police and the ruling party were closely linked. Managing the secret police machinery became an important stepping stone on the road to higher office. Yuri Andropov, who headed the KGB in the Soviet Union for 15 years before becoming General Secretary of the Communist Party in 1982, is one example. Heading the surveillance machinery was a political appointment and supreme loyalty to the party was demanded of secret police officials.

The use of the police to silence opposition is not limited to communist states. It has been a feature of the police in authoritarian regimes generally. Often organized on para-military lines, the police played a key role in political repression under military rule in Latin America. Between 1973 and 1990, under the dictatorship of Pinochet in Chile, about 15 000 people were assassinated, more than 2 200 political detainees 'disappeared' and over 150 000 prisoners were held in concentration camps. After General Videla came to power in Argentina in 1976, state kidnapping, torture and murder of political opponents became systematic. Little attempt was made to hide the extent of the operation, with most victims arrested in front of witnesses. This was state terrorism in the classic manner (Gilbert, 1995).

In some postcommunist countries the security services continue to play a major role. Although the KGB (Committee for State Security) in Russia has been subject to numerous reorganizations, the security apparatus remains an autonomous force, an organized power in a disorganized country. The security forces provided a power base for Gorbachev and have been reorganized but not contained by President Yeltsin. The members of this 'state within a state' still operate as a powerful and unaccountable force in Russia's postcommunist politics. The security forces include a large parallel army of about 70 000 internal troops and, together with the other power ministries such as the military, they were largely responsible for the disastrous invasion of Chechnya. Senior Kremlin officials accept that they are probably kept under surveillance by their own security service (Sakwa, 1996, p. 73). Corruption is endemic and the security apparatus, as well as being available for hire, also forms a powerful alliance with criminal gangs. The continuing power of the secret police throws a shadow across Russia, holding back the development of a civil society on which future stability and prosperity depend (Waller, 1994).

The legacy of the police state caused major difficulties for all postauthoritarian societies. The Nuremberg question was raised again: to what extent should the personnel of police states be brought to book, as some Nazis were after the Second World War? (Sakwa, 1996, p. 74). In Latin America the relatives of 'the disappeared' wanted police and military murderers identified and tried, but the generals would be less likely to support a new democracy if the price was jail for themselves or their underlings. In South Africa many past injustices remain uncorrected but questions remain over whether Bishop Tutu's Truth and Reconciliation Commission is the most prudent way forward. Either Truth or Reconciliation may be feasible but achieving both may be impossible. The danger of selectively raking over the past is that it lengthens the arduous journey to a harmonious future.

> **Definition**
> **Lustration** is literally the process of purifying through religious rituals. In postcommunist politics it refers to how former communists were dealt with, particularly those linked to the security apparatus. Many states passed lustration laws which released the names of such people or prevented them from working in the public sector.

The problems of coping with the past are equally acute in postcommunist states. Some postcommunist leaders wanted to draw a thick line under the past; in Russia, Yegor Yakolev (a former communist and adviser of Gorbachev, turned democrat) argued that 'democracy is not thirsty for revenge'. President Yeltsin agreed but for pragmatic reasons: he realised that former communists remained a powerful and knowledgable group, many of whom were needed to run the postcommunist system. In police states such as East Germany or Romania, it becomes impractical to try every informer; a population cannot convict itself. But other postcommunist leaders adopted a more vigorous approach to decommunization. Lithuania established a special commission which exposed several MPs as collaborators with the KGB. Czechoslovakia and Poland, among others, passed lustration laws which publicly exposed past collaborators in a way which amounted to judging people guilty without a trial. Revenge is always a messy, selective and arbitrary process.

Key reading

> **Next step:** *Finer (1988, first pub. 1962) is a classic and accessible study of the military in politics.*

Huntington (1957) remains the starting point for studying civilian control of the military; see also Nordlinger (1977). Decalo (1990) is a major study of coups. For studies of military rule, see Baynham (1986) and Pinkney (1990). On military withdrawal see Danopoulos (1988, 1992); Zagorski (1992) for Latin America and Sundhaussen (1985) for both the conditions of withdrawal and the persistence of military rule in South East Asia. Studies of the military in regime transitions include Aguero (1995), Barany (1993) and Luckham (1996). Zartman (1995) is an outstanding collection which includes the role of the military in collapsed states. For the military after communism, see Bebler (1997). Millett and Gold-Biss (1996) examine the position of the armed forces in Latin America after military rule. On the police, Brewer *et al.* (1996) is a good comparative study of the police and public order. Mawby (1990) places the Anglo-American model of policing in a broader perspective. Roach and Thomancek (1985) examine policing in Europe, while Cawthra (1993) examines the interesting case of South Africa. Waller (1994) discusses the 'secret empire' of the KGB in postcommunist Russia.

PART 4

POLICY AND METHOD

Politics matters. In one country, government actions may be the principal cause of human misery. In another, public policies may help to create the conditions under which people can fulfill their potential. In chapter 15, therefore, our focus shifts from the structures and processes of government to the policies that governments pursue. We explore the changing agendas confronting rulers and the concepts used in policy analysis. The final chapter serves both as a conclusion and as a foundation for more advanced work using the comparative method. Using examples from the preceding chapters, we discuss the strategies and techniques involved in undertaking comparative political research.

The policy process

Policies and politics are interwoven. We want to understand the institutions of government not merely for their own sake but because of the policies which emerge (or fail to emerge) from them. Consider, for instance, two areas of domestic policy which most concerned government in the twentieth century: building a welfare state and maintaining a competitive economy. Welfare policy illustrates the capacity of governments to improve the security of people's lives. In both Western democracies and the communist world, twentieth-century states introduced policies which offered ordinary people insurance against the scourges of illness, old age and unemployment. Public welfare on this scale was an intended result of public policy, requiring a massive commitment of resources: it was probably the major achievement of government in the twentieth century.

Competition policy tells a different story. It shows how governments can be forced, often against their instincts, to introduce policies which seem to work against people's immediate interests. By the 1990s, Western democracies were seeking to construct national economies which could prosper in an era of global competition. This meant that the welfare state, so expensively built to provide insurance against difficult times, began to be dismantled. The United States, never the most generous government in supplying welfare, reduced its provision. Several European countries did not and discovered instead a growing problem of unemployment. In postcommunist states the policy of freeing markets led to even greater insecurity in the short term, producing massive suffering. By the mid-1990s, most Russians were living below the official poverty level. Russian life expectancy fell below the level of India and policy-makers spoke ominously of the need 'to write off a generation' (Standing, 1996, p. 235).

The shift from the welfare state to the competition state was the big story in public policy in the final decades of the twentieth century. Yet to understand this enormous agenda shift we must search beyond the institutions of government (Cerny, 1990). After all, the transformation took place in the West within a stable framework of democratic political institutions. It was objectives that changed, not institutions. So in examining public policy we must raise such questions as: how do policy agendas evolve? Why do some governments respond more to changing agendas than others? Why does policy often fail to achieve its aims? And how do we tell whether a policy has succeeded or failed?

The policy focus: rational and incremental models

The task of policy analysis is to understand 'what governments do, why they do it and what difference it makes' (Dye, 1984). In addressing this agenda, modern policy analysis is informed by two models of decision-making – the rational or synoptic model associated with Simon (1983), and the incremental model associated with Lindblom (1979). The key difference between them is this: the rational model views policy as emerging from a systematic search for the most efficient means of achieving defined goals; while by contrast, the incremental model sees policy as resulting from a compromise between actors who have ill-defined, or even contradictory, goals (Box 15.1).

An example will clarify the contrast. Suppose we were in charge of education policy. If we adopted a rational approach we would first specify the outcomes sought, such as the number and level of student qualifications. Then we would consider the most efficient means of maximizing that goal; should we invest in new schools, more teachers or some combination of the two?

Definition

A **policy** is a more general notion than a decision. A policy covers a bundle of decisions, and it involves a predisposition to respond in a specific way. When a government says, 'our policy favours public transport', it is merely stating an intention to make specific decisions with this attitude in mind. In fact, the practical 'decisions' may never arrive at all; some policies are just window-dressing.

An incremental approach, however, begins with a different starting point. We would engage in regular consultation with all the organized interests: teacher unions, parents' associations, educational researchers. We would hope that from these discussions a consensus would slowly emerge on how best to spend extra resources. The long-term goals of this expenditure might not be measured or even specified, but we would assume that a policy acceptable to all is unlikely to be bad policy. Such an approach is policy-making by evolution, not revolution; hence the word 'incremental' (small steps).

Certainly, the incremental approach is less demanding than the rational model. According to the rational model, policy-makers must rank all their values, formulate clear options, calculate all the results of choosing each option and select the alternative which achieves most values. This is an unrealistic counsel of perfection. It requires policy-makers to foresee the unforeseeable and measure the unmeasurable. It can lead to enormous disasters. Even so, several techniques have been developed in an attempt to implement aspects of the rational model (Carley, 1980; Nigro, 1984). By considering one of these, cost-benefit analysis (CBA), we can obtain a flavour of how the rational approach works when attempts are made to apply it.

BOX 15.1

Rational and incremental models of policy-making

Rational model	Incremental model
Goals are set before means are considered	Goals and means are considered together
A 'good' policy is the most appropriate for the desired ends	A 'good' policy is one on which all main actors can agree
Analysis is comprehensive; all effects of all options are addressed	Analysis is selective; the object is good policy, not the best policy
Theory is heavily used	Comparison with similar problems is heavily used

Sources: Modified from Lindblom (1959, p. 81) and Parsons (1995, p. 285).

CBA involves giving a monetary value (positive or negative) to every consequence of choosing each option and then selecting the option with the highest net benefit. Take an example from Britain. In 1971 the Roskill Commission on the Third London Airport was assigned the task of working out the best site for this new project. To produce a defensible analysis it sought to quantify all the costs and benefits of locating the airport at each of four short-listed sites. Every foreseeable effect of selecting each site was quantified. For instance, the effect of airport noise on local residents was brought into the analysis by assessing its impact on house prices. The policy-makers' response to this elaborate analysis? They decided not to decide; perhaps wisely, they shelved the issue of the third London airport altogether for another 15 years.

CBA does have strengths. It brings submerged assumptions to the surface and can benefit those interests which would otherwise lack political clout. However it also has weaknesses. It underplays 'soft' factors such as fairness and the quality of life. It is also cumbersome and expensive – a CBA of CBA might yield negative results.

The incremental model was developed by Lindblom (1959) as part of a reaction against the rational model. Lindblom's starting point is that policy is continually remade in a series of minor adjustments, rather than as a result of a single, com-

EXHIBIT 15.1

Using cost benefit analysis to balance economic gain and environmental loss

The chemical industry is essential to a modern economy, but it is also environmentally sensitive. Deciding whether to permit or ban a particular chemical involves a difficult balance between economic and environmental considerations. Some environmentalists claim that all chemicals should be banned until they are shown to be free from negative effects ('the precautionary principle'). However, this would preclude using chemicals which do more good than harm: for instance, fire retardants which inhibit fires but give off dangerous fumes once alight.

Here is an example of part of a cost benefit analysis (CBA) by the British government of tributyl tin (TBT), a chemical used in wood preservatives and marine anti-fouling paints:

Costs of banning TBT

Costs to the wood industry of using another preservative	£800 000 (about $1.2m) per year.
Costs to the shipping industry (extra dry docking of ships and slower speed due to more drag from marine life on hulls).	£10m ($15m) per year plus one-off conversion cost of £9m ($13.5m).

Benefit of banning TBT

The main gain would be to end the damage caused to shellfish. Quantifying this benefit is virtually impossible (does a healthy shellfish have intrinsic value?) but commercial shellfish farms would make increased profits and these can be measured.

Assessment

CBA cannot make the political decision about whether the benefits to shellfish farmers (and to the environment!) outweigh the costs to the wood and shipping industries. Further, the focus of CBA is on *net* gains and losses, without concern to their distribution. But CBA can clarify the options for the decision-maker and contribute to transparent policy-making by forcing decision-makers to account for policies where costs exceed benefits. In other words CBA can help to keep policy makers honest. This is why in the USA, CBA is used on any regulatory proposal expected to have an impact on the economy exceeding $100m.

Further reading: Luesby (1996).

---

prehensive plan. Incrementalism represents what Lindblom calls the 'science of muddling through'. This approach may not lead to achieving grand objectives but it does at least avoid making huge mistakes. In incremental policy-making, what matters is not that those involved should agree on objectives but that agreement should be reached on the desirability of following a particular policy, even when objectives differ. Hence policy emerges from, rather than precedes, negotiation with interested groups. If the rational policy-maker resembles investors who seek the highest return on their money, incrementalists are more like savers whose first object is to avoid losing all their money, even at the cost of a lower return.

What assessment should we give of these two models? To address this question let us apply the

models to the development of the welfare state, which we have described as the major achievement of Western (especially European) states in the twentieth century. At first glance it would seem that the universal benefits which we associate with the welfare state – covering public pensions, unemployment benefit, medical care, education and income maintenance – are the outcome of a single rational plan. And indeed the politicians and bureaucrats who built this edifice over the first three-quarters of the twentieth century did sense that their work formed part of the development of a modern, progressive society (Esping-Andersen, 1996). So there was certainly a strategic, rational element to the welfare state 'project'.

But the detailed history of the welfare state shows that benefits were introduced incrementally and

Table 15.1 Introduction of social insurance, selected countries

	Industrial accident	Health	Pensions	Unemployment benefit	Family allowances
Australia	1902	1945	1909	1945	1941
Austria	1887	1888	1927	1920	1921*
Canada	1930	1971	1927	1940	1944
Denmark	1898	1892	1891	1907	1952
Finland	1895	1963	1937	1917	1948
France	1898	1898	1895	1905*	1932
Germany	1871*	1883*	1889*	1927	1954
Italy	1898	1886	1898	1919	1936
Netherlands	1901	1929	1913	1916	1940
New Zealand	1900	1938	1898	1938	1926
Norway	1894	1909	1936	1906	1946
Sweden	1901	1891	1913	1934	1947

* innovator.

Source: Pierson (1991, Table 4.1).

only gradually extended to a higher proportion of the population (Table 15.1). The first benefits were introduced before the First World War, but universal provision of all major services was not achieved in most European countries until the 1970s. Indeed several non-European democracies, notably Japan and the United States, never developed a European-style welfare state at all. So the development of the welfare state reflected both strategic and incremental elements. As with the extension of the suffrage, it was a classic example of a transformation in small steps.

As a general account of how policy is actually made, there is little doubt that Lindblom's incremental account is more accurate than the rational model. Incrementalism is more sensitive to the politics of policy-making, whereas the synoptic model is really an idealized account of individual rather than collective decision-making. However, incrementalism cannot be accepted as a model of how policy should be made in all areas. As Lindblom (1977) himself came to recognize, incremental policy-making works to the advantage of those interests which benefit most from the status quo, particularly large corporations.

Even more important, incremental decision-making deals with existing problems rather than with avoiding future ones. It is politically safe but unadventurous; public policy becomes remedial rather than innovative. But the threat of ecological disaster, for instance, has arisen precisely from human failure to consider the long-term, cumulative impact of industry upon the environment. So incrementalism is an inadequate reponse to complex global issues. The trick is to find ways of dealing with such problems which do not fall victim to the shortcoming of the rational model, namely demanding more of policy-makers than they can deliver (Lindblom, 1990).

From plans to markets?

As a more detailed case study of rational versus incremental approaches to public policy, we can compare the planned economies of the communist world with the market economies of the West. While history has judged the market superior, it is important to explore why the seemingly unplanned market approach did prove more successful than state planning. The answer tells us much about the nature and limits of public policy in modern conditions.

EXHIBIT 15.2

China's Great Leap Forward ... into starvation

As an illustration of how planning can go wrong, consider the disaster of China's Great Leap Forward launched by Mao Zedong in 1957.

Mao believed that if the masses were motivated to support a project, there was nothing they could not achieve. Where the capitalist world had developed by relying on capital equipment, expertise and professionalism, China would utilize ideological commitment, mass mobilization and organization. In the countryside the peasants were put into large communes. To aid industrial development the rural population was exhorted to produce its own steel. In 1958, as the Great Leap Forward got under way, everything appeared to be progressing well. In particular the grain harvests were far better than expected, apparently breaking record after record. Believing that the country was awash with grain, the central planners ordered peasants to grow more cash crops (such as cotton and tobacco) and transferred large amounts of grain to urban centres.

But the success was all a sham. Spurred on by the desire to prove their revolutionary commitment, party officials throughout the country had exaggerated their grain production figures. Furthermore, much of the iron ore produced in backyard steel furnaces was so poor as to be unusable.

The Great Lie came home to roost in 1959 and 1960. In the space of two years, half of all the cultivated land in China was affected by drought or floods. Food consumption had increased during 1958 when it appeared that there was more than enough to go around, so peasants had few or no stockpiles to fall back on. It also became evident that when property was being pooled in 1957 and 1958, many peasants had slaughtered and ate their livestock rather than allow it to be turned over to the communes.

The exact extent of the famine that followed is unknown. Coale's (1981) estimate of 16.5 million deaths between 1958 and 1961 is one of the lowest figures. At the other extreme, Mosher (1984) suggests that as many as 30 million may have died in 1960 alone. The total figure for the period 1958–63 was probably in the region of 40 million deaths – a phenomenal price to pay for a plan that went tragically wrong.

Further reading: Coale (1981), Mosher (1984).

Communist states were planned societies, seeking a new 'rational' way of organizing the economy which would overcome the anarchic weaknesses of capitalism. Within the communist grouping, the Soviet Union was the most planned economy the world has ever seen. Gosplan, the State Planning Committee, drew up annual and five-year plans which were given the status of law once they had received political approval. Implementation was the responsibility of ministries which controlled individual enterprises through a complex administrative network. Detailed planning was the essence of a command economy. A factory could not buy its components on the market because there was no market. Instead arrangements had to be made for another factory to manufacture the parts and deliver them on time – and that factory in turn had to be supplied with raw materials.

In theory, the Soviet economy was a massive exercise in rational planning. But there was an obvious flaw. For anything to go right everything had to go right – but inevitably something went wrong! Because the right components did not arrive at the right time, all sorts of informal and often illegal deals had to be cooked up to ensure that arbitrary production quotas were met. Further, the whole system was dominated by remote planners and indifferent producers, not customers. Gosplan, not the consumer, decided how many goods should be produced and at what price they should be sold. If the price was too low, demand was restricted by rationing; no mechanism existed for prices to go up so as to encourage new suppliers to enter the market. Shortages were so acute that people joined queues without even knowing what the line was for; they just assumed someone further up had been tipped off that new supplies were coming in. Shortages encouraged the development of a massive black market which further reduced supply to ordinary people who lacked connections.

There was no development of brands or sensitivity to market niches: consumers bought the model supplied or they went without. Production targets were based on quantity, not quality. As a result, goods were shoddy when they were produced at all; spare parts were often unavailable. Local managers could not use their initiative, even though they were often in the best position to see what needed to be done. In the end the planned economy just produced an indifferent shrug of the shoulders from a population resigned to the absurd results of the supposedly 'rational' plan.

So was the planned economy an unmitigated disaster? In many communist states it did succeed in building the foundations of industrial development, albeit at a sizable human price. Heavy industry was the great success of the planned economy. For instance, Stalin's big push on industrialization meant that between 1928 and 1938 industrial production in the Soviet Union rose from 7 to 45 per cent of American output. Massive changes such as these could never have resulted from incremental policy-making as practised in liberal democracies. However, the big push was focused, not rational, planning. Absolute priority was given to a single goal and blow the other consequences – such as damage to the environment. Objectives determined budgets rather than vice versa. The big push was a deliberately blinkered approach which was completely foreign to the careful accounting techniques of rational policy-making.

Once the heavy industrial base had been constructed, the planned economy began to reveal its flaws. It proved far less successful in generating light industrial and consumer goods and in delivering high-quality services. With their contours distorted by massive military spending, the planned economies had run their course by the early 1980s, at least in industrial societies. Most of the communist states that had built their economies on a planned system were already turning towards the market. In Eastern Europe, movements to introduce market mechanisms and break down central planning were underway long before the revolutions of 1989. In Hungary, for instance, the 'communist' state relinquished many of its direct controls over economic enterprises and allowed market forces to

set the prices of some products. The planned economy had been discredited, and to an extent dismantled, before communism's collapse as a system of political rule.

Galbraith (1990) argues that the socialist system did succeed in attaining its initial goals but failed to adapt to the new challenges and requirements placed upon it: 'capitalism in its original or pristine form could not have survived. But under pressure it did adapt. Socialism in its original form and for its first tasks did succeed. But it failed to adapt'. Where the closest comparisons can be made – as between East and West Germany, South and North Korea or Taiwan and the People's Republic – the market proved superior. What then is the source of the adaptability of market economies? Essentially it is that they operate in an incremental way. Decision-making is devolved to thousands of producers and millions of consumers, all of whom have a self-interest in using their resources wisely. No Gosplan attempts the impossible task of drawing up plans for all the goods and services found in an advanced economy. Because prices more accurately reflect supply and demand, the market interaction of consumers and producers yields more sensitive production plans than was possible in a command economy where such decisions were made by central planners using inaccurate, out-of-date information.

Yet today, even posing the question of economic organization in terms of 'plans or markets?' is too simple. The issue facing all modern governments is not whether to plump for a planned or a market economy – that 'choice' was central to the politics of the twentieth century but is too simple for a new era. Today, the policy question is whether governments can plan *for* markets, ensuring national prosperity in an era of global competition. This brings us to the idea of the 'competition state', a term which refers to the role of governments in ensuring the success of the national economy in a global market (Cerny, 1990). The function of the competition state is essential but narrow: to create the conditions for economic success while also leaving detailed business decisions to private firms. In essence, the competition state reconciles state planning and market incrementalism: not either/or but each in its place. The East Asian tigers, such as Malaysia, offered one form of a competition state suitable for developing countries but even devel-

Country profile NEW ZEALAND

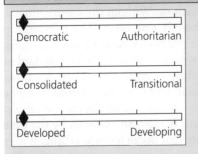

Democratic — Authoritarian

Consolidated — Transitional

Developed — Developing

Population: 3.7m.

Gross domestic product per head: $18300.

Form of government: a unitary parliamentary democracy in which the British monarch serves as sovereign, with formal powers delegated to the Governor General. Like Britain, New Zealand has no codified constitution.

Legislature: the unicameral assembly contains 120 members elected for a short maximum tenure of three years. Parliament is the key institution of democratic accountability.

Executive: the cabinet of about 20 ministers forms the apex of decision-making. The prime minister is 'first among equals' but is losing some autonomy now that coalition governments are becoming inevitable following electoral reform.

Judiciary: based on English law and headed by a Court of Appeal. Parliamentary sovereignty has limited judicial assertiveness but this increased slightly with the passage of the Bill of Rights Act 1990.

Electoral system: additional member system, termed mixed member proportional (MMP) in New Zealand. In the 1996 election, the first fought under this new system, no party won a majority. Some seats (five in 1996) are allocated to Maori voters.

Party system: the two strongest parties are National and Labour, and the party caucus (meeting of MPs) is a dominant force within these parties. Three newer parties, New Zealand First, the Association of Consumers and Taxpayers (ACT) and the Alliance (itself a coalition) have gained ground. New Zealand First formed a governing coalition with National after the 1996 election.

At several points in this book, New Zealand has served as a remarkable example of political and economic reforms occurring in the context of a consolidated democracy in the late twentieth century. These changes included electoral reform, the reorganization of the bureaucracy, privatization and policies to expose a protected economy to greater international competition. Together, these reforms give New Zealand far greater significance for students of politics than its small population would imply. What, then, explains this outbreak of new zeal in New Zealand? Why has the country reinvented itself?

Part of the answer is that New Zealand was an outlier in the first place. Politically, New Zealand was a pure example of a two-party system operating in a disciplined, adversarial fashion. Governments could do as they wished, with few constraints on their power, and they chose to do a large amount. The economy was highly protected and included a substantial public sector. The state supplied a comprehensive system of welfare. Special interests (such as farmers) exerted considerable influence. For liberal advocates of free markets and a smaller state, New Zealand was an ideal patient awaiting treatment.

And the treatment was what it got, imposed by a small, technocratic, cross-party élite. The advocates of reform included not just business associations such as the Business Roundtable, but also politicians and civil servants in the Treasury and Reserve Bank (central bank). Fuelled by faith in their own prescriptions, the reformers skilfully exploited the considerable powers of the political system to implement a package of radical reforms.

Yet many voters never accepted the new liberal agenda. For them, the new New Zealand is a less comfortable and predictable place. Further, the manner of change – in effect, an élite conspiracy – hardly helped in selling the reforms to a sceptical population accustomed to a benign state. The result of public disillusionment was majority support for electoral reform in referendums held in 1992 and 1993. And, as the 1996 election showed, the new additional member system is likely to deliver coalition governments which will probably be unable to summon the political will for radical innovations in the future. Thus the long-term and unforeseen effect of the reform package may prove to be indecisive governance. Certainly, in the twenty-first century New Zealand's traditionally strong and competitive parties will have to adjust to the need for compromise with their new partners in power.

Further reading: Mulgan (1997).
www.govt.nz/govt_info
www.govt.nz/nzgo_admin

oped states – including the resolutely free market United States – must assess the wider social conditions of economic progress.

Stages of the policy process

We can distinguish between the five stages of the policy process shown in Figure 15.1. These divisions are analytical, not chronological, meaning that in real policy-making they are often considered together:

- *Initiation* – the decision to make a decision in a particular area; also called agenda-setting.
- *Formulation* – the detailed development of a policy into concrete proposals.
- *Implementation* – putting the policy into practice.
- *Evaluation* – appraising the effects and success of the policy.
- *Decision* – continuation, revision or termination?

Initiation

Why did governments expand welfare policy for the first three decades after 1945 and then reduce it thereafter? Why did many Western governments take companies into public ownership after the war and then start selling them back to the private sector in the 1980s? These are questions about policy initiation – about the decision to make (or, just as important, not to make) policy in a particular area. Initiation emerges from the political agenda. In any complex society the agenda cannot be controlled by a single group; it is the product of debate between a variety of competing though often unequal forces. Except for regimes which set out to transform society, policy agendas are fluid and fast-flowing because they are made by events rather than by politicians or planners. Hence 'policy initiation' is too rational a word for the mysterious process by which issues first float to the top of the agenda and then sink back into the murky bog of non-issues.

We can identify three general influences on policy initiation – science, technology and the media:

Science, first, is clearly one driver of public policy.

The current concern with global warming, for instance, rests primarily on scientific assessments of its future implications. Without the science, no one would know there is a problem. The relationship between science and policy raises thorny questions, though. One problem is knowing what standard of evidence is needed to justify new policy. Scientists work to a high standard of proof but prudence may justify new policy before the results are conclusive. The environment is again an example: by the time we know for sure that ocean levels are rising, it may be impossible to make them go down again. But committing resources to solve problems which may not even exist, and where the science is still unclear, is politically demanding. President Clinton discovered this problem in his attempts to make the United States more environmentally-conscious. Corporate interests, in particular, were quick to exploit the uncertainties in his case. The danger is that policy initiation is deferred and risk is left to accumulate. The long-run result, suggests Beck (1995), will be catastrophe. An additional complexity arises from the origins of scientific knowledge itself. Governments commission as well as consume science, and ministers' power over the production of knowledge helps them to keep uncomfortable issues off the policy agenda. The British

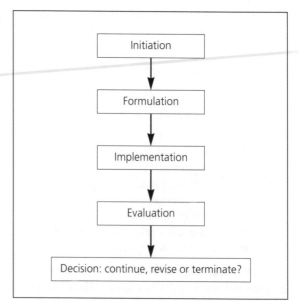

Figure 15.1 Stages of the policy process

government, for instance, was unduly slow in commissioning research into mad cow disease which swept through the country's herds (and into the brains of at least a few of its people) in the 1990s. Proactive policies can just heighten awareness of problems.

Applications of science – that is, *technology* – also influence policy initiation. Governments have an incentive to encourage new technology; it encourages economic competitiveness and prompt introduction allows a country to steal a march on its competitors. But many new technologies involve regulation. Designs for nuclear power stations must be assessed for safety; frequencies for mobile telephones must be allocated; new drugs must be examined for side-effects; and the effects of allowing genetically-altered plants, fish and animals into the environment must be considered. In all these cases technological innovation forces policy initiation from government. Again, the danger is that governments will approve those 'advances' which offer clear short-term gain at the cost of intangible, long-term risk. Nuclear energy is arguably an example.

Third, the ability of the *media* to highlight issues means they are also a significant influence on policy initiation. A single and perhaps unusual incident is often taken up by one outlet and then, through pack journalism, amplified by other media until politicians are forced to respond to what has suddenly become a serious social problem. Common topics of such media-induced moral panics are food scares, teenage hooligans, gang wars, welfare scroungers, mad dogs, infectious diseases, drug crazes and crime waves (Henshel, 1990). These balloons of concern often burst as quickly as they are inflated; in only a few cases are the media turning their searchlight on a problem where public policy does indeed need to be initiated.

Formulation

Once a decision has been taken to address a specific problem, policy must be formulated, and translating a feeling that something should be done into precise legislation or administrative proposals is a core political craft. Like bringing a ship into harbour, many decisions must be made correctly and in sequence if the goal to be achieved. The three tasks here are when, what and how:

- Knowing *when* to proceed – the question of identifying the ripe moment
- Knowing *what* to propose – the question of understanding the problem so that the proposals will work
- Knowing *how* to proceed – the question of building a political consensus around the proposals.

A crucial and often-ignored influence on policy formulation is the policy discourse, which refers to the climate of ideas within which a problem is addressed. Analysing policy discourse helps in exploring hidden presuppositions in the approach to policy. In France, for example, the Channel Tunnel was presented as a state-inspired achievement which symbolized modernity and the march to European unity. In Britain, the privately-financed tunnel was seen as a financial as well as a physical black-hole (Howarth, 1995). The way issues are framed also evolves over time, reflecting broad changes in political thinking. For instance, a debate about 'extending welfare rights' in the 1960s had become a discussion of how to 'reduce the dependency culture' by the 1990s.

Equally, had the HIV virus emerged in the nineteenth century, it would have been viewed not as a problem to be solved but as a scourge to be accepted – or even as a punishment to be endured. As Kingdon (1984, p. 119) notes, 'for a condition to become a problem, people must become convinced that something should be done to change it'. Thus a crucial aspect of the policy discourse is whether it links government to the policy issue in question. Just to complicate matters, public responsibility for problems is itself the subject of continued party debate. For conservatives, the responsibility for urban riots rests with the participants themselves; for liberals, the cause lies in a poor social environment. Thus the policy discourse is the ideological battleground of politics, where the prize is influence over how issues are addressed and, as a result, what policies are formulated.

> **Definition**
> **Policy discourse** refers to the way issues are framed, defined and discussed. Controlling the discourse (*how* issues are addressed) is the next best source of influence to controlling the agenda itself (*what* issues are discussed).

Professional experts come into their own in policy formulation. Just as science and technology help to drive the policy agenda, so too do policy specialists help to firm up policy options. The professional or academic expert does not have all the answers but can at least provide a detached view of the options. But in matters of public policy even the experts rarely agree completely (and even when they do they are often later shown to be wrong!). Policy-makers know full well that experts are often over-committed to their own theories and are not always as neutral as they appear. Indeed the hired guns known as advocacy analysts are paid by interest groups precisely to come up with selective facts, statistics and arguments to support their client's case. Money can easily buy a plausible case.

The policy-forming environment echoes with opinions and politicians must seek to uncover the signal of good sense which enables them to identify a way forward. The danger is that bad policy analysis drives out good, as decision-makers take shelter under their own prejudices from a shower of conflicting specialist opinions. The babble of opinions is certainly one reason why politicians proceed incrementally, preferring to get everyone on board rather than risk their own independent judgments. But in the end, as Parsons (1995, p. 393) comments,

> academic scribblers – and others in the advice game – cannot resolve arguments so much as provide arguments and evidence which can be deployed to persuade.

Implementation

Probably the main achievement of policy analysis has been to direct attention to problems of implementation. Traditional political science stopped at the point where a government took a decision. Putting the policy into practice was once regarded as a technical matter of administration but that was much too simple. The British government's failure to prevent mad cow disease from crossing the species barrier to humans in the late 1980s is a classic instance of implementation failure. Official committees instructed abattoirs to remove infective material (such as the spinal cord) from slaughtered cows but initially took no special steps to ensure these regulations were carried out carefully. As a result of incompetence in slaughter-houses, the disease agent continued to enter the food chain.

Three conditions must be met if a policy is to be carried out successfully:

- There must be enough time and resources for the policy to be delivered. Often a policy-maker will mandate the goals but not the resources to achieve them, hoping the problem will go away once a policy has been introduced. The political imperative is to introduce a scheme, rather than for the scheme to achieve results. For example, in 1972 Congress approved $100 million for a nutrition programme for elderly people. The implementing department worked out that this seemingly large sum was only enough to cover 5 per cent of the intended beneficiaries. At the time, the cost of all the department's programmes reaching every eligible person would have been $250 billion, more than the total federal budget.
- There should be few 'stations' where the policy has to sit awaiting clearance from a variety of different groups before it can be put into effect. In the United States, again, a range of agencies at federal, state and local level are involved in any substantial innovation, delaying and complicating the process of implementation.
- Those in authority must be able to achieve compliance from their subordinates who may already be fully committed to their own pet projects (Hogwood and Gunn 1984, Ch. 11).

Yet even when all these criteria are fulfilled, the policy may still fail because of changes in circumstances (bad luck) or because the policy is not based on valid assumptions about how to achieve its goals (bad policy). The above conditions are based on a rational or 'top-down' view of implementation. The problem is conceived as one of facilitating democ-

EXHIBIT 15.3

Policy fiascos: the Heysel Stadium tragedy of 1986

On 29 May 1986, 39 football supporters died and more than 400 were injured after fighting among supporters triggered a crowd surge at the Heysel stadium in Brussels, Belgium, before the European Cup soccer final between Liverpool and Juventus. By any standard, this was a policy fiasco, a concept defined by Bovens and Hart (1996, p. 15) as

> a negative event that is perceived by a socially and politically significant group of people in the community to be at least partially caused by avoidable and blameworthy failures of public policymakers.

In investigating fiascos, the top-down approach would begin with the presumption of implementation failure. The starting-point would be that someone, or more likely some people, failed to do their job. The bottom-up approach adopts a different perspective. It seeks to identify the proximate causes of the fiasco and then to trace these back to the strategic, higher-level errors which created the possibility for lower-level mistakes to develop into disaster.

Adopting the bottom-up approach, Bovens and Hart note the significant failure of a platoon commander of the Belgian *Gendarmerie* to call quickly and on his own authority for reinforcements to come to the section of the stadium where the tragedy was unfolding. Rather than taking decisive action himself, the commander obeyed strict military hierarchy and spent several minutes attempting to contact his superior, who was outside the ground investigating a robbery. Communication equipment proved faulty; reinforcements arrived too late.

The next question is strategic: why was a rigid military force assigned to the sensitive task of policing English soccer hooligans, particularly in an old stadium where, through errors of ticket allocation, Italians were placed next to the English section? The answer reveals an organizational conflict between the *Gendarmerie* and the Brussels municipal police, a dispute only resolved by the astonishing political compromise of allocating half the stadium to each force. On the night, only three out of nine increasingly urgent warning messages from the Brussels police reached the *Gendarmerie*; none was acted on immediately.

So the policy fiasco of Heysel reveals strategic errors which go far beyond the actions of a single platoon commander or the failure of one piece of equipment. Yet it is precisely the strategic, higher-level problems which are least likely to be addressed. Over ten years after Heysel, poor coordination between Belgium's police forces remains commonplace.

Further reading: Bovens and Hart (1996).

racy by giving politicians the means of to control unruly subordinates. But what if circumstances have changed since the policy was formulated? And what if the policy is just poorly designed? Writers in the 'bottom-up' tradition (for example Barrett and Fudge, 1981) argue that policy is more likely to succeed if its executors have flexibility over application and therefore content. At street level (the point where the policy is put into effect), policy emerges from interaction between local bureaucrats and affected groups. Here, at the sharp end, the goals of policy can often be best achieved by adapting it to local conditions. For example, education, health care and policing must surely differ between the rural countryside and multicultural areas in the inner city.

This bottom-up approach reflects a more incremental view of policy-making in which implementation is seen as policy-making by other means; it is more in tune with the contemporary emphasis on governance.

Some Western democracies have been experimenting with new modes of implementing policy, particularly contracting out tasks to the voluntary and profit-making sectors. Whether or not these deliver value for money, the key political outcome is clear enough. Changes in delivery systems produce a new, complex network of organizations resistant to direct political control. Indeed these self-governing networks may be a model for governance in the twenty-first century. The key point about them is that they can be directed only, if at all, by persuasion (Rhodes R., 1996). In this respect most Western countries are becoming more like the federal USA, where Washington bureaucrats have long struggled to influence how policy is applied in the states and cities of a large country. So implementation is everywhere becoming more about persuasion and less about orders: hierarchies are giving way to networks.

Evaluation

The job of policy evaluation is to work out whether a policy has achieved its goals. Like the famous recipe for political stew which begins 'first catch your rabbit', this neatly sidesteps initial difficulties. As we have seen, the motives behind a policy are often multiple, unclear and sometimes contradictory. This 'mushiness of goals', to use Fesler and Kettl's phrase (1996, p. 287), means that policymakers' intent is often a poor benchmark for evaluation. Working out the objectives of policy is no easy task.

Until the 1990s wave of public sector reform, few governments had made much headway in building evaluation studies into the policy process. Sweden is a typical example. In the postwar decades a succession of Social Democratic governments concentrated on building a universal welfare state without even conceiving of a need to evaluate the effectiveness with which services were delivered by an expanding bureaucracy. Yet without some evaluation of policy, governments will fail to learn the lessons of experience. Even an unsuccessful policy offers hints on how *not* to proceed in the future.

In the United States, Jimmy Carter (President, 1977–81) did insist that at least 1 per cent of the funds allocated to any project should be devoted to evaluation. The vast number of reports required meant a bonanza for photocopier makers but did not noticeably improve the effectiveness of public policy. However, evaluation has now returned to the fore. To take the USA again, the Government Performance and Results Act (1993) requires each agency to perform an annual programme evaluation which is then intended to be used by the government to revise plans and budgets. Throughout the Western world, public officials are beginning to

think, often for the first time, of the outcomes their policies are supposed to achieve.

Policy evaluation requires outcomes (what government achieves, including unintended consequences) to be distinguished from outputs (what government does). The link between the two is often tenuous. In 1966, for example, the US government published the results of the Coleman report, a massive sociological study of American secondary schools. This study found that outputs such as teachers' salaries and educational expenditure had little effect on the ultimate outcome of education: children's learning. The main influence on outcomes (that is, childrens' educational success) was the family background of the child and its peers. Children from a lower-class background were likely to underperform even if they were placed in a well-resourced school.

> **Definition**
>
> **Policy outputs** are what government does; **policy outcomes** are what government achieves. Outcomes are the activity; outcomes are the effects, both intended and unforeseen. Outputs are measured easily enough: for instance, so many new prisons built or a specified increase in the state pension. Outcomes are harder to ascertain: for instance, a reduction in recidivism or in the number of elderly people living in poverty.

Just as policy-making in accordance with the rational model is an unrealistic goal, so judging policy effectiveness against precise objectives is an implausibly scientific approach to evaluation. A more bottom-up, naturalistic view is that evaluation should simply gather the opinions of all the stakeholders affected by the policy. As Parsons (1995, p.567) describes this approach,

> evaluation has to be predicated on wide and full collaboration of all programme stakeholders: agents (funders, implementers); beneficiaries (target groups, potential adopters); and those who are excluded ('victims').

In a naturalistic evaluation, the varying objectives of different interests are welcomed rather than dismissed as a barrier to objective scrutiny of policy. This is a more incremental approach because the

EXHIBIT 15.4

Policy delivery: rediscovering the voluntary sector

What delivery systems should be used to translate policy into practice? Traditionally, the answer was simple: the government made the decision and the bureaucrats put it into practice. The welfare state, for instance, required an army of public servants to administer programmes with complex eligibility rules. The inevitable result was to marginalize the private, voluntary and charitable third sector which had traditionally provided services to the needy (called 'the third sector' because it is neither public nor profit-making). Today, however, the ethos is that the state should set policy but not deliver services:

Public sector
(the state)

Private for-profit
sector
(firms)

Private not-for-profit
sector (voluntary
organizations)

Figure 15.2 Policy delivery sectors

'rather than hiring more public employees, governments make sure other institutions are delivering the services and meeting the community's needs' (Osborne and Gaebler, 1992, p. 32).

But what exactly are these 'other institutions'? The answer is a mixture of for-profit and not-for-profit organizations. In welfare policy, for example, the profit-making sector playes a growing role, with firms in some American states contracted to prepare welfare recipients for employment – and paid by their results. In education, too, for-profit companies provide specialist services to schools and sometimes even take over the management of failing schools completely. But many governments rely more on the voluntary, not-for-profit sector to deliver state-funded services to clients. For example, the needs of a disabled person may be assessed by a public agency which then contracts with a charity to deliver these services. In theory, such private providers are cheaper and more flexible than a public bureaucracy. In catholic countries the Church has always played a strong role in welfare provision. However, in protestant countries where the state became a major provider of welfare – Scandinavia especially but also the UK – we can expect the voluntary sector to reemerge more strongly, working alongside but maintaining its organizational independence from the state. Thus policy delivery increasingly depends on negotiation between the three points on the triangle shown in Figure 15.2.

Further reading: p. 181, 228–31

---

stakeholders might agree on the success of a policy even though they judge it against different standards. We see here, then, how the rational and incremental models of policymaking also offer contrasting approaches to evaluation; and we conclude that the more incremental, naturalistic approach can offer superior results.

Continuation, revision, termination

Once a policy has been evaluated, or even if it has not, the three possibilities are: to continue, to revise or to terminate. Most policies, along with the agencies set up to carry them out, continue with only minor revisions. Organizations rarely fold up when their job is done. In 1996, 27 years after Neil Armstrong stepped onto the moon, the space agency NASA seized on dubious reports that life may once have existed on Mars as a source of new goals to justify its continued existence. There is, it has been said, nothing so permanent as a temporary government organization. The intriguing question is: why is policy termination so rare? Bardach (1976) suggests five reasons:

- Policies are designed to last a long time
- Termination brings conflicts which leave too much blood on the floor
- No-one wants to admit the policy was a bad idea
- Termination may affect other programmes
- Politics rewards innovation rather than tidy house-keeping.

The conclusion here is that introducing new policies is simplicity itself compared to ending old ones.

The welfare state is probably the most important example of the modern state seeking to revise, though not to terminate, its provision. The crisis of the welfare state reflected extra costs caused by ageing populations (especially in Japan) and growing unemployment (especially in Europe). Even Helmut Kohl, Chancellor of Germany, finally admitted in 1997 that 'we have arrived at the limit of what is possible' with the welfare state. In the 1980s and 1990s, benefits were reduced; eligibility rules were tightened, especially by raising the pension age; charges were introduced for services such as medical treatment; few new commitments were taken on; and the state made an effort to revive the voluntary sector, such as charities and the church. While some of these reforms could be presented as cutting back on 'welfare scroungers', others were difficult to sell to populations which had grown accustomed to the cushion of social solidarity provided by the welfare state. In 1995, the French government's plans to reduce social benefits led to the country's worst riots for at least 20 years. This is an example of how governments experience more difficulty in paring existing programmes than in creating new ones.

Global agendas, national styles

The study of public policy has traditionally focused on single countries or comparisons between them. But we must now inject a global dimension into policy analysis. Problems spillover from one country to another, and the agenda of policy knows no boundaries – ideas flow freely across borders. Yet, by and large, it is still national governments which formulate a response even to shared problems. And

national institutions, traditions and histories still shape the way countries respond to such problems. Public policy is neither global nor national; rather, it is a product of the interaction between the two.

Economic policy is one of the more 'globalized' sectors. Because the global market pits country against country, governments have a clear incentive to copy innovations which improve economic performance. Britain's pioneering policy of privatization is now being emulated by many other states with a traditionally large public sector. Indeed the shift to the competition state has led to some convergence in industrial policy in the Western world. On the one hand, those countries where the state traditionally directed national economic strategy (for example France and Japan) have tended to leave more decision-making to the private sector. On the other hand, those countries where the state adopted a hands-off attitude to the private sector (for example Britain and the USA) have begun to address problems of national economic competitiveness, for example by seeking to improve education standards. Even right-wing parties have been forced to acknowledge the role of governments in creating the competition state. Similarly, parties on the left have come under pressure to abandon traditional nostrums and adopt more market-friendly policies.

Countries developing at a similar rate tend to experience the same problems at a similar time. Many developed countries, for example, are coping with the ageing of the population which flows from affluence and public health successes. Some solutions, such as encouraging people to save for their own pension, are likely to be considered, though not necessarily adopted, by countries sharing the same problem. The mass media and international conferences between experts encourage the diffusion of policy across national boundaries. However politicians tend to be keener on lesson-drawing when existing policy is clearly failing; otherwise, complacency wins and existing national approaches tend to continue.

As Rose (1993) notes, searching for lessons across countries was a practice known to America's Founding Fathers. They studied the British constitution to avoid the faults of governance which led to their revolt against the Crown. The American presidency, for instance, was an attempt to produce an executive which, unlike Britian's monarchy, would

EXHIBIT 15.5

Comparing attitudes to the welfare state

The response of national decision-makers to the crisis of the welfare state illustrates the power of national tradition in shaping policy even in a global era. When a group of policy-makers from Britain, Germany and the US met in 1996 to discuss the future of welfare, the American delegates gasped at the generosity of German income support (about $1500 a month for a typical family). One member of Congress described Germany's scheme as 'a scrounger's charter' and noted a connection with Europe's high unemployment, about twice the rate of America's. But underlying the German support for social insurance is a belief that it protects against disorder. Welfare policy is about more than handouts for the poor; it is a tangible expression of committment to solidarity and political stability. As a German minister said, 'People in Germany know from experience that social security is stabilizing – without the social state and the legal state there is no social peace'. Slowly but surely, global economic competition is putting that assumption to the test.

Yet it was the turn of the Germans to be amazed when the Americans ran through their own ideas for workfare. 'This is going back to the Middle Ages – beggary on the one hand and private charity on the other', said a German MP. The American welfare discourse is far removed from Germany's. In the USA, the failure to achieve self-reliance is considered a sign of individual culpability rather than social failure. As for the Britons, they favoured an intermediate position, neither as lavish as Germany nor as ruthless as the United States. 'I don't like the American model but …', said the Conservative Minister for Employment. Governments differ, then, in their response to the problems confronting the welfare state but global pressures have forced the issue onto each country's agenda.

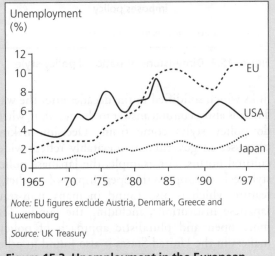

Note: EU figures exclude Austria, Denmark, Greece and Luxembourg

Source: UK Treasury

Figure 15.3 Unemployment in the European Union, USA and Japan, 1965–97

Further reading: Adonis (1996), Taylor-Gooby (1996).

be accountable to the people's representatives. Today American federalism remains a laboratory of experiment as programmes in one city or state are examined elsewhere in the country. But precisely because of its leading position in the world, the United States to some extent lost the art of drawing lessons from other countries. As Heald (1988, p. 13) wrote,

In the US until recently, our nearly self-contained continental market and culture were the international success story. This very success makes our new task – the adaptation of state and local, public and private institutions – more challenging and difficult than for countries with a longer history of operating in an international context.

Dominant states are often the last to adapt to global change; this indeed is one cause of their downfall.

Yet it is still national policy-makers who must implement national solutions, operating in their own specific political system. For instance, one solution to America's escalating spending on medical care would be to introduce a British-style National Health Service (NHS) where total public spending on health care is capped each year by the government. Yet that is as inconceivable as Britain switching to an American-style private health insurance scheme. The agenda may be international but policies must still work in national settings, both building on the administrative capital invested in existing programmes and accepting the constraints of policy discourse in a particular country.

The term 'policy styles' directs attention to some of these contrasts between nations. This idea refers not to what policies governments make but to how they make them. For example, Britain has a predilection for consultation, especially with entrenched interests. Sweden also consults widely but as part of a more rational search for solutions to problems. The French policy style reflects secrecy and limited consultation, with a (diminishing?) penchant for grand designs.

> ### Definition
> A **policy style** is a preferred way of making policy ('a procedural ambition'). It presumes that countries can be characterized according to their own national way of reaching decisions. Dimensions of policy style include: how much consultation is there? How open is the policy process? Is policy made in the context of an overall strategy or is it *ad hoc* and reactive?

Richardson (1984) suggests the two main dimensions of policy style are first, whether the government has an anticipatory attitude towards policy-making (Sweden) or adopts a reactive, fire-brigade role (UK); and second, whether the government seeks a consensus with organized groups (USA) or is willing to impose decisions. These dimensions yield the possibilities shown in Figure 15.4. Most liberal democracies are concentrated on the right-hand side of the diagram, reacting to rather than anticipating problems. Compared to authoritarian governments, democracies also tend to congregate in the upper half, seeking to construct a consensus rather than impose policy.

Where does a country's policy style come from? The answer is partly from its experience with crises; emergencies call forth new procedures which then become part of a country's habitual response to problems. For example, the depression of the 1930s forced most Western governments to adopt a stronger role in the management of the economy. Equally, the second world war called forth national planning on a grand scale – it created close consultation between governments and producer groups,

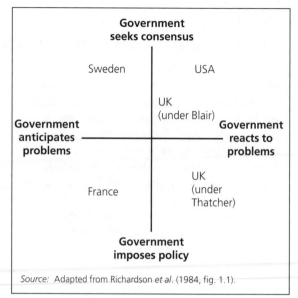

Source: Adapted from Richardson *et al.* (1984, fig. 1.1).

Figure 15.4 Dimensions of national policy style

links which solidified in the decades after the war. There is also a cultural answer to the question, where do policy styles come from? Decision-making processes in government inevitably reflect wider cultural norms. For example, the Japanese policy style seeks to suppress the open display of conflict, a feature which is also found in many non-state Japanese institutions, including the family. The more open and pluralistic approach of policy-makers in the United States is also found in other aspects of American life. By contrast, the chronic secrecy of British government reflects (and is reflected in) other institutions, not least the country's universities.

Key reading

> **Next step:** *Parsons (1995) is a comprehensive introduction to policy analysis.*

Dunn (1994) or Anderson (1984) are alternatives to Parsons. Hogwood and Gunn (1984) or Bobrow and Dryzek (1987) remain excellent discussions of the concepts used in the field. For studies of public policy in America specifically, see Peters (1993) and Rushefsky (1990). Kingdon (1984) is an innovative account of agenda-setting. Comparative studies based on examination of particular sectors include Heidenheimer, Heclo and Adams (1990) and Harrop (1992). Rose (1993) is a comparative study of lesson-drawing in public policy; Bovens and Hart (1996) is a thoughtful discussion of policy fiascos. On policy styles, Richardson (1984) is the main source, though restricted to Western Europe. The starting-point on implementation is the classic American study by Pressman and Wildavsky (1973). Barrett and Fudge (1981) is an influential British work. Mazmanian and Sabatier (1989) offer an overall perspective on implementation.

The comparative method

A family of methods

In this concluding chapter, we seek to articulate the nature of the enterprise called 'comparative politics' and we outline the main research strategies employed in the field. Our purpose is not to repeat the advantages of studying politics comparatively (p. 12). Rather, our goal is to draw on the bank of comparisons established earlier in the book in order to outline the main techniques which constitute the craft of comparative political research.

'But what exactly do you do when you study comparative politics?' ask our colleagues from other disciplines, disconcertingly. This question hardly arises with those who specialize in the politics of a single country. Everyone knows (or thinks they know) what is involved in studying American, Australian or Dutch politics. Further, it is often assumed that no special expertise in research design is needed to investigate politics within a single, or at least one's home, country. In the comparative arena, however, the answers to our colleagues' question are less clear-cut. The content and boundaries of comparative politics are poorly defined, partly because the 'field' is an ambiguous compound of method and subject area. As Evans (1995, p. 2) says, comparative politics has 'a messy center'.

Broadly (and breadth is really the point), the goal of comparative politics is to encompass the major political similarities and differences between countries. The task is to develop some perspective on the mixture of constants and variability which characterizes the world's governments and the contexts in which they operate. Sometimes an awareness of diversity provides the starting point for a comparative enquiry. As Mackenzie wrote, 'political science has its beginning when an observer notes that another people is not governed as we are. Why?' (quoted in Rose, 1991). For instance, the concepts which underpin this book – democratic/authoritarian, consolidated/transitional, developed/developing – all draw attention to dimensions on which countries vary. In other cases, comparative understanding emerges from considering a thesis about similarities. A brave scholar advances a 'universal' proposition: say, that government is giving way to governance, or that legislatures are concentrating more on committee work. But whether the initial focus is on differences or similarities, the task of comparative politics is to comprehend the complexity of the political world.

In this chapter, we conceive of the comparative method very simply, as the family of techniques employed in comparative political research. Grander definitions are of course available. With some justification, the comparative method can be regarded as the 'master strategy' for drawing inferences about causes in any field of study. After all, experiments and statistical analysis designed to uncover relationships of cause and effect necessarily involve a comparison between observations. All explanatory research is, by nature, comparative (Holland, 1986). But the reverse does not apply, at least not in politics. It would be misleading to assume that all comparative political research either

---

BOX 16.1
The family of methods in comparative politics

	Number of cases	Case- or variable-centred?	Strategy
Case studies	One	Case	Intensive study of a single instance
Focused comparisons	A few	Case	Intensive comparison of a few instances
Truth tables	Intermediate	Primarily variable	Qualitative assessment of the impact of variables
Statistical analysis	Large or all	Variable	Quantitative assessment of the impact of variables

---

does or should focus on explanation. As students of comparative politics, our goals are often more modest if still challenging: to encompass and to comprehend but not necessarily to explain. The task of getting to grips with crossnational similarities and differences is demanding enough without imprisoning ourselves in a straitjacket called 'explanation'.

Box 16.1 lists the four main members of the family of methods used in comparative politics: case studies, focused comparisons, truth tables and statistical approaches. In this chapter, we examine these techniques one by one. However, underlying all these methods is a contrast between case-oriented and variable-oriented research. In case work, the object is to provide a detailed account of an episode or theme falling into a wider category: say, a study of a specific military coup or an examination of a particular revolution. The focus is on how the factors at work in the example interact to form a particular configuration or conjuncture. By contrast, variable-oriented research examines the relationship between political forces applying across cases: say, the impact of inequality on political instability. As Ragin (1994a, p. 302) notes, statistical work treats cases as little more than 'sites for the measurement of variables'. Histories and conjunctures give way to a statistical approach in which the object is to explain maximum variation in the variable of interest. Much methodology is premised on variable-oriented research but case analysis is just as useful for comprehending general political developments. We need to take King, Keohane and Verba's dictum (1994, p. 44) seriously: 'good description is better than bad explanation'.

> **Definition**
> **Case-oriented** research aims to provide a detailed description of a specific topic. While still searching for significance beyond the case, the focus is on how variables interact and evolve in a particular setting. By contrast, **variable-oriented** research aims to establish a relationship between factors which are measured across a series of cases, for example the impact of electoral systems on party systems.

General pitfalls

Whichever techniques we use, several problems arise in putting the comparative approach to work. But Sartori (1970) has warned against the dangers of over-conscious thinking which leads only to the conclusion that all comparisons have overwhelming difficulties. So we will describe these problems in order to be aware of the difficulties, not to present a case against the comparative method.

Conceptual stretching

Countries must be compared against a common concept but the meaning of that concept may itself vary between the countries under study. Conceptual traveling is the application of concepts to new cases; conceptual stretching is the distortion of understanding that can result (Collier and Mahon, 1993). This 'traveling problem' can arise at the deep level of the conceptual framework within which politics is understood in a particular setting. For example, terms such as bureaucracy, the state, social solidarity, left and right are more meaningful, and are viewed more positively, in most of continental Europe than in the United States. To understand how the political discourse varies across countries is not merely a preliminary to a comparative project; it is itself an underused form of comparative research (Howarth, 1995). More specifically, the stretching problem can be seen in the difficulties of translation. A questionnaire which is translated from Spanish to English, and then independently translated back into Spanish, will end up differing from the way it started out. Similarly, in analyzing political behaviour across countries, it is important to remember that the meaning of an action depends on the conventions of the country concerned. When members of Australia's House of Representatives vote against their party, their act is far more significant than when an American legislator departs from the party line in the less disciplined Congress. To treat the acts as equivalent would be a mistake.

To take a final illustration, Western observers were sometimes shocked by the apparent indifference with which military coups were greeted in developing countries. They failed to recognize that coups had become a regular – and fairly peaceful – mechanism for the circulation of elites. In a sense, coups had become the functional equivalent of elections in the West (at least as far as elite replacement was concerned) and should have been compared accordingly. Particularly when different institutions perform the same underlying function, comparing like with like is not always straightforward; concepts cannot be exchanged across countries as simply as currencies. If they could, comparative politics would be less challenging – and less valuable.

Definition

Two institutions or processes are **functionally equivalent** when they fulfil the same role within the political system. Institutions with the same label do not necessarily perform exactly the same functions; monarchs may rule with a rod of iron or just dispense medals to worthy citizens. Also, the same function can be performed by different processes; compare elections and revolutions as devices for replacing the governing elite (Myers and O'Connor, 1998).

Selection bias

This problem arises when the choice of what to study, or even how to study it, produces unrepresentative results. It is an inherent risk in a generalizing subject such as comparative politics in which any one study usually covers only a small number of countries. The danger often arises as an unintended consequence of a haphazard process of case selection. We choose to study those countries which speak the same language, or which have good exchange schemes, or in which we feel safe. One result is that the findings of comparative politics (and therefore of this book) are weighted toward consolidated developed democracies, a rare form of polity in the expanse of human history. Large, powerful countries also receive more attention than small, powerless ones – a justifiable bias, perhaps, but one which leads to an understatement of interdependence. One virtue of designs covering a large number of countries is that they reduce the risk of selection bias. Indeed, if the study covers all countries, selection bias disappears.

But, alas, the problem may just resurface in another form, through an unrepresentative selection of variables rather than countries. Much statistical research in comparative politics relies on existing data collected by governments and international bodies with different interests to our own. Their priorities tend to be financial, economic, social and political – in that order. So financial and economic variables may receive more attention than they justify, and politics runs the risk of becoming a branch of economics. Thus a large body of research examines the relationship between changing economic conditions and the popularity of national governments as reported in regular opinion polls (p. 108). This work has produced worthwhile findings but its sheer quantity reflects the ready availability of statistical information more than the intrinsic significance of the topic for the development of comparative politics.

Too many variables, too few countries

This is a major problem for scholars who emphasize the theory-testing function of the comparative method. Even though the United Nations now has 185 member states, it is rare to find a country which is identical to another in all respects except for that factor (say, the electoral system) whose effects we wish to detect. This means that comparison in political science can never become a full equivalent of the experiments conducted in the natural scientist's laboratory. We just do not have enough countries to go round. The crucial comparisons are rarely possible; we just run out of countries.

Interdependence

In reality, far fewer than 185 cases are available to the student of comparative politics. Countries learn from, copy, compete with, influence and even invade each other in a constant process of interaction. Even the states which provide the units of our subject did not develop separately; rather, the model of statehood diffused outwards from its proving ground in Europe (p. 6). As Dogan and Pelassy (1990, p. 1) say, 'there is no nation without other nations'. The major transitions of world history – industrialization, colonialism and decolonization, democratization, marketization – unfolded on a world stage; in that sense we have one world system rather than 185 independent states (Wallerstein, 1974, 1979). As globalization accelerated in the late twentieth century, so Galton's problem (as the task of separating diffusion from other causes of similarities between states is called) ran wild. Specific institutional forms also reflect diffusion: the communist model was often imposed by force of Soviet arms; the presidential system in Latin America was imported from the United States; and the ombudsman was a device copied from Sweden. The development of supranational and intergovernmental bodies also creates denser connections between states as well as creating more complex patterns of 'multi-level governance'. Of course, Galton's problem is also an opportunity; studying diffusion, after all, necessarily involves comparison. Further, a natural comparative design is to examine how member states respond to the demands of international organizations of which they are all members (for example the European Union). But it is clear that any comparative study which assumes that cases are independent – and much statistical analysis proceeds on precisely this assumption – must seek to justify a dubious starting point.

> **Definition**
> **Galton's problem** refers to the difficulty of testing whether similarities between nations are caused by diffusion across countries or, alternatively, by parallel but independent development. For example, how many times did communism collapse: once or once in each state which is now postcommunist?

The problems of comparison, then, are real enough. Practicing comparative politics is inherently a challenging enterprise. Yet as Ziman (1978, p. 41) says about science in general, 'what is remarkable is not that each of us makes so many mistakes but that we have made such remarkable progress together'. And amid the technical difficulties of comparison, we should always remember the deeper truth espoused by Dogan and Pelassy (1990): knowledge of self is gained through knowledge of others.

Case studies

Case studies offer a useful answer to the implicit question raised by students considering whether to undertake a comparative project. The doubt is this: why compare two or more countries in a single project when this is more difficult, and leads to no more credit, than just studying the one? There are of course several answers here. One is that the task of comparison forces reflection which will (we stress: will) result in a more interesting and theoretically-informed report. But there is more to it than that. It is perfectly possible to practice comparative politics by studying a single country. And the device which enables us to achieve this seemingly impossible goal is both the most common and the most under-estimated research strategy used in comparative politics: the case study.

The term 'case study' is often used loosely, as an impressive but redundant synonym for 'study'. But the difference between a case study and a study is methodologically significant. Indeed, the distinction helps to clarify the nature of comparative politics itself. A case is an instance of a more general category. To conduct a case study is therefore to investigate something which has significance beyond its boundaries. For instance, lawyers study cases which are taken to define a legal principle with wide applicability; anthropologists study particular communities to cast light on general issues in their discipline. A project turns into a case study only when it becomes clear what the study is a case of.

By contrast, a study is undertaken for its own sake, without any pretence at wider relevance. Most historical research (including the best) consists of studies, not case studies. Historians study the French Revolution, or the First World War, or the presidential administration of John Kennedy, because they believe these are important and interesting topics which do not require further justification. By the same token, political scientists who devote their professional lives to the study of specific countries do not regard their expertise as necessarily having wider applicability. They are students of countries, not cases.

Because of their concern to encompass general trends, students of comparative politics prefer case studies to studies. They want their investigations to cumulate rather than just to accumulate. As Scarrow (1969, p. 7) pointed out, case studies make a contribution to general knowledge of politics if 'the analysis is made within a comparative perspective which mandates that the description of the particular be cast in terms of broadly analytic constructs'. In other words, a single case can offer a detailed illustration of a theme of wider interest, whether we take Russia as an example of presidentialism, Japan as an instance of electoral reform or Australia as an illustration of republicanism. Thus cases are deliberately chosen, or can at least be written up, as examples of broader phenomena. In this book, for instance, we have looked briefly at Thailand as a case of how East Asian countries responded to the financial crisis of the late 1990s (p. 52), at Benin as an early example of democratization in Africa (p. 89), and at the internet as an illustration of the problem of crime control in a global world (p. 250).

In a case study, we seek to deepen our understanding of processes which have already been accepted within the discipline as significant. Thus one practical advantage of conducting a case study is that there is sure to be some interest in the findings. Compared with studies, case studies provide intellectual gearing, making a contribution to a wider debate as well as offering a rounded account of a particular subject. They offer a double return on the research investment.

Definition

Path dependence describes a process which can lead to several stable outcomes, depending on options selected early in the process. For example, the success of democratization may depend critically on the details of the constitution established during the transition from the old regime. However, if underlying factors (for example strong elite support for democracy) mean that the new democracy will consolidate come what may, the process is **path-independent**. Case studies often exaggerate path-dependence but statistical studies generally ignore it altogether.

While case studies are sometimes treated as a weak sibling in the family of research strategies, it would be pretentious for comparative politics to adopt such a lofty attitude (Yin, 1994). Politics is an untidy subject, in which cases are continually changing in path-dependent ways, often influencing each other as they evolve. By nature, our subject is data-rich and theory-poor; for this reason, cases are and will remain the major route to understanding. Unlike, say, economics, we do not have a single theoretical model to underpin our research. We must proceed by inspecting cases rather than by making deductions from first principles. In consequence, much comparative political analysis takes the form not of relating cases to abstract theory, but simply of drawing analogies between the cases themselves. How did the process of state-building differ between postcolonial states of the twentieth century and the states of early modern Europe (p. 7)? What are the similarities and differences between the Russian and Chinese revolutions (p. 93)? Reflecting this pragmatic approach, Khong (1992) suggests that much political reasoning, especially in foreign policy, is by analogy. Decision-makers and analysts look for earlier crises which resemble the current one, so that lessons can be learned and errors avoided. In the absence of overarching theory, case studies are the building blocks from which we construct our understanding of the political world.

Case studies are a strategy for selecting a topic more than a technique for conducting research. In practice, they are normally multimethod, using the range of techniques in the political scientist's toolkit: reading the academic literature, examining sec-

---

BOX 16.2
Some types of case study

Type	Definition	Example
Representative	Typical of the category	Poland's transition from communism
Prototypical	Expected to become typical	de Tocqueville's study of democracy in America
Deviant	An exception to the norm	Military rule in Nigeria
Crucial	Tests a theory in the least favourable conditions	Seeking democratizing trends in Saudi Arabia
Archetypal	Creates the category	French revolution

---

ondary documents (for example newspapers), searching for primary material (for example unpublished reports) and ideally conducting interviews with participants and other observers. Scholars of cases engage in 'soaking and poking, marinating themselves in minutiae' (King, Keohane and Verba, 1994, p. 38). Case studies aim to provide a description which is both rounded and detailed, a goal which the anthropologist Clifford Geertz (1993, first pub. 1973) famously defined as 'thick description'. Because of this rounded character, case studies are often contrasted with research using a single, systematic technique. Sample surveys, for instance, offer one particular form of evidence on the topic. Compared to the single slice of data provided by a survey, case students look through multiple lenses, mixing history and analysis, specific detail and wider implications, in an often compelling combination.

Happenstance is and will remain the main reason for selecting a particular case. Contacts, linguistic skills, accessibility, grants – all must and should enter into the calculus of choosing what to study. But, contrary to the beliefs of the inexperienced researcher, a case may have powerful intellectual significance even if this importance is not realised on selection. We should not confuse the personal history behind the selection of a case with its intellectual value. Indeed, intellectual order can be honourably imposed on a case even after the information about it has been collected. Box 16.2 sets out some ways in which cases can be given wider significance.

Representative cases

The first and most common form of case study is the representative case – the study of a typical, standard example of a wider category. This is the workhorse of case study designs, as useful as it is undramatic. As Peters (1998) says, 'one very valid reason for doing a case study is to collect information on the topic in question, especially while the case is still in progress …. Examining the political process while it is still in progress may be especially valuable in comparative politics, given that the researcher may be less familiar with the national setting of the case than he or she would be for their own country.'

Prototypical cases

The second type of case study is the prototypical form. Here a topic is chosen not because it is representative but because it is expected to become so: 'their present is our future' (Rose, 1991, p. 459). Studying an early example may help us to understand a phenomenon of growing significance. Thus we have looked closely in this book at the new public management in New Zealand, since that country has travelled furthest down the road of bureaucratic reform (p. 229). In the nineteenth century, de Tocqueville (1954, first pub. 1835) studied America because of his interest in the new politics of democracy; 'my wish has been to find there instruction by which we may ourselves profit'. Today, Europeans still look to the United States as a forerunner of trends, especially in the economy, which are expected to cross the Atlantic in due course. The danger with the prototypical case is that it involves a bet on the future: what if the prototype turns into a dud? Also, innovators are by nature unrepresentative; they often possess unusual enthusiasm and experience additional difficulties to those confronting their imitators. Yet by the same token, the prototypical case study does offer opportunities for lesson-drawing: later adopters can learn from the mistakes of the innovator (Rogers, 1971). Here the prototype still exerts influence but in a negative rather than a positive way.

Deviant cases

Deviant case studies are based on a different logic from both representative and prototypical designs. The purpose of a deviant case study is to cast light on the exceptional and the untypical: the countries which remain communist, or which are still governed by the military, or which seem to be immune from democratizing trends. For example, Rhodes (1994) sought to explain why Britain did not develop a powerful central bureaucracy until the middle of the nineteenth century, much later than most other countries of Western Europe. His answer was that Britain's island character and secure borders meant that it had no need of a large standing army and the bureaucracy needed to support it. As this illustration shows, deviant cases are often used to tidy up our understanding of exceptions and anomalies. In the same way, curiosity led us to consider why India is an exception to the thesis that democracy presupposes prosperity (p. 29). Normal science, suggests Kuhn (1970), proceeds in exactly this way, with researchers seeking to show how apparent paradoxes can be resolved within a dominant intellectual tradition.

But deviant cases can also be of considerable value in identifying underlying causes (Kazancigil, 1994, p. 214). This is because they can provide the variation without which well-founded explanation is impossible. If we want to argue that X causes Y, we must come up with cases of not-X and show that they lead to not-Y. For instance, European scholars may long have suspected that the need to service a permanent military force was a reason for the early development of bureaucracies. However the deviant British case adds greatly to our confidence in the hypothesis; it introduces vital variance by giving us an example of 'not-X'. While deviant cases always attract interest, the danger is that they become overstudied; the exceptional is always more exotic than the typical.

Crucial cases

The crucial case study is sometimes commended, but less often used, in comparative politics. The idea here is that if a proposition can be shown to work when conditions are least favourable to its validity, it is likely to be valid in all other circumstances as well. If democracies are now consolidating in countries which have no previous experience of that form of rule, we can be sure that the modern move toward democracy is significant. Alternatively, a proposition which fails to work even in the most favourable conditions can quickly be dismissed. If postmaterial values are nowhere to be found among graduates in the wealthiest countries, then the theory of postmaterialism is no good (p. 67). Depending on expectations, we can set out either to prove a theory by showing its value in unfavourable conditions (a 'least favourable' design) or to disprove a theory by showing it fails even in favourable circumstances (a 'most favourable' design).

> *Definition*
> The **least favourable** design seeks to test a theory in the crucial circumstances where it is least likely to hold up. The **most favourable** design seeks initial support for a theory by testing it in favourable conditions.

In comparative politics, the more powerful 'least favourable' design is occasionally encountered. In *Political Parties* (1949, first pub. 1911), the German sociologist Robert Michels (1876–1936) sought to develop his thesis that all organizations become dominated by a ruling elite. In what amounted to a crucial case, he chose to examine socialist parties, organizations committed to the norm of internal democracy. If oligarchy could be found there (as it was), it was also likely to apply to other organizations lacking a democratic culture. Or take a more recent example. If privatization is politically successful in Britain, where public support for the market mechanism remains muted, it is likely to work in countries such as the United States or even Canada, where the ideological environment is more favourable.

Eckstein (1975, p. 127) is a strong advocate of crucial case studies. He suggests that 'a single crucial case may certainly score a clean knockout over a theory'. But his thesis is limited in three ways. First, common sense suggests we should not place too much weight on any one case, no matter how crucial it appears to be. For this reason, King, Keohane and Verba (1994, p. 210) doubt that 'a crucial case study can serve the explanatory purpose Eckstein assigns to it'. Second, the crucial case design assumes a narrow theory-testing role for case studies which, as we have suggested, is often inappropriate for comparative politics. Third, crucial case studies involve a risky bet on the results. If the findings run counter to expectations, we have learned nothing at all of significance beyond the case. Suppose Michels had discovered, contrary to his expectations, that socialist parties were properly democratic after all. Then he would have been criticised for producing an obvious finding. When the results come out 'wrong', the crucial test dissolves into insignificance.

Archetypal cases

Our final form of case study is the archetypal case. The idea here is that in comparative politics a case often generates the category of which it is then taken, in a somewhat misleading way, as representative. Take the French Revolution. We suggested that this episode altered the whole concept of revolution, reconstructing the idea as a progressive, modernizing force (p. 92). In this way, the French Revolution made possible all the modern revolutions which followed. To regard the French experience of 1789 as just a representative example of a wider category is to understate its significance. It was not just a prototype (an early model) but also an archetype (a defining case). In similar fashion, the American presidency does far more than illustrate the presidential system of government; it is the model which influenced all later attempts to create similar systems, notably in Latin America (p. 203). Seisselberg's concept of the 'media-mediated personality party' owes much to the archetypal case of Berlusconi's Forza Italia (p. 136). The archetypal case is the basis, and not just an illustration, of a theory – and hence can should not be used to 'prove' the theory. There is a certainly a grain of truth in the proposition that some 'models' in comparative politics are just archetypal cases with the proper names taken out.

Quasi-experiments

Although not necessarily a form of case study, we should mention quasi-experimental design here. This technique is useful for both studies and case studies. The idea is to ascertain the effects of a variable, typically an institutional reform, through a before-and-after comparison. What has been the impact of Israel's switch to a directly-elected Prime Minister on the cohesion of its executive (p. 210)? Did the switch to a mixed member electoral system in Japan reduce the role of money in Japanese elections (p. 105)? The advantage of the before-and-after approach is that it holds most other factors constant, allowing an unusually pure measure of the impact of the specific factor in which we are interested. The findings from before-and-after studies can certainly contribute to wider debates in comparative politics. Examining the statistical correlation between the plurality method and two-party systems across all democracies is one thing; observing whether a change away from the plurality method leads to the collapse of an existing two-party system provides additional, and perhaps more crucial, leverage on the vexed question of the relationship between electoral and party systems (p. 103).

> *Definition*
> In an **experiment**, subjects are pre-tested and then randomly assigned to a treatment group or a control group. In a post-test, the two groups are compared to ascertain the impact of the treatment. True experiments must be constructed but comparative politics can occasionally take advantage of naturally-occurring **quasi-experiments** to draw inferences about the impact of a particular variable (for example electoral reform).

Note, however, that the before-and-after approach should ideally include some control cases for comparison. This comparative element is needed to help answer the question of what changes might have been expected in the main case even if a specific reform had not been enacted. For example, would we have expected more parties to have gained representation in New Zealand's parliament even if that country had not switched to a more proportional electoral system? Such 'what–if' questions should always be raised before causal inferences are drawn; and the answers, often tentative but usually worthwhile, always involve comparison with other cases (Przeworski, 1995). In the example at hand, we could trace New Zealand's party system back in time. Was the party system beginning to fragment even before electoral reform? Alternatively, we could examine a comparable country, such as Britain, to see if its two party system was beginning to weaken even in the absence of electoral reform. In examples such as these, we can see how comparative politics can exploit the natural experiments offered by political and specifically institutional innovation. Just occasionally, the world can indeed serve as our laboratory.

Focused comparisons

Focused comparisons fall between case studies and statistical analysis. They are 'small N' studies which concentrate on the intensive analysis of an aspect of politics in a small number of countries ('N' stands for number of cases). Most often, the number of countries is two, a paired or binary comparison, or three, a triangular comparison. The emphasis should be on the comparison at least as much as on the cases; otherwise, the design would be a multiple case study rather than a focused comparison.

To illustrate the technique, consider some examples. First, in a classic study Heclo (1974) compared the origins of unemployment insurance, old age pensions and earnings-related supplementary pensions in Britain and Sweden. In both countries, he concluded, the bureaucracy was the main agency of policy formulation in these areas. Second, Kudrle and Marmor (1981) compared the growth of social security programmes in the United States and Canada. They argued that the presence of elements of left-wing and Tory paternalistic ideology in Canada explained its higher levels of spending and programme development. Third, Lipset (1990) also compared the political cultures of the United States and Canada, tracing contemporary contrasts back to America's origins as a revolutionary society committed to individual freedom.

Small N studies have proved to be the success story of comparative politics in recent decades (Collier, 1991). They have been applied not just to policy studies but also to historical questions such as the origins of revolutions (p. 95). Focused comparisons remain sensitive to the details of particular countries and policies while also forcing the intellectual discipline which inheres in the comparative enterprise. The dimensions of comparison must be addressed, similarities and differences sorted out and some effort made to account for the contrasts observed. Focused comparisons work particularly well when a few countries are compared over time, examining how they vary in their response to common problems such as the transition to democracy. Unlike much statistical analysis, focused comparisons remain sensitive to the historical dimension. If it is difficult to produce a poor case study, it is virtually impossible to deliver an uninteresting report using focused comparison.

How should countries be selected for a focused comparison? Again, considerations of substance and practicality should trump purely methodological factors. Indeed, in much small N research countries are selected not as 'cases' but for their intrinsic interest; in our terminology, many focused comparisons are comparative studies rather than comparative case studies. But two obvious strategies suggest themselves: either to select contrasting cases or alternatively to examine similar ones. The first strategy consists in taking a few countries which vary on the topic of interest and asking, what accounts for the difference? For instance, why has the economy of communist China grown much faster than that of democratic India (p. 35)? Why did Britain manage a more peaceful transition to democracy than did Germany? Why is the United States Congress more autonomous from the executive than the Canadian parliament? Taking contrasting cases is consistent with Peters' rule (1998) of 'maximizing experimental variance' – that is, ensuring there is good variation in the phenomenon we seek to understand.

If the countries which vary on the factor of interest are otherwise similar, we have a 'most similar' design. This approach can rule out some potential explanations for the difference we seek to explain. Specifically, all ways in which two countries are the same cannot account for a contrast between them. For instance, a comparison of the Scandinavian countries automatically holds constant the ways in which these countries resemble each other. Elements of history and culture are shared, ruling out these factors as explanations of remaining differences. However, the most similar design cannot take us any further than excluding some potential explanations. The problem is that with a small N the most similar design is incapable of separating out the many possible explanations of a difference between two countries. Any difference between the countries is a potential explanation and we have no purchase on which factor is the correct explanation. In statistical language, we have more variables than cases; our dependent variable is over-determined.

An example will clarify the point. Suppose we took two consolidated developed democracies – Sweden and the United States – and asked why Sweden developed a welfare state but the United States never did. One answer might be that in a federal country such as the United States, it is much harder to agree on national standards for welfare provision. Another answer is cultural: Americans favour self-reliance whereas Swedes support a more collective interpretation of society. The problem is that our research design does not allow us to separate the impact of these two variables. To pursue the analysis further, we would need to look at more countries. We would need to go hunting for federal countries with a collective culture, and unitary states with an individualistic culture. In effect, small N would have to give way to larger N.

Definition

A **most similar** design takes similar countries for comparison on the assumption, as Lipset (1990, p. xiii) puts it, that 'the more similar the units being compared, the more possible it should be to isolate the factors responsible for differences between them.' By contrast, the **most different** design seeks to show the robustness of a relationship by demonstrating its validity in a range of contrasting settings (Przeworski and Teune, 1970). Most large N research implicitly adopts a 'most different' approach.

An alternative approach to selecting cases for a focused comparison is to choose similar rather than contrasting cases. The task is then to explore these cases to uncover how much they have in common in their origins, character and effects. Many area studies take this form. For instance, we could compare the welfare states in Scandinavia in terms of their evolution and their contemporary viability in an era of lean government. But similar cases do not have to be contiguous. We could take some examples of attempts to develop regional links – say, the European Union and NAFTA – in order to understand the motivations that underlay these efforts, the contrasting forms they have taken and the extent to which they have achieved their goals (p. 47).

This technique of comparing several instances of a phenomenon is entirely defensible for the descriptive purpose of broadening our perspective. But the strategy holds traps for those unwise enough to use the method as a sole strategy of explanation. The problem is that the research design does not permit any assessment of how often the explanatory factors do **not** produce the phenomenon under study. Perhaps regional integration is motivated by the desire to achieve mutual gains from increased trade. But this motivation presumably applies to any group of adjacent countries. Our hypothesis – regional integration as mutual back-scratching – therefore fails to explain why regional integration is attempted in only a few cases where shared benefits could be achieved.

The underlying problem here is known as selection on the dependent variable. As King, Keohane and Verba (1994, p. 129) note, 'the literature is full of work that makes the mistake of failing to let the dependent variable vary; for example, research that tries to explain the outbreak of wars with studies only of wars, the onset of revolutions with studies only of revolutions, or patterns of voter turnout with interviews only of nonvoters'. For instance, Porter's study (1986) of the common features of internationally successful industries identified the importance of a geographical cluster of highly specialized firms working in the sector. But how often do such clusters exist yet fail to become internationally competitive? Perhaps such clusters are even stronger in declining industries! By failing to include less competitive industries in his design, Porter was unable to show to what extent the clustering of firms and international competitiveness covaried. He offended against Peters' principle of maximizing the experimental variance.

Skocpol's (1979) study of revolutions in France, Russia and China is another example of selection on the dependent variable. Her research design allowed her to identify common features in these revolutions, such as the declining international and domestic effectiveness of the old regime (p. 95). However, she was unable to say how often a failing regime was followed by a revolution. Like Porter, she had selected on the dependent variable and was restricted to positive cases. She was therefore unable to assess how far government ineffectiveness and revolutions covaried (however, Skocpol did reduce the problem by including some limited assessment of other 'moments of revolutionary crisis' in her study). At best, studies which select on the dependent variable can identify necessary conditions of the phenomenon under study. They cannot identify sufficient conditions.

> **Definition**
> **Selection on the dependent variable** occurs when only similar (usually positive) cases of a phenomenon are selected. By eliminating variation, there is no contrast left to explain. For example, a study just of countries which have democratized successfully can tell us nothing about the conditions of successful democratization. Those conditions can only be identified through a comparison with failed democratizations.

History plays a trick on us by selecting on the dependent variable through evolution. For instance, in our discussion of the origins of the modern European state, we noted that their emergence owed much to the efforts by monarchs to mobilize men and materials for war (p. 6). However this tells us nothing about how many monarchs failed in the task, with the result that their protostates disappeared into the waste-bin of history. In other words, the states surviving now are a biased sample of the protostates existing then. Przeworski (1995, p. 19) offers another example of this easily-overlooked problem of selection by history. He notes that even if democracies do achieve higher rates of economic growth than authoritarian regimes, this may arise just because low-growth democracies become unstable, eventually turning into dictatorships. So by looking just at the surviving democracies, we are skewing our results in democracy's favour. Always remember, the best research never forgets the patients who died!

We should not be carried away on a wave of methodological perfectionism. The studies by Porter and Skocpol are major success stories in comparative research, offering insights which could then be tested by more systematic means. Further, selecting on the dependent variable can lead to the identification of necessary conditions – those which are always present in the phenomenon under study. So we can legitimately test the proposition, 'the declining capacity of the state is a necessary condition of revolution' by looking only at revolutions. Although necessary conditions may be rare, so too are revolutions; indeed, Dion (1998) suggests that searching for necessary conditions may be particularly sensible when examining rare events such as revolutions.

Selecting similar cases is also entirely legitimate when the research task is descriptive rather than explanatory. Many focused comparisons are concerned with the question 'how?' rather than 'why'? and they are none the worse for that. In comparative politics, the task is often to obtain more perspective on the topic, not to test a premature and inappropriately precise theory. For instance, we might want to identify common features in how the revolutionary process develops, or to understand the problems rulers typically experience in privatizing industries, or to identify what steps governments have taken to implement agreed targets on pollution emissions. Despite their limited explanatory value, focused comparisons are also useful for generating ideas. After all, we cannot design a project to test our independent variables until we have some ideas about what those variables are.

Truth tables

The analysis of truth tables, termed qualitative comparative analysis by Ragin (1994a and b), is an intriguing method for seeking out causal inferences from a series of case studies. As such, it forms a bridge between qualitative and quantitative analysis. Truth tables operate on yes/no variables (for example whether a country is democratic or authoritarian), rather than the numerical variables associated with statistical analysis (for example a country's national income). Although a truth table sets out the information from which inferences can be drawn about the relationships applying across the cases, these conclusions are expressed not in statistical correlations but in the language of conditions: for example,

BOX 16.3
Necessary and sufficient conditions

X is a *necessary condition* of Y = all cases of Y show feature X.

Example: The plurality method is a necessary condition of a two party system if two party systems occur only when the plurality method is used.

X is a *sufficient condition* of Y = all cases of X show feature Y.

Example: The plurality method is a sufficient condition of a two party system if two party systems occur whenever the plurality method is used.

X is a *necessary and sufficient* condition of Y = Y occurs if and only if X also occurs.

Example: The plurality method is a necessary and sufficient condition of a two party system if two party systems occur only and whenever the plurality method is used.

necessary and sufficient conditions (Box 16.3). In this way, truth tables direct our attention to the configuration(s) of variables found in the cases. They direct our attention to conjunctures, to the combination of factors operating in a particular example. Although the full rigours of Ragin's method may be too demanding for most research situations in comparative politics, the truth table itself can be a useful device for presenting the main features of a research project with a medium number of cases. Alternatively, a truth table can be used to summarize the results obtained from reviewing a series of existing case reports.

A truth table simply sets out each possible combination of the values of the main variables included in the study (Box 16.4). Each possible combination is represented as a row in the table. Several cases may share the characteristics of a particular row; other rows may be empty, representing possible but not actual configurations. As with other forms of explanatory analysis, one variable is dependent – that which we seek to explain. The others are independent or explanatory – those factors which may affect the dependent variable (Box 16.5). In the example in Box 16.4, the dependent variable is whether, over a specific period, the government has

BOX 16.4
Hypothetical truth table on the introduction of independent government agencies

Independent variables			Dependent variable	(Number of countries)
Large government deficit?	Administrative fiasco?	Government by right-wing party?	Independent government agencies introduced?	
Y	Y	Y	Y	(3)
Y	Y	N	N	(4)
Y	N	Y	Y	(4)
Y	N	N	N	(3)
N	Y	Y	Y	(2)
N	Y	N	N	(–)
N	N	Y	N	(1)
N	N	N	N	(2)

Note: Y = yes, N = no. For an example using real data on new public management, see Peters (1998, Ch.7).

BOX 16.5
Dependent, intervening and independent variables

Type of variable	Definition	Example
Dependent variable	the factor we seek to explain	party voted for
Independent variable	the factor believed to influence the dependent variable	social class
Intervening variable	a factor through which the independent variable influences the dependent variable	attitudes to party leaders

---

introduced any new public agencies operating independently of the government itself (such agencies are a feature of the new public management, p. 228). The three independent variables, all of which might be expected to encourage administrative reform, are (1) whether there has been a large government deficit in the period, (2) whether there have been any administrative fiascos and (3) whether the government has been led by parties of the right. Note that the size of the government's deficit would originally be a number which would have to be reduced to a two-category variable in order to fit the truth table discipline. The final column shows the number of countries falling into each configuration; in the table, this varies from none to four. All countries with the same configuration of independent variables share the same outcome on the dependent variable; if this is not the case, the model is incorrectly specified and in theory additional independent variables should be sought.

From inspection of Box 16.4, we can observe a strong if complex pattern. Among these made-up cases, only right-wing governments introduce independent agencies but not all of them do so; the ideology of the government is necessary but not sufficient for introducing the reform. Right-wing governments also need the stimulus provided by either a large budget deficit or an administrative fiasco. In other words, two sets of conditions – two 'conjunctures' – are sufficient to account for the introduction of independent agencies: (1) a right-wing government and a large funding deficit, (2) a right-wing government and an administrative fiasco. This emphasis on combinations of variables, and the ability to pick out different routes to the same outcome, are characteristics of the truth table layout. Note too how we have expressed the relationships in qualitative fashion, using the terms 'and'

and 'or', rather than statistical measures such as a correlation; this too is a characteristic of the approach.

The preparation and inspection of a truth table is itself a valuable feature. In practice, it helps to begin by constructing a 'data table' in which each row represents a case rather than a particular combination of independent variables. But once a truth table has been built, and given a thorough visual inspection, it is possible to proceed to more systematic analysis. We can conduct a formal analysis of the data to identify necessary and sufficient conditions; special software is available for the purpose (Ragin, 1994a). The idea here is to process truth table information in a quasi-experimental fashion, testing combinations of variables and eliminating a particular variable from a specific combination if it makes no difference to the outcome. Using this method, Wickham-Crowley (1992, p. 320) was able to isolate a series of conditions necessary for the success of revolutionary movements in Latin America between 1956 and 1990.

Peters (1998) offers a balanced assessment of truth table analysis. He concludes that the technique is useful for cumulating case studies and also for eliminating potential causes. But truth tables offer 'no magic bullet' for the comparative scholar. In particular, the method 'depends on the existence of relatively clear conditions of necessity and sufficiency among the variables ... unfortunately, however, few things in the social sciences are so sharply defined'. Especially where variables can be scored on a numerical scale, statistical techniques may offer results which are both more precise and more sensitive.

Statistical analysis

Statistics can enter into many studies, including case studies. For instance, case studies of specific states often include some reworking of existing statistics about the country, frequently drawn from official figures (originally, 'statistics' meant the science dealing with facts about the state). However, our focus in this section is on the use of statistical analysis as a primary research strategy. In such variable-oriented research, the object is to explore the covariation between variables, at least some of which are usually measured quantitatively. Examples of statistical work in comparative politics include the debate on whether democracy helps or hinders economic growth (p. 35); efforts to measure the impact of a country's levels of affluence and education on its population's commitment to postmaterial values (p. 68) and cross-national surveys of the effect of social status on political participation (p. 82) and electoral choice (p. 107).

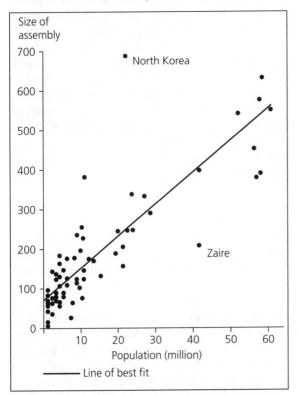

Figure 16.1 Population and assembly size from fig. 11.1 (p. 185), showing the line of best fit and highlighting two outliers.

As a straightforward illustration of the statistical approach, consider the relationship between a country's population and the number of members in its national assembly. A scatterplot, as in Figure 16.1, displays all the information about these two variables for the countries surveyed. However, the content of the graph can be usefully summarized by calculating a regression line which gives the best fit to the data. This line, also shown in the figure, is defined by an equation linking the variables. Given such an equation, we can use the population of any particular country to predict its assembly size; indeed, these predictions can easily be made from the regression line using a ruler.

We could extend this basic regression analysis in various directions. One useful procedure is to calculate the deviation of each country's assembly size from its predicted value, producing a number known as the residual. Countries with high residuals form deviant cases, called outliers in statistics, for which special explanations can be sought, thus providing a link to case analysis. In our example, North Korea's Supreme People's Assembly is far larger than would be expected for a country with a population of just 23 million. Conversely, Zaire has a high negative residual – a smaller assembly than would be anticipated, given its population. More systematically, we could calculate the residual for each country in our study and try to account for the residuals using additional variables. For example, North Korea is a communist state with a unicameral parliament; both factors are probably linked to larger-than-predicted assemblies. In this way additional independent variables can be incorporated into a regression model. If we extended the analysis to all the world's countries, we might also want to consider the possibility of a curved regression line, since assembly size may cease to increase once population extends beyond the 60 million level which serves as a cut-off for the diagram and the linked equation. Note, however, that increasing statistical complexity often produces diminishing returns; strong findings generally surface straight away.

But the real question concerns the intellectual value of the estimates produced by techniques such as regression analysis. At issue is the status of such equations as explanations of the phenomenon under study. Some of the problems here are technical. A strong correlation between two variables may arise

BOX 16.6

Regression analysis

The form of the simplest *regression equation* is:

$$Y = a + bX$$

where Y is the dependent variable, a is the intercept, b is the regression coefficient and X is the independent variable.

The *intercept* is the point at which the line is projected to cross the vertical axis; in the example in Figure 16.1, the intercept is 75.6. In this example, the intercept holds no substantive interest.

The *regression coefficient* states the slope of the line and indicates how sharply the independent variable impinges on the dependent variable.

The regression equation corresponding to the scatterplot in Figure 16.1 is $Y = 75.6 + 8.0X$, where Y is the number of members in the assembly and X is population size (in million).

The regression coefficient of eight indicates that, on average, the membership of an assembly increases by eight for an increase of one million in population.

A country with a population of 10 million would therefore be expected to have an assembly size of $75.6 + 8.0(10) = 155.6$ which rounds to 156.

The residual is the difference between the actual and the predicted value. Observations with high residuals are called *outliers*.

The *correlation coefficient* measures the accuracy of such predictions. Specifically, the square of the correlation coefficient indicates the proportion of the variation in the dependent variable which can be accounted for by the independent variable. In our case, the correlation is 0.86, indicating that population can account for 74 per cent (0.86×0.86) of the variation in assembly size.

Definition

A **spurious correlation** exists between two variables when their values both result from those of a third variable. When all three variables are measured, statistical analysis can help to determine whether a correlation is spurious. Even so, correlation does not finally prove causation.

Yet even if a relationship is genuine, the direction of causation remains to be established. Suppose we find that democracies have higher growth rates than authoritarian regimes. Is this because democracies facilitate economic growth or because a high rate of growth fosters a stable democracy? A case can be made both ways and by itself a correlation will not tell us the answer. In interpreting an equation, we always run the risk of repeating the error made by the child who asked its mother to stop the trees from waving their branches because they were making the wind get up. In general, correlations obtained by nonexperimental methods can never finally prove causation. However, even a spurious correlation may be a useful if risky basis for prediction.

At a more philosophical level, it would clearly be naive to equate 'variance explained' with 'causes understood'. Returning to the example of assembly size, the obvious tack to adopt in explaining the size of a specific legislature is to discover the reasoning of the people who set it up in the first place. Why did they make the membership neither larger nor smaller but just so? Regression equations based on large numbers of cases do not seem to enter into our intuitive idea of what is involved in explaining a specific case. Further, the cross-sectional nature of much statistical analysis, with all variables drawn from the same point in time, excludes time itself from the analysis, thereby losing the purchase which we obtain from applying the axiom that causes necessarily come before their effects.

Yet even accepting these limits to statistical analysis, we should retain the genuine benefits which it can provide. As Peters (1998) wisely says, 'statistical analysis may not be everything but it is certainly something'. In particular, the ability to predict, even with the limited accuracy typically found in comparative politics, is well worth having. And even simple descriptive statistics – how many semi-presidential executives are there? what was the

simply because both depend on a third, unmeasured variable. This is 'spurious correlation'. For example, a relationship between ethnic minority status and low turnout might disappear (or even go into reverse) when social status is taken into account. That is, the correlation between ethnicity and turnout may result just from the concentration of minorities among the poor. In principle, the solution to this problem is simple: include all relevant variables in the analysis, for statistical techniques can effectively control for such problems. In practice, not all the relevant variables will be known; so spurious correlation is a continuing danger.

probability that an authoritarian regime in 1980 would become democratic by 1990? – are essential means for comprehending the variability of the political world. Indeed, straightforward counting is probably the most under-used statistical technique in comparative politics. Statistics may be an exercise in simplification but, precisely for that reason, they help us with our core task of encompassing politics at a comparative level. As King, Keohane and Verba (1994, p. 42) rightly say, 'simplification has been an integral part of every known scholarly work'.

Key reading

> **Next step:** *Peters (1998) is a thorough and balanced discussion of comparative techniques by an experienced practitioner.*

Dogan and Pelassy (1990) is a challenging account of the comparative approach, more philosophical than Peters but insightful even so. For general overviews, Lijphart (1971), Rose (1991), Collier (1991), Keman (1993) and Mair (1996) are all worth reading. King, Keohane and Verba (1994) explore how qualitative designs can lead to valid causal inferences; they have much to contribute to comparative research design. Dogan and Kazancigil (1994) mix comparative approaches and examples in a stimulating way. On specific techniques, Yin (1994) is a useful account of case studies from a broad social science perspective. For small N studies, whether focused comparisons or truth table analysis, see Ragin (1994a) and Ragin, Berg-Schlosser and de Meur (1996). On statistics, Lewi-Beck (1995) is our recommended introduction; Jackson (1996) is a more advanced treatment. Janoski and Hicks (1994) contain good discussions and examples, without becoming too technical.

References

Aberbach, J. *et al.* (1981) *Bureaucrats and Politicians* (Cambridge, Mass.: Harvard University Press).

Abramson, P. and Inglehart, R. (1992) 'Generational Replacement and Value Change in Eight Western Societies', *British Journal of Political Science* (22) 183–228.

Acherson, N. (1995) 'Postcommunism Triumphs by Default', *Independent on Sunday*, 26 November 1995, p. 14.

Adonis, A. (1996) 'Two Faces of Welfare', *Financial Times*, 3 July 1996, p. 12.

Agh, A. (ed.) (1994) *The Emergence of East Central European Parliaments* (Budapest: Hungarian Centre of Democracy).

Agh, A. (1996) 'Democratic Parliamentarism in Hungary: The First Parliament (1990–94) and the Entry of the Second Parliament' in *The New Parliaments of Central and Eastern Europe*, ed. D. Olson and P. Norton (London: Frank Cass) pp. 16–39.

Agocs, S. (1997) 'A Dispirited Army' in *Civil–Military Relations in Postcommunist States: Central and Eastern Europe in Transition*, ed. A. Bebler (Westport, Conn. and London: Praeger) pp. 86–92.

Aguero, F. (1995) 'Democratic Consolidation and the Military in Southern Europe and South America' in *The Politics of Democratic Consolidation: Southern Europe in Comparative Perspective*, ed. R. Gunther, P. Diamandouros and H. Puhle (Baltimore, Md. and London: Johns Hopkins University Press) pp. 124–65.

Alesina, A., Spolare, E. and Wacziarg, R. (1996) *Economic Integration and Political Disintegration* (Chicago: National Bureau of Economic Research).

Almond, G. and Bingham Powell, G. (1996) *Comparative Politics Today: A World View* (N.Y.: HarperCollins) 5th edn.

Almond, G. and Verba, S. (1963) *The Civic Culture* (Princeton, N.J.: Princeton University Press).

Almond, G. and Verba, S. (eds) (1980) *The Civic Culture Revisited* (Princeton, N.J.: Princeton University Press).

Anderson, C. and Ward, D. (1996) 'Barometer Elections in Comparative Perspective', *European Journal of Political Research* (15) 447–60.

Anderson, J. (1984) *Public Policy-making* (Orlando, Fla.: Holt, Rinehart & Winston).

Anderson, M. (1989) *Policing the World: Interpol and the Politics of International Police Cooperation* (Oxford and N.Y.: Clarendon Press).

Anderson, M. *et al.* (eds) (1995) *Policing the European Union: Theory, Law and Practice* (Oxford and N.Y.: Oxford University Press).

Andeweg, R. (1991) 'The Dutch Prime Minister: Not Just Chairman, Not Yet a Chief?', *West European Politics* (14) 116–32.

Andeweg, R. (1997) 'Collegiality and Collectivity: Cabinets, Cabinet Committees and Cabinet Ministers' in *The Hollow Crown: Countervailing Trends in Core Executives*, ed. P. Weller, H. Bakvis and R. Rhodes (London: Macmillan and N.Y.: St Martin's Press) pp. 58–83.

Andeweg, R. and Irwin, G. (1993) *Dutch Government and Politics* (London: Macmillan).

Arblaster, A. (1994) *Democracy* (Milton Keynes: Open University Press and Minneapolis: University of Minnesota Press).

Arendt, H. (1970) *On Violence* (London: Penguin).

Arian, A. (1996) 'The Israeli Election for Prime Minister and the Knesset', *European Journal of Political Research* (15) 447–60.

Arian, A. (1997) *The Second Republic: Politics in Israel* (Chatham, N.J.: Chatham House).

Asher, H. (1988) *Presidential Elections and American Politics* (Pacific Grove, Calif.: Brooks/Cole).

Astin, A. (1977) *Four Critical Years: Effects of College on Beliefs, Attitudes and Knowledge* (San Francisco, Calif.: Jossey-Bass).

Baer, M. (1993) 'Mexico's Second Revolution: Pathways to Liberalization' in *Political and Economic Liberalization in Mexico: At a Critical Juncture?*, ed. R. Roett (Boulder, Colo. and London: Lynne Reinner) pp. 51–68.

Bagehot, W. (1963) *The English Constitution* (London: Fontana) first pub. 1867.

Ball, T. and Dagger, R. (1995) *Political Ideologies and the Democratic Ideal* (N.Y.: HarperCollins), 2nd edn.

Barany, Z. (1993) 'Civil–military Relations in Comparative Perspective: East-Central and Southeastern Europe', *Political Studies* (41) 594–610.

Bardach, E. (1976) 'Policy Termination as a Political Process', *Policy Sciences* (7) 123–31.

Bardacke, T. *et al.* (1997) 'Thai Bailout: Self-interest Makes for Cooperation', *Financial Times*, 12 August 1997, p. 6.

Barnes, S. and Kaase, M. (1979) *Political Action: Mass Participation in Five Western Democracies* (Thousand Oaks, Calif. and London: Sage).

Barrett, S. and Fudge, C. (1981) *Policy and Action* (London: Methuen).

Bartolini, S. and Mair, P. (1990) *Identity, Competition and Electoral Availability: The Stabilization of European Electorates 1885–1985* (Cambridge and N.Y.: Cambridge University Press).

Batley, R. and Stoker, G. (eds) (1991) *Local Government in Europe: Trends and Developments* (London: Macmillan).

Batt, J. (1993) 'The Politics of Economic Transition' in *Developments in East European Politics*, ed. S. White, J. Batt and P. Lewis (London: Macmillan) pp. 205–24.

Bayart, J.-F. (1993) *The State in Africa: the Politics of the Belly* (Harlow and N.Y.: Longman).

Bayley, D. (1982) 'A World Perspective on the Role of the Police in Social Control' in *The Maintenance of Order in Society*, ed. R. Donelan (Ottawa: Canadian Police College) pp. 27–39.

Baylis, T. (1996) 'Presidents Versus Prime Ministers: Shaping Executive Authority in Eastern Europe', *World Politics* (48) 297–322.

Bayne, N. (1997) 'What Governments Want from International Economic Institutions', *Government and Opposition* (32) 361–79.

Baynham, R. (ed.) (1986) *Military Power in Black Africa* (London: Croom Helm).

Bean, C. (1997) 'Parties and Elections' in *New Developments in Australian Politics*, ed. B. Galligan, I. McAllister and J. Ravenhill (South Melbourne: Macmillan) pp. 102–26.

Bebler, A. (ed.) (1997) *Civil–Military Relations in Postcommunist States: Central and Eastern Europe in Transition* (Westport, Conn. and London: Praeger).

Beck, U. (1995) *Ecological Politics in an Age of Risk* (Cambridge: Polity).

Beer, S. (1982) *Britain against Itself* (London: Faber & Faber).

Beetham, D. and Boyle, K. (1995) *Introducing Democracy: 80 Questions and Answers* (Cambridge: Polity).

Bekke, H., Perry, J. and Toonen, T. (1996) *Civil Service Systems in Comparative Perspective* (Bloomington, Ind.: Indiana University Press).

Bell, D. *et al.* (eds) (1995) *Towards Illiberal Democracy in Pacific Asia* (London: Macmillan).

Bell, J. (1991) 'Administrative Law' in *The Blackwell Encyclopaedia of Political Science*, ed. V. Bogdanor (Oxford and Cambridge, Mass.: Blackwell) pp. 9–12.

Bennett, J. (1991) *International Organizations* (Englewood Cliffs, N.J.: Prentice-Hall), 5th edn.

Bentley, A. (1908) *The Process of Government* (Chicago, Ill.: University of Chicago Press).

Benyon, J. (1996) 'Policing the Union: European Supranational Law Enforcement' in *Policing Public Order: Theoretical and Practical Issues*, ed. C. Critcher and D. Waddington (Aldershot and Brookfield, Vt.: Avebury) pp. 237–58.

Benyon, J. *et al.* (1995) *Police Forces in the New European Union: A Conspectus* (Leicester: Centre for the Study of Public Order).

Berger, A. (1991) *Media USA* (N.Y.: Longman).

Berrington, H. (1995) 'Political Ethics: The Nolan Report', *Government and Opposition* (30) 429–51.

Bill, J. and Springborg, R. (1994) *Politics in the Middle East* (N.Y.: HarperCollins), 4th edn.

Blais, A. and Massicotte, L. (1996) 'Electoral Systems' in *Comparing Democracies: Elections and Voting in Global Perspective*, ed. L. LeDuc, R. Niemi and P. Norris (Thousand Oaks, Calif. and London: Sage) pp. 49–82.

Blais, A., Massicotte, L. and Dobrzynska, A. (1997) 'Direct Presidential Elections: A World Summary', *Electoral Studies* (16) 441–455.

Blake, D. and Walters, R. (1992) *The Politics Of Global Economic Relations* (Englewood Cliffs, N.J.: Prentice Hall).

Blau, P. and Meyer, M. (eds) (1987) *Bureaucracy In Modern Society* (N.Y.: Random House) 3rd edn.

Blondel, J. (1973) *Comparative Legislatures* (Englewood Cliffs, N.J.: Prentice Hall).

Blondel, J. (1993) *Consensus Politics and Multiparty Systems* (Australian National University: Conference on Consensual Policymaking and Multiparty Politics).

Blondel, J. (1995) *Comparative Government: An Introduction* (Hemel Hempstead: Prentice Hall/Harvester Wheatsheaf) 2nd edn.

Bobrow, D. and Dryzek, J. (1987) *Policy Analysis by Design* (Pittsburgh, Pa.: Pittsburgh University Press).

Bogason, P. (1996) 'The Fragmentation of Local Government in Scandinavia', *European Journal of Political Research* (30) 65–86.

Bogdanor, V. (1988) 'Introduction' in *Constitutions in Democratic Politics*, ed. V. Bogdanor (Aldershot: Gower) pp. 1–13.

Boldt, M. (1993) *Surviving as Indians: The Challenge of Self-Government* (Toronto and Buffalo, N.Y.: University of Toronto Press).

Boston, J. (ed.) (1995) *The State Under Contract* (Wellington: Bridget Williams).

Boulding, K. (1989) *Three Faces of Power* (Thousand Oaks, Calif. and London: Sage).

Bovens, M. and Hart, P. (1996) *Understanding Policy Fiascos* (New Brunswick, N.J. and London: Transaction Publishers).

Bratton, M. (1997) 'Deciphering Africa's Divergent Transitions', *Political Science Quarterly* (112) 67–93.

Bratton, M. and van de Walle, N. (1997) *Democratic Experiments in Africa: Regime Transitions in Comparative Perspective* (Cambridge and N.Y.: Cambridge University Press).

Breuilly, J. (1993) *Nationalism and the State* (N.Y.: St Martin's Press) 2nd edn.

Brewer, J. *et al.* (1996) *The Police, Public Order and the State* (London: Macmillan) 2nd edn.

Brooker, P. (1995) *Twentieth-Century Dictatorships: The Ideological One-Party States* (London: Macmillan).

Broughton, D. (1995) *Public Opinion Polling and Politics in Britain* (Hemel Hempstead: Harvester Wheatsheaf).

Brown, A. (1989) 'Ideology and Political Culture' in *Politics, Society and Nationality inside Gorbachev's Russia*, ed. S. Bialer (Boulder, Colo. and Oxford: Westview) pp. 15–32.

Brown, A. (1996) *The Gorbachev Factor* (Oxford and N.Y.: Oxford University Press).

Brubaker, R. (1996) *Nationalism Reframed: Nationhood and the National Question in the New Europe* (Cambridge and N.Y.: Cambridge University Press).

Brunold, G. (1994) *Africa Does Not Exist (translated title)* (Frankfurt: Eichborn Verlag).

Bryce, J. (1921) *Modern Democracies* (N.Y.: Macmillan).

Brzezinski, Z. (1997) 'The New Challenge to Human Rights' *Journal of Democracy* (8) 3–8.

Budge, I. (1996) *The New Challenge of Direct Democracy* (Cambridge: Polity).

Budge, I. and Newton, K. *et al.* (1997) *The Politics of the New Europe: Atlantic to Urals* (N.Y.: Addison Wesley and Harlow: Longman).

Budge, I., Robertson, D. and Hearl, D. *et al.* (1987) *Ideology, Strategy and Party Change* (Cambridge and N.Y.: Cambridge University Press).

Bukst, J. (1993) 'Interest Groups in Denmark' in *Pressure Groups*, ed. J. Richardson (Oxford and N.Y.: Oxford University Press) pp. 100–12.

Bull, H. (1977) *The Anarchical Society: A Study of Order in World Politics* (London: Macmillan).

Bunce, V. (1997) 'Presidents and the Transition in Eastern Europe' in *Presidential Institutions and Democratic Politics: Comparing Regional and National Contexts*, ed. K. von Mettenheim (Baltimore, Md. and London: Johns Hopkins University Press) pp. 161–76.

Burgess, M. and Gagnon, A. (eds) (1993) *Comparative Federalism and Federation: Competing Traditions and Future Directions* (Hemel Hempstead: Harvester Wheatsheaf).

Burnham, W. (1970) *Critical Elections and the Mainsprings of American Politics* (N.Y.: Norton).

Bush, G. (1980) *Local Government and Politics in New Zealand* (Northcote, Auckland: Allen & Unwin).

Butler, D. (1989) *British General Elections* (Oxford and Cambridge, Mass.: Blackwell).

Butler, D. (1996) 'Polls and Elections' in *Elections and Voting in Global Perspective*, ed. L. LeDuc, R. Niemi and P. Norris (Thousand Oaks, Calif. and London: Sage) pp. 236–53.

Butler, D. and Ranney. A. (eds) (1994) *Referendums around the World: The Growing Use of Direct Democracy* (Washington, D.C.: American Enterprise Institute and London: Macmillan).

Campbell, A. (1996) 'City Government in Russia' in *Transformation from Below: Local Power and the Political Economy of Postcommunist Transitions*, ed. J. Gibson and P. Hanson (Aldershot and Brookfield, Vt.: Edward Elgar) pp. 37–56.

Campbell, A. *et al.* (1960) *The American Voter* (N.Y.: Wiley).

Campbell, C. and Wilson, G. (1995) *The End of Whitehall: Death of a Paradigm?* (Oxford and Cambridge, Mass.: Blackwell).

Canel, E. (1992) 'Democratization and the Decline of Urban Social Movements in Uruguay: A Political Institutional Account' in *The Making of Social Movements in Latin America: Identity, Strategy and Democracy*, ed. A. Escobar and S. Alvarez (Boulder, Colo. and Oxford: Westview) pp. 276–90.

Carey, J. (1996) *Term Limits and Legislative Representation* (Cambridge and N.Y.: Cambridge University Press).

Carley, M. (1980) *Rational Techniques in Policy Analysis* (London: Heinemann).

Case, W. (1996) 'Can the "Halfway House" Stand? Semi-democracy and Élite Theory in Three Southeast Asian Countries', *Comparative Politics* (28) 437–64.

Cawthra, G. (1993) *Policing South Africa: The SAP and the Transition from Apartheid* (London and Atlantic Highlands, N.J.: Zed).

Cerny, P. (1990) *The Changing Architecture of Politics* (Thousand Oaks, Calif. and London: Sage).

Chalmers, D. (1990) 'Dilemmas of Latin American Democratization: Dealing with International Forces' in *Papers on Latin America No.18* (N.Y.: Columbia University Institute of Latin American and Iberian Studies).

Chandler, J. (1993) *Local Government in Liberal Democracies: An Introductory Survey* (London and N.Y.: Routledge).

Chazan, N. (1993) 'Between Liberalism and Statism: African Political Cultures and Democracy' in *Political Culture and Democracy in Developing Countries*, ed. L. Diamond (Boulder, Colo.: Lynne Reinner) pp. 67–105.

CIA (1997) *Handbook of the Nations* (Washington, D.C.: Gale).

Cigler, C. and Loomis, B. (eds.) (1991) *Interest Group Politics* (Washington, D.C.: Congressional Quarterly Press).

Clapham, C. (1982) *Private Patronage and Public Power: Political Clientelism in the Modern State* (London: Pinter).

Clapham, C. (1985) *Third World Politics: An Introduction* (Beckenham: Croom Helm).

Clapham, C. and Philip, G. (1985) 'The Political Dilemmas of Military Regimes' in *The Political Dilemmas of Military Regimes*, ed. C. Clapham and G. Philip (Beckenham: Croom Helm) pp. 1–26.

Close, D. (ed.) (1995) *Legislatures and the New Democracies in Latin America* (Boulder, Colo. and London: Lynne Reinner).

Coale, A. (1981) 'Population Trends, Population Policy and Population Studies in China', *Population and Development Review* (7) 85–97.

Collier, D. (1991) 'The Comparative Method: Two Decades of Change' in *Comparative Political Dynamics: Global Research Perspectives*, ed. D. Rustow and K. Erickson (N.Y.: HarperCollins) pp. 7–31.

Collier, D. and Mahon, J. (1995) 'Conceptual "Stretching" Revisited: Adapting Categories in Comparative Analysis', *American Political Science Review* (87) 845–55.

Colton, T. (1990) 'Perspectives on Civil–Military Relations in the Soviet Union' in *Soldiers and the Soviet State: Civil–Military Relations from Brezhnev to Gorbachev*, ed. T. Colton and T. Gustafson (Princeton, N.J.: Princeton University Press) pp. 3–43.

Comstock, W. *et al.* (1971) *Religion and Man: an Introduction* (N.Y.: Harper & Row).

Conover, P. and Searing, D. (1994) 'Democratic Citizenship and the Study of Political Socialization' in *Developing Democracy: Essays in Honour of J. F. P. Blondel*, ed. I. Budge and D. McKay (Thousand Oaks, Calif. and London: Sage) pp. 24–55.

Conradt, D. (1996) *The German Polity* (N.Y. and London: Longman), 6th edn.

Cook, M., Middlebrook, K. and Horcasitas, J. (eds) (1994) *The Politics of Economic Restructuring: State-Society Relations and Regime Change in Mexico* (San Diego, Calif.: Center for US-Mexican Studies).

Cornelius, W. (1996) 'Politics in Mexico' in *Comparative Politics Today: A World View*, ed. G. Almond and G. Bingham Powell (N.Y.: HarperCollins) pp. 492–555. 5th edn.

Coulson, A. (ed.) (1995) *Local Government in Eastern Europe* (Cheltenham and Brookfield, Vt.: Edward Elgar).

Cox, T. (1993) 'Democratization and the Growth of Pressure Groups in Soviet and Post-Soviet Politics' in *Pressure Groups*, ed. J. Richardson (Oxford and N.Y.: Oxford University Press) pp. 71–85.

Crawford, K. (1996) *East Central European Politics Today* (Manchester: Manchester University Press and N.Y.: St Martin's Press).

Crespi, I. (1989) *Public Opinion, Polls and Democracy* (Boulder, Colo. and Oxford: Westview).

Crick, B. (1992) *In Defence of Politics* (Harmondsworth: Penguin).

Cronin, T. (1989) *Direct Democracy: The Politics of Initiative, Referendum and Recall* (Cambridge, Mass. and London: Harvard University Press).

Crouch, H. (1996) *Government and Society in Malaysia* (Cornell, N.Y.: Cornell University Press).

Cumings, B. (1987) 'The Origins and Development of the Northeast Asian Political Economy: Industrial Sectors, Product Cycles and Political Consequences' in *The Political Economy of the New East Asian Industrialism*, ed. F. Deyo (N.Y.: Cornell University Press) pp. 44–83.

Curtice, J. and Jowell, R. (1997) 'Trust in the Political System' in *British Social Attitudes, the 14th Report: The End of Conservative Values?*, ed. R. Jowell *et al.* (Aldershot and Brookfield, Vermont: Ashgate) pp. 89–110.

Cutler, L. (1980) 'To Form a Government', *Foreign Affairs* (59) 126–43.

Dahl, R. (1957) 'The Concept of Power', *Behavioral Science* (2) 201–15.

Dahl, R. (1989) *Democracy and its Critics* (New Haven, Conn. and London: Yale University Press).

Dahl, R. (1991) *Modern Political Analysis* (Englewood Cliffs, N.J.: Prentice Hall).

Dahl, R. (1993) 'Pluralism' in *The Oxford Companion to Politics of the World*, ed. J. Krieger (N.Y. and Oxford: Oxford University Press) pp. 704–7.

Dalton, R. (1994) *The Green Rainbow: Environmental Groups in Western Europe* (New Haven, Conn. and London: Yale University Press).

Dalton, R. (1996) 'Political Cleavages, Issues and Electoral Change' in *Elections and Voting in Global Perspective*, ed. L. LeDuc, R. Niemi and P. Norris (Thousand Oaks, Calif. and London: Sage) pp. 319–42.

Dalton, R. and Kuechler, M. (1990) *Challenging the Political Order: New Social and Political Movements in Western Democracies* (Cambridge: Polity).

Dalziel, P. (1993) 'The Reserve Bank Act: Reflecting Changing Relationships between State and Economy in the Twentieth Century' in *State and Economy in New Zealand*, ed. B. Roper and C. Rudd (Auckland and Oxford: Oxford University Press) pp. 74–90.

Damgaard, E. (ed.) (1993) *Parliamentary Change in the Nordic Countries* (Oxford and N.Y.: Oxford University Press).

Danopoulos, C. (ed.) (1988) *Military Disengagement from Politics* (London and N.Y.: Routledge).

Danopoulos, C. (ed.) (1992) *From Military to Civilian Rule* (London and N.Y.: Routledge).

Davidson, R. (ed.) (1992) *The Postreform Congress* (N.Y.: St Martin's Press).

Davies, J. (1962) 'Toward a Theory of Revolution', *American Sociological Review* (27), 5–18.

Dawson, R., Prewitt, K. and Dawson, K. (1977) *Political Socialization* (Boston, Mass.: Little Brown).

De Villiers, B. (ed.) (1995) *Evaluating Federal Systems* (Dordrecht: Martinus Nijhoff).

Decalo, S. (1990) *Coups and Army Rule in Africa* (New Haven, Conn. and London: Yale University Press).

Deegan, H. (1998) *South Africa Reborn: Building a New Democracy* (Basingstoke: Taylor & Francis).

Dehousse, R. (1997) 'European Integration and the Nation-State' in *Developments in West European Politics*, ed. M. Rhodes, P. Heywood and V. Wright (London: Macmillan) pp. 37–56.

Dehousse, R. (1998) *The European Court of Justice* (London: Macmillan).

Dellenbrant, J. (1993) 'Parties and Party Systems in Eastern Europe' in *Developments in East European Politics*, ed. S. White, J. Batt and P. Lewis (London: Macmillan) pp. 147–62.

Dempsey, J. (1993) 'East European Voices' in *Developments in East European Politics*, ed. S. White, J. Batt and P. Lewis (London: Macmillan) pp. 280–8.

Denver, D. (1994) *Elections and Voting Behaviour in Britain* (Hemel Hempstead: Philip Allan) 2nd edn.

Derbyshire, J. and Derbyshire, I. (1996) *Political Systems of the World* (Oxford: Helicon).

Diamandouros, P. (1995) 'Conclusion' in *The Politics of Democratic Consolidation: Southern Europe in Comparative Perspective*, ed. R. Gunther, P. Diamandouros and H. Puhle (Baltimore, Md. and London: Johns Hopkins University Press) pp. 389–414.

Diamond, L. (1992) 'Economic Development and Democracy Reconsidered' in *Reexamining Democracy: Essays in Honor of Seymour Martin Lipset*, ed. G. Marks and L. Diamond (Thousand Oaks, Calif. and London: Sage) pp. 93–131.

Diamond, L. (1993) 'Introduction: Political Culture and Democracy' in *Political Culture and Democracy in Developing Countries*, ed. L. Diamond (Boulder, Colo. and London: Lynne Reinner) pp. 1–36.

Diamond, L. (1997) 'Democracy in the Americas', *Annals of the American Academy of Political and Social Sciences* (550) 12–41.

Diamond, L., Kirk-Greene, A. and Oyediran, O. (eds) (1997) *Transition Without End: Nigerian Politics and Civil Society under Babanginda* (Boulder, Colo. and London: Lynne Reinner).

Diamond, L., Linz, J. and Lipset, S. (eds) (1989) *Democracy in Developing Countries* (Boulder, Colo. and London: Lynne Reinner) 3 volumes.

Diamond, L., Linz, J. and Lipset, S. (1995) 'Introduction: What Makes For Democracy?' in *Politics in Developing Countries: Comparing Experiences with Democracy*, ed. L. Diamond, J. Linz and S. Lipset (Boulder, Colo. and London: Lynne Reinner) pp. 1–33.

Diamond, L. and Lipset, S. (1995) 'Legitimacy' in *The Encyclopaedia of Democracy*, ed. S. Lipset (London and N.Y.: Routledge) pp. 747–51.

Diamond, L. and Plattner, M. (eds) (1996) *The Global Resurgence of Democracy* (Baltimore, Md. and London: John Hopkins University Press) 2nd edn.

Dicey, A. (1959) *Introduction to the Study of the Law of the Constitution* (London: Macmillan) first pub. 1885.

Dion, D. (1998) 'Evidence and Inference in the Comparative Case Study', *Comparative Politics* (30) 127–45.

Di Palma, G. (1990) *To Craft Democracies: An Essay on Democratic Transitions* (Berkeley, Calif. and Oxford: University of California Press).

Dodge, L. and Raundalen, M. (eds) (1987) *War, Violence and Children in Uganda* (Oslo: Norwegian University Press).

Dogan, M. and Kazancigil, A. (eds) (1994) *Comparing Nations: Concepts, Strategies, Substance* (Cambridge, Mass. and Oxford: Blackwell).

Dogan, M. and Pelassy, D. (1990) *How to Compare Nations: Strategies in Comparative Politics* (Chatham, N.J.: Chatham House) 2nd ed.

Donnelly, C. (1992) 'Evolutionary Problems in the Soviet Armed Forces', *Survival* (34) 28–42.

Donovan, M. (1995) 'The Politics of Electoral Reform in Italy', *International Political Science Review* (16) 47–64.

Doran, C. and Babby, E. (eds) (1995) *Being and Becoming Canada* (Thousand Oaks, Calif. and London: Sage).

Dowding, K. (1995) *The Civil Service* (London and N.Y.: Routledge).

Downs, A. (1957) *An Economic Theory of Democracy* (N.Y.: Harper).

Downs, G., Roche, D. and Baroom P. (1996) 'Is the Good News About Compliance Good News About Cooperation?', *International Organization* (50) 379–406.

Dreyfus, F. (1990) 'The Conseil d'État' in *Developments in French Politics*, ed. P. Hall, J. Hayward and H. Machin (London: Macmillan) pp. 133–51.

Dreze, J. and Sen, A. (1989) *Hunger and Public Action* (Oxford and N.Y.: Clarendon Press).

Dryzek, J. (1990) *Discursive Democracy: Politics, Policy and Political Science* (Cambridge and N.Y.: Cambridge University Press).

Du Fresne, K. (1989) 'Lobbying New Zealand Style' in *New Zealand Politics in Perspective*, ed. H. Gold (Auckland: Longman Paul) pp. 312–19.

Duchacek, I. (1970) *Federalism: The Territorial Dimension of Politics* (N.Y.: Holt, Rinehart & Winston).

Duchacek, I. (1973) *Power Maps: The Comparative Politics of Constitutions* (Santa Barbara, Calif.: ABC Clio).

Duchacek, I. (1991) 'Constitutions/Constitutionalism' in *The Blackwell Encyclopaedia of Political Science*, ed. V. Bogdanor (Oxford and Cambridge, Mass.: Blackwell) pp. 142–4.

Dunleavy, P. (1997) 'The Constitution' in *Developments in British Politics 5*, ed. P. Dunleavy *et al.* (London: Macmillan and N.Y.: St Martin's) pp. 129–54.

Dunleavy, P. and O'Leary, B. (1987) *Theories of the Liberal Democratic State* (London: Macmillan).

Dunn, W. (1994) *Public Policy Analysis: An Introduction* (Englewood Cliffs, N.J.: Prentice Hall).

Duverger, M. (1954) *Political Parties* (London: Methuen).

Duverger, M. (1980) 'A New Political System Model: Semi-presidential Government', *European Journal of Political Research* (8) 165–87.

Dye, T. (1984) *Understanding Public Policy* (Englewood Cliffs, N.J.: Prentice Hall) 5th edn.

Easter, G. (1997) 'Preference for Presidentialism: Postcommunist Regime Change in Russia and the NIS', *World Politics* (49) 184–211.

Easton, D. (1965a) *A Framework for Political Analysis* (Englewood Cliffs, N.J.: Prentice-Hall).

Easton, D. (1965b) *A Systems Analysis of Political Life* (N.Y.: Wiley).

Eatwell, R. (1996) *Fascism: a History* (London: Chatto & Windus).

Eatwell, R. (ed.) (1997) *European Political Cultures: Conflict or Convergence?* (London and N.Y.: Routledge).

Eckstein, H. (1975) 'Case Study and Theory in Political Science' in *Handbook of Political Science, Vol. 7: Strategies of Inquiry*, ed. F. Greenstein and N. Polsby (Reading, Mass.: Addison-Wesley) pp. 79–137.

Edelman, M. (1964) *The Symbolic Uses of Politics* (Urbana, Ill.: University of Illinois Press).

Edelman, M. (1995) 'Israel' in *The Global Expansion of Judicial Power*, ed. C. Tate and T. Vallinder (N.Y. and London: New York University Press) pp. 403–16.

Eisenstadt, S. and Lemarchand, R. (eds) (1981) *Political Clientelism, Patronage and Development* (Thousand Oaks, Calif. and London: Sage).

Elazar, D. (1996) 'From Statism to Federalism: A Paradigm Shift', *International Political Science Review* (17) 417–30.

Elgie, R. (1995) *Political Leadership in Liberal Democracies* (London: Macmillan).

Elkit, J. and Roberts, N. (1996) 'A Category of its Own: Four PR Two-tier Compensatory Member Electoral Systems', *European Journal of Political Research* (30) 217–40.

Emy, M. and Hughes, O. (1991) *Australian Politics: Realities in Conflict* (South Melbourne: Macmillan).

Epstein, L. (1986) *Political Parties in the American Mold* (Madison, Wis.: University of Wisconsin Press).

Escobar, A. and Alvarez, S. (eds) (1992) *The Making of Social Movements in Latin America: Identity, Strategy and Democracy* (Boulder, Colo. and Oxford: Westview).

Esping-Andersen, G. (1996) 'After the Golden Age? Welfare State Dilemmas in a Global Economy' in *Welfare States in Transition: National Adaptations in Global Economies*, ed. G. Esping-Andersen (Thousand Oaks, Calif. and London: Sage) pp. 1–31.

Esposito, J. (1997) *Political Islam: Revolution, Radicalism or Reform?* (Boulder, Colo. and London: Lynne Reinner).

Evans, P. (1995) 'The Role of Theory in Comparative Politics: A Symposium' *World Politics* (48) 2–10.

Farcau, B. (1996) *The Transition to Democracy in Latin America: The Role of the Military* (Westport, Conn.: Praeger).

Farrell, D. (1997) *Comparing Electoral Systems* (Hemel Hempstead: Prentice Hall).

Fenno, R. (1978) *Home Style: House Members in their Districts* (Boston: Little Brown).

Fernando, J. and Heston, A. (1997) 'NGOs Between States, Markets and Civil Society', *Annals of the American Academy of Political and Social Sciences* (554) 8–20.

Fesler, J. and Kettl, D. (1996) *The Politics of the Administrative Process* (Chatham, N.J.: Chatham House).

Finer, S. (1974) *Comparative Government* (Harmondsworth: Penguin).

Finer, S. (1988) *The Man on Horseback: The Role of the Military in Politics* (Boulder, Colo.: Westview).

Finer, S. (1997) *The History of Government from the Earliest Times* (Oxford and N.Y.: Oxford University Press) three volumes.

Fiorina, M. (1981) *Retrospective Voting in American National Elections* (New Haven, Conn.: Yale University Press).

Fitzmaurice, J. (1991) *Austrian Politics and Society Today* (London: Macmillan).

Fitzmaurice, J. (1996) *The Politics of Belgium: A Unique Federalism* (London: Hurst).

Flammang, J. *et al.* (1990) *American Politics in a Changing World* (Pacific Grove, Calif.: Brooks/Cole).

Flanagan, S. and Reed, S. (1996) 'Politics in Japan' in *Comparative Politics Today: A World View*, ed. G. Almond and G. Bingham Powell (N.Y.: HarperCollins) pp. 326–79, 5th edn.

Flynn, N. and Strehl, F. (1996) *Public Sector Management in Europe* (Englewood Cliffs, N.J. and Hemel Hempstead: Prentice Hall).

Forsyth, M. (1989) *Federalism and Nationalism* (Leicester: Leicester University Press).

Fox, E. (1988) 'Media Politics in Latin America: An Overview' in *Media and Politics in Latin America: the Struggle for Democracy*, ed. E. Fox (Thousand Oaks, Calif. and London: Sage) pp. 6–35.

Frank, A. (1969) *Capitalism and Underdevelopment in Latin America* (N.Y.: Monthly Review Press).

Franklin, B. (1994) *Packaging and Politics: Political Communication in Britain's Media Democracy* (London: Edward Arnold and N.Y.: Routledge, Chapman & Hall).

Franklin, D. and Baun, M. (eds) (1995) *Political Culture and Constitutionalism: A Comparative Approach* (Armonk, N.Y. and London: M. E. Sharpe).

Franklin, M. (1992) 'The Decline of Cleavage Politics' in *Electoral Change: Responses to Evolving Social and Attitudinal Structures in Western Countries*, ed. M. Franklin, T. Mackie and H. Valen (Cambridge and N.Y.: Cambridge University Press) pp. 383–405.

Franklin, M. (1996) 'Electoral Participation' in *Elections and Voting in Global Perspective*, ed. L. LeDuc, R. Niemi and P. Norris (Thousand Oaks, Calif. and London: Sage) pp. 216–35.

Franklin, M., Mackie, T., Valen, H. *et al.* (1992) *Electoral Change: Responses to Evolving Social and Attitudinal Structures in Western Countries* (Cambridge and N.Y.: Cambridge University Press).

Fried, R. (1990) *Nightmare in Red: The McCarthy Era in Perspective* (N.Y. and Oxford: Oxford University Press).

Friedrich, C. (1937) *Constitutional Government and Politics* (N.Y.: Harper).

Fukuyama, F. (1989) 'The End of History?', *National Interest* (16) 3–18.

Fukuyama, F. (1995) *Trust* (N.Y. and London: Free Press).

Furley, O. (1995) Child Soldiers and Youths in African Conflicts: International Reactions (Coventry University: Africa Studies Centre).

Gabriel, O. (1996) 'Political Culture in East Germany After Unification', *ECPR News* (8) 6–9.

Galbraith, J. (1992) *The Culture of Contentment* (London: Sinclair-Stevenson).

Gallagher, M. (1997) 'Electoral Systems and Voting Behaviour' in *Developments in West European Politics*, ed. M. Rhodes, P. Heywood and V. Wright (London: Macmillan) pp. 114–30.

Gallagher, M., Laver, M. and Mair, P. (1995) *Representative Government in Modern Europe* (N.Y.: McGraw-Hill) 2nd edn.

Gallagher, M. and Uleri, P. (eds) (1996) *The Referendum Experience in Europe* (London: Macmillan).

Gamble, A. and Payne, A. (1996a) 'The New Regionalism' in *Regionalism and World Order*, ed. A. Gamble and A. Payne (London: Macmillan) pp. 247–64.

Gamble, A. and Payne, A. (eds) (1996) *Regionalism and World Order* (London: Macmillan).

Geertz, C. (1993) 'Thick Description: Toward an Interpretative Theory of Culture' in *Interpretation of Cultures*, ed. C. Geertz (London: Fontana) pp. 1–33, first pub. 1973.

Gerth, H. and Mills, C. (1948) *From Max Weber* (London: Routledge & Kegan Paul).

Gibson, J. and Hanson, P. (eds) (1996) *Transformation from Below: Local Power and the Political Economy of Postcommunist Transitions* (Aldershot and Brookfield, Vt.: Edward Elgar).

Gilbert, P. (1995) *Terrorism, Security and Nationality* (London and N.Y.: Routledge).

Gilbert, R. (1998) *The Mortal Presidency: Illness and Anguish in the White House* (N.Y.: Fordham University Press).

Gills, B. (1997) 'Whither Democracy? Globalization and the "New Hellenism"' in *Globalization and the South*, ed. C. Thomas and P. Wilkin (London: Macmillan and N.Y.: St Martin's Press) pp. 60–75.

Gills, B., Rocamora, J. and Wilson, R. (eds) (1993) *Low Intensity Democracy: Political Power in the New World Order* (Boulder, Colo. and London: Pluto).

Gilmour, I. (1970) *The Body Politic* (London: Hutchinson).

Ginsberg, B. (1982) *The Consequences of Consent* (Reading, Mass.: Addison Wesley).

Giol, J. (1990) 'By Consociationalism to a Majoritarian Parliamentary System: The Rise and Decline of the Spanish Cortes' in *Parliament and Democratic Consolidation in Southern Europe*, ed. U. Liebert and M. Cotta (London: Pinter) pp. 92–131.

Gladden, E. (1972) *A History of Public Administration* (London: Frank Cass) Vol. 1.

Goban-Klas, T. and Sasinka-Klas, T. (1992) 'From Closed to Open Communication Systems' in *Democracy and Civil Society in Eastern Europe*, ed. P. Lewis (London: Macmillan and N.Y.: St Martin's Presss) pp. 76–90.

Goldsmith, M. and Klausen, K. (eds) (1997) *European Integration and Local Government* (Aldershot and Brookfield, Vt.: Edward Elgar).

Goldstone, J. (1991) 'An Analytical Framework' in *Revolutions of the Later Twentieth Century*, ed. J. Goldstone, T. Gurr and F. Moshiri (Boulder, Colorado and Oxford: Westview) pp. 37–51.

Goldstone, J., Gurr, J. and Moshiri, F. (eds) (1991) *Revolutions of the Later Twentieth Century* (Boulder, Colorado and Oxford: Westview).

Gould, R. and Jackson, C. (1995) *A Guide for Election Observers* (Aldershot and Brookfield, Vt.: Dartmouth).

Green, D. and Shapiro, I. (1994) *Pathologies of Rational Choice Theories* (New Haven, Conn. and London: Yale University Press).

Greenberg, D. *et al.* (eds) (1993) *Constitutionalism and Democracy: Transitions in the Contemporary World* (N.Y. and Oxford: Oxford University Press).

Grofman, B. (1996) 'Political Economy: Downsian Perspectives' in *A New Handbook of Political Science*, ed. R. Goodin and H. Klingemann (Oxford and N.Y.: Oxford University Press) pp. 691–701.

Grugel, J. and Hout, W. (1998) 'Globalization, Regionalism and the State in the Semi-periphery' in *Regionalism across the North–South Divide: State Strategies in the Semi-periphery*, ed. J. Grugel and W. Hout (London and N.Y.: Routledge).

Guehenno, J.-M. (1995) *The End of the Nation-State* (Minneapolis, Mn. and London: University of Minnesota Press).

Gundle, S. and Parker, S. (eds) (1996) *The New Italian Republic: From the Fall of the Berlin Wall to Berlusconi* (London and N.Y.: Routledge).

Gurr, T. (1980) *Why Men Rebel* (Princeton, N.J.: Princeton University Press).

Hadenius, A. (ed.) (1997) *Democracy's Victory and Crisis* (N.Y. and Cambridge: Cambridge University Press).

Hall, J. (ed.) (1995) *Civil Society: Theory, History, Comparison* (Cambridge: Polity).

Hall, P. and Ikenberry, G. (1989) *The State* (Milton Keynes: Open University Press).

Hames, T. (1994) 'The Changing Media' in *Developments in American Politics 2*, ed. G. Peele *et al.* (London: Macmillan) pp. 335–47.

Hannay, D. (1996) 'The UN: Mission Impossible', *Prospect* (February) 75–9.

Hansen, T. (1993) 'Intermediate-Level Reforms and the Development of the Norwegian Welfare State' in *The Rise of Meso Government in Europe*, ed. L. Sharpe (Thousand Oaks, Calif. and London: Sage) pp. 154–82.

Harrison, M. (1984) *Corporatism and the Welfare State* (Aldershot: Gower).

Harriss, J. (1995) 'A Time of Troubles: Problems of Humanitarian Intervention in the 1990s' in *The Politics of Humanitarian Intervention*, ed. J. Harriss (London and N.Y.: Pinter) pp. 1–15.

Harrop, M. (1987) 'Voters' in *The Media in British Politics*, ed. J. Seaton and B. Pimlott (Aldershot: Gower) pp. 45–63.

Harrop, M. (1990) 'Political Marketing' *Parliamentary Affairs* (43) 277–91.

Harrop, M. (ed.) (1992) *Power and Policy in Liberal Democracies* (Cambridge and N.Y.: Cambridge University Press).

Harrop, M. and Miller, W. (1987) *Elections and Voters: A Comparative Introduction* (London: Macmillan).

Haugerud, A. (1995) *The Culture of Politics in Modern Kenya* (Cambridge and N.Y.: Cambridge University Press).

Havel, V. (1985) *The Power of the Powerless* (London: Hutchinson Education).

Hayek, F. (1960) *The Constitution of Liberty* (Chicago: University of Chicago Press).

Haynes, J. (1993) *Religion in Third World Politics* (Buckingham and Philadelphia, Pa.: Open University Press).

Haynes, J. (1996) *Religion and Politics in Africa* (London and Atlantic Highlands, N.J.: Zed Books).

Hazan, R. (1996) 'Presidential Parliamentarism: Direct Popular Election of the Prime Minister, Israel's new Electoral and Political System', *Electoral Studies* (15) 21–37.

Hazan, R. (1997a) 'The 1996 Election in Israel: Adopting Party Primaries', *Electoral Studies* (16) 95–102.

Hazan, R. (1997b) 'Legislative–Executive Relations in an Era of Accelerated Reform: Reshaping Government in Israel', *Legislative Studies Quarterly* (22) 329–50.

Heady, F. (1996) *Public Administration: A Comparative Perspective* (N.Y.: Marcel Dekker).

Heald, A. (1988) 'Merchandising Ideas: Continent to Community', *The Entrepreneurial Economy Review* (7) 13–6.

Heclo, H. (1974) *Modern Social Policies in Britain and Sweden* (New Haven, Conn.: Yale University Press).

Heclo, H. (1978) 'Issue Networks and the Executive Establishment' in *The New American Political System*, ed. A. King (Washington, D.C.: American Enterprise Institute) pp. 87–124.

Heidenheimer, A., Heclo, H. and Adams, C. (1990) *Comparative Public Policy: The Politics of Social Choice in Europe and America* (London: Macmillan).

Held, D. (1996) *Models of Democracy* (Cambridge: Polity) 2nd edn.

Henkin, L. (1968) *How Nations Behave: Law and Policy* (London: Pall Mall).

Henshel, R. (1990) *Thinking About Social Problems* (N.Y.: Harcourt Brace Jovanovich).

Hernnson, P. (1994) 'American Political Parties: Growth and Change' in *Developments in American Politics 2*, ed. G. Peele *et al.* (London: Macmillan) pp. 67–84.

Hesse, J. and Wright, V. (eds) (1996) *Federalizing Europe? The Costs, Benefits and Preconditions of Federal Political Systems* (Oxford and N.Y.: Oxford University Press).

Heywood, A. (1998) *Political Ideologies* (London: Macmillan), 2nd edn.

Heywood, P. (1995) *The Government and Politics of Spain* (London: Macmillan).

Heywood, P. and Wright, V. (1997) 'Executives, Bureaucracies and Decision-making' in *Developments in West European Politics*, (ed.) M. Rhodes, P. Heywood and V. Wright (London: Macmillan) pp. 75–94.

Hirst, P. and Thompson, G. (1996) *Globalization in Question: The International Economy and the Possibilities of Governance* (Oxford and Cambridge, Mass.: Blackwell).

Hobsbawn, E. (1990) *Nations and Nationalism Since 1780* (Cambridge and N.Y.: Cambridge University Press).

Hodder-Williams, R. (1996) *Judges and Politics in the Contemporary Age* (London: Bowerdean).

Hoetjes, B. (1993) 'The European Tradition of Federalism: The Protestant Dimension' in *Comparative Federalism and Federation: Competing Traditions and Future Directions*, ed. M. Burgess and A. Gagnon (Hemel Hempstead: Harvester Wheatsheaf) pp. 117–37.

Hoffman, S. (1995) 'The Politics and Ethics of Military Intervention', *Survival* (37) 29–51.

Hogwood, B. and Gunn, L. (1984) *Policy Analysis for the Real World* (Oxford: Oxford University Press).

Holland, K. (1991) 'Introduction' in *Judicial Activism in Comparative Perspective*, ed. K. Holland (London: Macmillan) pp. 1–11.

Holland, R. (1986) 'Statistics and Causal Inference', *Journal of the American Statistical Association* (81) 945–60.

Holmberg, S. (1994) 'Party Identification Compared Across the Atlantic' in *Elections at Home and Abroad: Essays in Honor of Warren E. Miller*, ed. K. Jennings and T. Mann (Ann Arbor, Mich.: University of Michigan Press) pp. 93–122.

Holmes, L. (1997) *Postcommunism: an Introduction* (Cambridge: Polity).

Holmes, S. (1996) 'Cultural Legacies or State Collapse? Probing the Postcommunist Dilemma' in *Postcommunism: Four Perspectives*, (ed.) M. Mandelbaum (N.Y.: Council on Foreign Relations) pp. 22–76.

Holmstrom, B. (1995) 'Sweden' in *The Global Expansion of Judicial Power*, ed. C. Tate and T. Vallinder (N.Y. and London: New York University Press) pp. 345–68.

Hood, C. (1996) 'Exploring Variations in Public Management Reform in the 1990s' in *Civil Service Systems in Comparative Perspective*, ed. H. Bekke, J. Perry and T. Toonen (Bloomington, Ind.: Indiana University Press) pp. 268–87.

Hoogvelt, A. (1997) *Globalization and the Postcolonial World* (London: Macmillan).

Horowitz, D. (1996) 'Comparing Democratic Systems' in *The Global Resurgence of Democracy*, ed. L. Diamond and M. Plattner (Baltimore, Md. and London: Johns Hopkins University Press) pp. 143–9.

Horrie, C. and Chippindale, P. (1990) *What is Islam?* (London: W. H. Allen).

Horton, C. (1995) *Policing Policy in France* (London: Policy Studies Institute).

Howard, A. (ed.) (1993) *Constitution-making in Eastern Europe* (Washington, D.C.: Woodrow Wilson Center Press).

Howard, A. (1993) 'How Ideas Travel: Rights at Home and Abroad' in *Constitution-Making in Eastern Europe*, ed. A. Howard (Washington, D.C.: Woodrow Wilson Center Press) pp. 9–20.

Howarth, D. (1995) 'Discourse Theory' in *Theory and Methods in Political Science*, ed. D. Marsh and G. Stoker (London: Macmillan) pp. 115–33.

Hrebenar, R. and Scott, R. (1990) *Interest Group Politics in America* (Englewood Cliffs, N.J.: Prentice Hall).

Hughes, O. (1994) *Public Management and Administration: An Introduction* (London: Macmillan).

Hunter, W. (1997) 'Continuity or Change? Civil–Military Relations in Democratic Argentina, Chile and Peru', *Political Science Quarterly* (112) 453–75.

Huntington, S. (1957) *The Soldier and the State: The Theory and Practice of Civil–Military Relations* (Cambridge, Mass.: Harvard University Press).

Huntington, S. (1991) *The Third Wave: Democratization in the Late Twentieth Century* (Norman, Okla. and London: University of Oklahoma Press).

Huntington, S. (1993) 'Clash of Civilizations', *Foreign Affairs* (72) 22–49.

Huntington, S. (1996) *The Clash of Civilizations and the Making of World Order* (N.Y.: Simon & Schuster).

Huntington, S. and Nelson, J. (1976) *No Easy Choices: Political Participation in Developing Countries* (Cambridge, Mass.: Harvard University Press).

Hurrell, A. (1995) 'Explaining the Resurgence of Regionalism in World Politics', *Review of International Studies* (21) 331–58.

Hyden, G. (1997) 'Democratization and Administration' in *Democracy's Victory and Crisis*, ed. A. Hadenius (Cambridge and N.Y.: Cambridge University Press) pp. 242–62.

Ignati, P. (1992) 'The Silent Counter-revolution: Hypotheses on the Emergence of Extreme Right-wing Parties in Europe', *European Journal of Political Research* (22) 3–35.

Inglehart, R. (1971) 'The Silent Revolution in Europe: Inter-generational Change in Post-industrial Societies', *American Political Science Review* (65) 991–1017.

Inglehart, R. (1988) 'The Renaissance of Political Culture', *American Political Science Review* (82) 1203–30.

Inglehart, R. (1990) *Culture Shift in Advanced Industrial Society* (Princeton, N.J.: Princeton University Press).

Inglehart, R. (1997) *Modernization and Postmodernization: Cultural, Economic and Social Change in 43 Societies* (Princeton. N.J. and London: Princeton University Press).

Inkeles, A. (1990) 'On Measuring Democracy', *Studies in Comparative International Development* (25) 3–6.

International Labour Office (1997) *Labour Report 1997* (Geneva: International Labour Organisation).

Jackson, J. (1996) 'Political Methodology: An Overview' in *A New Handbook of Political Science*, ed. R. Goodin and H. Klingemann (Oxford and N.Y.: Oxford University Press) pp. 714–48.

Jackson, J. (1998) *The World Trade Organization* (Herndon, Va. and London: Cassell).

Jackson, R. (1989) *Quasi-states: Sovereignty, International Relations and the Third World* (Cambridge and N.Y.: Cambridge University Press).

Jackson, R. and Rosberg, C. (1982) *Personal Rule in Black Africa: Prince, Autocrat, Prophet, Tyrant* (Berkeley, Calif.: University of California Press).

Jacobs, F. and Corbett, R. (1992) *The European Parliament* (London and N.Y.: Longman).

Jacobsen, A. (1994) 'Transitional Constitutions' in *Constitutionalism, Identity, Difference and Legitimacy: Theoretical Perspectives*, ed. M. Rosenberg (Durham, N.C. and London: Duke University Press) pp. 413–22.

Jacobson, H. (1985) *Networks of Interdependence: International Organizations and the Global System* (N.Y.: Alfred Knopf).

Jaensch, D. (1992) *The Politics of Australia* (South Melbourne: Macmillan).

Jacquette, J. (1997) 'Women in Power: From Tokenism to Critical Mass', *Foreign Policy* (108) 23–36.

Janoski, T. and Hicks, A. (eds.) (1994) *The Comparative Political Economy of the Welfare State* (Cambridge and N.Y.: Cambridge University Press).

Jayanntha, D. (1991) *Electoral Allegiance in Sri Lanka* (Cambridge and N.Y.: Cambridge University Press).

Johnson, C. (1987) *Japan: Who Governs? The Rise of the Developmental State* (N.Y. and London: Norton).

Johnson, R. and Schlemmer, L. (eds) (1996) *Launching Democracy in South Africa: The First Open Election, April*

1994 (New Haven, Conn. and London: Yale University Press).

Jones, B. (1993) 'Sweden' in *Local Government in Liberal Democracies: An Introductory Survey*, ed. J. Chandler (London and N.Y.: Routledge) pp. 118–37.

Jones, B. and Keating, M. (eds) (1995) *The European Union and the Regions* (Oxford and N.Y.: Oxford University Press).

Jones, C. (1994) *The Presidency in a Separated System* (Washington, D.C.: The Brookings Institution).

Jones, G. (ed.) (1991) *West European Prime Ministers* (London: Frank Cass).

Jones, M. (1995a) *Electoral Laws and the Survival of Presidential Democracies* (Notre Dame, Ind.: University of Notre Dame Press).

Jones, M. (1995b) 'A Guide to the Electoral Systems of the Americas', *Electoral Studies* (14) 5–21.

Jones, P. (1994) *Rights* (London: Macmillan and N.Y.: St Martin's Press).

Joseph, R. (ed.) (1998) *State, Conflict and Democracy in Africa* (Boulder, Colorado and London: Lynne Reinner).

Juegensmeyer, M. (1993) *The New Cold War: Religious Nationalism Confronts the Secular State* (Berkeley, Calif. and Oxford: University of California Press).

Junnosuke, M. (1995) *Contemporary Politics in Japan* (Berkeley, Calif. and London: University of California Press).

Kahler, M. (1995) *International Institutions and the Political Economy of Integration* (Princeton: Princeton University Press).

Karasimeonov, G. (1996) 'The Legislature in Post-Communist Bulgaria' in *The New Parliaments of Central and Eastern Europe*, ed. D. Olson and P. Norton (London: Frank Cass) pp. 40–59.

Karl, T. (1991) 'Dilemmas of Democratization in Latin America' in *Comparative Political Dynamics: Global Research Perspectives*, ed. D. Rustow and K. Erickson (N.Y.: HarperCollins) pp. 163–91.

Karvonen, L. and Selle, P. (eds) (1995) *Women in Nordic Countries: Closing the Gap* (Aldershot: Dartmouth).

Kashfir, N. (1976) *The Shrinking Political Arena: Participation and Ethnicity in African Politics with a Case-Study of Uganda* (Berkeley, Calif. and London: University of California Press).

Kashyap, S. (1979) 'Committees in the Indian Lok Sabha' in *Committees in Legislatures: A Comparative Perspective*, ed. J. Lees and M. Shaw (Durham, N.C. and London: Duke University Press) pp. 288–326.

Katz, R. (1996) 'Party Organizations and Finance' in *Elections and Voting in Global Perspective*, ed. L. LeDuc, R. Niemi and P. Norris (Thousand Oaks, Calif. and London: Sage) pp. 107–33.

Katz, R. and Mair, P. (eds) (1994) *How Parties Organize: Change and Adaptation in Party Organization in Western Democracies* (Thousand Oaks, Calif. and London: Sage).

Katz, R. and Mair, P. (1995) 'Changing Models of Party Organization and Party Democracy: The Emergence of the Cartel Party', *Party Politics* (1) 5–28.

Katzenstein, P. (1996) 'Regionalism in a Comparative Perspective', *Cooperation and Conflict* (31) 123–60.

Kazancigil, A. (1994) 'The Deviant Case in Comparative Analysis: High Stateness in Comparative Analysis' in *Comparing Nations: Concepts, Strategies, Substance*, ed. M. Dogan and A. Kazancigil (Cambridge, Mass. and Oxford: Blackwell) pp. 213–38.

Keating, M. (1991) *Comparative Urban Politics: Power and the City in the United States, Canada, Britain and France* (Aldershot and Brookfield, Vt.: Edward Elgar).

Keating, M. (1993) *The Politics of Modern Europe* (Aldershot and Brookfield, Vt.: Edward Elgar).

Keddie, N. (1991) 'The Revolt of Islam and its Roots' in *Comparative Political Dynamics: Global Research Perspectives*, ed. D. Rustow and K. Erickson (N.Y.: HarperCollins) pp. 292–308.

Keeler, J. and Schain, M. (1997) 'Institutions, Political Poker and Regime Evolution in France' in *Presidential Institutions and Democratic Politics: Comparing Regional and National Contexts*, ed. K. von Mettenheim (Baltimore, Md. and London: Johns Hopkins University Press) pp. 84–108.

Kegley, C. and Wittkopf, E. (1997) *World Politics: Trend and Transformation* (London: Macmillan and N.Y.: St Martin's Press) 6th edn.

Kellas, J. (1991) *The Politics of Nationalism and Ethnicity* (London: Macmillan).

Keman, H. (ed.) (1993) *Comparative Politics: New Directions in Theory and Method* (Amsterdam: VU University Press).

Keohane, R. (1994) 'International Institutions: Two Approaches' in *International Organization: A Reader*, ed. F. Kratochwil and E. Mansfield (N.Y.: HarperCollins) pp. 44–60.

Kesselmann, M., Krieger, J. and Allen, C. (1987) *European Politics in Transition* (Lexington, Mass.: D.C. Heath).

Kettl, D. (1986) *Leadership at the Fed* (New Haven, Conn. and London: Yale University Press).

Khaidagala, G. (1995) 'State Collapse and Reconstruction in Uganda' in *Collapsed States: The Disintegration and Restoration of Political Authority*, ed. I. Zartman (Boulder, Colo. and London: Lynne Reinner) pp. 33–48.

Khatani, H. (1992) 'The Preservation of Civilian Rule in Saudi Arabia' in *Civilian Rule in the Developing World: Democracy on the March?*, ed. C. Danopoulos (Boulder, Colo. and Oxford: Westview) pp. 53–72.

Khong, Y. (1992) *Analogies at War: Korea, Munich, Dien Bien Phu and the Vietnam Decisions of 1965* (Princeton: Princeton University Press).

King, A. (1981) 'The Rise of the Career Politician in Britain – and its Consequences', *British Journal of Political Science* (11) 249–85.

King, A. (1994a) '"Chief Executives" in Western Europe' in *Developing Democracy: Comparative Research in Honour of J. F. P. Blondel*, ed. I. Budge and D. McKay (Thousand Oaks, Calif. and London: Sage) pp. 150–64.

King, A. (1994b) 'Ministerial Autonomy in Britain' in *Cabinet Ministers and Parliamentary Government*, ed. M. Laver and K. Shepsle (Cambridge and N.Y.: Cambridge University Press) pp. 203–25.

King, A. (1997) *Running Scared: Why American Politicians Campaign Too Much and Govern Too Little* (N.Y. and London: Free Press).

King, G., Keohane, R. and Verba, S. (1994) *Designing Social Inquiry: Scientific Inference in Qualitative Research* (Princeton: Princeton University Press).

Kingdon, J. (1984) *Agendas, Alternatives and Public Policy* (Boston, Mass.: Little Brown).

Kingsley, J. (1964) 'Bureaucracy and Political Development, with Particular Reference to Nigeria' in *Bureaucracy and Political Development*, ed. J. LaPalombara (Princeton, N.J.: Princeton University Press) pp. 301–17.

Kircheimer, O. (1966) 'The Transformation of the Western European Party Systems' in *Political Parties and Political Development*, ed. J. LaPalombara and M. Weiner (Princeton, N.J.: Princeton University Press) pp. 177–200.

Kirkpatrick, J. (1993) 'The Modernizing Imperative', *Foreign Affairs* (72) 22–27.

Klapper, J. (1960) *The Effects of Mass Communication* (N.Y. and London: Free Press).

Knox, P. and Taylor, P. (eds) (1995) *World Cities in a World-System* (Cambridge and N.Y.: Cambridge University Press).

Knutsen, O. (1990) 'Materialist and Postmaterialist Values and Structures in the Nordic Countries', *Comparative Politics* (23) 85–101.

Kobach, K. (1997) 'Direct Democracy and Swiss Isolationism', *West European Politics* (20) 185–211.

Kohn, R. (1997) 'How Democracies Control the Military', *Journal of Democracy* (8) 141–53.

Kommers, D. (1994) 'The Federal Constitutional Court in the German Political System', *Comparative Political Studies* (26) 470–91.

Konrad, G. (1984) *Antipolitics: An Essay* (N.Y. and London: Harcourt, Brace, Jovanovich).

Kopecki, P. (1995) 'Developing Party Organizations in East-Central Europe: What Type of Party is Likely to Emerge?', *Party Politics* (1) 515–34.

Krasner, S. (1994) 'International Political Economy: Abiding Discord', *Review of International Political Economy* (1) 13–20.

Kratochwil, F. and Mansfield, E. (eds) (1994) *International Organization: A Reader* (N.Y.: HarperCollins).

Kratochwil, F. and Ruggie, J. (1994) 'International Organization: A State of the Art or an Art of the State?' in *International Organization: A Reader*, ed. F. Kratochwil and E. Mansfield (N.Y.: HarperCollins) pp. 4–19.

Kresl, P. and Gappert, G. (eds) (1995) *North American Cities and the Global Economy: Challenges and Opportunities* (Thousand Oaks, Calif. and London: Sage).

Kudrle, R. and Marmor, T. (1981) 'The Development of Welfare States in Europe and America' in *The Development of Welfare States in Europe and America*, ed. P. Flora and A. Heidenheimer (New Brunswick, N.J. and London: Transaction Books) pp. 187–236.

Kuhn T. (1970) *The Structure of Scientific Revolutions* (Chicago: Univesity of Chicago Press).

Kuhn, T. (1997) 'The Media and Politics' in *Developments in West European Politics*, ed. M. Rhodes, P. Heywood and V. Wright (London: Macmillan) pp. 263–80.

Kumar, K. (ed.) (1997) *Rebuilding Societies after Civil War: Critical Roles for International Assistance* (Boulder, Colorado and London: Lynne Reinner).

Kumar, K. (ed.) (1998) *Postconflict Elections, Democratization and International Assistance* (Boulder, Colorado and London: Lynne Reinner).

Kux, S. (1996) 'From the USSR to the Commonwealth of Independent States: Confederation or Civilized Discourse?' in *Federalizing Europe? The Costs, Benefits and Preconditions of Federal Political Systems*, ed. J. Hesse and V. Wright (Oxford and N.Y.: Oxford University Press) pp. 325–58.

L'Etang, H. (1980) *Fit to Lead?* (London: Heinemann).

Lacqueur, W. (1989) *The Long Road to Freedom* (N.Y.: Scribner's).

Laffin, M. (1994) 'Reinventing the Federal Government' in *Developments in American Politics 2*, ed. G. Peele *et al.* (London: Macmillan) pp. 172–99.

Landes, R. (1995) *The Canadian Polity: A Comparative Introduction* (Scarborough, Ontario: Prentice-Hall Canada).

LaPalombara, J. (1987) *Democracy Italian Style* (New Haven, Conn. and London: Yale University Press).

Laponce, J. (1994) 'Democracy and Incumbency: The Canadian Case' in *The Victorious Incumbent: A Threat to Democracy?*, ed. A. Somit *et al.* (Aldershot and Brookfield, Vt.: Dartmouth) pp. 122–49.

Laundy, P. (1989) *Parliaments in the Modern World* (Aldershot and Brookfield, Vt.: Gower).

Laver, M. (1983) *Invitation to Politics* (Oxford: Martin Robertson).

Laver, M. and Hunt, W. (1992) *Policy and Party Competition* (London and N.Y.: Routledge).

Laver, M. and Shepsle, K. (eds) (1994) *Cabinet Ministers and Parliamentary Government* (Cambridge and N.Y.: Cambridge University Press).

Lawson, C. (1997) 'Mexico's New Politics: The Elections of 1997', *Journal of Democracy* (8) 13–27.

Lawson, K. (ed.) (1994) *How Political Parties Work: Perspectives from Within* (Westport, Conn. and London: Praeger).

LeDuc, L., Niemi, R. and Norris, P. (eds) (1996) *Elections and Voting in Global Perspective* (Thousand Oaks, Calif. and London: Sage).

LeDuc, L., Niemi, R. and Norris, P. (1996) 'Introduction' in *Elections and Voting in Global Perspective*, ed. L. LeDuc, R. Niemi and P. Norris (Thousand Oaks, Calif. and London: Sage) pp. 1–48.

Lemarchand, R. (1995) 'African Transitions to Democracy' in *The Encyclopaedia of Democracy*, ed. S. Lipset (London and N.Y.: Routledge) pp. 40–47.

Lenin, V. (1963) *What Is To Be Done?* (Oxford: Clarendon Press) first pub. 1902.

Lesch, A. (1996) 'Politics in Egypt' in *Comparative Politics Today: A World View*, ed. G. Almond and G. Bingham Powell (N.Y.: HarperCollins) pp. 608–67, 5th edn.

Levine, S. and Roberts, N. (1994) 'The New Zealand Electoral Referendum and General Election of 1993', *Electoral Studies* (13) 240–53.

Lewis, P. (1996) 'Introduction and Theoretical Overview' in *Party Structure and Organization in East-Central Europe*, ed. P. Lewis (Aldershot and Brookfield, Vt.: Edward Elgar) pp. 1–19.

Lewis, P. (ed.) (1996) *Party Structure and Organization in East-Central Europe* (Aldershot and Brookfield, Vt.: Edward Elgar).

Lewis-Beck, M. (1995) *Data Analysis: An Introduction* (Thousand Oaks, Calif. and London: Sage).

Leys, C. (1996) *The Rise and Fall of Development Theory* (Bloomington, Ind.: Indiana University Press and London: James Currey).

Liebert, U. (1990) 'Parliament in the Consolidation of Democracy: a Comparative Assessment of Southern European Experiences' in *Parliament and Democratic Consolidation in Southern Europe*, ed. U. Liebert and M. Cotta (London: Pinter) pp. 249–272.

Liebert, U. and Cotta, M. (eds) (1990) *Parliament and Democratic Consolidation in Southern Europe* (London: Pinter).

Lieberthal, K. (1995) *Governing China: From Revolution Through Reform* (N.Y. and London: Norton).

Liebman, C. (1993) 'Religion and Democracy in Israel' in *Israeli Democracy Under Stress*, ed. E. Sprinzak and L. Diamond (Boulder, Colo. and London: Lynne Reinner) pp. 273–92.

Lijphart, A. (1971) 'Comparative Politics and the Comparative Method', *American Political Science Review* (65) 682–93.

Lijphart, A. (1977) *Democracy in Plural Societies: A Comparative Exploration* (Berkeley, Calif.: University of California Press).

Lijphart, A. (1984) *Democracies: Patterns of Majoritarian and Consensual Government in Twenty-One Countries* (New Haven, Conn. and London: Yale University Press).

Lijphart, A. (ed.) (1992) *Parliamentary versus Presidential Government* (Oxford and N.Y.: Oxford University Press).

Lijphart, A. (1994) *Electoral Systems and Party Systems* (New Haven, Conn. and London: Yale University Press).

Lijphart, A. (1997) 'Unequal Participation: Democracy's Unresolved Dilemma', *American Political Science Review* (91) 1–14.

Lijphart, A. and Crepaz, M. (1991) 'Corporatism and Consensus Democracy in Eighteen Countries: Conceptual and Empirical Linkages', *British Journal of Political Science* (21) 235–46.

Lindblom, C. (1959) 'The Science of Muddling Through', *Public Administration* (19) 78–88.

Lindblom, C. (1977) *Politics and Markets* (N.Y.: Basic Books).

Lindblom, C. (1979) 'Still Muddling, Not Yet Through', *Public Administration Review* (39) 517–26.

Lindblom, C. (1990) *Inquiry and Change: The Troubled Attempt to Understand and Shape Society* (New Haven, Conn. and London: Yale University Press).

Linz, J. (1970) 'An Authoritarian Regime: The Case of Spain' in *Mass Politics: Studies in Political Sociology*, ed. E. Allardt and S. Rokkan (N.Y. and London: Free Press) pp. 251–83.

Linz, J. (1978) 'Crisis, Breakdown and Re-equilibration' in *The Breakdown of Democratic Regimes*, ed. J. Linz and A. Stepan (Baltimore, Md. and London: Johns Hopkins University Press) pp. 1–124.

Linz, J. (1990) 'The Perils of Presidentialism', *Journal of Democracy* (1) 51–69.

Linz, J. and Stepan, A. (eds.) (1978) *The Breakdown of Democratic Regimes* (Baltimore, Md. and London: Johns Hopkins University Press).

Linz, J. and Stepan, A. (1996) *Problems of Democratic Transition and Consolidation: Southern Europe, South America and Postcommunist Europe* (Baltimore, Md. and London: Johns Hopkins University Press).

Linz, J. and Valenzuela, A. (eds) (1994) *The Failure of Presidential Democracy* (Baltimore, Md.: Johns Hopkins University Press).

Lippman, W. (1922) *Public Opinion* (London: Allen & Unwin).

Lipset, S. (1983) *Political Man* (N.Y.: Basic Books), first pub. 1960.

Lipset, S. (1990) *Continental Divide: The Values and Institutions of the United States and Canada* (N.Y. and London: Routledge).

Lipset, S. (1994) 'Binary Comparisons: American Exceptionalism – Japanese Uniqueness' in *Comparing Nations: Concepts, Strategies, Substance*, ed. M. Dogan and A. Kazancigil (Cambridge, Mass. and Oxford: Blackwell) pp. 153–212.

Lipset, S. and Rokkan, S. (1967) 'Cleavage Structures, Party Systems and Voter Alignments' in *Party Systems and Voter Alignments*, ed. S. Lipset and S. Rokkan (N.Y. and London: Free Press) pp. 1–65.

Little, W. (1997) 'Democratization in Latin America 1980–95' in *Democratization*, ed. D. Potter *et al.* (Cambridge: Polity) pp. 174–94.

Loader, B. (1997) *The Governance of Cyberspace* (London and N.Y.: Routledge).

Lockard, D. (1976) *The Perverted Priorities of American Politics* (N.Y.: Macmillan).

Loewenberg, G., Patterson, S. and Jewell, M. (eds) (1985) *Handbook of Legislative Research* (Cambridge, Mass.: Harvard University Press).

Longley, L. and Davidson, R. (eds) (1998) *The New Roles of Parliamentary Committees* (London: Frank Cass).

Loughlin, J. and Mazey, S. (eds) (1995) *The End of the French Unitary State?* (London: Frank Cass).

Lowi, T. (1969) *The End of Liberalism* (N.Y.: Norton).

Luckham, L. (1996) 'Faustian Bargains: Democratic Control over Military and Security Establishments' in *Democratization in the South: The Jagged Wave*, ed. R. Luckham and G. White (Manchester and N.Y.: Manchester University Press) pp. 119–77.

Luckham, R. and White, G. (eds) (1996) *Democratization in the South: The Jagged Wave* (Manchester and N.Y.: Manchester University Press).

Lucy, R. (1989) *The Australian Form of Government: Models in Dispute* (South Melbourne: Macmillan).

Luesby, J. (1996) 'Framework for Decisions', *Financial Times*, 26 September 1996, p. 12.

Lukes, S. (1974) *Power: A Radical View* (London: Macmillan).

Lukes, S. (ed.) (1986) *Power* (Oxford and Cambridge, Mass.: Basil Blackwell).

Macdonald, F. (1996) *Dodging Democracy: An Investigation into Regime Manipulation of the Democratization Process in Subsaharan Africa* (University of Newcastle upon Tyne: M.Phil).

Machel, G. (1996) *Children and War* (N.Y.: United Nations).

Machiavelli, N. (1961) *The Prince* (Harmondsworth: Penguin), trans. G. Bau, first pub. 1531.

Mackenzie, W. (1958) *Free Elections* (London: Allen & Unwin).

Maddex, R. (1997) *Constitutions of the World* (London and N.Y.: Routledge).

Magyar, K. (1992) 'Military Intervention and Withdrawal in Africa: Problems and Perspectives' in *From Military to*

Civilian Rule, ed. C. Danopoulos (London and N.Y.: Routledge) pp. 230–48.

Mahalingam, R. (1997) 'Self-determination in the UN Era: A Response to Peter Sproat', *Terrorism and Political Violence* (9) 109–123.

Mahler, G. (1992) *Comparative Politics: An Institutional and Cross-national Approach* (Englewood Cliffs, N.J.: Prentice Hall).

Mainwaring, S. (1992) 'Presidentialism in Latin America' in *Parliamentary versus Presidential Government*, ed. A. Lijphart (Oxford and N.Y.: Oxford University Press) pp. 111–17.

Mainwaring, S. and Scully, T. (eds) (1995) *Building Democratic Institutions: Party Systems in Latin America* (Stanford, Calif.: Stanford University Press).

Mainwaring, S. and Shugart, M. (1997a) 'Juan Linz, Presidentialism and Democracy: A Critical Appraisal' *Comparative Politics* (29) 449–72.

Mainwaring, S. and Shugart, M. (eds) (1997b) *Presidentialism and Democracy in Latin America* (Cambridge and N.Y.: Cambridge University Press).

Mair, P. (ed.) (1990) *The West European Party System* (Oxford and N.Y.: Oxford University Press).

Mair, P. (1994) 'Party Organizations: From Civil Society to the State' in *How Parties Organize: Change and Adaptation in Party Organizations in Western Democracies*, ed. R. Katz and P. Mair (Thousand Oaks, Calif. and London: Sage) pp. 1–22.

Mair, P. (1996) 'Comparative Politics: An Overview' in *A New Handbook of Political Science*, ed. R. Goodin and H. Klingemann (Oxford and N.Y.: Oxford University Press) pp. 309–35.

Mair, P. (1997) 'E. E. Schattschneider's "The Semi-Sovereign People"', *Political Studies* (45) 947–54.

Maley, W. (1997) *Fundamentalism Reborn? Afghanistan under the Taliban* (London: Hurst).

Manin, B. (1997) *The Principles of Representative Government* (Cambridge and N.Y.: Cambridge University Press).

Mann, T. and Orren, G. (eds) (1992) *Media Polls in American Politics* (Washington. D.C.: The Brookings Institution).

Mansbach, R. (1997) *The Global Puzzle: Issues and Actors in World Politics* (Boston, Mass.: Houghton Mifflin).

March, J. and Olsen, J. (1995) *Democratic Governance* (N.Y. and London: Free Press).

Marks, G. and Diamond, L. (eds) (1992) *Reexamining Democracy: Essays in Honour of Seymour Martin Lipset* (Thousand Oaks, Calif. and London: Sage).

Markus, G. and Converse, P. (1979) 'A Dynamic Simultaneous Equation Model of Electoral Choice', *American Political Science Review* (73) 1055–70.

Marody, M. (1995) 'Three Stages of Party System Emergence in Poland', *Communist and Postcommunist Studies* (28) 263–70.

Marsh, A. (1990) *Political Action in Europe* (London: Macmillan).

Marsh, D. and Rhodes, R. (eds) (1992) *Policy Networks in British Government* (Oxford and N.Y.: Oxford University Press).

Marshall, G. (1984) *Constitutional Conventions* (Oxford and New York: Clarendon Press).

Matthews, T. (1989) 'Interest Groups' in *Politics in Australia*, ed. R. Smith and L. Watson (Sydney: Allen & Unwin) pp. 211–27.

Mavrogordatos, G. (1987) 'Downs Revisited', *International Political Science Review* (8) 333–42.

Mawby, R. (1990) *Comparative Policing Issues: The British and American Experiences in International Perspective* (London and Winchester, Mass.: Unwin Hyman).

Mayall, J. (1996) *The New Interventionism, 1993-1994: United Nations Experience in Cambodia, Former Yugoslavia and Somalia* (Cambridge and N.Y.: Cambridge University Press).

Mayhew, D. (1974) *Congress: The Electoral Connection* (New Haven, Conn. and London: Yale University Press).

Mazey, S. and Richardson, J. (eds) (1993) *Lobbying in the European Community* (Oxford and N.Y.: Oxford University Press).

Mazmanian, D. and Sabatier, P. (1989) *Implementation and Public Policy* (Lanham, Md. and London: University Press of America).

McAllister, I. (1996) 'Leaders' in *Elections and Voting in Global Perspective*, ed. L. LeDuc, R. Niemi and P. Norris (Thousand Oaks, Calif. and London: Sage) pp. 280–98.

McCauley, M. and Carter, S. (eds) (1986) *Leadership and Succession in the Soviet Union, Eastern Europe and China* (London: Macmillan).

McDonough, P. (1995) 'Identities, Ideologies and Interests: Democratization and the Culture of Mass Politics in Spain and Eastern Europe', *Journal of Politics* (57) 649–76.

McGregor, J. (1996) 'Constitutional Factors in Politics in Postcommunist Central and Eastern Europe', *Communist and Postcommunist Studies* (29) 147–66.

McGrew, A. (1992) 'Conceptualizing Global Politics' in *Global Politics: Globalization and the Nation-State*, ed. A. McGrew, P. Lewis *et al.* (Cambridge: Polity) pp. 1–30.

McKay, D. (1997) *American Politics and Society* (Oxford and Cambridge, Mass.: Blackwell), 4th edn.

McPhail, B. (1995) *NAFTA Now! The Changing Political Economy of North America* (Lanham, Md.: University Press of America).

McWhinney, E. (1981) *Constitution-Making: Principles, Process, Practice* (Toronto and London: University of Toronto Press).

Medhurst, K. (1991) 'Politics and Religion in Latin America' in *Politics and Religion in the Modern World*, ed. G. Moyser (London and N.Y.: Routledge) pp. 189–221.

Medvedev, R. (1972) *Let History Judge: The Origins and Consequences of Stalinism* (London: Macmillan).

Meier, K. (1993) 'Representative Bureaucracy: A Theoretical and Empirical Exposition', *Research in Public Administration* (2) 1–35.

Meny, Y. (1990) *Government and Politics in Western Europe: Britain, France, Italy, West Germany* (N.Y. and London: Free Press).

Mershon, C. (1996) 'The Costs of Coalition: Coalition Theories and Italian Government', *American Political Science Review* (90) 534–54.

Meyer, A. (1983) 'Cultural Revolutions: The Uses of the Concept of Culture in Comparative Communist Studies', *Studies in Comparative Communism* (16) 1–8.

Mezey, M. (1979) *Comparative Legislatures* (Durham, N.C.: Duke University Press).

Michels, R. (1949) *Political Parties* (Glencoe, Ill.: Free Press) first pub. 1911.

Milbrath, L. and Goel, M. (1977) *Political Participation: How and Why Do People Get Involved in Politics?* (Chicago, Ill.: Rand McNally) 2nd edn.

Mill, J. (1991) 'Considerations on Representative Government' in *Collected Works of John Stuart Mill*, ed. J. O'Grady and B. Robson (Toronto: University of Toronto Press and London: Routledge) pp. 371–577, first pub. 1861.

Miller, D. (1991) 'Politics' in *Blackwell Encyclopaedia of Political Thought*, ed. V. Bogdanor (Oxford and Cambridge, Mass.: Blackwell) pp. 390–1.

Miller, W. *et al.* (1990) *How Voters Change: The 1987 British Election Campaign in Perspective* (Oxford and N.Y.: Oxford University Press).

Millett, R. (1996) 'The Future of Latin America's Armed Forces' in *Beyond Praetorianism: The Latin American Military in Transition*, ed. R. Millett and M. Gold-Biss (Miami, Fla.: North–South Center Press) pp. 291–300.

Millett, R. and Gold-Biss, M. (eds) (1996) *Beyond Praetorianism: The Latin American Military in Transition* (Miami, Fla.: North–South Center Press).

Mishra, S. (1994) 'Party Organization and Policy Making in a Changing Environment: The Indian National Congress' in *How Political Parties Work: Perspectives from Within*, ed. K. Lawson (Westport, Conn.: Praeger) pp. 153–79.

Mitra, S. (1996) 'Politics in India' in *Comparative Politics Today: A World View*, ed. G. Almond (N.Y.: HarperCollins) pp. 668–729. 6th edn.

Mitrany, D. (1975) *The Functional Theory of Politics* (London: LSE).

Moe, T. (1980) *The Organization of Interests* (Chicago, Ill.: University of Chicago Press).

Molotoch, H. (1976) 'The City as a Growth Machine: Toward a Political Economy of Place', *American Journal of Sociology* (82) 309–31.

Montesquieu, C.-L. (1949) *The Spirit of the Laws* (N.Y.: Hafner), ed. F. Neumann, first pub. 1748.

Moore, B. (1966) *Social Origins of Dictatorship and Democracy: Lord and Peasant in the Making of the Modern World* (Boston, Mass.: Beacon).

Moore, M. (1996) 'Is Democracy Rooted in Material Prosperity?' in *Democratization in the South: The Jagged Wave*, ed. R. Luckham and G. White (Manchester and N.Y.: Manchester University Press) pp. 37–68.

Morlino, L. (1995) 'Italy's Civic Divide', *Journal of Democracy* (6) 173–7.

Morris, P. (1994) *French Politics Today* (Manchester: Manchester University Press and N.Y.: St Martin's Press).

Mortimer, E. (1997) 'Prevention Zone', *Financial Times*, 21 September 1997, p. 18.

Morton, F. (1995) 'The Living Constitution' in *Introductory Readings in Canadian Government and Politics*, ed. R. Wagenberg (Mississauga, Ontario: Copp Clark) pp. 41–72.

Mosher, S. (1984) *Broken Earth: The Rural Chinese* (N.Y. and London: Free Press).

Moyser, G. (ed.) (1993) *Politics and Religion in the Modern World* (London and N.Y.: Routledge).

Müller, W. (1994) 'The Development of Austrian Party Organizations in the Post-war Period' in *How Parties Organize: Change and Adaptation in Party Organizations in Western Democracies*, ed. R. Katz and P. Mair (Thousand Oaks, Calif. and London: Sage) pp. 51–80.

Mulgan, R. (1997) *Politics in New Zealand* (Auckland: Auckland University Press) 2nd edn.

Munck, R. (1989) *Latin America: The Transition to Democracy* (London and Atlantic Highlands, N.J.: Zed).

Mundt, R. and Aborisade, O. (1996) 'Politics in Nigeria' in *Comparative Politics Today*, ed. G. Almond and G. Bingham Powell (N.Y.: HarperCollins) pp. 730–83. 6th edn.

Myers, A. (1975) *Parliaments and Estates in Europe to 1789* (London: Thames & Hudson).

Myers, D. and O'Connor, R. (1998) 'Support for Coups in Democratic Political Culture: A Venezuelan Explanation', *Comparative Politics* (30) 193–212.

Nadel, F. and Rourke, F. (1975) 'Bureaucracies' in *The Handbook of Political Science*, ed. F. Greenstein and N. Polsby (Reading, Mass.: Addison-Wesley) pp. 373–440.

Neustadt, R. (1980) *Presidential Power: The Politics of Leadership from FDR to Carter* (N.Y.: Wiley).

Nicholson, B. (1989) Increasing Women's Parliamentary Representation: The Norwegian Experience (University of Newcastle upon Tyne: Centre for Scandinavian Studies)

Nickson, R. (1995) *Local Government in Latin America* (Boulder, Colo. and London: Lynne Reinner).

Nigro, L. (ed.) (1984) *Decision Making in the Public Sector* (N.Y.: Marcel Dekker).

Niskanen, W. (1971) *Bureaucracy and Representative Government* (Chicago, Ill.: Aldine Atherton).

Nordlinger, E. (1977) *Soldiers in Politics: Military Coups and Governments* (Englewood Cliffs, N.J.: Prentice Hall).

Norpoth, H. (1996) 'The Economy' in *Elections and Voting in Global Perspective*, ed. L. LeDuc, R. Niemi and P. Norris (Thousand Oaks, Calif. and London: Sage) pp. 299–318.

Norris, P. (1993) 'Comparing Legislative Recruitment' in *Gender and Party Politics*, ed. J. Lovenduski and P. Norris (Thousand Oaks, Calif. and London: Sage) pp. 309–30.

Norris, P. (1995) *Comparative Models of Political Recruitment* (Bordeaux: ECPR Workshop on Political Recruitment).

Norris, P. (1996) 'Legislative Recruitment' in *Elections and Voting in Global Perspective*, ed. L. LeDuc, R. Niemi and P. Norris (Thousand Oaks, Calif. and London: Sage) pp. 184–215.

Norris, P. (1997) *Electoral Change in Britain since 1945* (Oxford and Cambridge, Mass.: Blackwell).

Norton, A. (1991) 'Western European Local Government in Comparative Perspective' in *Local Government in Europe: Trends and Developments*, ed. R. Batley and G. Stoker (London: Macmillan) pp.21–40.

Norton, A. (1994) *International Handbook of Local and Regional Government* (Aldershot and Brookfield, Vt.: Edward Elgar).

Norton, P. (ed.)(1990a) *Legislatures* (Oxford and N.Y.: Oxford University Press).

Norton, P. (ed.) (1990b) *Parliaments in Western Europe* (London: Frank Cass).

Norton, P. (1993) *Does Parliament Matter?* (Hemel Hempstead: Harvester Wheatsheaf).

Norton, P. (1994) *The British Polity* (Harlow and N.Y.: Longman) 3rd edn.

Norton, P. (1997) 'Parliamentary Oversight' in *Developments in British Politics 5*, ed. P. Dunleavy *et al.* (London: Macmillan and N.Y.: St Martin's Press) pp. 155–76.

Norton, P. and Olson, D. (1996) 'Parliaments in Adolescence' in *The New Parliaments of Central and Eastern Europe*, ed. D. Olson and P. Norton (London: Frank Cass) pp. 231–44.

Nousiainen, J. (1994) 'Finland: Ministerial Autonomy, Constitutional Collectivism and Party Oligarchy' in *Cabinet Ministers and Parliamentary Government*, ed. M. Laver and K. Shepsle (Cambridge and N.Y.: Cambridge University Press) pp. 88–105.

Nugent, N. (1994) *The Government and Politics of the European Union* (London: Macmillan) 3rd edn.

Nurmi, H. (1990) 'A Theoretical Review of the Finnish Parliamentary and Presidential System' in *Finnish Democracy*, ed. J. Sunberg and S. Berglund (Helsinki: Finnish Political Science Association) pp. 51–64.

Nye, J. (1990) *Bound to Lead: the Changing Nature of America's Power* (N.Y.: Basic Books).

Nye, J., Zelikow, P. and King, D. (eds) (1997) *Why People Don't Trust Government* (Cambridge, Mass.: Harvard University Press).

O'Brien, D. (1993) *Storm Center: The Supreme Court in American Politics* (N.Y.: Norton).

O'Donnell, G. (1996) 'Delegative Democracy' in *The Global Resurgence of Democracy*, ed. L. Diamond and M. Plattner (Baltimore, Maryland and London: Johns Hopkins University Press) pp. 94–110.

O'Donnell, G. and Schmitter, P. (1986) *Transitions from Authoritarian Rule: Tentative Conclusions from Uncertain Democracies* (Berkeley, Calif. and Los Angeles, Calif.: University of California Press).

O'Donnell, G., Schmitter, P. and Whitehead, L. (eds.) (1986) *Transitions from Authoritarian Rule: Prospects for Democracy*, (Baltimore, Md. and London: Johns Hopkins University Press).

O'Sullivan, N. (1986) *Fascism* (London: Dent).

O'Toole, B. and Chapman, R. (1995) 'Parliamentary Accountability' in *Next Steps: Improving Management in Government?*, ed. B. O'Toole and G. Jordan (Aldershot and Brookfield, Vt.: Dartmouth) pp. 118–41.

O'Toole, B. and Jordan, G. (eds) (1995) *Next Steps: Improving Management in Government?* (Aldershot and Brookfield, Vt.: Dartmouth).

OECD (1993) *Managing With Market Type Mechanisms* (Paris: OECD).

Offe, C. (1996) 'Institutions in East European Transitions' in *The Theory of Institutional Design*, ed. R. Goodin (Cambridge and N.Y.: Cambridge University Press) pp. 199–226.

Olson, D. (1994) *Legislative Institutions: A Comparative View* (Armonk, N.Y.: M. E. Sharpe).

Olson, D. and Norton, P. (eds) (1996) *The New Parliaments of Central and Eastern Europe* (London: Frank Cass).

Olson, M. (1968) *The Logic of Collective Action: Public Goods and the Theory of Groups* (N.Y.: Schocken Books).

Olson, M. (1982) *The Rise and Decline of Nations* (New Haven, Conn. and London: Yale University Press).

Osborne, D. and Gaebler, T. (1993) *Reinventing Government: How the Entrepreneurial Spirit Is Transforming the Public Sector* (N.Y. and London: Penguin).

Ostrogorski, M. (1902) *Democracy and the Organisation of Political Parties* (London: Macmillan).

Page, E. (1992) *Political Authority and Bureaucratic Power: A Comparative Analysis* (Hemel Hempstead: Harvester Wheatsheaf) 2nd edn.

Palan, R. and Abbott, J. (1996) *State Strategies in the Global Economy* (London and N.Y.: Pinter).

Panebianco, A. (1988) *Political Parties: Organization and Power* (Cambridge and N.Y.: Cambridge University Press).

Park, B. (1986) *The Impact of Illness on World Leaders* (Philadelphia, Pa.: University of Pennsylvania Press).

Parkin, S. (1989) *Green Parties: An International Guide* (London: Heretic Books).

Parry, G., Moyser, G. and Day, N. (1992) *Political Participation and Democracy in Britain* (Cambridge and N.Y.: Cambridge University Press).

Parsons, T. (1967) 'On the Concept of Political Power' in *Sociological Theory and Modern Society*, ed. T. Parsons (N.Y. and London: Free Press) pp. 286–99.

Parsons, W. (1995) *Public Policy: An Introduction to the Theory and Practice of Policy Analysis* (Brookfield, Vt. and Aldershot: Edward Elgar).

Peele, G. (1984) *Revival and Reaction: The Right in Contemporary America* (Oxford and N.Y.: Clarendon Press).

Peeler, J. (1998) *Building Democracy in Latin America* (Boulder, Colorado and London: Lynne Reinner).

Peretz, D. and Doron, G. (1997) *The Government and Politics of Israel* (Boulder, Colo. and Oxford: Westview).

Pesic, J. (1994) 'The Cruel Face of Nationalism' in *Nationalism, Ethnic Conflict and Democracy*, ed. L. Diamond and M. Plattner (Baltimore, Md. and London: John Hopkins University Press) pp. 132–6.

Peters, B. Guy (1993) *American Public Policy: Promise and Performance* (Chatham, N.J.: Chatham House) 3rd edn.

Peters, B. Guy (1995) *The Politics of Bureaucracy* (White Plains, N.Y.: Longman) 4th edn.

Peters, B. Guy (1998) *Comparative Politics: Theory and Methods* (London: Macmillan and N.Y.: New York University Press).

Petersson, O. (1989) *Maktens Natverk* (Stockholm: Carlssons).

Petracca, M. (1992) 'The Rediscovery of Interest Group Politics' in *The Politics of Interests: Interest Groups Transformed*, ed. M. Petracca (Boulder, Colo. and Oxford: Westview) pp. 3–31.

Petro, N. (1995) *The Rebirth of Russian Democracy: An Interpretation of Political Culture* (Cambridge, Mass. and London: Harvard University Press).

Pierre, J. (ed.) (1995) *Urban and Regional Policy* (Aldershot and Brookfield, Vt.: Edward Elgar).

Pierson, C. (1991) *Beyond the Welfare State?* (Oxford: Polity).

Pinkney, R. (1990) *Right-wing Military Government* (London: Pinter).

Pogany, I. (1996) 'Constitution Making or Constitutional Transformation in Postcommunist Societies?', *Political Studies* (44) 568–91.

Pomper, G. *et al.* (1997) *The Election of 1996: Reports and Interpretations* (Chatham, New Jersey: Chatham House).

Porter, B. (1994) *War and the Rise of the Modern State: the Military Foundations of Modern Politics* (N.Y. and London: Free Press).

Porter, M. (1990) *The Competitive Advantage of Nations* (London: Macmillan).

Post, J. and Robins, R. (1993) *When Illness Strikes the Leader: The Dilemma of the Captive King* (New Haven, Conn. and London: Yale University Press).

Potter, D. *et al.* (eds) (1997) *Democratization* (Cambridge: Polity).

Pressman, J. and Wildavsky, A. (1973) *Implementation* (Berkeley, Calif.: University of California Press).

Preston, P. (1990) *The Politics of Revenge* (London: Unwin Hyman).

Price, R. and Mancuso, M. (1995) 'Ties That Bind: Members and Their Constituencies' in *Introductory Readings in Canadian Government and Politics*, ed. R. Krause and R. Wagenberg (Mississauga, Ontario: Copp Clark) pp. 211–36.

Pridham, G. (1990) 'Political Parties, Parliaments and Consolidation in Southern Europe: Empirical and Theoretical Perspectives' in *Parliament and Democratic Consolidation in Southern Europe*, ed. U. Liebert and M. Cotta (London: Pinter) pp. 225–48.

Pridham, G. (ed.) (1995) *Transitions to Democracy* (Brookfield, Vermont and Aldershot: Dartmouth).

Pross, A. (1993) 'Canadian Pressure Groups: Talking Chameleons' in *Pressure Groups*, ed. J. Richardson (Oxford: Oxford University Press) pp. 145–58.

Prosser, T. (1996) 'Understanding the British Constitution', *Political Studies* (44) 473–87.

Przeworski, A. (1991) *Democracy and the Market: Political and Economic Reforms in Eastern Europe and Latin America* (Cambridge and N.Y.: Cambridge University Press).

Przeworski, A. (1995) 'The Role of Theory in Comparative Politics: A Symposium', *World Politics* (48) 16–21.

Przeworski, A. and Limongi, F. (1993) 'Political Regimes and Economic Growth', *Journal of Economic Perspectives* (7) 51–69.

Przeworski, A. and Limongi, F. (1997) 'Modernization: Theories and Facts', *World Politics* (49) 155–83.

Przeworski, A. and Teune, H. (1970) *The Logic of Comparative Inquiry* (N.Y.: Wiley).

Pusey, M. (1991) *Economic Rationalism in Canberra: A Nation-building State Changes Its Mind* (Cambridge and N.Y.: Cambridge University Press).

Putnam, R. (1976) *The Comparative Study of Political Élites* (Englewood Cliffs, N.J.: Prentice Hall).

Putnam, R. (1993) *Making Democracy Work: Civic Traditions in Modern Italy* (Princeton, N.J.: Princeton University Press).

Putnam, R. (1995) 'Bowling Alone: America's Declining Social Capital', *Journal of Democracy* (6) 65–78.

Putzel, J. (1997) 'Why has Democratization been a Weaker Impulse in Indonesia and Malaysia than in the Philippines?' in *Democratization*, ed. D. Potteret *et al.* (Cambridge: Polity) pp. 240–68.

Pye, L. (1985) *Asian Power and Politics: The Cultural Dimensions of Authority* (Cambridge, Mass.: Harvard University Press).

Pye, L. (1995) 'Political Culture' in *The Encyclopaedia of Democracy*, ed. S. Lipset (London and N.Y.: Routledge) pp. 965–9.

Qualter, T. (1991) 'Public Opinion' in *The Blackwell Encyclopaedia of Political Science*, ed. V. Bogdanor (Oxford and Cambridge, Mass.: Blackwell) p. 511.

Raadschelders, J. and Rutgers, M. (1996) 'The Evolution of Civil Service Systems' in *Civil Service Systems in Comparative Perspective*, ed. H. Bekke, J. Perry and T. Toonen (Bloomington, Ind.: Indiana University Press) pp. 67–99.

Ragin, C. (1994a) 'Introduction to Qualitative Comparative Analysis' in *The Comparative Political Economy of the Welfare State*, ed. T. Janoski and A. Hicks (N.Y. and Cambridge: Cambridge University Press) pp. 299–319.

Ragin, C. (1994b) *Constructing Social Research* (Thousand Oaks, Calif.: Sage).

Ragin, C., Berg-Schlosser, D. and de Meur, G. (1996) 'Political Methodology: Qualitative Methods' in *A New Handbook of Political Science*, ed. R. Goodin and H. Klingemann (Oxford and N.Y.: Oxford University Press) pp. 749–68.

Randall, V. (ed.) (1988) *Political Parties in the Third World* (Thousand Oaks, Calif. and London: Sage).

Randall, V. (1997) 'Why have the Political Trajectories of India and China been Different?' in *Democratization*, ed. D. Potter *et al.* (Cambridge: Polity) pp. 195–218.

Ranson, S. and Stewart, J. (1994) *Management for the Public Domain: Enabling the Learning Society* (London: Macmillan).

Ray, J. (1992) *Global Politics* (Boston, Mass.: Houghton Mifflin).

Remmer, K. (1989) *Military Rule in Latin America* (Boston, Mass.: Unwin Hyman).

Reynolds, A. (1994) *Election '94 South Africa: The Campaigns, Results and Future Prospects* (London: James Currey and N.Y.: St Martin's Press).

Rhodes, M. (1996) 'Globalization and West European Welfare States: A Critical Review of Recent Debates', *Journal of European Social Policy* (6) 305–327.

Rhodes, R. (1994) 'State-building Without a Bureaucracy: The Case of the United Kingdom' in *Developing Democracy: Essays in Honour of J. F. P. Blondel*, ed. I. Budge and D. McKay (Thousand Oaks, Calif. and London: Sage) pp. 165–88.

Rhodes, R. (1996) 'The New Governance: Governing Without Government', *Political Studies* (44) 652–67.

Rich, P. (ed.) (1994) *The Dynamics of Change in South Africa* (London: Macmillan and N.Y.: St Martin's Press).

Richardson, J. Gustaffson, G. and Jordan, G. (1982) 'The Concept of Policy Style' in *Policy Styles in Western Europe*, ed. J. Richardson (London and Boston, Mass.: Allen & Unwin), pp. 1–16.

Richardson, J. (ed.) (1984) *Policy Styles in Western Europe* (London: Allen & Unwin).

Richardson, J. (ed.) (1993) *Pressure Groups* (Oxford and N.Y.: Oxford University Press).

Riker, W. (1962) *The Theory of Political Coalitions* (New Haven, Conn. and London: Yale University Press).

Riker, W. (1975) 'Federalism' in *The Handbook of Political Science*, ed. F. Greenstein and N. Polsby (Reading, Mass: Addison-Wesley) pp. 93–172.

Riker, W. (1996) 'European Federalism: The Lessons of Past Experience' in *Federalizing Europe? The Costs, Benefits and Preconditions of Federal Political Systems*, ed. J. Hesse and V.

Wright (Oxford and N.Y.: Oxford University Press) pp. 9–24.

Ritchie, E. (1992) 'Law and Order' in *Power and Policy in Liberal Democracies*, ed. M. Harrop (Cambridge and N.Y.: Cambridge University Press) pp. 195–217.

Roach, J. and Thomaneck, J. (1985) *Police and Public Order in Europe* (London: Croom Helm).

Rocher, F. and Smith, M. (eds) (1995) *New Trends in Canadian Federalism* (Peterborough, Ontario: Broadview Press).

Rogers, E. (1971) *Communication of Innovation: A Cross-Cultural Approach* (N.Y.: Free Press and London: Collier-Macmillan).

Rokkan, S. (1970) *Citizens, Elections, Parties* (N.Y.: McKay).

Rose, R. (1989) *Politics in England: Change and Persistence* (London: Macmillan).

Rose, R. (1991) *The Post-Modern President* (Chatham, N.J.: Chatham House).

Rose, R. (1991) 'Comparing Forms of Comparative Analysis' *Political Studies* (39) 446–62.

Rose, R. (1993) *Lesson-Drawing in Public Policy* (Chatham, N.J.: Chatham House).

Rose, R. (1995) 'Mobilizing Demobilized Voters in Post-communist Societies', *Party Politics* (1) 549–63.

Rosenau, J. (1989) 'The State in an Era of Cascading Politics: Wavering Concept, Widening Competence, Withering Colossus or Weathering Change?' in *The Elusive State: International and Comparative Perspectives*, ed. J. Caporaso (Thousand Oaks, Calif. and London: Sage) pp. 17–48.

Rosenau, J. (1992) 'Governance, Order and Change in World Politics' in *Governance without Government: Order and Change in World Politics*, ed. J. Rosenau and E.-O. Czempiel (Cambridge: Cambridge University Press) pp. 3–6.

Rosenau, J. (1996) 'The Rise of the Virtual State', *Foreign Affairs* (75) 45–61.

Rosenfeld, M. (ed.) (1994) *Constitutionalism, Identity, Difference and Legitimacy: Theoretical Perspectives* (Durham, N.C. and London: Duke University Press).

Rostow, W. (1971) *The Stages of Economic Growth: A Non-Communist Manifesto* (Cambridge and N.Y.: Cambridge University Press) 2nd edn, first pub. 1960.

Rostow, W. (1987) *Rich Countries and Poor Countries: Reflections on the Past, Lessons for the Future* (Boulder, Colo. and Oxford: Westview).

Rousseau, D. (1994) 'The Constitutional Judge: Master or Slave of the Constitution?' in *Constitutionalism, Identity, Difference and Legitimacy: Theoretical Perspectives*, ed. M. Rosenfeld (Durham, N.C. and London: Duke University Press) pp. 261–83.

Rueschemeyer, D., Stephens, E. and Stephens, J. (1992) *Capitalist Development and Democracy* (Cambridge: Polity).

Rummel, R. (1997) *Death by Government* (New Brunswick, N.J. and London: Transaction Books).

Rush, M. (1992) *Politics and Society: An Introduction to Political Sociology* (Hemel Hempstead: Harvester Wheatsheaf).

Rushefsky, M. (1990) *Public Policy in the United States: Towards the Twenty-First Century* (Pacific Grove, Calif.: Brooks/Cole).

Rustow, D. (1970) 'Transitions to Democracy', *Comparative Politics* (2) 337–63.

Sakwa, R. (1996) *Russian Politics and Society* (London and N.Y.: Routledge) 2nd edn.

Salisbury, R. (1992) *Interests and Institutions: Substance and Structure in American Politics* (Pittsburgh, Pa.: University of Pittsburgh Press).

Salvatore, D. (1993) 'Introduction' in *Protectionism and World Welfare*, ed. D. Salvatore (N.Y. and Cambridge: Cambridge University Press) pp. 1–15.

Sandel, M. (1996) *Democracy's Discontent: America in Search of a Public Philosophy* (Cambridge, Mass. and London: Harvard University Press).

Saro-Wiwa, K. (1995) *A Month and a Day: A Detention Diary* (London and N.Y.: Penguin).

Sartori, G. (1970) 'Concept Misformation in Comparative Politics', *American Political Science Review* (54) 1033–53.

Sartori, G. (1976) *Parties and Party Systems: A Framework for Analysis* (Cambridge and N.Y.: Cambridge University Press).

Sartori, G. (1994) *Comparative Constitutional Engineering: An Inquiry into Structures, Incentives and Outcomes* (London: Macmillan).

Scarrow, H. (1969) *Comparative Political Analysis* (N.Y.: Harper & Row).

Scharpf, F. (1996) 'Can there be a Stable Federal Balance in Europe?' in *Federalizing Europe? The Costs, Benefits and Preconditions of Federal Political Systems*, ed. J. Hesse and V. Wright (Oxford and N.Y.: Oxford University Press) pp. 361–73.

Schattschneider, E. (1942) *Party Government* (N.Y.: Farrar & Reinhart).

Schmid, A. (1989) 'Terrorism and the Media: The Ethics of Publicity', *Journal of Terrorism and Political Violence* (1) 539–65.

Schmidt, V. (1991) *Democratizing France* (Cambridge and N.Y.: Cambridge University Press).

Schöpflin, G. (1990) 'Why Communism Collapsed', *International Affairs* (66) 3–17.

Schöpflin, G. and Hosking, G. (eds) (1997) *Myths and Nationhood* (London: Hurst).

Schumpeter, J. (1943) *Capitalism, Socialism and Democracy* (London: Allen & Unwin).

Schwarz, B. (1960) 'The Legend of "the Legend of Maoism"', *China Quarterly* (2) 35–42.

Schwarz, R. and Miller, J. (1964) 'Legal Evolution and Societal Complexity', *American Journal of Sociology* (70) 159–69.

Scott, S. (1997) 'Australia and International Institutions' in *New Developments in Australian Politics*, ed. B. Galligan, I. McAllister and J. Ravenhill (South Melbourne: Macmillan) pp. 271–90.

Scruton, R. (1996) *A Dictionary of Political Thought* (London: Macmillan), 2nd edn.

Searing, D. (1994) *Westminster's World: Understanding Political Roles* (Cambridge, Mass. and London: Harvard University Press).

Seisselberg, J. (1996) 'Conditions of Success and Political Problems of a "Media-mediated Personality Party": The Case of Forza Italia', *West European Politics* (19) 715–43.

Senelle, R. (1996) 'The Reform of the Belgian State' in *Federalizing Europe? The Costs, Benefits and Preconditions of*

Federal Political Systems, ed. J. Hesse and V. Wright (Oxford and N.Y.: Oxford University Press) pp. 266–324.

Seymour-Ure, C. (1991) *The British Press and Broadcasting since 1945* (Oxford and Cambridge, Mass.: Blackwell).

Shain, Y., Berat, L. and Linz, J. (1995) *Between States: Interim Government and Democratic Transitions* (Cambridge and N.Y.: Cambridge University Press).

Shanks, C., Jackobson, H. and Kaplan, J. (1996) 'Inertia and Change in the Constellation of Intergovernmental Organizations', *International Organization* (50) 593–627.

Shapiro, M. (1990) 'The Supreme Court from Early Burger to Early Rehnquist' in *The New American Political System*, ed. A. King (Washington, D.C.: American Enterprise Institute) pp. 47–86. 2nd version.

Shapiro, M. and Stone, A. (1994) 'The New Constitutional Politics of Europe', *Comparative Political Studies* (26) 397–420.

Sharpe, L. (ed.) (1993) *The Rise of Meso Government in Europe* (Thousand Oaks, Calif. and London: Sage).

Shi, T. (1997) *Political Participation in Beijing* (Cambridge, Mass. and London: Harvard University Press).

Shively, W. (1995) *Power and Choice: An Introduction to Political Science* (N.Y. and London: McGraw-Hill) 4th edn.

Shugart, M. and Carey, J. (1992) *Presidents and Assemblies: Constitutional Design and Electoral Dynamics* (Cambridge and N.Y.: Cambridge University Press).

Sigmund, P. (1993) 'Christian Democracy, Liberation Theology and Political Culture in Latin America' in *Political Culture and Democracy in Developing Countries*, ed. L. Diamond (Boulder, Colo. and London: Lynne Reinner) pp. 329–46.

Simon, H. (1983) *Reason in Human Affairs* (Oxford and Cambridge, Mass: Blackwell).

Sithole, M. (1993) 'Zimbabwe: In Search of a Stable Democracy' in *Democracy in Developing Countries: Africa*, ed. L. Diamond, J. Linz and S. Lipset (Boulder, Colo. and London: Lynne Reinner: pp. 217–58.

Sjolin, M. (1993) *Coalition Politics and Parliamentary Power* (Lund: Lund University Press).

Skene, G. (1989) 'Parliament: Reassessing its Role' in *New Zealand Politics in Perspective*, ed. H. Gold (Auckland: Longman Paul) pp. 182–98.

Skidmore, T. (1993) 'Politics and the Media in a Democratizing Latin America' in *Television, Politics and the Transition to Democracy in Latin America*, ed. T. Skidmore (Baltimore, Md. and London: Johns Hopkins University Press) pp. 1–22.

Skocpol, T. (1979) *States and Social Revolutions: A Comparative Analysis of France, Russia and China* (Cambridge and N.Y.: Cambridge University Press).

Skocpol, T. (1992) *Protecting Soldiers and Mothers: The Political Origins of Social Policy in the United States* (Cambridge, Mass. and London: Harvard University Press).

Slaughter, M. (1994) 'The Multicultural Self: Questions of Subjectivity, Questions of Power' in *Constitutionalism, Identity, Differences, and Legitimacy: Theoretical Perspectives*, ed. M. Rosenfeld (Durham, N.C. and London: Duke University Press) pp. 369–82.

Smith, D. (1970) *Religion and Political Development* (Boston, Mass.: Little Brown).

Smith, G. (1989) *Politics in Western Europe* (Aldershot: Gower) 5th edn.

Smith, G. (1995) *Federalism: The Multiethnic Challenge* (Harlow and N.Y.: Longman).

Smith, G., Paterson, W. and Padgett, S. (eds) (1996) *Developments in German Politics 2* (London: Macmillan).

Smith, M. (1995) *Pressure Politics* (Manchester: Baseline Books).

Somit, A. (1994) '. . . And Where We Came Out' in *The Victorious Incumbent: A Threat to Democracy?*, ed. A. Somit *et al.* (Aldershot and Brookfield, Vt.: Dartmouth) pp. 11–18.

Sorensen, G. (1993) *Democracy and Democratization* (Boulder, Colo. and Oxford: Westview).

Sorensen, G. (1997) 'An Analysis of Contemporary Statehood: Consequences for Conflict and Cooperation' *Review of International Studies* (23) 253–70.

Sprizak, E. and Diamond, L. (eds) (1993) *Israeli Democracy under Stress* (Boulder, Colo. and London: Lynne Reinner).

Sproat, P. (1997) 'The United Nations' Encouragement of Aggression and Ethnic Cleansing: Time to Abandon the Right to Self-Determination?', *Terrorism and Political Violence* (8) 93–113.

Standing, G. (1996) 'Social Protection in Central and Eastern Europe: A Tale of Slippery Anchors and Torn Safety Nets' in *Welfare States in Transition: National Adaptation in Global Economies*, ed. G. Esping-Andersen (Thousand Oaks, Calif. and London: Sage) pp. 225–55.

Steen, A. (1995) *Change of Regime and Political Recruitment: The Parliamentary Élites in the Baltic States* (Bordeaux: ECPR Workshop on Political Recruitment Patterns).

Stepan, A. and Skach, C. (1993) 'Constitutional Frameworks and Democratic Consolidation: Parliamentarism versus Presidentialism', *World Politics* (46) 1–22.

Stevens, A. (1996) *The Government and Politics of France* (London: Macmillan and N.Y.: St Martin's Press) 2nd edn.

Stimson, J. (1991) *Public Opinion in America: Moods, Cycles and Swings* (Boulder, Colo. and Oxford: Westview).

Stouffer, S. (1966) *Communism, Conformity and Civil Liberties* (N.Y.: Wiley).

Strange, S. (1994) *States and Markets* (London and N.Y.: Pinter).

Strom, K. (1990) *Minority Government and Majority Rule* (Cambridge and N.Y.: Cambridge University Press).

Stubbs, R. and Underhill, R. (eds) (1994) *Political Economy and the Changing Global Order* (London: Macmillan).

Sturgess, G. (1996) 'Virtual Government: What Will Remain Inside the Public Sector?', *Australian Journal of Public Administration* (55) 59–73.

Sturm, R. (1994) 'The Chancellor and the Executive' in *The Development of the German Chancellorship*, ed. S. Padgett (London: Hurst) pp. 42–53

Sullivan, J., Pierson, J. and Marcus, G. (1982) *Political Tolerance and American Democracy* (Chicago, Ill.: Chicago University Press).

Sundhaussen, U. (1985) 'The Durability of Military Regimes in South-East Asia' in *Military-Civilian Relations in South-East Asia*, ed. Z. Ahmad and H. Crouch (Singapore and Oxford: Oxford University Press) pp. 269–86.

Szacki, J. (1995) *Liberalism after Communism* (Budapest: Central European University Press).

Taras, R. (ed.) (1997) *Postcommunist Presidents* (Cambridge and N.Y.: Cambridge University Press).

Tarrow, S. (1989) *Democracy and Disorder* (Oxford and N.Y.: Oxford University Press).

Tarrow, S. (1994) *Power in Movement: Social Movements, Collective Action and Politics* (Cambridge and N.Y.: Cambridge University Press).

Tate, C. and Vallinder, T. (eds) (1995) *The Global Expansion of Judicial Power* (N.Y. and London: New York University Press).

Taylor, C. (1993) *Reconciling the Solitudes: Essays on Canadian Federalism and Nationalism* (Montreal and Kingston: McGill-Queen's University Press).

Taylor-Gooby, P. (1996) 'Eurosclerosis in European Welfare States: Regime Theory and the Dynamics of Change', *Policy and Politics* (24) 109–24.

Teune, H. (1995a) 'Preface', *Annals of the American Academy of Political and Social Sciences* (540) 8–10.

Teune, H. (1995b) 'Local Government and Democratic Political Development', *Annals of the American Academy of Political and Social Sciences* (540) 11–23.

Thomas, C. (ed.) (1993) *First World Interest Groups: A Comparative Perspective* (Westport, Conn.: Greenwood Press).

Thomas, C. (1997) 'Globalization and the South' in *Globalization and the South*, ed. C. Thomas and P. Wilkin (London: Macmillan) pp. 1–17.

Tilly, C. (1975) 'Reflections on the History of European State-making' in *The Formation of National States in Western Europe*, ed. C. Tilly (Princeton, N.J.: Princeton University Press) pp. 3–83.

Tipton, E. (1990) *The Japanese Police State: The Tokko in Interwar Japan* (London: Athlone Press).

Tismaneanu, V. (ed.) (1995) *Political Culture and Civil Society in Russia and the New States of Eurasia* (N.Y.: M. E. Sharpe).

Tivey, L. (ed.) (1981) *The Nation-State: The Formation of Modern Politics* (London: Martin Robertson).

Tocqueville, A. de. (1954) *Democracy in America* (N.Y.: Vintage Books) first pub. 1835.

Tocqueville, A. de. (1966) *The Ancien Regime and the Revolution in France* (London: Fontana) first pub. 1856.

Touraine, A. (1997) *What Is Democracy?* (Boulder, Colo. and Oxford: Westview).

Tsebelis, G. and Money, J. (1997) *Bicameralism* (Cambridge and N.Y.: Cambridge University Press).

Tuck, R. (1979) *Natural Rights Theories* (Cambridge and N.Y.: Cambridge University Press).

Tumarkin, N. (1997) *Lenin Lives! The Lenin Cult in Soviet Russia* (Cambridge, Mass. and London: Harvard University Press).

Turner, K. (1989) 'Parliament' in *Politics in Australia*, ed. R. Smith and L. Watson (Sydney: Allen & Unwin) pp. 65–84.

UBS (1997) *The UBS Guide to the Emerging Markets* (London: Bloomsbury).

Uhr, J. (1997) 'Parliament' in *New Developments in Australian Politics*, ed. B. Galligan, I. McAllister and J. Ravenhill (South Melbourne: Macmillan) pp. 68–84.

United Nations (1992) *An Agenda for Peace* (Washington, D.C.: United Nations).

United Nations (1993) *World Investment Report: Transnational Corporations and Integrated International Production* (N.Y.: United Nations).

United Nations (1995) *Supplement to an Agenda for Peace* (N.Y.: United Nations).

United Nations Industrial Development Organization (1997) *The Globalization of Industry: Implications for Developing Countries Beyond 2000* (Vienna: UNIDO).

Vainshtein, G. (1995) 'The Authoritarian Idea in the Public Consciousness and Political Life of Contemporary Russia', *Journal of Communist and Transition Politics* (11) 272–85.

van Eijk, R. (1997) 'The United Nations and the Reconstruction of Collapsed States', *African Journal of International and Comparative Law* (9) 543–72.

van der Meer, F. and Roborgh, R. (1996) 'Civil Servants and Representativeness' in *Civil Service Systems in Comparative Perspective*, ed. H. Bekke, J. Perry and T. Toonen (Bloomington, Ind.: Indiana University Press) pp. 119–33.

Vanhanen, T. (1997) *Prospects of Democracy: A Study of 172 Countries* (London and N.Y.: Routledge).

Vartola, J. (1988) 'Finland' in *Public Administration in Developed Democracies: A Comparative Study*, ed. D. Rowat (N.Y.: Marcel Dekker) pp. 117–32.

Vatikiotis, M. (1993) *Indonesian Politics Under Suharto: Order, Development and Pressure for Change* (London and N.Y.: Routledge).

Vatikiotis, M. (1996) *Political Change in Southeast Asia: Trimming the Banyan Tree* (London and N.Y.: Routledge).

Ventner, D. (1995) 'Malawi: the Transition to Multi-Party Politics' in *Democracy and Political Change in Sub-Saharan Africa*, ed. J. Wiseman (London and N.Y.: Routledge) pp. 152–92.

Verba, S. (1987) *Élites and the Idea of Equality: A Comparison of Japan, Sweden and the United States* (Cambridge, Mass. and London: Harvard University Press).

Verba, S. and Nie, N. (1972) *Participation in America: Political Democracy and Social Equality* (N.Y.: Harper & Row).

Verba, S., Nie, N. and Kim, J. (1978) *Participation and Political Equality: A Seven-Nation Comparison* (Cambridge and N.Y.: Cambridge University Press).

Verba, S., Schlozman, K. and Brady, H. (1995) *Voice and Equality: Civic Voluntarism in American Politics* (Cambridge, Mass. and London: Harvard University Press).

Vereshchetin, V. (1996) 'New Constitutions and the Old Problem of the Relationship between International Law and National Law', *European Journal of International Law* (7) 29–41.

Vickers, J. and Yarrow, G. (1988) *Privatization: An Economic Analysis* (Cambridge, Mass.: MIT Press).

Volgyes, I. and Barany, Z. (1995) *The Legacies of Communism in Eastern Europe* (Baltimore, Md. and London: Johns Hopkins University Press).

von Beyme, K. (1985) *Political Parties in Western Democracies* (Aldershot: Gower).

von Mettenheim, K. and Rockman, B. (1997) 'Presidential Institutions, Democracy and Comparative Politics' in *Presidential Institutions and Democratic Politics: Comparing Regional and National Contexts*, ed. K. von Mettenheim (Baltimore, Md. and London: Johns Hopkins University Press) pp. 237–46.

Walker, D. (1991) 'American Federalism in the 1990s' in *Political Issues in America Today*, ed. P. Davies and F. Waldstein (Manchester and N.Y.: Manchester University Press) pp. 119–32.

Wall, D. (1997) 'Policing the Virtual Community: the Internet, Cyberspace and Cybercrime' in *Policing Futures: the Police, Law Enforcement and the Twenty-First Century*, ed. P. Francis, P. Davies and V. Jupp (London: Macmillan and N.Y.: St Martin's Press) pp. 208–36.

Waller, J. (1994) *Secret Empire: The KGB in Russia Today* (Boulder, Colo. and Oxford: Westview).

Wallerstein, I. (1974, 1979) *The Modern World System* (N.Y.: Academic Press) two vols.

Wallis, M. (1989) *Bureaucracy: Its Role in Third World Development* (London: Macmillan).

Warwick, P. (1994) *Government Survival in Parliamentary Democracies* (Cambridge and N.Y.: Cambridge University Press).

Waters, M. (1995) *Globalization* (London and N.Y.: Routledge).

Watson, S. (1990) *Playing the State: Australian Feminist Interventions* (London and N.Y.: Verso).

Watt, E. (1982) *Authority* (London: Croom Helm).

Watts, R. (1996) 'Canada: Three Decades of Periodic Federal Crises', *International Political Science Review* (17) 353–72.

Weaver, R. and Rockman, B. (eds) (1993) *Do Institutions Matter? Government Capabilities in the United States and Abroad* (Washington, D.C.: The Brookings Institution).

Webber, M. (1997) 'States and Statehood' in *Issues in World Politics*, ed. B. White, R. Little and M. Smith (London: Macmillan and N.Y.: St Martin's Press) pp. 24–44.

Weber, M. (1957) *The Theory of Economic and Social Organization* (Berkeley, Calif.: University of California Press) first pub. 1922.

Weber, M. (1968) *Economy and Society* (N.Y.: Bedminster Press), first pub. 1925.

Weber, M. (1990) 'The Advent of Plebiscitarian Democracy' in *The West European Party System*, ed. P. Mair (Oxford and N.Y.: Oxford University Press) pp. 31–7.

Weigel, G. (1990) 'Catholicism and Democracy: The Other Twentieth Century Revolution' in *The New Democracies: Global Change and U.S. Policy*, ed. B. Roberts (Cambridge, Mass.: MIT Press) pp. 20–25.

Weiler, J. (1994) 'A Quiet Revolution: the European Court of Justice and its Interlocutors', *Comparative Political Studies* (26) 510–34.

Weiss, T. and Gordenker, C. (1996) 'Pluralizing Global Governance' in *Nongovernmental Organizations, the United Nations and Global Governance*, ed. T. Weiss and C. Gordenker (Boulder, Colo. and London: Lynne Reinner) pp. 17–50.

Weller, P. (1985) *First Among Equals: Prime Ministers in Westminster Systems* (Sydney: Allen & Unwin).

Weller, P., Bakvis, H. and Rhodes, R. (eds) (1997) *The Hollow Crown: Countervailing Trends in Core Executives* (London: Macmillan and N.Y.: St Martin's Press).

Westerlund, D. (ed.) (1996) *Questioning the Secular State: The Worldwide Resurgence of Religion in Politics* (London: Hurst).

Wheare, K. (1963) *Federal Government* (Oxford and N.Y.: Oxford University Press) 4th edn.

Wheare, K. (1968) *Legislatures* (Oxford: Oxford University Press).

White, G. (1991) 'Functions of the House of Commons' in *Politics: Canada*, ed. P. Fox and G. White (Toronto: McGraw-Hill Ryerson) pp. 407–17, 7th edn.

White, S. (1979) *Political Culture and Soviet Politics* (London: Macmillan).

White, S. (1993) 'Eastern Europe after Communism' in *Developments in East European Politics*, ed. S. White, J. Batt and P. Lewis (London: Macmillan) pp. 2–15.

White, S. (1994) 'From Communism to Democracy?' in *Developments in Russian and Post-Soviet Politics*, ed. S. White, A. Pravda and Z. Gitelman (London: Macmillan) pp. 1-21.

White, S. (1997) 'Russia: Presidential Leadership under Yeltsin' in *Postcommunist Presidents*, ed. R. Taras (Cambridge and N.Y.: Cambridge University Press) pp. 38–66.

White, S., Batt, J. and Lewis, P. (eds) (1993) *Developments in East European Politics* (London: Macmillan).

White, S., Gill, G. and Slider, D. (1993) *The Politics of Transition: Shaping a Post-Soviet Future* (Cambridge and N.Y.: Cambridge University Press).

White, S., Pravda, A. and Gitelman, Z. (eds) (1994) *Developments in Russian and Post-Soviet Politics* (London: Macmillan).

White, S., Pravda, A. and Gitelman, Z. (eds) (1997) *Developments in Russian Politics* (London: Macmillan).

Whitehead, L. (1993) 'A Latin American Perspective' in *Prospects for Democracy: North, South, East, West*, ed. D. Held (Cambridge: Polity) pp. 312–29.

Whitehead, L. (1996) *The International Dimensions of Democratization: Europe and the Americas* (Oxford and N.Y.: Oxford University Press).

Wickham-Crowley, T. (1991) *Guerillas and Revolution in Latin America: A Comparative Study of Insurgents and Regimes since 1956* (Princeton, N.J.: Princeton University Press).

Wilcox, K. (1989) 'Australian Federalism' in *Politics in Australia*, ed. R. Smith and L. Watson (North Sydney: Allen & Unwin) pp. 140–53.

Williams, C. (1995) 'A Requiem for Canada?' in *Federalism: The Multiethnic Challenge*, ed. G. Smith (Harlow: Longman) pp. 31–72.

Williams, F. (1997) 'Foreign Investment Builds Up', *Financial Times*, 22 September, p. 4.

Williamson, O. (1975) *Markets and Hierarchies* (N.Y. and London: Free Press).

Williamson, P. (1985) *Varieties of Corporatism: A Conceptual Discussion* (London: Macmillan).

Wilson, G. (1990) *Interest Groups* (Oxford and Cambridge, Mass.: Blackwell).

Wilson, J. (1973) *Political Organization* (N.Y.: Basic Books).

Wilson, J. (1997) *American Government* (Boston, Mass.: Houghton Mifflin) 4th edn.

Wiseman, J. (1995) 'Introduction' in *Democracy and Political Change in Sub-Saharan Africa*, ed. J. Wiseman (London and N.Y.: Routledge) pp. 1–10.

Wiseman, J. (1996) *The New Struggle for Democracy in Africa* (Aldershot and Brookfield, Vt.: Avebury).

Wolinetz, S. (ed.) (1997) *Political Parties* (Aldershot and Brookfield, Vt.: Ashgate).

Womack, B. and Townsend, J. (1996) 'Politics in China' in *Comparative Politics Today*, ed. G. Almond and G. Bingham Powell (N.Y.: HarperCollins) pp. 438–91. 6th edn.

Woodhouse, D. (1996) 'Politicians and the Judges: A Conflict of Interest', *Parliamentary Affairs* (49) 423–40.

World Bank (1992) *Governance and Development* (Washington, D.C.: International Bank for Reconstruction and Development).

World Bank (1993) *The East Asian Miracle: Economic Growth and Public Policy* (Oxford and N.Y.: Oxford University Press).

World Bank (1997) *World Development Report: The State in a Changing World* (Oxford and N.Y.: Oxford University Press).

World Trade Organization (1996) *Annual Report* (Washington, D.C.: World Trade Organization).

Woshinsky, O. (1995) *Culture and Politics: An Introduction to Mass and Élite Political Behavior* (Englewood Cliffs, N.J.: Prentice Hall).

Wright, V. (1989) *The Government and Politics of France* (London: Unwin Hyman) 3rd edn.

Wright, V. (1997) 'La fin du dirigisme?', *Modern and Contemporary France* (5) 151–5.

Wyatt-Walter, H. (1995) 'Regionalism, Globalization and World Economic Order' in *Regionalism and World Politics: Regional Organization and International Order*, ed. L. Fawcett and A. Hurrell (Oxford and N.Y.: Oxford University Press) pp. 74–121.

Wyman, M. (1994) 'Russian Political Culture: Evidence from Public Opinion Surveys', *Journal of Communist Studies* (10) 25–54.

Yin, R. (1994) *Case Study Research: Design and Methods* (Thousand Oaks, Calif. and London: Sage) 2nd ed.

Yishai, Y. (1994) 'Interest Parties: The Thin Line between Groups and Parties in the Israeli Electoral Process' in *How Political Parties Work: Perspectives from Within*, ed. K. Lawson (Westport, Conn.: Praeger) pp. 197–226.

Zagorski, P. (1992) *Democracy versus National Security: Civil-Military Relations in Latin America* (Boulder, Colo. and London: Lynne Reinner).

Zariski, R. (1993) 'Italy' in *Politics in Western Europe*, ed. M. Hancock *et al.* (Chatham, N.J.: Chatham House and London: Macmillan) pp. 293–381.

Zartman, I. (ed.) (1995) *Collapsed States: The Disintegration and Restoration of Political Authority* (Boulder, Colo. and London: Lynne Reinner).

Ziman, J. (1978) *Reliable Knowledge: An Exploration of the Grounds for Belief in Science* (Cambridge and N.Y.: Cambridge University Press).

Index

Entries in **bold** indicate a definition box.